BASIC MANUAL
FOR THE LEGAL PROFESSIONAL

FIFTEENTH EDITION

Prepared by
NALS®. . . *the association for legal professionals*

Edited by
Text Development Committee

Cathy A. Zackery, CLP, Kalamazoo, Michigan
Barbara LeCaptain, PLS, Manitowoc, Wisconsin
Kristin Messick, PP, Oklahoma City, Oklahoma
Emily Walterscheid, PP, PLS, Lubbock, Texas
Paula Steffey, PP, CLP-SC, CWCP, Kalamazoo, Michigan
Sharolyn C. Sayers, Ph.D., Professor, Milwaukee, Wisconsin
Maureen Jones, PP, PLS Cadillac, Michigan
Helene Wood, PP, PLS, TSC-RE, Houston, Texas

Maria Easterly, NALS National Certification and Education Manager

For Customer Assistance Call 1-800-328-4880

Mat #42478485

© Thomson Reuters 1962 - 2019

ISBN 978-1-539-23081-6

ACKNOWLEDGMENTS

The Text Development Committee thanks the following for their time, contributions and assistance in the revision of the *Basic Manual for the Legal Professional*, Fifteenth Edition.

Cathy A. Zackery, CLP, Kalamazoo, Michigan
Barbara LeCaptain, PLS, Manitowoc, Wisconsin
Kristin Messick, PP, Oklahoma City, Oklahoma
Emily Walterscheid, PP, PLS, Lubbock, Texas
Paula Steffey, PP, CLP-SC, CWCP, Kalamazoo, Michigan
Sharolyn C. Sayers, Ph.D., Professor, Milwaukee, Wisconsin
Maureen Jones, PP, PLS Cadillac, Michigan
Helene Wood, PP, PLS, TSC-RE, Houston, Texas

Maria Easterly, NALS National Certification and Education Manager

The NALS® Text Development Committee is comprised of NALS® members who worked closely with their respective attorneys to revise and update the *Basic Manual for the Legal Professional*, Fifteenth Edition. On behalf of NALS® . . . *the association for legal professionals*, we would like to thank the following for their support of the committee members.

Levine & Levine, Attorneys at Law
Kalamazoo, Michigan

McWhorter, Cobb & Johnson, LLP
Lubbock, Texas

Matthew Harris Law, PLLC
Lubbock, Texas

Goidosik Morse Disability Law Group
Kalamazoo, Michigan

Whyte, Hirschboeck & Dudek
Madison, Wisconsin

Milwaukee Area Technical College
Milwaukee, Wisconsin

McCurdy, Wotila & Porteous, P.C.
Kalmazoo, Michigan

Deming PLLC
Kalamazoo, Michigan

Lewis, Reed & Allen, PC

Kalamazoo, Michigan

Godfrey Kahn SC
Milwaukee, Wisconsin

Norton, Rose, Fulbright US LLP
Houston, Texas

Sloan Firm
Houston, Texas

Davis & Kuelthau
Milwaukee, Wisconsin

Steimle Birschbach
Manitowoc, Wisconsin

Without the support offered by the firms listed above, this project would not have been successful. Thank you for your continued professional courtesies and generosities extended throughout the development of this edition and for your support of the committee members.

Staying current in such a rapidly changing field is a challenge. As the law evolves, so do our texts and accompanying materials.

NALS® ... *the association for legal professionals*, would like to thank the following attorneys/individuals for their contributions to this project:

Aviva Kaiser, Esq., Wisconsin State Bar Association
Gwynn P. Martin, Esq., McWhorter, Cobb & Johnson, LLP
James L. Stevens, Esq., McWhorter, Cobb & Johnson, LLP
Carrie A. Harris, Esp., Matthew Harris Law, PLLC
Kayla R. Wimberley, Esq., Matthew Harris Law, PLLC
Fernando M. Bustos, Esq., Bustos Law Firm, PC
D. Gene Valentini, Lubbock County Office of Dispute Resolution
Honorable Carl Ashley, Milwaukee County Circuit Court
Ann M. Maher, Esq., Husch Blackwell, LLP
James K. Walsh, Esq., Wiswall & Walsh, PC
Gina Carter, Esq., Husch Blackwell, LLP
Brianna M. Schonenberg, Esq., Husch Blackwell, LLP
Andrew J. Steimle, Esq., Steimle Birschbach, LLC
Richard Dietz, Esq., Foster Swift Collins & Smith, PC
Michael Liddane, Esq., Foster Swift Collins & Smith, PC
Sarissa K. Montague, Esq., Levine & Levine
Rachel L. Gruetzner, Esq., Levine & Levine
Tyler Stewart, Esq., Levine & Levine
Garold A. Goidosik, Esq., Goidosik Morse Disability Law Group

Special thanks to the proofreading team:

Mary Lemmond, EdD, ED-IT: A Proofreading Service, LLC
Maria Easterly, NALS National Certification and Education Manager
Andrea D. Griffin, PP, PLS, Chair, Lubbock, Texas
Tami Dodd, PP, PLS, ALP, Vice-Chair, Jonesboro, Arkansas

ACKNOWLEDGMENTS

The assistance of these individuals was invaluable to this project. Thank you.

PREFACE

NALS® believes continuing education is vital to every successful career in the legal profession. This Manual, the Fifteenth Edition, is geared toward those persons entering or returning to the legal field.

We believe this text will provide a useful tool for all legal support personnel, regardless of title, job description, or experience. Even as we remind you that the *Basic Manual for the Legal Professional* remains a general reference and not a specific map for your practice, we encourage you to rely on this manual for basic knowledge and guidance.

HOW TO USE THIS TEXTBOOK

The *Basic Manual for the Legal Professional* is presented by NALS® as part of a training course for legal support personnel. It is also the official text for the NALS® Legal Training Course and Independent Course of Study.

It is intended for use as a training aid for people who are entering or have recently entered the legal field. It does not attempt to teach the law.

The content of the text is general, because it is geared for a broad audience. The accompanying Student Study Guide and Instructor's Manual offer many suggestions on the application of general subject matter to local needs.

This text is not intended as a legal authority and should not be used in such a manner. The intent is purely informational. The examples in the text are illustrative in nature and should be used in an office only at the direction of the lawyer. Legal procedures change daily, and legal support personnel, as well as lawyers, should maintain a knowledge of current procedures in their local practice area.

Summary of Contents

Appendices

Table of Contents

CHAPTER 1. THE LAWYER'S ASSISTANT

CHAPTER 2. ETHICS

CHAPTER 3. THE LAW OFFICE

CHAPTER 4. COMPUTERS IN THE LAW OFFICE

CHAPTER 5. BILLING AND BASIC ACCOUNTING PROCEDURES

CHAPTER 6. WRITTEN COMMUNICATIONS

CHAPTER 7. PREPARATION OF LEGAL DOCUMENTS

CHAPTER 8. THE LAW LIBRARY

CHAPTER 9. THE COURTS

CHAPTER 10.   ADMINISTRATIVE AGENCIES

CHAPTER 11.   LITIGATION

CHAPTER 12.   CONTRACTS

CHAPTER 13. TORTS

CHAPTER 14. CRIMINAL LAW AND PROCEDURE

CHAPTER 15. FAMILY LAW

CHAPTER 16. BUSINESS ORGANIZATIONS

CHAPTER 17. REAL ESTATE

CHAPTER 18.   ESTATE PLANNING

CHAPTER 19.   ESTATES AND GUARDIANSHIPS

CHAPTER 20.   BANKRUPTCY

APPENDICES

Chapter 1

The Lawyer's Assistant

KeyCite®: Cases and other legal materials listed in KeyCite Scope can be researched through the KeyCite service on Westlaw®. Use KeyCite to check citations for form, parallel references, prior and later history, and comprehensive citator information, including citations to other decisions and secondary materials.

---

§ 1.1   A professional career

There are many different ways to describe the staff that assists the lawyer, including assistant, administrative assistant, lawyer's assistant, legal assistant, legal secretary, paralegal, and secretary. The job description and the title of the position vary with the employer. Regardless of the title, job description, or employer, however, the role of the legal support professional remains the same: to assist one or more lawyers. Because the term "legal assistant" in certain parts of the country indicates a person with paralegal duties, to avoid confusion, the term *lawyer's assistant* will be used throughout this text to indicate the support person who serves a lawyer in a secretarial capacity, perhaps with expanded duties as detailed later in this chapter and throughout this text.

The legal profession requires skills and support of the highest quality in order for the lawyer to give the best service possible to clients. It follows that the lawyer's support staff is the heart of the law office.

Lawyers all differ in personality and work style. All lawyers, however, have certain things in common. The formal education required in order to become a lawyer is extensive, and that education continues with each new case and client. The lawyer is dedicated to the public and the service of justice. This often is reflected in personal activities—community service, charity, and **pro bono** work all allow the lawyer to donate time and service to the benefit of the public. Lawyers believe in the right of representation of all people in spite of frailties, gross misjudgments, even flagrant violations of the law. A lawyer is also held to the strictest standards of moral and ethical conduct, in both professional and personal life.

A lawyer's assistant contributes significantly to the image and public perception of the lawyer. The assistant must convey respect for the lawyer and the law. Clients and members of the legal community can sense an assistant's respect for the lawyer and the lawyer's work. Sometimes professionalism is a matter of how the work is done, and sometimes it is a matter of how things look. For example, in many offices, the staff uses the lawyer's first name. In some situations, this practice may portray a casual or unprofessional image. The lawyer's assistant should avoid addressing the lawyer or clients by their first names in front of clients unless instructed otherwise.

Another aspect of professionalism is the necessity for acting within the ethical constraints that are placed upon both the lawyer and staff. The details of ethical behavior are explored in Chapter 2, Ethics.

A lawyer's assistant should neither criticize nor condone criticism of the lawyer or the firm. The lawyer's assistant may not always understand the lawyer's decisions. In dealing directly with clients, the lawyer's assistant has a very weighty responsibility. To the clients, the assistant is an extension of the lawyer. It is important that clients understand that the lawyer's assistant cannot offer legal advice regardless of the circumstances. This is one of the most important, and often one of the most difficult, tests of the integrity of the lawyer's assistant.

Perhaps the most important way to express professionalism to the lawyer, the firm, and the clients, however, is for the lawyer's assistant to believe in himself or herself and in the assistant's ability to accomplish the work that needs to be done. The only way to build that kind of confidence is through training and experience. Occasional discouragement is natural. Everyone makes mistakes, and the learning involved in legal work is endless, but when a job this difficult is well done, the confidence gained is tremendous.

The most important attribute of a successful lawyer's assistant is the assistant's attitude toward self and career. Attitude is reflected in every contact with others and in completion of work assignments, often under difficult and pressure-filled conditions. The valued lawyer's assistant has learned to remain consistently composed and efficient under the most trying circumstances, knowing that conflicts and deadlines are inevitable. Legal work is a career, not just a job, and each experience is an investment in the assistant's future.

The second basic ingredient in the development of the lawyer's assistant and a by-product of proper attitude is initiative. The assistant can make an appreciable difference in the firm's productivity by requesting additional assignments after completing work and by recognizing and completing unassigned tasks. The lawyer's assistant should let the lawyer know he or she is serious about the career and eager to contribute by asking relevant questions, inquiring about appropriate reading material, and requesting periodic evaluations. There are excellent training courses and educational materials available through national, state, and local legal professional associations, as well as from vocational schools and universities, that will help enhance the lawyer's assistant's knowledge and skills. Continuing education is an investment that produces dividends in direct relation to the assistant's time and effort. Also, some law firms offer extensive skill training, and the lawyer's assistant should take advantage of this added benefit to further develop the assistant's skill set.

Development of the proper attitude and strong initiative will result in the self-confidence that is the third vital factor in the makeup of the professional lawyer's assistant. Real confidence is not automatic—it is developed over a period of time through experience. The lawyer's assistant gains self-confidence by satisfactorily accomplishing tasks that initially seemed too difficult to complete. The lawyer's assistant can know that he or she has acquired self-confidence when the assistant can allow someone else to be given credit for the assistant's idea or work product; can accept sound, constructive criticism graciously and gratefully; and can admit mistakes honestly without searching for an excuse.

Confidence is required for honest self-evaluation. In a candid and objective self-appraisal, the lawyer's assistant should ask himself or herself whether he or she fulfills the assistant's key responsibilities, presents a professional image, and supplies genuine support for the lawyer.

§ 1.2 Beginning the career of lawyer's assistant

The image of the professional lawyer's assistant is composed of many facets and often begins with the visual one. The assistant's attitude, imagination, and enthusiasm for the career should shine through. It should be obvious to everyone that the assistant likes the work and takes pride in doing it well.

Many law offices have dress codes. The underlying goal should be to create a picture of professionalism that will foster the client's confidence in the assistant, the lawyers, and the firm. The first step is reading, understanding, and upholding the firm dress code. The next step is to explore what constitutes business casual or business attire in the community where the lawyer's assistant works. Lawyers like to inspire confidence by looking prosperous—in their person, in their office furnishings, and in their staff—so any clothing that is worn, faded, or visibly mended should not be worn to work.

Jewelry, makeup, hairstyles, and, for men, neat and trimmed beards and mustaches in the law office should be in good fashion and tasteful. Avoid extremes, with elegance, modesty, and good taste being the goal.

§ 1.2.1 Beginning the career of lawyer's assistant—Applying for the job

The first active step in becoming a lawyer's assistant is the creation of a professional résumé. The résumé is the lawyer's first impression of the assistant's work, so it must be perfect. Proofread it as if it were worth $35,000, $45,000,* or more, because it may be. Always have someone else proofread it as well. A second set of eyes may help identify errors that were overlooked and identify additional ways to improve the resume overall. Study books and Internet sites on the creation of the perfect résumé. Every fact in the résumé must be true. Present information in the best possible light, but do not exaggerate.

The next step is the job interview. The lawyer's assistant should positively state his or her qualifications, but remain dignified and professional. The assistant should bear firmly in mind that he or she is prepared to bring commitment, professionalism, enthusiasm and determination to the job. Whether the lawyer realizes that or not in this interview, the right lawyer will realize it and put the lawyer's assistant to work. A courteous, dignified, pleasant, and professional manner is essential to a successful lawyer's assistant and to a successful interview.

The successful applicant will act naturally and present him or herself honestly during the interview. Good working relationships depend on good chemistry, so it is important that the applicant be honest. The applicant should wear the best clothes he or she would normally wear to work—a suit for either men or women, a dress for women and dress pants and shirt for men or women are all possibilities. The applicant needs to have a tidy appearance, including pressed clothing, neat style, conservative make-up for women, and a good shave or trimmed facial hair for men.

The applicant should learn as much as possible about the position before and during the interview. It will be helpful to know what will

---

[Section 1.2.1]

*Salaries for lawyer's assistants vary across the country and also depend on the size of the firm.

be expected of the employee and what the employee can expect from the employer. It is very possible the applicant may discover he or she is not compatible with the position or with the employer. Do not expect the interviewer to indicate immediately whether the job will be offered. The interviewer may have to consult with others or may have other interviews scheduled. In addition, nearly all legal positions require an interview with the attorneys to whom the assistant will be assigned before a hiring decision is made. Many firms interview prospective employees more than once, sometimes two or three times. It is appropriate to inquire when to expect to hear from the firm. If the firm does not contact the applicant by the indicated time, the applicant should call and ask whether he or she is still being considered.

Know when the interview is over and leave. Be as dignified in exiting as in arriving. Final impressions are also important. Every applicant should send a letter to the interviewer thanking them for taking the time to meet and expressing the applicant's interest in the position. The tone of the thank-you letter should be polite and to the point, but the applicant should mention some key quality that he or she can offer the prospective employer. The smart lawyer's assistant will not skip the follow-up letter, as many interviewees fail to send them—and it can make the difference in being hired or not. It can also create a lasting impression of professionalism, should the interviewer be encountered later in a different role.

§ 1.2.2 Beginning the career of lawyer's assistant—On the job

A new lawyer's assistant may not understand some methods the lawyer uses. The best way to learn is by asking and taking notes for future reference. The new lawyer's assistant should have a notebook handy and be ready to use it. The new employee should let the lawyer know that the job will be easier and the results better if the assistant understands the tasks at hand. Ideally, the assistant's notebook should be organized by classification. Then, every time something new comes along, it can be added to the notebook. Even if the law firm has a procedures manual, it may not cover some of the basics needed in the first few days or weeks. If learning the new information is hard, take the notes home and review them. Besides the day-to-day tasks, the notebook can become a resource including client and case information sheets, billing information, information needed to manage administrative tasks for the lawyer, commonly used phone numbers, and so forth. Additionally, this notebook would become an invaluable aid to a floater or temp filling in for the assistant.

One of the most difficult—and sometimes terrifying—tasks for the new lawyer's assistant is dealing with the client who calls or comes into the office to ask about the client's case. The client may be upset or irate and may expect the lawyer's assistant to be able to give up-to-date and detailed information. It is entirely possible the client and the details of the case are unknown to the assistant, making the situation even more upsetting. Remember that the assistant's relationship with the client is that of maintaining communication between lawyer and client. Routine information—court dates or the information that a document was recently mailed—should be given if known or obtained quickly if not. Legal details need to come from the lawyer, and it is appropriate for the assistant to remind the client that the assistant cannot give out legal information. A pleasantly stated, truthful assurance that the lawyer will be able to contact the client within a stated time is fine.

Once the assurance is given, someone with the authority to discuss the case must contact the client within the time stated. Be sure the attorney receives the message and find out how to handle the situation. The attorney may give a message to relay to the client or may opt to contact the client directly. Over time, if every client request is fielded politely and efficiently, the client will come to know that the lawyer's assistant can be trusted. The lawyer's assistant should strive to treat each client as a special person with an individual problem or situation. Such an attitude is further evidence that the lawyer also regards the client and the client's circumstances as special and deserving of attention.

It is a truism that one can never afford to offend anyone in the local legal community—coworkers, bosses, opposing counsel, court clerks, and so forth. The smart lawyer's assistant tries to be pleasant to everyone, knowing that help from that person may be needed later. It is particularly important to promote mutual respect with other staff members by refusing to participate in office politics or gossip.

§ 1.3   The career of lawyer's assistant

One of the great benefits of a career in the legal field is the incredible diversity of possible areas of practice, job settings, and positions. In the following section, the potential opportunities available to the lawyer's assistant will be explored.

§ 1.3.1   The career of lawyer's assistant—The small firm

Looking for a challenge? The lawyer's assistant in a small law office, with perhaps one or two lawyers, probably receives a more rounded education on the job than in any other type of legal position and may have to be everything to everybody, an expert in all areas of office relations and office work.

A lawyer's assistant in a small office deals with the public and is usually the first person with whom the client or prospective client speaks, in person or on the telephone. The lawyer's assistant sets the mood for the entire relationship. Therefore, the assistant needs all of the abilities of a good receptionist, an arbitrator, and a psychologist. The lawyer's assistant should make an effort to be interesting and interested.

The small-firm lawyer's assistant gets the mail and distributes it, wraps parcels, posts the mail, takes care of postage expenses, collects return receipts, and performs a myriad of other postal duties. The assistant must know the postal system thoroughly and how to make it meet the firm's needs. An excellent online reference for U.S. Postal information is www.usps.com.

The small-firm lawyer's assistant may also keep the books, write checks, deposit receipts, send out bills (and rebillings), and may need to be familiar with the banking procedures as well. The assistant may handle trust and estate accounts and have to be able to verify everything done in these accounts. The small-firm lawyer's assistant must keep accounting records in order to expedite tax reporting and filing. So the small-firm assistant may need to be competent at accounting and accounting procedures as well as the preparation of legal documents.

The small-firm lawyer's assistant orders supplies and maintains office equipment, requesting repairs when needed. The small-firm assistant needs to know what equipment and supplies provide the required performance affordably. The assistant will need to find a place for everything and keep it well-marked for the convenience of everyone in the office.

(All updates are now available online through Westlaw or Lexis). It is likely that the lawyer's assistant may need to assist with Internet research, too. Law libraries have now transformed into research and materials found on the Internet. The two largest resources for legal research are Westlaw and Lexis.

Over time, as the lawyer's assistant in the small firm prepares everything that leaves the office, the assistant will come to know the proper forms for communications, pleadings, and all other documents. The assistant needs to proofread everything at least once, make all corrections carefully and neatly, and be familiar with the copying requirements for each type of document.

The small-firm lawyer's assistant is likely to compose a great deal of correspondence for the lawyer's signature and will learn to prepare correspondence that reflects the lawyer's writing style. The assistant will know the components of a successful business letter and have a thorough knowledge of English, both in word choice and mechanics.

In a small firm, the lawyer's assistant is usually responsible for filing every document that comes into or leaves the office. The assistant will need to maintain files that are orderly, current, and organized in a system the lawyer can also use.

As the lawyer's assistant becomes more adept at the job, the assistant will learn everything he or she can about the details of the lawyer's practice and relieve the lawyers of any work the assistant can do.

A key point for the lawyer's assistant in the small firm over time is that the assistant knows everything that is happening, where everything is, what forms to use, what progress is being made in each case, what procedures to follow, and what comes next. It is vitally important that this information is recorded in the proper files as it relates to clients and cases and in an office manual as it relates to procedures. The professional lawyer's assistant will make it possible for someone to step into the job with the least disruption necessary if an emergency should ever arise.

The job of a small-firm lawyer's assistant can be profoundly challenging. A large firm may not give the breadth of experience that would be gained in a small firm practice. The small-firm assistant is truly well-rounded, and although the assistant may not realize it, is steadily gaining the skills necessary to obtain the designation of PLS® . . . an advanced certification for the legal professional. (See § 1.5.2.)

§ 1.3.2 The career of lawyer's assistant—The large firm

The lawyer's assistant in a large law firm will focus almost exclusively on legal work. Large law firms offer many amenities, including departments that provide support to lawyers and staff throughout the firm for non-legal functions. The following are some of the common support departments and functions.

File clerk. Large firms may have a special procedure for setting up new files and checking for conflicts. These processes are sometimes quite complicated, but most firms find them necessary to ensure that no conflicts of interest go unidentified. The lawyer's assistant should learn the procedures and become aware of the time lapse that may exist between submission of paperwork and approval of a new file.

Accounting. The lawyer's assistant in the large firm must learn to use the computer programs for time entry and billing as they apply to the assistant's position. Large firms will also have forms and established procedures for requesting checks. The assistant must be aware of the turnaround time involving checks since it may take more than one day to receive them. Office expenses such as postage, copying, long distance calls, faxes, and other out-of-pocket expenses will be billed to clients or administrative files. The assistant will need to learn and abide by the procedures for these billing items.

Word processing. Longer or more complex documents such as briefs, wills, trusts, profit sharing plans, and so forth, may be prepared in the word processing department, freeing the lawyer's assistant to do other work for the lawyer. Typically the lawyer's assistant will prepare a form with instructions for the word processing staff and deliver the materials to the department.

Copying and Scanning. Many firms now have staff who either do all of the copying and scanning for the office or who are available to assist with large projects. Some firms outsource this function through vendors who operate on-site at the law firm. Additionally, many firms now have several types of copying machines used for different purposes. When the lawyer's assistant is responsible for doing copying and scanning, the assistant will have to learn which type of equipment to use for which type of project and who maintains the machines in the event of a malfunction. Most larger firms have a procedure for billing copies to clients that the lawyer's assistant will need to learn.

Librarian. The law library will probably be kept up to date by a librarian or by one specific person in the office who Internet research sites and other reference materials. In many large firms, the librarian may also be responsible for assisting with legal research. It is the lawyer's assistant's responsibility to learn how to use the office library and in which situations the librarian may be able to help.

Mail room. Each firm generally has its own procedure for handling incoming and outgoing mail. It is important to learn this procedure so that mail will go out on time. It is also important to learn what role the mail room staff plays in handling tasks such as certified or registered mail, overnight deliveries, courier requests, and the like.

Faxes. Facsimile receipts and transmissions are sometimes handled by a separate department, such as telecommunications, support services, a facsimile software program, or by receptionists or other designated staff members. The lawyer's assistant should learn the firm's procedures for sending and receiving faxes and know how to send a fax when department personnel are not available.

Errands. Generally, in larger firms, errands will be handled by an in-house messenger or an outside delivery service. Learn the requirements for requesting messenger service and what it takes to get items delivered correctly and on time. In addition to whatever training the large firm may give on these office functions, the procedures are likely also outlined in an office procedures manual available to all employees.

Most larger firms prefer their correspondence and legal documents to be prepared uniformly. The firm's training sessions or office procedures manual will provide instructions on how to set up documents.

What the small-firm lawyer's assistant gains in breadth of knowledge, the large-firm lawyer's assistant will likely gain in depth of knowledge in one, two, or three specific practice areas, depending on how attorney assignments are managed. Over time, the large-firm litigation assistant may not only develop knowledge of the procedures utilized in many of the state courts but may also have opportunities to prepare briefs on appeal. In addition to filing routine Chapter 7 bankruptcy cases, the bankruptcy assistant may have the opportunity to prepare complex pleadings for cases involving large companies with securities interests. Generally, while small-firm experience provides a good basic background, large-firm experience is valuable as well.

§ 1.3.3   The career of lawyer's assistant—The corporate environment

In the corporate environment, the legal department is usually an arm of top management and, as such, reaches out into every phase of the company's operations. The primary function of the legal department is the practice of preventive law in an effort to perceive, analyze, and correct legally related problems within the organization before they result in litigation. This is a noble goal, but no large corporation is without Equal Employment Opportunity complaints, workers' compensation claims, unemployment and Department of Labor hearings, union-labor problems, complex contract claims, and liability issues. Corporate legal issues range from small-dollar problems to the defense of lawsuits involving millions of dollars. The matter is further complicated if the corporation is under primary contract to the government and thus subject to the never-ending rules and regulations that have been promulgated to enforce applicable laws and statutes. These laws have been primarily enacted to assure fairness, equal opportunity, protection of the government's interests, and to absolve the government of any appearance of conflict of interest, corruption, or wrongdoing. The paperwork and effort required to comply are added responsibilities.

The lawyer's assistant is vital to the proper and effective operation of a corporate legal office. The lawyer's assistant must have excellent secretarial skills, a working knowledge of legal terminology, and good communication skills, both oral and written. In addition, the assistant must have a thorough understanding of the corporate structure and the responsibilities of the lawyers in the office in order to direct requests for information to the appropriate lawyer best able to assist. The lawyer's assistant must also be sensitive to political issues within or outside the company, as good public relations are essential to the smooth operation of the legal department and the corporation. Finally, the lawyer's assistant is often called upon to assist with legal research, which requires a basic knowledge of the legal resources most frequently consulted by the legal department.

The role of the corporate lawyer's assistant is both administrative and clerical. Corporate legal work is often more general than private legal work, and management-related duties often consume as much time as legal duties. A lawyer's assistant position in a corporate legal department is challenging, offering opportunities for learning, as well as variety, high visibility, and frequently a close relationship with top management.

§ 1.3.4   The career of lawyer's assistant—The clerk in the court system

When asked to express his understanding of the duties and functions of a court clerk, one judge said:

> It must be borne in mind that the designation court clerk is a complete misnomer, and that the duties of court clerks, regardless of what court they may be in, go far beyond the connotation of clerk, typist, or similar position. The court clerk has great responsibility not only to the court and lawyers but also to the public generally. It is the primary responsibil-

ity of these individuals to see that the courts run smoothly and that the work is done properly and expeditiously. They are required to have a reasonable understanding of the law, rules of civil and criminal procedure, and other matters that bind the court in its daily work. This is not to say that they must be legally trained, but the clerks certainly must be able to understand statutes and case law as told to them by either the judge or the lawyer involved. Therefore, it must be kept in mind that the position of court clerk is one of more responsibility than a clerk, typist, or even a secretary.

Court records are of vital importance to the general public. It is essential that a court clerk have the training and ability to organize and maintain complete, accurate files and dockets. This can, at times, be repetitious and boring; however, the variety offered in court work more than compensates. The courts handle many kinds of cases, including criminal, juvenile, civil, adoptions, divorces, traffic, and so forth. The court clerk is responsible for these cases from beginning to end. The clerk assists the court by swearing in witnesses; operating an electronic recorder; taking orders and motions from the judge verbatim; and receiving, marking, and safeguarding exhibits. The clerk prepares, compiles, and files minutes of court hearings and trials; issues bench warrants under direction of the judge for persons who do not appear or who fail to pay fines imposed by the court; receives and accounts for fines imposed by the court; maintains a calendar and status file on each active case; prepares forms, legal documents, and correspondence as directed by the court; compiles and tabulates statistical data and caseload reports; and performs secretarial work for the judges.

A court clerk must have the ability to exercise judgment in the proper dissemination of information and to provide good public relations in stressful, sensitive situations. The job is challenging, rewarding, and fascinating. Excellent skills are important, but above all, a court clerk is required to be understanding, compassionate, and dedicated to serving the public.

§1.3.5 The career of lawyer's assistant—The federal government

The duties of lawyer's assistants in federal service are similar to those of civil service secretaries with GS ratings. A federal service lawyer's assistant is normally accorded confidence in all matters relating to the office in which they are employed, and the work is closely identified with the viewpoint and responsibilities of the particular agency or department. An office manager is directly answerable to the agency head or member of Congress, and the lawyer's assistant works under the direction of the office manager.

A lawyer's assistant performs or supervises the performance of a variety of tasks including:

- Performing telephone and receptionist duties
- Keeping calendars and scheduling appointments and conferences

- Performing liaison duties as necessary between the office manager and other office personnel, as well as with other offices
- Receiving and distributing incoming mail and preparing replies
- Arranging for recording of proceedings of conferences or hearings
- Reviewing and channeling outgoing mail
- Maintaining records and files
- Making travel arrangements for staff members
- Assembling and disseminating information
- Transmitting staff instructions
- Performing miscellaneous clerical, stenographic, and secretarial duties

Lawyer's assistant positions may or may not require stenographic, word processing, or dictation machine transcription skills.

There are significant differences in civil service and federal service jobs. With federal service there is no job security, and salaries may vary a great deal, according to the wishes of the employer, the amount available in the clerk hire fund of the particular office, or ceilings of grades for certain positions. Service to constituents is the primary reason for hiring of staff in congressional offices. There is a great deal of research and contact with various governmental agencies to resolve problems. Because of these contacts, a certain amount of glamour and prestige is attached to federal service jobs. Many support staff positions, however, require longer hours than regular civil service jobs or jobs in private industry. No overtime is paid, but in some cases, compensatory time off is allowed.

Most federal service assistants do not come from the civil service registry but are recruited by advertisement or word of mouth. An employment service is also provided for the use of the members of Congress. Abilities are tested and evaluated in the same manner used by private industry employment agencies. Lawyer's assistant skills are much in demand. Usually, the assistant's training has included language skills, such as obtaining information for and composing correspondence as well as reviewing outgoing correspondence for correct grammar, spelling, and format. The advancement of the assistant depends on many factors, including length of time in the position, improved job skills, and the ability to work without direct supervision. Other traits essential to the performance of duties are:

- Effectiveness in getting along with others
- Loyalty, integrity, and discretion
- Capacity and willingness to accept responsibility
- Judgment, initiative, and resourcefulness
- Poise, personal dignity, neatness, and good grooming

§ 1.3.6 The career of lawyer's assistant—Specialized practice

Lawyers in general practice handle all types of cases. The lawyer might be involved in the defense of a criminal matter one day and in a personal injury trial the next. General practice firms do not limit their practices to trial work. They may also handle a large volume of work such as property transactions, contracts, estate planning, and tax work. The lawyer's assistant in a general practice, therefore, must be especially versatile and knowledgeable about many aspects of the law.

Some lawyers thrive on the excitement and challenge of trial. Some criminal defense lawyers specialize in white-collar crime cases. Some civil trial legal practices emphasize personal injury, tax matters, domestic relations, bankruptcy, or other types of civil actions.

Other lawyers specialize in one particular practice area, such as estate planning, property law, probate law, tax law, corporate law, admiralty law, patent law, domestic relations law, and so forth. For the lawyer's assistant who works for a specialist, there is the particular challenge of also becoming a specialist in that particular area of law.

§ 1.4 Career advancement

What constitutes advancement varies a great deal from firm to firm, from lawyer to lawyer, and from lawyer's assistant to lawyer's assistant. One assistant may start out working for a lawyer so compatible and agreeable that the assistant never chooses to change jobs. Another may work his or her way up from a small firm with limited challenges to a position in a big firm working for a firm manager or lawyer whose work is nationally known. An assistant can be fired from one firm and find the job of a lifetime at another firm within a month. The qualities that are needed to make any career successful, though, are generally the same everywhere. The lawyer's assistant's attitude is crucial. The assistant who is eager to learn; who can take instruction and criticism gracefully; who can stay current with changing equipment, forms, and formats; and who can keep an open mind about what the job demands is likely to do well on the job. Whether advancement means an improvement in benefits, pay, job title, or responsibilities, attitude plays a key role.

To prepare for career advancement, regardless of how that may be perceived, the lawyer's assistant must maintain and increase his or her knowledge base. Seminars and workshops offer continuing legal education for the lawyer's assistant, just as they do for the lawyer. Certification is another option, with the designation of **Accredited Legal Professional (ALP®)**, or if preferred, is also designated as **Certified Legal Professional (CLP®)** available to those in their first three years of legal work; **Professional Legal Secretary (PLS®)** available to those with three or more years of legal experience, and the **Professional Paralegal (PP®)**, available for those with five years of experience in paralegal or legal assistant work. Further, NALS® offers a Specialty Certificate Program for the lawyer's assistant who is a Certified PP or PLS. This Specialty Certificate is received after obtaining continuing legal education credits in any of the three designated specialty tracks: Litigation/Civil Law, Corporate Law, or Estate Planning/Family Law. The lawyer's assistant should keep abreast of what is happening in the firm, in the local legal community, and in the world. If the lawyer is aware the assistant is actively involved in and seeking out continuing legal education or certification, it can often make a difference.

Some lawyers hesitate to promote the assistant into a different position because they feel the lawyer's assistant is indispensable. One answer is to have the job so well organized with an office manual, a forms file, a procedures manual, and systematic training of backup personnel that the lawyer need not be concerned about training someone new. The skilled lawyer's assistant can be of even more help to the lawyer in an advanced capacity than in a purely assistant role.

§ 1.5 NALS® Programs

NALS® . . . *the association for legal professionals*, began in 1929 as the National Association of Legal Secretaries. A young legal secretary, Eula May Jett, in Long Beach, California, was encouraged by a court clerk to talk with other legal secretaries about correct preparation of legal documents. As a result of that challenge, NALS® was formed. Today NALS® is a tri-level organization with membership available in local chapters, state associations, and on the national level.

NALS® encourages the personal and professional growth of its members through education and the promotion of professional standards and ethics. Members support and abide by the Code of Professional Responsibility of the American Bar Association as well as the NALS® Code of Ethics and Professional Responsibility. Membership is available to all persons engaged in work of a legal nature, such as law office administrators, lawyer's assistants, legal assistants, stenographers, or employees of public and private institutions. Lawyers, judges, and educators may join NALS® as associate members, and there is a special class of membership available to students.

NALS®, local chapters, and state associations offer many educational materials and programs, such as:

- Textbooks and handbooks to provide helpful how-to information for the everyday use of lawyer's assistants in both general and specialty practices.
- Manuals to assist law offices in developing their own procedures and systems as well as tests for hiring qualified support staff.
- Training courses and independent study courses to provide basic and advanced instruction for lawyer's assistants and study groups to assist them in preparing for the certification examinations.
- Educational conferences, seminars, and webinars held throughout the nation, year-round.

- *@LAW*, the quarterly magazine containing educational articles and information on career development, seminars, and other educational opportunities.

- The *NALSdocket*, a monthly email that includes information about topics covered on legal blogs and Twitter, along with industry related articles and association news directly from the Resource Center Staff.

- The NALS® blog feature, *inside NALS*, which provides blog postings from NALS® officers and staff, as well as items from the NALS® website.

- The NALS® Community, with a presence on Facebook, Twitter, LinkedIn, and its own online social network, provides the up-to-date information on NALS® events and its members.

- NALS® affinity programs provide members with discounts on a variety of goods and services.

- The NALS® Online Learning Center is a great source for those preparing to take their NALS certification exams. NALS holds a series of WebEd sessions with coverage over all parts of the exam as well as exam-specific reviews for the ALP, PLS, and the PP and as well as general exam test taking tips.

- The NALS® WebEd program is the place where NALS hosts webinars on various topics of interest to its members and others in the legal support industry. Sessions are expert-driven with both a visual and audio presentation to give the attendee an all-around great experience. NALS members enjoy a number of free WebEd sessions and receive a discount on all other sessions offered in this format.

- NALS® offers an online Legal Training Course hosted by Stetson University. Check the NALS® website at http://www.nals.org for more information.

- The NALS® OnDemand Library offers members a valuable education resource. The OnDemand Library holds a listing of past webinars and podcasts available for download, 20+ presentations from the most popular conference sessions, a catalog of Jett Award winning chapter project outlines, the Ethics Series, The NALS Guide to Model Competencies for Legal Secretaries, and full issues of past @LAW magazines in PDF format. Members can download the materials to their mobile devices and tablets.

- Through the NALS® Career Center, education and career services are now combined to deliver the ultimate platform built with the tools to meet members' professional learning objectives. The NALS Career Center is part of the Legal Job Exchange, which gives its members' résumés more exposure to aid in a more comprehensive job search. Members can post résumés, receive job alerts via email, and apply for jobs online!

§ 1.5.1 NALS® Programs—Accredited Legal Professional (ALP®) certification

One way to demonstrate one's preparedness for the demanding field of law is by becoming an Accredited Legal Professional (ALP®). This certification is awarded after passing a four-hour, three-part examination that covers:

1. Written Communication
2. Office Procedures and Legal Knowledge
3. Ethics, Human Relations, and Judgment

This exam was formerly known as Accredited Legal Secretary (ALS). In order to more fully embrace the diversity of legal professionals entering the workforce and provide those individuals with certifications reflecting that diversity, NALS has adapted the name of its Accredited Legal Secretary certification to Accredited Legal Professional (ALP). As of May 1, 2013, any persons who attain or have attained this certification may use either the ALS or ALP designation.

§ 1.5.2 NALS® Programs—Certified Legal Professional (CLP®) or Professional Legal Secretary (PLS®) certification

CLP® is the designation for the lawyer's assistant who wants to be identified as exceptional. It certifies a lawyer's assistant as an individual who possesses the foundation to perform substantive legal tasks; demonstrates a mastery of office and people skills; and has the ability to interact on a professional level with lawyers, clients, secretaries, lawyer's assistants, legal assistants, office administrators, judges, and court officials. Working under the direct supervision of a practicing lawyer or judge, the CLP® certified legal professional is expected to assume responsibility, exercise initiative and judgment, and make decisions within the scope of assigned authority. The certified legal professional has a working knowledge of procedural law and the law library and is capable of drafting correspondence, legal documents, and court documents under the direct supervision of an attorney.

The full-day examination includes four areas of testing:

1. Written Communication
2. Office Procedures and Technology
3. Ethics and Judgment
4. Legal Knowledge and Skills

This exam was formerly known as Professional Legal Secretary (PLS). In order to more fully embrace the diversity of legal professionals entering the workforce and provide those individuals with certifications reflecting that diversity, NALS has adapted the name of its Professional Legal Secretary certification to Certified Legal Professional (CLP). As of June 1, 2016, any persons who attain or have attained this certification may use either the PLS or CLP designation.

§ 1.5.3 NALS® Programs—Professional Paralegal (PP®) certification

PP® (Professional Paralegal) certification is an attainable goal for paralegals or legal assistants who wish to be identified as exceptional in all areas of law. The certificate is received after passing a one-day, four-part comprehensive paralegal certification examination. Any person who has five years of experience performing paralegal or legal assistant duties may take the exam. A candidate may receive a partial waiver of one year if the candidate has a post-secondary degree, other certification, or a paralegal certificate; a candidate with a paralegal degree may receive a two-year partial waiver.

This full-day examination covers four areas:

1. Written Communications
2. Legal Knowledge and Skills
3. Ethics and Judgment Skills
4. Substantive Law

§ 1.5.4 Membership in NALS®—The certification examinations

The ALP®, CLP®, and PP® examinations are administered concurrently nationwide on the first Saturday in March and the last Saturday in September. Each exam is also offered at special times for schools and colleges. Applications and fees must be postmarked by January 1 for the March examination and by August 1 for the September examination. The ALP® examination is now available online.

§ 1.5.5 NALS® Programs—Specialty Certificate

The Specialty Certificate, available to a Certified CLP/PLS or Certified PP, is received after obtaining 50 continuing legal education credit hours in one of the specialty tracks designated by NALS®: Litigation/Civil Law, Corporate Law, or Estate Planning/Family Law.

§ 1.5.6 NALS® Programs—NALS® contact information

Anyone interested in membership or information on programs and available products is encouraged to write or call:

NALS, Inc.
PO Box 470348
Tulsa, OK 74147
918/582-5188 (Telephone)
918/582-5907 (Facsimile)
http://www.nals.org (Website)

Information may also be obtained from local or state chapter membership or education chairpersons.

Chapter 2

Ethics

KeyCite®: Cases and other legal materials listed in KeyCite Scope can be researched through the KeyCite service on Westlaw®. Use KeyCite to check citations for form, parallel references, prior and later history, and comprehensive citator information, including citations to other decisions and secondary materials.

---

§ 2.1   Definition

Ethics are principles of conduct that govern an individual or profession. In law, the ethics principles that govern the practice of law also apply to the work of nonlawyer employees or contractors.

§ 2.2   ABA Code of Professional Responsibility and Canons of Judicial Ethics

In 1908, the American Bar Association (ABA) adopted the Canons of Professional Ethics. This set of guidelines left many questions unanswered, and in 1969, the ABA adopted the Code of Professional Responsibility and Code of Judicial Conduct to replace them. The Code of Professional Responsibility also left unanswered questions and had limited disciplinary application. In 1983, the ABA adopted the Model Rules of Professional Conduct to replace the Code of Professional Responsibility. The Model Rules of Professional Conduct with current amendments can be accessed on the Internet at http://www.ab anet.org/cpr/mrpc/model_rules.html. Most states have adopted the

Model Rules of Professional Conduct or rules patterned after them with revisions by the state. Lawyer's assistants should consult the rules of professional conduct of the state in which they are employed. Links to the state rules of professional conduct and other state ethics materials are provided on the ABA website.

§ 2.3   Ethical considerations and disciplinary procedures

While the Code of Professional Responsibility (Code) and the Model Rules of Professional Conduct (Model Rules) are similar, there are significant differences. The Code consists of canons that defined standards of professional conduct, ethical considerations that interpreted the canons, and mandatory disciplinary rules. The Model Rules offer disciplinary guidelines, but disciplinary action is determined by the state. The model rules also are not intended to assess civil liability against the lawyer.

Under the Model Rules, there is greater emphasis on professional functions and responsibilities, regulation of trust accounts, potential conflicts of interest, and a requirement for written consent and waivers of conflicts. Disclosure of client confidences, solicitation and advertising, and fees and fee splitting are also addressed. The Model Rules also concern disabled clients; the lawyer as advisor or intermediary; the lawyer as author; relatives in competing firms; successive government and private employment; disqualifications; organizations as clients; supervision of associates, junior lawyers, and paralegals; and reporting misconduct. The ABA has also adopted the Model Code of Judicial Ethics.

The lawyer employer is responsible for the conduct of office staff and can be disciplined for an employee's violation of the state code of ethics. Although the lawyer's assistant cannot be disciplined by their state bar, civil lawsuits, loss of employment, and criminal charges may result from a failure to uphold state ethical codes.

The Model Rules are divided into eight sections. The ABA has also included comments that aid in understanding practical application of the rules and frequently issue ethical opinions to guide attorneys in the rapidly developing areas of law.

§ 2.4   Client-lawyer relationship

The "Client-lawyer Relationship" section of the Model Rules governs all aspects of the client-lawyer relationship, including competence, scope of representation, representation with due diligence, and regular communication with the client. Additionally, this section provides rules regarding the reasonableness of fees, confidentiality, conflicts of interest, disqualification, representing an organization or individual under a disability, and the safekeeping of client property. Of particular importance to the lawyer's assistant are the rules governing competence (Rule 1.1), confidentiality (Rule 1.6), and conflicts of interest (Rules 1.7 to 1.12).

In order to assist a lawyer in their requirements under Rule 1.1 (Competency) a lawyer's assistant should maintain and upgrade skills often to assist the lawyer in competently representing the client.

Client information is confidential and must be kept confidential. Information learned at work should not be discussed outside of the office, no matter how tempting it may be. If an assistant is put in a situation where work is going to be discussed outside the office, the assistant should first present the situation to the supervising attorney before giving out information. It is always better to err on the side of nondisclosure.

Regular communication with clients is extremely important. One of the most common bar complaints is lack of communication from the lawyer. The lawyer's assistant often acts as liaison between client and lawyer. It is helpful to encourage the lawyer to return client phone calls promptly and prepare periodic status reports.

The lawyer's assistant can greatly assist the lawyer in identifying conflicts of interest. If the assistant has knowledge of a potential conflict, the lawyer's assistant should immediately bring the potential conflict to the lawyer's attention. For instance, the lawyer's assistant may have done business with an actual or potential client, may have worked on the same matter elsewhere, or may have worked on another matter involving a potential client. Lawyers need such information to evaluate the existence of real or perceived conflicts of interest. The lawyer's assistant can also assist the lawyer in maintaining an accurate, up-to-date list of current and former clients so the lawyer can run a conflicts check before representation.

§ 2.5 Counselor

Rules in this section require the lawyer to exercise judgment and regulate when acting as (1) an advisor to a client, (2) providing an evaluation of a matter affecting a client for the use of someone other than the client, and (3) when providing third-party neutral services as a mediator or arbitrator.

§ 2.6 Advocate

Rules in this section define the lawyer's responsibilities when acting in a judicial proceeding or before a legislative or administrative tribunal. The rules address the filing of unmeritorious claims or the use of delay tactics. The rules also require candor to the court and fairness to opposing parties and counsel. Finally, the rules govern trial and pretrial publicity, define when a lawyer may act as a witness, and contain specific rules for prosecutors.

The lawyer's assistant should not talk to the media at all. Calls from the press should be routed to the lawyer or to the firm's designated media contact, following firm policy exactly.

The lawyer's assistant often becomes a sounding board for the lawyer to vent frustration with a client, judge, or opposing counsel. Regardless of how the lawyer has described them or how the assistant feels, the assistant must be polite and respectful when dealing with these people.

§ 2.7   Transactions with persons other than clients

Lawyers must be truthful and must disclose material facts if necessary to avoid a client's criminal or fraudulent act that may seriously injure another. Lawyers must also be cautious in dealing with unrepresented persons and cannot communicate with an adverse party that the lawyer knows is represented by counsel. The lawyer must also show respect for the rights of third parties.

§ 2.8   Law firms and associations

This section defines the responsibilities of lawyers and nonlawyers. The rules regulate the independence of the lawyer and prohibit the unauthorized practice of law. The lawyer is responsible for the conduct of all firm employees. The lawyer's assistant should become familiar with how *unauthorized practice of law* is defined in the state where the assistant is employed. For instance, a lawyer's assistant may be asked to draft a simple will for a relative. The lawyer's assistant has typed hundreds of wills, has the basic format on the computer, and only has to change the names. In some states this is unauthorized practice of law, whether the assistant is paid or not. In other states, it may be permissible. The unauthorized practice of law can also create civil liability and have criminal consequences.

§ 2.9   Public service

The Model Rules of Professional Conduct encourage the lawyer to render public service. The term "pro bono" comes from the Latin *pro bono publico*, which means "for the public good." The ABA describes the parameters of *pro bono* for practicing lawyers in Model Rule 6.1, which states that lawyers should aspire to render at least 50 hours of *pro bono* legal services per year, with an emphasis that these services be provided to people of limited means or nonprofit organizations that serve the poor. This rule also defines the lawyer-client relationship when the lawyer is a member of a legal services organization or law reform group.

§ 2.10   Information about legal services

Rules in this section regulate how a lawyer may describe the lawyer's practice area, advertise, solicit business directly, and use firm names and letterhead. The United States Supreme Court ruled that a complete ban on lawyer advertising was a violation of First Amendment rights, but states are free to regulate the manner and extent of advertising and solicitation of business. A lawyer may claim to specialize in a field of law under limited circumstances that vary significantly from state to state. A lawyer can disclose licensing to appear before government agencies—e.g., the Patent and Trademark Office, the Federal Communications Commission, or the Internal Revenue Service—to prospective clients.

The lawyer's assistant's friends and relatives will often ask about the lawyer's specialty. The assistant should feel free to respond to these questions but be careful not to promote the employer's capabilities or compare the lawyer's qualifications with those of other lawyers. The assistant's opinion may carry inappropriate weight because the assistant is considered "in the know." The lawyer's assistant also must not violate Canon 6 of the NALS® Code of Ethics and Professional Responsibility, which prohibits solicitation of business on a lawyer's behalf.

§ 2.11 Maintaining the integrity of the profession

Rules in this last section define professional misconduct and require lawyers to comply with information requests from disciplinary boards. The lawyer is prohibited from making false statements about the qualifications or integrity of a judge or political candidate. The lawyer is also required to report misconduct or a possible rule violation by another lawyer to the appropriate body.

This section's purpose is to enhance the public perception of the integrity of the legal profession. The lawyer's assistant can help in this goal by acting with honesty and integrity both professionally and personally and by avoiding disparaging the legal profession and the judicial system.

§ 2.12 NALS® Code of Ethics and Professional Responsibility (with discussion)

Members of NALS® are bound by the objectives of this Association and the standards of conduct required of the legal profession.

Every member shall:

- Encourage respect for the law and the administration of justice;
- Observe rules governing privileged communications and confidential information;
- Promote and exemplify high standards of loyalty, cooperation, and courtesy;
- Perform all duties of the profession with integrity and competence; and
- Pursue a high order of professional attainment.

Integrity and high standards of conduct are fundamental to the success of our professional association. This Code is promulgated by NALS® and accepted by its members to accomplish these ends.

Canon 1.	***Members of this association shall maintain a high degree of competency and integrity through continuing education to better assist the legal profession in fulfilling its duty to provide quality legal services to the public.***

The purpose of continuing legal education, supported by NALS®, is to expand the knowledge of NALS® members, to increase member self-esteem, and to help members better deliver legal services. NALS® encourages continuing education by offering institutes, seminars, and courses.

NALS® encourages every lawyer's assistant to obtain the designation of ALP® . . . a basic certification for the legal professional, PLS®/CLP® . . . an advanced certification for the legal professional, and PP®, Professional Paralegal (for paralegals and legal assistants). Certification is a standard of excellence that signifies above-average skills and abilities, initiative, good judgment, and dedication to the profession.

The growth of a profession and the attainment and maintenance of individual competence requires ongoing incorporation of new concepts and techniques. Continuing education enables law office staff to become aware of new developments and improve skills used in delivery of legal services. A NALS® member recognizes the importance of continuing legal education. Professional competence is each member's responsibility.

A NALS® member also recognizes the necessity of membership and participation in a professional association. One of the hallmarks of any profession is its professional association, founded to provide standards and guidelines for the growth and development of the profession. Through professional association, a NALS® member is able to promote cooperative effort with others in the legal community.

For a comparison to other rules of professional responsibility and ethics, see ABA Model Rules of Professional Conduct Rule 1.1. See also Preamble [4], Rule 1.16, Comment [1].

Canon 2.	***Members of this association shall maintain a high standard of ethical conduct and shall contribute to the integrity of the association and the legal profession.***

Ethical conduct and integrity are the backbone of the legal profession. Because of the close professional relationship of lawyer and NALS® member, it is essential that the member maintain an equally high standard of conduct. The client expects and deserves ethical conduct and integrity from the lawyer and all nonlawyer staff members.

For a comparison to other rules of professional responsibility and ethics, see ABA Model Rules of Professional Conduct Rules 8.1, 8.2, 8.3, and 8.4. See also Rules 5.1, 5.3, and 5.5.

> **Canon 3.** *Members of this association shall avoid a conflict of interest pertaining to a client matter.*

Loyalty is an essential element in the lawyer's relationship to a client. A member of NALS® acting as a legal assistant or paralegal must disclose any conflict of interest to the lawyer before representation is undertaken. In the event a conflict occurs after representation has begun, the member must disclose that to the lawyer immediately.

For a comparison to other rules of professional responsibility and ethics, see ABA Model Rules of Professional Conduct Rules 1.7(b), 1.8, 1.9, 1.10, 1.11 and 1.12.

> **Canon 4.** *Members of this association shall preserve and protect the confidences and privileged communications of a client.*

The obligation of a NALS® member to preserve the confidences of a client continues after the client stops employing the lawyer and after the member leaves the lawyer's employ. Although it may seem extreme, these confidences are held forever. A client must feel free to discuss anything with the lawyer, and the lawyer must be equally free to ask for additional information. The normal operation of a law office exposes nonlawyer employees—particularly those with access to files—to confidential client information. None of the lawyer's assistant's responsibilities is more important than preserving client confidences. If there is any doubt about what information may be disclosed, the assistant should seek advice from the lawyer. It is best to say, "I'll have to check with the lawyer" before giving information to a client, another lawyer, or a third party. It is always better to ask questions before an error is made.

For a comparison to other rules of professional responsibility and ethics, see ABA Model Rules of Professional Conduct Rule 1.6, 1.9, and 1.18.

> **Canon 5.** *Members of this association shall exercise care in using independent professional judgment and in determining the extent to which a client may be assisted without the presence of a lawyer and shall not act in matters involving professional legal judgment.*

It is permissible—and often occurs—that lawyers delegate tasks to members of the law office staff. An important ABA ethical opinion held:

> A lawyer can employ lay secretaries, lay investigators, lay detectives, lay researchers, accountants, lay scriveners, nonlawyer draftsmen, or nonlawyer researchers. In fact, he/she or the attorney may

employ nonlawyers to do any task for him/her except counsel clients about law matters, engage directly in the practice of law, appear in court, or appear in formal proceedings as part of the judicial process, so long as it is he who takes the work and vouches for it to the client and becomes responsible to the client.

ABA Comm. on Professional Ethics, Formal Op. 316 (1967).

For a comparison to other rules of professional responsibility and ethics, see ABA Model Rules of Professional Conduct Rules 2.1, 5.3, and 5.5(b).

Canon 6.	***Members of this association shall not solicit legal business on behalf of a lawyer.***

A lawyer should be selected on an informed basis. Advice and recommendation of relatives, friends, acquaintances, business associates, or other lawyers and information about the lawyer and practice area may help. A layperson is best served if the recommendation is disinterested. For the recommendation to be disinterested, the lawyer should not solicit business, and the lawyer's assistant should not solicit business on the lawyer's behalf, either because the lawyer requested it or independently.

For a comparison to other rules of professional responsibility and ethics, see ABA Model Rules of Professional Conduct Rule 7.3.

Canon 7.	***Members of this association, unless permitted by law, shall not perform legal functions except under the direct supervision of a lawyer and shall not advertise or contract with members of the general public for the performance of paralegal functions.***

See discussions under Canons 5, 8, and 9 and the comparisons to other rules of professional responsibility and ethics referred to in those discussions.

For a comparison to other rules of professional responsibility and ethics, see ABA Model Rules of Professional Conduct Rules 5.3 and 5.5.

Canon 8.	***Members of this association, unless permitted by law, shall not perform any of the duties restricted to lawyers or do things which lawyers themselves may not do and shall assist in preventing the unauthorized practice of law.***

Canon 8 is similar to Canon 9, but Canon 8 specifically states that members may not do what lawyers are not permitted to do. Canon 8 highlights that the lawyer's assistant should not give legal advice to clients, as that is the lawyer's exclusive province.

Canon 9.	*Members of this association not licensed to practice law shall not engage in the practice of law as defined by statutes or court decisions.*

The definition of unauthorized practice of law varies from state to state. A NALS® member should determine the appropriate definition and work to ensure that neither the assistant nor the lawyer violates it.

A NALS® member may perform tasks assigned by a lawyer so long as the lawyer maintains a direct client relationship, supervises the work, and has complete professional responsibility for the work product. Maintenance of the lawyer's direct client relationship does not preclude a law office staff member from meeting with the client to carry out duties assigned by the lawyer. The lawyer's assistant should ensure, at the start of any client meeting, that the assistant's status as a lawyer's assistant is known by the client. Ideally, the lawyer will have disclosed the role of the assistant at the first client meeting or in prior communications. Nevertheless, the lawyer's assistant should not assume the client is aware of or remembers this and should verbally identify the assistant's status at the start of each client meeting.

In general, a lawyer's assistant can perform any task delegated by the lawyer, so long as there is no prohibition by statute, court rule, decision, or other rule or regulation. These tasks include, but are not limited to: interviewing and maintaining client contacts as long as the client is aware of the lawyer's assistant's status; locating and interviewing witnesses, so long as the witness is aware of the assistant's status; performing statistical and legal research for the attorney; drafting legal documents, correspondence, and pleadings for attorney review and signature; summarizing depositions, interrogatories, and testimony for attorney review; and attending execution of wills, real estate closings, and administrative or court hearings with the attorney. The lawyer's assistant may also write and sign letters, so long as the assistant's status is clear and the letter does not contain independent legal opinions or advice.

Some states have adopted requirements for the practice of paralegals or legal assistants. Any NALS® member employed as, or whose duties include those of, a paralegal or legal assistant should consult the appropriate state requirements. This canon is intended to protect the public from receiving legal services from unqualified individuals.

For a comparison to other rules of professional responsibility and ethics, see ABA Model Rules of Professional Conduct Rule 5.5(b).

Canon 10.	*Members of this association shall do all other things incidental, necessary, or expedient to enhance professional responsibility and participation in the administration of justice and public service in cooperation with the legal profession.*

§ 2.13 Summary

If a lawyer's assistant adheres to the NALS® Code of Ethics and Professional Responsibility, neither the lawyer nor the firm should receive disciplinary action for state ethical code violations based on the assistant's acts or omissions.

Simply stated, the lawyer's assistant should:

- Work continually to upgrade skills and knowledge.
- Be honest and forthright in and out of the office, display exemplary conduct, and inspire public confidence in the legal system.
- Not solicit business for the lawyer or firm.
- Not practice law by any means, including giving legal advice or preparing documents without attorney supervision.
- Not discuss any client or case outside the office or discuss a client's case with the client or opposing counsel unless authorized to do so.
- Be certain to advise the lawyer or firm if he or she knows any of the opposing parties in a matter being handled in the office.
- Do all work competently.
- Follow instructions concerning client funds.

Working in an atmosphere where lawyers and support staff alike are required to adhere to a strict code of ethics, including requirements to continue learning and to uphold the judicial system, is challenging and rewarding.

Chapter 3

The Law Office

KeyCite®: Cases and other legal materials listed in KeyCite Scope can be researched through the KeyCite service on Westlaw®. Use KeyCite to check citations for form, parallel references, prior and later history, and comprehensive citator information, including citations to other decisions and secondary materials.

---

§ 3.1   Getting to know the law firm

There are three areas of focus that will help the lawyer's assistant who is new on the job. First, an office policy and procedures manual will spell out the day-to-day operations of the law firm and what is expected of the staff. In some firms, there may not be a policy and procedures manual. In others, the manual is well thought out and given to each new employee on the first day of work. Regardless of the format, it is a good place to begin, and each new lawyer's assistant is responsible to find and study it.

The lawyer's assistant who is new to a firm also needs to know who the boss is—hopefully, this was covered in the interview—and who the boss's boss is. Where does the lawyer fall in the chain of command? What is the lawyer's department? The new lawyer's assistant also needs to know who runs things. The firm CEO, the managing partner, the person who runs the file room, the person who runs the copy center and mail room, the head of personnel, and the secretarial supervisor are all must-know players in the new lawyer's assistant's work life. It may take a little effort to find out who these people are, but it is well worth the trouble. Once the lawyer's assistant has been introduced, the assistant should practice ten-foot attitude with these people. When any of them come within ten feet and are not engaged in conversation with anyone else, the lawyer's assistant should smile and greet them by name. It is important to establish a positive relationship early on with management. If a negative event should occur later, management will remember the assistant as having been cooperative and friendly and will tend to interpret the negative event in the assistant's favor.

Finally, in a perfect world, every lawyer's assistant's desk would have a job description available on the first day of work. However, the information available to new employees varies enormously from firm to firm.

In the following sections, the most frequent duties of a lawyer's assistant will be explored in detail, along with information about the general operation of a law firm.

§ 3.2 Law firm personnel

The following are the personnel one will typically see in a law firm, although in a small firm, one individual may fill several roles, while other roles are considered optional or are outsourced:

- Lawyers
- Paralegals/legal assistants
- Receptionists
- Lawyer's assistants/secretaries
- File coordinator/file clerks
- Bookkeepers/accountants
- Law clerks
- Office administrator/office manager
- Administrative secretaries
- Word processing personnel
- Computer/information technology personnel
- Human Resources/benefits personnel
- Marketing personnel

§ 3.3   Job requirements

The basic requirements for the lawyer's assistant are good skills in typing, spelling, composition, grammar, machine transcription, proofreading, and sometimes speedwriting or shorthand. In addition to these, strong computer skills are necessary in word processing and, depending on the job, in spreadsheet, presentation, calendaring-docketing, time-billing, or database programs.

§ 3.3.1   Job requirements—Accuracy

When transcribing dictation or making document revisions, do so as accurately as possible. Obvious errors can be corrected. If instructions are difficult to follow, ask the lawyer for clarification. Documents should be proofread before turning them over to the lawyer. While it is rarely the case that a single error will cause a catastrophe, legal work is exacting and sometimes a small error will cause big problems. It is the assistant's responsibility to provide the highest quality work possible to reduce the risk that something important will be missed.

§ 3.3.2   Job requirements—Getting the job done

Much of the work in law offices is performed under pressure. Meeting deadlines is a way of life for most lawyers and their support staff. Emergencies are not uncommon, and at times there is simply too much to do. The pressure can be reduced by attending to routine tasks when the office is less busy. Check with each lawyer on each assignment to make sure the deadline is known and organize the work in order of urgency. Supplies, frequently used telephone numbers and addresses, and reference tools should be kept within easy access. The desk should be kept free of clutter to avoid mixing stray materials into correspondence or pleadings while they are being prepared.

§ 3.3.3   Job requirements—Keeping an organized work area

In addition to keeping the work area neat and ready for work, the assistant may also be responsible for keeping the lawyer's desk or office neat and orderly, as well as any conference rooms the lawyer uses. Obviously, this is done with the lawyer's consent, but putting the lawyer's area in order can promote efficiency. Client files and law books should be returned to their proper places when no longer needed. Some lawyers need help, too, in organizing materials that need to be filed.

§ 3.3.4   Job requirements—Personal habits

Attorneys and law firms demand a high level of professionalism and social etiquette from their staff. In addition, some clients may have strong preferences about the personal behavior of the lawyer's support staff. Office behavior that does not fit with that standard can cause problems. Three areas that can cause trouble are chewing gum, smoking, and swearing.

While chewing gum occasionally to freshen the breath is not likely to offend, it should be avoided when clients or lawyers are present. The level of language permitted in a law office varies a great deal. The best approach for the staff is to talk in a manner that is professional and courteous. People are rarely offended by language that omits swear words and fairly often offended when they are used. Additionally, when attending events where community lawyers or clients of the law firm might be present, what is said should be said carefully.

§ 3.3.5 Job requirements—Interoffice relationships

Work relationships should be enjoyable for all involved and it takes effort on everyone's part. A key component to good working relationships is the ability to be nonjudgmental and recognize and respect other people's beliefs, views, and practices.

If the assistant's workload is light and someone else is getting behind, the assistant should offer to help. The professional lawyer's assistant will not entertain a "that is not my job" attitude. On the other hand, while friendly helpfulness is appropriate, personal conversation should be curtailed to avoid disturbing others (particularly the lawyers).

If another employee is not completing work assignments, talking excessively on the phone, coming to work late or leaving early, or performing low quality work, the lawyer's assistant should avoid drawing attention to the problem unless it has a direct effect on the assistant's work. Other people will have noted the problem, so no action is necessary. If what the other employee does impacts the assistant's work, the assistant should talk to the person directly. If, after addressing the problem directly with the co-worker, the problem persists, then the lawyer's assistant can talk to the office manager or lawyer.

§ 3.3.6 Job requirements—Punctuality and attendance

Punctuality and good attendance are traits every lawyer looks for in an assistant. The world is divided into two kinds of people: people who are nearly always on time, and people who often are not. There's no evidence to suggest that the punctual are necessarily superior in any other way, but they are present when they are needed, and lawyers care about that. If timeliness is a problem, many firms will allow adjusted hours, and some lawyers prefer to work later in the afternoon. If this option is not available, the assistant will need to make adjustments.

It is very important not to create the impression that one's presence at work is an occasional or casual thing. The assistant who successfully keeps office hours, arrives on time, keeps the set lunch period, and does not leave early sends the message that the assistant is serious about the job. In addition, the assistant who shows up at work every day and plans ahead for appropriate time off as much as possible demonstrates the job is the most important thing on the assistant's plate. Such people are likelier to last in a law office than those who do not.

§ 3.3.7   Job requirements—Handling personal matters

Personal telephone calls and personal business should be taken care of on the assistant's own time. If personal business of an urgent nature must be taken care of during office hours, it should be handled so as not to interfere with the smooth and efficient operation of the office. It is best that personal phone calls not be overheard by other staff members or the lawyers or clients. If it is possible to remove oneself from the work area for such calls, that is a smart move. The use of a personal cellphone in a public area telegraphs the personal nature of the call to everyone nearby. Again, try to move to a private area.

§ 3.4   Client relations

Next to the lawyer, the most important human component of the job is the client. Having positive interactions with the client, maintaining confidentiality, and correctly handling client files are all essential to a successful career in a law firm.

§ 3.4.1   Client relations—Meeting clients

At the initial meeting, a client generally does not yet know the lawyer. The client may have been referred or may have selected the lawyer's name randomly from a directory. The client's first impression of the lawyer is also affected by the lawyer's staff. The lawyer's assistant should have a professional attitude that reflects the good public image the lawyer deserves.

Every effort should be made to see that client appointments are kept on time. If the lawyer is going to be late, call the client or inform the client immediately upon arrival so the client can do something else until the lawyer is available. The client may choose to wait or to reschedule. When the choice is to wait, make the client comfortable by offering a beverage, magazine or newspaper, and, if needed, a telephone or wi-fi access.

Before the conference, the lawyer's assistant should locate the client's file and give it to the lawyer. When the client arrives, the assistant should escort the client to the lawyer's office or conference room, introduce the client, and close the door on the way out. The lawyer's assistant should avoid overhearing the lawyer's conversation with the client, as attorney-client privilege is often destroyed when the conversation includes a third person. The assistant should remain available during the conference to provide any needed materials or perform requested services. If the client is a repeat visitor, the lawyer's assistant should know the client's name and be generally familiar with the case.

The lawyer's assistant should avoid interrupting the lawyer and the client during the meeting. If it is absolutely necessary to interrupt, the lawyer's assistant may call the lawyer in the conference room or may write the message on a note, knock gently on the door, enter and hand the lawyer the note. The assistant should wait briefly to see what the lawyer would like done and then leave quietly. The best practice is to discuss with the lawyer at the beginning of employment how the lawyer wants such situations handled.

§ 3.4.2 Client relations—Confidentiality and privileged communications

The lawyer never discusses a client's business with outsiders. In fact, statements made between the lawyer and the client are protected from forced disclosure to other parties. The information a client gives the lawyer is considered privileged communication. Under most circumstances, the work done on behalf of the client is protected under the work product doctrine or attorney-client privilege.

Information the lawyer's assistant receives from a client in the course of work may also be privileged. Serious consequences may result from revealing information concerning a legal matter or a client's circumstances inappropriately. It is mandatory that the lawyer's assistant not discuss office or client business outside the office.

It is also important not to state to outsiders, including family members and friends, that a certain person was in the office or is a client. The very fact that the lawyer represents a given client may reveal inappropriate information to the public. If a well-known person is known to consult a divorce lawyer, this can be a problem. If a corporate CEO is known to consult a bankruptcy lawyer, this can cause problems not only for the CEO but also for the company.

The client's confidentiality must also be protected in the office. The client's case should not be discussed on a public elevator or near the reception area. Even when lunching with co-workers, it is important not to discuss the case within hearing of other people not involved in the case. The lawyer's assistant should not talk to a client on the telephone about the client's case if the assistant is sitting where others can hear the conversation.

The lawyer's assistant should avoid discussing the client's case with the client except to take a message for the lawyer. As a nonlawyer, the lawyer's assistant cannot give legal advice and should not be seen appearing to do so. The lawyer's assistant should only share information regarding the client's case with the client when specifically instructed to do so by the lawyer.

§ 3.4.3 Client relations—Privacy of client files

If the lawyer's assistant sits in an area where clients or persons who do not work on the same matters approach the desk to talk, the assistant should be sure there are no open files or documents on the desk. If the assistant is working on a document when someone approaches, the assistant should cover the material so that it cannot be read by the person standing there.

§ 3.4.4   Client relations—Client access to documents and files

Some offices make a practice of sending copies of all letters and legal documents relating to a client's case to the client. Others send copies of only certain letters and documents. The best practice is to ask the lawyer at the start of employment what procedures the lawyer prefers to use when sending out correspondence and documents. The lawyer's assistant should also check with the lawyer when correspondence or documentation seems to warrant special handling.

The lawyer's assistant must have the lawyer's permission to show a file to a client. It is usually permissible to remove personal papers such as a marriage certificate or filed tax return and let the client review these papers in the lawyer's assistant's presence. The client should not have access to documents, letters, notes, or the lawyer's work product without the lawyer's permission. The client should never remove anything from the office without prior consent of the lawyer.

All files released from the office should be noted in a release file which includes the name of the person to whom the file was released, the date the file left the office, and the name of the lawyer authorizing release of the file. The person taking the file should sign a receipt for it and the receipt should be placed in the release file. This protects the office in the event of future questions on the file.

§ 3.5   Public relations in the law office

In the course of business, the lawyer's assistant may have dealings with a variety of people who are not clients but may also require special handling.

Judges. Judges should receive immediate attention. The lawyer's appointment should be interrupted; the lawyer should be tracked down and made to answer the phone. If the lawyer is absolutely unavailable, a message should be taken, the lawyer should be located, and the call should be returned at the earliest possible moment.

Clerks of court. Clerks of court are accorded most of the same respect that would be given a judge, because they are the judge's direct representative. The difference is a clerk of court will typically call on some practical or technical aspect of a case—an additional filing is needed, the filing that was sent is incomplete or incorrect, the filing fee was for the wrong amount—and very often the lawyer's assistant may field the clerk of court's request. Those requests are taken seriously and responded to immediately, because if it is important enough for a clerk to call about it, it is something that can prevent the case from going forward.

It is wise to treat every clerk with unfailing courtesy. Clerks have a great deal of power and can make a case go well or poorly simply by the way they choose to do their jobs. Clerks can also be a rich source of information about court business and how various processes are conducted, so the lawyer's assistant in litigation practice will be calling the clerks fairly often. If one clerk cannot answer a question satisfactorily, pleasantly wish the clerk a good day and try calling back later, in hopes of getting a different clerk who can provide the needed help.

Opposing counsel. Opposing counsel come in all flavors. Some are friendly and helpful. Some are bullying. Some are very stern and businesslike. Avoid giving them information that has not been preapproved by the lawyer. Take messages or offer voicemail. The lawyer's assistant should try to avoid conversations with opposing counsel; they may glean information the assistant did not intend to give, or they may attempt to manipulate the assistant. Should opposing counsel express any kind of threat in an attempt to get a quicker response, simply take a message or forward the call to voicemail and assure the opposing counsel the lawyer will be advised of the call as quickly as possible.

Opposing counsel's staff. Opposing counsel's staff may call to request a copy of a pleading, an electronic copy of a discovery document, or some other favor regarding the paperwork of the case. Generally, such requests should be accommodated pleasantly—clear it with a lawyer first if there is any question—as long as they are public documents (already filed in court) or documents that have already been exchanged among the parties. The assistant may need a favor in return later in the case; courtesy is the best choice. Such documents should be mailed or emailed directly to the opposing counsel's secretary; the lawyer may not know what to do with them. If opposing counsel's assistant or paralegal calls requesting information about the lawyer's plans for some aspect of the case, those queries should be deferred to the lawyer, either for instructions on how the assistant should respond or for the lawyer to respond directly.

The press. The lawyer's assistant should review the firm's policy on relations with the media during the first week of work and keep it where it can easily be located later. The firm policy should be followed to the letter when the press contacts the lawyer through the lawyer's assistant. If there is no policy, the lawyer's assistant should make no comments whatsoever about any firm business to the press and take a message or forward the call to voicemail for the lawyer to handle.

The lawyer's family. The lawyer's assistant should learn from the lawyer how to handle calls from family and follow those instructions. Make an extra effort to be pleasant to the lawyer's family, even if the lawyer occasionally acts annoyed at receiving their calls.

The lawyer's friends. Most lawyers have lawyer friends, and some of them may call often. It is important to be friendly, but it is also important to avoid giving them information about a case by accident. Big cases sometimes involve half the lawyers in a smaller city. It is difficult to be certain who is working on a case and in what capacity. The lawyer's nonlawyer friends are often also clients, so again, it is important the lawyer's assistant neither discuss someone else's case nor the client's case, to avoid giving the impression the assistant might be careless about confidential information.

§ 3.6 Lawyer relations

A lawyer may unconsciously play hide-and-seek with the assistant. The lawyer leaves the office and disappears without leaving any clues as to the lawyer's whereabouts. It is essential the lawyer's assistant be able to reach the lawyer on matters that might arise in the lawyer's absence. To provide good client service, the lawyer's assistant should ask where the lawyer is going and when the lawyer will be back in the office. If the lawyer is going out of town, the lawyer's assistant needs a full itinerary, including lodging and a list of daytime meetings. The lawyer should understand that the lawyer's assistant is not checking up; the assistant just wants to be prepared for any emergency that might occur.

The lawyer's assistant may find when opening a new client file that all of the necessary information is not available, such as complete names, addresses, ages, phone numbers, and so on. This might be just an oversight. If it occurs often, the assistant may want to arrange with the lawyer to sit in on the latter part of the initial client interview to obtain the information. In the alternative, the assistant might prepare a checklist or client interview sheet for the lawyer to use during the initial interview.

Many lawyers prefer to maintain a businesslike relationship with their support staff. It is useful to discover the time of day when the lawyer is most likely to be receptive to questions about the practice and preferences regarding office procedures and take advantage of those times to increase one's grasp of how the job should ideally be done. It is helpful to gradually develop a personal rapport with the lawyer, and such a rapport may make a difference in how long the lawyer's assistant remains employed with the law firm. That rapport can be developed by taking an interest in the lawyer's practice and personal preferences and, if appropriate, by taking an interest in the lawyer's family, children, or hobbies. However, the assistant should be cautious about revealing much detail about the assistant's personal life to the lawyer, particularly if one's personal life might seem troubled to an outsider. If the lawyer wants a more personal connection, the lawyer will ask those questions. Some lawyers do not care for an emotional connection, and it is best to let the relationship unfold gradually.

The good lawyer's assistant complements the lawyer by filling in any gaps. The lawyer and assistant work as a team and everyone benefits. The word *synergy* implies a whole that is greater than the sum of its parts. In the law office, one good lawyer and one good lawyer's assistant working as a team can generate work output greater than the total of what each could do separately.

§ 3.7 Answering the telephone

Often the first impression the client gets of a law firm comes from the voice of the person answering the telephone. If that voice is pleasant and the caller hears a smile, the impression will be a positive one. It is a good practice to hesitate a second before picking up the phone, smile, and then answer with a patient and relaxed voice. The professional lawyer's assistant treats each caller with full attention, courtesy, and concern.

§ 3.7.1 Answering the telephone—Rules to follow

Answering the phone badly can create an unfavorable impression on clients, people in the legal community, and the general public. Follow these rules in answering the phone:

- The phone should always be attended.
- Answer the phone by the second ring whenever possible.
- Do not answer the phone while chewing gum or food.
- Use a pleasant, positive voice.
- Do not talk too quickly or too quietly.
- Take time to get the correct spelling of names and verify phone numbers.
- Place the person on hold when leaving the desk to get information, so the caller does not overhear background conversations.
- Always ask the caller if it is permissible to place the caller on hold before doing so,
- When transferring, let the caller know (1) the call is being transferred, (2) to whom, and (3) the extension number.
- Help the client *without* giving legal advice.
- Do not tell the caller where the lawyer is, except when the lawyer is in court, unless specifically instructed otherwise by the lawyer on a case-by-case basis.
- Do not promise a time when the lawyer will return calls.
- Do not quote fees or discuss a caller's case.
- Be attentive and listen without interrupting.
- Talk quietly and calmly to callers that are upset.
- Avoid slang.
- Convey courtesy, sincere interest, and understanding by vocal tone and words.
- Conclude the phone call with a friendly "thank you" or "goodbye."

§ 3.7.2 Answering the telephone—Incoming calls

Procedures for handling incoming calls vary in firms where there is a central receptionist, an operator, or direct dialing. In some firms, calls coming through the receptionist or operator are forwarded directly to the lawyer. In others, the calls are referred to the lawyer's assistant first. The lawyer's assistant can then get any file the lawyer might need for the call or handle the call if the lawyer is unable to take it.

Most firms have direct dial numbers for lawyers and staff as well as a general number which is answered by a receptionist or operator. Direct-dialed calls will usually ring three times at the lawyer's phone before going into voicemail. If there is no answer by either the lawyer or the lawyer's assistant, the call will automatically be routed to the voicemail system, where the caller can leave a message or press zero to speak with a receptionist or operator.

Voicemail allows the caller to leave a digitized message that can be stored on computer media. This allows the receiver to hear the message later and, if desired, add comments and forward the message to someone else. Sometimes the lawyer will opt to have an important message transcribed and placed in a client file.

§ 3.7.3 Answering the telephone—Screening calls

Telephone etiquette suggests that calls be answered by the person to whom they are directed, and few lawyers have all calls screened as a normal procedure. There will be circumstances, however, when it is necessary to screen calls.

The assistant must be careful not to be rude in an effort to determine who is calling. A simple "May I tell him who is calling?" is usually sufficient. By knowing in advance who is calling, the lawyer can get any information needed to handle the call efficiently. When a call has been screened and the lawyer does not wish to take the call, the lawyer's assistant must be tactful. "Ms. Smith is unable to take a call right now" is a polite approach. Then the lawyer's assistant should offer to direct the call to voicemail or take a complete message and assure the caller that the message will be given to the lawyer as soon as possible. Some lawyers are very good about returning calls; others are not. If the lawyer needs to be reminded to return calls, the assistant can keep a record of messages given to the lawyer. Message pads that make carbonless copies are very useful for this purpose.

Never promise the lawyer will call; promise only that the message will be delivered promptly. If the lawyer has a reason for not wanting to return the call, the lawyer is then free to make the choice. Avoid giving a false reason for a lawyer's unwillingness to take a call, in case the lawyer wishes to make an excuse later in a different way.

§ 3.7.4 Answering the telephone—Helping the client

The client does need to feel that someone is concerned. Whether the lawyer is out of the office or just unavailable, the lawyer's assistant can always ask if there is some way the assistant can help. The assistant can then evaluate whether to contact the lawyer away from the office, interrupt what the lawyer is doing, or refer the client's problem to another member of the firm.

Calls from any irate client should be transferred as quickly as possible to the lawyer. In the absence of the lawyer, the lawyer's assistant should listen and give the angry client an opportunity to clear the air. When it is apparent, as it usually will be, that the assistant cannot give any immediate assistance, the assistant should tell the caller that the message will be delivered to the lawyer as quickly as possible and follow through to make sure that happens.

§ 3.7.5   Answering the telephone—When the caller is on hold

When a call is on hold, check back frequently and remind the lawyer if it is taking too long to answer the call. If it appears the lawyer is going to be tied up for a while, ask the caller if it is possible to take a message and have the lawyer call back.

§ 3.8   Outgoing telephone calls

Procedures for outgoing telephone calls address long-distance service, conference calls, placing calls for the lawyer, and maintaining lists of frequently called numbers.

§ 3.8.1   Outgoing telephone calls—Calling long distance

Follow firm procedures for identifying client-chargeable long-distance calls. Many offices have telephone systems which require the caller to input the client-matter number prior to placing the call. Other law firms use handwritten logs which include the date, the phone number called, a brief description, and the client-matter number. When calling long distance, the lawyer's assistant should also check the time zone before placing the call to be sure the other office will be open.

§ 3.8.2   Outgoing telephone calls—Conference calls

Conference calls (a telephone conversation among more than two persons) can be initiated in three ways. Some in-house phone systems allow the caller to keep adding participants to a conference call by pushing a button, entering the next phone number, and pushing the conference call button again. Some in-house conference call phone systems only allow three participants; others allow six or more.

The second way to institute a conference call is to call a commercial telephone service, provide names and phone numbers for the participants, the approximate length of the call, and the date and time. At the designated time, the carrier then calls each participant and adds that person to the call.

The third method also uses a commercial service. The service is advised of the date and time, the number of participants, the approximate length of the call, and the name and company of the person initiating the call. The initiating caller is given a call-in telephone number and sometimes a conference-call code to provide to each participant.

Conference calls are time consuming to arrange. With the near-universality of email and the capability of contacting everyone at once, email requests for participants' availability and follow-up emails with conference time and call-in information, if needed, are likely the most efficient approach.

Conference call technology is much richer than it once was. In addition to the simple audio conference call, today video conferencing using computer support and television cameras, or webcams is possible. The lawyer's assistant should learn what kinds of video conferencing are available in the law firm and how to set up video conference calls.

§ 3.8.3 Outgoing telephone calls—Placing the lawyer's calls

Telephone etiquette suggests that calls be placed by the person actually making the call. However, some lawyers prefer to have their assistants place their calls for them. If the lawyer prefers to have the assistant place the call, the assistant should put the lawyer on the call as soon as the call is being connected with the person being called. The person initiating the call should do the waiting, and the assistant should be sure the lawyer is aware of adverse reactions by people who have been kept waiting.

§ 3.8.4 Outgoing telephone calls—Frequently called numbers

The lawyer's assistant should keep an accurate, up-to-date record of names, addresses, and phone numbers of clients and others who are commonly contacted by the lawyer or the lawyer's assistant. These can be kept in a card file, in a notebook, or on the assistant's computerized contact list. It should include numbers of the courts, process servers, court reporters, insurance adjusters and agents, tax bureaus, office supply firms, home phone numbers of office employees, and so forth. This may also be a good place to note the lawyer's social security number and bar registration number.

One very convenient way of maintaining phone numbers and client information in one location where they can all be easily accessed is to create a client contact sheet for each new client and a matter contact sheet for each new matter. Each contact sheet should include information regarding the client such as address and phone numbers. The client's secretary or staff members can be added if they are contacted periodically. The contact sheet becomes very useful in litigation matters, where it contains client contact information; contact information on the opposing party and, if represented, opposing party's counsel; any other parties to the litigation or their counsel; court address, case name, judge's name, and clerk's name as needed; expert witness contact information; fact witness contact information; and a list of all firm attorneys active in the case. The contact sheet can be adapted to any type of matter. The only rule is that each and every piece of useful information should be added to the contact sheet, labeled so anyone using the sheet can tell what it is, and organized so it can be found. The contact sheet remains on the computer for computer access and revisions as needed, and it can be printed out for inclusion in a desk reference notebook.

§ 3.9   Facsimile or fax

Facsimile or fax machines are electronic machines used to transmit reproduced images of documents or photographs over standard phone lines. The machine optically scans the document to be sent and converts the image into digitized data transmitted over the phone by modem to a fax machine on the receiving end, which converts the data back into its original image. Some firms use computer systems that allow faxes to be sent or received on the user's computer.

There are confidentiality issues associated with the use of the fax machine. First, it may be necessary to fax a document to a client at a fax machine in a public area at the client's business. If so, a courtesy call to the client or the client's secretary before the fax is sent is a must. The second concern is transmittal of a facsimile concerning the client's case to a public place, such as a hotel at which a lawyer may be staying on business. If the client owns a business near the hotel, the client's name and identifying information should be *redacted* (whited out, blacked out, or removed) before sending the facsimile to a public fax machine. The client's private business is unlikely to remain private for long if handled by hotel staff in the client's home town.

Finally, it is often necessary to send a hard copy to follow up a faxed document. Check with the lawyer for the lawyer's preference or check for a firm policy.

§ 3.10   Handling incoming mail

Following are the steps in handling incoming mail:

1. Sort the mail into stacks of expedited and Certified Mail, First-Class letters, routine mail, and advertising or junk mail. Begin processing the mail with the expedited and Certified Mail.

2. Be careful when opening envelopes not to slit material in the envelope.

3. Empty each envelope completely; check carefully to see that everything has been removed.

4. Fasten any enclosures to the letter. If the enclosures are small, they should be attached to the front of the letter; larger enclosures are attached to the back of the letter. If any enclosures mentioned in the letter are missing, make a note of this on the front of the letter.

5. Before destroying the envelope:
   a. Be sure the return address and name of the sender are on the letter; if not, staple the envelope to the back of the letter.
   b. If the date of the letter is more than one day earlier than the postmark or a certificate of mailing states a date that is different from the postmark, attach the envelope to the back of the letter.

6. Mend the letter or other contents with tape if they have been damaged in the process of opening the envelope.

7. Date-stamp the letter. Also date-stamp copies of documents received from other lawyers, but do not date-stamp any original document (other than letters).

8. Do not open mail marked "Personal and Confidential" or any other mail that is obviously personal. If personal mail is opened accidentally, return it to the envelope unread.

§ 3.10.1   Handling incoming mail—Special touches

The lawyer's assistant may be asked to read the mail, underlining or highlighting important points, especially dates. It is advisable to highlight a copy of the letter, not the original. This method saves the lawyer time because only a quick review of the letter is necessary. Enter any important dates in the lawyer's and the lawyer's assistant's calendar and inform the person responsible for the firm's docket control system of all pertinent dates.

Some lawyers prefer to have the assistant make a note of estimated time to read and respond to the mail. These notes can be added to the lawyer's calendar or timesheet along with notes on the time spent on appointments, hearings, and so forth. The lawyer then reviews the estimated time entries and revises or adds to them as needed.

When appropriate, the lawyer's assistant may draft a response to correspondence for the lawyer's review and signature, if the likely response is known. The mail and the draft response are placed together on the lawyer's desk. This level of service is often considered a paralegal or legal assistant's task and can be billed to the client, if the lawyer approves.

§ 3.11   Preparing outgoing mail

Procedures for handling outgoing mail vary greatly. Large firms often have a central mail department. In small firms, mail is often the responsibility of the lawyer's assistant.

Each lawyer's assistant should be responsible for folding and inserting the correspondence into envelopes. When inserting letters into envelopes, verify that the letter has been signed, all enclosures are included, and all items are placed in the proper envelope. If a document accompanies the letter, make sure the lawyer has signed the document, too.

Because familiarity with the correspondence going out is so important in avoiding mailing errors, the person who prepared a letter or document should also prepare the document for mailing. It is tempting on a busy afternoon to ask someone else to take care of copying and stuffing envelopes, but if this is done, great care must be taken to be sure the person helping knows precisely what goes where.

§ 3.11.1 Preparing outgoing mail—Express mail

Many law offices use Express Mail services. Express Mail provides delivery service 365 days a year. Express Mail packaging supplies (envelopes, boxes, tubes) are available free from the local post office. Express Mail rates are based on the weight of the piece, without regard for how far the piece travels; however, there is also a flat rate for anything mailed in the special flat rate envelope provided by the United States Postal Services (USPS). A list of the cities in which Express Mail services are available can be obtained from the post office.

§ 3.11.2 Preparing outgoing mail—Overnight delivery

Several commercial services offer next day delivery. These services include United Parcel Service, Federal Express (FedEx), and DHL, among others. Overnight deliveries are typically sent in the carrier's packaging. Pickups may be scheduled daily, or special pickups may be scheduled for Saturday pickup or pickup at other than the usual pickup times. If a pickup time is missed and a special pickup cannot be scheduled, it is important to know where the package or envelope can be dropped off for same-day handling. Pickups can usually be scheduled on the carrier's website, and information about drop-off points should also be available there.

There are times when overnight delivery, regardless of cost, is preferable. Mail going to any member of Congress since September 11, 2001, will be held up for several weeks in security checks. Anything that needs to be delivered quickly to a member of Congress must be sent by overnight delivery. A letter that does not need to be received in hard copy can be sent by email to the member's chief of staff or other senior aide.

§ 3.11.3 Preparing outgoing mail—First Class and Priority Mail

First-Class Mail consists of letters, postcards, greeting cards, business reply mail, bills, and checks. Certain items, including handwritten or typewritten material, bills, statements of account or invoices, credit cards, and all matter sealed or otherwise closed against inspection must be mailed by First-Class Mail. First-Class Mail that weighs more than 13 ounces is handled as *Priority Mail*.

Priority Mail provides air mail service for First-Class Mail weighing over 13 ounces and under 70 pounds. The maximum length and girth combined is 108 inches. The rate is determined by the distance the letter is to travel and by the weight of the letter. The actual fee can be calculated using the Rate Calculator on the USPS website. Priority Mail can be insured, registered, certified, or sent COD for an additional charge.

§ 3.11.4 Preparing outgoing mail—Standard Mail, periodicals, and package services

Standard Mail is used primarily by retailers, catalogers, and other advertisers who have large mailings. Printed matter, flyers, circulars, advertising, newsletters, bulletins, and catalogs, small parcels, and commercial First-Class Mail can be sent with Standard Mail rates. Eligible nonprofit organizations can also apply to the USPS for non-profit rates for large mailings. Standard Mail also includes rates for individual parcels that weigh less than one pound.

Periodicals mail is designed for newspapers, magazines, and other periodical publications whose primary purpose is transmitting information to an established list of subscribers or requesters.

Package services include Parcel Post, bound printed matter, Media Mail and library mail. Parcel Post is used for mailing merchandise, books, circulars, catalogs, and other printed matter. Bulk rates are available for large quantities of Parcel Post. Bound printed matter includes advertising, promotional, directory, and editorial materials. Media Mail is most often used for books, film, printed music, printed test materials, sound recordings, play scripts, printed educational charts, loose-leaf pages and binders consisting of medical information, and computer-readable media. Library mail is used by libraries, schools, zoos, and research facilities.

§ 3.11.5 Preparing outgoing mail—Certificate of Mailing

A *Certificate of Mailing* is a receipt issued by the USPS that shows evidence of mailing. It can only be purchased at the time of mailing and is used with First-Class Mail, Priority Mail, Parcel Post, bound printed matter, and Media Mail. Insurance coverage and proof of delivery are not provided with this certificate.

§ 3.11.6 Preparing outgoing mail—Certified Mail

Certified Mail is used for First-Class Mail or Priority Mail for which proof of delivery is desired. No insurance is provided, but this service enables the mailer to have a receipt as evidence that the material has been mailed and, for an extra fee, receive a card (return receipt) showing the mail was received or picked up by either the addressee or addressee's agent. It is also possible to stipulate that the letter be given to only the addressee and for the return receipt to show the address of delivery. See Illustrations 3-1, 3-2, and 3-3 for the receipt and return receipt card. Law offices use Certified Mail a great deal, and the lawyer's assistant should keep the necessary forms handy. A program is available online to allow the preparation of the receipt and return receipt card from a data entry form that includes the recipient, address, and file or billing code. The documents are then peeled off the backing of the form, the return receipt card is folded, and they are attached to the mail as usual. See Illustration 3-4 for the computer form.

When sending Certified or Registered Mail, the lawyer's assistant should keep the receipt in a follow-up file until the return receipt card comes back or the assistant is notified of receipt.

Illustration 3-3

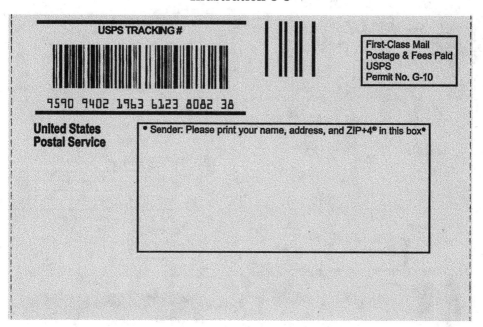

Illustration 3-4

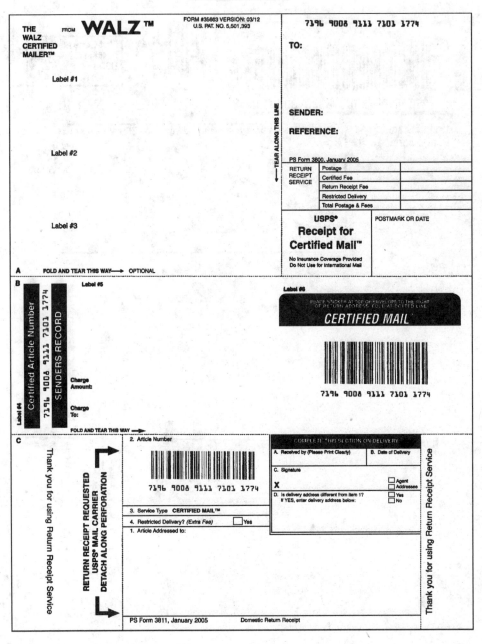

WALZ
POSTAL SOLUTIONS™

WALZ Form No:35663
Version:03/12

To reorder forms, *contact us at:*

sales@walzgroup.com

(800) 882-3811

www.walzgroup.com

WALZ SOLUTIONS:

- **WALZ CERTIFIED MAILERS™:** Patented forms and software to automate your in-house process

- **WALZ CONVERGENT COMMUNICATIONS®:** Comprehensive outsourcing solution including critical mailings, imaging, telephony, email, fax and text messaging

- **TRACKRIGHT®:** Tracks USPS® Delivery events, images and updated status

- **STORERIGHT®:** Return Receipt and Unclaimed Mail storage and records management system

Since 1985, Walz has been a pioneer and the nationwide leader in providing Certified Mail™ solutions. We offer significant domain expertise in Certified Mail™ and the leading solutions in the industry.

- Walz currently services 34 of the Fortune 100 companies and 86 of the AmLaw 200

- 80% of the top mortgage companies are our clients along with over 3,500 organizations such as government, legal, healthcare, and insurance

- Over the past twenty years, Walz has created unique Certified Mail™ solutions for over 200 million mailings

WALZ REFERRAL PROGRAM

- Do you know someone who could benefit from using our forms?

- Mention our forms to a friend, and tell them to mention your name when they call. Both you and your friend will receive **10%** off of your next orders (limit of 10% off per order).

Promotional Code R1

Label 1: Addressee label

Label 2: Additional addressee label or optional return address label when using the Walz Certified Macro

Label 3: Return address label

Label 4: Sender's record of the Certified Article Number

Label 5: Additional label for customer files

Label 6: PS Form 3800 Certified sticker (affix at the top of the envelope with the perforation mark on the edge)

Return Receipt: Proof of delivery that provides recipient signature, delivery date and forwarded address of delivery, if applicable

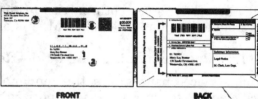

FRONT   BACK

UNITED STATES POSTAL SERVICE®

PRINT YOUR NAME, ADDRESS AND ZIP CODE™ BELOW

First Class Mail®
US Postage Paid
Permit No. G - 10

PEEL BACK TO EDGE

PEEL BACK TO EDGE

DO NOT BEND VERTICAL PERF

DO NOT BEND VERTICAL PERF

§ 3.11.7   Preparing outgoing mail—Registered Mail

When sending money and valuable papers such as stocks, bonds, or bids, Registered Mail is often used. *Registered Mail* is the most secure mail service provided by the USPS and is used with First-Class or Priority Mail. Additional fees are required for return receipt and restricted delivery services. Insurance on Registered Mail can also be purchased. The current limit is $25,000 for domestic Registered Mail; international coverage varies. The return receipt can only be signed for by the addressee and shows the date and address of delivery.

Occasionally when contracts are drafted, the question may come up whether to require contractual notices to be given by Certified or Registered Mail. Certified Mail can be prepared and handled routinely by the office staff and, depending on whether one desires to have a stamped receipt, can even be handed to the mail carrier during a regular pickup. Registered Mail requires a separate trip to the post office, and most offices do not have the Registered Mail form on hand to prepare in advance. A requirement that notice be sent by Registered Mail, therefore, forces both parties to the contract to go to considerable trouble to comply. Certified Mail is an easier choice for everyone.

§ 3.11.8   Preparing outgoing mail—Restricted delivery

This service ensures that the sender's mail is delivered only to a specific addressee or a person authorized in writing to receive the addressee's mail. However, restricted mail can be delivered to an agent without the addressee's written authorization if it is addressed to government officials, members of the legislative and judicial branches of federal and state governments, members of the diplomatic corps, minors, and individuals under guardianship. This service is available only for First-Class Mail, Priority Mail, Parcel Post, bound printed matter, and Media Mail sent Certified, COD, insured for more than $50, or Registered.

§ 3.11.9   Preparing outgoing mail—Insured mail

Insurance can be purchased against loss or damage up to $5,000 for First-Class Mail, Priority Mail, Parcel Post, bound printed material, and Media Mail. For materials insured for more than $50, a delivery receipt is signed by the recipient and filed at the delivery post office. Items cannot be insured for more than their value, and insured mail must be presented to a retail employee at a post office or to a rural carrier.

§ 3.11.10   Preparing outgoing mail—Additional postal information and services

Additional information regarding preparation of mail and other mail services provided by the USPS can be obtained from the local post office or by writing to Consumer Advocate, U.S. Postal Service, 475 L'Enfant Plaza SW, Room 5821, Washington, DC 20260-2200. The name of the publication is "Consumer's Guide to Postal Services and Products." Information about domestic and international mail services, as well as postage calculators, can be found on the web at www.usps.com.

§ 3.11.11 Preparing outgoing mail—Email

Electronic mail or *email* is made possible through computer-based communications equipment. Messages or documents can be sent almost instantaneously from one email address to another, within the office, down the street, or around the world. The efficient lawyer's assistant will be able to add and delete names from email address lists, attach files to an email, sort emails into folders and use the various features that are found in most email software. Email is extremely popular for sending drafts of documents since it is fast and is not subject to postage.

However, despite its popularity, the use of email to send privileged documents has some security hazards. In addition, sending conventional correspondence by email requires special procedures to ensure quality and accuracy of handling. See § 4.15 for more information regarding the security issues and proper handling of email correspondence.

§ 3.12 Scheduling travel

Some lawyers rarely travel; some travel all the time. Therefore, whether a lawyer's assistant has to make travel arrangements will vary. Whether the lawyer makes the arrangements or leaves them to the lawyer's assistant, the lawyer (or the firm) is very likely to have preferences about whether to use a website or a travel agent to set up travel.

It should be noted that while airlines may offer bargain rates online, the ability to have tickets refunded when schedules change is sometimes problematic. A travel agent is more likely to be able to set up truly refundable flights, usually at reasonable prices, and can coordinate exchange or replacement of tickets when travel is changed or cancelled. Travel agents often have after-hours services that can assist with travel changes even at night or on the weekends. Travel agents are also good at coordinating hotel stays and other necessities, such as car rentals, at the location of the airport or the site where the attorney will be visiting or working.

Many international hotels and air trips can be located and booked online, and maps to assist in locating international hotels and other sites of interest can often be obtained online. When the lawyer's assistant is not sure what can be found, the best first step is to start searching and see what comes up.

§ 3.13　Calendaring and docket control

There are two types of input to calendars and docket control systems that must be considered. The first concerns critical dates; the second concerns case review and management. The term *docket* is used in the court systems to refer to the court's calendar and various hearing and trial dates. In the lawyer's office, the term *docket* is used more loosely to refer to the day's agenda, including a to-do list of cases to be reviewed or worked on, as well as the calendar of appointments, hearing dates, and the like.

A *docket control system* is a reminder system. It provides a means of keeping track of deadlines and court dates for both litigation and nonlitigation matters, as well as scheduled appointments. Ideally, the docket control system should serve not only as a reminder system but also as a means of file control, scheduling, and planning to ensure that work is done in the ordinary course of business rather than at the last minute.

There are those who argue that regardless of the size of the firm, there should be only one system—a firm-wide system—encompassing all calendar dates and all docket control items. Such people argue correctly that every single file must have an entry in the docket control system. What they do not address in an ideal fashion is the problem of maintaining a system of calendar dates that also contains review dates for every file in a firm spread out over several cities with dozens of attorneys and thousands of active files. The docket system should contain as much depth as possible. If it is possible to maintain one calendar with court dates, deadlines, and appointments and include file review and work schedule dates as well, then it should be done as one. In most larger firms, it is not believed that such a system is possible, and it rarely is done.

What should be contained on a firm-wide docket or calendar without fail is all critical dates. Missed deadlines are the source of many malpractice claims. Malpractice insurance carriers, in an effort to reduce claims, review docket control systems carefully before issuing insurance. Since malpractice coverage rates are also escalating and coverage is more difficult to obtain, firms are paying much more attention to firm-wide docket control as an effective loss prevention technique.

It is important for the lawyer's assistant to determine what type of docketing or calendaring system is in place—whether firm-wide or individual—and to determine how such a calendar has been maintained, whether it needs to be beefed up to ensure that no dates are missed, and what needs to be done to make it an effective reminder system for the lawyer.

§ 3.13.1　Calendaring and docket control—Responsibility for the docket control system

Although the primary responsibility for the docket control system rests with the lawyer, the lawyer's assistant is responsible for getting the information into the system. To the extent the lawyer's assistant has access to calendar or docket items, the assistant is often expected to make entries into the system without specific instructions from the lawyer. The lawyer's assistant must be resourceful, consistent, and timely in determining and entering important dates.

§ 3.13.2   Calendaring and docket control—Double calendar systems

Some firms employ double calendar systems, and malpractice insurance carriers just love them. Two calendar entries are made for each transaction or date which requires a reminder. One entry is made on a calendar kept by the lawyer responsible for meeting the deadline, and the other entry is made on a calendar kept by the lawyer's assistant or a central calendar kept by a docket clerk. Both the lawyer and the lawyer's assistant are responsible for checking the calendar each day to be sure all deadlines are met and appointments kept.

§ 3.13.3   Calendaring and docket control—What to put on the calendar

Any type of future commitment belongs on the calendar. Examples are:

- All litigation dates, including statute of limitation dates, due dates for pleadings and briefs, deadlines for notices of appeal and renewals of judgments, deposition dates, due dates for discovery production, dates by which subpoenas must be issued and served, and trial and hearing dates.
- Dates by which adverse parties in litigation have agreed to provide material, data, or information.
- Dates by which service of process is expected to be made.
- Filing and hearing dates for various estate matters, such as federal income and estate tax returns, state inheritance tax returns, notice dates required by law, and dates of annual and final accountings.
- Follow-up dates for annual reports, minutes of meetings, etc., provided for corporate clients.
- Dates by which clients must meet the requirements of a contract provision.
- Proof of publication from newspapers on notices required in various types of actions.
- Appointments.
- Professional and personal commitments.

Additional entries that should be added to make a fully functional docket control system would include:

- Dates by which receipt of documents or requested information from third parties is expected.

- Follow-up dates for work in progress on all files.
- Follow-up dates for review of inactive files or files labeled for destruction.
- Accounting and administrative deadlines, such as personnel and expense accounting, tax returns and other tax-related reports, supply ordering, lease renewals, maintenance contract renewals, insurance policy renewals, and so forth.

§ 3.13.4 Calendaring and docket control—Types of docket control systems

Several types of docket control systems have been used in law offices over the years. The days of perpetual calendars and ticklers managed with index cards in card files are gone now, with very rare exceptions. Virtually every firm with a well-known email program also has a calendar program that can be used to maintain a docket. Whether a standard calendar program or some other system is used, it is important that there be a system in writing and that it be used and maintained daily. In addition, it is a smart move to run a hard copy of any electronic calendar at least weekly to ensure that, in the event of system failure, the calendar is not lost.

§ 3.13.5 Calendaring and docket control—Using automated calendars

Many firms have software with records management capabilities. Reminder dates and pertinent information are fed into the computer, recorded, and later retrieved by date, lawyer, or file. At regular intervals, a master or office calendar is printed for each lawyer and for the entire firm. Friday is a popular day for distributing the calendar, since it is useful in planning the coming week. The calendar lists every future commitment of all firm lawyers. In most firms, file review items are not included on the master calendar.

For attorneys who like to maintain complex docket follow-up calendars, computer programs are available that allow for lengthy daily to-do lists, listing each file and listing specific appointments and calendar items on a facing page. Docket items can be prioritized, reprioritized, moved to new dates, or deleted as they are completed.

§ 3.13.6 Calendaring and docket control—Docket coordinator

Some offices entrust the docket control system to one individual (often referred to as a *docket clerk* or *docket coordinator*) who is responsible for reminding all lawyers of deadlines in advance. All lawyer's assistants and lawyers are required to furnish pertinent information to the docket coordinator. In some firms all mail and pleadings (whether coming into or leaving the firm) are routed to the docket coordinator to ensure that all critical dates are entered into the system. The docket coordinator then sends written reminders of all deadline dates. Lawyers responsible for the work must then notify the docket coordinator that the work has been completed.

The final responsibility for reminding the lawyer of deadlines rests with the lawyer's assistant. Even if there is a central reminder system, the lawyer's assistant must monitor it carefully and make sure the lawyer receives the reminders and the work has been done.

§ 3.13.7   Calendaring and docket control—Calendaring mail

For the system to be effective, all incoming mail must be opened and processed by the lawyer's assistant. Under no circumstances should any mail be removed from the assistant's desk prior to processing. The lawyer is equally responsible for seeing that any items in the mail requiring calendar or docket notations are properly handled. Any piece of mail not marked as having been calendared should be returned to the lawyer's assistant for processing.

The lawyer's assistant sets up docket and calendar entries from all incoming mail that notifies a lawyer of any court appearance or deadline. It is a good practice for the lawyer's assistant to use a stamp or write a note on the item indicating that it has been calendared, by whom and when. This provides documentation that items were properly and timely calendared.

Prompt calendaring is essential. Any calendar entry should be made as soon as the date is known. Calculate the return time on summonses, interrogatories, and so forth, and enter them in the calendar (the attorney can explain how to calculate these times). When preparing notices, interrogatories, or material requiring a response by a certain date, calendar these in both the assistant's and the lawyer's calendar. Deciding how much or how little to enter on a desk calendar is a matter of judgment that the lawyer's assistant will acquire with experience. Appointments, meetings, court dates, birthdays, anniversaries, and any deadline dates should all be entered on the calendar. The firm's docket coordinator must also be advised of all pertinent dates.

§ 3.13.8   Calendaring and docket control—Calendaring
telephone calls and conferences

Often a hearing date or other matter requiring a calendar entry results from a telephone call or conference. The lawyer scheduling a hearing or other appointment gives the assistant the hearing or due date, so it can be calendared promptly. It may be helpful to supply the lawyer with forms to note calendar items, or it may work just as well to have the lawyer send the assistant an email.

§ 3.13.9   Calendaring and docket control—Setting
appointments

Many lawyers prefer to make their own appointments. If the lawyer does ask the assistant to schedule appointments, coordination is essential. When making an appointment, if the lawyer is not available to confirm, the assistant must get the client's name and telephone number and make the appointment tentative. The lawyer's assistant should learn the lawyer's specific preferences regarding time of day or day of week for appointments. Once the appointment has been scheduled, it should be calendared on both the assistant's and the lawyer's calendars, and the docket coordinator should be notified of the appointment.

§ 3.13.10   Calendaring and docket control—Calendaring unscheduled appointments

If a client drops in without an appointment, the lawyer's assistant should make note of it on the lawyer's calendar because it may later be necessary to verify that the client was in the lawyer's office on that day. If the assistant also notes this information on the calendar, the assistant can check with the lawyer to see what work must be done for the client.

§ 3.13.11   Calendaring and docket control—How to calendar reminder dates

Prior to noting a calendar item, the lawyer's assistant should determine whether additional lead time will be needed. For instance, any calendar item that will require a written document or personal appearance will require several reminders—the last of which is the due date.

EXAMPLES:

Statute of limitations
- No less than five reminders are set up:
    Three months prior to expiration of the statute
    Two months prior to expiration
    One month prior to expiration
    One week prior to expiration
    Date of expiration

Answer date
- No less than four reminders are set up:
    Fifteen days prior to answer date
    Ten days prior to answer date
    Five days prior to answer date
    Answer date

Hearing dates
- There must be at least three reminders:
    One for a date sufficiently ahead of the hearing date to allow for preparation

One for the day before the hearing

One for the date of the hearing

When a document is being prepared for a calendared event, one to two full working days should be allowed, depending on the anticipated size of the document. For particularly lengthy briefs, contracts, and so forth, much more time may be needed—consult with the attorney for an estimate. If a document requires outside printing, sufficient time should be allowed. The due date means that the lawyer's work product must be completed and the final document out of the office by that date.

§ 3.13.12   Calendaring and docket control—Reminder system

A formal reminder system should be established, as should a good working rapport with the lawyer. Some lawyers postpone projects until the last minute. This means the lawyer's assistant will be putting in a lot of overtime unless the assistant develops the knack of getting the lawyer to do the work sooner. The lawyer's assistant can leave reminders on the lawyer's desk or chair, taped to the lawyer's briefcase, or taped to the telephone or dictation equipment. Use bright paper so the message will be obvious. The important thing is to get action.

§ 3.13.13   Calendaring and docket control—Daily checking of calendars

The first thing the lawyer's assistant should do in the morning and the last thing to be done at night is to compare the assistant's calendar with the lawyer's. Computerized calendars are very popular and allow the lawyer's assistant to have access to the lawyer's calendar at all times. It often turns out the lawyer has made appointments without notifying the assistant, or the assistant has made appointments without entering them on the lawyer's calendar. The two calendars should match. By checking the calendars a few days ahead, the lawyer's assistant can more easily plan ahead.

§ 3.13.14   Calendaring and docket control systems—Retention of calendars

At the end of the year, calendars should be retained with the accounting records. Calendars serve as a handy reference to determine who was in when and what business transpired. If the lawyer keeps a computerized calendar, it should be saved in hard copy or on a disk. Many lawyers have had to go back to their calendars to recreate a sequence of events for a client. A malpractice claim may also more easily be defended with documents such as calendars and timesheets from the time period in question.

§ 3.14   Lawyer's assistant as receptionist

In many small and midsize firms, the lawyer's assistant may be called upon to sit in for an absent or lunching receptionist. The lawyer's assistant must always keep in mind the lasting effect of first impressions and realize that a client's attitude may be largely influenced by the initial contact with the receptionist.

Since the receptionist is constantly under public scrutiny, the desk and work area must be kept neat. The receptionist should avoid chewing gum, personal grooming, eating, visiting with other staff, and spending time on personal calls at the front desk. However, it should be remembered that the receptionist is typically not allowed to leave the desk for any reason and probably needs to call for a substitute in order to take a break, use the restroom, or take lunch. The lawyer's assistant can be a big help by agreeing to cover the reception area when the receptionist needs to get up for a few minutes.

§ 3.14.1   Lawyer's assistant as receptionist—Incoming phone calls

In many firms, the receptionist is expected to manage not only incoming visitors but also incoming telephone calls on the firm's main telephone line. The receptionist who also answers the telephone must be pleasantly assertive to route calls efficiently. The instinct of the caller who is not experienced with law firms is to start telling the story to the first person who picks up the phone. The receptionist is experienced in communicating, quickly and kindly, that the right person to speak to would be the lawyer.

§ 3.14.2   Lawyer's assistant as receptionist—Greeting visitors

The receptionist must also have a professional appearance and a pleasant manner to deal with the people who walk through the front door—in many firms there is a constant stream of traffic consisting of delivery persons, clients, salesmen, opposing counsel, and other visitors. Clients and others who must wait to see their party should be offered a comfortable chair, a beverage, and some reading material.

The receptionist should promptly announce the arrival of the visitor to the lawyer's assistant or lawyer. This assures the visitor that business is being handled. The receptionist should address and announce visitors by titles such as "Mr., Mrs., Ms., or Dr." unless they request otherwise. The lawyer's assistant then immediately notifies the lawyer that the visitor has arrived.

Many people who visit lawyers have serious concerns, and visitors may be anxious, upset, or nervous. For some, it is the first visit to a lawyer, which only intensifies the anxiety. The pleasant, helpful attitude of the receptionist can do much to relieve the visitor's fears. If a visitor is tearful or obviously upset, the receptionist should arrange to have the visitor taken to a private area to wait.

A professional receptionist will use good judgment to determine which clients the lawyer will see without appointments, which should be seen by another lawyer, and which can be taken care of by someone else in the office, such as the lawyer's assistant or office manager. When a visitor comes into the office without an appointment, the receptionist should check with the lawyer or lawyer's assistant to see if the visitor can be seen. If not, the receptionist should ask whether an appointment should be scheduled. Unless the receptionist is empowered to schedule appointments, the request for an appointment should be fielded by the lawyer's assistant. Drop-in visits are nearly always inconvenient, but the receptionist should be courteous in dealing with the visitor while protecting the lawyer from interruption. Note that salesmen are usually seen by the office manager and by appointment only.

§ 3.14.3 Lawyer's assistant as receptionist—Working with the lawyer

Another function of the receptionist is to know whether the lawyer is out and how long the lawyer is expected to be gone. As the lawyer is leaving, the receptionist should ask the lawyer about a return time and remind the lawyer of any scheduled appointments for that day or early the next day (assuming the receptionist has access to the calendar).

§ 3.15 Lawyer's assistant as notary public

The lawyer's assistant may be requested by the employer to become a notary public. A *notary public* is a person authorized by law to administer oaths, attest to and certify depositions, and take acknowledgments of signatures on deeds, mortgages, liens, powers of attorney, and other instruments in writing.

§ 3.15.1 Lawyer's assistant as notary public—Legal requirements

The position of notary public is one of great responsibility. The requirements vary from state to state but usually require a person to be a resident of the state for a stated period of time, to be 18 years of age or older, and to have good moral character. Some states administer examinations to applicants; others require only an application and a bond.

The notary public can be liable for damages resulting from improper performance of duties. Therefore, upon receiving the appointment, the notary should carefully read all information and become familiar with all terms relating to the duties and responsibilities of a notary in that state's jurisdiction.

§ 3.15.2   Lawyer's assistant as notary public—Terms

Administration of oath. The notary public administers an ***oath***, which is a solemn or official declaration of the statements that the person has just made or is about to make are true.

Affirmation. *Affirmation* is similar to an oath in meaning and importance but for religious reasons does not include an appeal to God or any supreme being. An affirmation may be requested either by a person who is not religious or by a person whose religious beliefs forbid such oaths. It is inappropriate to ask why an affirmation is requested.

Affidavit. An ***affidavit*** is a written statement sworn to as being true before a notary public. The affidavit contains the certification of the notary public that the statement was sworn to or affirmed and signed in the notary's presence by the ***affiant*** (the person who is making the affidavit).

Acknowledgment. An ***acknowledgment*** is required for some documents, such as deeds and mortgages, and consists of a statement that the person who signed the document declared to and before the notary public it was the person who signed the document. The notary public then signs and dates the acknowledgment, and stamps or affixes the seal, if required.

§ 3.15.3   Lawyer's assistant as notary public—Proper identification of affiant

In order to perform the duties properly, the notary public must be familiar with the person who appears or must be presented with adequate identification. If adequate identification cannot be produced, the notary should refuse to take the acknowledgment.

§ 3.15.4   Lawyer's assistant as notary public—Necessity of personal appearance of signer

The notary public should take no acknowledgments by telephone. The person whose signature is on the document and acknowledging such signature should appear personally to make the acknowledgment and sign the document. Where an oath is required, the notary should check the affiant's identification, administer the oath, have the person sign, and then the notary should sign and affix a seal, if applicable. Some notaries are reluctant to go through the formality of the oath, but in those instances where the document reads "sworn to before me" or similar wording, it is essential that the notary perform this function.

§ 3.15.5   Lawyer's assistant as notary public—Maintaining ethical and legal boundaries

The notary public cannot act in an official capacity when personally involved or interested. For example, the notary could not notarize signatures on a will of which the notary is a beneficiary. The notary is also not permitted to function outside the appointed territorial limits, whether for county or state, depending upon state law.

It is not unusual for an affiant to ask a notary to backdate an acknowledgment. The date on which the instrument is signed before the notary is the date that must appear on the acknowledgment. To do otherwise is illegal and could result not only in loss of the notary commission but also in a malpractice action against the law firm.

In some offices, a lawyer may come to the notary public with a document signed by a client in front of the lawyer but away from the office and ask that the document be notarized. Obviously, the document must be signed in the presence of the notary. Likewise, documents that have been mailed in with signatures cannot be notarized; the lawyer's assertion that the signature is the client's is not enough. If the lawyer's assistant believes a steady stream of inappropriate requests will be experienced and does not feel able to manage this, then the assistant should not become a notary. The job is not for everyone.

§ 3.16   Setting up a brief bank

A *brief bank* is designed to preserve legal research, briefs, and forms. Not only does it save time in document preparation or legal research, but it also saves time spent looking for a form "used in that Jones case two years ago." Legal work received from other law firms may also be put into the system for future reference. By gathering this type of information in one place, lawyers and legal staff can easily find particular forms and legal opinions about a particular topic.

The key to an effective, useful retrieval system is a good index with extensive cross-indexing. Most such systems are indexed by major practice area categories and then by subtopics. Some are tied to the West Key Number System, although the Key Number topic system may be too detailed to adapt easily to the brief bank.

There are two options in maintaining a brief bank. One is to maintain a physical bank of documents in folders, notebooks, or files. The other is to scan the documents onto the computer system and maintain them in a directory there. The imaged documents can be printed and revised; it may also be possible to use OCR scanning to put the documents into format for direct word processing.

Should the lawyer working on a brief bank item feel it is obsolete or poor work product, the lawyer should either weed out the document or attach a note indicating that the document may no longer be useful. In a small firm, all lawyers contribute items, update material, and even weed. In larger firms, however, one individual—a lawyer or librarian—is given the responsibility for maintenance of the system.

§ 3.17   Opening new files

The process of opening new files is one of the most complex administrative procedures undertaken in the law office. It begins with the filing of a new matter report and proceeds through a check for conflicts of interest. The conflicts check can result in a clean bill of ethical health for a new matter, can proceed through a course of attempted conflict resolution, or can stop the new file dead in its tracks. When conflicts are cleared or resolved, new file numbers are assigned, files and subfiles are prepared and labeled, and the file is routed to the lawyer, the lawyer's assistant, or the central file room, depending on firm procedure. Most of the steps in opening a new file have some complexities to be considered and dealt with, as will be explained below.

§ 3.17.1 Opening new files—New matter report

When a lawyer accepts a new matter, the lawyer's assistant will be given the information needed to prepare a new matter report. Typically, the new matter report provides not only pertinent information to the firm for accounting purposes but also provides a brief description of the work to be performed by the firm, perhaps the fee arrangement under which the work will be performed, and the information needed to run a conflict of interest check, as well as any critical deadlines to be entered in the docket control system.

Illustration 3-5
NEW MATTER REPORT

Prepared by: _____ Date: ____ File No. _____
Billing Lawyer: _____
Responsible Lawyer(s): _____
Case name: _____ Client No. ____ Matter No. _____

Court: _____   Docket No.: _____
CLIENT INFORMATION _____
New client _____
Present client _____

Client: _____
Address: _____

Business phone: _____
Home phone: _____   Fax number: _____
Cell phone: _____   Email Address: _____
AFFILIATES OF CLIENT: _____

Person to contact: _____
OPPOSING OR OTHER PARTY INFORMATION

Name: _____   Lawyer: _____
Address: _____   Address: _____
Phone No.: _____   Phone No.: _____
Fax No.: _____   Fax No.: _____

Email Address: _____   Email Address: _____

INSURANCE CARRIER: _____

COVERAGE DISPUTE: ☐ YES   ☐ NO

ADVERSE OR POTENTIALLY ADVERSE PARTIES: _____
OTHER PERSONS OR ENTITIES THAT MIGHT BE INTERESTED,
AFFECTED, OR INVOLVED: _____
MATTER INFORMATION Case Received by: _____
Case Assigned to: _____
File Name: (Client name first) _____
Description of case: _____
Subject indexing: _____

STATUTE OF LIMITATIONS, ANSWER OR   Area of
                                                 Practice
OTHER CRITICAL DATE TO TICKLE *[specify]*: _____   Code:

                                                 _____

IF APPLICABLE: DATE OF LOSS: DATE OF
                                         ACCIDENT:
CLAIM NO.:   POLICY NO.:   COURT:
CASE TYPE:

FEES AND BILLING INFORMATION   Hourly Rate of $____
☐ Contingency fee of: _____
☐ Other *[specify]*: _____
  Has retainer agreement been prepared? ____ Yes ____ No
☐ Standard billing (bill fees quarterly and costs monthly)
☐ Other billing agreement *[specify]*: _____
☐ Joint Bill   ☐ Send Reminder Statement

CLIENTS TO BE CHARGED FOR:	YES	NO	RATE
Computerized Research	X		Standard
Facsimiles		X	
Photocopies	X		¢¢/page
Messenger Services	X		Standard

REMARKS (Note additional cross-references or other special instructions in this space):

_____

_____

_____

Names to be run in   Additional Names to be
Conflicts System: Cross-referenced:

                                _____

                                _____

_____   _____
_____   _____

Conflicts System run by: _____
Date of Conflicts System run: _____

§ 3.17.2 Opening new files—Definition of conflict of interest

In a law office, a conflict of interest generally arises when the law firm (or the individual lawyers in the firm) places itself in the position of representing parties in adverse positions. What is difficult about conflicts of interest is that a conflict may be created by a lawyer's representation of a client years before the current situation. What is even more difficult is that these guidelines apply to all lawyers in the firm. It is assumed that representation by one lawyer in the firm is the same as representation by all, even if they are in different cities.

> EXAMPLE: Mrs. Jane Baker sees a lawyer in the firm about filing for a divorce against her husband, David Baker. Another lawyer in the firm has already agreed to represent David Baker.
>
> EXAMPLE: The firm is general counsel for XYZ Insurance Company; Jane Baker asks a lawyer in the firm to file a claim against XYZ Insurance Company.
>
> EXAMPLE: The firm is general counsel for XYZ Insurance Company. Jane Baker sues XYZ Insurance Company and Todd Jones for damages she sustained in an accident in which Todd Jones was driving the car which hit Jane Baker's car. The XYZ Insurance Company is Todd Jones's insurer. XYZ Insurance Company must provide a defense for Todd Jones, but it intends to take the position that Todd Jones violated the conditions of his insurance policy, so the coverage does not apply. In other words, the interests of XYZ Insurance Company and Todd Jones are at odds.

Before undertaking representation of a client, the lawyer must make certain that the law firm does not already represent another client whose interests are at odds with those of the potential client. It is critical, therefore, for every firm to have an index of all clients, present and past, and to check the index before it accepts new work. Unfortunately, it is not always simple to determine whether or not a potential conflict exists, and the decision is often a subjective one.

> EXAMPLE: The firm handled an incorporation for XYZ Corporation. One of the firm's clients wants the firm to handle a claim against Jerry Hunt, the vice president of XYZ Corporation. Is there a conflict?

Only the lawyer or lawyers in the firm can decide whether there is a potential conflict. Even if the firm does not have a conflict, the lawyers may decide that they do not want to accept work as a matter of business practice. From a business standpoint, there are some people against whom the firm will not want to be in an adverse position.

Conflicts of interest are a real problem in some firms. Some do not have effective systems for checking new clients for potential conflicts. There are a number of reasons why, but in most instances the lack of a conflict of interest system results from the failure of the firm to develop such a system when it was small enough to do it easily. As the firm grows, the job becomes more overwhelming, and the result is that one day the firm finds itself in the embarrassing position either of representing clients with conflicting interests, or worse, with a malpractice claim. It is much easier to develop a system when the firm is small. Even if there is only one lawyer, there should be a conflict of interest system.

§ 3.17.3   Opening new files—Information for conflicts checks

Information for conflict of interest purposes is critical. This is true not only for checking the new matter for any potential conflicts when the file is opened, but also for future references. If the lawyer does not provide the information, the lawyer's assistant should ask if there are names in addition to those listed in the file name that must be indexed.

> EXAMPLE: If the firm is representing the estate of a decedent, the name of the personal representative or trustee as well as the names of all heirs and beneficiaries should be indexed.

If the firm is handling a real estate transaction for a development company, the names of the principals of the company should also be indexed. If the development has a project name, the project name should be indexed. For example, if the developer is The Build-it-Fast Company and the firm is doing the legal work involved in the development of the Josey Ranch Shopping Plaza, Josey Ranch Shopping Plaza should be listed as a related party in the firm's conflict system.

If the firm represents a bank, the names of the bank officers should be indexed.

If the firm is incorporating a small business, the names of each of the shareholders, directors, and officers should be indexed.

In order for the law firm's conflict records to be complete, the client's name should be listed in full; any parents, subsidiaries, or other affiliated firms should be listed on the Affiliated Companies line of the form; the opposing party and any known affiliates should be listed under Adverse or Potentially Adverse Parties; corporate officers should be listed under Names to Be Run in Conflicts; and any other parties that may be significantly involved should be listed on the line labeled Other Persons or Entities that Might Be Interested, Affected, or Involved. Some conflicts indexes also require the city and state of the people or entities indexed.

After the lawyer's assistant prepares the new matter report, it is sent to the file coordinator for processing. The file coordinator in a smaller firm may be the office manager. In a very small firm, a paralegal or lawyer's assistant may serve as file coordinator.

§ 3.17.4   Opening new files—Running the conflicts check

The *conflicts check* is performed at the beginning of the file opening process. Before the file coordinator assigns a number to the file, all indexed names appearing on the conflicts line of the new matter report are checked against the computer conflicts system. These systems can work in a couple of different ways. Some systems integrate accounting and file management systems, and a conflict query is run against client names and matter names or subfile titles to pick up the adverse parties. The system can include, either in addition to or instead of a client-matter-subfile search, a bank of names that is entered and maintained permanently with indicators as to the role the party played in the previous matter. The computer generates a list of existing possible conflicts that the lawyer can review.

The file coordinator is trained to identify situations that might present potential conflicts. For example, if the firm is opening a new matter for an existing client, that client's name will appear in the index. This is not a problem. If, on the other hand, the person to be sued was a former client, the file coordinator would notify the lawyer immediately for further instruction. The lawyers determine whether or not a potential conflict exists based on judgment acquired after a good deal of experience. The file coordinator initials the new matter report to indicate that the conflicts check has been run. The new file information should also be emailed to all lawyers for a final check to ensure that nothing has been missed in the computer search.

§ 3.17.5   Opening new files—When conflicts occur

If a conflict is discovered, two different approaches can be taken. Some conflicts are insurmountable—for example, an active matter involving an existing client would typically forbid any action that might list the client as an adverse party. Some conflicts may be capable of resolution. In order to resolve a conflict such as one in which a former client is an interested but not necessarily adverse party represented by a different lawyer, the lawyer seeking to open the file (or a lawyer who knows the former client better in some cases) would call or write the client to seek a waiver allowing the firm to accept the new matter despite the conflict. A waiver of this type must be made in writing, and typically if a waiver is needed from a former client, a waiver will also be needed from the potential new client as well. If the parties agree to sign waivers, then when the waiver or waivers are returned by the parties, the new file can be opened.

§ 3.17.6   Opening new files—Assigning file numbers

Once the conflict of interest check has been run, the file coordinator can assign the file number (client and matter number). In some firms, assignment is made by the accounting department. Some computerized systems assign numbers automatically. If the client already has a number, only a matter number need be assigned.

§ 3.17.7   Opening new files—Preparing file jackets

The file coordinator prepares the file jacket, which contains subfiles and a copy of the new matter report. The file is sent directly to the lawyer's assistant. Some firms with stronger centralized storage may retain the file until it is requested by the lawyer or lawyer's assistant. If the file is not routinely sent to the lawyer or lawyer's assistant, another means of notifying the lawyer and assistant that the file has been opened can be used. A copy of the initialed and finalized new matter form can be returned, an email notification can be sent, or the firm can devise some other system.

§ 3.17.8   Opening new files—Setting up subfiles

A common complaint in many law firms is that everyone uses a different system for subfiles, so the subfile names do not easily identify subfile contents. Another is that no record is kept on subfiles, so a subfile could be misplaced and no one would ever know it was missing. To overcome these problems, many firms have adopted standardized categories for subfiles by practice area. A sample list of possible standard subfiles for litigation and corporate files is shown below.

Litigation
    Correspondence
    Lawyer's Notes
    Client Documents
    Pleadings
    Discovery
    Evidence
    Damages
    Legal Research
    Briefs and Legal Memoranda

Miscellaneous

General Corporate

    Correspondence

    Lawyer's Notes

    Client Documents

    Corporate Documents

    Miscellaneous

Each subfile should carry the file number and name and can also be assigned a letter, number, or other identifier to designate the subfile. The correspondence subfile for File No. 00129-700 might be 00129-700(a); the pleadings file, 00129-700(b); and so forth. Subfiles are not numbered for recognition by accounting software, but a master list that includes all subfiles should be kept to prevent the loss of a subfile.

When standard subfiles are used, they are created when the new file is opened. Additional subfiles can be requested as needed. Some file coordinators like to have a form for creation of a special subfile; in other firms, a simple email is sufficient. Some file management programs include programming for requesting subfiles through the file management system. The newly created subfiles are inserted in the new file folder. If the new file is routed to the lawyer's assistant, that location is noted in the file management program; if it is kept in central storage, that location is noted instead.

§ 3.17.9   Opening new files—Preparing file labels

Most computerized files management systems can also print file labels with appropriate color coding, if desired. Where labels are still being prepared manually, the name on the label should be placed very close to the top of the label right below the color coding so that it will be visible when materials are placed in the file. Begin at the first or second space from the left edge of the label so that all labels will be uniform. If the label contains more than one line, indent the second and third lines three spaces so the name on the first line will stand out. Whether labels are prepared in all capital letters or in title case (initial capitals only) is a decision for the individual firm, and the chief criterion is readability. Insert the file number on the label as well as the name, leaving at least three spaces between the number and words so that the number will stand out.

§ 3.17.10   Opening new files—Checklists for opening files

The new file opening process is relatively complex. The file coordinator may prefer to use a checklist to ensure that each step is completed as a new file is opened.

§ 3.18   File management

File management in the law office receives perhaps the least attention, although it may be the most important of all clerical functions.

Client files are the inventory and the memory of the law office, and they contain all work in progress—a major asset of the firm. In addition, they often contain important client documents, as well as the work product of the firm, and are seldom easily replaceable. Regardless of its importance, however, files management is not popular. Assistants tend to put off filing because most find it tedious. It is equally difficult to convince law firms that both time and personnel must be allocated for adequate file management.

Although a lawyer's assistant may encounter a firm with no real filing system in some newer and smaller firms, generally the file room will already be set up when the assistant starts work with the law firm. No two filing systems are the same—even if they use the same computer program to manage the filing system.

§ 3.18.1   File management—Definition

File management is the control of each file in the office from the time it is opened to the time when it is ultimately closed or destroyed. It is a crucial area of legal practice because handling a file efficiently affects profitability. Effective file management also provides many of the quality control mechanisms that are essential to ensure that work is properly handled. Many malpractice claims are generated by poor file management.

File management is much more than filing documents in a file. It also includes checking for conflicts of interest before the file is opened; ensuring that work progresses appropriately by using a docket control system; ensuring all deadlines are met; preserving new work product for future use; ensuring that anyone in the office can find the file or any document that belongs in the file; closing the file once work has been completed; and destroying the file once it serves no further useful purpose.

§ 3.18.2   File management—Centralized and decentralized systems

The major categories of filing systems are *centralized* and *decentralized*. Under a highly formalized central filing system, files are removed only to be worked on and are returned to the filing cabinets at the end of each day, regardless of whether work remains to be done. A centralized system also includes controlled access. No one can remove a file from the filing system without signing for it. In a completely decentralized system, the lawyers store files in their own work areas and have total responsibility for and control of the files. Barcoding is often used in large law firms to track the location of files.

§ 3.18.3   File management—Centralized control and decentralized storage

A totally centralized system is difficult to achieve in a law office. Most lawyers like to keep active files in their work areas rather than returning them to the central file room at the end of the day.

Centralized control, however, is important. This means that regardless of where files are physically kept, there is a central control system to maintain the ability to locate all files. The most important criterion in judging the effectiveness of a file system is findability. In most law firms a centralized control system means files not being used frequently are kept in the active files area, usually a central file room.

A fairly common form of decentralized storage is one in which a practice group maintains its files in a separate location. It is quite common for the estate planning group to store estate planning files in a vault to protect the documents against fire or in a separated area where the risk of loss can be minimized. The litigation section of a firm with a large corporate practice might find it easier to maintain files if they are not mixed in with the corporate files. A practice group may have access to a work room which lends itself to segregated storage. Where this type of storage is well organized and used consistently, it need not be problematic. If, on the other hand, a practice group keeps some files in separated storage and not others, the work of locating a missing file is doubled.

§ 3.18.4 File management—Classification of files

In most firms there are several classifications of files. They include:

Active. These constitute the firm's work in progress. They are the files in which there is work to be done and for which there may be unbilled time.

Inactive. These are usually files in which there will be no activity for some time and for which all time has been billed. Additional work is anticipated at some point in the future. In a centralized system, it might not be necessary to differentiate between active and inactive files, as all files are stored together. If this is done, however, there should be a system for following up on inactive files to determine whether they can be closed or when they should be pulled for review.

Closed. These are usually files in which all work has been done and the file has been billed, collected, culled, and marked for destruction, if it can be destroyed, or for permanent retention if it cannot.

While this is relatively straightforward, some common problems arise in law firm file rooms:

- In some firms, there are both permanent and inactive files because different lawyers use different words to identify the same type of file. Terminology differences must be resolved to avoid confusion.
- If a file involves a matter in which there may or may not be further action, is it an active file or an inactive file? In some states, a lawsuit in which there has been no activity for a specified period of time is automatically dismissed. Therefore, in many situations in which a law firm represents the defendant, once a responsive pleading is filed and the services are billed, the

lawyer hopes the plaintiff will lose its case file. At what point does that active file become inactive? This situation requires the assignment of a review date after which the file can be declared inactive or closed.

- Is each closed file automatically set for destruction at the time it is closed, or is there review at a later date? A clear firm policy needs to be articulated and enforced.
- Which files should be destroyed, and which should be permanently retained? A firm policy determining what files are permanently retained needs to be developed.

Written guidelines can prevent confusion and save time in locating files. The firm's office policy and procedures manual should include a detailed explanation of the filing system and the procedures in place. If the filing procedures have not been documented, the lawyer's assistant should check with the office manager to see if plans for documenting the procedures exist. If no one has been assigned the task, the lawyer's assistant can offer to draft a files management procedures document. If that project is approved, the lawyer's assistant should ask for input from the office manager, lawyers, and co-workers to make sure the filing procedures are workable for everyone in the office. If the lawyer's assistant is working in an office that has no filing system, the lawyer's assistant could offer to develop one, discuss the proposed system with lawyers and staff, and implement the system, if approved.

§ 3.18.5   File management—Filing systems

Three types of filing systems commonly used in law offices are *alphabetic*, *numeric*, and *alpha-numeric*. Although some are more effective than others, the right one depends upon the needs of the firm.

Alphabetic. Under an alphabetic system, files are labeled and stored in alphabetical order, generally by the name of the client, following standard filing procedures. Although many law firms still use alphabetic filing systems, they are the least efficient because of the necessity of constantly reshuffling files to make room for additional files. Additionally, people rarely interpret filing rules the same way.

Alphabetic filing probably works best in small firms that have a number of short-term matters, such as traffic or low-level criminal matters. The relatively short lives of the files make assignment of individual client numbers more cumbersome, and it is harder to remember client and matter numbers when billing time or costs. Where the number of files stored is relatively fewer, as in a small firm, it is typically easier to locate files in alphabetical storage. The problem of continually shuffling the files can be somewhat overcome by frequently culling older files that should be moved to closed storage.

In some firms, the litigation files are filed alphabetically by the name of the plaintiff, regardless of whether the firm's client is the plaintiff, the defendant, or another party to the action. Filing under this system makes controlling and finding files more difficult. A good cross-index would be very helpful.

Numeric. Under a numeric system, files are assigned a number, are identified by that number, and are stored in numerical order. If, as is now generally the case, the files management system is maintained on a computer, there is no need to create cross-index entries, as the computer systems offer the option of searching by name as well as number. In systems that are not maintained on a computer, an alphabetic cross-index will be needed. As manual filing systems are increasingly rare and typically individualized for the needs of the office, they will not be discussed in detail here.

Numeric filing alleviates the problem of reshuffling files, because new files are added at the end of the storage area. Another big advantage to a well-designed numeric system is that the same numbering system can be used both for files and accounting. A well-designed computerized numbering system can also generate management reports to assess profitability and store and manipulate data for long-range planning and marketing.

Consecutive filing and *terminal-digit filing* are the two primary types of numeric filing systems.

Under a consecutive-number system, numbers are assigned in straight sequential order and are filed in straight sequence, one behind the other, so that the most recent number assigned is the last in the file drawer or on the shelf.

With terminal-digit filing, numbers are broken down into groups of two digits and are filed in numerical order by the last two digits. (Numbers are read from right to left.) For example, File No. 112233 would be read as 33 22 11 and would be filed in Drawer 33, Section 22, Folder 11. The next consecutive file number would be 112234 and the file would be stored in Drawer 34, Section 22, Folder 11. Many terminal-digit filing systems are also color coded for increased ease in filing. One advantage of terminal-digit filing is that material is evenly distributed through the file storage area so that each drawer or each shelf grows at the same rate. The big disadvantage of this system is the inability to accommodate client numbers as well as matter numbers. This disadvantage can be overcome by using a unique matter number and filing only by matter number. Terminal-digit filing is particularly good where confidentiality is an issue and is most commonly seen in doctor's offices. It is less often seen in law firms.

Alpha-numeric. An alpha-numeric system is a combination of an alphabetic filing system and a numeric system. Under this type of system, numbers assigned to files are in blocks according to the letter of the alphabet which identifies the client. The purpose of such a system is to achieve alphabetic filing. Since the number blocks are filed together, the files are also more or less in alphabetic order. In such a system, however, there is still the potential problem of having to reshuffle files constantly to provide for growth.

Other file identification systems include:

Subject. A subject system is one in which files are filed alphabetically by subject matter. The firm's general administrative files (accounting, personnel, equipment, insurance, and other files concerning the firm's business affairs) can be filed by subject matter in a locked area of the file room. Often, the more current administrative files are located in the departments that use them. Forms files and retrieval systems are also usually filed by subject matter.

Geographic. A geographic system is one in which filing is done by geographic area, such as a state or a region. Geographic filing would be rare in a law office, except that an office that had branch locations might file its general administrative files by geographic location of the office and then by subject. In corporate law departments that work extensively with branch offices or subsidiaries, a geographic system is not unusual. The geographic system may also encompass a numeric system, but it may be necessary to access files by city, for example.

§ 3.18.6   File management—Using a numeric filing system

Although some firms continue to use alphabetic systems for filing, most firms have converted to numeric filing systems, which are easier to expand and afford more confidentiality. The use of computers to index files is also common and allows law office support personnel to manage files more efficiently. A numeric system also provides an easier system of correct physical filing—the precise location of a numbered file is more specific than an alphabetic one.

§ 3.18.7   File management—Client numbers

In most law office numeric filing systems, a file number should consist of a client number and a matter number. Under this type of system, each client is assigned a unique client number when the firm begins to represent the client. The client retains the same client number no matter how many different matters the firm may handle for the client.

§ 3.18.8   File management—Sequential matter numbers by client

If a firm finds it useful to know how many files it has opened for a particular client, it will often choose to assign unique client numbers, but the matter numbers for all clients are simply numbered from 001 or 0001, continuing under each client in numerical order.

§ 3.18.9   File management—Unique matter numbers

Some firms find it more practical to issue a new matter number for each new matter, regardless of whether the matter is for an existing client or a new one. Each new matter opened is numbered sequentially. The matters are filed under the client number and in numeric order by matter. There are a number of advantages to unique matter numbers, including the ability to refer to the case by matter number alone for billing and time entry, the ability to gauge the rough age of a matter by its number, and the ability to label word processing or other documents using fewer numbers. In addition, unique matter numbers avoid confusing two cases with the same matter number and a similar client number.

§ 3.18.10   File management—Master file index

Computerization has greatly simplified files management. A master file index of existing files can easily be generated by the computer program. An alphabetical cross-index can be generated using a sorting function. Most computerized files management systems also have the capability of maintaining a list of all subfiles generated under each matter, and the location of each file can be entered into the program and changed when the file location changes. A computerized system can also sort files by designations such as *active, inactive,* or *closed.*

Some firms still using noncomputerized filing systems may opt to generate a spreadsheet or database listing all files. Such a list can still be sorted by various fields, such as the numeric field or the name field to generate a workable master index or cross-index.

§ 3.18.11   File management—Files inventory

At regular intervals, the file coordinator should check lawyers' offices to verify that the file records are correct. This usually entails checking the locations listed in the records against the physical locations where the files are kept. Where files have been barcoded, if a file is found in a location other than the one recorded, it is a simple matter to check the file in at its new location.

§ 3.18.12   File management—Lawyer case lists

While it may not always be necessary, most lawyer's assistants find it helpful to maintain a list of active cases for each lawyer they work with. Such a list simplifies time entry and cost billing and is also a valuable resource when a substitute sits at the assistant's desk. Such a list can be quite simple, listing client, matter, a case nickname, if it differs from the matter name, and the numerical codes needed for filing and billing (both numbers if different).

§ 3.18.13   File management—New files list

As part of the file opening process, a list of all new files should be prepared periodically (weekly or daily in large firms) and distributed to all lawyers. This can serve as an additional conflict of interest check and also keeps lawyers informed.

§ 3.19 Maintaining individual files

One of the most hated tasks of the law office is document filing. Done poorly and seldom, filing can be at the root of lost documents, missed deadlines, and poor efficiency. Done daily and with care, it can help support strong performance and good results for the clients.

§ 3.19.1 Maintaining individual files—Using file numbers

Once the file has been opened and assigned a file number, that number should be shown on all correspondence, statements, and other file documentation. The lawyer's assistant should note the file number on all pleadings, so the file clerks will have no problem identifying the document for filing. If there are subfiles, the proper subfile identification should also be included. If the document should not be defaced, the file number should be written on an adhesive note attached to the document. It is the responsibility of the lawyer's assistant to see that proper file numbers are noted on all filing material. The lawyer's assistant is often in a position to do filing for the lawyers and should do so as much as possible since it is very cost-effective.

§ 3.19.2 Maintaining individual files—Lawyer's approval on filing

Incoming mail should always be reviewed by the lawyer before it is filed. Some offices require a lawyer's initials on all materials coming into the office before they are filed in the client folders. Some lawyers like to have a working copy of all correspondence and pleadings. If this is the case, the lawyer's assistant would make a copy of the incoming correspondence and pleadings and place the original in the file with a notation indicating the lawyer had received a working copy.

In addition to maintaining a working copy of incoming correspondence, many lawyers like to have their assistants maintain a file of *readings* documents. This file includes a copy of all outgoing correspondence maintained in chronological or reverse chronological order. This makes it possible to locate a missing outgoing document by date and makes it easy to retain documents for which there is no file. The readings file is maintained in addition to the file copies routed to individual files.

§ 3.19.3 Maintaining individual files—Preparing material for filing

Sort documents by category (client, personal, general correspondence). After documents have been sorted by category, sort within the category, placing them in numerical or alphabetical order, whichever is appropriate. Mark the document with the filing notation, such as the file number in numerical filing, or underline the name on the document that indicates in which file it should be placed. (This is known as **coding**.) If it goes in a subject file, write the subject in the upper right-hand corner. Carefully punch holes at the top of the document. Be sure that documents placed in the file folder are not crowded into the fold of the folder. When placing material in the folder, verify the number and name.

It is tempting when the workload is very heavy to leave the filing until later. Unfortunately, if it waits long at all, the lawyer can no longer rely on the file to reflect the matter's current status. Typically, if a key document is missing, the lawyer will know it, and hopefully it can be located quickly, but the quickest way to locate needed documents is in the file. The time that is spent on daily filing is far less than the time that will be spent locating lost documents that have never been properly filed.

Filing should be done by the lawyer's assistant most familiar with the file (or by trained file room personnel), not by a part-time clerk or by the newest assistant in the office. The lawyer's assistant should do the filing daily in those files stored in the nearby area or the lawyer's work area; file room personnel should do the filing in the files located in the central file room. The lawyer's assistant is responsible, however, for providing sufficient accurate information to ensure that the filing is done properly.

§ 3.19.4   Maintaining individual files—Organizing the files

Keep the files neat and orderly. To the extent possible, all materials should be filed in reverse chronological order (with the most recent date on top). Attorneys' notes should be dated (if it is possible to get the attorneys to do so). With the exception of clients' personal documents and pleadings that may need to be filed later, every piece of paper should be fastened into the file.

§ 3.19.5   Maintaining individual files—Assigning files to other lawyers

In a firm where lawyers frequently assign work to other lawyers, it is beneficial to have a system for notifying the file room that another lawyer has the file. Some file room managers like to have a transfer slip; others are content with a quick email. Unless the firm's file management structure is very elaborate, a quick note to the person responsible for noting the location of files should be sufficient.

Typically, the lawyer will not think about notifying the file coordinator that the location of the file has changed. The lawyer's assistant can save everyone time and trouble by handling that without being formally asked to do so. The lawyer should be encouraged to tell the assistant when assigning a file to someone else, so the change of location can be noted.

§ 3.19.6   Maintaining individual files—Sending active files to central file room

With centralized storage, a lawyer has the option of storing many files in the central file room. When central storage is arranged effectively, it makes sense to keep as few files as possible in the lawyer's or assistant's work area.

Files should not be sent to the central file room without first noting a review date in the docket control system. In some firms, that date is noted on the file folder as well. In some firms with tighter file management, when a file is sent to the central file room without a review date, it is returned to the lawyer.

§ 3.19.7 Maintaining individual files—Retrieving files from the central file room

For a more effective files management system, controlled access to the central file room is important. *Controlled access* means that only the file coordinator and file room staff members remove files from the file room. The lawyer or lawyer's assistant tells the file coordinator which file is needed, and the file coordinator checks the file out. The new location of the file is noted in the computer system. Thus, the file coordinator knows where files are if they are not in the file room. Controlled access does not usually exist in small firms. Even in firms where there is controlled access, it is impossible for the file coordinator to be in the file room at all times. Some firms prohibit access to the file room at such times. In other firms, lawyers and assistants are free to help themselves to files after hours. Problems may arise if check-out procedures are not followed. In larger firms, a member of the file room staff can be present at all times during working hours.

§ 3.19.8 Maintaining individual files—Closing files

In many law firms, lawyers feel that it is not necessary to close files. The crunch comes when sufficient filing space is no longer available. By then the task is often so monumental that outside help is needed. This is another area where the lawyer's assistant can be of invaluable assistance. When a file is ready to be closed, the lawyer's assistant should review the contents of the file and remove extra copies of documents, legal pads, ballpoint pens, and other extraneous material. Before closing the file, the lawyer must decide the eventual disposition of the files.

Some firms renumber files when they are closed. Typically, if a file needs to be reopened, it will be requested by its original number, so if new closing numbers are issued, a cross-index will be needed. Whether a renumbering system is helpful or not depends on the needs of the firm. Where closed files are renumbered, many numbering systems are available. One that works well is to include the year when the file is closed in the new number. Once any renumbering has been done, the file can be moved to the closed file area or stored off-site, according to firm policy.

One aspect of file renumbering is inevitable, however. Particularly in larger metropolitan areas, firms are storing closed and permanent files in commercial file storage facilities. In some instances, commercial storage is less expensive than on-premises storage. When stored off-site, the closed file will likely have a location number associated with its off-site storage location. That number will need to be noted in the files management system, at least for the use of the file room personnel.

§ 3.19.9   Maintaining individual files—Destroying files

Some law firms have never destroyed files. Some files are 50 to 100 years old. Most of these firms are now changing their philosophies about the necessity to maintain these files perpetually. Storage of files that will never be used again is expensive. Some firms are taking the position that they are not a depository for clients' documents—tax returns, wills, etc.—and are now putting the burden of maintaining these documents on the clients. What must be retained from a legal standpoint is a subjective decision that only the firm's lawyers can make. Generally, firms are keeping only those documents that cannot be replaced, are not in a court record, or for which they are not protected under the statute of limitations. Some firms first transfer selected or all contents of the file to CD or DVD, or tape archive before closing or destroying the files.

As part of the file destruction process, the firm must develop guidelines by which files that must be retained permanently can be selected. A retention timetable should be developed by area of practice.

§ 3.19.10   Maintaining individual files—Returning files to clients

One way to avoid storage of unnecessary documents is to purge the file of client documents when the file goes into inactive or closed status. The file is often composed in large part of documentation furnished by the client for a particular matter. Once the file is ready for inactive status, there is no reason not to return these documents to the client. Many firms offer the file to the client when the file comes up for destruction.

§ 3.20   Filing supplies and equipment

Filing supplies and equipment should be selected based on utility. Filing supplies should be chosen that will operate well in the existing file storage areas; special color coding or labeling features may be helpful. Filing equipment is chosen based upon the law firm's facilities and the amount and type of storage needed.

§ 3.20.1   Filing supplies and equipment—Color coding

In firms where there is continuous movement of files among various lawyers, color-coded file folders can be helpful in locating missing files. Color coding can increase accuracy, speed up filing, and lessen the time spent hunting for missing files. For example:

- Use a different color for different types of cases, e.g., green for real estate, red for domestic relations, blue for probate.
- Different colors can be used to designate different types of files and subfiles, such as correspondence, briefs, client documents, and so forth.
- In numerical filing, a different color can be used for different digits. Each numeral is a different color. Thus, all files between 4310 and 4319 will look alike, except for the last digit. That makes it very easy to spot the misplaced 5312 on the same shelf.

§ 3.20.2 Filing supplies and equipment—Filing equipment

Generally, the types of filing equipment available include:

Vertical file drawers. These are the traditional office file cabinets. They are the least efficient and are cumbersome to use.

Lateral file drawers. The files are arranged laterally, providing more space than vertical file cabinets. It is also easier to insert and remove files.

Open-shelf filing. Open-shelf filing is also lateral filing, but files are placed vertically on open shelves, which are usually seven feet high. There are no drawers. Open-shelf filing is more efficient than either lateral file cabinets or vertical file drawers.

Retractable shelves. Open shelves are placed on tracks so that an aisle is not required between each row of shelves. From a safety standpoint, any firm purchasing this type of equipment should make certain that it is equipped with a slip clutch. This slip clutch causes the unit to stop when it makes contact with an object. Some manufacturers also feature an optional safety bar that physically crosses the open aisle. The bar locks the equipment and also serves as a visual reminder that the aisle is in use.

Before a final decision can be made on selection of filing equipment, it must be determined that the floor load capacity of the area will accommodate the added weight of loaded files.

§ 3.21 Copying equipment

There are too many types of copiers to describe here, but generally, the copiers used by a firm include some or all of the following features:

- Automatic stapling
- Duplex copying (double-sided copy)
- Color copies
- Automatic tri-folding of brochures
- Saddle binding (stapling along the binding or center of the folded-in-half booklet)
- Collating copies
- Reduction or enlargement of originals
- Oversized document copying

- Automatic lightening or darkening of originals for clearer copies
- Automatic two-hole and three-hole punching of copies
- Image scanning

§ 3.22 Dictation equipment

Dictation equipment permits document origination much more quickly than by any other method. Dictating material to an assistant, who takes it down in shorthand and then transcribes it, requires the time of two persons. Handwriting can be difficult to decipher. Using machine dictation, the lawyer can dictate whenever there is an opportunity without relying upon anyone else to be available.

§ 3.22.1 Dictation equipment—Types of dictation equipment

Three basic categories of dictation equipment are desktop models, portable models, and central units. In addition, two types of technology—analog and digital—are available.

§ 3.22.2 Dictation equipment—Desktop models

Desktop models are usually located at both the author's desk and the transcriber's desk. The author's unit provides for dictation and is equipped with a microphone; the transcriber's unit provides for transcription and is equipped with a headset and a foot pedal. Most desktop units use cassettes because cassettes are easy to handle and offer good sound quality.

§ 3.22.3 Dictation equipment—Portable models

Portable models are used principally by persons who dictate while they are away from the office. They can be purchased in many sizes; some are small enough to fit into a shirt or coat pocket and weigh as little as five ounces. They are particularly valuable for persons who spend a lot of time in cars, planes, or remote locations; are useful for recording seminars and speeches; and are also useful in interviewing witnesses.

§ 3.22.4 Dictation equipment—Central dictation systems

A central recording system is a dictation system with the recorder located in one main area, but with dictating and transcribing units in many locations.

§ 3.22.5 Dictation equipment—Analog equipment

This is the type of equipment most lawyer's assistants are used to seeing and using. An analog unit is basically a tape recorder that uses cassette tapes. Analog equipment is typically reasonably priced. The dictation units are available in many sizes, from desktop units to wallet-size models. Standard-size audio cassettes or microcassettes are used with analog equipment. Because of the popularity of computer-based dictation systems, analog transcription units are increasingly difficult to obtain, with some manufacturers and units dropping out of the market entirely. Local suppliers may, however, have reconditioned used units for sale, and some units remain available new.

§ 3.22.6 Dictation equipment—Digital equipment

State-of-the-art digital dictation systems record sound digitally, store it directly onto a computer's hard drive, and play back the voice file. Dictation units can be handheld units which feed the completed dictation to a designated computer directory and send an e-mail to the transcriptionist. Some computer dictation is controlled through the firm telephone system. Transcription functions are managed through a computer program and a foot feed similar to those used with analog equipment. Digital equipment can be placed at individual workstations or networked for a central dictation system. Storage capacity demands on usage, and number of phone lines necessary for link-up to the system are a few of the factors to be considered before purchasing this type of equipment. The technology is rapidly changing, so new features should be investigated thoroughly before purchase. Sometimes people who have not used computer-based dictation equipment have fears about how the system will function, relative to the equipment they are used to. There are very few practical differences in the way dictation is given or transcribed.

§ 3.22.7 Dictation equipment—Special features of dictation equipment

Following are some of the features available on dictation equipment. Features available vary from unit to unit.

Automatic measured review. An automatic measured review is provided on many systems. The dictator can set the machine to back up a set distance automatically after an interruption.

Conference recording. The conference recording feature picks up all the voices in the room rather than minimizing background noise.

Indexing. Some units have electronic indexing, which indicates by audible sound the end of the recording or special instructions from the dictator.

Privacy lockout. A privacy lockout is available for central systems. This ensures that material dictated by one individual is not heard by anyone queuing into the system after the dictator has finished.

Telephone input. By using a telephone input system, the dictator can call into the system from any distance away from the firm. Material can be dictated at any hour of the day or night to be transcribed by the assistant while the dictator is away from the office. No media needs to be delivered from the dictator to the assistant.

Voice activation. Systems can be equipped with voice activation. These relays stop operation of the unit when the dictator is silent and reactivate the unit at the sound of a voice. This is particularly helpful when the dictator pauses to gather thoughts or to answer a phone call. Without it, the unit continues running and uses up valuable dictation space on the media.

§ 3.22.8 Dictation equipment—Selecting dictation equipment

Information on the types and sizes of equipment, as well as storage media and equipment feature, can be found through vendors or through the Internet. In determining which dictation equipment should be purchased by the firm, the amount and type of dictation should be considered. The need for out-of-office call-in dictation should also be considered. In the current, rapidly changing technological climate, a careful review of system requirements and features available should be made before purchase.

§ 3.23 Office supplies

The assistant is often responsible for ordering supplies and maintaining an inventory of supplies. The lawyer's assistant can periodically visit local dealers to learn what is new on the market. The office files should contain a list of local dealers with phone numbers and addresses. A word of caution—beware of phone solicitors offering to sell office supplies at a large discount because of a closeout, a refused order, a bankrupt business, or an erroneous shipment. When the order is received, the bargain supplies may be old, stale, or defective.

A reputable supplier will replace defective merchandise. Do not order in quantities unrealistic for the firm. Discounts for buying in quantity are available, but the shelf life of the supplies must be considered before placing a bulk order.

An inventory should be kept in the supply area listing the minimum amount to be kept on hand so that more can be ordered to maintain that amount. New supplies should be placed behind older supplies so they will be used last. A well-organized supply area can save both money and time.

Chapter 4

Computers in the Law Office

> **KeyCite®:** Cases and other legal materials listed in KeyCite Scope can be researched through the KeyCite service on Westlaw®. Use KeyCite to check citations for form, parallel references, prior and later history, and comprehensive citator information, including citations to other decisions and secondary materials.

§ 4.1 Introduction

Computers have become the law office's primary tool for providing efficient, cost-effective, flexible services to its clients. In the late 1970s and early 1980s, dedicated word processors—computers that performed only the function of word processing—revolutionized the law office. Today's computers are used by lawyer's assistants, paralegals, lawyers, and clients to communicate, exchange and process data, and to connect to worldwide resources, in addition to word processing.

This chapter provides an overview of computer components, discusses the major features of word processing, and introduces other computer applications commonly used in the legal environment, such as email, scheduling and docketing, spreadsheets, database management, image scanning, and computer-assisted legal research. The chapter concludes with a description of the Internet, discussion of computer security issues, recommendations for selecting a computer system, and a discussion of trends.

§ 4.2 Components of computer systems

Computer systems are comprised of hardware (the physical components) and software (the instructions that operate the computer). Hardware and software are linked by the operations and calculations performed by the *central processing unit* (CPU). The CPU is the part of the computer system where all computations, sorting, selecting, and data manipulation takes place; oversees the use of the main memory; and monitors input and output operations.

Hardware includes the keyboard, a monitor, a printer, a modem, a scanner, and a tactile control, which may comprise a joystick, a track pad, or a "mouse." Inside the case are components such as power supply, memory, and hard drives. The CPU is situated on an electrical board usually referred to as the motherboard. Also housed in the case are memory and storage devices called disks or **hard disc drives**. External hardware includes monitors, printers, and scanners. Hardware is categorized as input devices, output devices, and memory components.

Software is a set of instructions written by programmers that directs the computer to manipulate or change data to accomplish the program's function. Operating system software contains the instructions that connect and coordinate hardware to software. Application software contains instructions that transform a computer into a practical tool, such as a word processor, spreadsheet, database manager, or scheduler.

§ 4.2.1   Components of computer systems—Input devices

An *input device* is a means of getting information or data from the operator into the computer. Keyboards, mice, scanners, touch screen monitors, and voice recognition systems are all input devices.

Keyboard. The computer keyboard includes alpha/numeric/symbol keys, a tab key, caps lock and shift keys, a backspace key, and an enter or return key. The computer keyboard also has cursor movement keys, such as left, right, up, and down arrows; and home, end, page up, and page down keys. Other keys found on the keyboard are escape, insert, and delete, which are used to perform editing tasks, and function keys F1 through F12 on the top row.

Special characters not found on the keyboard, such as the section mark (§); paragraph symbol (¶); degree (°); and registered (®), trademark (™) or copyright (©) notations can be inserted into a document. Check under special characters in the software manual or simply open insert in the word processing program and check under symbol.

Mouse, trackball, and track pad. The mouse is an input device that is rolled across the desktop to position the cursor on the screen. The cursor's shape can change from an I-beam into an arrow, hourglass, or hand while the operator is working within a document. The mouse usually has two or three buttons on top that can be clicked or double clicked to perform certain operations or held down to drag the cursor across the screen to select text. Some mice now have a button which allows scrolling with a touch of the finger. A mouse can be adapted for use by left- or right-handed people, and products are available to make the mouse and keyboard easier to use for people who have motion, hearing, or visual limitations. A grammatical note about the plural of mouse: Both mouses and mice are considered acceptable by most sources.

A *trackball* is a pointing device with a ball on top that is rolled with the fingertips to move the cursor while the base of the trackball device remains stationary. The stationary trackball can reduce strain on the operator's wrists and hands and requires less desk space to control the cursor.

A *trackpad* is often found on laptops and allows fingertip control of cursor movement.

Scanner. Scanners are available in desktop, copier-based, or handheld versions. Many of them feature automated document handling that feeds the scanned document a page at a time and scans the document electronically, creating an electronic image that is sent electronically to the operator's email or to a storage directory. The stored image is processed either into an imaged document or converted into characters for word processing. See § 4.14 for more detail about this important technology.

Bar code scanner. This is a small scanner that reads a bar code (or UPC-type code). Law firms often use this technology to label client files so the file's location can be monitored with minimal effort.

Voice recognition systems. This technology recognizes speech and translates spoken words or commands into digital sound that can be interpreted by the computer. The person using this system speaks words and commands into a microphone attached to the computer. The computer analyzes the sounds until the computer can recognize the speech pattern of the operator. Voice recognition is affordable, and its use is becoming more common. Voice recognition documents require careful proofreading because of the possibility of computer misinterpretation of vocal signals.

Webcams. *Webcams* are cameras that send live images over the Internet or capture video to file. Some law firms use them for video conferencing.

Digital cameras. Digital cameras format photographs into files computer programs can use. They are now used in nearly every context that requires still photography, including many aspects of litigation.

§ 4.2.2 Components of computer systems—Output devices

An *output device* is used to get information or data out of the computer and back to the operator. The two most common output devices are the monitor and the printer. After data is input and then processed, the operator can view the data on screen or print the output on paper. A printout is sometimes called a hard copy.

Monitor. The monitor is an output device that displays data that has been processed by the CPU. Monitors come in a variety of screen sizes. The monitor's clarity or resolution is measured in *pixels*, the small dots that create a picture on the screen, and in dots per pitch, the distance between each pixel measured in millimeters. The smaller the dot pitch, the better the screen's resolution. Because of their slim design and reduced energy needs, laptop computers use liquid crystal display (LCD) and can use light-emitting diode (LED) as a backlight to illuminate the LCD.

Printers. Printers vary in speed, print quality, and price. They include laser or inkjet and print in black and white or color.

Laser printers use technology similar to that of a photocopier to produce printed text and graphics. Because of their relatively low price, speed, and excellent print quality, they are widely used in law firms.

Color printers are increasingly affordable and have a very practical place in a law office. They can be used to produce client newsletters and in-house marketing brochures, thus eliminating the cost of outside printing services. Litigation support staff can also create effective, inexpensive trial documents and exhibits.

Copier-based printer functions have been incorporated into many copier models. By linking the copier to an office network, print jobs can be sent to the copier, where the job may either print directly or, in some copiers, may be stored in a special operator-specific directory and printed at the operator's convenience. Copier-based printing takes advantage of the speed of the copier and also allows a printed document to be hole-punched, stapled, or double-sided with ease. Both black and white and color copiers now have the capability of being linked to an office network as printers. Copier-based printing systems also allow the client to be billed for large print jobs using billing software or hardware already attached to the copier for copy charging.

Follow me printing has become more recently adopted in law firms particularly because of the added security and flexibility benefits. This solution allows the operator to initiate a print job from any workstation and then execute that print job only once physically present at the designated printer using an authentication method such as a username and password or ID card.

§ 4.2.3 Components of computer systems—Communication devices

Communication devices are considered both input and output hardware. Computer users exchange data from computer to computer using a *network card*, which allows data to be transmitted wirelessly, through cabling, fiberoptics, or satellite links. A communication link is necessary for email and Internet. It also is needed to connect with online legal research services, such as lexisnexis.com and Westlaw. Law offices are usually connected to the Internet by a router.

Wireless cards are very common and allow computers to connect to networks without cables. Wireless Service includes *WiFi*, which connects to a wireless router and 3G or 4G LTE wireless offered by cellular phone companies that can be used anywhere a cellphone signal can be received.

A *MiFi* taps into 3G or 4G mobile phone networks and uses this connection to create a mini wireless broadband cloud or hotspot. This can then be shared between mobile internet-enabled devices such as smartphones, laptops, and tablets that are within range of its signal.

§ 4.2.4   Components of computer systems—The CPU and internal memory

The CPU directs the flow of information, performs all calculations, and controls all the components of the computer system. While it is processing, there is a continual exchange of data between the CPU and the internal and external memory storage areas. The internal memory area stores the programs the CPU is actively using. The external memory area is used for longer-term data storage.

When a computer is switched on, the CPU begins by accessing Basic Input Output System (BIOS) or read-only memory (ROM) instructions that are permanently stored on the circuit board located inside the computer. These instruction routines summon the operating system software instructions.

What is displayed on the screen, are stored in the internal memory storage area called *random access memory* (RAM). The CPU can quickly access, process, change, and replace the data, and as this occurs, the screen changes. This type of memory is volatile—all the data that it holds will be lost when the electricity is turned off. In order to retain the contents of the screen, it must be saved to an external memory device. Backup is a second copy of computer data made to avoid data loss in the event of a computer outage.

§ 4.2.5   Components of computer systems—External memory

Processed data can be permanently stored externally on magnetic disks or other storage media. *External* storage reflects storage not included on the motherboard or CPU, and includes drives that may be permanently installed in the computer chassis. Storage media memory capacity is gauged in terms of bytes. The term *byte* refers to the amount of space required to store one character of information. One byte is the equivalent of one letter, number, or punctuation mark. A one-page double-spaced document is approximately 2,000 to 3,000 bytes. Instead of referring to bytes singly, they are grouped by thousands (kilobytes), millions (megabytes), billions (gigabytes), and 1,000 billion (terabytes). There are a number of forms of external memory media now in use.

USB drives. Over the last few years, *USB drives*, smaller versions of which are often called memory sticks, flash drives, or thumb drives, have come into common use. These have made CD-ROMs and zip drives obsolete. These very small devices plug into USB ports and contain memory that functions as a hard drive. The term *USB drive* covers a broad variety of devices and also includes larger devices that are integrated into hardware much like a hard drive. USB drives can now hold terabytes of data. There are security issues associated with USB drives, since vast amounts of data can be easily copied from a computer very quickly. USB drives can also be used to boot the computer to a different operating system, typically not for legitimate purposes. The best practice for using USB drives is to use password-protected encryption to avoid loss of confidential data should the drive be misplaced.

It's worth noting that with tablets' popularity on the rise, many do not have USB ports to share data. Instead these tablets have SD and microSD cards slots.

Internal hard disk drive. The internal hard disk drive is nonremovable and located in the case of the computer. The internal hard disk drive housed in the case of a computer usually stores up to about two terabytes, and technology continually changes, so the amount of data that can be stored will undoubtedly continue to increase.

External hard disk drive. The external backup drive is a portable drive that connects into an outside port of the computer, such as the USB port. As with USB drives, it is a best practice to encrypt the drive with a password to protect against unauthorized use.

§ 4.3   Operating systems

The ***operating system*** is software, usually installed in the computer at the time of purchase, that must be in place before any other software can be operated. The operating system tells the computer how to store a file, controls the flow of information to and from the CPU, coordinates input and output devices, and does a variety of other tasks. It also performs housekeeping chores such as allocating resources to software applications. The majority of law firms are now using a version of Windows. While the Macintosh is well respected, the perceived difficulty of integrating it with Windows programs has made it less popular in law offices. Macintosh technology is often chosen for design and art applications, where its programming is considered especially good, and Macintosh is very competitive in the market for higher-end—more expensive and better designed—computers.

§ 4.3.1   Operating systems—Windows

Windows operating system (Windows OS), or simply Windows, is the dominant operating system in the personal computer (PC) realm. Windows has gone through dozens of upgrades since its inception in the 1980's. The current version is Windows 10. Rather than using character-based commands, Windows provides a graphical user interface or GUI (pronounced "gooey") to display menus and choices. Windows is easy to learn because it uses icons, or pictures, which are considered user-friendly. All the programs written for the Windows environment have similar menus and basic commands, such as saving, printing, editing, and displaying documents, that are performed in the same way. Windows provides for multitasking, so a user can be working on a word processing document, a spreadsheet document, and a presentation document at the same time. Information in one program can be moved or copied from one application to another.

Data and graphics can be linked to or embedded in another Windows program or application, and if the data is updated in one program, it will automatically be updated in the other program.

One of the most helpful features of Windows is that information is presented in WYSIWYG fashion, or "what you see is what you get"; the screen displays exactly what will be printed. It is very easy to use graphics and fonts to make attractive documents.

§ 4.3.2 Operating systems—Windows XP, Vista, Windows 7, Windows 8, and Windows 10

Windows XP (2001), Vista (2006), Windows 7 (2009), Windows 8 (2012), and Windowns 10 (2015) are examples of Windows operating system releases overtime. They are graphical user interfaces; they use icons and have a WYSIWYG screen. They also have multiple windows (display screens) that can run separate programs simultaneously. These systems require progressively faster processing units. The newest version, Windows 10, has several new features such Timeline, which displays recent activity such as browsing or files so you can quickly resume working on previously used sites or documents. Windows 10 also includes Focus assist, which creates distraction-free work times by blocking notifications, sounds, and alerts. Additionally, Windows 10 offers Nearby sharing to provide the ability to share videos, photos, documents, and websites instantly using Bluetooth or WiFi with other compatible PCs.

§ 4.4 Computer size classifications

Generally, computers are classified into four sizes: mainframes, minicomputers, microcomputers, and portables.

Mainframe computers are large, very expensive, high-speed machines that require trained operators and special temperature environments.

Minicomputers are midsized, powerful computers often used as network servers. Large law firms that have branch offices and desire to share data and programs generally use this class of computers. Individual computer workstations (much less costly than the minicomputer) are linked or networked to the minicomputer or *server.*

Microcomputers are small-sized computers known as personal or desktop computers (PCs). They are very affordable, easy to use, and require only a small area of desk space. PCs can work individually or they can be networked so data and *peripherals*, such as printers and scanners, can be shared with other PCs on a system. Microcomputers can be part of a *local area network* (LAN) or part of a *wide area network* (WAN). A LAN connects computers that are located close together (in the same building) and are joined by cables or with a wireless connection. A WAN connects computers that are located farther apart, for instance, in another city. A WAN uses high-speed data lines and communications-satellite linkage. Computer technicians are usually required to maintain LANs and WANs, which are complex systems.

Portable computers include notebooks, laptops, handheld, tablets, and even smart phones.

§ 4.5 Software applications

The term *application* refers to the specific tasks a computer can do and the jobs it can perform. The most common application is word processing. The operator uses word processing software to produce letters, memoranda, reports, pleadings, and many other legal documents. To create more complex documents, such as newsletters, catalogs, marketing materials, and business reports, the operator can use word processing software to enter the text, a graphics program to create pictures and other visual enhancements, and then use the page layout capabilities of desktop publishing software to make a document that is camera-ready for printing on laser printers or typesetting equipment.

Many law firms use spreadsheet software to analyze financial and statistical data. A spreadsheet is similar to a manual worksheet or an accountant's ledger but is not limited to the size of a piece of paper. It can contain hundreds of columns and thousands of rows, and when data is changed in one place, the rest of the calculations will automatically update. Another type of software commonly used in law firms is database software that is used to keep track of personnel, clients, and projects and can be used in litigation to organize and provide quick access to discovery documents. Litigation support staff also use presentation software to assemble, organize, and create persuasive trial presentations.

§ 4.6 Word processing programs

In the following sections, the features and functions of word processing programs are described. These are features every operator should master, regardless of the word processing program in use.

§ 4.6.1 Word processing programs—Basics

Default settings. To make word processing easy, program default settings are used. When an operator starts with a clear screen and begins to enter text, the document automatically uses the settings for a standard sheet of paper, has one-inch margins, begins in single line spacing, and has tab settings every half inch.

Screen. The screen commonly displays areas such as status line, rulers, and menu selection bars. The status line, usually at the bottom or top of the screen, displays such information as the page number, the vertical and horizontal position of the cursor, and the document's file name.

For successful word processing, the operator needs to be able to visualize how the document on the screen will look when printed. The operator can look at the status line and relate the numerical values displayed to those on a sheet of paper or, more easily, on most contemporary word processing software, simply preview the printed document.

Cursor or insertion point movements. The flashing square or bar on the screen is called the *cursor*, and it indicates where the next character will appear or the next edit will take place. There are a number of shortcuts that can be used to search to the beginning or end of the document, beginning or end of the line, to move from paragraph to paragraph, page to page, word to word, and so forth. Check the Help feature (search for shortcut keys), computer manuals, or reference books to learn more about these shortcuts.

Word wraparound. In word processing, as text reaches the end of the line, it automatically wraps to the next line so the operator can continue entering text without worrying about where the lines will end. This feature, word wraparound, is one of the features that initially made word processing so popular.

At least one popularly used word processing program does not have an easy method to create and number the typical pleading style paragraph, which has a five-space indent followed by a number and period, followed by a five-space indent, where text begins. These paragraphs wrap back to the left margin on the second and following lines. Inexperienced operators sometimes choose to use a hanging indent paragraph, which is much easier to invoke. Check a computer manual or reference book or talk with a trainer or experienced operator to learn the correct formatting structure for a pleading paragraph. In an emergency, the formatting can be copied from a paragraph in a different pleading that is correctly structured. Just copy the paragraph and type in the new text over the old. To start a new paragraph with the same formatting, hit enter at the end of the previous paragraph to bring up existing formatting and, if used, automatic paragraph numbering. These concepts are equally applicable to the preparation of motion briefs, appellate briefs, and contracts, which may also require cross-reference to a table of contents.

Paper size. The page format or page setup options allow the operator to select a paper size other than the standard 8 1/2 × 11 sheet of paper. Choices include legal (8 1/2 × 14 inches), executive (7 1/4 × 10 1/2 inches), envelope (4 × 9 inches), numerous label sizes, and custom sizes. The operator may also choose the direction of printing on the page. Portrait orientation prints text down the length of the page; landscape orientation prints text across the width of the paper. Some less sophisticated printers do not support landscape printing.

Portrait and Landscape Orientation

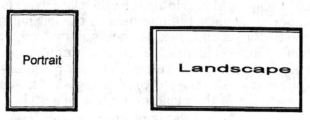

Pleading paper. Some courts require paper with left and right ruled margins. Some local courts require the California format, which uses line numbering to place the numbers on the left margin, graphics to place the vertical rule lines next to the line numbers, and footers to place law firm's name, address and phone numbers on the bottom right corner of each page. Because creating numbered lines and ruled margins requires advanced word processing skills, some software includes options to select the pleading format as a style or template.

Margins. The standard default top and bottom margins are one inch, and the left and right margins are either 1 or 1 1/4 inches depending on the software. Margins can be changed either before or after entering text. To fit more text on a page, decrease the margins. Decreasing the bottom margin from 1 inch to 1/2 inch often allows three more lines of text on a page.

Line spacing. The default setting for line spacing is single spaced. The operator can change text to any line spacing—double, triple, or any fixed increment—either before or after the text is entered. Pleadings, agreements, and other legal documents may require several line spacing changes within the same document. For example, most briefs require double spacing with quotations cited within the brief being single spaced. As to line spacing, local court rules should always be checked to make sure that spacing requirements are met.

Tabs. The tab key has two functions. First, it is used to align columns of text or numbers instead of pressing the spacebar to push characters into columns. When the spacebar is used, the text may look aligned on the screen but may print misaligned. When tabs are used to align text, all the entries in any one column can be readjusted simply by moving the tab setting rather than adjusting each row.

Most word processing programs have four types of tab alignments: left, center, right, and decimal alignment. The chart below demonstrates each of these types of alignment.

Date	Provider of Service	Amount Due	Status
10/15/02	County Hospital	$12,223.00	Pending
10/15/02	Anesthesiologists	1,700.00	Paid
10/18/02	Nursing Services	3,333.04	Paid
10/21/02	Nursing Services	2,752.11	Not billed
↑	↑	↑	↑
Left	**Center**	**Decimal**	**Right**

The tab key's second function is to move the cursor or insertion point forward through user menu choices or options that are displayed in various software programs and to move the cursor or insertion point around in tables created in word processing and spreadsheet tables. A shift + tab key combination moves the cursor or insertion point backwards in menus and tables. To override the tab's cursor movement in a table, the operator must use a special key combination such as home + tab, control + tab, or shift + tab. Often tables without borders are used instead of tabs because they are more flexible.

Indent. The indent key is sometimes called a temporary left margin. It is used to push text in from the left margin. Each time the indent key is pressed, it moves the paragraph of text over one more tab stop, usually 1/2 inch. This way the operator can quickly set off subsections of a document so the document is easier to read and understand. The indent key (with other paragraph formatting commands) can make formatting numbered paragraphs, bullet points, and quoted material simple.

Another type of indent is hanging indent. The first line hangs out to the left and the second and consecutive lines are indented under the first line. This format is used to format bibliography entries, glossary terms, and, in some programs, bulleted and numbered lists.

Justification. Justification refers to the four types of text alignment. When text aligns only on the left margin with a ragged right margin, it is left justified. When text is distributed between margins aligned on both left and right, it is called full justification. The software automatically adds extra space between the words so that each line is the same length (a process called kerning). When the operator selects center, the cursor moves to the center of the screen and the text is centered between the left and right margins. When the operator selects right justification, the cursor is placed on the far right margin, and as the text is entered, it is aligned on the right-hand side.

Left Justification	Center Justification	Right Justification	Full Justification
Word processing systems should be fast, user friendly, and easy to learn. The first word processing systems were slow, required the use of many codes, and were difficult to learn.	Word processing systems should be fast, user friendly, and easy to learn. The first word processing systems were slow, required the use of many codes, and were difficult to learn.	Word processing systems should be fast, user friendly, and easy to learn. The first word processing systems were slow, required the use of many codes, and were difficult to learn.	Word processing systems should be fast, user friendly, and easy to learn. The first word processing systems were slow, required the use of many codes, and were difficult to learn.

Which type of justification to use depends on the style chosen by the law firm. Left justification tends to be easier to read and therefore easier to proofread, but newsletters and marketing materials may use full justification for a more polished look, and some firms prefer the typeset appearance of full justification for letters and pleadings. Also, some courts may require full justification.

Fonts. The term **fonts** refers to the style or design of a collection of letters, numerals, symbols, and punctuation marks. The fonts available depend on the software program and the capabilities of the printer. The ability to see the actual font shape and size on the computer screen is dependent on the type of word processing program. Windows-based programs display most fonts on screen as they will print out.

There are two kinds of fonts: serif, which has small extensions at the bottom and top of many characters called serifs, and sans serif, which does not have the extensions. Below are examples of serif and sans serif fonts in three point sizes:

This is a sample of a serif font, Times New Roman, 8 pt.

This is a sample of a serif font, Times New Roman, 12 pt.

This is a sample of a serif font, Times New Roman, 16 pt.

This is a sample of a sans serif font, Arial, 8 pt.

This is a sample of a sans serif font, Arial, 12 pt.

This is a sample of a sans serif font, Arial, 16 pt.

Some guidelines for using fonts in a document:

1. Keep the number of font types to three per page—more than that may make the document appear busy.

2. Headings and subheadings are sometimes presented in sans serif fonts, such as Arial, while the body of the document is in serif fonts, such as Times New Roman. (Note that this kind of combination is not formal enough for many kinds of legal documents.)

3. Point sizes for headings should be balanced and proportional to the point size of the body of the document. Main headings may be 2 to 4 point sizes larger than subheadings, while subheadings could be 2 to 4 point sizes larger than the body of the document. Again, this much variation in point size is not common in formal documents such as pleadings and would not be permitted in appeal documents, which have strict font type and size requirements.

4. For a contemporary professional look, use bold or italics to emphasize text. Larger font size may also be used in less formal applications. Underlining has fallen somewhat out of fashion and may give the appearance that the document's author is technologically out-of-date (although it is still acceptable in pleadings for case citations in most courts).

5. Use the style feature to apply formatting to headings, subheadings, and paragraphs. This feature, discussed below, allows the operator to quickly make font changes in similar levels of text.

§ 4.6.2 Word processing programs—Editing tools

Selecting text. Text can be changed or formatted before or after it is entered. Once text is entered, however, the operator must select the text and then perform the needed command. When text is selected, it appears in reverse video or in a different color. There are a number of shortcuts that can be used to select text more efficiently. Computer manuals or reference books can provide details on these shortcuts.

Inserting text. There are two modes for inserting text. Automatic insert is the normal mode. The operator places the cursor where text needs to be inserted and then begins to enter text. The existing text automatically moves to the right, making space for the newly entered text. Typeover or overtype, a second type of insert function, is destructive: when the operator begins to enter text, the new letters are inserted over the old characters, wiping out the text that was previously entered.

Deleting text. The operator presses backspace to delete characters to the left of the cursor and presses delete to delete characters to the right of the cursor or insertion point. There are a number of shortcuts to delete words, paragraphs, and sections of text more efficiently. One of the largest practical differences between Word and Word Perfect is the direction in which text is deleted when certain shortcuts are used.

However, if the operator is using a MacIntosh computer, there is only backspace, no delete. The operator should consult computer manuals or reference books to learn the correct deletion shortcuts for the program in use.

Keyboard shortcuts. Keyboard shortcuts are usually one or two keys, alone or in combination, which tell the computer program to do a certain task. They are used to replace actions found in a menu using a pointing device.

Moving and copying text. One of the most common word processing tasks is moving or copying text. Moving text means that selected text is deleted from its original position and moved to a new location in the same document or to an entirely different document. Copying text means that the selected text is duplicated at another place in the document or in another document.

Windows-based word processing has a feature called *drag and drop* that simplifies the moving or copying procedure and is used when the text is being moved to a close location in the same file. Using the mouse, text is selected and then, while holding down a mouse key (or control plus the mouse key when copying), the operator drags the text to a new location, releases the mouse button, and drops the text in its new position. The text that is copied or moved is placed in a temporary memory area called the clipboard. Once text is in the clipboard, it can easily be moved or copied to other applications or documents.

Append and spike. Two features that are related to move and copy are **append and spike**. Append allows the operator to gather or collect, in order, each item deleted and then insert them as a group in another location or document. Note that the clipboard can sometimes be used to collect and paste multiple items from different programs. Spike allows the operator to select text and copy it to the end of an existing document without opening or retrieving that document to the screen.

Search. The search feature allows the operator to quickly find a specific word or code in a document. Searches can be performed through some or all of the document. The term search string refers to the actual text or code that is being searched for and matched. If the search string is entered in upper case letters, only upper case letters will be matched. If the string is entered in lower case letters, both upper case and lower case letters will be matched. The ability of the search function to match upper and lower case words is referred to as case sensitivity, and each word processing program has its own guidelines.

Search and Replace. Search and replace allows the operator to search for text, special symbols, and formatting and replace them with other text, codes, and formats. For example, if the operator spells Hansen with an "en" throughout a document and then finds out the name should be spelled with an "on", the search and replace feature can be used to quickly make the correction.

Always save the document before searching and replacing. It is easy to make a mistake in the search and replace string and change the document incorrectly. For example, if the operator searched for spaces and replaced them with nothing, all words would become one continuous string. If a mistake occurs during search and replace, the operator should click on the undo icon, which will reverse all occurrences of the replacement.

§ 4.6.3   Word processing programs—Formatting tools

Headers and Footers. Headers place text and graphics at the top of each page, and footers place text and graphics at the bottom of each page. Automatic page numbering codes can be inserted in headers and footers so each page is numbered consecutively. Some programs allow the operator to insert codes in the header or footer that give the document's file name and path and the date and time the file was created and saved.

Headers should be used to create continuation page headings in long letters, memos, and reports, rather than manually keying in the header on each page. The header should be placed at the beginning of the document and formatted so it does not print on the first page. With headers, the document can be edited and the page headings will automatically adjust when text is inserted or deleted or spacing is changed.

Footers are used in pleadings to place the title and page number of the pleading on each page, in wills and other estate planning documents, and real estate documents. Footers are especially useful for identifying documents that are to be compared and redlined.

Footnotes and endnotes. Footnotes are created by placing the cursor at the end of the word, phrase, or sentence where the footnote number should appear. Then the operator chooses a menu option to create the footnote, and typically, a separate window appears where the operator types the footnote text. When that window is closed, the program places a superscripted number or symbol in the main text, adds a 2 1/2 inch line to separate the main text from the footnote text, and places the text of the footnote at the bottom of the page. When footnotes are deleted, inserted, or moved, the numbering (or in some cases, symbolic) sequence is automatically updated. The footnote text may not appear on the regular screen, and in order to see how the footnotes will look when printed, the operator may have to preview the document. Footnote continuation notes can also be inserted. Endnotes work exactly like footnotes, but when the endnote is entered, the operator chooses endnote placement.

Columns. Text can be formatted into columns that allow the operator to create newsletters, advertising brochures, catalogs, phone lists or other multicolumn documents. To create newspaper-style columns, the operator defines the number and width of columns needed. Column width can be equal or unequal. As the text is entered, it wraps within the column. When the text reaches the bottom of the page, it automatically continues at the top of the next column. The operator can start a new column before the text reaches the bottom of the page with a simple keystroke combination. An entire document or a selected part of the text can be formatted in columns, and the columnar format can be applied after the text is entered. Sometimes a vertical line or rule is placed between columns to give a professional look to the document.

Tables. A table is composed of vertical columns and horizontal rows that form cells. To create a table, the operator identifies the number of vertical columns and horizontal rows needed. Once a table is created, columns and rows can be added or deleted, the widths of the columns can be adjusted, and columns or rows can be moved or copied with just a few keystrokes.

The operator then enters text in each cell and makes formatting decisions about the appearance of the table. For example, the text can be boldfaced, italicized, set in various font types and sizes, centered, left-aligned, right-aligned, or aligned on the decimal point. The table itself can be enhanced by using a variety of styles of vertical or horizontal lines called borders and cells can be shaded in a number of colors.

Tables without borders can also be used to present text side by side. For example, a résumé is often formatted with side headings on the left margin of the paper with the descriptive text set off to the right side. This table format has two columns and as many rows as there are side headings. The left column is narrower than the right column, and no border lines are used.

Some legal usages that can be set up in a table format without border lines are multiple address blocks placed in letters or in certificates of mailing, deposition and medical summaries, pleading captions, side-by-side signature blocks, notary blocks, and client/case information lists.

§ 4.6.4 Word processing programs—Proofreading tools

Spell checker. Most word processing programs have a spelling function that can be left on while typing to flag spelling errors as they are typed or can be invoked after a document is completed. The word processing program compares each word on the screen to the words in its internal dictionary, which may contain over 100,000 words. If a match is not made, the word is highlighted so that the operator can check its spelling. The operator can choose to correct the word, ignore the word, or add the word to a custom dictionary.

A spell checker finds not only misspelled words but also double occurrences of words, irregular case, and words that contain both alphabet and numeric characters. The pitfall of the spell checker is that it does not find all mistakes. For example, it will not find a misspelling that is also a correct spelling in other circumstances, such as

"Untied" States, or an incorrect word choice, such as "there" instead of "they're".

Thesaurus. This word processing tool is used to find synonyms, or words with similar meanings, and antonyms, or words with opposite meanings. It can also be used to help determine the meaning of a word. For example, for the word "egregious", the thesaurus would list the synonyms "gross, outrageous, flagrant". The thesaurus can also be used to determine correct word choice and to differentiate between words that sound alike.

Grammar checker. Some grammar checkers run at the same time as the spell checker and identify both spelling and grammatical errors. The grammar checker assists in identifying verb-subject disagreement, sentence fragments, misplaced punctuation, extra spaces between words, and a number of other grammatical and typographical issues. The programs often suggest potential corrections for the identified problems. Some grammar checkers may also evaluate writing for formal, business, or casual writing style; provide readability statistics; and offer suggestions on how to improve the writing. Be careful when using grammar checker as legal writing is not always accurate—always proofread.

§ 4.6.5 Word processing programs—Automating word processing tasks

Automatic paragraph numbering. This feature allows the operator to enter a special code to automatically number paragraphs of text. When the operator moves, inserts, or deletes paragraphs, the paragraphs will automatically renumber sequentially. Pleadings, business and commercial agreements, real estate documents, and estate planning documents commonly contain numbered paragraphs.

Styles. A *style* is a number of formatting choices bundled together and given a name to make it easy to apply that look to multiple paragraphs or the same look to something else. Styles can help give a professional look to a document. For example, in this book, all the main headings are bold and use the same font type and size; the subheadings for each topic use the identical font and paragraph numbering; and the tables of contents at the beginning of each chapter look alike. The tool used to create this consistent appearance in a word processing document, while reducing keystrokes required to format the document, is called styles. The codes that will be used in each section are saved with style names, such as "Main Heading, Subheading 1, Subheading 2," and "Text Body." The operator selects the text to be formatted and then chooses a style name from a menu and applies it to the selected text.

This feature also makes it effortless to experiment with different formats before deciding on the best one for the document. After applying styles to the document, the operator simply changes the style code, for instance, for all headings, and immediately all the headings are updated with the new formatting choices. The same procedure can be used to change formatting in paragraph text.

Another advantage of styles is that once a particular set of styles is created and saved, it is available for use in every document and by every user. Many law firms use styles because lawyers, paralegals, and assistants can all use them, providing uniformity in firm documents. Styles can also save time, because the users do not have to learn how to do complex formatting.

Macros. This feature allows the operator to record keystrokes and then play them back with just a few keystrokes. For example, creating a footer may require eight keystrokes. Using a macro, the operator can access the footer screen with perhaps only two keystrokes. Some common tasks that are automated using macros are:

- Letter format and dateline
- Memo openings
- Letter signature blocks
- Pleading signature blocks
- Creating captions
- Retrieving captions
- Standard language used in pleadings
- Changing directories
- Formatting
- Creating and editing headers and footers
- Printing commands

The process for creating a macro usually includes:
1. Giving the macro a name and description;
2. Turning on the recording process;
3. Recording the keystrokes; and
4. Turning off the recording process.

Once the macro is created, it can be used at any time. Macros can be assigned to shortcut keys or icons or listed in menus so they are easy to access.

Complex macros that include programming language to make menus and customized screen options are most often created by expert in-house programmers or by outside consultants. However, the lawyer's assistant should learn how to make simple macros. The simplification of routine tasks is well worth the effort.

Autocorrect. The autocorrect function can be used to create very simple automated functions. The original purpose of the autocorrect function is to correct common misspellings as they are typed, but it can also be used to automate typing long or complicated character strings. Input a short syllable that will not commonly be used in normal typing, such as "mx", into the autocorrect list. When prompted for the text to replace the character string, the operator should type in the desired phrase, add it to the list when prompted, and exit the autocorrect screen. The next time the syllable is typed, the system will automatically replace it with the longer text string. This technique can also be used temporarily, deleting the autocorrect syllable from the list when the need for it no longer exists.

Table of authorities. Legal briefs contain citations referring to case law, statutes, rules, and other legal authorities. Some courts require that these citations be listed or indexed, including a page number reference, in a table at the beginning of the document. Sophisticated word processing programs have a feature that allows the operator to mark each citation and authority, categorize it as case law, statutes, etc., and then generate a list of the authorities. When changes are made to the document, the table of authorities can be corrected and updated quickly.

Form documents. It is a good practice to save any document that may be used again as a form. The most basic form document is a document filled with blanks that can be copied and used over again by deleting the blanks and filling in the pertinent information. More complex documents incorporate a model form called a "template", which includes macro and merge features. Many lawyer's assistants maintain a form file that includes a hard copy of each form marked with its computer filename so it can be accessed efficiently.

Document assembly. Document assembly is the process of creating several short, separate documents that can be used over and over again. The small documents, sometimes referred to as standard paragraphs or boilerplate paragraphs, can be combined to make one large document. For example, this process could be used to tailor a will by selecting from a group of previously stored required and optional paragraphs that might reflect such possibilities as the existence or nonexistence of a surviving spouse or children, the statutory requirements in different states of domicile, the presence or absence of specific bequests, and possible use of a testamentary trust.

Document comparisons. This feature allows the user to compare two versions of a document. Additions in the new version are marked with redline underscoring (called redline because the changes are often shown in red) and deletions in the new version are marked with strikeout or strikethrough, making it easy to see the changes between the original and new versions. Document comparisons done with redlining are often called redlines, or when the ink used is black, sometimes blacklines. Word processing programs are able to compare documents, but for larger or more complex comparisons, specialized software is desirable.

Merging. Merging is the process of combining data from two files to make a third document. The first file contains a form letter, an envelope, or label format. This file is called the main document or primary file. The second file contains a set of names, addresses, phone numbers, and other types of individual information. This file is called the data source or secondary file. Codes that match the fields in the data source are placed in the form letter, memorandum, table, chart, list, and envelope. The operator then performs a sequence of commands that combines or merges the primary and data source files. The merge process creates a third file containing personalized letters, usually separated by page breaks, envelopes, or labels for each separate name in the data source. The resulting document of individual letters can be edited, saved, and printed just as if the operator had typed the entire text.

The data source includes fields and records. A field is one piece of information about a person or business. It can be a person's title (Mr., Mrs., Ms., Dr.), a person's first name and last name, a business name, address, phone number, or any other piece of information. A record is made up of all the fields relating to that one person or business. Because the data source file can be used over and over again with various main documents or primary files, it should contain information for current and future use. For example, a data source file listing possible witnesses might include a field for the witness's phone number. The phone number may never be used in a letter, but it might be used to create a call-back or follow-up list for the lawyer's assistant.

§ 4.6.6 Word processing programs—Troubleshooting

Help. Most word processing programs have a help feature that can be accessed to explain what a feature does and how it works. In Windows-based programs, the help feature is comprehensive, and the user is able to print the help topics shown on the screen.

Undo. In Windows-based word processing programs, there is a feature that allows the user to undo a previous command. If the operator makes a mistake, simply click on undo and the last steps are reversed. This feature is important; it can allow the instant reversal of very large mistakes.

Reveal codes. Some word processing programs use reveal codes. For those, word processing operators must know how to determine what codes have been inserted into a document and to analyze their placement and why or how they are working. Codes are classified as either open or paired. *Open codes*, such as line spacing, margins, tab sets, font changes, justification, and page numbering, affect only the text to the right of the code. *Paired codes*, such as underline, bold, italics, and the styles on and off codes, affect only the text inserted between a pair of codes. The location and use of the reveal codes function varies dramatically from program to program. Check the user's manual for more information.

Ctrl+Alt+Delete. If a computer freezes, this combination of keystrokes allows the operator to end a task or shut down or restart the computer if necessary. Note that some data may be lost.

Printing. Printers occasionally stop working, and there are several places to check for proper operation. First, be familiar with the error messages and lights that indicate such things as paper out, paper jam, off line, low ink, and so forth. Second, make sure all cords are plugged in and that there is a good cable connection between the computer and printer. Third, look at the menus relating to printing to see if the proper printer type and location are selected and change the settings if they are not correct.

§ 4.6.7   Word processing programs—Converting file formats

When a document is created and saved, it is embedded with codes that distinguish its file format, which is determined by the operating system type, the word processing software type, and the version of the software program. Special conversion steps must be taken to change the file's format into one that is compatible with other software. Software conversion programs are available to assist in converting file formats, and some programs have built-in conversion software.

When different versions of the same software are used, documents created and saved in an older version of the software can be used in newer versions without any additional steps. Documents created and saved in a newer version have to be converted down to the older version using special steps. The user manual will explain how to convert documents as needed.

§ 4.7   Document management

A well-defined method for naming and controlling files saves time and energy in locating documents, provides consistency and uniformity throughout an office, is easy to learn, and is essential for easy file identification. Many offices have a systematic method of naming documents and routinely place a document name and path in a small font on the last page or in a footer in the document, making the document easy to locate.

The first part of a **document path** identifies the external storage area where the document is saved. For example, a document can be saved on A:, the first disk drive slot; on B:, the second disk drive slot; on C:, the hard drive; or on F: to Z:, indicating locations on a network.

The second part of a file name is called the path. The C: drive and network drives are divided into subdirectories or folders (in Windows-based programs) created and named by the operator. A subdirectory, folder, or a combination of subdirectories or folders make up the path to the document. A file can be referred to by its document name or by its full path name.

The last part of the document path is the document name. Windows-based programs allow for lengthy, descriptive document names, which can include the name of the document, the recipient, the matter, or other identifiers. All letters and numbers and many symbols can be used in the creation of a file name. If the operator inadvertently chooses an inappropriate symbol, the computer will likely reject the chosen name. To save time and potential trouble, the operator should consult the user manual to determine which symbols can be used.

Windows associates extensions with applications. For example, any document or file with a ".wpd" extension will be opened with WordPerfect, and any document or file with a ".doc" extension will be opened with Microsoft Word. If it is necessary to rename a document, do not alter endings such as ".wpd,.doc," or ".pdf", which tell the computer how to open and run the documents.

Some standard ways of organizing subdirectories or folders in a law office are:

- Client name or number and then subdividing by matters
- Lawyer
- Practice area
- Types of documents
- Combinations of the above

§ 4.7.1   Document management—Document management systems (DMSs)

To help with the naming of documents and file management, some law firms purchase document management software that takes the job of naming the files away from the operator and automatically assigns file names according to standardized programming instructions. The *document management system* or DMS creates a unique document number that is typically inserted into a footer or other location in the document so the document can be easily recalled.

Document management systems are continually evolving. Contemporary systems are designed to allow more flexibility in document storage and access. Some programs allow separate documents to be related together so that, for a project containing multiple documents, all documents can be accessed at once, simplifying email, printing, and other tasks. Some systems allow the system administrator to create storage fields designed to meet specific needs—product codes for retail clients, statutory references for research, and so forth. Another feature appearing in some of today's document management systems is a comments screen with text that is searched at the same time as the document name, allowing for information at a glance without opening the document and document location using a much broader range of search terms.

§ 4.8   Spreadsheet programs

A computerized spreadsheet is an electronic worksheet like an accounting ledger that gives the operator tools to store, calculate, manage, analyze, and manipulate numbers. Using spreadsheet software, data can be displayed graphically using bar graphs, line graphs, pie charts, or stacked bar graphs. In the past, spreadsheets were often only used by law office management to produce financial and accounting records and by lawyers who specialized in finance-related practice areas like bankruptcy, tax law, real estate, and estate planning. Because today's Windows-based programs are easier to learn and use and can be linked with word processing documents, lawyer's assistants are quickly identifying new ways to use spreadsheets. Some legal applications include tracking case costs, calculating claims for damages, calculating child support and alimony, dividing assets in divorce cases, calculating and analyzing lost wages, and creating professional-looking trial exhibits.

§ 4.9 Database management systems

Database management system software is used to collect, store, and organize data into a database. Once a *database* is created and saved, the fields can be alphabetized or sorted. Each record can be searched or queried for key words or specific information. New information can be added to the database; incorrect information can be modified. The information in a database can be used to create a variety of reports. The data can also be merged with merge documents in word processing programs.

Lawyer's assistants can use database software in a variety of ways. It can be used to keep track of a law firm's clients. An assistant can use the database software to index discovery documents, including when a particular document was created, who created it, why it was created, who got copies of it, and so on. Some assistants organize the information contained in medical summaries, including the name of the doctor or provider of a service, date of service, medications given, prognosis notes, and so forth. Law librarians can use database software to keep track of the brief bank. The fields in this database might include the name of the brief, the author, the case, or key words.

§ 4.10 Time and billing software

Time and billing software is used to track billable and nonbillable time, calculate charges and costs, and then create the statements and invoices that are sent to the clients. Some programs have features that enable the user to start and stop a timer for accurate time reporting. The lawyer's assistant often inputs attorney time into the billing software, and the accounting department generates the bills. In small law firms, the lawyer's assistant may manage the entire billing system, including adding and editing client data, billing rates, special rates, etc. Time and billing software is also capable of generating work-in-progress (WIP) reports and billable and nonbillable time reports by timekeeper.

§ 4.11 Calendaring/docket programs

One of the most critical aspects of a lawyer's assistant's job is to keep track of critical dates for the client and lawyer. (See Chapter 3,

The Law Office). Many law offices now use electronic calendars and docket programs to monitor activities, to schedule events, and to bring up reminders of upcoming deadlines. Hard copies of the master calendar can be prepared and distributed as needed, and reminders may be programmed into desktop computers, smartphone, Blackberry or similar unit.

§ 4.12 Personal information management software, smartphones, and more

The concept of personal information management surfaced in the late 1980s and, for a time, products directed at these needs were referred to as PIMs. In 2002, the first personal digital assistant (PDA) was released, and the terminology began to change. Personal information management software is intended to provide resources such as address books, lists (including to-do lists), calendar, reminders, email and instant messages, and voice mail.

Today, smartphones, such as iPhones, as well as notebooks, laptops, and handheld computers all provide many of these resources and then some, with text messaging, full Internet access, and specialty applications for everything from searching movie theater directories to purchasing a home. iPhone, and other smartphones, in particular, have become quite popular and in some firms are provided to all attorneys, because mobile device management allows individuals to receive firm information on their device such as e-mail, the firm address book, and even time and billing systems when out of the office.

§ 4.13 Presentation software

Presentation software helps organize information for presentation to an audience. This software can be used to create slides that can be displayed on a computer screen or projected onto a large screen. Slides using text, charts, graphics, scanned photographs, animations, shapes, and sounds are used to make an impact on the audience. Examples include Microsoft PowerPoint and Prezi. These programs include automated coordination of slides, handouts, and speaker's notes.

The trial lawyer may find presentation software such as Trial Director or Sanction extremely effective—both in cost and the ability to persuade an audience. A judge and members of a jury will often comprehend complex ideas more quickly when they are presented through visual aids.

§ 4.14 Imaging technology

In the 1980s, at about the same time the U.S. Post Office began using *optical character recognition* (OCR) equipment to scan addresses and machine-route mail, the possibility of scanning documents in hard copy onto word processing drives became very attractive—a great many businesses still had many documents that documents in hard copy onto word processing drives became very attractive—a great many businesses still had many documents that had not been word processed and had to be typed from scratch when needed. The limitations of OCR scanning at first were severe due to technical limitations and high cost.

Today, however, scanning capability is built into copiers or provided in small desktop units that are priced more like desktop printers, and portable handheld scanners are even available for use out of the office. A significant portion of the programming used to create and manage imaged documents is available free on the Internet. Really superior programs that allow for the manipulation of the scanned image—for better quality; to highlight, label, or add small amounts of text; or to mask information that should not be shown—are now available. Image scanning now is much more common than OCR scanning.

Document scanning can simplify mundane tasks and save time. Commonly used documents can be scanned instead of copied, and the scanned image can then be sent to the printer when a reprint is needed. Scanning documents and sending them by email to other coworkers who may need the same material is typically faster than making multiple copies and routing them through office mail. Word processed letters can be signed and sent by email, saving postage and providing very rapid, cost-free delivery.

§ 4.14.1 Imaging technology—Image scanning

Imaging is used to provide computer storage for key legal documents such as executed settlement agreements or contracts. Word processing documents are converted to pdf (portable document format) documents to electronically file pleadings in federal court (and a few state courts); electronic filing also includes electronic service; and the imaged pleadings are available to all participants online for printing or review whenever needed. An imaged document can safely be sent to opposing counsel without fear of alteration and without risk to the original document. Programming exists to create, store, and process a variety of imaged documents, such as pdfs, jpegs, tiffs, and bitmaps (bmps).

Imaging technology has made the use of color in document creation easier and cheaper. Color desktop scanners or color copiers with scanning functions can scan color photographs or images, which can then be saved in the appropriate computer application. Advertising flyers and colorful newsletters can be produced very cheaply in-house and then sent to a very wide distribution list as cheaply as to a handful of people.

The technology involved in imaging can be very complex, and the work of imaging large volumes of material can be very time-consuming. Legal vendors who once specialized in copying documents for litigation now offer imaging services along with copying—discovery documents that once would have taken dozens of boxes to deliver—

can be stored electronically. Imaging technology is increasingly important in the creation of very professional litigation exhibits, and vendors often have the expertise to make first-rate exhibits using advanced imaging software. The use of an outside vendor is often more cost-effective than imaging large volumes of documents in-house or attempting to create complex documents with the limited software options available in some firms.

Imaging, however, now goes far beyond scanned documents. Logos and pictures can be copied from Internet sites and inserted into emails and word processing documents, creating individualized documents such as employee or procedures manuals for clients, for example. The skills involved in this sort of maneuver are often second nature to lawyer's assistants who grew up playing and working on personal computers at home and at school, but may elude their older counterparts. The savvy lawyer's assistant of every age makes it a point to trade technology tips with coworkers whenever possible and to stay current with the techniques used in the law firm where he or she works. The lawyer's assistant who has technology skills may even be able to introduce new techniques to improve the law firm's work product.

§ 4.14.2 Imaging technology—OCR scanning

Despite the burgeoning importance of imaged documents, OCR scanning is not obsolete. The quality of optical character scans has improved a great deal. Most fonts used in business practice are scannable. It is still possible for a character to be misread—a "1" may be read as "!", for example, depending on the quality of the original being scanned—and OCR-scanned material must be proofread carefully. Large firms with word processing departments often ask the word processing staff to do OCR scanning and proofread the document before it is routed to the lawyer's assistant for revisions. This approach allows for a minimum investment in OCR software, the processing of OCR documents by operators who are familiar with the process and know the hazards, and the processing of OCR documents with less time pressure than is often present at a lawyer's assistant's desk. When documents from outside the firm must be revised, OCR scanning remains a strong option to save time and create a document that can be revised or redlined as needed.

§ 4.15 Email

Email is a system of delivering and receiving messages electronically through computer networks such as the internet. Both the sender and the receiver must have an email address. Email is vital in legal practice, as clients and lawyers are able to send documents, messages, and letters instantly by email.

There are two approaches to email transmission of correspondence. The first is simply to write an informal email. When a situation calls for more formal correspondence, a memo or letter can be prepared as usual, revised and finalized, and attached to an email for transmission. A formal letter with signature can be scanned to a pdf document and attached to the email, or a memo can be attached in regular word processing format. Correspondence to adversaries, such as opposing counsel in litigation, should always be scanned or converted to pdf before emailing.

It is important to record legal counsel via e-mail, or other written documentation, when that counsel is given by phone, text or instant message (IM) so that there is a record of that correspondence which can easily be tracked or referenced as needed. Federal discovery rules on electronic storage require that electronic documents of significance be retained according to a set firm policy, so keeping records of emails sent to clients or on their behalf cannot be overlooked. Learn and follow the firm policy for storing these documents on the computer. Many law firms today utilize a document management system (DMS) as a way to provide a very well-organized client and matter-based electronic storage system.

Another aspect to keep in mind when working with email are email "best practices." Problems can occur with carbon copies (CCs) or blind carbon copies (BCCs), attachments, and general email etiquette. Email, unlike regular correspondence, email can be sent at the touch of a button, and it is easy to make mistakes. It is crucial for the lawyer's assistant to develop a process that prevents errors such as omitting recipients to be copied, mis-sending letters to similar addresses (because email often calls up an address from memory based on the first few letters typed), forgetting attachments, and so forth. A correction can be sent, but the professional image of the firm suffers when corrections are necessary.

One safeguarding technique is to fill in the "to" line last, after attachments have been added and checked, copies and blind copies have been noted on the email, text has been entered in the email and proofread (most email programs have spell checkers, and some operate automatically). Until the email is addressed, it cannot accidentally be sent anywhere with incomplete attachments, spelling errors, or other problems. Another important safeguard is to check each attachment to make sure it is the correct attachment before the email is sent.

Another hazard in emailing documents is the use of Track Changes or other, similar text comparison programs. It may sometimes be desirable to exchange documents with clients showing redlined changes so the client can see the changes that are made, perhaps make some changes of their own and return them to the lawyer, and so forth. But if a document has been created with Track Changes for office use— perhaps a contract that was used for Sunshine Products has been modified for a new client, Radiant Light—then all tracked changes must be accepted before the document is sent. It is not enough to set the document to "Final" display, because it can easily be reset to "Final Showing Markup," which will show that the document was modified from an existing document, possibly calling into question the time billed to create the document, exposing another client's confidential business, and running the risk of offending the new client as well.

As a recipient of an email, it is important to pay attention to all the individuals included on the blind copy. Do not Reply All unless absolutely necessary. This will help avoid long email chains from spiraling out of control and plugging up other people's inbox of whom the message is no longer relevant. If you need to send an off-topic message to a particular individual in an email chain, be courteous and start a new email message with an accurate subject line and key words in the message body so that the recipient can easily search for it again later. Watch out for confusing abbreviations, poor grammar, and other mistakes that distract from your message. A well-worded message is read more smoothly and accurately by your recipient.

The final risk in emailing a word processing document is the existence of metadata. *Metadata* is data stored in the computer that shows who created, accessed, or revised a document, what changes were made and by whom, and the dates and times when all of this occurred. All of this information can be accessed by a person with sufficient training and the right equipment and software. This is a more sophisticated electronic exploration than simply turning on the Track Changes display, but where security or confidentiality are at stake (and in any major litigation), it must be considered. Some email programs automatically provide the option of scrubbing or cleaning out all metadata before a document is sent, and for offices that send many documents by email, such a program is a good investment.

§ 4.16　Computer-assisted legal research

Computer-assisted legal research can locate case law, statutes, citations, and other legal information. Some programs are updated on a daily basis with the most recent case law available to provide lawyers and their assistants with the most up-to-date information. Westlaw and lexisnexis.com are two of the best-known legal research programs, but the computer-assisted legal research market is growing, and other sources are also available. See Chapter 8, The Law Library, for more information about these important tools.

§ 4.17　Internet

The Internet connects computers worldwide and allows computer users to receive and transfer text, programs, graphic images, and sounds. The Internet was launched in 1969 and for many years was used primarily by the government and the scientific and academic communities. In 1989, scientists introduced the Worldwide Web and software tools called web browsers. These new developments provided the general public with a simple way of accessing the Internet and its resources. The Internet is made up of millions of documents that are written in a special language called HyperText Markup Language (HTML). Each individual document is called a web page or website and ranges from one to many screens in length. The opening page of a website is called the home page. Within each of the web pages are links (also known as hypertext, hyperlinks, hotspots, and jumps) that associate one web page to another. By clicking on a hyperlink, the user can quickly move from one location or topic to another. Each website and hyperlink has an address called a ***Universal Resource Locator*** (URL) code on the Internet.

To connect with the Internet, the computer user connects through a LAN or WAN and then through a service provider. There are many commercial internet service providers (ISPs). Once the user is connected, a *web browser*, such as Microsoft Internet Explorer, Mozilla, or several others, accesses websites using their URL. The URL contains three parts:

1. The protocol used, which can be considered the language of the transmitted computer information. Common protocol types are http (HyperText Transfer Protocol), ftp (File Transfer Protocol), and Gopher (a specialized transfer protocol).

2. The ***domain***, which indicates the computer system that stores the information or a group of people who maintain a server. Domains are divided into categories: ".com" (commercial), ".edu" (education), ".org" (nonprofit organizations), ".gov" (government), ".mil" (military), and ".net" (network), to list a few.

3. The actual location of an item on the server.

The Internet is a required tool in law offices since most courts and agencies require efiling. Court rules, form documents, and much more up-to-date information is available. As the assistant finds helpful websites, the bookmark feature in the web browser can be used to add the site to a personal list.

Many law firms block certain websites due to security vulnerabilities. Always keep "safe surfing" in mind when browsing the internet or performing online research. Avoid visiting unfamiliar websites or downloading software from an unverified source. By sticking with legitimate websites you can trust, you will avoid the risk of accidentally clicking on a malware infested website. Utilizing Google alerts, for instance, is a great way to stay apprised of firm, competitor and client news. If you are redirected to click on link, always hover over that link to check the URL. If you do not recognize it or are suspicious, always err on the side of caution.

§ 4.17.1   Internet—The law firm and social media

Because electronic communications reach people as easily at home— thanks to the smartphone and the Internet—as they do at work, more and more people are communicating through social milieu such as

Facebook, Twitter, LinkedIn and so forth. The line between work and socializing is beginning to blur. An attorney writes a blog on a client's website responding to a joking accusation that the client violated a local liquor law. The blog is funny, charming, pleasant, and written on behalf of the client, but it is carefully crafted by the lawyer, because the liquor laws are nothing to joke about, and the city may be watching. The trend of keeping a presence on social media website has and will continue to grow exponentially.

It is important to keep in mind that negative public exposure can put a law firm at risk, and firms are crafting company policies that seek to curtail the more excessive personal expressions of employees in their hours away from work. Lawyer's assistants—and lawyers— everywhere will be assessing what they can reveal of themselves in public online venues without putting their work at risk. In particular, it is not a good career move to criticize one's employer online. Lawyers are especially sensitive about public image. In fact, as a general best practice, you should avoid revealing too much personal information, such as your firm's name, in your social media accounts. Be sure to review your firm's social media policy prior to accessing social media platforms in the workplace or mentioning your firm by name in your personal social media use.

§ 4.18   Law firm websites

Almost all law firms have a website on the Internet, although the sites may vary in quality depending upon the size of the firm. Websites can provide links to a firm-generated newsletter, a schedule of seminar events for client education or training, or a series of essays on specialty programs the firm can provide for clients. A newsletter or blog that focuses on a hot topic with legal implications that touch on a firm specialty might be featured. Many websites contain some type of page listing employment opportunities for lawyers, staff, or both. A website can contain useful links that connect clients and visitors with sites providing general information about the firm's areas of practice. Much of the same material that would go in a firm résumé or marketing packet could appear as web pages, too. Law firm websites, like other business websites, are now trying to customize what is presented on the webpage based on who is viewing the website.

The law firm website is a very important computer application used by the lawyer's assistant. Job applicants routinely research company websites before drafting their cover letters, tailoring their résumés, or attending their interviews. There's no better way to match up the lawyer's assistant's experience with the needs of the law firm or to determine which areas of the assistant's experience deserve the most focus. The law firm website continues to be useful after starting work as well. It can offer insight into a firm's programs and treatment of legal issues. It can provide general education about the areas of firm specialization. The website also often lists specific information about individual members or associates which can be helpful as well.

§ 4.18.1 Law firm websites—Intranet

Larger firms are also designing **Intranet**, or in-house online web pages, for their firms. Intranet sites can serve the purposes of a company newsletter, without wasting paper. They can provide employee phone lists, birthday calendars, and news on employees' new babies or recent family deaths. There may also be client specific pages that includes information regarding the matters, timekeepers, client contacts, documents, and financials. Intranets can replace email traffic seeking general information with a centralized bulletin board or document repository. Human resources, accounting, and intake forms can be posted online for easy reference. Jobs listings can be made available before they are advertised to the public.

News regarding employees' special accomplishments or public recognition can be featured. Special firm events can be advertised ahead of time. All the information that can be posted on the Intranet frees up the email system for work; saves paper, printing costs, and the environment; and makes information readily accessible to the entire firm, regardless of the number of offices or the rank or physical location of the employee. In those firms with Intranet sites, the Intranet may replace policy and procedures and training manuals. Documents, such as phone lists, which were once routinely circulated through office mail when updated, may be posted to the Intranet, and it becomes the lawyer's assistant's responsibility to monitor them for updates. Intranet sites should also post use policies to limit dissemination of in-house information outside the firm and to prevent the posting of inappropriate items.

§ 4.19 Electronic filing and case management

Electronic filing (efiling) is a system used by courts, government agencies, attorneys, and the public to reduce paperwork and electronically file documents over the Internet using a standard web browser. Word processing and other types of files are converted to pdf documents and then authorized users can file or transmit and access them on the court's website.

In 2001, the federal district court system initiated the **Case Management/Electronic Case Filing** (**CM/ECF**) program to allow case management, case filing, and document access online to federal courts. The program started with bankruptcy courts. District courts began to join the program in 2002, and the appellate courts began to join in 2005. As of May 2009, the bankruptcy courts in all fifty states, the District of Columbia, Guam, Puerto Rico, and the Virgin Islands were all fully operational under CM/ECF, and the bankruptcy court in the Northern Mariana Islands was being brought on line. The district courts in all fifty states, the District of Columbia, Guam, Puerto Rico, the Virgin Islands, and the Northern Mariana Islands are all participating in CM/ECF. The Court of International Trade and the Court of Federal Claims are both participating in CM/ECF. All of the appellate courts are participating except the Eleventh Circuit. Increasingly, state and municipal courts are also implementing electronic filing, although the requirements and structure of such systems are not as uniform as those in the federal system.

Documents filed electronically are available to judges at their bench or in chambers; attorneys and their staff have access to documents in the federal CM/ECF system. (Availability of documents in state court efiling systems varies.) Electronic case filing systems allow electronic service of pleadings and court orders; service lists can easily be updated. This new use of Internet technology is and will continue to be revolutionary in litigation practice. Always check the local court rules for efiling requirements such as fonts, page lengths, and margins to comply with filing rules.

§ 4.20 Backup

To prevent costly loss of data, the law firm should routinely make a *backup* copy of all data stored on the computer and place that duplicate in a separate location. Small law offices using stand-alone computers or individuals who use laptops should purchase backup software or use an Internet-based backup service consistently to back up software and data stored on the computer. Networked computer systems require efficient, systematic backup procedures usually performed daily by trained staff members.

Copies or originals of all software in use and an updated copy of all data stored on the computer should be stored on a backup disk. An inventory of the software is also helpful. In the event the computer crashes, the computer and backup software disks can be taken to a computer store, where the computer can be repaired and the software reinstalled. See § 3.19.9 on record retention and deleting client data.

§ 4.21 Computer security

Law firms must protect the computer systems from unauthorized access by technical penetration into their systems, telephone access, or by physical intruders in the office. Intensified security of user identification passwords and higher levels of authentication are two areas increasingly being used to protect law firm systems. Keeping computing resources secure is everyone's responsibility, not just that of the information technology department. It is important that you remain vigilant and act as the first line of defense in protecting confidential data.

§ 4.21.1 Computer security—Viruses and malware

Before jumping into ways you can mitigate computer or cybersecurity risks, you should be familiar with the security issue of *viruses*. A virus is a computer code that can be copied into an existing computer program and make itself known by flashing an innocuous message on the screen or doing something as serious as destroying data, disabling the operating system, or stealing data. The first virus was detected in the early 1980s. The term *virus* was adopted due to the ability of the foreign code to replicate itself and infect other computers. Computer viruses can spread through infected diskettes, email or email attachments, shared computer software, through an online service, or through a network. Many varieties of *malware* (viruses, Trojans, keyboard scanners, and many others) are now attacking unprotected computers. New types of malware are invented daily that attack newly discovered computer vulnerabilities, so computer security is critical and must be maintained and updated continuously.

Virus scanners are available to check for viruses and remove them from the system. It is important to select a software package that will scan email attachments in addition to other files found on the hard drive. Regularly updating virus signatures to detect the most recent viruses is crucial. Because new viruses are introduced all the time, no system is totally safe. Modern antivirus software also scans the websites that the operator visits for spyware and spam. In addition, some include a firewall to keep out hackers. For instance, Windows include firewalls in the operating system and Microsoft Internet Explorer has security settings that can make Internet use safer. Individual users must be educated about computer security and make common-sense decisions when linking to resources outside the user's computer.

§ 4.21.2 Computer security—Social engineering and phishing

You should always be aware of suspicious emails; this is true also with social networking sites, phone calls or individuals who you do not recognize. Cyber security criminals will attempt to trick you into divulging personal information such as banking information, usernames and passwords, or ID badges. These various manipulative techniques are referred to as *social engineering*.

If you receive an email attachment or link in an email that you are not expecting or seems suspicious for any reason, you should avoid clicking on it and follow your firm's procedures to notify the correct individual of this occurrence. Known as *phishing,* scams like this can spread viruses or malware through files attached to email messages or use a faulty link to steal sensitive data such as your password. Often times, Phishers prey on heightened emotions of fear or curiosity like "Warning" or "Act Now" to trick you into opening an infected file or link, so don't fall victim to that sense of urgency.

§ 4.21.3 Computer security—Passwords

Some system administrators have a policy to change passwords routinely on a specific date. Passwords should be as many digits as possible and should not be obvious for security reasons. The following types of passwords are easily decoded and should be avoided:

- Ascending digits (e.g., 1234)
- Same digits (9999)
- Digits corresponding to employee's name (e.g., 5646 for John)
- Current year
- Same number as phone extension
- Reverse phone extensions
- Numbers that identify the owner (social security, employee identification, room number, birth date)
- Pets, children, family members

Always memorize passwords and never write them down or share them with others.

§ 4.21.4   Computer security—Physical security

Another tip for protecting your firm's computer security is to lock your screen or shut down your system when not in use. You should never leave devices unattended unless they are physically secure, such as using a cable lock for a laptop. You can also use a screen protector on a laptop screen or desktop monitor to prevent preying eyes from reading the data on your screen.

§ 4.22   Selecting equipment

The task of selecting equipment for a law office requires time and energy, and if a law practice is larger than four or five lawyers or if a network is going to be installed, technical assistance from computer vendors or system consultants may be needed. In small firms, the following points should be considered:

- The current and future needs of the law office
- Current equipment and replacement costs
- Storage needs and the possibility of upgrading the system as needed
- Costs of peripherals and software
- Referrals from people who have recently purchased equipment
- Vendor demonstrations of potential equipment choices
- Availability of warranty and after-purchase support

§ 4.23   Ergonomics

Ergonomics involves adjusting equipment and behavior modification techniques that aid in the prevention or reduction of repetitive strain injuries. Because of the widespread use of computers, today's workforce faces problems associated with constant keyboard work, such as muscle aches, tension, and pain in the hands, arms, neck, and back. These conditions are referred to as **repetitive strain injuries, repetitive stress injuries**, or RSI. Some ways of preventing RSI without buying new equipment or furniture are listed below.

- Look away from the screen to something in the distance every 10 to 15 minutes to refocus and rest the eyes and take one- to five-minute screen breaks every hour, getting up and stretching, walking, and moving around.
- Rotate tasks between heavy keyboarding and walking, moving, or other desk activity in which the arms are frequently changing position.
- Use an adjustable chair that can be positioned so the operator can sit comfortably with the spine up and straight, not curved or twisted to the right or left or hunched forward.
- Adjust the desk and keyboard to the proper height and sit in front of the keyboard with the arms bent at the elbow, parallel to the floor; the keyboard should be positioned at the same height as the bent arms.
- Place the monitor directly in front of the operator, with the operator's eyes level with the top of the screen.
- Touch the keyboard lightly, not hammering the keys, and keep the wrists 1/2 inch above the keyboard so they do not rest on anything. Keeping the wrists in a fixed position is a major cause of carpal tunnel syndrome and other RSIs.

§ 4.24   Getting additional help

The knowledge required for using computers changes rapidly. Some of the programs, technologies, and companies mentioned here may not still exist when this textbook is updated two years from now, and new ones will have appeared in their place. There are many resources to help the lawyer's assistant obtain the basic skills required to produce correspondence and documents or to continue updating, refining, and learning new skills. Community colleges offer short-term, inexpensive computer classes. Some firms provide in-house training programs and others purchase reference manuals, training workbooks, or videos to help users in self-guided training efforts. Valuable information can be found by reading periodicals and journals dealing with computers in general or specific software applications. An excellent way to develop knowledge is to share ideas with coworkers or other computer users, formally at meetings or seminars or informally during lunch or breaks. Do not overlook the benefit of attending state and national NALS® seminars and local NALS® meetings, which often provide technology updates. Most important, however, is the lawyer's assistant's awareness of the importance of the computer in the law office and the need to keep an open, willing, exploratory attitude towards the systems in use.

Chapter 5

Billing and Basic Accounting Procedures

> **KeyCite®:** Cases and other legal materials listed in KeyCite Scope can be researched
> through the KeyCite service on Westlaw®. Use KeyCite to check citations for form,
> parallel references, prior and later history, and comprehensive citator information,
> including citations to other decisions and secondary materials.

§ 5.1 Introduction

Very early in the law office work experience, it becomes obvious
that as a service business, the time of the lawyers and staff is a valu-

able commodity. Law offices sell time the way a music shop sells CDs. In the modern mid- or large-sized law firm, an accounting department will handle the more specialized aspects of accounting, including billing; generation of checks; payment of law firm expenses; maintenance of the firm checking account, including deposits and withdrawals; generation of business reports; and preparation of payroll (payroll is often outsourced to companies that specialize in payroll accounting). This chapter deals with the limited accounting tasks that fall to the lawyer's assistant in the typical modern firm, including entry of attorney and staff time records, generation of cost records, basic payment methods, and checking account management, the basics of trust accounts, and the use of a petty cash fund. Although today's law firms are computerized and most all of the accounting tasks in this chapter are fully automated, the lawyer's assistant should have a working knowledge of these accounting tasks in the event the need arises to manually perform any accounting task.

§ 5.2　Basic principles

Accounting is the process of analyzing, recording, classifying, summarizing, reporting, and interpreting financial transactions and events. The five basic accounting elements are assets, liabilities, equity, revenues, and expenses. Assets and expenses are debit accounts; liabilities, equity, and revenues are credit accounts. The fundamental *accounting equation* is *assets = liabilities + equity*. The value of these elements is increased or decreased when the firm realizes revenue or pays expenses.

Every transaction affects two (or more) accounts. For example, the receipt of fees affects both revenue and cash; the payment of a bill affects both an expense account and cash. This is the basis of double-entry bookkeeping: every event gives rise to two equal and offsetting entries on the books, a debit and a credit.

§ 5.2.1　Basic principles—Debits and credits

Every double entry recorded in a journal is made up of one or more *debits* and one or more *credits*. The total debits must always equal the total credits. To debit an account means to record an amount on the left or debit side of the account. To credit an account means to record an amount on the right or credit side of the account. The difference between the total debits and total credits posted to an account is called the *balance*. Any account may have either a debit or credit balance.

§ 5.3　Time entries

The first aspect of law office accounting the lawyer's assistant is likely to see is time entry. Time is reported in a variety of ways. In the modern law office, a time entry is entered into a computer where it can be sorted by client and matter and processed into bills that can be sent to the client, usually monthly. An important element is the designation of separate projects of a given client or *matters.* A long-term client may come to the attorney for help with a variety of different projects. Typically those separate projects are billed as separate matters, so the client can easily see how much time (and money) has been spent on a given project.

How time entries get into the computer varies from firm to firm and lawyer to lawyer. Commonly, the lawyer dictates or handwrites the time entries, and the lawyer's assistant makes those entries into a time processing program. Some lawyers make their own entries directly into the program.

Time is reported most often by tenths of an hour (six minutes per tenth). Like many cellphone companies, law firms do not round down. If an action takes any time at all, it is billed for six minutes or one-tenth of an hour. If a lawyer works quickly and consistently and happens to cover many small actions, he or she can wind up billing more time in a day than he or she actually spent at work. More often, time is spent on larger actions that may take an hour or more and the slight advantage of rounding up in time entry does not amount to much. In some firms, time is billed by the quarter hour, rather than by tenths.

Lawyers are not the only members of the law firm who bill time. While lawyer's assistants or secretaries generally do not bill their time, paralegals, researchers, analysts, investigators, and others usually do bill their time when work is done on behalf of a client. If a lawyer's assistant performs paralegal duties, he or she may also bill time for those specific duties.

§ 5.3.1   Time entries—Nonbillable time

Since time is money in a law office, time is accounted for even when it is not directly billable. This is known as nonbillable time. If a lawyer performs work on contingency—in which the lawyer is paid only if the client's case is won—he or she still must account for the time spent on the case, as such time may have tax implications and is certainly helpful in evaluating the profitability of the attorney, the department, or the firm. A *contingency fee* is a fee that is a percentage of the amount obtained in negotiation or litigation with another party.

Time is also captured for other nonbillable activities, such as *pro bono* work, in which the lawyer does community service without being compensated; client development, in which new business is sought; time spent on firm administration; and time spent attending continuing legal education seminars, to name a few. The results of this type of time entry allow a law firm to consider the relationship between billable and nonbillable time for each attorney. Such time entries document the time spent working on getting new business or conducting firm management activities. It is particularly important for new or younger attorneys to document nonbillable as well as billable activities, so firm members, partners, or managers can see that the new attorney is working all day, even when some of the work is unbillable.

§ 5.3.2   Time entries—Discounting time

Like any other business, a law office must remain competitive to hang onto its customers and bring new ones in. This sometimes results in the manipulation of billed time to make a bill more acceptable to the customer. Time is sometimes **written down** (reduced), or removed from the bill, to create a discounted bill. Time may be written down when a senior attorney believes that too much time was spent on a specific project, or it may simply be written down because the supervising attorney believes the amount of fees will be unacceptable. Attorneys and paralegals are often either compensated based on their billable hours (frequently through annual bonus programs) or required to produce a specific number of hours annually to maintain good standing in the firm. Frequent discounting of billable time for younger attorneys and paralegals can become a significant sore spot for those employees affected, but it can also signal to senior management that an employee is not able to complete work efficiently.

§ 5.3.3   Time entries—Issues in reporting time

Because of the problems of reconstructing a day's activities after the fact, most firms have programs that attempt to enforce frequent reporting of time by the attorneys. In fact, it is not unusual for a firm to have attorneys who routinely fail to produce time records before the end of the month (when billing is usually compiled and prepared for mailing). To combat this tendency, some firms use disciplinary approaches in which those who fail to turn their time in when expected may be fined or experience some other negative consequence. Some firms use reward programs, particularly when timely billing is very important, such as at year-end. Often, the lawyer's assistant is responsible for reminding the attorney to turn in time entries. The best-case scenario is for an attorney to keep a time log on the desk and record every new event—a telephone call, reading a letter, drafting a pleading—as it occurs. Then not even small amounts of time will be accidentally forgotten.

§ 5.3.4   Time entries—Making time entries

There are a number of *time entry programs* that allow for the efficient entry of attorney and paralegal or other staff time. Time entry programs record and store information about time worked and hold that information until it has been reviewed, approved, and released for entry into the accounting system, where fees are allocated to client bills. A time entry includes several key components. The person who performed the activity being recorded is represented, usually by initials or by an employee number. The date of the activity is recorded.

The length of time spent on the activity is recorded. A description of the activity is given. Some clients require special codes that allow them to analyze how legal time is spent. For example, there may be a code that indicates that an action was a communication, involved drafting a document, required a court appearance, and so forth. There may also be a subcode that indicates, for example, for whom or to whom a communication was made. These codes often differ from client to client. Insurance companies are particularly fond of these special codes. Once time entries are made, most firms require that they be checked by the billing attorney or staff member before they are finalized and released to the accounting system for inclusion in bills. Illustration 5-1 shows a sample time entry as it might appear on a time entry printout.

Illustration 5-1

Attorney	Date	Client-Matter	Code-Subcode	Hours
AMM	10/20/10	12345 26718	A202 L113	3.5
Description:	Court appearance; conference with client; examination of possible evidentiary materials; confer with court clerk.			

§ 5.3.5 Time entries—Client billing requirements

In recent years, corporate clients have become very watchful regarding legal costs. Different activities may not be permitted to be billed— for example: communication between attorneys at the same firm; file organization or management; and research may not be billable. Sometimes what is objected to by the client may be a matter of how the item is worded, rather than what took place. Experienced lawyer's assistants are often able to assist the lawyer in breaking up block billings and avoiding time descriptions that are likely to provoke a negative reaction from the client.

§ 5.3.6 Time entries—Proper style of time entries

Most law firms have specific stylistic rules for time entries. Certain abbreviations may be required or, alternately, forbidden. Time entries must be in a consistent tense—either past or present tense, depending on firm preferences. A string of related activities for the same client and on the same matter may be put together in a block entry with semicolons between separate activities, with the time entry ending in a period. This type of entry is sometimes referred to as *block billing*, and some clients demand that every activity be billed separately so they can more accurately track how much time various activities require. A downside, of course, is that time is not rounded down, and the decision to bill many related items separately may end up costing the client more.

§ 5.4 Cost entries

In addition to billing the time spent in providing legal services, every law firm has certain costs that it bills to the client. Common items are phone calls, faxes, copier costs, litigation filing fees, court reporter costs, consultation with specialists, travel expenses, and fees for expert witnesses.

Costs are billed in a variety of ways. The costs of phone calls are often captured by using programming that requests a client and matter code when making a long-distance phone call or sending a facsimile. Client or matter codes may be required when using copiers. These costs are processed through a computer directly to the client's account.

Some types of cost—such as those where a check must be requested to pay an expense or to pay an invoice submitted—must be entered into the system in a cost entry program. Typically these cost entries are done in the accounting department, but in smaller firms, the lawyer's assistant may be responsible for making cost entries. The typical requirements for a cost entry are date the cost was incurred, to whom a payment was made, who authorized the cost, and the reason for the expenditure.

§ 5.4.1 Cost entries—Accounting forms

Most law firms use cost entry forms for certain types of cost items. For example, when an attorney travels and wants to bill a client or be reimbursed by the firm, there is likely a travel form that organizes the types of charges the attorney might want to report, such as parking, airfare, mileage, meals, seminar fees for Continuing Legal Education (CLE), and so forth. Another type of cost form that is commonly used is a check request form. The check request form specifies billing codes—either client-matter numbers or firm codes that categorize nonbillable requests—and requires documentation to be attached for the files. These forms are usually developed in-house to meet the needs of the accounting staff and to coordinate with the type of accounting software in use. Typically they are relatively easy to learn and use.

§ 5.5 Billing format

Illustration 5-2 shows a sample billing statement (a statement that itemizes fees and costs billed on a given matter or to a client). The elements in this sample bill are common: address, phone number, federal I.D. number (essential in order to be paid any time a bill is presented to a company, as opposed to an individual), inside address, invoice number, date of invoice, client account number, fees, costs, and a summary of attorneys and their rates and time expended. Greater or less detail can be given with respect to fees: sometimes the number of hours is omitted; sometimes the rate is included on the line with the hours; special coding may be inserted on each entry. Most computer programs that structure billing statements allow the user to select the elements to be included or omitted from fees entries. Discounts for prompt payments, statements advising that credit card payments are accepted, and other information may also be included. Some clients require back-up for costs, so the statement may include copies of travel receipts, phone bills, and so forth.

Illustration 5-2

COUNSEL, JUDGE & FINCH, P.C.
Attorneys at Law
1234 Mina Street
Eaglesville, New York 00232
(213) 554-1204

Federal I.D. No. 46-123578

John Q. Client   Invoice #4501   August 25, 2012
3434 Thrush Street
Eaglesville, New York
00235

Your Account No.
2535
Matter No. 33421

FEES

Attorney	Date	Description	Hours	Amount
ABC	8/13	Court appearance	1.0	$200.00
HHJ	8/15	Review of new evidence from opposing counsel.	2.0	$300.00
AXF	8/16	Confer with opposing counsel regarding scheduling.	1.0	$150.00
		TOTAL FEES		$650.00

DISBURSEMENTS

8/13	Long distance phone	$2.35
8/16	Postage	$1.44
	TOTAL COSTS	$3.79
	TOTAL DUE	$653.79

Attorneys

<u>DISBURSEMENTS</u>

Arnold B. Counsel @ $200 per hour—1 hour

Harry H. Judge @ $150 per hour—2 hours

Atticus Finch @ $150 per hour—1 hour

§ 5.6   Handling the firm checking account

In smaller firms, even an entry-level lawyer's assistant may be responsible for some aspects of the use or maintenance of the firm's checking account. Most businesses make payments by checks drawn on local commercial banks. A check is a written order directing the **drawee**, the person to whom a check is written, (the bank) to make payment to the **payee** (the person to whom a promissory note, bank draft, or check is issued) from the account balance of the **drawer** (the person by whom a check is written and upon whose funds the check is drawn).

When a checking account is opened, each person authorized to sign checks completes a signature card. A deposit slip is used to list items to be added to the account, including checks received from others, such as fees collected from clients.

Each check deposited must be endorsed. Endorse a check in ink across the reverse left end (never across the right end) within the space indicated. Endorse it exactly as the name appears on the face, even though incorrect. If incorrect, write the correct signature immediately below. It is not necessary to write the explanation of the two signatures; they will be understood by the bank. Do not write the correct signature first and the incorrect one below in parentheses. This violates the banking rule that the last endorser must be the person to whom the money is paid. There are several types of endorsements:

1. <u>Endorsement in blank</u>. This is a simple signature of the payee, which makes the check payable to bearer. It should be cashed or deposited immediately.

2. <u>Special (or Full) endorsement</u>. This states to whom a check is to be paid, i.e., "Pay to the order of. . ." above the payee's signature. This requires the designated person's endorsement but is still negotiable.

3. <u>Restrictive endorsement</u>. This limits the further purpose or use of the check. One type of restrictive endorsement includes only the words "Pay to (name)" below the payee's signature. The check is then nonnegotiable—it must be paid to the designated person and no one else. Another restrictive endorsement marks the check "for deposit only" with a bank account number.

4. <u>Qualified endorsement</u>. The endorser assumes no legal responsibility for payment should the drawer have insufficient funds

to honor the check by using the words "Without recourse" written above the payee's signature in the endorsement. This relieves the endorser of any future liability on the check.

The deposit only restrictive endorsement should be used on checks to be deposited. The blank endorsement should be used only when presenting a check for cash.

Checks for deposit by a firm are preferably endorsed with a rubber stamp that includes the account number assigned by the bank. The date is also carried on some rubber stamps. In the absence of a rubber stamp, type "For deposit only" and below it the payee's name. All checks for deposit should be endorsed immediately to safeguard them in case they are lost before or while being taken or mailed to the bank.

When preparing to write a check, be sure the stubs are completed first, showing all information; then complete each check using pen and ink or a typewriter. The check should be signed with indelible ink. When making deposits, be sure to enter the deposit on the check stub and carry the balance forward. The check stubs can be used to prepare the journal entries. With the proper software, it is possible to produce computer-generated checks.

§ 5.6.1 Handling the firm checking account—Certified check

When a check is deposited, the bank credits the account subject to collection of the check. To ensure that a check is good, one can ask the drawer to have the check certified by their bank. To certify a check, the teller stamps "Certified" and the date on the check, and the certification is then signed by an authorized bank officer. After the check is certified, the bank reduces the drawer's account by the amount of the check and holds the funds for payment. The bank then becomes responsible for the payment of the certified check.

In reconciling the bank balance, an outstanding *certified check* is listed separately from the other outstanding checks because it has already been charged to the account by the bank and deducted as a payment. Certified checks are recorded like ordinary checks by both drawer and payee in the cash journal.

§ 5.6.2 Handling the firm checking account—Cashier's check

A check drawn by a bank on its own funds is called a *cashier's check*. If the depositor's credit is not established, the cashier's check will be accepted as payment where the depositor's personal check may not be. Cashier's checks are recorded as ordinary checks by both buyer and seller in the cash journals.

§ 5.6.3 Handling the firm checking account—Bank draft

A *bank draft* is a check issued by a bank upon its funds in another bank, usually located in some other city. The bank draft is used chiefly in buying goods from an out-of-town business with which the buyer has no credit but from which the buyer wishes immediate delivery. If the purchaser had sent a personal check in payment, the seller would not ship the goods until the check was honored, a procedure that could take several days. The seller will generally make immediate shipment against a bank draft because the bank is responsible for its payment.

To obtain a bank draft, the buyer draws a check to the order of the bank for the amount needed plus the bank charge for the service. The bank then prepares a bank draft for the required amount, drawn on a bank in the city where the seller resides. The bank draft should be made payable to the buyer, who then endorses it in full to the seller. This procedure makes it easy to secure the canceled bank draft from the bank as evidence of payment.

§ 5.6.4 Handling the firm checking account—The money order

If a person does not have a checking account and wants to make a payment other than in currency, this can be done by purchasing a *money order* at a United States post office, bank, and many stores. The money order is purchased with cash. The amount for which a money order can be bought is limited. Money orders are accounted for in the same manner as ordinary checks.

§ 5.6.5 Handling the firm checking account—Reconciling the bank statement

When a bank statement is received, the bookkeeper should check it immediately with the balance record on the check stubs or the bank account in the general ledger. This procedure, known as *reconciling the bank statement*, ensures the record of the bank and the record of the depositor (the check register) are in agreement. The balances may not be the same for one or more of the following reasons:

- Some of the checks issued during the period may not have been presented to the bank for payment by the date the statement was prepared (outstanding checks).
- Deposits made may not have been recorded in time to appear on the bank's statement (outstanding bank deposits).
- Bank services charged to the depositor may not yet appear on the depositor's record. The bank statement is usually the source document for such charges unless a carbon copy of such debit has already been received and journalized.
- Errors may have been made by either party.

Most bank statements contain a form on the reverse side for the depositor's use in reconciliation, and after completion, these forms are filed in the depositor's office.

A suggested procedure for reconciliation of a bank statement is:

1. Check the amount of each deposit on the bank statement with the check stubs, duplicate deposit tickets, or the cash receipts journal. If any outstanding deposits are found, they should be enumerated and added to the bank's total.
2. Check the amount of each canceled check and the numbers of the checks which have been paid by the bank, as indicated in the bank statement, to be sure all checks issued have been paid and the amounts entered properly in the check stubs and cash disbursements journal. Any checks not paid should be enumerated as outstanding and deducted from the bank's balance shown on the statement. The current trend is for banks not to return the physical check to the business but to send a scanned copy of the check. The scanned copy is considered as good as the original for legal purposes, but when an amount is in dispute, it is important to obtain a front-and-back scanned copy from the bank as soon as possible. It is also still possible to have the original checks returned with the bank statement from some banks for a fee.
3. Any bank service charges or debits to the depositor not already shown on check stubs or in the accounts must be enumerated and deducted from the depositor's record total.

After these adjustments are entered on the reconciliation form, the two balances should be in agreement. If not, the depositor's records should first be checked for errors in addition, subtraction, and posting (such as a transposition of figures). If the error still cannot be found, a check of the bank's statement may reveal an error. Bank errors must be reported to the bank at once; banks will correct errors only if reported within a certain amount of time. If a depositor still is unable to reconcile the bank statement, it should be reported to the bank immediately. (Note: Errors in transposition are divisible by 9. Divide the amount out of balance by 9, and if it is divisible evenly, the problem very easily could be a transposition error.)

§ 5.7   Law firm trust accounts

Under the ethical rules governing legal representation in every state, the lawyer must have a separate *trust account* in which to deposit and maintain client funds that have been entrusted to him or her. The ABA Model Rules of Professional Conduct spell out in detail how client funds and property are to be handled. The recordkeeping associated with a trust account must be perfect. The law firm or lawyer's money cannot be deposited with the client funds in the trust account (with the exception of the amount of money required to cover bank charges for maintenance of the account). A failure to handle client funds properly often results in disciplinary action against the attorney—even if the staff created the problem.

The best safeguard for a new lawyer's assistant is never to

undertake any activity regarding the trust account without the attorney's direct supervision and permission. In simple terms, any time a client pays a *retainer* (an advance payment that covers some of the expected costs of a legal action) or makes an advance payment for expected costs such as filing fees, fines, court costs, or other costs, that money needs to be deposited to the trust account and a careful record of the client's identity and the purpose for depositing the client's funds should be made.

Money is paid out of the trust fund during monthly billing, when retainers are used to pay client bills, or when a case is settled, allowing distribution of proceeds to the attorney and client according to a carefully prepared settlement accounting that itemizes costs paid, the agreed-upon attorney's fee (often a percentage of the total payment after deduction of costs), and the money due to the client. Where a client has given the attorney a retainer or an advance payment for expected costs, it is important that monthly billings reflect any retainer funds withdrawn and how they were applied to the bill.

§ 5.8　Petty cash fund

Many law firms maintain a **petty cash** fund which is used to pay small amounts for which a firm check is not appropriate, either because requisitioning a check may take too long, or because there may be a need to make a payment where a check would not be accepted. The usual procedure is that any employee may request petty cash but must provide documentation or an explanation of what is being purchased. Usually one person in the firm maintains the petty cash account so the money is maintained securely, and expenditures can be accounted for accurately. It may be necessary for the requester to fill out a voucher before receiving petty cash funds. The petty cash fund is sometimes referred to as an imprest fund.

§ 5.9　Payroll

There is absolutely no margin for error in payroll accounting. The first step in determining the amount to be paid an employee is to calculate the total or gross earnings, including any overtime pay. The second step is to determine the deductions required either by law or agreement. The third step is to pay the employee the difference between the two, the net pay.

§ 5.9.1　Payroll—Determination of total earnings

An employee in a law office will be paid an hourly, weekly, semimonthly, or monthly rate. The *Fair Labor Standards Act* (minimum wage laws) governs wages by the hour. An employee may be entitled to overtime pay in some cases. Wage and hour cases usually involve time cards and time clocks or a computer-based timekeeping system in larger firms. Regardless of the method that the employer uses to determine pay scales and dates, the bookkeeper must maintain an accurate record of the gross amount paid, the itemized deductions, and the net amount paid.

§ 5.9.2 Payroll—Deductions from total earnings

With few exceptions, employers are required to withhold portions of each employee's total earnings for federal income tax, Social Security, and Medicare taxes. Many states and cities also require income or earnings tax withholding by employers. Besides those deductions, an agreement between employer and employee may call for amounts to be withheld for any one or more of the following reasons:

- To pay life, accident, or health insurance premiums for the employee
- To pay the employee's union or other professional dues
- To add to a pension or profit sharing plan
- To pay to some charitable organization, such as United Way
- To repay a loan from the company or the company credit union
- To contribute to a company flex pay program

§ 5.9.3 Payroll—Social Security and employer's identification numbers

Each employee is required to have a Social Security number for payroll accounting purposes. Just as each individual must have a reporting number, so must the employer have a number with which to identify tax reports. All but the new employer will have these numbers. In the case of new employers, the bookkeeper must obtain *an employer identification number* by submitting an application form (SS-4) to the Internal Revenue Service (IRS). After the number is obtained, it must be used on all reports submitted to the IRS.

§ 5.9.4 Payroll—Circular E, Employer's Tax Guide and federal employment tax forms

The IRS publishes a booklet for the employer's use entitled *Circular E-Employer's Tax Guide, which can also be located online at http://www.irs.gov.* This booklet is revised periodically and supplemented regularly as tax laws change. The bookkeeper must obtain a copy of this booklet for the files. Once a mailing address is established with the IRS, the subsequent editions are automatically sent to the employer. Circular E provides the bookkeeper with the following information and instructions for performing the following tasks and completing the following forms:

- Income tax withholding and payment to the IRS
- Social Security and Medicare tax withholding and payment to the IRS
- Payment of employer's share of Social Security and Medicare taxes to the IRS

- Form W-4 (Employee's Withholding Allowance Certificate)
- Form 941 (Employer's Quarterly Federal Tax Return)
- Form 940 (Employer's Annual Federal Unemployment (FUTA) Tax Return)
- Charts of amounts to be withheld for both income tax and Social Security and Medicare taxes
- Tax withholding by the percentage method

The bookkeeper must be alert to the changes in these laws and should check periodically to see whether there have been revisions. Literature on Social Security and Medicare taxes is included in the booklet. The bookkeeper must be aware of the maximum amount that an employee is required to pay for the year and the current percentage rate for both the employee and the employer.

Federal Unemployment Tax Act (FUTA) taxes must be sent in at the close of each year, or quarterly if required, on the form provided. The government publishes an annual booklet entitled "Federal Employment Tax Forms" (Publication 393) that contains a supply of the routine forms needed to report taxes as well as an order blank for more forms. Instructions are included for filling out each type of form. These items are usually mailed to employers well in advance of the due dates, but the bookkeeper must be aware of the dates and should obtain a supply from the local IRS office if they have not been received.

In addition to all the federal withholding reporting and payment requirements, the law firm is faced with a myriad of state and local taxes with periodic reporting and payment requirements. These may include state personal income taxes, local property taxes, real property taxes, state unemployment taxes, workers' compensation insurance taxes, business license fees, and professional license fees. The bookkeeper must be able to handle all of these or ensure that the law firm's payroll vendor or accountants are doing so.

§ 5.9.5 Payroll—Payroll register

There are many types of payroll registers on the market in the bound, spiral, and looseleaf forms. As long as the form contains the necessary information, any type is satisfactory.

§ 5.10 Computing interest

There are three factors that must be considered when computing interest: (1) principal, (2) interest rate, and (3) time period.

The principal is the amount of money borrowed. The interest rate is usually given on the face of the note. If the note is interest bearing and the interest rate is not given on the face of the note, the legal rate must be used. The legal rate varies from state to state. The interest rate shown on the face of the note is always an annual percentage rate unless stated otherwise. The time period of the note is determined by the number of days or months from the date when the note is issued until the date of maturity. Interest computations are based on this time period. The principal amount × the interest rate × the period will give you the amount of interest due.

If the due date is specified on a note, the exact number of days from the date of the note through the due date or maturity date must be determined. For example, if a note is issued on January 1 and is due on March 17, the time period is computed as follows:

Days in January	31
Date of note, January 1	– 1
Days remaining in January	30
Days in February**	28
Days in March	17
Time period in days	75

** Do not assume February to be a leap year in your computations unless you are told to do so. Notice in the above computation that the date of maturity is included, but the date of the note is excluded. After determining the proper factors, interest is calculated using the following formula:

Principal × Rate × Time Period = Amount of Interest

EXAMPLE: $1,000 (principal) × 12% (rate) interest = $120, which is the amount of interest for an entire year. Divide $120 by 365 (the number of days in a year), and this gives you the daily interest rate, which in this case is 0.32876, rounded up is 33 cents per day. Multiply the daily interest rate by the number of days in the time period, 75 days – 75 days × .33 per day equals $24.75 in interest. Add the interest to the principal amount, and the amount required to pay off the note on March 17 is $1,024.75.

§ 5.11 Computerized accounting systems

Manual accounting processes have been made obsolete by the use of computers in virtually all offices. Many software programs are available for small business accounting as well as specific programs for professional service firms; they come with detailed instructions as well as technical help by telephone.

These programs, plus a good personal computer, perform the majority of the accounting procedures. Even though such a system will probably be in use wherever the lawyer's assistant works, it is helpful to understand the basic steps being performed by the system.

Chapter 6

Written Communications

> **KeyCite®:** Cases and other legal materials listed in KeyCite Scope can be researched through the KeyCite service on Westlaw®. Use KeyCite to check citations for form, parallel references, prior and later history, and comprehensive citator information, including citations to other decisions and secondary materials.

---

§ 6.1 Introduction

Over 70 percent of the business day is spent using language. Often business success is directly related to an individual's communication skills. Oral and written communications differ in emphasis. Oral communication tends to be more informal than writing. Many things are communicated in addition to words and their simple meanings: gestures and word choice also communicate warmth, authority, maturity, passion, integrity, and other qualities. Often a grammatically correct choice is not consistent with the desire to communicate factors other than the simple meaning of words. Writing, on the other hand, is preserved on paper or electronically and is more likely to communicate negatively if it is done carelessly or ungrammatically. Ungrammatical writing can imply indifference, lack of education, or lack of professionalism. Although both oral and written communications are important, this chapter deals with the stricter grammatical demands of written communications.

One of the basic means of mastering English is a study of grammar, which concerns itself with the study of words and their functions and relationships in sentences and the rules that govern proper use of the language. This chapter is not intended to offer a complete course in grammar. For those who need additional help, grammar references such as *The Gregg Reference Manual*, Internet sources, and college courses offer good options. A local college bookstore may offer suggestions about good handbooks. Every lawyer's assistant should have an up-to-date English usage reference and should consult it freely.

§ 6.2 The basics of English grammar

The eight parts of speech (names given to words according to their roles in sentences) are verbs, nouns, pronouns, adverbs, adjectives, prepositions, conjunctions, and interjections. The role the word plays in the sentence determines the form of the word that should be used.

§ 6.3 Verbs

A *verb* is a word or word group that tells what the subject does, what the subject is, or what happens to the subject. A sentence is not complete without a verb, and sentences may have more than one verb.

Verbs are sometimes described as action verbs or states of being. **Action verbs** show the action of a sentence. Some examples are *play*, *type*, *solves*, and *write*. Action verbs are categorized as transitive and intransitive. Verbs that do not express action express a state of being and are called linking verbs. Some linking verbs are *feels*, *appears*, *tastes*, *is*, *are*, *was*, *were*, *seems*, and *looks*.

§ 6.3.1 Verbs—Transitive verbs

A **transitive verb** is an action verb that needs a direct object to complete the meaning of the sentence. When a verb is transitive, the action passes from the doer (the subject) to a receiver of the action (the direct object). The **direct object** tells who or what receives the action of the verb.

> EXAMPLES: Mary *read* the book. ("Book" is the direct object and "read" is the transitive verb)

§ 6.3.2 Verbs—Intransitive verbs

An **intransitive verb** is an action verb that does not require a direct object. The verb does not express an action that passes over to a receiver. A verb may be transitive in one sentence and intransitive in another sentence.

> EXAMPLES: Chris called on the morning of August 6th.
> (Intransitive)
> Chris called the client on the morning of August 6th. (Transitive)
> Mike ran. (Intransitive)
> Mike ran a business. Transitive

§ 6.3.3 Verbs—Linking verbs

Some verbs express a state of being rather than an action. These are called **linking verbs**, and they link the subject to a word or words that identify or describe the subject. A noun, pronoun, or adjective complements the subject.

> EXAMPLES: Gerry *is* very efficient. (*Efficient* further describes *Gerry*.)
> Gerry *is* president of the organization. (*Gerry* and *president* are the same person.)

§ 6.3.4 Verbs—Regular verbs

A *regular verb* is one that forms its past tense and past participle by adding *d* or *ed* to the present tense of the verb.

§ 6.3.5 Verbs—Irregular verbs

Verbs that do not form their past tense and past participle in this manner are called *irregular*. Illustration 6-1 shows several of the irregular verbs in their three forms.

§ 6.3.6 Verbs—Verb tense

The *tense* of a verb refers to the time an action or event takes place or the time of the state of being.

The three sets of tenses are: *simple*, *perfect*, and *progressive*. The simple tenses are present, past, and future. The perfect tenses express actions that are completed, and progressive tenses express actions that are continuing.

Illustration 6-1

COMMONLY USED IRREGULAR VERBS		
Present Tense	Past Tense	Past Participle (have, has, had)
arise	arose	arisen
awake	awoke or awaked	awakened or awoken
beat	beat	beaten
become	became	become
begin	began	begun
bite	bit	bitten
blow	blew	blown
break	broke	broken
bring	brought	brought
burst	burst	burst
buy	bought	bought
choose	chose	chosen
cling	clung	clung
come	came	come
cost	cost	cost
do	did	done
drag	dragged	dragged
draw	drew	drawn
drink	drank	drunk
drive	drove	driven
eat	ate	eaten

COMMONLY USED IRREGULAR VERBS		
Present Tense	Past Tense	Past Participle (have, has, had)
fall	fell	fallen
fight	fought	fought
fling	flung	flung
fly	flew	flown
forget	forgot	forgotten
freeze	froze	frozen
get	got	got
give	gave	given
go	went	gone
grow	grew	grown
hang	hung	hung
hang (to execute)	hanged	hanged
hear	heard	heard
hit	hit	hit
hurt	hurt	hurt
know	knew	known
lay	laid	laid
lead	led	led
leave	left	left
let	let	let
lie (recline)	lay	lain
lie (fib)	lied	lied
lose	lost	lost
pay	paid	paid
put	put	put
read	read	read
ride	rode	ridden
ring	rang	rung
rise	rose	risen
run	ran	run
say	said	said
see	saw	seen
set	set	set
shake	shook	shaken
show	showed	showed or shown
sing	sang	sung
sink	sank or sunk	sunk
sit	sat	sat
sleep	slept	slept

COMMONLY USED IRREGULAR VERBS		
Present Tense	Past Tense	Past Participle (have, has, had)
speak	spoke	spoken
spring	sprang or sprung	sprung
steal	stole	stolen
swear	swore	sworn
swim	swam	swum
swing	swung	swung
take	took	taken
teach	taught	taught
tear	tore	torn
tell	told	told
think	thought	thought
throw	threw	thrown
wake	woke	woken
wear	wore	worn
wet	wet	wet
write	wrote	written

§ 6.3.7 Verbs—Present tense

Present tense refers to the present moment.

> EXAMPLES: The attorney *is* ready. (Shows state of being in the present.)
> The receptionist *answers* the phone. (Action is occurring now.)

In the present tense, to show that the action is continuous and moving forward (progressive), use the *ing* form of the verb and add the proper form of *be*.

> EXAMPLES: I *am* filing.   We *are* filing.
> You *are* filing.   You *are* filing.
> He *is* filing.   They *are* filing.

To emphasize the action taking place in the present tense, use the emphatic verb *do* as the helping verb.

> EXAMPLES: I *do* file.
> You *do* file.

He *does file.*

§ 6.3.8 Verbs—Past tense

Past tense shows that something took place in the past or that the state of being was in the past.

EXAMPLES: He *left* at five.
He *was* there all night.

To show past action that was continuous or moving forward, use the *ing* form of the verb (progressive form) with the past tense of *be*.

EXAMPLES: I *was filing.*   We *were filing.*
You *were filing.*   You *were filing.*
She *was filing.*   They *were filing.*

To emphasize the action in the past tense, add *did* to the verb.

EXAMPLES: I *did file.*   We *did file.*
You *did file.*   You *did file.*
He *did file.*   They *did file.*

§ 6.3.9 Verbs—Future tense

Future tense tells that the action or state of being will occur at some future time. To express future tense, use *shall* or *will* followed by a main verb. *Shall* is used in very formal writing with the first person (*I, we*). *Will* is more commonly used in contemporary English with the first person and is always used with the second and third person (*you, he, she, it, they*).

EXAMPLES: I *shall* be glad to answer any questions you may have.
They *will* leave tomorrow.

EXAMPLES: I *will be filing.*   You *will be filing.*
He *will be filing.*   They *will be filing.*

§ 6.3.10 Verbs—Present perfect tense

The present perfect tense indicates that the action or state of being is complete (perfect) in the present. This tense is always written with *has* or *have* preceding the past participle of the main verb.

EXAMPLES: Mary *has worked* all night.

Jon and Fred *have* already *left.*

§ 6.3.11   Verbs—Past perfect tense

The past perfect tense shows that the action or state of being was completed at some time in the past. It indicates action or a state of being began in the past and completed at or before some stated or implied past time. It is always formed by using *had* with the past participle of the main verb.

EXAMPLES: Sarah *had left* by the time I arrived.

By the time of the divorce, they *had lived* in separate homes for two years.

§ 6.3.12   Verbs—Future perfect tense

The future perfect tense shows that the action will be completed by a certain time in the future or before some other future event takes place. It is formed by using *shall have* or *will have* with the past participle of the main verb.

EXAMPLES: By the time I am 21, I *will have* bought my own car.

By the end of next year, they *will have* completed the merger.

§ 6.3.13   Verbs—Active and passive voice

Active voice refers to the use of active verbs in sentence structure. *Passive voice* refers to the use of passive verb forms, which consist of some form of *to be* plus the past participle of the primary verb. Active verbs direct the action of the sentence toward the object of the sentence. Passive verbs direct the action toward the subject.

EXAMPLES: Active: The secretary *typed* the letters very quickly.

Passive: The letters *were typed* very quickly by the secretary.

Sentences in the active voice are normally preferred because they are briefer, more direct, and more powerful. There is less risk of confusing the reader with the straightforward structure of active voice. As a practical matter, though, good writing requires variety. Every sentence should not have the same structure, and there are some things that are easier to do in passive voice. Passive verbs are properly used to emphasize the receiver of the action or to deemphasize the doer of the action.

§ 6.3.14 Verbs—Verb moods (subjunctive mood)

Verbs are categorized into three moods: *indicative*, *imperative*, and *subjunctive*. The *indicative mood* is used to state a fact or ask a question.

The *imperative mood* is used to give an order, a request, or a command.

The *subjunctive mood* is used to express conditions that are contrary to fact or doubtful. The subjunctive is also used in clauses following verbs that express a doubt, wish, request, suggestion, demand or proposal.

When forming the subjunctive, change the verb for the third person singular (*he, she, it*) by dropping the *-s* or *-es*. Also change the form of the verb *to be* to the word *be* in the present tense and *were* in the past tense, regardless of what the subject is.

EXAMPLES: Incorrect: I suggest that Terry *goes* to the court.

Correct: I suggest that Terry *go* to the court.

Incorrect: If Jamie *was* here, she would go to court with us.

Correct: If Jamie *were* here, she would go to court with us.

Incorrect: The attorney insisted that Sheila *is* allowed to go to the seminar.

Correct: The attorney insisted that Sheila *be* allowed to go to the seminar.

§ 6.3.15 Verbs—Subject-verb agreement

A subject must agree with the verb in person and number. A singular subject must have a singular verb. A plural subject must have a plural verb.

EXAMPLES: He *does* it. (singular)

We *do* it. (plural)

You always takes a plural verb even when only one person is meant.

EXAMPLES: *You* are the only secretary we need. (singular)

You are the only secretaries we need. (plural)

Two or more subjects connected by *and* take a plural verb.

> EXAMPLE: The director of marketing and the product
>   managers *are reviewing* the proposal.

Two or more subjects connected by *and* that refer to the same person or thing take a singular verb.

> EXAMPLE: Our secretary and treasurer *is* Mary Brown.

Two or more subjects connected by *and* that are preceded by *each, every, many a,* or *many an* take a singular verb.

> EXAMPLES: Every sweater, jacket, and hat *is* on sale.
>   Many a paralegal and secretary *has worked* on
>   pro bono cases.

Two or more singular subjects connected with *or* or *nor* take a singular verb.

> EXAMPLE: Either Sally or Mary *plans* to meet you there.

When a singular subject and a plural subject are joined by *or* or *nor,* the plural subject should directly precede the verb, and a plural verb should be used whenever this can be done without sacrificing the emphasis desired.

> EXAMPLE: Either Mary or the boys *plan* to meet you
>   there.

When the subject is made up of different grammatical persons, the verb should agree in person (*I, we, you*) and number (*has, have*) with the nearer subject.

> EXAMPLES: Neither you nor she *has* the time to take the
>   case.
>   Neither she nor you *have* the time to take the
>   case.

A collective noun (see § 6.4.3) requires a singular verb if the noun is a single unit. A plural verb should be used if the persons or things are being considered as individuals within the unit. It is often necessary to add a word referencing the individuals specifically to avoid an awkward construction.

EXAMPLES: The jury *delivers* its verdict to the judge. (singular)
The jury *members are* hopelessly deadlocked. (plural)

When *number* is preceded by *the,* a singular verb is used. If *a* precedes *number*, a plural verb is used.

EXAMPLES: The number of entries *was* large this year. (singular)
A number of entries *were* duplicates. (plural)

· A sum of money used as a subject requires a singular verb.

EXAMPLE: Fifty dollars *is* the required filing fee.

§ 6.3.16 Verbs—Verbals

There are three types of verbals: ***infinitives, gerunds***, and ***participles***. A verbal is not a verb but a form of a verb used as a noun, adjective, adverb, or as part of a noun phrase or adjective phrase. In the sentence, "*Trying a case may be very expensive,*" *Trying* is a gerund functioning as the subject of the sentence; it is not a verb.

§ 6.3.17 Verbs—Infinitives

An ***infinitive*** is created by placing the word *to* in front of the verb as in *to go.* An infinitive may be used as a noun, an adjective, or an adverb. It may be modified by adverbs and may have subjects and objects just as a verb has. The infinitive phrase consists of the infinitive and the word or words closely related to the infinitive.

EXAMPLE: *To read* a book is an interesting pastime. (*Book* is the direct object of the infinitive *to read.*)

Try to avoid splitting infinitives, which occurs when a modifier is placed between *to* and the verb.

EXAMPLES: Incorrect: To *slowly improve.*
Correct: To *improve slowly.*
Incorrect: You have the right *to not see it.*
Correct: You have the right not *to see it.*

However, it should be noted that while it is preferable to keep the infinitive phrase together, it is acceptable to split an infinitive for emphasis, clarity, or readability.

Split infinitives are often the result of awkward or wordy writing. A concerted effort to focus the writing into simpler and clearer sentences will often resolve the problem.

§ 6.3.18 Verbs—Gerunds

A *gerund* is the present participle form of the verb used in the sentence as a noun or part of a noun phrase.

> EXAMPLE: *Writing* gives me great pleasure. (*Writing* is a gerund and is the subject of the sentence.)

A gerund phrase consists of the gerund and the adverbs, adjectives, and words closely associated with it. It can take an object and an indirect object.

> EXAMPLE: *Writing Alice a letter* was a generous gesture. (*Writing* is the gerund; *Alice* is the indirect object; and *letter* is the direct object of the gerund. The gerund phrase, *Writing Alice a letter,* is the subject of the sentence.)

When a noun or pronoun precedes the gerund, the possessive case of the noun or pronoun is generally used.

> EXAMPLES: Incorrect: I *look forward* to him going.
> Correct: I *look forward* to his going.
> Incorrect: *I objected* to Mary leaving.
> Correct: *I objected* to Mary's leaving.

§ 6.3.19 Verbs—Participles

A *participle* is a verb form that cannot stand by itself. It must have a helping verb in order to function. The participle may also act as an adjective.

The ***past participle*** is the third principal part of the verb. In regular verbs, the past participle ends in *ed, d,* or *t* (*walk, walked, walked*). In irregular verbs there is no consistency in forming the past participle. Consult the irregular verb chart (Illustration 6-1) for past participles of irregular verbs.

A fourth verb form is the ***present participle***, which is formed by adding *ing* to the present form of the verb. The ***perfect participle*** is formed by adding *having* or *having been* to the past participle.

A participle may function as an adjective when it is used without a helping verb.

EXAMPLES: The *tired* old woman walked slowly. (*Tired* is the past participle.)

The *dancing* bear stole the show. (*Dancing* is the present participle.)

The watch, *having been broken,* no longer worked accurately. (*Having been broken* is the perfect participle.)

A *participle phrase* consists of the participle and words closely associated with it. The phrase should be placed close to the word it modifies. When it is incorrectly placed, it distorts the meaning of the sentence and is known as a dangling participle.

EXAMPLES: Incorrect: *Talking loudly,* the attorney observed the witnesses. (It incorrectly appears that the attorney is talking.)

Correct: The attorney observed the witnesses *talking loudly.* (The witnesses are talking.)

§ 6.4 Nouns

A *noun* is a word that names a person (*secretary*), place (*city*), thing (*desk*), or idea (*justice*).

§ 6.4.1 Nouns—Common nouns

A *common noun* is a name given to a general class of person, place, thing, or idea.

§ 6.4.2 Nouns—Proper nouns

A *proper noun* is the name of a particular person (*Susan*), place (*Utah*), or thing (*Talking Elmo*). Proper nouns are **_always_** capitalized.

§ 6.4.3 Nouns—Collective nouns

A *collective noun* is one that names a group of persons or things, (*faculty, orchestra, jury, family*), and takes a singular verb. (See § 6.3.15, Subject-verb agreement.)

§ 6.4.4 Nouns—Plurals of nouns

When forming the plural of a noun, use one of the following guidelines or consult the dictionary.

- Add *s* to most common nouns (*cat/cats, boy/boys, plate/plates*).
- Add *es* to nouns ending in *s, x, ch, sh,* or *z* (*glass/glasses, box/boxes, crutch/crutches, wish/wishes, waltz/waltzes*).
- When nouns ending in *o* have a consonant preceding the *o*, add

es to the noun (*potato/potatoes, veto/vetoes*); many exceptions to this rule are nouns from foreign languages, such as those dealing with music (*piano/pianos, solo/solos*); *memo/memos* is another exception.

- When nouns ending in *o* have a vowel preceding the *o*, add *s* to the noun (*studio/studios, ratio/ratios*).
- When nouns ending in *y* have a consonant preceding the *y*, change the *y* to *i* and add *es* (*fly/flies, company/companies, secretary/secretaries*).
- When nouns ending in *y* have a vowel preceding the *y*, leave the noun the same and add *s* (*attorney/attorneys, key/keys, gray/grays*).
- When forming the plural of abbreviations and letters, add apostrophe and *s* to lower case letters and abbreviations (*p's* and *q's, r.p.m.'s, c.o.d.'s*) and upper case letters where confusion may result (*A's, I's, U's*); however, for other capital letters and abbreviations ending in capital letters, just add *s* (*M.D.s, Ph.D.s, ABCs*).
- Nouns ending in *f* or *fe* are made plural by changing the *f* to *v* and adding *es* (*wife/wives, life/lives*); exceptions are *chief/chiefs* and *belief/beliefs*.

There are exceptions to these rules, such as *man/men, woman/women, child/children, mouse/mice, sheep/sheep, tooth/teeth, foot/feet, corps/corps*. Most of the exceptions are well known. When in doubt, consult the dictionary.

§ 6.4.5   Nouns—Compound nouns

Compound nouns are typically composed of two words, one of which functions as a noun and one of which functions as an adjective. To make the matter more confusing, often both words are capable of acting as nouns, and it can take some work to analyze the compound to make a correct plural.

There are four types of compound nouns. The first is a compound which is a single word, e.g., *billboard* or *paycheck*. (Note that bill, board, pay, and check are all nouns in normal usage. *Bill* modifies *board*, the primary noun; *pay* modifies *check*.) The majority **but** not all words are made plural with the simple addition of "s" and require no further analysis. *Passersby* is one of the few exceptions here.

Two other forms of compound nouns include those composed of two words, either joined by a hyphen or standing as separate words. The rule for each of these two types is the same. To form the plural of compound nouns such as *attorney general* or *senator-elect*, make the word which serves as a **noun** plural. For example, *general* describes the type of attorney and serves an adjective role. In this case, then, add *s* to *attorney*. In the example, "*senator-elect*", *senator* is the noun, and *elect* is adjectival or descriptive, so the plural is *senators-elect*.

Finally, some compounds are made up of a noun and a short prepositional phrase that serves a descriptive or adjective function, e.g., *mother-in-law* or *bill of lading*. In this case, again, add *s* to the noun to make the plural, e.g. *mothers-in-law* and *bills of lading*.

Contemporary usage tends toward the practice of making the last word in any compound plural, but the rules given above are generally more appropriate for formal writing. Again, consult the dictionary when in doubt.

§ 6.5 Possessive nouns

To show ownership or possession, use an apostrophe with the noun. There are three basic rules governing the form of possessives.

§ 6.5.1 Possessive nouns—Singular possession

Add an apostrophe and an *s* to the end of a singular noun (*Mary's, typist's, today's*). However, when a proper noun ends in *s* and the addition of *'s* would make the word hard to pronounce, only an apostrophe is added (*Moses'*). Obviously, application of a rule based on the way a word sounds will be subjective. When in doubt, add *'s*.

> EXAMPLES: The glass's rim is chipped.
> Moses' sister Miriam is Rachel's heroine.

§ 6.5.2 Possessive nouns—Plural possession

First, make the word plural; then look at the end of the word. If it ends in *s*, add only an apostrophe. If it does not end in *s*, add *'s* just as in the singular (*boy / boys / boys', child / children / children's*).

> EXAMPLES: The *judges'* calendars were posted on the Internet.
> The *women's* voices were loud.

§ 6.5.3 Possessive nouns—Three steps to forming possession

1. Is the apostrophe necessary? Does the word actually show possession?
2. If yes, then spell out the singular or plural noun first.
3. Apply the rules in §§ 6.5.1 and 6.5.2 above.
   Some additional rules for forming possessive nouns include:
   - To show singular possession, add an apostrophe and *s* to the last word of a compound noun (*brother-in-law's* house).
   - To show plural possession of a hyphenated or multiple-word compound noun, make the plural first, then add apostrophe and *s* to the end of the compound (*mothers-in-law's* birthdays).

- To show separate ownership of two or more things, add an apostrophe and *s* to each name (*Sue's and Mary's* cards).
- To show joint ownership, add apostrophe and *s* only to the last owner (*Fred and Robyn's* house).
- On personal and company names, add the apostrophe and *s* at the end of the name (*John Q. Smith III's, Stacy & Stacy's*).

§ 6.6 Pronouns

A ***pronoun*** is a word that replaces a noun or a name in order to avoid awkward repetitions. Instead of writing "*John answered John's phone and talked to John's client,*" one would write, "*John answered **his** phone and talked to **his** client.*" Pronouns can be classified as personal, possessive, reflexive, relative, indefinite, interrogative, demonstrative, and reciprocal.

§ 6.6.1 Pronouns—Personal pronouns

Personal pronouns are used for the person speaking, the person spoken to, and the person spoken about.

> EXAMPLE: *He* told *her* about *me.*

§ 6.6.2 Pronouns—Person and case

Pronouns are classified as first person (person doing the speaking), second person (person being spoken to), and third person (person being spoken about).

First person pronouns are *I, we, me, us, my, mine, our, ours.*

Second person pronouns are *you, your, yours.*

Third person pronouns are *he, she, it, they, him, her, them, his, hers, its, their, theirs.*

There are three case forms of personal pronouns: *nominative* (also known as *subjective*), *objective,* and *possessive.* Illustration 6-2 shows the pronouns in each case. The position in which the pronoun appears in the sentence determines the case. Note that in the possessive case there are two forms of pronouns. When the pronoun precedes a noun, it acts as an adjective. When it stands alone and shows possession, it is a possessive pronoun.

Illustration 6-2

CASES AND FUNCTIONS OF PRONOUNS				
Nominative	**Objective**	**Possessive**		
I, we	me, us	my	mine	
		our	ours	
you	you	your	yours	

CASES AND FUNCTIONS OF PRONOUNS

Nominative	Objective	Possessive	
he, she	him, her	her, his	hers, his
it, they	it, them	its, their	its, theirs

FUNCTIONS IN THE SENTENCE

1.	Subject *She* is home.	1.	Direct object Ray told *her.*	1.	Possessive pronoun as adjective
2.	Predicate nominative (subject complement)	2.	Indirect object Ray told *me* the news		This is *your* book.
				2.	Possessive pronoun
	The owner is *he.*	3.	Object of preposition Give the food to *him.*		Is the book *yours?*
		4.	Object of infinitive Jay wanted to send *me* instead of Alice		
		5.	Subject of infinitive The teacher wanted *them* to do the acting.		
			(Pronouns preceding and following an infinitive are in the objective case.)		

§ 6.6.3 Pronouns—Possessive pronouns

Possessive pronouns never contain apostrophes. *Its* is a possessive pronoun; *it's* is a contraction for *it is. Your* and *their* are possessive pronouns. *You're* and *they're* are contractions. *Her's* is simply wrong.

§ 6.6.4 Pronouns—Reflexive pronouns

A ***reflexive pronoun*** ends in *-self* or *-selves,* e.g., *myself, ourselves.* Reflexive pronouns are used only to refer back to a noun in the sentence meaning the same person. They are typically used to emphasize the subject's lone role in an action.

EXAMPLES: I gave *myself* a haircut. (*Myself* refers to I.)
Incorrect: Mary and myself went shopping.

Correct: Mary and I went shopping. (In the incorrect sentence there is no one to whom the pronoun *myself* can reflect back.)

§ 6.6.5   Pronouns—Relative pronouns

A ***relative pronoun*** joins a dependent clause to an independent clause. It begins the dependent clause and is related to another word or idea in the sentence. It also serves as the subject, direct object, or object of the preposition in the dependent clause.

EXAMPLES: The file clerk *who* types fastest will get the job. (*Who* is a relative pronoun and is the subject of the verb *types*.)
The file clerk *whom* you hired is very efficient. (*Whom* is a relative pronoun and is the direct object of the verb *hired*.)
The file clerk to *whom* you refer is my sister. (*Whom* is a relative pronoun and is the object of the preposition *to*.)

In each of the above examples the dependent clause is related to *the file clerk* by the relative pronoun.

Illustration 6-3 shows the relative pronouns.

Illustration 6-3

RELATIVE PRONOUNS		
Pronoun	Use in Sentence	Examples
Who	*Nominative case* Used as a subject of a clause	The girl *who* gave you the package left quickly.
Whom	*Objective case* Used as a direct object Used as an object of the preposition	The teacher *whom* I knew well quit teaching. The lady to *whom* I gave your name will call you tomorrow.
Whose	*Possessive case* Used as an adjective (Note: *who, whom* and *whose* refer to persons only.)	The man *whose* dog was lost lives on your street.

RELATIVE PRONOUNS		
Pronoun	Use in Sentence	Examples
Which	Refers to animals or things Used for nonessential (nonrestrictive) clauses Used as a subject	 The desk *which* was broken was sold.
	Used as an object of a preposition	The chair on *which* I stood fell.
That	Refers to persons, animals, or things Used for essential (restrictive) clauses Used as a subject	 I think *that* will do for now.
	Used as a direct object	The movers *that* I know will do it for you.

§6.6.6 Pronouns—Indefinite pronouns

Indefinite pronouns do not stand for a particular person or thing. Some of them are always singular; others are always plural; others may be either singular or plural depending upon the noun to which they refer. (See Illustration 6-4.)

Illustration 6-4

INDEFINITE PRONOUNS		
Use a Singular Verb	Use a Plural Verb	Use Either a Plural or Singular Verb
another, anybody, anyone, each, everybody, everyone, either, neither, someone, somebody	both, few, many, others, several	all, any, more, none, some

§6.6.7 Pronouns—Interrogative pronouns

Interrogative pronouns are used in asking questions. *Who, whom, whomever, which, what,* and *whose* are the most common ones. Do not confuse *whose* with *who's. Who's* is a **_contraction_** of *who is; whose* is possessive.

EXAMPLES: Whose car is that?
What are you doing?
Who is going with me?

Whom shall I appoint?
Which of the books do you want?

§ 6.6.8   Pronouns—Demonstrative pronouns

Demonstrative pronouns are used to modify a noun or take the place of a noun. They serve as indicators or pointers.

Singular	**Plural**	
This	These	Refer to objects near at hand.
That	Those	Refer to objects at either a slight or great distance.

§ 6.6.9   Pronouns—Reciprocal pronouns

Reciprocal pronouns relate specifically to another person, i.e., *each other* and *one another*.

§ 6.6.10   Pronouns—Agreement of pronouns and antecedents

The word to which a pronoun refers must be clear to the reader. Maintain a consistent viewpoint by making sure the pronoun agrees in number, whether singular or plural, with the word to which it refers.

EXAMPLES:

Incorrect: *Students* learning to type must be careful to type *his* papers accurately.

Correct: *Students* learning to type must be careful to type *their* papers accurately.

Incorrect: *Alice* wants to know where *you* can buy a set of striped seatcovers.

Correct: *Alice* wants to know where *she* can buy a set of striped seatcovers.

When the pronoun refers to two words, if they are connected by *and*, use a plural pronoun; if they are connected by *or*, use a singular pronoun.

EXAMPLES: Sonia *and* Dave say *they* will attend.
Either Matt *or* Charlie could bring *his* book.

When the pronoun refers to two words, one of which is plural and one of which is singular, place the plural subject closer to its pronoun, if possible.

EXAMPLES: Neither Mr. Wilson nor his employees *have* reached the quota.

Neither the employees nor Mr. Whipple *has* reached the quota.

Indefinite pronouns pose a special challenge. See Illustration 6-4 to determine whether the pronoun is singular or plural. Be sure that any reference back to the indefinite pronoun is also singular or plural.

EXAMPLES:

Incorrect: *Everyone* going to the picnic should bring *their* lunch.

Correct: *Everyone* going to the picnic should bring *his or her* lunch.

Incorrect: All *employees* working on the night shift should be sure to bring *his* lunch.

Correct: All *employees* working on the night shift should be sure to bring *their* lunches.

or

Each employee working on the night shift should bring *his or her* lunch.

When a pronoun is used to refer to a person of undetermined sex practicing a traditionally male profession, it is particularly important to choose pronouns that do not suggest that only men can occupy that profession. This is a situation in which the traditional use of "he" to refer to all people of either sex is particularly offensive. It is equally offensive to many to use a female pronoun to describe a person of undetermined sex occupying a traditionally female profession. Three ways to write in gender-neutral language are (1) make the subject plural, (2) omit the pronouns and use "a" or "an," or (3) refer to both feminine and masculine forms. In an extended work concerning a single profession, masculine and feminine forms can be alternated throughout the text. Regardless of the approach used, it is still incorrect to use the plural possessive *their* with a singular noun.

EXAMPLES:

Gender-biased:	An employee has *his* schedule to follow.
Incorrect pronoun agreement:	An employee has *their* schedule to follow.
Corrected:	Employees have their schedules to follow.
	An employee has a schedule to follow.

An employee has his or her schedule to follow.

§ 6.7   Adverbs

Adverbs are words that describe or limit a verb, an adjective, or another adverb. They also modify verbals (infinitives, gerunds, and participles). They answer the questions of:

Where?	He works *downtown*.
When?	Mother left *today*.
To what degree?	She worked *considerably harder* than Judith.
How?	The snow melted *quickly*.
Why?	She worked *so she would not starve*. (adverb clause)

§ 6.7.1   Adverbs—Comparison of adverbs

Illustration 6-5 shows the three degrees of comparison of adverbs.

The *simple adverb* expresses no comparison.

> EXAMPLE: The law student studied *diligently*.

The *comparative adverb* compares two persons, places, or things.

> EXAMPLE: The law student studied *more diligently* than his friend.

The *superlative adverb* compares three or more persons or things.

> EXAMPLE: Of the three law students, Jack studied *most diligently*.

Illustration 6-5

COMPARISON CHART FOR ADVERBS		
Simple	Comparative	Superlative
No comparison	Compares two persons or things.	Compares three or more persons or things.

COMPARISON CHART FOR ADVERBS		
Simple	Comparative	Superlative
	Add *er* to simple form.	Add *est* to the simple.
	Use the word *more* before the simple form.	Use the word *most* before the simple.
	Use the word *less* before the simple form.	Use the word *least* before the simple.
EXAMPLES		
efficiently	more efficiently	most efficiently
efficiently	less efficiently	least efficiently
soon	sooner	soonest
obvious	more obvious	most obvious
much	more	most
bad	worse	worst
slow	more slowly	most slowly

§ 6.8 Adjectives

Adjectives are words that modify, describe, or limit nouns, pronouns, and gerunds. They answer questions such as:

Which one?   The *red* car is mine.
How many?   The *two* books are his.
What kind?   The *wooden* chair is broken.

Most people are familiar with adjectives preceding nouns such as those in the examples above. There are also adjectives that follow linking verbs (*be, appear, seem*). These are called **predicate adjectives**.

EXAMPLES: The dress is *beautiful.*
              She seems *happy.*
              He appears *exhilarated.*

Occasionally an adjective follows a noun.

EXAMPLES: His wife found the restaurant *dirty.* (*Dirty* modifies restaurant.)
              A dress *six inches longer* would not look nice on her.
              (*Six inches longer* modifies dress.)

165

Adjectives are sometimes created from proper nouns. These are called ***proper adjectives***.

> EXAMPLES: An *English* actor is appearing in the local theater.
> A *European* car was seen in the used car showroom.

Some proper adjectives are no longer capitalized because they are no longer associated with the proper names from which they were derived.

> EXAMPLES: pasteurized milk (Louis Pasteur)
> herculean task (Hercules)

§ 6.8.1   Adjectives—Compound adjectives

Compound adjectives are those that consist of two or more words that function as a unit and express a single thought. The words in a compound adjective are hyphenated when they occur directly before the noun. When they occur elsewhere in the sentence, they may or may not be hyphenated depending on how they are used.

> EXAMPLES: This is a *first-class* restaurant.
> The *up-to-date* report was given to the manager.

When compound adjectives follow the noun, they are not hyphenated.

> EXAMPLES: The restaurant was *first class*.
> The report was *up to date*.

Sometimes what looks like a compound adjective is in reality an adverb-adjective combination. The adverb often ends in *ly*. These should never be hyphenated. The test is to see if the word immediately preceding the noun can be omitted and still leave a combination that sounds correct.

> EXAMPLES: The *friendly-acting* man sold teapots.
> The *privately owned* yacht was luxurious.

Since *friendly man* sounds correct, a hyphen is needed. Because *privately yacht* does not make sense without *owned*; the hyphen is not needed. The reasoning behind this is that the "*ly*" adverb ending shows the relationship of the two words without the hyphen. But two adjectives that function as one thought, as in *"worldly-wise person,"* need the hyphen to tie the two words together. (See also § 6.14.11.)

A noun followed by a gerund (*profit-taking, price-cutting*) needs a hyphen when it is used to modify a following noun.

> EXAMPLES: She did her *letter writing* late at night.
> He entered the *letter-writing* contest.

Most words ending in *ing, ed, d, en,* or *n,* are hyphenated when used in compound modifiers.

> EXAMPLES: Far-reaching
> Old-fashioned
> Soft-spoken
> Half-grown

The general rule is that if the phrase is out of its normal order, it should be hyphenated.

> EXAMPLES: The coat *looked old.*
> The *old-looking* coat was still useful.
> The statement was *off the record.*
> The *off-the-record* statement upset some employees.

If compound adjectives need to be hyphenated, they are still hyphenated in the comparative or superlative forms.

> EXAMPLES: a *low-priced* house   a *lower-priced* house
> a *slow-burning* fire   the *slowest-burning* fire

§ 6.8.2   Adjectives—Comparison of adjectives

Adjectives are compared in the same manner as adverbs—*simple, comparative*, and *superlative.*

Simple—pretty, graceful

Comparative—prettier, more graceful

Superlative—prettiest, most graceful

Some words, such as certain, perfect, correct, true, right, complete, round, unique, and dead, cannot be compared logically. For example, a unique item cannot be compared, because by definition it is one of a kind. While most readers will know what is meant when one dress is said to be more perfect than another, some will be disturbed by the lack of clear thinking such an expression suggests, especially in formal writing. When it is necessary to compare two things in these categories, change the descriptive terms to nonabsolutes. For example, try "Joann's dress is more magnificent than Mary's," or "Fred is already dead, but John is expected to die very soon."

§ 6.8.3   Adjectives—Distinguishing between adverbs and adjectives

Adverbs are often formed by adding "ly" to adjectives (courteous/courteously, direct/directly, real/really). Occasionally, when the adjective ends with "y" preceded by a consonant, the "y" is changed to "i" and "ly" is added (ready/readily, happy/happily).

Some commonly used adverbs and adjectives are irregular in form and confusing to use. *Good* is an adjective and *well* is an adverb, except in matters of health, where well is an adjective. *Bad* is an adjective and *badly* is an adverb; be sure that you use the correct word, especially in discussing the five senses.

> EXAMPLES: I smell *bad*. (The person has a bad odor.)
> I smell *badly*. (The person does a poor job of sniffing.)
> I feel *bad*. (I am not well.)
> I feel *badly*. (I do a poor job of touching.)

Real is an adjective; *really* is an adverb. Neither real nor really is a good substitute for very. Real is an ungrammatical usage; really can unintentionally convey the meaning of actually rather than very.

> EXAMPLES:
> Incorrect: I worked *real* hard.
> Correct: I worked *very* hard.
> Incorrect: She is a *real* happy person.
> Acceptable: She is a *really* happy person.
> Correct: She is a *very* happy person.

Some adjectives form their degrees in an irregular manner. The following are some of the common irregular adjectives:

Simple	Comparative	Superlative
bad, ill	worse	worst
good, well	better	best
little	littler, less, lesser	littlest, least
many, much	more	most

Simple	Comparative	Superlative
far	farther, further	farthest, furthest

Most adjectives that end in "-ful" or "-less" and all adjectives of more than two syllables form their degrees by adding "more" or "less" for the comparative and "most" or "least" for the superlative.

§ 6.8.4 Adjectives—Commonly confused adjectives

Farther and *further* are the comparatives for *far*. *Farthest* and *furthest* are the superlatives for *far*. *Farther* and *farthest* are used when referring to measurable distance; *further* and *furthest* refer to degree or quantity.

Later is used to refer to time; *latter* means near the end or the second of two items.

Less and *least* are used to describe nouns that are concerned with amount and quantity; *fewer* and *fewest* are used to emphasize number by actual count. *Fewer* refers to number and is used before plurals (*fewer books*); *less* refers to degree or amount and is used before singular words (*less noise*).

§ 6.9 Prepositions

A *preposition* is a word used to show the relationship of the noun or pronoun that follows it to some other word in the sentence. The prepositional phrase consisting of the preposition and its object may be used to modify other words in a sentence. It helps connect the thoughts in a sentence and offers clearer writing. The object of a preposition is never the subject of a sentence. For example, in the sentence "The list of exhibits was ready," the word *list*, not *exhibits*, is the subject; the prepositional phrase, including *exhibits*, describes the subject *list*.

COMMONLY USED PREPOSITIONS

about	except
above	for
according to	from
after	in
against	in addition to
along with	into
among	of
around	off
as well as	on
at	over
before	regarding

below	through
beside	to
between	under
but	up
by	upon
concerning	until
during	with

Note: *But* is usually a conjunction, although it may also serve as a preposition meaning *except*, e.g., Everyone left *but* him.

§ 6.10   Conjunctions

A **conjunction** is used to connect two or more words, phrases, or clauses.

§ 6.10.1   Conjunctions—Coordinating conjunctions

Coordinating conjunctions connect words, phrases, and clauses of equal value. The common coordinating conjunctions are *and, but, or,* and *nor.*

§ 6.10.2   Conjunctions—Subordinating conjunctions

Subordinating conjunctions join dependent clauses (subordinate clauses) to independent clauses.

Following is a list of subordinate conjunctions:

after	when
although	while
as	where
as if	whether
as though	whereas
because	unless
before	than
in order to	provided
if	inasmuch as
since	so that
until	

§ 6.10.3   Conjunctions—Conjunctive adverbs

Conjunctive adverbs also join clauses, words, and phrases that are grammatically equal. The following is a list of conjunctive adverbs:

however	moreover	thus
therefore	nevertheless	too
consequently	likewise	hence

§ 6.10.4 Conjunctions—Correlative conjunctions

"Either/or" and "neither/nor" are the *correlative conjunctions*. They also join equal sentence elements.

§ 6.11 Interjections

An *interjection* is a word used to express strong feeling or emotion. It does not change the basic meaning of the sentence. It is usually followed by a comma or exclamation mark.

EXAMPLE: Help! I'm being robbed!

§ 6.12 Sentence structure

The correct use of pronouns in direct and indirect objects, subject-verb agreement, correct placement and punctuation of adverbs and adjectives, and correct punctuation all rely on the ability to analyze and correct sentence structure.

§ 6.12.1 Sentence structure—The sentence

A *sentence* expresses a complete thought; it contains a *subject* and a *predicate* (verb plus associated words). The subject is the person, place, or thing being told about or doing the action. The predicate tells something about the person, place, or thing.

§ 6.12.2 Sentence structure—The simple sentence

The *simple sentence* contains a subject and a verb.

EXAMPLE: Allen   sings.
           S   **V**

A simple sentence may contain a *compound subject* (more than one person, place, thing, or concept) and a *compound verb* (more than one action or state of being). What makes a simple sentence simple is the existence of just one independent clause that requires no additional clauses to complete its meaning.

EXAMPLE: Fred and   danced and   in the show.
           Agnes   sang
           S   **V**

(*Fred and Agnes*=subject; *danced and sang*=verb)

A simple sentence may also contain a direct object, indirect object, predicate nominative, predicate adjective, and other parts of speech.

The *direct object* is the person, place, or thing receiving the action.

> EXAMPLE: Jamie   pounded   the table.
>   **S**   **V**   **DO**

The *indirect object* is the person, place, or thing receiving the direct object.

> EXAMPLE: Rosalie sold Anita the necklace.
>   **S**   **V**   **IO**   **DO**

A *predicate nominative* means the same thing as the subject and is connected to the subject by a linking verb. In simple terms, a predicate nominative identifies or names the subject. The sentence can be reversed without changing the meaning.

> EXAMPLE: Mrs. Smith   is   the teacher.
>   **S**   **V**   **PN**
>
>   The teacher   is   Mrs. Smith
>   **S**   **V**   **PN**

A *predicate adjective* describes the subject and is connected to the subject by a linking verb.

> EXAMPLE: The sunflow-   are   yellow.
>   ers
>   **S**   **V**   **PA**

§ 6.12.3   Sentence structure—The compound sentence

The *compound sentence* consists of two or more independent clauses (simple sentences) connected in one of the following ways:

- By a coordinating conjunction preceded by a comma

> EXAMPLE: Devon typed the letter, and Terry organized the notebooks.

- By a semicolon

EXAMPLE: Devon typed the letter; Terry organized the notebooks.

- By a conjunctive adverb preceded by a semicolon and followed by a comma

EXAMPLE: Devon typed the letter; however, Terry organized the notebooks.

If there are more than two independent clauses and they are short, they may be joined with commas.

EXAMPLE: Devon typed, Nicki proofread, Jamie copied, and Terry delivered the documents. (Note the coordinating conjunction preceding the last clause.)

If a stronger break between clauses is desired, use semicolons between each clause. Place a semicolon followed by *and* between the last two independent clauses.

EXAMPLE: Devon and Nicki went to court in the morning; Jamie and Terry copied the documents; and they prepared exhibits later that evening.

Use a semicolon to separate items in series if the individual items contain commas.

EXAMPLE: The meetings will be held in Kansas City, Missouri; Butte, Montana; and Cleveland, Ohio.

However, if no misreading is likely, it is acceptable to use commas to separate the items.

Do not join two independent clauses with only a comma (omitting a conjunction). If more complicated punctuation is undesirable, make the two clauses into separate sentences.

§ 6.12.4 Sentence structure—The complex sentence

The ***complex sentence*** consists of one independent clause and one or more dependent clauses.

The ***dependent clause*** contains a subject and a verb; it may also contain any or all of the other sentence parts, but it cannot stand by itself. It needs the independent clause to complete its meaning.

EXAMPLE: While the lawyer was in   Sarah did the filing.
                             court,
                        Dep. Cl.   **Indep. Cl**.

Dependent clauses can serve as nouns, adverbs, or adjectives in relation to the main clause.

A **noun clause** functions as a noun; it serves as the subject, direct object, or object of the preposition.

EXAMPLES: *Who is going to be president* is anybody's guess.
                        (The noun clause is the subject of the sentence.)
                        Jack said *that Tony would not be here today.*
                        (The noun clause is the direct object of the verb *said.*)
                        Please give the promotion to *whomever you choose.*
                        (The noun clause is the object of the preposition *to.*)

There is no punctuation separating the noun clause from the remainder of the sentence.

An **adverb clause** functions in the same manner as an adverb; it modifies or limits verbs, adjectives, or other adverbs. It answers the questions of where? when? how? and why? It is connected to the main clause by a subordinating conjunction. See § 6.10.2 for a list of subordinating conjunctions.

If an adverb clause precedes the independent clause, the two clauses are separated by a comma. When an adverbial clause ends the sentence, check to see if it is restrictive (essential to the meaning) or nonrestrictive. If it is nonrestrictive, place a comma between it and the main clause.

EXAMPLES: Please decide if you wish to purchase the suit, *inasmuch as we have other interested buyers.*
                        If we cannot agree, we must submit to arbitration.
                        We must submit to arbitration *if we cannot agree.*
                        Before the painter gets here, she wants to leave.
                        She wants to leave *before the painter gets here.*

Adjective clauses are generally introduced with *relative pronouns* (*who, whom, whose, which,* and *that*). They modify, limit, or describe nouns and gerunds. They are directly related to a noun or gerund in the sentence.

EXAMPLE: She worked quickly because the deadline *that she made* was fast approaching. (This has two dependent clauses in it: *that she made* is part of the dependent clause beginning with *because. That she made* modifies *deadline.*)

§ 6.12.5 Sentence structure—The compound-complex sentence

A *compound-complex sentence* consists of two or more independent clauses and one or more dependent clauses.

EXAMPLE:

They hired a new software technician	who had excellent training,
IC	DC

but he came in late every morning.
                     IC

§ 6.12.6 Sentence structure—Phrases

A *phrase* is a group of words. Phrases usually serve as modifiers in the sentence, but infinitive and gerund phrases can also serve as nouns. Probably the most common phrase is the prepositional phrase. It can serve as an adverb or adjective in the sentence. It consists of the preposition and its object (a noun or pronoun); it may also contain several related words that serve as modifiers in the phrase itself.

EXAMPLES:

During	the long,	extended	trial,	she	worked	continuously.
PREP	**ADJ**	**ADJ**	**OB PREP**	**S**	**V**	**ADV**

He	gave	it	to	the	very	competent	assistant.
S	**V**	**DO**	**PREP**		**ADV**	**ADJ**	**OB PREP**

§ 6.13 Review of sentence structure

Here are some basic steps for identifying parts of speech:

1. Locate the verb or verbs with tense in the sentence (*eat, ate, has eaten*).
2. Identify a subject for each verb (who is doing what?).
3. Find the direct object and indirect object, if any (on what is the action focused?).

4. Locate the predicate nominative or predicate adjective, if there is one (the descriptive language following the verb).

5. Determine the correct case for Items 3 and 4 above (singular or plural; nouns, pronouns, or verbs).

6. Look for the prepositions and the nouns following them. (Some people prefer to locate the nouns in the sentence and check to see if they are preceded by a preposition.)

7. Then look for the adverbs, adjectives, and connecting words.

8. With sentences containing *who* or *whom,* it may be necessary to rearrange the sentence in order to identify the case correctly.

> EXAMPLES: The man (who/whom) I gave it to was very handsome.
> The man to *whom* (object of preposition) I gave it was very handsome.
> *Who/Whom* are you going to call?
> You are going to call *whom?* (object of the infinitive *to call*)

9. It can be helpful to replace *who* or *whom* with a pronoun to decide which one to use:

> EXAMPLES: Tim is the one who lives on Denver Street.
> *He* lives on Denver Street.
> With whom are you working?
> I am working with *him*.

COMMON ERRORS TO AVOID

- A prisoner is *hanged*, not hung. A picture is *hung*.
- There is a difference between a *house* and a *home*. A home is not sold. A house can be sold.
- The phrases *kind of* and *sort of* are appropriate only in informal writing. In formal writing, use *rather* or *somewhat*.
- *Injury* refers to persons; *damage* refers to objects.
- A resolution is *adopted*. An ordinance is *passed*.
- Do not say a person *broke* his arm unless he did so deliberately. Instead say his arm *was broken*.
- A person does not *sustain* a fatal injury. *Sustain* means to bear up under; to support by adequate proof. Instead, say a person *suffered* a fatal injury.
- *All right* is all right. *Allright* and *alright* are not.
- It is permissible to refer to a newly married couple as *bride and*

groom. When mentioning the man alone, he is the *bridegroom*—unless he takes care of horses.

- An event that has not been arranged or planned *occurs*. A wedding, a party, or a conference *takes place*.
- *Afterward, forward, toward,* and similar words with the suffix *ward* do not end in *s*.
- Go a short *way*, not a short *ways*.
- *Headquarters, molasses,* and *whereabouts* all take singular verbs.
- Mrs. Jones is the widow of John Jones, not the late John Jones. He *leaves* his widow; his widow *survives*.
- A person died *of* pneumonia, not *from* pneumonia.
- The word *per* is a Latin term with fairly specific—and frequently misunderstood—meaning. In formal writing, reserve the use of *per* for Latin structures like *per diem*. Refer to miles *an* hour, not miles *per* hour. However, if it is necessary to abbreviate miles per hour, use *per* when the phrase is written out and *mph* as the abbreviation. *Per* is often used in technical writing to indicate calculation by division.
- It was *proved*, but it has been *proven*.
- Collective nouns generally take singular verbs, but there are exceptions. The pair *were* married. The American people *are* dependable.
- A *scholar* is a learned person. A child in school is a *pupil*. A person attending high school or college is a *student*.
- *Heart disease* is a general term describing any one of several chronic heart conditions. *Heart failure* is a specific heart event that often ends in death. Do not describe heart disease as heart failure.
- *Murder* is a technical term indicating a degree of guilt; use the term advisedly.
- Not all real estate brokers are Realtors®. A Realtor® is an active member of the local real estate board having membership in the National Association of Real Estate Boards. Do not use the term Realtor® unless the broker's status is known.
- *Character* is what one really possesses; *reputation* is the character one is believed to possess.
- *Round table* is two words.
- Many well-known organizations are usually identified only by their initials, e.g., *YWCA*. Such abbreviations are written without periods or spaces in all capitals. Certain professional designations are also written in this way. In describing "PLS . . . an advanced certification for the legal professional®," use the full description for the first reference, then shorten to *PLS*® for brevity in later references.
- A turkey is *red-headed*, but a person is *red-haired*.
- *Compare to* refers to different things (life *compared to* a movie). *Compare with* refers to similar things (Congress *compared with* Parliament).

177

- When itemizing, use *first, second,* and *third* or, since there is no *firstly*, use *initially, next*, and *finally*.
- Use *regardless* or *irrespective*. Although *irregardless* is a word with its own place in the dictionary, it is nonstandard English and sounds little better than *ain't* to most audiences.

§ 6.14 Punctuation

The purpose of punctuation is to assist the reader in understanding written material. When a person is speaking, they lower or raise their voice and pause for emphasis or clarity. Punctuation accomplishes the same function for the reader.

§ 6.14.1 Punctuation—Period

The *period* indicates a full stop. It is used:
- At the end of a sentence
- In abbreviations, except when several initials are commonly used together and do not require periods (*YMCA, AAA, NALS*)
- After initials in a name
- Between dollars and cents ($1.89)
- To indicate a decimal (10.9 inches)

In a web address, the punctuation before the suffix (*com, net, org, edu, gov*) is called a *dot*, not a period.

§ 6.14.2 Punctuation—Comma

The *comma* is a partial stop. It gives pause and helps clarify the meaning of the sentence. Commas should be used only when there is a reason for using them. The comma is used:
- To separate words, phrases, or short clauses in a series of three or more. Generally, a comma is placed before the *and*; however, some writers prefer to omit the comma preceding *and*. It is essential to be consistent within any single document. Try to avoid causing confusion. For example, are "whisky, vodka, gin and tonic" three drinks or four?

> EXAMPLE: A lawyer's assistant needs to be prompt, efficient, and trustworthy.

In the names of business firms, do not use a comma before an ampersand in a firm name.

> EXAMPLE: Jackson, Hall, Roe & Stone

- To separate independent clauses connected by coordinating conjunctions unless they are short and closely related.

EXAMPLES: The lawyer was in court all day, and the
assistant had to work late.
Kristen rowed and Robyn bailed.

- To set off a subordinate clause that precedes the main clause.

    EXAMPLE: Since he locked his key in the car, he could
    not open the door.

- After an introductory phrase that contains a verb form.

    EXAMPLE: After skiing all day, he was too tired to go to
    a movie.

- To set off a nonessential (nonrestrictive) clause from the rest of
  the sentence.

- To set off parenthetical and transitional words from the rest of
  the sentence when pauses are clearly indicated. The following is
  a list of some of these expressions or words.

accordingly	more or less
all in all	namely
also	needless to say
as a matter of fact	of course
by and large	otherwise
by the way	so it seems
for example	therefore
however	though
if possible	too
in brief	unfortunately
meanwhile	usually

Most of the time, a pause is indicated and the comma is used.

- To set off an intervening phrase or clause that breaks the continuity of the sentence.

    EXAMPLE: These men, even though they were very
    hungry, gave the food to the children.

- To set off contrasting phrases or clauses.

        EXAMPLE: What we need is justice, not just trite promises.

- To set off explanatory words or phrases that mean the same as the preceding word.

        EXAMPLE: Indexing, or coding, of the material to be filed is necessary.

- To separate two or more parallel adjectives.

        EXAMPLE: The tall, lovely woman came to my table. No comma is used when the adjectives modify one another: The dark red dress was stunning.

- To set off names used in direct address.

        EXAMPLE: Do you believe, Dr. Jones, that I will live?

- To set off appositives, phrases, or words that further identify a preceding word when they are not essential to the meaning.

        EXAMPLES: My mother, Madeline, was here this evening.
                        George Washington, the first president, was born on February 22, 1732.

- To set off quotations from the rest of the sentence.

        EXAMPLE: Charlie said, "Don't count on me for more money."

- To set off words such as *Inc.* and *Jr.,* (when preferred by the individual), names of states when used with the city name, and the year when used with the month and day. Many lawyers believe the following comma after the year or state should be omitted, although the use of the following comma is standard in every major style book. When in Rome, act Roman.

        EXAMPLES: I will be there on August 11, 2016, to see you perform.
                        Mason & Jones, Inc., is open for business.
                        Did you go to Denver, Colorado, on your birthday?

Lee James, Jr., is not my husband.

- To set off *etc.,* a comma is placed before and after it.

  EXAMPLE: Paper, pencils, pens, etc., will be sent tomorrow.

- To separate a title or degree from a name.

  EXAMPLE: John Jones, Ph.D., will speak at our next luncheon.

§ 6.14.3   Punctuation—Semicolon

The **semicolon** is used between parts of a sentence to separate phrases, clauses, and enumerations. It is used:

- To separate independent clauses joined by a conjunction when one or more of the clauses contain internal commas and a strong break between clauses is desired.

  EXAMPLE: The shipment of coats, suits, and skirts will be ready tomorrow; and they will be sent air express.

- To separate two independent clauses when no connective is used.

  EXAMPLE: I plan to leave at nine on the plane; I will be in New York by ten.

- To set off a phrase when words are missing but understood, a comma may also be used, but if there are other commas, a semicolon makes the meaning clearer.

  EXAMPLE: To some teachers, it was a catastrophe; to others, a minor nuisance.

- Between independent clauses of a compound sentence that are joined by a conjunctive adverb (*however, therefore,* etc.).

  EXAMPLE: We had car trouble; therefore, we did not arrive on time for the depositions.

§ 6.14.4 Punctuation—Colon

The *colon* is used:

- After the salutation in a business letter.

  EXAMPLE: Dear Mr. Jones:

- In stating clock time.

  EXAMPLE: 12:10 p.m.

- After introductory expressions preceding an enumeration, such as *the following, thus, as follows.*

  EXAMPLE: Please order the following:

- In a web address, following *http.*

  EXAMPLE: To search for anything related to government, go to http:\\www.whitehouse.gov

- The colon may follow a verb, preposition, or conjunction when it introduces a list, but in running text, no colon is used.

  EXAMPLES: Among those present were:
  Sam Brown
  George White
  James Black
  Among those present were Sam Brown, George White, and James Black.

- To introduce a long quotation, typically presented in block format.

  EXAMPLE: Lincoln's Gettysburg Address read: "Fourscore and seven years ago . . .."

§ 6.14.5 Punctuation—Question marks

The *question mark* is used in the following ways:

- After a direct question.

  EXAMPLE: When are you sending my discovery requests?

A question mark is not used if the question is rhetorical or communicates an order rather than a request.

> EXAMPLE: Will you please send me a corrected bill.

- After each of a series of questions in a single sentence.

> EXAMPLE: How do you feel about *Time? Newsweek? Fortune? Good Housekeeping?*

§ 6.14.6 Punctuation—Exclamation point

The **exclamation point** may be used internally in a sentence or at the end of a sentence. It is used after a word or group of words expressing a strong command, strong feeling or emotion, or an excited exclamation.

> EXAMPLE: Help! He stole my purse!

§ 6.14.7 Punctuation—Dash

There are two types of dash in contemporary word processing and printing—the **en dash** and the **em dash**. Typographically, the en dash is the width of an *n* in type, while the em dash is the width of an *m*. Neither dash has a space on either side of it in text. The em dash is more commonly used, and when the em dash symbol itself is not available, two hyphens are used instead. There is no space on either side of the two hyphens, nor is there a space between them. The dash is used:

- To set off a single word or expression for emphasis.

> EXAMPLE: His work lacked only one thing—accuracy.

- To set off a change of thought or side comment from the rest of the sentence.

> EXAMPLE: His whole unlucky life—or so it seemed to me—was wasted on that woman.

- To take the place of parentheses.

> EXAMPLE: The five senses—smell, touch, sight, hearing, and taste—are gems of great value.

- To substitute for a colon where the word *namely* has been omitted.

> EXAMPLE: There are two urgent needs—prevention of crime and a balanced economy.

- To set off a repetition, variation, explanation, or summary of what has gone before.

> EXAMPLES: Give money—dollars and cents—right now.
> They have acquiesced—given in—to our demands.
> I went to that movie—one I had seen before—and sat through it again.
> To give your money and your life for a cause—that is dedication.

- For emphasis (as in sales letters).

> EXAMPLE: This is not the same offer we made last year—it is a brand new plan especially created for the consumer of today.

§ 6.14.8   Punctuation—Parentheses

Parentheses are a strong mark of punctuation used when it is necessary to separate certain information from the rest of the sentence. All marks of punctuation, such as the ending period, question mark, exclamation point, or semicolon, should be placed outside the parentheses, except when the material contained in the parentheses requires its own internal or ending punctuation. If the sentence in the parentheses stands alone and is not a part of another sentence, a period is used within the parentheses.

- Place in parentheses only material that could be removed from the sentence without impairing the meaning.
- A complete sentence in parentheses that is part of another sentence should not start with a capital letter or end with a period.

> EXAMPLE: His luck was running out (he lost all the money he had), and he had to sell his car.

- Parentheses are used when writing figures after words.

EXAMPLE: We are enclosing a check for Twenty-five Dollars ($25).

- Use both opening and closing parentheses when enumerating in running text.

EXAMPLE: There are three kinds of ending punctuation marks: (1) period, (2) question mark, and (3) exclamation point.

- Use parentheses around explanatory or illustrative words or phrases.

EXAMPLES: The three assistants (Miss Jones, Mrs. Smith, and Ms. Bills) were at the meeting. Water (H_2O) is essential to all human beings.

§ 6.14.9   Punctuation—Quotation marks

When using **quotation marks**, the writer needs to know both how to use the quotation marks and how to punctuate around them. Certain punctuation marks are written inside the final quotation mark; others are written outside. The period and comma always go inside the quotation marks.

- When a quotation mark is used with a semicolon, colon, or dash, the quotation mark comes before the punctuation.

EXAMPLE: She was told, "A stitch in time saves nine" she did not believe it.

- A question mark or exclamation point should be placed after the quotation mark unless the quoted material itself ends in a question mark or exclamation point.

EXAMPLES: She asked, "Where did you buy the blouse?" Why didn't she ignore his "idiosyncrasies"?

- Only one ending punctuation mark should come at the end of the sentence, either before or after the quotation mark. If the quotation ends in a period, question mark, or exclamation point and is followed by a quotation mark, no further punctuation is needed.
- When there is a quotation within another quotation, single quotation marks are used for the internal quote.

- Quotation marks are used to indicate conversation. A new paragraph should be made each time the speaker changes.

  EXAMPLES: "I would like to see Ms. Mason," said the client.
  "She is in court today. May I make you an appointment for tomorrow?" asked the assistant.
  "No," answered the client, "because I will be in the hospital tomorrow."

- Quotation marks are sometimes placed around slang or coined words if they might give a poor impression. The reader is thus made aware that the writer knows the words are poor but is using them for effect. However, use of quotation marks may make it appear that the writer is apologizing for the word choice—and this can also create a poor impression. This use of quotation marks should be infrequent.

  EXAMPLE: Granny says things "ain't" like they used to be.

- Words referred to as words may be placed in quotation marks to identify them as words and not part of the sentence. Italics or underlining can also be used.

  EXAMPLE: Place the comma before "and" in a compound sentence.

- Use quotation marks to indicate the title of a published article. Book titles are typically underlined or italicized.

§ 6.14.10   Punctuation—Apostrophe

The *apostrophe* is used:

- To form contractions of words and figures. The apostrophe is used in place of omitted letters or figures.

  EXAMPLES:
is not	isn't	wherever	where'er
cannot	can't	you have	you've
'76	'50s		

- To form possessives. Never use an apostrophe with pronouns showing possession.

  EXAMPLES: Robyn's hair looks very nice.

Its color is red.

- To form plurals of lower case letters and upper case letters when the lack of an apostrophe may create confusion.

    EXAMPLES: Be sure to dot your *i's* and cross your *t's*. Her *A's* and *I's* were written in a European style.

- To set off quoted material that appears within a larger quotation.
- In names with the prefix *O*, such as *O'Brien* and *O'Connor*.

§ 6.14.11 Punctuation—Hyphen

There is a great deal of disagreement about when **hyphens** should be used. Many words that were once hyphenated are now joined as one word, and that trend continues, particularly with computer terminology. The following is a list of general usage rules. The principle is that a hyphen pulls words together into a single thought.

- Use the hyphen for one-thought expressions (two or more words functioning as one word).

    EXAMPLE: He has the know-how to do the job.

- Use the hyphen to join two or more words that modify a noun and act as a single thought.

    EXAMPLE: She had blue-green eyes.

- When two or more words modify a noun and are not in their normal order, they are hyphenated. To check, place them after the noun to see if the words then have separate force. If so, then they are not hyphenated after the noun and are hyphenated before the noun.

    EXAMPLES: an up-to-date proce-   the procedure was
    dure   brought up to date

- Three or more words serving as a single modifier are usually hyphenated.

    EXAMPLE: change-of-address cards

- An adverb ending in *ly* preceding an adjective is not connected to the adjective with a hyphen. To test to see if it is an adverb, try to use it with a noun without the adjective. If it cannot be used with the noun alone, then do not use the hyphen.

> EXAMPLES: a highly respected em- (a highly employee)
> ployee
> a friendly-looking girl (a friendly girl)

- Use the hyphen when verbs are composed of two or more words (not including helping verbs) and have a single thought.

> EXAMPLE: She cross-referenced the material.

- Suspended hyphens are used when two or more words share an additional word with a hyphen. Each of the words must have a hyphen following it.

> EXAMPLES: the five- and ten-cent store
> at three-, six-, and twelve-month intervals

- When the prefix *re-* is added to a word and the resulting word means to do something *again,* add a hyphen between the *re* and the word if the unhyphenated word would be confused with another word.

> EXAMPLES: recover re-cover (cover again)
> reform re-form (form again)
> resign re-sign (sign again)

- Words preceded by the prefixes *ex-, self-,* and *quasi-* are hyphenated.

> EXAMPLES: *ex-wife, self-sacrificing, quasi-legal*

- A civil or military title that stands for a single office should not be hyphenated.

> EXAMPLES: Vice President Attorney General
> Secretary of State

- When an office consists of two functions, it is hyphenated.

> EXAMPLE: secretary-treasurer

- A letter meant to designate shape before a word is hyphenated to the word.

EXAMPLES: An S-curve   L-shaped   T-square

- A hyphen can be used to clarify meaning.

EXAMPLES: fifty one-dollar bills
one half-cooked chicken or
one-half cooked chicken

§ 6.14.12   Punctuation—Ellipses

Ellipses are used to indicate omission of a word or words in quoted material.

- If the quoted material is in the middle of the sentence, three periods with intervening spaces (. . .) are used. If the quoted material ends with a period, leave one space and follow it with three periods with intervening spaces. If another sentence follows, leave one or two spaces after the ellipses, depending on the style used following sentences throughout the document.
- To indicate that an unfinished sentence trails off, use three periods with intervening spaces.
- In quoted material, omissions of paragraphs are indicated by inserting and centering three or four periods or asterisks with intervening spaces on a new line.
- On most modern word processing equipment, character sets are available that allow the insertion of ellipses as one character. However, the prescribed intervening spaces are omitted (as is often the case in professional typesetting). A more conservative approach would be to type the ellipses manually, rather than using the character insertion, so the spaces between the periods can be retained. The best option is the one the lawyer prefers.

§ 6.15   Capitalization

The following selected rules of capitalization may be helpful.

§ 6.15.1   Capitalization—Common usage

The most common usages of capitalization are:

- The first word of every sentence is capitalized.
- The first word of a complete direct quotation is capitalized.
- The first word of a salutation and all nouns used in the salutation are capitalized.
- The first word—and only the first word—in a complimentary close is capitalized.
- The first word of each item displayed in a list or outline is capitalized.

§ 6.15.2   Capitalization—First word after a colon

Capitalize the first word after a colon only when the colon introduces a complete passage or sentence having an independent meaning.

> EXAMPLE: In conclusion I wish to say: "The survey shows that . . ."

If the material following a colon is dependent on the preceding clause, the first word after the colon is not capitalized.

> EXAMPLE: I present the following three reasons for changing: the volume of business does not justify the expense; we are short of people; the product is decreasing in popularity.

§ 6.15.3   Capitalization—Capitalizing names

- Capitalize the names of associations, buildings, churches, hotels, streets, organizations, and clubs.

> EXAMPLES: The Business Club, Merchandise Mart, Central Christian Church, Peabody Hotel, Seventh Avenue, Administrative Management Society, Chicago Chamber of Commerce

- All proper names should be capitalized.

> EXAMPLES: Great Britain, John G. Hammitt, Internet

- Capitalize names derived from proper names.

> EXAMPLES: American, Chinese, English, Chinese noodles, English grammar, Italian spaghetti

Do not, however, capitalize words derived from proper nouns that have developed a special meaning.

> EXAMPLES: pasteurized milk, china dishes, morocco leather

- Capitalize special names for regions and localities.

> EXAMPLES: North Central states, the Far East, the East Side, the Hoosier State

- Capitalize names of government boards, agencies, bureaus, departments, and commissions.

    EXAMPLES: Civil Service Commission, Social Security Board, Bureau of Navigation

- Capitalize names of and pronouns relating to the Deity, books of the Bible, holy days, and religious denominations.

    EXAMPLES: God, Allah, Abba in His kingdom, Easter, Genesis, Church of Christ

- Capitalize the names of holidays.

    EXAMPLES: Memorial Day, Labor Day

- Capitalize words used before numbers and numerals, with the exception of common words such as *page, line, paragraph,* and *verse.*

    EXAMPLES: He found the material on page 3, line 3, Part 3 of Chapter X.
    The reservation is Lower 6, Car 27.
    The class will meet in the Fine Arts Building, Room 114.

Do not capitalize the noun when the noun and number are separated in the sentence.

    EXAMPLE: The number of the room where we will meet is 932.

- Capitalize names of the days of the week and months; do not capitalize names of seasons unless they are personified.

    EXAMPLES: I can arrange for a showing of fall styles on Tuesday, August 28.
    Old Lady Winter's bitter smile graced the fields.

§ 6.15.4   Capitalization—Capitalizing titles used in business and professions

The following are rules for capitalizing titles in business and professions.

- Any title that signifies rank, honor, and respect and immediately precedes an individual's name is capitalized.

> EXAMPLES: Kelly asked President Terry G. Sanders to preside.
> Kelly accompanied Dr. Alex Richards.

- Academic degrees are capitalized when they precede or follow an individual name.

> EXAMPLES: Constance R. Collins, Ph.D., was invited to direct the program.
> Marion R. Benson, Master of Arts

- Capitalize titles of high-ranking government officers when the title is used in place of the proper name in referring to a specific person.

> EXAMPLES: Our Senator invited us to visit her in Washington.
> The President will return to Camp David soon.

- Capitalize military and naval titles signifying rank.

> EXAMPLES: Captain Meyers, Lieutenant White, Lieutenant Commander Murphy

§ 6.16   Word division

Whenever possible, avoid dividing a word at the end of a line. The printed document should flow for easy reading, and a divided word may cause the reader to become confused or have to slow down in reading.

§ 6.16.1   Word division—How to divide words

- Divide between syllables only. The addition of the past tense does not necessarily add an extra syllable.

> EXAMPLE: *guessed*

- Put enough of the word to be divided on the first line to suggest what the completed word will be.

- As a rule, divide between a prefix and the letter following it.

  EXAMPLE: *pre-sumed*

- Divide a word with a suffix as follows:

  1. When a root word ends with the double consonant, separate the suffix from the root word.

  EXAMPLE: *express-ing*

  2. When a consonant is doubled before a suffix, the added consonant goes with the suffix.

  EXAMPLE: *stop-ping*

  3. For a word ending in *cian, cion, gion, sion, sive,* or *tion,* divide between the stem of the word and the suffix.

  EXAMPLE: *progres-sion*

- When a word containing three or more syllables is to be divided at a one-letter syllable, divide as follows:

  1. For most words, keep the one-letter syllable on the first line.

  EXAMPLE: *sepa-rate*

  2. For words to be divided at a point where two vowels pronounced separately come together, divide between the vowels.

  EXAMPLE: *gradu-ation*

  3. For a word ending in such terminations as *able, ible,* or *ical,* divide between the stem of the word and the suffix.

  EXAMPLE: *remov-able*

  Note: This rule applies only when the vowel is typed correctly as a syllable by itself and does not apply to such a word as *feasible* (feasi-ble) in which the vowel is a part of the syllable *si.*

- Divide hyphenated words and compounds at the hyphen only.

  EXAMPLE: *self-explanatory*

§ 6.16.2   Word division—When not to divide words

- Do not divide a word of one syllable.
- Do not divide a two-syllable word of four letters.
- Do not separate a single-letter syllable at the beginning or end of a word.

> EXAMPLE: *around, steady*

- Do not separate a two-letter syllable at the end of a word.

> EXAMPLE: *difficulty*

- Avoid separating a two-letter syllable at the beginning of a word.

> EXAMPLE: *defended*

- Do not separate a syllable that does not contain a vowel from the remainder of the word.
- Do not divide contractions.
- Do not divide abbreviations.

§ 6.16.3   Word division—Word divisions to avoid

- Do not divide words at the ends of more than two consecutive lines.
- Do not divide a word at the end of the first line of a personal or business letter if it is possible to avoid it.
- Do not divide the last word on a page.
- Do not divide a five- or six-letter word.
- Do not divide a proper name if it is possible to avoid it, and do not separate titles or initials.

> EXAMPLE: Dr. John C. Crosby

- Do not separate numbers.

> EXAMPLES: 13,000,000
> $2,419.56

- Do not separate dates. If the division cannot be avoided, retain the numeral representing the day of the month with the whole name or a syllable division of the month.

EXAMPLES: March 7, 2005; September 23; January 15, 2006

§ 6.17 Compound words for legal use

There are numerous compound words used by the legal profession. Give careful attention to their proper usage. They offer exact reference with the use of a minimum of words.

aforesaid	Stated before or stated earlier in this document
foregoing	What precedes or has gone before
hereafter	After this point in time
hereby	By this or by this document
hereinabove	Within this document; however, before this point in this document
hereinafter	Within this document; however, after this point in this document
hereof	Of this
hereto	To this
heretofore	Before now or prior to this point
hereunder	Under the conditions in this document; following this point in this document
hereunto	To this
herewith	With this document or enclosed with this document
notwithstanding	Regardless or however
thenceforth	Following that condition or that time
thereafter	After that condition or that time
therefor	For it
therefore	Because
therefrom	From that
thereof	Of that
thereon	On that or on it
thereto	To that
undersigned	One who signed at the end of a document (under the document)
whatsoever	What or whatever
whereas	Considering or when in fact
wherefore	For those reasons or for that reason
wheresoever	A place or where it is
wherewithal	Resources, means, or money
whomsoever	Whomever

whosoever   Whoever

Be cautious with these common legal compound terms:
- Inasmuch as
- Insofar as
- A lot (not one word)
- Cannot (one word)

§ 6.18 Spelling

Here are some rules to avoid spelling mishaps.

- Be sure to complete the root word before adding a suffix beginning with a consonant (ly, less, ful, ment).

EXAMPLES:	EXAMPLES:	EXCEPTIONS:
additional-ly	financial-ly	tru-ly
accurate-ly	grate-ful	argu-ment
agree-ment	immense-ly	acknowledg-ment
accidental-ly	immediate-ly	judg-ment
achieve-ment	incidental-ly	
adjust-ment	install-ment	
advertise-ment	misstate-ment	
allot-ment	occasional-ly	
approximate-ly	sincere-ly	
arrange-ments	undoubted-ly	
develop-ment	force-ful	
final-ly		

- Remember, "*I* before *e* except after *c,* or when sounded like *a*, as in *neighbor* and *weigh*."

EXAMPLES:	EXAMPLES:	EXCEPTIONS:
anxiety	cashier	either
audience	fierce	neither
believe	grief	financier
boundaries	niece	weird
convenience	pier	species
efficiently	pierce	seize
grievous	relieve	leisure
necessities		forfeit
ninetieth	EXCEPT AFTER C:	ancient
siege	ceiling	foreign

EXAMPLES:	EXAMPLES:	EXCEPTIONS:
sieve	conceive	height
achieve	deceit	their
apiece	deceive	
chief	receive	

- A word ending in silent *e* generally drops the *e* before a suffix beginning with a vowel.

EXAMPLES:

admire	admiration	arrive	arriving
arrange	arranging	believe	believing
desire	desirous	reconcile	reconcilable

- Words ending in *ce* or *ge* to which are added a suffix beginning with *a* or *o* (*able* or *ous*) retain the silent *e* in order to preserve the soft sound of the *c* or *g*.

EXAMPLES:

advantage	advantageous	notice	noticeable
change	changeable	peace	peaceable
courage	courageous	service	serviceable

- Of the words that end with a syllable that sounds like *seed,* only *supersede* ends in *sede*. Three words end in *ceed*: *exceed, proceed, succeed*. The rest end in *cede*.

EXAMPLES:

accede	cede	concede
precede	recede	intercede

- In words of one syllable and words accented on the last syllable ending in a single consonant preceded by a single vowel, double the final consonant before adding a suffix beginning with a vowel unless adding the suffix will change the accented syllable.

EXAMPLES:

Suffix begins with a vowel (one syllable)

cut	cutting
plan	planning
stop	stopped
quit	quitting

197

(Accent on last syllable)

admit	admitted	equip	equipped
begin	beginning	commit	committed
remit	remitted	occur	occurred
confer	conferring	compel	compelled

(No accent on last syllable)

prefer	preference	benefit	benefited
refer	reference	marvel	marvelous
happen	happened		

(Suffix begins with a consonant)

glad	gladness
fat	fatness
man	manhood

§ 6.18.1   Spelling—Words frequently misspelled

absorbent
accessible
accidentally
accommodate
accumulate
acknowledge
acknowledgment
announced
apparent
appearance
argument
assistance
athletic
attendance
auxiliary
bankruptcy
believable
benefited
camouflage
canceled
cannot
category
cemetery

circuit
clinically
coliseum
concede
consensus
defendant
definitely
develop
disappointed
disastrous
dissatisfaction
drastically
eligible
embarrass
exaggerate
existence
extension
extraordinary
facetious
familiar
February
forfeit
forty

fulfill
gauge
governor
grammar
grievous
guarantee
harass
hemorrhage
impugn
incidentally
indict
inoculate
innocuous
insistence
intercede
investor
jeopardize
judgment
justifiable
knowledgeable
labeled
laid
liaison
lien
license
likelihood
maintenance
manageable
mathematics
minuscule
miscellaneous
mischievous
ninety-ninth
occasionally
occurred
occurrence
ophthalmology
parallel
permissible
personal
personnel
perseverance

phenomenal
precede
prerogative
principle
privilege
procedure
proceed
protein
prominence
punitive
questionnaire
recommend
referring
relevant
rescind
rhythm
resistance
safety
salable
scissors
sergeant
seize
separate
similar
singular
soluble
superintendent
supersede
surreptitious
threshold
totaled
transferable
traveled
unforeseen
usage
vacuum
various
vicinity
weird
wholly
withhold
wrought

yacht

§ 6.19   Vocabulary improvement

English has about half a million words. It may not be possible to learn them all, but most people can benefit by adding new words to their vocabulary from time to time. Here are strategies that can help:

- Look up the meaning of any unknown word, including its etymology (history).
- Where there is doubt about the spelling of any word, use the dictionary.
- Do not mispronounce words—check the dictionary.
- Learn how to use and pronounce unfamiliar words that might be useful in the law office.
- Use a specialized legal dictionary, such as *Black's Law Dictionary*, to explore legal vocabulary.
- Learn the vocabulary of a variety of hobbies or professions. Plan recreational reading to embrace as many new areas of experience as possible.
- Keep current with the news.
- Make use of one of the fine books available on vocabulary development.
- Consider seeking NALS® certification, which can aid the lawyer's assistant in matching up legal practice with specific necessary vocabulary.

§ 6.20   Spelling—Confusing words

accede	To express approval or give consent as a result of urging
exceed	To be greater than; to go beyond a set limit
	EXAMPLES: He *acceded* to the demands of his public and ran for office.
	His vote total *exceeded* that of his opponent.
adapt	To make, fit, adjust, conform
adopt	To take as one's own; to take by choice into a relationship
	To accept formally and put into effect
	EXAMPLE: The child found it hard to *adapt* to the decision of his parents to *adopt* a second son.
adverse	Harmful, hostile
averse	Opposed to

advise	To give information; to inform or recommend; (always used as a verb)
advice	Recommendation; information given (always used as a noun)
	EXAMPLE: I *advise* you to take your lawyer's *advice*.
affect	To produce an influence upon or alteration in; to act upon (*affect* is very rarely used as a noun meaning the appearance or physical expression of emotion)
effect	noun: Result of a change or influence; result, consequence, outcome
	verb: To cause to come into being
	EXAMPLE: The new office manager will *effect* a change in office procedures that will *affect* all secretaries. Hopefully, the *effect* of the change will be good.
aid	verb: To give help
aide	noun: Assistant
	EXAMPLE: The teacher's *aide* tried to *aid* the child in reading.
all ready	All prepared
already	By this time; prior to some specified or implied time
	EXAMPLE: The packages are *all ready* for mailing; the letters have *already* been mailed.
altogether	Wholly, thoroughly, in all
all together	Collectively
	EXAMPLES: They are *altogether* too frail. Were the school children *all together*?
among	Used when three or more persons or things are involved
between	Used when two persons or things are involved
	EXAMPLE: The cake was divided *among* the four boys, and the pie was divided *between* the two girls.
ante-	A prefix that means *before* when added to the beginning of a word
anti-	A prefix that means *against* when added to the beginning of a word
	EXAMPLES: An *ante*cedent is a word that is referred to by a following word.

An *anti*coagulant is a substance that hinders (works against) the clotting of the blood.

anyone	Any person at all; anybody
any one	Any individual person

EXAMPLE: The winner can be *any one* of the three candidates, but not just *anyone* can win.

anxious	Worry or anxiety
eager	Enthusiastic or impatient
appraise	To set a value on; to evaluate the worth, significance, or status
apprise	To give notice; to tell; to inform

EXAMPLE: Please *apprise* the lawyer of the value of the estate. He is the one who will *appraise* the assets.

approximate	Nearly correct or exact
proximate	Very near, close

EXAMPLE: The *proximate* cause of the accident was that he was traveling *approximately* 120 miles an hour.

beside	At or to the side; by the side of; disjoined from
besides	Over and above; moreover, else, in addition to

EXAMPLE: She sat *beside* the road, but that is *beside* the point. *Besides* that, she was hurt.

biannual	Occurring twice a year
biennial	Occurring every two years
bimonthly	Occurring every two months; also occurring twice a month (*semimonthly* also means "occurring twice a month," and may be used instead of bimonthly to avoid confusion)

EXAMPLES: The *biennial* meetings will be held in 2010 and 2012; however, the board meetings will be held *biannually* in January and July.

The *bimonthly* newsletter will be published in January, March, May, July, September, and November. The meetings will be *bimonthly* (or *semimonthly*) on the first and third Monday.

capital	Chief in importance or influence; related to money; seat of government; a city serving as a seat of government
capitol	A building in which a legislative body meets

	EXAMPLE:	The legislature voted a *capital* appropriation of $750,000 to refurbish the *Capitol* Building.

compliment
: An expression of esteem, respect, affection, or admiration

complement
: Something that fills in, completes, or makes perfect; one of two mutually completing parts; counterpart

	EXAMPLES:	The dark blue tie *complemented* the light blue shirt.
		Everyone likes to receive a sincere *compliment*.

continual
: Successive or one after another

continuous
: Without interruption

courtesy
: Refers to manners

curtesy
: Interest a husband has in the property of his wife

	EXAMPLE:	He had the *courtesy* to give up his *curtesy* in her property.

council
: A committee's board of directors

counsel
: A giver of advice; an attorney

decent
: Fitting, worthy, honorable

descent
: A downward step, as in station or value; a derivation from an ancestor; process of descending from a higher to a lower level

dissent
: Disagree

	EXAMPLE:	There was *dissent* that her *descent* down the stairs on her hands was the *decent* thing to do.

defuse
: To make less harmful; to make less tense

diffuse
: Wordy; badly organized

descendant
: One descended from another (having to do with family)

decedent
: A deceased person

	EXAMPLE:	The *descendant* of the *decedent* was his only grandchild.

device
: A scheme to deceive; a piece of equipment or mechanism designed to serve a special purpose or function

devise
: The act of giving or disposing of real property in a will; property devised by will; to plan to obtain or bring about

	EXAMPLE:	A will is a *device* by which a person can *devise* his real property to his heirs.

discreet	Having or showing good judgment in conduct and speech; capable of preserving silence
discrete	Individually distinct; constituting a separate entity
	EXAMPLES: The assistant should be very *discreet* when discussing clients.
	Magnetic cards and diskettes are *discrete* media.
disburse	To give out, to pay out
disperse	To scatter randomly
	EXAMPLE: Once the raffle prizes were *disbursed*, the winners *dispersed*.
elusive	Baffling; hard to catch
illusive	Misleading; unreal
eminent	Prominent, standing out, distinguished
imminent	Ready to take place; hanging threateningly over one's head
	EXAMPLE: The *eminent* senator believed death to be *imminent*.
envelop	To enfold or enclose completely
envelope	A container, usually for a letter
	EXAMPLES: The fog threatened to *envelop* the airport.
	She forgot to put the letter in the *envelope*.
guarantee	To assure the fulfillment of a condition; to promise performance
guaranty	Something given as security; a pledge to answer for the payment of a debt; an assurance of performance
warranty	A binding legal covenant or assurance of facts
	EXAMPLES: Can you *guarantee* the merchandise? Is the *guaranty* in writing?
	You have my *warranty* on the property.
illicit	Illegal
elicit	To draw forth or bring out
	EXAMPLE: Did the detective *elicit* any information from the man about *illicit* activities?
imply	To involve or indicate by inference, association, or necessary consequence rather than by direct statement; to suggest
infer	To derive as a conclusion from facts or premises

	EXAMPLE: From what you say, I *infer* that you mean to *imply* she is incapable.
insure	To make certain by taking necessary precautions or steps; to obtain or give insurance on (this term almost always involves the payment of money for an insurance policy)
ensure	To make sure, certain, or safe
assure	To make safe from risks; to inform positively
	EXAMPLE: I *assure* you that I have *ensured* your safety by carefully checking your parachute; however, the company has refused to *insure* you when you are jumping.
interstate	Between two or more states
intrastate	Within one state
	EXAMPLE: He runs an *interstate* trucking service in the Pacific Northwest; his brother has an *intrastate* service in Idaho.
liable	Obligated according to law; responsible (do not use *liable* for *likely*)
libel	A written defamation or attack of another person
	EXAMPLE: Newspapers are *liable* if they publish a *libel* of a person.
precedents	Something done or said that may serve as an example or rule to authorize or justify an act of similar nature. In law, those previous court decisions that influence all later cases of a similar kind
precedence	Priority of importance
	EXAMPLE: The case that took *precedence* on the calendar was based on *precedents* established in California.
principle	A rule or code of conduct; a fundamental law, doctrine, or assumption; the laws or facts of nature
principal	A person who has controlling authority; a chief or head, man or woman; one who employs another to act for him or her; a capital sum placed at interest; the corpus of an estate
	EXAMPLE: The school *principal* invested her *principal* at five percent interest because she was devoted to the *principle* of saving money.

proceeding	A form of the verb *proceed* meaning to go forward; move along a course
	A noun meaning events, happenings; a legal action
preceding	A form of the verb *precede* meaning to be, go, or come ahead or in front of; to be earlier than
	EXAMPLE: The criminal *proceeding* will *precede* the civil trial.
pro rata	An adverb or adjective meaning according to a precise calculable formula
prorated	A verb meaning evenly distributed
rebut	To argue in opposition
refute	To prove wrong
specially	In a special manner
especially	Particularly; usually great or significant
	EXAMPLE: The *specially* prepared foods were a delight to the palate, *especially* since the cook had so little experience.
stationary	Fixed
stationery	Writing materials

§ 6.21 Abbreviations

In business writing, abbreviations are appropriate in business forms, catalogs, and routine memos and letters between business offices, where the emphasis is on communicating data in the briefest form. In writing of a more formal nature, use abbreviations sparingly. In formal communications, the following are acceptable:

- The title that precedes a person's name is abbreviated.

    EXAMPLES: Ms., Mrs., Mr., Dr.

- Titles or degrees written after names are abbreviated.

    EXAMPLES: Esq., Jr., B.A., M.D., PLS

- Titles before surnames are never abbreviated.

    EXAMPLES: Governor Tomlinson, Professor Garrett

- Titles before full names can be abbreviated.

    EXAMPLES: Gov. Guy Tomlinson, Prof. Sara Garrett

- Titles of respect or dignity are never abbreviated.

    EXAMPLES: The Honorable Guy Tomlinson, the
    Reverend Doctor Bennett

- Firm names are not abbreviated unless the company prefers the abbreviation and uses it in its communication.
- Names of agencies, organizations, or associations are abbreviated using the first letter of each word in the title. These are generally written with no space or punctuation between letters to form an initialism or acronym.

    EXAMPLES: FBI, IRS

- Technical terms such as chemical symbols or formulas that are used many times in business communications are abbreviated with no punctuation.
- When letters are substituted for names, punctuation is unnecessary.

    EXAMPLES: Mr. A, Exhibit D, Mister X

- Certain words that have been shortened through usage are not followed by punctuation.

    EXAMPLES: *Ad* for advertisement, *lab* for laboratory,
    gym for gymnasium

- Always abbreviate *A.D.* and *B.C.* in dates and use the punctuation. Use *a.m.* and *p.m.* to designate morning and afternoon or evening.
- Use *No.* or *Nos.* before numerals except when they occur at the beginning of a sentence; then spell out *Number.* If the numeral is specifically identified, *No.* or *Nos.* should be omitted, e.g., *Room 314, Check 784.*
- *Fort, Point, Port* as parts of place names should never be abbreviated.
- Directions written out in text should not be abbreviated, but *N, NE, NNE,* for example, can be used in legal descriptions.
- Terms of measurement should not be abbreviated except in technical writing, invoices, etc. This rule applies to weight, length, capacity, area, volume, temperature, and time.
- If possible, the following words should be spelled out in full:

    president   building   street

superintendent	association	boulevard
honorable	department	avenue
reverend		east
professor		west
		south
		north

- Generally, city and state names should be spelled out completely; however, in the inside address the two-letter postal state abbreviation may be used to match the address on the envelope if it is followed by the ZIP code.
- When an abbreviation is followed by a period, the period should be retained even if other punctuation follows the abbreviation. If the abbreviation ends the sentence, however, only one period is necessary. The plurals of abbreviations are generally formed by adding an *s* to the abbreviation before the period, but note these exceptions:
  - *in* for inch or inches
  - *mi* for mile or miles
  - *oz* for ounce or ounces
  - *pp.* for pages
  - *ll.* for lines
- As a rule, contractions are only used in informal writing and in tables where space is limited.
- Abbreviations of academic degrees and religious orders require a period after each element in the abbreviation but no internal space.

§ 6.21.1   Abbreviations—Commonly used abbreviations

A list of commonly used abbreviations follows:

@	at
ab init.	from the beginning (Latin *ab initio*)
A.D.	in the year of the Lord (Latin *Anno domini*)
acct., a/c, A/C	account
addl., add.	additional
ad fin.	to the end (Latin *ad finem*)
Adm.	administration, administrative, Admiral
Admr.	Administrator, Administratrix
agt.	agent
a.m.	before noon
amt.	amount
anon.	anonymous
app.	appendix

approx.	approximate
appt.	appointment
Apt.	Apartment
arr.	arranged
art.	article
ASAP	as soon as possible
Assn.	Association
assoc., asso.	associates
Asst.	Assistant
Attn.	Attention
Atty.	Attorney
Atty. Gen.	Attorney General
Ave.	Avenue
avg.	average
bal.	balance
bbl.	barrel(s)
bf.	boldface
B/L, BL	bill of lading
bldg.	building
Blvd.	Boulevard
bu	bushel(s)
bus.	business
Bus. Mgr.	Business Manager
bx.	box
C.	Celsius (centigrade), hundred
c	copy
cc	carbon copy, or computer copy
cap.	capital, capacity
caps	capital letters
Capt.	Captain
cat.	catalog
C/D, CD	Certificate of Deposit; compact disk
cert.	certificate, certification, certified
cf.	compare (Latin *confer*)
cfm, cfs	cubic feet per minute, per second
chg.	charge, change
ck.	check
cm	centimeter
c/o	in care of, carried over
Co.	Company; County
COD, c.o.d.	cash on delivery
com., comm.	committee, commission

Corp.	Corporation
C.S.T., CST	central standard time
depo	deposition
dept.	department
D.S.T., DST	Daylight Savings Time
E.	East
ea.	each
e.g.	for example (Latin *exempli gratia*)
enc.	enclosure
EOM, e.o.m.	end of month
Esq.	Esquire
et al.	and others (Latin *et alia, et alii*)
E.S.T., EST	eastern standard time
etc.	and so forth (Latin *et cetera*)
Ex.	Exhibit
F., Fahr.	Fahrenheit
fax	facsimile
f.b.o., FBO	for the benefit of
fig.	figure
f.o.b., FOB	free on board
ft	foot, feet
fwd.	forward
FY	fiscal year
FYI	for your information
g	gram(s)
GAAP	Generally Accepted Accounting Principle
gal	gallon(s)
govt.	government
gr. wt.	gross weight
guar., gtd.	guarantee, guaranteed
HQ	headquarters
hp, HP	horsepower
hr.	hour(s)
ht.	height, heat
ibid.	in the same place (Latin *ibidum*)
id.	the same (Latin *idem*)
i.e.	that is (Latin *id est*)
Ill., illus.	illustration, illustrated
in	inch(es)
Inc.	Incorporated
inv.	invoice
ital.	italics

J.D.	Doctor of Jurisprudence (Latin *juris doctor*)
K	thousand, karat, contract
kc	kilocycle
kg	kilogram(s)
km	kilometer
kw	kilowatt
L	liter(s)
l., ll.	line, lines
lb	pound(s)
L/C	Letter of Credit
l.c., lc.	lowercase
liq.	liquid
LL.B.	Bachelor of Laws (Latin *legum baccalaureus*)
L.L.C., LLC	Limited Liability Company
LL.D.	Doctor of Laws (Latin *legum doctor*)
loc. cit.	in the place cited (Latin *loco citato*)
L.S.	place of the seal (Latin *locus sigilli*)
ltr.	letter
M	1,000
m	meter(s)
mdse.	merchandise
memo	memorandum
Messrs.	plural of Mr. (F. Messieurs)
mfg.	manufacturing
mi.	mile(s)
min.	minute(s)
misc.	miscellaneous
Mlle.	Mademoiselle
mo., mos.	month, months
M.S.T., MST	mountain standard time
Mt.	mount, mountain
mtg.	mortgage, meeting
n/30	net in 30 days
N.	North
No., Nos.	number(s) (use before figures only)
obs.	obsolete
op. cit.	in the work cited (Latin *opere citato*)
oz	ounce(s)
p., pp.	page, pages
P.C.	Professional Corporation
pd.	paid
PBX	Private Branch Exchange (telephone systems)

pkg.	package
p.m.	after noon (Latin *post meridiem*)
prox.	of the next month (Latin *proximo*)
P.S.T., PST	pacific standard time
qt	quart(s)
recd.	received
retd.	returned
rev.	revised, revision
R.F.D.	Rural Free Delivery
rm.	ream, room
R.N.	Registered Nurse
R.S.V.P.	please reply (French *respondez s'il vous plait*)
Rte., Rt.	Route
Ry.	railway
S.	South
SASE	self-addressed, stamped envelope
sec.	section
seq.	the following (Latin *sequens*)
sic	so written, thus (Latin)
sq ft	square foot (feet)
Sr.	Senior
SS.	To-wit (Latin *scilicet*)
St.	Street, Saint, Strait, Statute(s)
Ste.	Sainte (feminine for St.), Suite
Supt.	Superintendent
Twp.	township (pl. Tps., Twps.)
TWX	teletypewriter exchange
u.c.	upper case
Univ.	University
viz.	namely (Latin *videlicet*)
vol	volume(s)
v.	versus
whsle.	wholesale
wk., wks.	work, week, weeks
wpm	words per minute
wt.	weight
yd	yard(s)
yr, yrs	year, years

§ 6.21.2   Abbreviations—State names

STATE ABBREVIATIONS

Alabama	Ala.	AL	Montana	Mont.	MT
Alaska	Alaska	AK	Nebraska	Nebr.	NE
Arizona	Ariz.	AZ	Nevada	Nev.	NV
Arkansas	Ark.	AR	New Hampshire	N.H.	NH
California	Calif.	CA	New Jersey	N.J.	NJ
Canal Zone	C.Z.	CZ	New Mexico	N. Mex.	NM
Colorado	Colo.	CO	New York	N.Y.	NY
Connecticut	Conn.	CT	North Carolina	N.C.	NC
Delaware	Del.	DE	North Dakota	N. Dak.	ND
District of Co-lumbia	D.C.	DC	Ohio	Ohio	OH
			Oklahoma	Okla.	OK
Florida	Fla.	FL	Oregon	Oreg.	OR
Georgia	Ga.	GA	Pennsylvania	Pa.	PA
Guam	Guam	GU	Puerto Rico	P.R.	PR
Hawaii	Hawaii	HI	Rhode Island	R.I.	RI
Idaho	Idaho	ID	South Carolina	S.C.	SC
Illinois	Ill.	IL	South Dakota	S. Dak.	SD
Indiana	Ind.	IN	Tennessee	Tenn.	TN
Iowa	Iowa	IA	Texas	Tex.	TX
Kansas	Kans.	KS	Utah	Utah	UT
Kentucky	Ky.	KY	Vermont	Vt.	VT
Louisiana	La.	LA	Virgin Islands	V.I.	VI
Maine	Maine	ME	Virginia	Va.	VA
Maryland	Md.	MD	Washington	Wash.	WA
Massachusetts	Mass.	MA	West Virginia	W. Va.	WV
Michigan	Mich.	MI	Wisconsin	Wis.	WI
Minnesota	Minn.	MN	Wyoming	Wyo.	WY
Mississippi	Miss.	MS			
Missouri	Mo.	MO			

*The two-letter postal abbreviations are used with ZIP codes; the other abbreviations are generally used only in citations.

§ 6.22 Number usage

- Spell out a number beginning a sentence. If the number is large, it is best to rearrange the sentence.
- Spell out approximate numbers given in even units.

> EXAMPLE: There were approximately *five hundred* people at the wedding.

- Numbers ten and below are spelled out; numbers above ten are written in figures.
- When two numbers follow each other in a sentence, use numbers for the larger one and spell out the smaller number. If both numbers contain three or more numerals, use figures for both.

EXAMPLES: He ordered *12 two-piece* suits from his client in New York City.
They sent us *175 500-page* manuals.

- Use figures for dimensions, measurements, distances, weights, and capacities.

EXAMPLES: 8 inches × 11 inches   4 ft. 3 in or 4'3"
2 lbs 15 oz   6 mi.

- If a weight or capacity is written before a noun, the quantity in numeral form is hyphenated to the unit spelled out in singular form. If it follows the word, the quantity and unit are not hyphenated, and the unit is plural.

EXAMPLE: a *15-gallon* jug
a jug holding *15 gallons*

- Use figures for page numbers and divisions of books.
- Use figures for temperatures, election returns, and chemical terminology.
- When entering mixed numbers, do not insert a space or a hyphen to separate the whole number from the fraction. If the fractional unit has to be composed (typed using a diagonal line), add a space between the whole number and the fraction to avoid misreading.

EXAMPLES: $9\frac{2}{3}$ or 9 2/3.

- Fractions used without whole numbers are spelled out except when used in a series.

EXAMPLES: Two-thirds of a mile. Measurements of $\frac{1}{48}$, $\frac{1}{24}$, and $\frac{1}{12}$.

- Fractions one fourth and one half should be written the same as other fractions when mixed:

EXAMPLES: $\frac{1}{4}$, $\frac{1}{2}$, $\frac{2}{3}$, $\frac{3}{4}$ or *1/4, 1/2, 2/3, 3/4.*

- Columns of whole numbers are aligned on the right; decimals are aligned on the decimal point; roman numerals and ordinal numbers are aligned on the right; dates and words are aligned on the left; and mixed items are aligned on the left or centered.
- Use figures before the word *percent* or the percent symbol. The

symbol should be used only in tables or in technical writing. Spell out *percent* in all formal writing.

> EXAMPLE: He gave me a *20 percent* discount on the damaged goods.

- Spell out numbers referring to decades and centuries.

> EXAMPLE: twentieth century

- Use figures for a series of numbers in a sentence when some of the numbers are above ten.

> EXAMPLE: I sent 20 letters, 2 postcards, and 6 packages.

§ 6.22.1 Number usage—Dates

- When writing dates, use figures without ordinal endings (*st, nd, rd, d,* or *th*) unless the day precedes the month.

> EXAMPLE: We will send the money on January 25, 2010.

- When the name of the month is not given, spell out the date.

> EXAMPLE: He will be leaving for Europe on the *tenth*.

- Do not indicate the month in figures except in tables or charts.

> EXAMPLES: 8/11/10
> August 11, 2010

- Use ordinal numbers when the day precedes the month.

> EXAMPLE: the 8th of March.

- In formal invitations, spell out the dates.

> EXAMPLE: On the twelfth day of May, two thousand and ten.

§ 6.22.2 Number usage—Age

- When the age is definite and given as a statistic or for quick reference, use figures; if the age is indefinite or appears in formal writing, use words.

> EXAMPLES: He is dating a woman who is about thirty years old.
> Judge John J. Bell, 56, is an authority on family law.
> She will be 39 on her next birthday.

- When writing the age in years, months, and days, use figures and no commas. The whole phrase is considered one unit.

> EXAMPLE: His age is 87 years 9 months and 5 days.

§ 6.22.3   Number usage—Time

In stating time, the following rules apply:
- Use figures preceding *a.m.* and *p.m.*

> EXAMPLES: 10 a.m.
> 9 p.m.

- Use words or figures preceding o'clock.

> EXAMPLE: *ten o'clock* or *3 o'clock*

Words are more commonly used.
- To express noon or midnight, do not use *a.m.* or *p.m.* Instead use *12 noon* or *12 midnight* when used with other times in the same sentence, or *noon* or *midnight* when used alone.
- Do not use *morning* or *evening* and *a.m.* or *p.m.* in the same phrase.

> EXAMPLES:
> *Incorrect:*   I will see you this morning at 10:30 a.m.
> *Correct:*   I will see you this morning at 10:30.
> *Correct:*   I will see you at 10:30 a.m.

- Do not use *a.m.* or *p.m.* with *o'clock.*
- When using an even hour, it is not necessary to add the colon and two zeros unless the time appears in a table. Use *3 a.m.* or *8 p.m.* rather than *3:00 a.m.* or *8:00 p.m.*

§ 6.22.4   Number usage—Money

- In legal documents amounts of money are often written in words and figures. Be careful that the figures in the parentheses are an exact summary of the words.

  EXAMPLES:
  Incorrect: Twenty-five Dollars ($25.00). (Incorrect because the No/100 was not included before the parentheses.)
  Correct: Twenty-five Dollars ($25)
  Incorrect: Twenty-five and No/100 ($25.00) Dollars. (Incorrect because-dollars must come before the parentheses.)
  Correct: Twenty-five and No/100 Dollars ($25.00).

- In correspondence, amounts of money are written in figures, when the amounts are indefinite, e.g., a *few million dollars*.

  EXAMPLES: The estimated fee for processing your claim is $585.
  The decimal and following zeros are unnecessary for even dollar amounts, e.g., $25, not $25.00.

- Separate hundreds from thousands with a comma. It is now considered acceptable to omit the comma for amounts under 10,000 in many places. Retain the comma between hundreds and thousands in formal uses or with an audience likely to be conservative.

  EXAMPLE: His annual membership fee was reported to be $1,800.

- Spell out an amount of money if it occurs at the beginning of a sentence.

  EXAMPLE: Sixty cents is really a trifling amount.

§ 6.22.5 Number usage—Addresses

- Spell out numbered street names from one through ten; use figures for numbered streets over ten.

  EXAMPLE: 15550 Eighth Street

- Use a hyphen between a house or building number and a numbered street to prevent misreading.

EXAMPLE: 234-44th Street

- Do not use # or No. in addresses. When an apartment number is needed, use the abbreviation *Apt.* after the street address.

EXAMPLE: 600 Lake Shore Drive, Apt. 280 or
1400-B College Drive

- Never use commas in address numbers.

§ 6.22.6   Number usage—Roman numerals

The rules for reading roman numerals are as follows:
- A repeated letter multiplies the value.

EXAMPLES: II = 2   XX = 20

- A letter occurring *after* one of higher value is added to the preceding one.

EXAMPLES: VI = 5 + 1 = 6   LX = 50 + 10 = 60

- A letter occurring *before* one of higher value is subtracted from the higher letter.

EXAMPLES: IV = 5 – 1 = 4   XL = 50 – 10 = 40

A symbol may be used only three consecutive times. Then the symbol changes to a different symbol. Example: I, II, III, IV, V, VI, VII, VIII, IX. The numbers and corresponding roman numerals are as follows:

1	I	11	XI
2	II	12	XII
3	III	13	XIII
4	IV	14	XIV
5	V	15	XV
6	VI	16	XVI
7	VII	17	XVII
8	VIII	18	XVIII
9	IX	19	XIX
10	X	20	XX

30	XXX	300	CCC
40	XL or XXXX	400	CD or CCCC
50	L	500	D
60	LX	600	DC
70	LXX	700	DCC
80	LXXX or XXC	800	DCCC
90	XC or LXXXX	900	CM or DCCCC
100	C	1000	M
150	CL	1500	MD
200	CC	2000	MM

§ 6.23   The creative aspects of written communications

Writing is a process. It is likely to be easier to do if it is done in the following stages:

Stage I.   Thinking and planning
Stage II.   Researching, organizing, and writing
Stage III.   Revising
Stage IV.   Proofreading

§ 6.23.1   The creative aspects of written communications— Stage I—Thinking and planning

Always be concerned with public relations in organizing and clarifying ideas for written communications. Some people interpret this first process as worrying rather than thinking, but it is a vital step. Analyze the audience and the purpose for writing. Determine the level of language to use—technical, formal, or informal. Think about how the audience will react to the message—neutrally, positively, or negatively. Use brainstorming, listing, mapping, and diagramming strategies to generate ideas. Once the thinking phase is completed and ideas are collected, start planning.

§ 6.23.2   The creative aspects of written communications— Stage II—Researching, organizing, and writing

Before beginning to write, collect data informally or formally to explain and support the ideas generated. Talk to those in the know, look in files, conduct a simple survey or conduct formal research using books, magazine, official reports, interviews, and the Internet.

Organizing consists mainly of examining all ideas, eliminating the irrelevant ones, and arranging the others in a clear, logical order. Ideas can be grouped by time sequence, by importance, by logical sequence, or by other methods. Whether to write an informal outline or merely jot down ideas on a scrap of paper is up to the writer.

The writing process is self-explanatory. Concentrate on formulating sentences instead of being concerned with thinking of ideas and trying to organize them. Write quickly to get thoughts down in the first draft. The first two stages are the preparatory work and will take about as much time as the next stage, which is revising.

§ 6.23.3   The creative aspects of written communications— Stage III—Revising

Few are so talented that they can express themselves clearly and concisely in a first draft. Expert writers know that they must and will revise. Examine the writing objectively so it can be revised effectively. Be eager to find fault and look for ways to increase the writing's clarity, conciseness, coherence, and for ways to improve the content and readability. Improve the structure of sentences, rearrange the text, add headings, use bold, underlining, or italics for emphasis, and find concise, correct words to use. To help achieve paragraph coherence, use transitional expressions for time association (before, after, first, second, next, until), contrast (although, however, but, instead), illustration (for example, in this way), cause and effect (consequently, therefore), and to include additional ideas (furthermore, in addition, moreover). After revising the document, proofread.

§ 6.23.4   The creative aspects of written communications— Stage IV—Proofreading

The final task, although perhaps not as taxing as others, is just as vital. If words are missing or repeated, letters are transposed, sentences are incoherent, or words misspelled, a reader may be perturbed enough to ignore or resist the ideas or information. Carelessness in writing antagonizes readers and raises questions in their minds about the writer's competence. Once finished with the proofreading, it is sometimes helpful to read the message or writing aloud—often mistakes are overlooked with the eyes and are found with the voice. Proofreading will be discussed in depth later in this chapter. (See § 6.25.2 Proofreading.)

§ 6.24   The paragraph

Sentences grouped together with a controlling topic or idea make a paragraph. Each idea can be its own paragraph or ideas may be grouped in a logical combination. Following are some strategies for writing clear and coherent paragraphs.

1. Start with the topic used in the plan. Put it into sentence form. Develop the topic with a few sentences. Then, move on to the next topic and develop it the same way as in the first.
2. Keep paragraphs reasonably short. Short paragraphs make the reader's job easier. Try to make the first and last paragraphs in letters and memos short—not more than three or four lines.

Elsewhere, if a paragraph gets to be more than eight or nine lines (100 words), consider breaking it up. In informal writing, ignore the rule that a paragraph has to be more than one sentence.

3. Paragraphs should be developed adequately to clarify and back up points. Use explanations, facts, illustrations, and examples.

4. Make sure each paragraph is unified and coherent. Ideas in the same paragraph should be closely related. The topic sentence or a summary sentence helps to keep out the irrelevant.

5. Review the paragraph in context with the surrounding paragraphs. Use transitional words to move from one paragraph to the next. Use words such as *next, moreover, besides, nevertheless, on the other hand, first, second, third.* If ideas are logical, these words will not sound phony.

6. Examine the way the paragraphs are developed and the message is given to the reader—make sure the writing makes sense.

§ 6.24.1 The paragraph—Correctness

Some people have a distorted concept of the correctness principle. They think it just means proper grammar, punctuation, and spelling. The fact is that one can be correct grammatically and mechanically and fail to use the correct level of language. There are three levels of language: formal, informal, and substandard.

The first two—formal and informal language—are both correct, but they are quite different from one another, have different uses, and should not be interchanged.

The formal level of language is used for writing a scholarly dissertation, a legal document, or other material for which formality is expected. The expressions used are often long, unconversational, and impersonal.

In contrast, the informal level refers to the language of business— the language of letters, reports, and other business communications. Such language is alive and mutable. Instead of formal words one should use short, well known, conversational words:

Formal	Informal
domicile	home
deem	think (believe)
edifice	building
procure	get
remunerate	pay
Will attain the age of eighteen years	Will be 18 years old

§ 6.24.2 The paragraph—Conciseness

Many business executives believe conciseness is the most important writing skill because a wordy message requires more time (and money) to type and to read. Conciseness is saying what one has to say in the fewest possible words without sacrificing completeness and courtesy.

To achieve conciseness:

- Omit trite expressions
- Avoid unnecessary repetition and word expressions
- Include only relevant facts

Not this	But this
Enclosed herewith please find	Enclosed is; is enclosed
At this time	Now
Consensus of opinion	Consensus
Pursuant to your inquiry	As you requested
Please do not hesitate to write	Please write
The undersigned (the writer)	I, me, or we
Please be advised that	(four wasted words unless advice is truly to follow)
The above subject matter	Unnecessary. The subject line is enough.
According to our records	Implies that the other person is wrong. Reword.
Acknowledge receipt of	The answer itself is an acknowledgment.
Advise	Tell or inform
As per	According to
At an early date	Vague. Use a definite time period: within the next 10 days, for example.
At the present time	Unnecessary. A verb tense says the same thing.
At your earliest convenience	This could be never. State a date or definite time period.
By return mail	Meaningless. Say: right away or immediately
Under date of January 15	January 15
Do not hesitate to call	Please call
Due to the fact that	Because
For your information	Obviously the purpose of the communication; omit the phrase
Hoping to hear from you soon, I remain	Old-fashioned; poor grammar; do not use.

Not this	But this
I have your letter	Naturally, or you would not be answering. Do not use.
a check in the amount of $50	A check for $50
Kindly	Say: please
Our Mr. Jones	You do not own him. Omit "our."
Recent date	Use the specific date.
We take pleasure	We are glad.
We take the liberty	Do not use.
We take this opportunity	Obviously you are.
Thank you in advance	Presumptuous. We will appreciate.
Under separate cover	We are sending

Be sure to begin the letter directly with the subject. Avoid repeating what the reader has already said in previous correspondence.

Conciseness contributes to emphasis. By eliminating unnecessary words, one helps make important ideas stand out.

§ 6.24.3 The paragraph—Clarity

Clarity involves most of the other principles of business writing—especially correctness, conciseness, completeness, consideration, and concreteness. Clarity means getting across the message so the reader will not misunderstand what one is trying to convey.

Choose short, familiar, conversational words. Avoid professional jargon. The legal assistant's professional vocabulary contains many legal terms. Colleagues easily understand these terms, so it is all right to use them when talking or writing to coworkers. Avoid professional jargon when talking or writing to someone—such as a client—who is not acquainted with such words.

If it is necessary to use technical words the reader may not understand, define them briefly and clearly.

EXAMPLES:

Technical jargon	Expressions familiar to the layperson
Easement for ingress and egress	Agreement allowing passage in and out
Escrow account	Reserve account for taxes and insurance
Conveying title	Signing and recording a deed

In summary, make all writing clear by using words familiar to the reader.

§ 6.25　Writing letters, memos, and messages

Most writing done by the legal assistant will be in the form of letters, memos, facsimiles, and email messages. These messages usually fall into the categories of requesting information, responding to a request for information, making a claim (complaint), or responding to a claim (complaint).

Like all writing, the first step for letter, memo and message writing should begin with thinking and planning. Following are some specific questions to be asked and answered before beginning to write:

- What is the purpose of the letter, memo, or message?
- Will the reader react neutrally, positively, or negatively? Is a direct or indirect method of getting to the main point best?
- To whom is the writing addressed? Will the style be formal, informal, or technical?
- How much will the writing tell? Include enough information so the reader does not need to write or call for more information.
- What is the goal of this letter? When should it be accomplished?

In stage two of the writing process, the legal assistant researches, organizes and writes the letter, memo, or message. The answers to the questions above are the basis of a good outline. Also, it is helpful when replying to correspondence to refer to the letter while composing the response. Following are some points to keep in mind when organizing and writing the first quick draft of the letter, memo, or message:

- Use the direct method and start the first paragraph by stating the purpose of the letter in one or two sentences. Do not keep the reader guessing, or the letter may not be read. However, if conveying a message to which the reader may react to negatively, the first paragraph may need to state a goodwill message, and the principal message may need to be delivered indirectly.
- If answering a letter, refer to the date; the reader can then pull that letter.
- Write from the reader's point of view. Put the reader into it, not the writer or the writer's company. Visualize the reader's way of life. Write conversationally.
- Use the correct tone. Be positive—the reader will be more receptive. Be polite—it is an art to be agreeable when disagreeing or raising a concern. Be natural—try to write conversationally. The acid test is to read the letter out loud. The letter should sound as if it were written by a human being. Do not be cute or flippant. Avoid slang and colloquialisms.
- Distinguish opinions from facts. One may have the best opinion in the world, but opinions are not facts. The legal assistant owes it to the reader to stay within the facts and to keep opinions separate, and in legal writing, giving an opinion may create the risk of committing unauthorized practice of the law.

- Decide on a conclusion and make sure that no new ideas are raised in the last paragraph. Include exactly what should be done and set a deadline for completion.
- Use a simple close like *Sincerely* or *Very truly yours.*

Now the letter is ready for revision and putting on the finishing touches followed by thorough proofreading. The legal assistant should make the writing perfect or the reader may think the writer does not know better or does not care.

§ 6.25.1 Writing letters, memos, and messages—First aid for writing problems

A major fault in letter writing is a tendency to smother the reader with words. Repeating words and phrases is not good word economy.

There was a time when the language of letters was in a far different style from the spoken language. Modern writers make every attempt to write as they talk. When editing, weed out every trite expression. Be careful not to ramble.

Always accentuate the positive in letters. Every piece of correspondence can make friends or alienate clients.

Use the right words and spell them correctly. Master the spelling errors most commonly made in writing. Poor spellers should doubt everything and use the dictionary.

Along with spelling comes vocabulary improvement. Do not just stumble over new words; learn their meanings and use the words.

§ 6.25.2 Writing letters, memos, and messages—Proofreading

Poor proofreading results from failure to realize its importance, from inadequate time, and from improper effort.

To proofread well, focus on the words. Slow down reading speed, stare hard at the page, and search for trouble rather than a way to finish quickly.

If interruptions occur during proofreading, place a check in the margin where the interruption occurred. When resuming proofreading, reread the two or three sentences preceding the checkmark to pick up the flow of the words.

When proofreading numbers, difficult copy, or property descriptions, check the original copy carefully. Check dates with a calendar to be sure they are correct.

Carefully proofread routine letters, such as form letters. Make sure that no information for a previous recipient remains in the new version of the letter and that all blanks are filled in.

Following are several troublespots in proofreading:

- Headings, subheadings, and inside addresses often contain errors. The proofreader assumes they are correct and spends time on the body of the material. Headings in all capital letters or underlined are often skipped.

- Errors in proofreading often occur at the beginnings and ends of lines. There is a tendency to read more quickly at the end of a line, which may carry over to the beginning of the next line.

- Missed proofreading errors occur often at the bottom of the page. If things have gone well that far, the proofreader has a tendency to rush to finish and skips over errors.

- When proofreading, read for the sense of the sentence. The text should follow logically. If the proofreader is reading only for spelling or typographical errors, insertion or deletion errors may be missed.

- Another proofreading problem arises in long words. Readers have mental pictures of words, and the brain tends to recognize the words without looking at the spelling.

- Transposed letters are easy to skip over. Sometimes the transposed word creates another word that is correct, and it is easy to pass over it. "From" can be transposed to "form." The best option is to proofread slowly or do it twice.

- Errors often go undetected in footnotes.

- Always verify the spelling of proper names. An error may go undetected unless the proofreader checks the name against the source.

- In outlines and numbered paragraphs, check the continuity of the letters and numbers. It is not unusual to see a list of numbers such as, 1, 2, 3, 4, 4, 5. Check numbers both horizontally and vertically to find all errors.

- Number combinations cannot be proofread without checking them with the original source. Any number can look correct when in reality the numbers may be transposed.

- One of the most common errors in proofreading occurs with the repeated word or letter. It occurs in the middle of a line, as "and and." It occurs at the end of one line and the beginning of the next. It can occur in the middle of words, such as "bookkeeper."

- Check divided words carefully. It is easy to miss a mistake when half of the word is on one line and the other half at the beginning of the next line. Make sure the second half is there. Words can be divided incorrectly, or letters may be left out when they are divided.

Some professional proofreaders read each line backwards. Some enlarge the page so errors are more noticeable. Some proofreaders read the text in multiple passes, one pass each for mechanical errors, spelling problems, sentence structure, and the successful communication of ideas. Regardless of the technique, proofreading requires painstaking effort.

§ 6.25.3   Writing letters, memos, and messages—Mailability

The standard for preparation of all written communications is mailability. Mailability means that the letter or document is suitable to be sent through the mail. It is in a form that represents the high standards of the office. To judge mailability, use the following checklist:

- It is not always necessary to follow the dictator's words verbatim, but it is essential that the exact meaning be conveyed.
- Be sure to have the correct name, title, and address of the addressee. A reader is quick to notice a mistake here.
- Is the layout of the letter attractive, or is it too high or low on the page? Are the margins even? Are the paragraphs too long?
- Check the spelling. A spellcheck program will not highlight a correctly spelled word used incorrectly.

The letter is NOT able to be mailed if it has misspelled words or faulty punctuation.

§ 6.26   The letter bank

Lawyers, inevitably, are very busy. If the legal assistant can handle routine correspondence effectively, the lawyer will be available for other duties.

Once the lawyer's assistant has the attorney's approval to handle routine correspondence, the assistant will look for ways to streamline letter writing. A **letter bank**, which is a simple collection of form letters, memos, messages, and other documents used as templates, is one way to do so.

Break up the letter bank into categories such as appointments, collections, statements, lawyer's personal correspondence, or divisions of the areas of law in which the lawyer practices. As letters enter and leave the office, select the most useful and make a copy for the appropriate category of the letter bank. As the file grows, the lawyer's assistant's value may increase to the lawyer by taking on more of the letter writing tasks.

If certain form letters are used very frequently, put them through the tests of good writing. Polish them. Once the lawyer's assistant has created good form letters, letter writing will be easier and the results better.

§ 6.27   Parts of a business letter

Letters are formatted using open or mixed punctuation, and law firms choose from several standard business styles.

There are nine parts to a standard business letter:

1. Letterhead or return address
2. Date

3. Inside address
4. Salutation
5. Body
6. Complimentary closing
7. Signature line
8. Official title
9. Reference initials

A letter may also contain postal and addressee notations, an attention line, a subject line (placed above or below the salutation), typed firm or organization name, enclosure notation, copy notation, and postscript.

§ 6.27.1 Parts of a business letter—Punctuation in letters

Two common forms of punctuation used in letters are *open* punctuation and *mixed* (or *standard*) punctuation.

§ 6.27.2 Parts of a business letter—Open punctuation

In **open punctuation**, no punctuation is used following the salutation or the complimentary closing.

§ 6.27.3 Parts of a business letter—Mixed or standard punctuation

In **mixed punctuation**, a colon follows the salutation and a comma follows the complimentary closing. In informal correspondence, commas are used in place of the colon after the salutation.

§ 6.28 Letter styles

There are three standard letter styles in common business use. The first two styles are called Modified Block with Blocked Paragraphs and Modified Block With Indented Paragraphs. These are the two styles most often used in law offices. The third, Block Style, is quick and simple.

Each letter part is illustrated on the letter shown in Illustration 6-6. Three common styles of business letters follow in Illustrations 6-7, 6-8, and 6-9. It is important to remember that the letter style should match letters generated by the law firm exactly.

Illustration 6-6

COLVIN, MASON & NORMAN①

Kay Colvin
Jerry Mason
Scott Norman

Attorneys at Law
3005 East Skelly Avenue
Tulsa, Oklahoma 74105

Telephone (918) 749-6423
Facsimile (918) 749-6422

[Date]②

Office Supply Company③
Attention: Mr. S.E. Tedesco
3399 Notation Blvd.
Tulsa, OK 74105

RE: Purchase Order No. 8843

Dear Mr. Tedesco:④

Thank you for rushing to us our order for two secretarial desks and two posture chairs. They arrived yesterday in time for the opening of our new office.
⑤
There has been a mistake, however, in the order. We requested two posture chairs, Catalog A67D, with dark blue upholstery. The ones we received are listed as Catalog A68D; they have light blue upholstery.

These chairs will not be suitable as they do not match the color scheme of our offices. Do you have the chairs we ordered in stock? If so, would you please ship them to us immediately. We are enclosing a copy of our order form.

We appreciate your assistant in this matter. By copy of this letter, we are notifying your local sales representative of the problem.

Sincerely,⑥

COLVIN, MASON & NORMAN
⑦

P. M. Martell
Office Manager⑧

PMM:GD⑨
Enclosure

c: Sarah Wilkins

The chairs we received cost $12 more than the ones we ordered. We would appreciate your revising the billing.

§ 6.28.1   Letter styles—Modified block with blocked paragraphs

The date line, the complimentary close, and the signer's identification all begin at the center line. The remainder of the letter begins at the left margin. (See Illustration 6-7.) Some firms prefer the date to be centered under the firm name, aligned with the return address, or at the right margin. The subject line may be centered for emphasis.

Illustration 6-7

MODIFIED BLOCK WITH
BLOCK PARAGRAPHS

COLVIN, MASON & NORMAN

Kay Colvin	Attorneys at Law	Telephone
Jerry Mason	3005 East Skelly Avenue	Area Code 918
Scott Norman	Tulsa, OK 74105	749-6423

October 9, *[Year]*

Mrs. Jon Wilkinson
222 Mason Avenue
Rigby, ID 83221

Dear Mrs. Wilkinson:

RE: Modified Block With Blocked Paragraphs Letter Style

This letter is written in the modified block with blocked paragraph style. The first line of each paragraph begins at the left margin. Mixed punctuation is used. Note that a colon follows the salutation, and a comma follows the complimentary close.

The date and complimentary closing, as well as the writer's name and identification, begin at the horizontal center of the page.

The subject line may be typed even with the left margin, indented five spaces, or centered.

Sincerely,
COLVIN, MASON & NORMAN

Trema Kuchenbecker
Office Manager

mm
c   Kristen Saunderson

§ 6.28.2 Letter styles—Modified block with indented paragraphs

Modified Block with Indented Paragraphs is the same as Modified Block with Blocked Paragraphs except the first line of each paragraph is indented five spaces. (See Illustration 6-8.)

Illustration 6-8

MODIFIED BLOCK WITH
INDENTED PARAGRAPHS

COLVIN, MASON & NORMAN

Kay Colvin	Attorneys at Law	Telephone
Jerry Mason	3005 East Skelly Avenue	Area Code 918
Scott Norman	Tulsa, OK 74105	749-6423

June 26, *[Year]*

Mr. Joe Kelly, President
Ace Electronics
445 Tudor Square
Boise, ID 83702

Dear Mr. Kelly:

This is a modified block style letter with indented paragraphs. It is the same format as the modified block letter with blocked paragraphs except the paragraphs are indented five spaces. The date and closing information begin at the horizontal center.

If the letter contains an enclosure, the enclosure notation is placed one space below the reference initials. The copy notation should be placed one space below the enclosure notation.

Postscripts are not common in business letters, but when they do occur, they are used for after thoughts and placed at the end of the letter following the copy notation. The letters P.S. may be omitted.

Sincerely,
COLVIN, MASON & NORMAN

Lila Smith
Secretary to Jerry Mason

mm
Enclosure
c/enc Loren Siddell

§ 6.28.3　Letter styles—Block

Block style letter formatting is used in many offices because it is the easiest to format, and letters can be typed efficiently. Because of its clarity, Block has become quite popular. Each line begins at the left margin, including the date and signature lines. (See Illustration 6-9.)

Illustration 6-9

BLOCK

A.G. LAMBERT
Attorney at Law　　　　　　　　　　　　　Telephone
741 Main Street　　　　　　　　　　　(918) 749-5826
Tulsa, OK 74105

July 6, *[Year]*

Mr. Lee James
900 Spring Place
Rexburg, ID 83440

Dear Mr. James

RE: Block Style Letter

In this type of letter, all lines begin at the left margin. The letter can use either open or mixed punctuation. This letter uses open punctuation; there is no mark of punctuation after the salutation and complimentary close.
This form of letter saves typing time because no tab stops or indentations are required for paragraphs, datelines, or closings.
Sincerely

Sally Johnson
Office Manager

mm

§ 6.29　Letters of two or more pages

In preparing a multipage letter, leave at least two lines of a paragraph at the foot of the page and carry at least two lines to the next page. A single line at the bottom of a page is called an ***orphan***; a single line at the top of a page is called a ***widow***.

Use plain paper of the same color and quality as the letterhead for the second and subsequent pages of a letter. Some law firms have the firm name engraved on the continuation pages. Use the same margins and letter style used on the first page.

The second page should contain a heading giving the name of the addressee, the page number, and the date. This heading should start approximately six line spaces from the top. At least two lines should be left between the heading and the first line of the resumed letter.

There are generally two methods for heading continuation pages (although the firm's style should always be followed):

- Each line of information begins at the left margin.
- The addressee's name is at the left margin, the page number is centered, and the date ends at the right margin.

The page number can either precede or follow the date. The numeral is preferred to the word for the page number because it allows the use of automated page numbering and headers in letters longer than two pages, but some firms feel that spelling out the page number looks more refined.

Illustration 6-10

BLOCK STYLE OF SECOND-PAGE HEADING

William E. Kerr, Ph.D. Page 2 April 14, *[Year]* food is delicious, the fireplace is bright and warm in the evenings.

HORIZONTAL STYLE OF SECOND-PAGE HEADING

William E. Kerr, Ph.D.	2	April 14, *[Year]*

food is delicious, the fireplace is bright and warm in the evenings, and the fishing stories exchanged by the guests are among the best I have heard anywhere.

§ 6.30 Appearance of the letter

The appearance and mechanics of the letter are what the reader sees first. A pleasing appearance invites the reader to investigate the contents. Here are some dos and do nots.

- Make the letter look appealing. To project a good image, use good quality stationery. Keep it neat and use paragraphing, headings, bullets, enumerations, and fonts that make the document easy to read.

- Keep letters to one page if possible. Keep the paragraphs short.
- The side margins of the letter will depend on the kind of stationery, style and size of font, space taken by the letterhead, and the length of the message. The basic rule is the finished letter must look like it is sitting in a frame of white space.
- Plan to leave a bottom margin of at least six line spaces (or one inch). If the letter continues to a second page, the bottom margin can increase to about twelve line spaces.
- A short letter can be spread over a page using several techniques:
    Lower the date line
    Allow more space between the date and inside address
    Allow more space for the signature
    Put the signer's name and title on separate lines
    Lower the reference initials, copy notation, and enclosure notation
- Shorten a long letter using these techniques:
    Raise the date line
    Allow only two or three blank spaces between the date and inside address
    Allow only two or three spaces for the signature
    Raise the reference initials one or two lines
- Ordinarily, all letters should be single spaced. If the message is very short it may be double spaced.
- For personal correspondence without a letterhead, put the return address in the upper right-hand corner. Start nine line spaces from the top and either begin at the center or have the longest line of the address even with the right-hand margin. If using the full block style, start at line nine flush with the left-hand margin.
- The date line is never abbreviated. Do not use a numerical date format, such as 6/23/10. Military or international form—23 June 2010—is acceptable, although not common.
- With a letterhead, position the date line three line spaces below the letterhead (or more if necessary for a professional appearance).
- For a personal or confidential letter, enter the appropriate notation two lines above the inside address at the left margin. This notation should be in all capital letters.
- The inside address in a letter being sent to an individual's home should include name, street address, and city, state, and ZIP code. If the person lives in an apartment, the apartment number should appear after the street address on the same line. If the person lives in a small town and the address is only two lines, do not separate the city from the state to make three lines.
- For a letter going to a company, organization, or school, use the above arrangement. If possible, address it to a particular individual and place this above the company name along with that

person's title. If there is no specific name, address it to a title, such as *Personnel Director.*

- The inside address should begin between four to eight lines below the date line; use single spacing.
- If a letter is addressed to two people at different addresses, type each name and address either one under the other, with one blank line between, or side by side, with one address aligned at the left margin and the other at center.

EXAMPLES: Dr. J.W. Cooper
123 Mustard Avenue
Greenwood, MO 45983

Dr. Jane Melody
432 Levon Creek, Suite 22-B
Jefferson City, MO 45976

Dr. J.W. Cooper	Dr. Jane Melody
123 Mustard Avenue	432 Levon Creek,
Greenwood, MO	Suite 22-B
45983	Jefferson City, MO 45976

Dear Dr. Cooper and Dr. Melody:

- If a letter is addressed to two people at the same address, list each name on a separate line of the same inside address.

EXAMPLE: Dr. J.W. Cooper
Dr. Jane Melody
123 Mustard Avenue
Greenwood, MO 45983

- Use a form of address before the name of a person (*Mr., Mrs., Ms., Miss, Dr.*).
- Consult the original correspondence for a person's preference in spelling. Do not abbreviate names or omit initials.
- When *Jr., Sr.,* or a roman numeral is part of the name, omit the comma after the surname, unless the addressee prefers the use of a comma.
- Do not use a form of address before a name if *M.D.* or *Esq.* follows the name. Write either *Dr. John Jones* or *John Jones, M.D.* and *Mr. John Jones* or *John Jones, Esq.*
- Abbreviations of religious orders, such as *S.J.,* are typed after names and preceded by a comma. An appropriate title should precede the name even though the abbreviation follows the name:

> EXAMPLE: *Reverend Neil Cahill, S.J.*

- If a person's title is very short, it should be placed on the same line with the name. If the title is very long, put it on a separate line. In this case, be certain that the second line of the title is indented at least two spaces beyond the first line of the title:

> EXAMPLE: Vice President and General Manager

- If a letter cannot be sent to the addressee but must be directed through a third person, use *In care of* or *c/o* John Doe.
- When using the name of an organization in an inside address, follow the organization's letterhead style for spelling, punctuation, capitalization, spacing, and abbreviation. If there is no way to determine the official form, consult the phone book or check the Internet. If that does not solve the problem:

  Spell out the word *and*—do not use *&*

  Write *Inc.* for Incorporated and *Ltd.* for Limited

  Spell out *Company* or *Corporation*; however, if the name is extremely long, abbreviate Company as *Co.* or Corporation as *Corp.*

  Do not use *The* at the beginning of the name unless it is a part of the official name

- If an address contains a building name and a street address, type the building name on the line above the street address.
- The street address should always be on a line by itself on the line preceding the city, state, and ZIP code.
- Do not abbreviate directions that appear before a street name, but use abbreviations if directions represent a section of a city.

> EXAMPLES: 1668 Southeast Ninth Street
>   1668 Ninth Street, SE

- Use the word *and* and not *&* in a street address:

> EXAMPLE: Tenth and Maple Streets.

- Do not abbreviate *Street, Avenue,* or *Boulevard* in an inside address.
- A post office box number may be used in place of a street address. Use Post Office Box 521 or P.O. Box 521. A station name, if needed, should appear after the box number on the same line and before the line for city and state.
- If an address shows both a street address and a box number in

its mailing address, whatever information appears in the line preceding the city and state is where the mail will be delivered.

- The city, state, and ZIP code must always be typed on one line:

> EXAMPLE: Des Moines, IA 50322

- Use one space between the state abbreviation and the ZIP code.
- Never abbreviate the name of a city or words like *Fort* and *Mount* in an address.

> EXAMPLE: Fort Dodge, Mount Vernon

- Abbreviate the word *Saint* in names of American cities.

> EXAMPLE: St. Louis, St. Paul

- When an address is given in a sentence, insert a comma after the street address and after the city. Leave one space between the state and the ZIP code. Insert a comma after the ZIP code unless a stronger mark of punctuation is required.
- When addressing mail to foreign countries, type the name of the country in all capital letters on a separate line. Do not abbreviate the name of the country.
- An attention line can be used, but it is typically reserved for situations when the full name of the addressee is unknown. It is best to address the letter to a particular person named in the first line of the inside address. In the absence of a notation of *personal* or *confidential,* the communication will be presumed to be company business and may be handled by others.
- Make certain that the spelling of the name in the salutation is the same as the spelling in the inside address.
- There are a few instances when a person's title or gender is unknown.

> EXAMPLES: To a person with name known, gender
> unknown:
> Dear Pat Black, Dear C.L. Blue
>
> To a person with name and gender
> unknown:
> Dear Madam or Sir
>
> To a woman, title unknown:
> Dear Ms. Black or Dear Mary Black

> To an organization composed of all men or all women:
> Dear Gentlemen or Dear Ladies
>
> To an organization composed of both men and women:
> Ladies and Gentlemen

- When a subject line is used in a block or modified block style letter, it is placed on the second line above or below the salutation. In most cases it will start at the left margin for block letters or at the left margin or centered for modified block style.
- The term *Subject* or *Re* is typed either in all capital letters or in upper and lower case letters and is followed by a colon.
- The message will start on the second line below the subject line or salutation.
- All letters except the modified block with indented paragraph style will have paragraphs starting flush with the left margin. The modified block style with indented paragraphs should be indented five spaces. If the letter is double spaced, indent each paragraph.
- To insert a quotation or other material in a display, indent the material five spaces or the same as your paragraph, leaving a line above and below. The material should be centered in this space with even margins left and right.
- For a list of numbered items appearing in the body, leave a line before beginning the items and begin either at the left margin or at the point of paragraph indentation. Follow the item number with a period, and start the item even with the paragraph indentation or five additional spaces to the right. If any item requires more than one line, indent the second line so that it begins under the first word of the line above or leave a line between items.
- Capitalize only the first word of the complimentary closing. If using mixed punctuation, place a coma after the last word of the complimentary closing.
- The complimentary closing affects the tone of the letter. For a personal tone use *Sincerely, Sincerely yours,* or *Cordially.* The reader will feel a more formal tone with *Very truly yours*, or *Respectfully yours.* If an informal closing phrase is used (*Best wishes, Warmest regards,* or *See you next week*), follow it with a comma. If one of these phrases is used with a more formal complimentary close, insert the informal phrase at the end of the last paragraph or as a separate, final paragraph.
- Watch the pattern of closings in writing to the same people. In a later letter a more formal closing than previously used may make the reader wonder what has happened to the relationship.

- The company or firm name may be used after the complimentary close. Its use emphasizes the fact that the writer is acting as an agent of the company as a whole. If used, the name should be in all capitals on the second line below the complimentary close and beginning at the same point as the complimentary close.
- Generally, the writer's name is on the fourth line after the complimentary closing or company name, whichever is last, aligned with the complimentary closing.
- Professional titles or degrees may be typed after the writer's name but are not written as part of the signature.
- If a lawyer's assistant signs a letter at the lawyer's request, the lawyer's name is in the assistant's handwriting with initials penned underneath the last part of the lawyer's name.
- If a letter is to be signed by two people, type each name and title either one under the other, with three blank lines between, or side by side, with one name aligned at the left margin and the other aligned at the center.

> EXAMPLES: Sincerely,
>
> Ann A. Pitts
> Office Manager
>
> Joan D. Moseley
> Patient Representative
>
> Sincerely,
>
> Ann A. Pitts   Joan D. Moseley
> Office Manager   Patient Representative

- Reference initials of the writer are placed at the left margin on the second line below the writer's name and title, typed in all capitals and followed immediately by a slash or colon; the typist's initials follow in lower case without a space after the slash or colon. When using only the typist's initials, use lower case letters.
- In personal correspondence, do not include reference initials.
- If the letter mentions that one or more items are to be included with the correspondence, indicate this fact by typing *Enclosure, Enc., Check enclosed, Enc. 2,* or other appropriate identification at the left margin one space below the reference initials.
- If the letter is to be delivered in a special way, type in the appropriate notation two lines above the inside address or immediately following the dateline in capital letters.
- Copy notations let the reader know that one or more other persons will receive a copy of the letter. Use the initials *c* or *cc*

for a copy notation. Place the notation at the left margin under the mailing notation. If more than one person receives a copy, type *c* only once; then align the second name under the beginning of the first name. The names are placed either in order of rank or alphabetically.

- The initial *c* is not capitalized. A colon may, but need not, be placed after it. (See Illustrations 6-6, 6-7, and 6-8 for a sample of each.)

- When an addressee is not to know who received copies of the letter, insert *bc* on the copies to the individuals who will receive blind copies. This notation should be placed on a separate page following the last page of the letter so it can be detached from letters or copies to be sent to those who should not receive the blind copy notation. Beware, however, of including blind copy notations on letters that may be sent by email.

- Postscripts are used to express an afterthought. Type the postscript a double space below the last reference or notation line. Use the same style for the postscript as in the body of the letter. The letters *P.S.* may be omitted.

- At least two lines of the body of the letter should appear on the second page before the complimentary close.

- Leave a margin of from 6 to 12 lines at the bottom of each page, and try to have uniform bottom margins on each page except the last.

§ 6.31 Addressing envelopes

Single space and block the address lines. The bottom line must include the city and state names and the ZIP code in that order. Leave one space between the state name or abbreviation and the ZIP code. (See Illustration 6-11.)

When the ZIP code is known, use the two-letter postal state abbreviation in all caps without punctuation. If the ZIP code is unavailable, call the post office or check the Internet at http://www.usps.com.

For a small envelope, start the address lines 2 inches from the top and 2 1/2 inches from the left edge.

For a large envelope, start the address lines 2 1/2 inches from the top and 4 inches from the left edge. (See Illustration 6-11.)

§ 6.31.1 Addressing envelopes—Return address

Start the return address on the second line from the top and three spaces from the left edge.

§ 6.31.2 Addressing envelopes—Postal notations

Postal notations (such as *CERTIFIED MAIL*) are in all capital letters three lines below the stamp. (See Illustration 6-11.)

§ 6.31.3 Addressing envelopes—Addressee notations

Notations such as *HOLD FOR ARRIVAL, PERSONAL,* and *PLEASE FORWARD* are placed a triple space below the return address and three spaces from the left edge.

Illustration 6-11

COLVIN, MASON & NORMAN
Attorneys at Law
3005 East Skelly Avenue
Tulsa, OK 74106-6864

CERTIFIED MAIL

HOLD FOR ARRIVAL

ACCOUNTS PAYABLE
XYZ CORPORATION
10 ELM AVE
ANYTOWN ST 01234-5678

§ 6.31.4 Addressing envelopes—Automated mail processing

The United States Postal Service speeds up the processing of the mail by rapidly reading and sorting mail with an optical character reader.

Preparing mail for machine processing requires a few additional steps:

- **ZIP codes**
  ZIP codes must be included in addresses, return addresses, and on preaddressed business reply mail and should be placed right after the state name. An envelope address that lacks a ZIP code is put aside until a post office employee can look it up and add it. This can delay a letter for several days.

- **Addresses**
  1. Addresses should be in block form with a uniform left margin.
  2. Print the address in a sans serif font, preferably in uppercase letters without punctuation. Do not use italic, artistic, script, or proportionately spaced fonts.
  3. Include only the street address or box number on the next-to-last line (including a suite or apartment number if needed) and the city, state, and ZIP code on the last line. Suite and apartment numbers should not appear on a separate line and never below the street address.
  4. Spell street, city, and state names correctly. Some equipment depends on finding an exact match of names with those already stored in memory.
  5. Activate the delivery point bar code feature in the envelope printer program. This will automatically insert a postal bar

code above the addressee's name. The bar code is scanned by the postal service and sorted automatically for faster delivery to the correct destination.

§ 6.32　Forms of address

Addressee	Form of Address	Salutation
Federal, State, and Local Government Officials		
alderman or city council-man	The Honorable John Smith	Dear Alderman Smith:
cabinet officers (as the Secretary of	The Honorable John Smith Secretary of State Dear Mr./Ms. Smith:	Dear Mr./Madam Secretary
State and the Attorney General)	The Honorable John Smith Attorney General of the United States	
chief justice, Supreme Court	The Chief Justice of the United States	Dear Mr./Madam Chief Justice:
commissioner	The Honorable John Smith	Dear Mr. Smith:
former U.S. president	The Honorable John Smith	Dear Mr. Smith:
governor	The Honorable John Smith Governor of ___	Dear Governor Smith:
judge, federal	The Honorable John Smith United States District Judge	Dear Judge Smith:
judge, state or local	The Honorable John Smith Chief Judge of the Court of Appeals	Dear Judge Smith:
lieutenant governor	The Honorable John Smith Lieutenant Governor of ___	Dear Lieutenant Governor Smith:
mayor	The Honorable John Smith Mayor of ___	Dear Mayor Smith:
		Dear Mr. Mayor
president, U.S.	The President	Dear Mr./Madam President:
representative, state (same format for assemblyman) representative, U.S.	The Honorable John Smith House of Representatives State Capitol	Dear Mr. Smith:
		Dear Representative Smith:
	The Honorable John Smith	Dear Mr. Smith:
	The United States House of Representatives	Dear Representative Smith:
senator, state	The Honorable John Smith	Dear Senator Smith:
	The State Senate State Capitol	
senator, U.S.	The Honorable John Smith United States Senate	Dear Senator Smith:
		Dear Mr. Smith:
		Dear Senator:
speaker, U.S. House of Representatives	The Honorable John Smith Speaker of the House of Representatives	Dear Mr. Speaker:
vice-president, U.S.	The Vice President United States Senate	Dear Mr./Madam Vice President:
Clerical and Religious Orders		
archbishop	The Most Reverend Archbishop of ___ or The Most Reverend John Smith Archbishop of ___	Your Excellency: Dear Archbishop Smith:

Addressee	Form of Address	Salutation
bishop, Catholic	The Most Reverend John Smith Bishop of ___	Your Excellency: Dear Bishop Smith:
bishop, Protestant	The Reverend or The Right Reverend John Smith	Reverend Sir: Dear Bishop Smith:
cardinal	His Eminence John Cardinal Smith	Your Eminence: Dear Cardinal Smith
clergyman, Protestant	The Reverend John Smith	Dear Reverend Smith:
	or	
	The Reverend Dr. John Smith (if having a doctor's degree)	Dear Sir:
		or
		Dear Dr. Smith:
pope	His Holiness Pope ___	Your Holiness:
	or	or
		Most Holy Father:
priest	The Reverend John Smith	Reverend Father:
		Dear Father Smith:
rabbi	Rabbi John Smith	Dear Rabbi Smith:
sisterhood, member of	Sister Mary Angelica, S.C.	Dear Sister Mary Angelica:
		Dear Sister:
sisterhood, superior of	The Reverend Mother Superior, S.C.	Reverend Mother:
		Dear Reverend Mother:

College and University Officials

dean of a college or university	Dean John Smith	Dear Dean Smith:
		Dear Dr. Smith:
president of a college or university	President John Smith	Dear President Smith:
		Dear Dr. Smith:
professor at a college or university	Professor John Smith	Dear Professor Smith:
		Dear Dr./Mr./Ms. Smith:

Miscellaneous Professional Ranks and Titles

attorney	John Smith, Esq.	Dear Mr. Smith:
	or	
	John Smith Attorney at Law	
dentist	John Smith, D.D.S. *(office address)*	Dear Dr. Smith:
	or	
	Dr. John Smith *(home address)*	
physician	John Smith, M.D. *(office address)*	Dear Dr. Smith:
	or	
	Dr. John Smith *(home address)*	
veterinarian	John Smith, D.V.M. *(office address)*	Dear Dr. Smith:
	or	
	Dr. John Smith *(home address)*	

§ 6.33   The memo

Memos are the means organizations use to communicate internally. Put in a memo any matter that requires ongoing attention or for which there needs to be a written record.

The tone of the memo will depend upon the relationship between the writer and the recipient, the nature of the subject, and organization policy. In some organizations, memos are written in third person to avoid mixing facts with opinions. A memo addressed to top management should be more formal than to someone of equal rank with the writer.

In organizing the memo, brevity is the rule, but one should not be so brief as to sound curt. Memos need to be as courteous as letters. The message is selling a point of view or explaining a situation. State the purpose in the first paragraph. Deliver the message using the same rules as for a letter. Use separate paragraphs for each idea or point. In the last paragraph close with a request, a statement of future action or conclusions.

The subject line may not adequately cover the purpose of the memo. Always state the reason for writing, perhaps referring to a memo received, a meeting, or a telephone conversation.

An excellent method for stating the message briefly is to use numbered paragraphs. If there are several topics to discuss, bold side headings may announce each change of topic.

Using the same sentence and paragraph construction and other rules for writing letters will produce an excellent product.

§ 6.33.1   The memo—Memo format

Some organizations have memo forms printed, carrying the company's name and the designation that it is a memorandum. Many others have a variety of memo format templates for use by their computer users. If not, it is easy to format one for future use. There are four basic elements to include in the form:

TO:
FROM:
DATE:
SUBJECT:

These words should be in all caps followed by a colon. The arrangement is optional. The elements can be divided with two positioned on the left side and two at the center, or all four can be listed at the left margin. Double spacing should set them apart to allow space for long names, titles, addresses, etc.

Write dates just as in a letter.

To address the memo, use any appropriate professional title for the addressee, such as Dr., but Mr., Mrs., Ms., or Miss may be omitted. If the organization is large, add the addressee's title, room number, or other identification for faster delivery.

If the memo is addressed to a group, at the bottom of the memo, type *Distribution List* and list all individual names alphabetically below.

The subject line should contain the topic of the memo. Type the subject matter in either all capital or upper and lower case letters.

The body or message should start three or four lines below the subject line. Use single spacing unless the message is very short.

Complimentary closings are omitted in memos. The writer can initial the document either next to the name in the heading or at the end of the memo. If the writer's signature is required, place it at the bottom of the memo.

§ 6.34 The informal report

There will be many occasions when the lawyer's assistant will need to put in writing some information that the lawyer or others have requested. The practice of writing informal reports is also a form of self-protection. If the assistant tells lawyers something, they may forget; however, if the assistant writes a report, the information is preserved. Informal reports also stand as visible proof of efficiency, and efficiency is more tangible when the report is in writing.

There are essentially three parts to the report:

- In the introduction state the purpose with points to support it.
- In the body, refer to any background necessary for clarity, then begin a discussion of each of the major points, giving details, examples, and facts. Reports rely very heavily on descriptive data.
- The conclusion summarizes and gives results, findings or recommendations.

First, the writer should prepare an outline. This can be very short or very detailed depending upon the assignment. For example, the firm may need a report on the software each of 12 lawyer's assistants. The firm plans to include new software within a budget and needs prices also, so there are two issues to investigate.

- List software the lawyer's assistants are using, including program capabilities.
- Check and report on the prices of new software from two or more suppliers.

When the details are gathered, the facts should be placed in the two categories. The items in each group should be arranged in the order in which they will be presented.

An informal report of this type will be set up as a memo. A copy of any informal report should be kept, no matter how seemingly unimportant. The original could be misplaced or lost.

The report should be clear, correct, complete, and concise. Everything that needs to be said should be said as economically as possible, using the same rules of grammar, punctuation, spelling, etc., as for letter writing. In a report, accuracy of information is more important than formality of tone. The report should be fact-oriented and straightforward.

A very effective way to present information is to use a table, chart, or graph. The reader can see everything at a glance.

After all the research has been included in the report, it should be summarized. In this scenario, it may be appropriate to recommend keeping some of the older software and adding new software.

The lawyer's assistant may occasionally want to write an unsolicited report. Any idea that might increase efficiency and productivity is likely to be welcome. Put the idea in writing in a complete, logical, and effective manner.

The report should be directed to the person who has the authority to put it into effect.

The subject line should be chosen carefully to describe concisely what the report is about.

The wording in the report should be tailored to appeal to the reader's interest. The writer should plan as for an informal research report and rely on facts and not on personal judgment. Alternatives, good and bad, should be given, and the strong points backed up with facts. In the conclusion, the writer should reemphasize the strong points presented.

§ 6.35   The formal report

Formal business reports concern themselves with more complicated problems and may require weeks of extensive research. The finished product may contain anywhere from one or two pages to over a hundred. If a company is basing a decision concerning the expenditure of a great amount of money on this report, it must be very carefully and expertly done.

Before starting, the purpose and scope of the project must be set out. It will have more parts than an informal report: introduction, summary, body, conclusions, and recommendations, plus supplementary information such as an appendix and bibliography.

A formal report is made up of information from many sources. The writer should catalog the information on note cards or note sheets, using one sheet for each item along with its source. After collection of all information, the writer then studies the material and begins the task of organizing it into a logical sequence for presentation.

A good report writer is careful to avoid expressions that imply the writer's personal opinions are the basis for the evaluations presented in the paper. A successful business report separates reasoning from facts.

§ 6.36   Summary

Skilled writers are valuable in any business. The spoken word evaporates in air; the written word stands as permanent testimony. That is why in business where large sums of money hinge on people's understanding each other—to produce items, deliver goods, promote goodwill, or render services—accurate writing is essential.

Writing is affected by the writer's environment, education, and intelligence, but anyone can learn to write competently if he or she desires to do so, receives proper instruction and supervision, and then continues to practice the skill. The lawyer's assistant who does not seek to improve writing skills, however, may be limited in job growth by depending upon obsolete or inadequate skills and techniques. The lawyer's assistant should be curious, interested, and flexible enough to adapt to changes in forms, formats, and the mechanics of written communications in the law office.

Chapter 7

Preparation of Legal Documents

KeyCite®: Cases and other legal materials listed in KeyCite Scope can be researched through the KeyCite service on Westlaw®. Use KeyCite to check citations for form, parallel references, prior and later history, and comprehensive citator information, including citations to other decisions and secondary materials.

---

§ 7.1 Introduction

All documents created in the law office reflect on the lawyer's assistant, the lawyer, and the firm. Documents should be neat and attractively arranged, conform to court specifications, and contain no typographical, content, or format errors. Competent, detail-oriented lawyer's assistants note any errors and work with the lawyer to prepare the best documents possible.

A strong background in English grammar, punctuation and capitalization, and formatting requirements is important. Punctuation in legal documents should be logical and conform to general standards; however, lawyer's assistants may find that the rules and procedures are not always clear-cut. Locality, time, purpose, and preferences may influence the choice of the rule to apply. For example, in eastern states, the subject line in a letter is normally placed after the salutation; in western states, the subject line is placed above the salutation. In formal documents, the word "Street" is spelled out; in informal documents it may be abbreviated. In addition, some lawyers have strong preferences about English style, and the best approach is simply to do as the lawyer asks; ultimately, it is the lawyer's reputation at stake in the work product.

Most state courts and agencies have a prescribed procedure for the preparation of documents, and the lawyer's assistant should read these guidelines carefully. The lawyer's assistant should also become thoroughly familiar with standard business English and consult a good legal procedures book when needed. Good sources of English manuscript and business style can easily be found. Many offices have procedures and style manuals. Other reference books include *The Elements of Style* by William Strunk, Jr., and E. B. White; *The Chicago Manual of Style*, 15th edition; *A Course in Basic Writing* by Susanna K. Horn and Ken Pramuk; and *The Gregg Reference Manual* by William A. Sabin.

To keep legal documents error-free, the legal team should work together. The lawyer's assistant should be careful not to perpetuate errors just because the office "has always done it that way." If there is a strong basis for a correction, the correction should be made, but before making changes, the assistant should determine whether the error is a true error or just a style difference. The lawyer's assistant should not hesitate to point out obvious errors to an attorney (e.g., the lawyer dictated *defendant* when he or she meant *plaintiff*). The attorney will appreciate the additional assistance in maintaining the professional appearance in the documents.

Following are some general procedures used in preparing legal documents.

§ 7.2   Basic procedures

The following sections detail procedures that are common to most legal documents.

§ 7.2.1   Basic procedures—Paper and number of copies

After documents are entered into a computer, they are printed in draft or final mode. (I do not think many offices do this any longer)

Heavier bond paper is often used for the final document, and copies are made on less expensive paper. The usual practice is to prepare one original, have it signed, and make any needed copies. Most court systems now require all filings to be on 8½ by 11 paper, and most law offices now use 8½ by 11 paper for all legal documents. (I think all law offices use this. Not many courts or county offices require filings on legal paper any longer, or even bond.)

When filing court documents, determine the number of copies to be made as follows: original (and appropriate number of copies) for the court, a copy for each lawyer representing a party to the action, a file copy, and a copy for the client (unless the lawyer indicates one is not needed). Many courts are using efiling systems. This means that the original of the document is kept in the file, however, parties are served through the efiling system, and nothing is required to be mailed.

When preparing legal documents that will not be filed in court, prepare a copy for any party signing the documents, their attorneys (if requested), and a file copy. In some instances, it may be necessary for the parties to sign more than one copy. The original and one or more copies will be designated as originals. These copies will all be **executed** as originals and have the same legal force as an original. Copies are sometimes made after all signatures have been obtained on one original.

Final documents are always copied before they leave the office. When a lawyer asks an assistant to prepare a document, he or she may tell the assistant to make "two plus four" copies, meaning an original, a copy of the original to be used as a duplicate original, and four copies. Alternatively, the lawyer might ask for "one plus two," meaning an original and two copies. If a document such as a letter or pleading requires a signature, copies should generally not be made until after the document is actually signed.

§7.2.2 Basic procedures—Margins

Most documents are now created with default settings of one-inch top and bottom margins and one inch or one-and-a-quarter inch left and right side margins. (If a document is going to be recorded with register of deeds, it has at least two-inch top margin, depending on the county). Pleadings and documents to be recorded by the county recorder (does this mean register of deeds?) often have special margin requirements. Additional margin space may be required when documents are going to be bound, hole-punched, or stapled or when ruled legal paper (called *legal cap*) (I have asked around but am not finding anyone that still uses legal cap) is used. Temporary left and right margins can be set to type legal descriptions and quoted materials. This feature, sometimes called *Indent*, allows for word wrapping.

All pages should begin on the same line space from the top and end on the same line space from the bottom. This format should be followed for neater documents and to avoid questions about lines being inserted.

Law offices vary in document justification. Left justification is easier to read, but many offices prefer full justification. In either case, avoid excessive hyphenation. Do not hyphenate the last word on a page.

Check the court rules for specific requirements regarding font, line spacing, and margins and then make a note in the office manual for future reference.

§ 7.2.3   Basic procedures—Tab settings

A five-space paragraph indent is usually used on legal documents. Most computers have default tab settings at five-space or one-half-inch intervals. These stops are useful in typing subheadings, bulleted items, and numbered lists.

§ 7.2.4   Basic procedures—Spacing

Spacing is described as single, double, or triple spacing. In single spacing there is no blank line between the lines of text, in double spacing there is one blank line between the lines of text, and in triple spacing there are two blank lines between the lines of text. In law offices, correspondence is generally single spaced with a double space between sections and three blank lines in the signature block. Legal documents are generally double spaced, but some long leases and other agreements are single spaced with double spaces between sections.

Court pleadings are formatted according to court rules, local style, and electronic filing requirements. After entering the name of the court, double space to the caption. Enter the caption in single space, and after the caption, double space to the body of the pleading. The body is usually double spaced with five-space paragraph indents. Property descriptions, quotations, and deposition or trial transcript references are usually block indented and single-spaced. The spacing in signature blocks is a matter of style, but at least two blank lines should be included above the signature line. Acknowledgments or verifications at the end of documents may be single-spaced.

§ 7.2.5   Basic procedures—Incomplete pages

Simple correspondence and most pleadings are not sensitive with respect to page endings. In correspondence, a multiple-page document should end so that the signature and at least two lines of text are on the final page. Space can be added or deleted above or below the dateline, spaces can be deleted from the signature block (within limits), and font size and margins can be adjusted to get correspondence to fit when desirable.

Many agreements and contracts, however, should not have more than two inches of space at the bottom of a page. In these documents, a Z-line or other method of marking may be used to fill up the blank space at the bottom of a page. Another option may be to simply insert the phrase, "Remainder of page intentionally left blank."

In proofreading documents, the lawyer's assistant should specifically look for pagination errors. A paragraph that is divided at the bottom of a page should have at least two lines of the paragraph on the end of the page and at least two lines of the paragraph at the top of the next page. A three-line paragraph should not be divided. A word processing feature called **Widow-Orphan** can make these adjustments automatically. Headings that appear on the bottom line of a page can be adjusted with word processing features that keep heading and text together.

The problem of signature lines or signature blocks splitting between two pages or appearing on a page by themselves should be corrected by positioning the signature block and two lines of the preceding text on the last page. Some documents that require a number of signatures may have pages consisting of only signature lines. If the document being prepared has a **testimonium clause**, a paragraph just before the signatures that usually starts with the words "IN WITNESS WHEREOF", it must be placed on the page with the signatures. There are several ways to adjust the page or pages preceding the signatures to get the signatures on the page or some of the body of the document onto the page with the signatures:

- Use wider top and bottom margins.
- Widen the side margins slightly, thereby creating an additional line.
- If one line has only one word on it, move that word up to the line above by widening the side margins.
- If most of the document is double spaced, change spacing to an exact measurement just short of a true double space, such as 1.9 line spaces.
- Leave less space between the signatures or between the testimonium clause and the signatures.
- Put half of the signature lines on the left side of the page and half of them on the right side of the page rather than aligning them vertically on the right side of the page.

§ 7.2.6 Basic procedures—Signatures

The document itself indicates who will sign it. Prepare the proper number of signature lines. Usually two or three blank lines between signature lines are sufficient. The signature line should be about three inches long. The signature lines or blocks can be aligned vertically one below the other close to the left margin or centered on the page. They can also be placed in two columns.

Under each line, the designation of the signing party, such as *Seller*, *Lessee*, or other term is usually typed. Some offices prefer to have the name of the party typed below the line, along with their title or designation. The name can be aligned with the beginning of the line or centered under the line.

> EXAMPLE: _____
>
>   E.G. Smith, Lessor

This method prevents the people signing the document from signing on the wrong line.

The testimonium clause is the last paragraph on a legal document before the signatures.

EXAMPLE:

"IN WITNESS WHEREOF, the parties hereto have hereunto set their hands on the day and year first above written."

If the testimonium clause states that the parties have "set their hands and seals," you know that the document is to be imprinted with a seal.

EXAMPLE:

"IN WITNESS WHEREOF, the parties hereto have caused this instrument to be executed properly on the day and year first above written."

Not all states require corporations to have seals; therefore, if the corporation does not have a seal, only the signature of the person signing for the corporation will appear.

§ 7.2.7   Basic procedures—Date blanks

The exact date on which a document will be executed is not always known. The usual procedure is to leave a space sufficient to insert a date either with or without a line. Some firms prefer to underline the blank space because a blank space is hard to see and may be overlooked.

> EXAMPLE: the   day of July _[Year]_
>   or the ____   day of July _[Year]_

Six spaces are left so that there would be a space before the word _day_—four spaces for the day and ordinal ending and a space following. Twelve spaces are used for the month. If it is near the end of the month and the month the document will be executed is unknown, leave sufficient space for the name of the longer month.

§ 7.2.8   Basic procedures—Typing drafts

Many lawyers prefer draft documents to bear the word _DRAFT_ and the date at the top of the page. Some lawyers prefer to put draft information in the footer and remove or change it in the final document. When possible, double or triple spacing is used for drafts so that revisions and corrections can be made. Any material directly copied from another source, such as a citation or quotation, can be single-spaced.

Speed and accuracy are important on drafts. The lawyer expects to make changes, but also expects the draft to be accurate. Be careful about citations, numbers, names, descriptions, dates, and money amounts. When a second version is completed, mark it *SECOND DRAFT* or *DRAFT #2* and date it so the drafts can be distinguished. Word processing programs allow you to insert headers or footers that will automatically update the date and time of each draft. Remember to remove the draft designation before printing the final version.

§ 7.2.9   Basic procedures—Collating documents

Collating is the process of placing document pages in proper sequence. Documents can be copied in groups or collated in sets. Virtually all copiers will collate and staple multiple copies. Some documents or packets—such as income tax returns or government applications—may be created in sections that are copied separately and then assembled by hand. This process is also sometimes called collating or assembling.

§ 7.2.10   Basic procedures—Executing documents

The formal signing of a legal document is called **executing** the document. It includes the procedures of having the appropriate parties sign and date the document, affixing a seal (if required), acknowledgment, and notarization. The latter two steps are described in the section on notaries public in Chapter 3 The Law Office. Proper execution by a party or a duly authorized representative is one element required to make a document legally binding. Blue or black ink is traditionally used in the execution, acknowledgment, and notarization of documents. Some states as well as some financial institutions require the use of blue ink because it is easier to distinguish original signatures from copies. However, one needs to check the court or recorder's rules as well as with the financial institution (if applicable) regarding the acceptability of documents executed in blue ink. Red ink or some other type of "off-color" ink is NEVER acceptable in the execution, acknowledgment, or notarization of documents.

§ 7.2.11   Basic procedures—Conforming documents

Some documents are signed only in the original and *conformed* in all copies. A signature can be conformed in writing or by typing the symbol /s/ plus the signature. Electronically filed pleadings are signed with the conforming signature on the original, filed document. For the majority of documents, however, the lawyer's assistant will make a copy of the executed document and use it as the file copy.

Some law offices use the practice of marking all copies with a copy stamp, so copies will not be confused with the original executed document.

EXAMPLE: */s/ Sarah Bridger*

§ 7.2.12   Basic procedures—Law blanks (printed forms)

The use of printed forms or **law blanks** varies from state to state. All states use some printed forms and variable information is filled in on the form. Although law blanks are used less frequently with the advent of legal software forms, they are still used for documents such as simple deeds. Material on printed forms is generally single spaced with blanks left for information that may change, such as addresses, names, pronouns, and verbs that may change with the number of parties. Read through the form carefully, filling in all blanks. Remember to punctuate the law blank just as if it were a document entered on the computer.

§ 7.3   Capitalization

In general, capitalize the same words in legal documents that are capitalized in regular documents. However, litigation, in particular, has some specialized usages. The word "court" is capitalized when it refers to a specific court, and it is capitalized in pleadings when referring to the court where the pleading is filed. This is technically a reference to the judge of the court. The word "court" used to refer to other courts in the same pleading is not capitalized. The words "plaintiff" and "defendant" are capitalized less often than formerly, but some attorneys still prefer to capitalize them. In addition, in both pleadings and legal documents that may not be filed with the court, it is common to define a term as a shorthand reference. For example, the grantor in an agreement may have a long corporate name but be referred to as "Grantor" throughout the agreement. Defined terms may be capitalized, italicized, underlined, placed in all capital letters or boldface type, or some combination of those.

If capitalization rules have not been established by the law firm or attorney, collect and establish standard rules and follow them in all instances. This type of information should go in a procedures or style manual, and all staff members should follow the same guidelines.

In legal work, it is traditional that certain phrases and words are placed in all capital letters; however, some attorneys prefer initial capital letters only. Check with the lawyer to learn preferences, and, again, place this information in a style book. Some examples follow:

- IN WITNESS WHEREOF/THEREOF/HEREOF
- THIS INDENTURE
- FOR VALUE RECEIVED
- RESOLVED
- WHEREAS

- NOW, THEREFORE
- WHEREFORE
- KNOW ALL PERSONS BY THESE PRESENTS
- THIS AGREEMENT
- IT IS ORDERED

§ 7.4 Numbers and amounts of money

A lawyer may dictate that certain numbers be placed in "words and figures" when the lawyer wants the assistant to enter a number or amount of money in words followed by the figures in parentheses. If there is a discrepancy between the words and the figures, the words will prevail. Therefore, it is imperative that these numbers be double-checked for consistency.

EXAMPLE:

Under the age of twenty-one (21) years.

Payment amounts in settlement documents and some contracts are spelled out with the initial letter of the major words capitalized.

EXAMPLE:

Twenty-five Thousand Dollars ($25,000)

Twenty-five Thousand and No/100 Dollars ($25,000.00).

Twenty-five Thousand Dollars and zero cents ($25,000.00).

The material in the parentheses matches the numbers that precede the parentheses.

Incorrect: Twenty-five Thousand Dollars ($25,000.00) (The parentheses indicate the cents fraction but the preceding words do not.)

Incorrect: Twenty-five Thousand and no/100 ($25,000.00) Dollars (This is incorrect because the word "Dollars" comes after the parentheses.)

Comprehensive guidelines for number usage are provided in *The Gregg Reference Manual* or *The Chicago Manual of Style*.

§ 7.5 Legal citations

A *citation* is the written notation referring to primary and secondary legal authorities such as constitutions, statutes, cases, treatises, and legal encyclopedias. The legal citation provides an easy and uniform method for locating and referring to authority in written documents. Following are examples of citations by category:

Cases	*Brown v. Board of Education*, 347 U.S. 483 (1954)
	Kerr v. Farrey, 95 F.3d 472 (7th Cir. 1996)
	Clark v. Clark, 725 N.E.2d 100 (Ind. Ct. App. 2000)
	Allen v. Oklahoma City, 175 Okla. 421, 52 P.2d 1054 (Okla. 1935)

| Constitutions | U.S. Const. amend. XIV, § 1 |
| | N.D. Const. art. 8, § 147 |

| Statutes | 28 U.S.C. § 1254(1) |
| | Ariz. Rev. Stat. § 36-582 (1999) |

Rules	Fed. R. Civ. P. 54(b)
	Rule 9.130, Fla. R. App. Proc.
	Cal. Rules of Court, Rule 976

| Secondary Authority | 17 Charles Alan Wright, Arthur R. Miller & Edward H. Cooper, Federal Practice & Procedure § 4036 (2d ed. 1988) |

Timothy M. Cook, *The Americans with Disabilities Act: The Move to Integration*, 64 Temp. L. Rev. 393 (1991)

Restatement (Second) of Torts, § 218 (1965)

Many legal documents contain citations. Whenever attorneys want to support a position with legal authority, they will refer to that authority by citation. A lawyer's assistant will most commonly encounter citations when preparing opinion letters or briefs.

A *brief* is a memorandum of the material facts, issues, applicable law, and argument to show the court the case and how it applies to the facts supporting the client's position. A list of legal authorities cited in a brief will be compiled into a *table of authorities*. See § 7.5.2 for a comprehensive list of the proper order in which to place citations in a table of authorities.

The contents of a brief are the responsibility of the lawyer. The lawyer's assistant is responsible for preparing the brief attractively and accurately and must be knowledgeable regarding correct citation practices, including proper abbreviations, punctuation, and capitalization. Citations must be entered and checked very carefully. Typically, the lawyer will verify citations against the actual sources. A brief's effectiveness may be damaged if it contains an incorrect citation.

The most widely accepted guide on legal citations is *The Bluebook: A Uniform System of Citation* (20th ed., 2015), compiled by the editors of the Columbia Law Review, the Harvard Law Review, the University of Pennsylvania Law Review, and The Yale Law Journal (commonly called *The Bluebook*).

While *The Bluebook* is still an authoritative guide to citation, it no longer is the only one. The *ALWD Citation Manual: A Professional System of Citation* (Aspen Publishers) was created in 2000 by the Association of Legal Writing Directors (ALWD) and is now in its fourth edition. The *ALWD Citation Manual* is praised for teaching citation form at a more basic level than *The Bluebook* and is often considered easier to use.[1]

Some state courts have developed their own citation practices, which should be followed where appropriate. The important thing is to be consistent, particularly within any one brief. It should be noted, however, that case names must always be either italicized or underscored—and italics and underscoring for case names should not be mixed in one document.

To acquire the background for understanding and writing citations, the lawyer's assistant should read and study the information in Chapter 8 The Law Library and Chapter 9 The Courts. It is especially useful to understand the terms "official" and "unofficial" reporters and the structure of the National Reporter System.

§ 7.5.1 Legal citations—Citation sentences and introductory signals

When joining citations in a sentence—sometimes referred to as a string citation—begin with a capital letter, separate individual citations with a semicolon, and end with a period.

EXAMPLE:

McClanahan v. American Gilsonite Co., 494 F. Supp. 1334 (D. Colo. 1980); *Shibuya v. Architects of Hawaii, Ltd.*, 647 P.2d 276 (Haw. 1982); *Kallas Millwork Corp. v. Square D Co.*, 225 N.W.2d 454 (Wis. 1975); *Phillips v. ABC Builders Inc.*, 611 P.2d 821 (Wyo. 1980).

In citing a case, the writer will show that a certain case supports, is comparable to, contradicts, or gives background material on a proposition and will use *introductory signals* such as *See, See also, E.g., Accord, Cf., Contra, But, But see,* and *See generally* before the actual citation to indicate the importance of the case. When no signal is given, the cited authority directly supports the proposition, is the source of quoted material, or identifies the authority referred to in the text. Note that when *see* is used as a verb in text rather than a citation, it is not a signal and is not italicized or underlined.

§ 7.5.2 Legal citations—Order of citations

When authorities are placed in a string citation, they should be grouped by signal, and within each signal, the most persuasive or au-

---

[Section 7.5]

[1]Although The Bluebook and the ALWD Citation Manual are both referenced here, for those who are studying for the ALS®, PLS®, or PP® certifications, The Bluebook remains the official NALS® resource for citation style.

thoritative authority should be listed first. *The Bluebook* suggests the following order for citations:

1. Constitutions (federal, state [alphabetically], foreign [alphabetically by jurisdiction], and then foundational documents of the United Nations, the League of Nations, and the European Union)

2. Statutes (federal, state [alphabetically], and foreign [alphabetically by jurisdiction])

3. Treaties and other international agreements (in reverse chronological order)

4. Cases—arrange within a signal according to the courts issuing the cited opinions; cases decided by the same court are arranged in reverse chronological order
   a. Federal
      i. Supreme Court
      ii. Courts of appeals; bankruptcy appellate panels; Emergency Court of Appeals; Temporary Emergency Court of Appeals; Court of Appeals for the Federal Circuit
      iii. District courts; district bankruptcy courts; Court of International Trade
      iv. Judicial Panel on Multidistrict Litigation; Railroad Reorganization Court
      v. Court of Federal Claims; Court of Appeals for the Armed Forces; Tax Court
      vi. Administrative agencies (alphabetically)
   b. State
      i. Courts (alphabetically by state and then by rank within each state)
      ii. Agencies (alphabetically by state and then alphabetically by agency)
   c. Foreign
      i. Courts (alphabetically by jurisdiction and then by rank within each jurisdiction)
      ii. Agencies (alphabetically by jurisdiction and then by agency)
   d. International (International Court of Justice, Permanent Court of International Justice, then other international tribunals and arbitral panels [alphabetically])

5. Legislative materials
   a. Bills and resolutions
   b. Committee hearings
   c. Reports, documents, and committee prints
   d. Floor debates

6. Administrative and executive materials
   a. Federal

      i. Executive orders
      ii. Current Treasury regulations, proposed Treasury regulations
      iii. All others currently in force (in progressive order of C.F.R. title)
      iv. Proposed rules (in reverse order)
      v. All materials repealed (in reverse order of promulgation)
    b. State (alphabetically) currently in force, then repealed
    c. Foreign (alphabetically by jurisdiction) currently in force, then repealed
7. Resolutions, decisions, and regulations of intergovernmental organizations
8. Records, briefs, and petitions
9. Secondary materials
    a. Uniform codes, model codes and restatements
    b. Books, pamphlets, and shorter works in a collection
    c. Works in journals
    d. Book reviews not written by students
    e. Student-written law review materials, including book reviews
    f. Annotations
    g. Magazine and newspaper articles
    h. Unpublished materials not forthcoming
    i. Electronic sources
10. Cross-reference to the author's own material in text or footnotes

§ 7.5.3 Legal citations—Elements of case citations

A full case citation contains:
1. The name of the case, underlined or italicized.
2. The published sources in which it may be found.
3. The page upon which the cite begins.
4. In parentheses, the date of the decision and information which identifies the court making the decision: *Wyant v. SCM Corp.,* 692 S.W.2d 814 (Ky. Ct. App. 1985).

In addition, many citations include the following information:
- A *pinpoint cite* or *page cite* (page(s) particularly referred to): *Curtiss v. Hubbard,* 703 P.2d 1154, 1155 (Alaska 1985).
- A parallel citation—official reporter first: State v. Reed, 237 Kan. 685, 703 P.2d 756 (1985).
- Other parenthetical information regarding the decision: *State v. Story,* 646 S.W.2d 68 (Mo. 1983) (en banc); *State v. Brewer,* 247 N.W.2d 205 (Iowa 1976) (maximum age of 65 is reasonable limitation).
- Subsequent case history: *Daniel v. International Brotherhood of Teamsters,* 561 F.2d 1223 (7th Cir. 1977), rev'd on other grounds, 439 U.S. 551 (1979).

- Other related authority: *Memphis Bank & Trust Co. v. Garner*, 459 U.S. 392 (1983) (construing 31 U.S.C. § 742).

§ 7.5.4 Legal citations—Case names

The full case name appears at the beginning of an opinion in the official reporter. The full case name should be modified following conventions set forth in *The Bluebook* or as directed by court rule. Citations found in the context of a sentence, whether in the body of the document or in footnotes, should be changed as explained below. Citations that are preceded by a signal or are part of a string citation require additional abbreviated forms. Note that these additional forms of abbreviations are discussed in Rule 10.2.2 of *The Bluebook*.

If a case is a consolidation of two or more actions, cite only the first listed parties:

EXAMPLES:
Burman v. Holiday Inns, Inc.

Omit all parties but the first listed on each side but do not omit the first listed relator or any portion of a partnership name:

EXAMPLES:
Fry v. Mayor of Sierra Vista NOT *Fry v. Mayor and City Council of Sierra Vista*

Omit words indicating multiple parties, such as *et al.* Also omit alternative names given for the first-listed party on either side:

EXAMPLES:
Cheng v. Seinfeld NOT *Cheng, et al. v. Seinfeld d/b/a The Man, Inc.*

In bankruptcy and similar cases, include a procedural phrase such as *In re* or *ex rel.* before the nonadversary name.

EXAMPLES:
In re Drexel Burnham Lambert Group, Inc., 120 B.R. 724 (Bankr. S.D.N.Y. 1990)

Abbreviate *on the relation of, for the use of, on behalf of,* and so forth, to *ex rel.*

EXAMPLES:

State ex rel. Clark v. Pratt NOT *State v. Pratt* or *State ex rel. Clark, Wilson & West*

Abbreviate *in the matter of, petition of, application of,* and so forth, to *In re.*

EXAMPLES:
In re Cooper

When adversary parties are named, omit all procedural phrases except *ex rel.*

EXAMPLES:
Cooper v. Harris NOT *In re Cooper v. Harris* BUT *Idaho ex rel. Evans v. Oregon*

Do not abbreviate the first word of a party's name unless the full name of a party can be abbreviated by commonly known initials.

EXAMPLES:
Blackstone Co. v. NLRB NOT *Blackstone Co. v. National Labor Relations Board.*

Do not otherwise abbreviate words in case names except for *Ass'n, Bros., Co., Corp., Inc., Ltd., No.,* and *&.* If any of these begin a party's name, however, do not abbreviate it.

EXAMPLES:
Number Smart v. Hirsch NOT *No. Smart v. Hirsch*

Omit given names or initials of individuals except in names of business firms or where a party's surname is abbreviated.

EXAMPLES:
Mayer v. Gordon NOT *Jennifer Cannon Mayer v. Daniel S. Gordon*

Omit "The" as the first word of a party name except as part of the name of the object of an *in rem* action or in cases in which *The King* or *The Queen* is a party.

EXAMPLES:
The King v. Broadup

Do not omit any part of a surname made up of more than one word.

EXAMPLES:
Van der Velt v. Standing Horse

Given names that follow a surname should be retained. Retain the full name where the name is entirely in a language in which the surname is given first (this is common in Oriental languages). If in doubt about a foreign name, use the name under which it is indexed in the reporter.

EXAMPLES:
Chun Ming v. Kam Hee Ho

Omit *City of* and similar expressions unless the expression begins a party name.

EXAMPLES:
Johnson v. Mayor of Clarkston NOT *Johnson v. Mayor of City of Clarkson* BUT *Schmidt v. City of Clarkston*

Omit *State of, Commonwealth of,* and *People of* except in citing decisions of the courts of that state, in which case only *State, Commonwealth,* or *People* should be retained.

EXAMPLES:
People v. Lucky (when cited in California)
California v. Lucky (when cited outside California)

In business firm designations omit *Inc., Ltd., L.L.C., N.A., F.S.B.,* and similar terms if the name also contains a word such as *Ass'n, Bros., Corp., Co.,* and *R.R.,* clearly indicating the party is a business.

EXAMPLES:
Land v. Twin City Insurance Co. NOT *Land v. Twin City Insurance Co., Inc.*

Omit such terms as *administrator, appellee, executor, licensee, trustee,* and so forth, which describe a party already named.

EXAMPLES:
Gold v. Sullivan NOT *Gold, Trustee v. Sullivan, Executor*
Silkwood, Administrator v. Kerr-McGee Corp.

Include any introductory or descriptive phrases such as *Accounting of*, *Estate of*, and *Will of*.

EXAMPLES:
In re Estate of Freeburn

Phrases or party names that would aid in identification of the case may be appended in parentheses after the formal case name.

EXAMPLES:
ILGWU v. NLRB (Bernhard-Altmann Texas Corp.)

In a bankruptcy proceeding, there may be a nonadversary name in the case name.

EXAMPLES:
Morse v. Barnard (In re Ramsey)

Omit all prepositional phrases of location not following *City*, and so forth, unless the omission would leave only one word in the name of a party or the location is part of the name of a business.

EXAMPLES:
Hall v. Department of Human Resources NOT *Hall v. Department of Human Resources of State of Oregon*
Chavez v. Industrial Commission NOT *Chavez v. The Industrial Commission of Arizona*

Include designations of national or larger geographical areas except in union names, but omit *of America* after *United States*. Never abbreviate *United States* when it stands for *United States of America* as a party to an action.

EXAMPLES:
Smith v. Prudential Insurance Co. of America
United States v. Widgets of America

The Commissioner of the Internal Revenue Service is cited simply as *Commissioner*.

A union name should be cited exactly as given in the official report, except that only the smallest unit should be cited. All industry designations except the first full one should be omitted, and all prepositional phrases of location should be omitted. Widely recognized abbreviations (CIA, UAW, and so forth) may be used.

EXAMPLES:
International Brotherhood of Teamsters v. NLRB NOT
International Brotherhood of Teamsters, Chauffeurs,
Warehousemen & Helpers of America v. NLRB

Case names may be abbreviated more extensively in footnotes to save space. Acceptable abbreviations are listed in *The Bluebook.*

EXAMPLES:
Pennsylvania Nat'l. Mut. Casualty Co.

§ 7.5.5   Legal citations—Federal court cases

Federal court cases should be cited as follows:

- United States Supreme Court:

Hunter v. Erickson, 303 U.S. 385, 89 S. Ct. 557, 21 L. Ed. 2d 616 (1969). A recent unreported case may be cited as United States v. Leon, __ U.S. __ (No. 86-1771, decided July 5, 1987).

- United States Court of Appeals:

Haley v. United States, 739 F.2d 1502 (10th Cir. 1984).

- United States District Court:

Brady v. Hopper, 570 F. Supp. 1333 (D. Colo. 1983). A recent unreported case may be cited as *Hawks v. Ingersoll Johnson Steel Co., U.S. District Court, S.D. Ind., No. IP 82-793-C, Apr. 4, 1984,* OR Perry v. Rockwell Graphic Systems, __ F. Supp. __ (D. Mass. 1985).

§ 7.5.6   Legal citations—State court cases

In briefs and memorandums to be filed in state courts, federal and state cases should be cited to both the official reporter (e.g., *United States Reports, Vermont Reports, Oregon Reports*) and the unofficial reporter (e.g., *Supreme Court Reports, Lawyers' Edition, Atlantic Reporter, Pacific Reporter*).

EXAMPLE:

Quinn v. Southern Pacific Transportation Co., 76 Or. Ct. App. 617, 711 P.2d 139 (1986).

If a state does not publish opinions in an official reporter or has opted to report official opinions in the National Reporter System, the court must be identified in parentheses at the end of the citation, followed by the year of the decision.

EXAMPLE:

State v. Twoteeth, 711 P.2d 789, 794 (Mont. 1985).

When the court report identifies the state but not the court, the state abbreviation may be omitted in the parenthetical.

EXAMPLE:

Lang v. Lang, 109 Idaho 802, 711 P.2d 1322 (Ct. App. 1985).

Only the jurisdiction appears at the end of the citation if the court of decision is the highest court.

EXAMPLE:

Miller v. Ottman, 136 N.E.2d 17 (Ind. 1956).

If the jurisdiction is not the court of decision, cite as follows:

EXAMPLE:

Mathes v. Ireland, 419 N.E.2d 782 (Ind. Ct. App. 1981).

If the decision has just been filed and it does not appear in the state reporter, it may be cited in one of the following ways:

EXAMPLE:

Wing v. Martin, 688 P.2d 1172 (Idaho 1984), or

Wing v. Martin, __ Idaho __, 688 P.2d 1172 (1984), or

Wing v. Martin, 84 Idaho Supreme Court Reports [I.S.C.R. when cited in Idaho] 1117, 688 P.2d 1172 (Idaho 1984).

If the advance sheets are not yet available, cite as follows:

EXAMPLE:

Wing v. Martin, No. 14790, Idaho Supreme Court (Sept. 25, 1984), or

Wing v. Martin, __ Idaho __ (1984).

§ 7.5.7 Legal citations—Citation of constitutions, statutes, session laws, ordinances, rules, and other legal authorities

The following are accepted formats to cite to various authorities:

- **Constitutions**
  U.S. Const. Art. II, § 4, cl. 1.
  U.S. Const. amend. XIV, § 1.
  Idaho Const. art. I, § 3.
- **Federal Statutes**
  Official Code: 28 U.S.C. § 2105(a)(1) to (3) (1964).
  Uniform Commercial Code: U.C.C. § 4-109 (1962).
  Code of Federal Regulations: 24 C.F.R. § 202.13 (1949).
  Internal Revenue Code: I.R.C. § 12.
- **State Statutes**

Since the statutes are not cited the same way in all states, consult the most recent edition of *The Bluebook* for the correct way to cite state statutes. Examples of abbreviations for commonly cited state statutes should be placed in a procedures manual for future reference.

EXAMPLE:

> Wyo. Stat. § 7-13-904 (1977).

- **Federal Session Laws**
  United States Statutes at Large: Federal Land Policy and Management Act of 1976, 90 Stat. 2769, 43 U.S.C. § 1744 (1982).
- **State Session Laws**

Since the state session laws are not cited the same way in all states, consult the tables in *The Bluebook* for the correct way to cite individual state session laws and include the correct citation in a procedures manual for future reference. Always give the name of the statute and the public law or chapter number. If there is no official or popular name, identify the act with a full date.

EXAMPLES:

> Act of July 1, 1972, 535 ch. 202, 1972 Idaho Sess. Laws 535.
> Michigan Sesquicentennial Act of 1984, Pub. Act No. 266, 1984 Mich. Legis. Serv. 37 (West).

- **Ordinances**

Cite by name of code (including municipal unit, not abbreviated, followed by state, abbreviated), section, and year of publication of the code.

EXAMPLE:

> Chicago, Ill., Municipal Code § 155-1 (1931).

- **Miscellaneous Codes**
  Model Penal Code § 303.5 (1962).
- **Restatements**
  Restatement (Second) of Torts § 324A.
- **Federal Rules**
  Federal Rules of Civil Procedure: Fed. R. Civ. P. 23(b).
  Federal Rules of Criminal Procedure: Fed. R. Crim. P. 12.
- **State Rules**

Consult individual state codes to determine the correct way to cite the civil, criminal, and appellate rules in individual states and make a note in a procedures manual.

- **Jury Instructions**

Citation forms are usually suggested in the volumes cited. When citing a jury instruction in a foreign jurisdiction, a more detailed citation must be given for state jury instructions.

EXAMPLES:

> Ninth Circuit Court: Model Jury Instr., 9th Cir. 3.08.
> California Jury Instructions: BAJI (6th ed.) No. 4.01; CALJIC (4th ed.) No. 7.07.

Illinois Jury Instructions: IPI-Criminal 3d 20.02.

- **Legislative Materials**
  Bills
  Senate Bill: S. 507, 94th Cong., 1st Sess. § 311 (1975).
  House Bill: H.R. 507, 95th Cong., 1st Sess. (1977).
  Resolutions
  Senate Resolution: S. Res. 50, 99th Cong., 1st Sess. (1983).
  House Resolution: H.R. Res. 50, 98th Cong., 1st Sess. (1983).
- **Committee Hearings**

Give title of hearing (underlined or italicized) and add which Congress, which session, page, date, and attribution.
EXAMPLE:

Age Discrimination in Employment: Hearings on S. 830 and S. 788 before the Subcommittee on Labor of the Senate Committee on Labor and Public Welfare, 90th Cong., 1st Sess. 23 (1967) (statement of Sen. Javits).

- **Committee Reports**
  Senate Report: S.Rep. No. 583, 94th Cong., 1st Sess. 65 (1975).

EXAMPLES:

Criminal Code Reform Act of 1977: Report of the Committee on the Judiciary, United States Senate, to accompany S. 1437, S. Rep. No. 605, 95th Cong., 1st Sess. 911 (1977).

House Report: H.R. Rep. No. 1724, 94th Cong., 2d Sess. 62 (1976).

H.R. Rep. No. 805, 90th Cong., 1st Sess. 4 (1967), 123 Cong. Rec. 34295 (1977) (remarks of Sen. Williams).

H.R. Rep. No. 867, 97th Cong., 2d Sess. 7, *reprinted in* 1982 U.S. Code Cong. & Ad. News 3362.

- **Floor Debates**
  124 Cong. Rec. 8218–8219 (1978) (remarks of Sen. Javits).
- **Congressional Records (daily edition)**
  130 Cong. Rec. H1847–48 (daily ed. Mar. 21, 1984) (statement of Rep. Kindness).
- **Dictionaries**
  Black's Law Dictionary 912 (6th ed. 1991).
  Stedman's Medical Dictionary 783 (4th Unabridged Lawyers' Ed. 1976).
  Last Clear Chance, 7 Am. Jur. Proof of Facts (Supp. 1990 at 45).
  49 Am. Jur. 2d *Eviction* § 300 (1970).
  86 C.J.S., *Torts* § 61 n. 9.
- **Treatises**

Cite by volume (use arabic numerals); author (initial and last name); full title; serial number (if any); page, section, or paragraph; edition (if more than one); and year.

EXAMPLES:

R. Hunter, *Federal Trial Handbook* § 15.26 (1984).

2A A. Larson, *The Law of Workmen's Compensation* § 68.21 (1976).

● **Law Review Articles**

If written by a student, give a designation, such as *Note* or *Comment*, instead of a student author's name.

EXAMPLE:

Note, *Employee Handbooks and Employment-at-Will Contracts*, 1985 Duke L.J. 196 (1985).

Other authors are identified by last name only.

EXAMPLE:

Strauss, *Mining Claims on Public Lands: A Study of Interior Department Procedures,* 1974 Utah L. Rev. 185, 193, 215–19.

● **Services**

Services (cases, administrative materials, and brief commentaries that are published periodically in loose-leaf form) are cited by volume, abbreviated title, publisher, subdivision, and date.

EXAMPLES:

United States v. Leon, Search & Seizure L. Rep. (Clark Boardman) 53 (Aug. 1984).

O'Brien v. Dean Witter Reynolds, Inc., [Current Binder] Fed. Sec. L. Rep. (CCH) ¶ 91,509 (D. Ariz. 1984).

● **Periodicals**

Cite by author (last name only), title of article in full, volume number of periodical, name of periodical found on title page (abbreviated), page on which article begins (and page or pages specifically referred to), and year of publication.

EXAMPLE:

Rothstein, *Amendments to the Federal Rules of Criminal Procedure,* 69 A.B.A. J. 1938 (1983).

● **Annotations**

Give the date of the volume, not of the case.

EXAMPLES:

American Law Reports, Fourth Edition: Annot., 41 A.L.R. 4th 131 (1985).

American Law Reports, Federal: Annot., 74 A.L.R. Fed. 505 (1985).

§ 7.5.8 Legal citations—Citation style rules

The following are rules for citation abbreviations, spacing, punctuation, capitalization, numbers, quotations, sections and subdivisions, and underlining.

- **Abbreviations**

And is always abbreviated to &.

Abbreviations for states, months of the year, subdivisions, and some reporters are included at the end of this chapter. A table of frequently used American abbreviations is found in *The Bluebook*.

- **Spacing**

A space should precede and follow all abbreviations that consist of more than one letter and the ampersand; close up single capitals.

> EXAMPLES:
> Ariz. St. L.J. [Arizona State Law Journal].
> Fla. St. U.L. Rev. [Florida State University Law Review].

An exception to the spacing rule is when an entity is abbreviated by widely recognized initials and a combination of those initials with others would be confusing.

> EXAMPLE:
> A.B.A. J. [American Bar Association Journal].

There must be a space between the symbols $§$ and ¶ and a number.

- **Punctuation**

Periods may be omitted from widely recognized initials that are read out loud as initials (NLRB, CBS, IRS) in case names but not when they refer to reporters, codes, or courts. If initials are read as words (N.D., S.C.), the periods should not be omitted.

A comma should not precede *note*, *n.*, and *nn*.

A comma should not precede the symbols $§$ and ¶ unless preceded by a number.

Multiple citations in a sentence are separated by semicolons.

Commas and periods are always placed inside quotation marks. All other punctuation is placed outside unless it is part of the quoted material.

Citations should never appear within parentheses.

- **Capitalization**

Generally, follow the "Guide to Capitalization" in the *United States Government Printing Office Style Manual*.

Act, *bill*, *rule*, *statute*, and so forth, are capitalized only when used as part of a proper name given in full.

Court is capitalized only when naming a specific court, when referring to the United States Supreme Court, or when referring to the presiding judge in a specific action.

Circuit is capitalized only when used with a circuit number.

Constitution is capitalized only when used in the full name of a constitution or when referring to the Constitution of the United States. Parts of a constitution, such as amendments, are not capitalized.

Judge and *justice* are capitalized only when giving the name of the judge or justice or when referring to the Chief Justice of the United States Supreme Court.

The abbreviation for number (*No.*) is always capitalized.

When used alone, a word that refers to people or groups is capitalized only when it is used as the shortened form of a specific group or body.

> EXAMPLE:
> The Free-Thinkers Consolidated Dogmatists (the "Dogmatists")

• Numbers

Spell out the numbers zero to 99 in text and zero to nine in footnotes.

Spell out all numbers that begin a sentence.

Round numbers may be spelled out (e.g., *three hundred*).

Use numerals in a series that contain any numbers.

Use numerals for numbers that include decimal points.

Do not use periods after 1st, 2d, 3d, 4th, and so forth.

Pages may be cited as follows:

> EXAMPLES:
> Pages 416 through 433: 416–33
> Pages 1476 through 1517: 1476–517

Sections must be cited as follows:

> EXAMPLES:
> Sections 416 through 433: 416–33
> Sections 1476 through 1517: 1476–517

• Quotations

Quotations of 50 or more words are usually block indented, and quotation marks should not be used. Quotations of 49 or fewer words should be enclosed in quotation marks but not set off from the rest of the text. Commas and periods are always placed inside the quotation marks.

EXAMPLE:

> This is an example of how a quotation of 50 or more words should be block indented with no quotations marks.

When a letter in a quotation is changed from lower to upper case or from upper case to lower case, enclose it in brackets. All substituted words or letters and added material should be placed in brackets.

Do not use ellipses to begin a quotation or when a word is merely altered. An omission of language from the middle of a quoted sentence is indicated by three periods separated by spaces between them. A fourth period is used to indicate the end of a sentence. Do not indicate deleted material after a period or other final punctuation that ends the quotation.

Indicate paragraph structure by indenting the first line of a paragraph. If the quotation begins in the middle of a paragraph, do not indent the first line. Omission of one or more paragraphs is indicated by inserting and indenting four periods on a separate line. Mistakes in the original of quoted material should be followed by *[sic]*.

The citation following its source should not be indented. It should appear at the left margin immediately following the quotation. Omitted footnotes, omitted citations, and change in emphasis of certain words in a quotation should be indicated in a parenthetical after the citation.

- **Sections and Subdivisions**

The following demonstrates the proper way to cite sections and section subdivisions in citations (do not use section symbols in text).

> EXAMPLES:
> Section 1414: § 1414
> Section 1414 through section 1452: §§ 1414–1452
> Section 1414, subsections a and 3: § 1414(a)(3)
> Sections 2.15-312, 2.15-314, and 2.15-320:
> §§ 2.15-312, -314, -320 [drop identical digits preceding a common punctuation mark]

Subdivision designations should be enclosed in parentheses even if printed in the source without.

> EXAMPLE:
> § 145(a)(1)(iii)

- **Underlining**

In briefs and legal memoranda underline or italicize:
> Case names
> Book and treatise titles
> Titles of articles in periodicals and newspapers

Congressional publications (including committee hearings)

When referring to a publication rather than citing to it (*Yale Law Journal, Pacific Reporter,* and so forth)

Names of titles or topics within encyclopedias

Introductory signals (*e.g., See,* etc.)

Id. and *supra*

The letter *l* when it is used to identify a subsection so it will not be confused with the number *1*

Letters used to designate people in hypothetical situations (A filed suit against B)

Foreign words not incorporated into the English language

For emphasis

EXAMPLES:

Case name: *In re XYZ Corp.*

Book and treatise title: *Black's Law Dictionary*

Extend the underscore beneath the period ending an abbreviation. Do not extend the underscore beneath the period that ends a sentence.

§ 7.5.9   Legal citations—Abbreviations for reporters, states, months of the year, and subdivisions

The following are rules for abbreviations for reporters, states, months of the year, and subdivisions.

Reports

American Law Reports Annotated	A.L.R.
American Law Reports Annotated, Second Series	A.L.R.2d
American Law Reports Annotated, Third Series	A.L.R.3d
Atlantic Reporter	A.
Atlantic Reporter, Second Series	A.2d
Bankruptcy Reporter	B.R.
California Appellate Reports	Cal. App.
California Appellate Reports, Second Series	Cal. App. 2d
California Reporter	Cal. Rptr.
Court of Customs and Patent Decisions	Dec. Com. Pat.
Court of Customs and Patent Appeals Reports	C.C.P.A.
Federal Cases	F. Cas.
Federal Reporter	F.
Federal Reporter, Second Series	F.2d
Federal Rules Decisions	F.R.D.

Federal Supplement	F. Supp.
Lawyers' Edition, United States Supreme Court Reports	L. Ed.
Lawyers' Edition, United States Supreme Court Reports, Second Series	L. Ed. 2d
Lawyers Reports, Annotated	L.R.A.
Lawyers Reports, Annotated, New Series	L.R.A. (n.s.)
Negligence Cases (CCH)	Negl. Cas.
Negligence Cases, Second Series (CCH)	Negl. Cas. 2d
New York Criminal Reports	N.Y. Crim.
New York Supplement	N.Y.S.
New York Supplement, Second Series	N.Y.S.2d
North Eastern Reporter	N.E.
North Eastern Reporter, Second Series	N.E.2d
North Western Reporter	N.W.
North Western Reporter, Second Series	N.W.2d
Pacific Reporter	P.
Pacific Reporter, Second Series	P.2d
South Eastern Reporter	S.E.
South Eastern Reporter, Second Series	S.E.2d
South Western Reporter	S.W.
South Western Reporter, Second Series	S.W.2d
Southern Reporter	So.
Southern Reporter, Second Series	So. 2d
Supreme Court Reporter [United States]	S. Ct.
United States Supreme Court Reports	U.S.
United States Tax Cases	T.C.

States

Ala.	Mont.
Alaska	Neb.
Ariz.	Nev.
Ark.	N.H.
Cal.	N.J.
Colo.	N.M.
Conn.	N.Y.
Del.	N.C.
D.C.	N.D.
Fla.	Ohio
Ga.	Okla.

Haw.	Or.
Idaho	Pa.
Ill.	R.I.
Ind.	S.C.
Iowa	S.D.
Kan.	Tenn.
Ky.	Tex.
La.	Utah
Me.	Vt.
Md.	Va.
Mass.	Wash.
Mich.	W. Va.
Minn.	Wis.
Miss.	Wyo.
Mo.	

Months of the Year

Jan.	July
Feb.	Aug.
Mar.	Sept.
Apr.	Oct.
May	Nov.
June	Dec.

Subdivisions

The following terms are always abbreviated as indicated below in full citations, but never in text—except that *section* is written § in textual footnotes when followed by the number of the section and not the first word of a sentence:

amendment(s)	amend., amends.
appendix(es)	app., apps.
article(s)	art., arts.
book(s)	bk., bks.
chapter(s)	ch., chs.
clause(s)	cl., cls.
column(s)	col., cols.
folio(s)	fol., fols.
footnote(s)	n., nn.

number(s)	No., Nos.
page(s)	p., pp. [or, at]
paragraph(s), subparagraph(s)	para., paras., ¶ , ¶¶
part(s)	pt., pts.
section(s), subsection(s)	§ , §§ [space between § and number]
series, serial(s)	ser.
title(s)	tit., tits.
volume(s)	vol., vols.

§ 7.6   Citing electronic media and other nonprint resources

Commercial Electronic Databases. Cases found in Westlaw and LexisNexis should be cited, providing the case name, docket number, database identifier, court name, and full date of the most recent major disposition of the case. The database identifier must contain enough information for a reader to identify the database and find the case. If the database has identifying codes or numbers that uniquely identify the case, these must be given. Screen or page numbers should be preceded by an asterisk; paragraph numbers should be preceded by a paragraph symbol.

EXAMPLES:
United States v. Carlisle, No. 90-2465SI, 1991 U.S. App. LEXIS 5863, at *3 (8th Cir. Apr. 10, 1991) (per curiam).
Clark v. Homrighous, CIV.A. 90-1380-T, 1991 WL 55402, at *3 (D. Kan. Apr. 10, 1991).

When citing a code contained in an electronic database, give parenthetically the name of the database and information regarding the currency of the database as provided by the database itself. Also give the name of the publisher, editor, or compiler unless the code is published, edited, compiled by, or under the supervision of, federal or state officials:

EXAMPLES:
CAL. BUS. & PROF. CODE § 1670 (Deering, LEXIS through 1995 Sess.).
CAL. BUS. & PROF. CODE § 1670 (West, Westlaw through 1995 portion of 1995 to 96 Legis. Sess.).

When citing legislative, administrative, and executive materials contained in a commercial electronic database, give the name of the database and any identifying codes or numbers that uniquely identify the material as shown in the following list:

- Federal bill (unenacted)—H.R. 3781, 104th Cong. § 2(b) (1976), WL 1996 CONG US HR 3781.
- Federal report—H.R. Rep. No. 92098 (1971), reprinted in 1971 U.S.C.C.A.N. 1071, 1971 WL 11312.
- Congressional debate—142 Cong. Rec. H11460 (daily ed. Sept. 27, 1996) (statement of Rep. Tanner). LEXIS 142 Cong Rec H11452p*11460.
- Federal regulation cited to *Code of Federal Regulations*—FTC Credit Practices Rule, 16 C.F.R. § 444.1 (2000), WL 16 C.F.R. § 444.1.
- Administrative adjudication—Reichold Chems., Inc., 91 F.T.C. 246 (1978), WL 91 F.T.C. 246.
- Formal advisory opinion—39 Op. Att'y Gen. 484 (1940), 1940 US AG LEXIS 16.
- Revenue ruling—Rev. Rul. 86-71, 1986-1 C.B. 102, 1986 IRB LEXIS 189.

When citing secondary materials to a database, provide a complete citation, a citation to the database, and the unique identifier or code to each document within the database. When accessing a traditional source as well as a commercial electronic database, you may use *available at* to provide increased accessibility; if using only the commercial database, no explanatory note should be used.

Elements of Internet Citation. The citation of information to Internet sources should indicate clearly and unambiguously the source actually used or accessed by the author of the citing work. The general rules of citation and style apply to such citations, and they should be provided in the form and typeface applicable to that source, with the exception of the URL. The following elements should be included in such citations:

- Available information about the authority being cited
- Appropriate explanatory phrase to indicate which source actually used by the author
- The provider responsible for the Internet site, where not apparent from the Uniform Resource Locator (URL)
- The URL
- A date parenthetical
- Any explanatory parenthetical

If only the Internet is accessed, provide the traditional and Internet citations, such as *New York v. McArthur, No. N4-999-501* (N.Y. Ct. App. Sept. 28, 1999), http://www.courts.state.ny.us/library/archive/cta pun/9909/501.htm.

If material is found exclusively on the Internet, use the explanatory phrase *at*, such as J.T. Weiss, *Ethical Issues for the Millenium*, 6 RICH. J.L. & TECH. 5, ¶ 7 (2000), at http://www.richmond.edu/jolt/v 61l/weiss.html.

An accurate URL is necessary for citation of Internet information. The URL also may provide information that may not be available on the site itself. The URL should appear in regular roman typeface, without angled brackets. Following is a typical breakdown of a URL for an Internet source:

http protocol (Hypertext Transfer Protocol), followed by:// (colon, double slash).

www World Wide Web server, followed by a period.

edf the organization presenting the information (here Environmental Defense Fund), followed by a period.

org designation that the provider is an organization, followed by a slash where other information is provided. Other provider designators include *com* for commercial providers, *edu* for educational institutions, and *gov* for governmental organizations.

Constitutions, statutes, legislative material, administrative and executive materials must be cited first to a traditional source or electronic database. Books, journals, magazines and other secondary sources, such as news reports, newspapers, and other nonlegal publications should be cited first to a traditional source, except an Internet source may be cited where information is not available in a traditional source or electronic database.

Citation of email. In citing email messages, include the date of the message. Archival information may be included parenthetically, but the email addresses of the sender and recipient are not required. They may be included if there is a reason for doing so.

Microform citation. When a document is reproduced in microform, this fact need not be indicated unless it would otherwise be difficult for a reader to identify and obtain the source. If necessary to cite to material on microform, provide a complete citation to the original document and a citation to the microform, including a unique identifier or code if one has been assigned. Include the name of the publisher of the microform series in parentheses.

Citation of films, broadcasts, and videotape. If citing films, broadcasts, and noncommercial videotapes, cite films in large and small capitals, and television or radio broadcasts in italics, by exact date, including the name of the company or network that produced or aired the film or broadcast. Cite videotapes containing images that have not been commercially displayed or broadcast by the title of the tape, the name of the person or institution that produced the video, and the year of production.

Citation of audio recordings. Commercial audio recordings should be cited by artist and title, providing the name of the recording company and the date of release. For noncommercial audio recordings, use ordinary roman type and indicate where a copy may be obtained.

Short form citations. Short form of citations should be styled as follows:

- Commercial electronic databases—use a unique database identifier, if one has been assigned.

  EXAMPLES:
  Tierney v. Mace, CIV.A. 90-1830-T, 1991 WL 5530, at *1 (D. Kan. Apr. 1, 2001) BECOMES *Tierney*, 1991 WL 5530, at *1

- Microform—use the short form appropriate for the original document—it is not necessary to indicate the source once it has been given in the first full citation.
- Internet—use the short form appropriate for the original document, including the URL or Internet address.
- Films, broadcasts, and audio recordings—*id.* and *supra* may be used when citing films, broadcasts, and audio recordings.

§ 7.7 Summary

Initially, this material may seem difficult and overwhelming, but the more one studies, uses, and/or is exposed to legal citations and legal citation formats, the more competent and confident one will become in typing and writing them. Also, bear in mind that although the exhaustive lists covered in the previous sections address nearly every situation, one can work a lifetime and never encounter a citation more complicated than that used for case law. However, it is still worthwhile to have a broad general knowledge of the various citation formats in order to be prepared for any situation in which they may be needed.

Chapter 8

The Law Library

> **KeyCite®:** Cases and other legal materials listed in KeyCite Scope can be researched through the KeyCite service on Westlaw®. Use KeyCite to check citations for form, parallel references, prior and later history, and comprehensive citator information, including citations to other decisions and secondary materials.

§ 8.1 Legal research and the law library

The essential job of the lawyer is to answer the question, "How does the applicable law apply to my client's legal problem?" For example, the client may ask the lawyer, "Now that my daughter has turned 18 and no longer receives child support, can I get a court to order my ex-husband to help pay her college expenses?" Legal education and law practice equip the lawyer to find and interpret the law applicable to the question at hand. To help the client get help with her daughter's college expenses, the lawyer must find some basis in existing law for the court to award such support.

Finding the law requires access to any constitutional provisions, statutes, regulations, case law, or other legal authority that may apply. Traditionally, lawyers have relied on libraries of printed legal resources to provide access to such authorities. It is extremely expensive, however, for a lawyer to buy and maintain a comprehensive law library of all the federal and state statutes, regulations, and cases that may be needed. Accordingly, many lawyers rely heavily on evaluated free online resources, public or academic law libraries for access to legal resources. Increasingly, lawyers also subscribe to commercial online services (such as lexisnexis.com and Westlaw), and the Internet for access to federal, state, and local law. Lawyers will also network through local, state, and federal bar associations as an additional source of information.

§ 8.2 Authority

When a lawyer asks a court to rule in favor of the lawyer's client in a given matter, the lawyer argues on the basis of some form of legal authority. The universe of legal authority is divided into two classes: primary legal authority and secondary legal authority.

§ 8.2.1 Authority—Primary legal authority

Primary legal authority is the law itself, as it is given in constitutional provisions, statutes, administrative regulations, municipal and county codes, published judicial decisions, court rules, etc. Primary law can issue from any governmental body legally empowered to create rules governing the conduct of others.

Federal and state governments conduct themselves in accordance with their own written constitutions. The United States Congress and individual state legislatures enact statutes to order the affairs of the people to the extent permitted by the applicable constitution. Federal and state administrative agencies issue regulations on matters entrusted by statute to their supervision. Counties and cities enact ordinances by which to govern themselves. All of these documents are samples of primary law.

Appellate courts create *case law* or judge-made law, a special kind of primary law. Imagine a fictional court case:

> The state of Washington sues the federal government in the United States District Court for the Eastern District of Washington, claiming that, under the federal Clean Water Act, the federal government should have to pay for cleaning up groundwater contamination due to radioactive waste. The radioactive waste has migrated from the Hanford Nuclear Reservation to adjacent land owned by the state of Washington. The federal government claims that it is not subject to suit under the Clean Water Act and brings a motion to dismiss Washington's lawsuit. The federal district court grants the motion to dismiss and publishes a written opinion explaining its rationale. The state of Washington then appeals the case to the United States Court of Appeals for the Ninth Circuit, claiming that the district court misinterpreted the Clean Water Act. In a written opinion, the Ninth Circuit reverses the district court's order and holds that the federal government is, in fact, subject to suit under the Clean Water Act. The federal government then appeals the Ninth Circuit decision to the United States Supreme Court, which, in its own written opinion, reverses the Ninth Circuit's decision and reinstates the district court's opinion.

The written opinions prepared by each court in this example are referred to as *case law*. Case law is the primary law created by courts; it is an important guide to the interpretation of other forms of primary law because courts are so often called upon to interpret constitutional provisions, statutes, and regulations.

§ 8.2.2 Authority—Mandatory versus persuasive primary legal authority

In the context of a particular legal dispute, primary legal authority can be subdivided into two kinds: mandatory and persuasive.

Mandatory legal authority is the primary law that the court is obligated to follow. Thus, in an action for child support, a court may not award support beyond the child's 18th birthday if the applicable state statute clearly terminates the parent's support obligation when the child turns 18. That state statute is the mandatory legal authority applicable to the case, and the court must follow it, regardless of whether every other state in the country permits postmajority support. In researching any legal question, the lawyer's first obligation is to identify and understand the mandatory primary law applicable to the case.

The mandatory legal authority applicable to the case, however, may be ambiguous. In such cases, a court may look to *persuasive legal authority* as a guide in interpreting the applicable law. For example, a court may consider judicial interpretations of analogous federal or state statutes from other jurisdictions. The applicable child support statute may not speak directly to the issue of postmajority support. In such a case, the court might consider whether other similarly worded statutes from other states have been interpreted to permit child support beyond the child's 18th birthday. Generally speaking, a court is not bound by the statutes of other states, but judicial opinions construing them may be persuasive on the question of whether the statute at issue should be interpreted to permit postmajority support.

§ 8.2.3 Authority—Secondary legal authority

Secondary legal authority refers to published legal analyses that are about the law. Unlike primary law, secondary legal authority does not purport to be the law itself.

For example, a lawyer may wish to help a client understand the legal effect of a clause in a contract that the client is about to sign. The lawyer may consult a treatise on contracts for a discussion of judicial decisions interpreting similar contract terms. In addition to providing a better understanding of contract law, the treatise may help the lawyer find cases supporting an interpretation favorable to the client's interests in the matter. Ideally, the lawyer will find favorable cases from the highest court of the jurisdiction in question (which will be mandatory authority on the issue at hand). In this fashion, lawyers use secondary legal authority to find and understand the primary law relevant to a client's question.

Secondary authorities include legal encyclopedias, treatises, practice guides, sets of annotated statutes, law review articles, even short articles in local bar journals. Courts occasionally rule in accordance with the opinions expressed by authors of secondary legal material, especially when the author is well respected and there seems to be no rule of primary law directly applicable to the case. Courts are not required, however, to follow the opinions expressed in secondary legal material because such authority is persuasive rather than mandatory.

§ 8.3 The hierarchy of legal authority

Under the *supremacy clause* of the United States Constitution, the Constitution is the supreme law of the land. Neither Congress nor a state legislature may enact laws that conflict with the Constitution.

The states enjoy authority to adopt their own constitutions, statutes, and administrative regulations, as long as those laws do not contradict federal law. As at the federal level, there is a hierarchy of authority within state law: no state legislature has the power to enact a statute that violates that state's constitution; no state administrative agency has the power to promulgate a regulation that violates a state statute.

There is a similar hierarchy of judicial authority. If, for example, a court case raises a federal constitutional question, then the court will look first to any United States Supreme Court decisions concerning the constitutional provision in question. A Supreme Court case concerning the precise constitutional question at hand is mandatory. The court will simply apply the Supreme Court's analysis and dispose of the question accordingly. Case law from lower federal courts (a United States Court of Appeals or federal district court, for example) may be persuasive, but such opinions are not mandatory if the Supreme Court has already spoken to the issue. A parallel hierarchy exists at the state court level.

§ 8.3.1 The hierarchy of legal authority—Constitutions

The organization of the government—federal and state—and the rules for its operation are established by the U.S. and state constitutions.

§ 8.3.2 The hierarchy of legal authority—Statutes

The legislative branches of government enact statutes and codes. At the end of each legislative session—federal or state—the acts are published in chronological order.

After a legislative session has adjourned, the laws passed during that session are compiled in volumes called *session laws*. These books contain the full text of each new law. The acts appear in the session laws in the order in which they were passed during the session. The session laws enacted by Congress are called *Statutes at Large*. The session laws enacted by a state legislature are given titles such as *Laws of Washington, 1998*.

The laws published in the session law volumes are codified according to subject matter. Codification places or inserts the provisions of the new law in the existing state code according to the topic(s) that the new law addresses. Thus, Title 26 of the United States Code contains the Internal Revenue Code. A new law amending some aspect of the Internal Revenue Code will be codified in the pertinent section of Title 26. Frequently, different aspects of a particular session law will amend several different areas of the law. For example, a new session law amending the Internal Revenue Code may also include criminal enforcement provisions that belong in Title 18 ("Crimes and Criminal Procedure") of the United States Code. Accordingly, individual provisions of a particular session law may be assigned to a variety of titles within the pertinent code.

Codification enables the legal researcher to find the law relevant to a given legal question because codes organize legislation in a hierarchical fashion by subject matter. In addition to topical organization, federal and state codes have indexes and other tools to enable the researcher to find all of the provisions relating to a particular subject.

§ 8.3.3 The hierarchy of legal authority—Ordinances

Local *ordinances* are similar to state statutes. In fact, they can be thought of as local statutes. Towns and cities usually come into existence with state government approval, either under a specific act dealing with each municipality or under general authority which sets out the procedure for incorporation by a municipality. When a town or city is recognized as a municipality, that recognition carries with it the right to enact certain legislation. Usually, municipalities adopt their own traffic ordinances, zoning ordinances, tax ordinances, Sunday closing laws (blue laws), and other laws of that nature. They usually develop their own election procedures and their own licensing procedures as well.

§ 8.3.4　The hierarchy of legal authority—Administrative regulations

Federal and state administrative agencies develop and administer programs entrusted to them by statute. Thus, the Social Security Act created the Social Security Administration and authorized it to promulgate rules to carry out its statutory mandate. Legislative bodies lack the time and the expertise to enact statutes which are comprehensive enough to govern administrative agencies. So, Congress and state legislatures delegate rule-making authority to the agencies themselves. Administrative regulations are legally binding, despite the fact that such rules are not enacted by elected officials.

On the federal level, new administrative regulations appear in the *Federal Register*, which is published daily. Online access to the regulations is also available through the GPO's Federal Digital System (https://www.federalregister.gov/). Just as new session laws are ultimately organized by topic in the applicable code, federal regulations are then codified by subject matter within the *Code of Federal Regulations*. A parallel scheme exists on the state level: new administrative rules appear first in a register published by the state and then are organized by subject matter into an administrative code. To make sure that an existing regulation is current, the legal researcher must understand how to check the pertinent register for changes in the regulation that have occurred since publication of the most recent administrative code.

§ 8.3.5　The hierarchy of legal authority—Court rules

Each court may adopt rules for conducting business before the court. Usually these rules deal with the mechanical processes of prosecuting and defending a legal matter.

§ 8.3.6　The hierarchy of legal authority—Judicial decisions

Every federal and state appellate court issues judicial decisions. In general, trial courts at the state level do not publish written opinions. The federal district courts, the trial courts of the federal judiciary, however, do publish many of their decisions.

The decisions of a particular court are published in books called *reporters*. The decisions of the United States Supreme Court, for example, are published by the federal government in a series entitled the *United States Reports*. United States Supreme Court cases are also published by private legal publishers, notably the *Supreme Court Reporter* by Thomson Reuters and the *United States Supreme Court Reports, Lawyers' Edition* by Michie (LexisNexis). Decisions of the 13 United States circuit courts of appeal are reported in the *Federal Reporter* (citation abbreviation forms are F., F.2d, and F.3d). The *Federal Supplement* contains many reported decisions of the United States District Courts (cited as F. Supp. and F. Supp. 2d). The *Federal Appendix* contains selected unreported decisions of the U.S. District Courts (cited as F. App.) Federal district court cases dealing primarily with the construction of the federal rules are reported in *Federal Rules Decisions* (cited as F.R.D.).

At one time each state published its own reports, and those reports were known as official reports. Thomson Reuters published reports containing the same cases as unofficial reports. However, an increasing number of states have discontinued publishing their own reports and rely solely on the National Reporter System. Thomson Reuters does publish separately the official reports of some of the states, and about one-fourth of the states that no longer publish their own official reports have officially adopted or rely on the decisions reported in the Thomson Reuters regional reporters.

Thomson Reuters publishes all reported out-of-state appellate court decisions in the United States. These state appellate court decisions are published by Thomson Reuters in regional reporters. At present, the National Reporter System is comprised of seven regional reporters as follows:

> **Atlantic.** Maine, Vermont, New Hampshire, Connecticut, Rhode Island, Pennsylvania, New Jersey, Delaware, Maryland, District of Columbia;
> **North Eastern.** Illinois, Indiana, Massachusetts, New York, Ohio;
> **North Western.** North Dakota, South Dakota, Nebraska, Minnesota, Iowa, Wisconsin, Michigan;
> **Pacific.** Washington, Oregon, California, Idaho, Nevada, Montana, Wyoming, Utah, Arizona, New Mexico, Colorado, Kansas, Oklahoma, Alaska, Hawaii;
> **Southern.** Louisiana, Mississippi, Alabama, Florida;
> **South Eastern.** West Virginia, Virginia, North Carolina, South Carolina, Georgia;
> **South Western.** Texas, Missouri, Arkansas, Kentucky, Tennessee.

(See Illustration 8-1.)

For court opinions issued prior to the beginning of the National Reporter System in 1880, one must consult older volumes of official state reports or the set called *Federal Cases* for lower federal courts.

Illustration 8-1

States Included

Pacific: AK, AZ, CA, CO, HI, ID, KS, MT, NV, NM, OK, OR, UT, WA, WY

North Western: IA, MI, MN, NE, ND, SD, WI

South Western: AR, KY, MO, TN, TX

North Eastern: IL, IN, MA, NY, OH

Southern: AL, FL, LA, MS

South Eastern: GA, NC, SC, VA, WV

Atlantic: CT, DE, DC, ME, MD, NJ, PA, RI, VT

Regional Reporters (State Cases)

Pacific | North Western | South Western | North Eastern | Southern | South Eastern | Atlantic

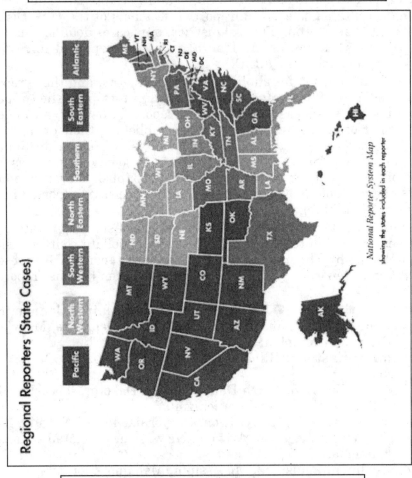

National Reporter System Map
showing the states included in each reporter

Current Reporter

Pacific: P.3d
(2000 – present)

Northwestern: N.W.2d
(1941 – present)

Southwestern: S.W.3d
(1999 – present)

North Eastern: N.E.2d
(1936 – present)

Southern: So.3d
(2009 – present)

South Eastern: S.E.2d
(1938 – present)

Atlantic: A.3d
(2010 – present)

The reporter listed next to the states includes all appellate decisions from those states.

§ 8.3.7   The hierarchy of legal authority—The decision

A *decision* published in a case law reporter is the opinion of the court, written by one of the judges. It is the decision of the court, resolving legal issues properly presented to it, which constitutes primary legal authority.

Rules of citation dictate how judicial decisions should be identified. When a lawyer wants to cite to a judicial decision in a brief, for example, the lawyer sets forth the name of the case, the volume of the reporter in which it appears, the page on which the decision begins, and the year the opinion was issued. For example, the United States Supreme Court opinion in *Roe v. Wade* begins at page 113 of volume 410 of the United States Reports. Thus, the citation for the case is *Roe v. Wade*, 410 U.S. 113 (1973). Please note some state and federal jurisdictions permit the citation of permitted unpublished decisions and citing these cases would not follow the format outlined above.

§ 8.4   The role of case citators in legal research

Case law is dynamic. For example, the United States Supreme Court may reverse a decision by a United States Court of Appeals. With the stroke of a pen, the Supreme Court can thus invalidate a decision in the Ninth Circuit. Persuasive or mandatory case law that has not been reversed or overruled is called *good law* and may be used to support arguments in pleadings. Once the case has been reversed or overruled, it is no longer good law, and it would be inappropriate for a lawyer to offer such a decision as authority before any court, although the history of the case may be discussed as being illustrative in some arguments.

Admittedly, most appellate decisions are never reversed (by a higher court) or overruled (by a subsequent court with appropriate authority). The meaning of an individual case may change dramatically, however, as subsequent judicial decisions discuss, interpret, refine, and apply that case in new circumstances. Thus, for example, to fully understand the United States Supreme Court's decision in *Roe v. Wade*, the careful legal researcher considers how that decision has been subsequently construed by the Supreme Court and by any lower court the decisions of which would be mandatory authority in the case at hand. Accordingly, a legal researcher must examine the subsequent history of any case they intend to cite as authority for a particular proposition.

Online publication tools called citators help the lawyer with this task by listing the citations to all of the judicial decisions that have cited a given case. Citators assign treatment codes to the subsequent citations, so that the lawyer can tell at a glance whether the case in question *followed, distinguished, explained, questioned, criticized,* or *overruled* the cited case.

§ 8.4.1   The role of case citators in legal research— Sheparding

The Shepard's Company, now owned by LexisNexis, is the oldest and best-known publisher of American legal citation services. Until quite recently, the Shepard's Company enjoyed a near monopoly in the publication of case citators. For this reason, generations of lawyers have referred to the process of researching the subsequent history of a case as *Sheparding*.

A Shepard's citator is published for each of the federal court reporters, Thomson Reuters regional reporters, and the individual state court reporters. Shepard's also offers citation services for federal and state constitutional provisions, statutes, administrative regulations, court rules, etc. These services provide lists of cases construing such provisions.

In addition to helping the legal researcher verify that a case remains good law, case citators identify subsequent decisions that may provide additional support for the position the lawyer wants to take. All things being equal, a recent decision from the United States Supreme Court reaffirming a principle established by an earlier decision is more powerful authority than the earlier decision standing alone.

§ 8.4.2   The role of case citators in legal research—Electronic citation services

Shepard's. *Sheparding* a case in the print volumes of Shepard's citators is a cumbersome, time-consuming task. Volumes of Shepard's citators do not cumulate. To Shepardize a case, the researcher must typically consult a bound volume of citations for the reporter in question as well as a series of supplements, each one more current than the last. To make a complete list of all cited cases, the researcher must: (1) find a library that has the Shepard's reports for the case reporter in question, (2) identify and collect all of the appropriate bound volumes and supplements, (3) mark the relevant pages, and (4) take them all to the copy machine. Then, there is the task of locating and reading the cases on the Shepard's cite-list.

The process of Sheparding cases became much easier when Shepard's created an electronic version of its library of citators. The Shepard's electronic service is only available on lexisnexis.com. Sheparding a case on lexisnexis.com involves little more than simply typing its citation. Only a mouse click is required to print the entire Shepard's report for a case. The electronic version of Shepard's also allows the researcher to customize the Shepard's report, limiting it, for example, to cases of a particular jurisdiction, cases published after a certain date, cases dealing with a specific aspect of the opinion, etc. The version of Shepard's available through lexisnexis.com even creates hypertext links between the citations listed on the Shepard's report and the cases themselves, enabling the legal researcher to move easily from the Shepard's report to the text of a case listed on the report and back again. These links are a valuable service for the lawyer who lacks convenient access to a comprehensive law library. Finally, the Shepard's service available through lexisnexis.com purports to be even more current than the print version.

Shepardizing cases online is so much faster, more current, and more reliable than Shepardizing cases using the books. Most new law school graduates lack any substantial experience with Shepardizing in the traditional way (law students typically enjoy unlimited free access to lexisnexis.com and Westlaw). In general, this is advantageous, because Shepardizing cases online is almost always more cost-effective than using the books. This lack of experience can represent a handicap, however, for new lawyers who find themselves in law offices that lack electronic access to Shepard's citation services.

However, in recent years, many law firms, law schools, and courts have discontinued their subscriptions to the print version of the Shepard's citators. This trend has influenced a growing number of law schools to discontinue teaching the use of the print process for Shepardizing.

§ 8.4.3   The role of case citators in legal research—Headnotes

When the publisher receives a decision from a court, its staff attorneys review it for the points of law decided in that case. A brief summary of each point of law is then written, and these summaries, called **headnotes**, appear at the beginning of each reported case.

§ 8.4.4   The role of case citators in legal research—Topic and Key Number System

The Topic and Key Number System is a master index of case headnotes. Thomson Reuters has devised a list of over 400 general areas of law and has further divided each of these topics into a numbered outline called *key numbers*. Every headnote composed by a Thomson Retuers editor is assigned a topic and key number. The headnotes appear at the beginning of the reported case with the topic and key number designation and are then collected by topic, or subject, in the digests. Once researchers have identified the pertinent topic and key number that collects headnotes on the point of law being researched, they can consult any unit of the American Digest System to locate additional cases on point. Key numbers provide a subject-based way to research case law and can be used in print digests or on Westlaw.

§ 8.4.5   The role of case citators in legal research—American Law Reports

American Law Reports (cited as A.L.R.), originally a selective approach to court reports, is used today for the annotations or legal memoranda following the reported case. Each annotation focuses on a specialized issue of law and summarizes pertinent cases and other authority from all jurisdictions. *American Law Reports* annotations are located through the *American Law Reports Index, American Jurisprudence*, Shepard's citators, and other cross-references.

Illustration 8-2

OUTLINE OF THE LAW

Digest Topics are arranged for your convenience by Seven Main Divisions of Law.
Complete alphabetical list of Digest Topics with topic numbers follows this section.

---

1. PERSONS
2. PROPERTY
3. CONTRACTS
4. TORTS
5. CRIMES
6. REMEDIES
7. GOVERNMENT

1. PERSONS

RELATING TO NATURAL PERSONS IN GENERAL

Civil Rights
Dead Bodies
Death
Domicile
Food
Health
Holidays
Intoxicating Liquors
Names
Seals
Signatures
Sunday
Time
Weapons

PARTICULAR CLASSES OF NATURAL PERSONS

Absentees
Aliens, Immigration, and Citizenship
Chemical Dependents
Children Out-of Wedlock
Convicts
Indians
Infants
Mental Health
Slaves
Spendthrifts

PERSONAL RELATIONS

Adoption
Attorney and Client
Child Custody
Child Support
Executors and Administrators
Guardian and Ward
Husband and Wife
Labor and Employment
Marriage
Parent and Child
Principal and Agent
Workers' Compensation

ASSOCIATED AND ARTIFICIAL PERSONS

Associations
Beneficial Associations
Building and Loan Associations
Clubs
Colleges and Universities
Corporations
Exchanges
Joint-Stock Companies and Business Trusts
Limited Liability Companies
Partnership
Religious Societies

PARTICULAR OCCUPATIONS

Accountants
Agriculture
Antitrust and Trade Regulation
Auctions and Auctioneers
Aviation
Banks and Banking
Bridges
Brokers
Canals
Carriers

VI

293

OUTLINE OF THE LAW

1. PERSONS — Cont'd

PARTICULAR OCCUPATIONS — Cont'd

Commerce
Consumer Credit
Credit Reporting Agencies
Detectives
Electricity
Explosives
Factors
Ferries
Gas
Hawkers and Peddlers
Innkeepers
Insurance
Licenses
Manufactures
Pilots
Public Amusement and Entertainment
Railroads
Seamen
Shipping
Steam
Telecommunications
Towage
Turnpikes and Toll Roads
Urban Railroads
Warehousemen
Wharves

2. PROPERTY

NATURE, SUBJECTS, AND INCIDENTS OF OWNERSHIP IN GENERAL

Abandoned and Lost Property
Accession
Adjoining Landowners
Confusion of Goods
Improvements
Property

PARTICULAR SUBJECTS AND INCIDENTS OF OWNERSHIP

Animals
Annuities
Automobiles
Boundaries
Cemeteries
Common Lands
Copyrights and Intellectual Property
Crops
Fences
Fish

Fixtures
Franchises
Game
Good Will
Logs and Logging
Mines and Minerals
Monopolies
Navigable Waters
Party Walls
Patents
Public Lands
Trademarks
Waters and Water Courses
Woods and Forests

PARTICULAR CLASSES OF ESTATES OR INTERESTS IN PROPERTY

Charities
Condominium
Dower and Curtesy
Easements
Estates in Property
Joint Tenancy
Landlord and Tenant
Life Estates
Perpetuities
Powers
Remainders
Reversions
Tenancy in Common
Trusts

PARTICULAR MODES OF ACQUIRING OR TRANSFERRING PROPERTY

Abstracts of Title
Adverse Possession
Alteration of Instruments
Assignments
Chattel Mortgages
Conversion
Dedication
Deeds
Descent and Distribution
Escheat
Fraudulent Conveyances
Gifts
Lost Instruments
Mortgages
Pledges
Secured Transactions
Wills

VII

3. CONTRACTS

NATURE, REQUISITES, AND INCIDENTS OF AGREEMENTS IN GENERAL

Contracts
Customs and Usages
Frauds, Statute of
Interest
Usury

PARTICULAR CLASSES OF AGREEMENTS

Bailment
Bills and Notes
Bonds
Breach of Marriage Promise
Champerty and Maintenance
Compromise and Settlement
Covenants
Deposits and Escrows
Exchange of Property
Gaming
Guaranty
Implied and Constructive Contracts
Indemnity
Joint Adventures
Lotteries
Principal and Surety
Public Contracts
Rewards
Sales
Subscriptions
Vendor and Purchaser

PARTICULAR CLASSES OF IMPLIED OR CONSTRUCTIVE CONTRACTS OR QUASI CONTRACTS

Account Stated
Contribution
Implied and Constructive Contracts

PARTICULAR MODES OF DISCHARGING CONTRACTS

Novation
Payment
Release
Subrogation
Tender

4. TORTS

Assault and Battery
Collision
Conspiracy

False Imprisonment
Forcible Entry and Detainer
Fraud
Libel and Slander
Malicious Prosecution
Negligence
Nuisance
Products Liability
Seduction
Torts
Trespass
Trover and Conversion
Waste

5. CRIMES

Abortion and Birth Control
Adulteration
Adultery
Arson
Bigamy
Breach of the Peace
Bribery
Burglary
Compounding Offenses
Controlled Substances
Counterfeiting
Criminal Law
Disorderly Conduct
Disorderly House
Disturbance of Public Assemblage
Embezzlement
Escape
Extortion and Threats
False Personation
False Pretenses
Fires
Forgery
Homicide
Incest
Insurrection and Sedition
Kidnapping
Larceny
Lewdness
Malicious Mischief
Mayhem
Neutrality Laws
Obscenity
Obstructing Justice
Perjury
Prostitution
Racketeer Influenced and Corrupt
  Organizations
Rape
Receiving Stolen Goods
Rescue
Riot

VIII

OUTLINE OF THE LAW

5. CRIMES—Cont'd

Robbery
Sodomy
Suicide
Treason
Unlawful Assembly
Vagrancy

6. REMEDIES

REMEDIES BY ACT OR AGREEMENT OF PARTIES

Accord and Satisfaction
Alternative Dispute Resolution
Submission of Controversy

REMEDIES BY POSSESSION OR NOTICE

Liens
Lis Pendens
Maritime Liens
Mechanics' Liens
Notice
Salvage

MEANS AND METHODS OF PROOF

Acknowledgment
Affidavits
Estoppel
Evidence
Oath
Records
Witnesses

CIVIL ACTIONS IN GENERAL

Action
Declaratory Judgment
Election of Remedies
Limitation of Actions
Parties
Set-Off and Counterclaim
Venue

PARTICULAR PROCEEDINGS IN CIVIL ACTIONS

Abatement and Revival
Appearance
Costs
Damages
Execution
Exemptions
Homestead
Judgment

Jury
Motions
Pleading
Pretrial Procedure
Process
Reference
Stipulations
Trial

PARTICULAR REMEDIES INCIDENT TO CIVIL ACTIONS

Arrest
Assistance, Writ of
Attachment
Bail
Deposits in Court
Garnishment
Injunction
Judicial Sales
Ne Exeat
Receivers
Recognizances
Sequestration
Undertakings

PARTICULAR MODES OF REVIEW IN CIVIL ACTIONS

Appeal and Error
Audita Querela
Certiorari
Exceptions, Bill of
New Trial
Review

ACTIONS TO ESTABLISH OWNERSHIP OR RECOVER POSSESSION OF SPECIFIC PROPERTY

Detinue
Ejectment
Entry, Writ of
Interpleader
Possessory Warrant
Quieting Title
Real Actions
Replevin
Trespass to Try Title

FORMS OF ACTIONS FOR DEBTS OR DAMAGES

Account, Action on
Action on the Case
Assumpsit, Action of
Covenant, Action of
Debt, Action of

IX

6. REMEDIES—Cont'd

ACTIONS FOR PARTICULAR FORMS OR SPECIAL RELIEF

Account
Cancellation of Instruments
Debtor and Creditor
Divorce
Partition
Reformation of Instruments
Specific Performance

CIVIL PROCEEDINGS OTHER THAN ACTIONS

Habeas Corpus
Mandamus
Prohibition
Quo Warranto
Scire Facias
Supersedeas

SPECIAL CIVIL JURISDICTIONS AND PROCEDURE THEREIN

Admiralty
Bankruptcy
Equity
Federal Civil Procedure

PROCEEDINGS PECULIAR TO CRIMINAL CASES

Double Jeopardy
Extradition and Detainers
Fines
Forfeitures
Grand Jury
Indictment and Information
Pardon and Parole
Penalties
Searches and Seizures
Sentencing and Punishment

7. GOVERNMENT

POLITICAL BODIES AND DIVISIONS

Counties
District of Columbia
Municipal Corporations
States
Territories
Towns
United States

SYSTEMS AND SOURCES OF LAW

Administrative Law and Procedure
Common Law
Constitutional Law
International Law
Parliamentary Law
Statutes
Treaties

LEGISLATIVE AND EXECUTIVE POWERS AND FUNCTIONS

Bounties
Census
Commodity Futures Trading Regulation
Customs Duties
Drains
Eminent Domain
Environmental Law
Highways
Inspection
Internal Revenue
Levees and Flood Control
Pensions
Postal Service
Private Roads
Public Contracts
Public Utilities
Schools
Securities Regulation
Social Security and Public Welfare
Taxation
Unemployment Compensation
Weights and Measures
Zoning and Planning

JUDICIAL POWERS AND FUNCTIONS, AND COURTS AND THEIR OFFICERS

Amicus Curiae
Clerks of Courts
Contempt
Court Commissioners
Courts
Federal Courts
Judges'
Justices of the Peace
Removal of Cases
Reports
United States Magistrates

CIVIL SERVICE, OFFICERS, AND INSTITUTIONS

Ambassadors and Consuls
Asylums and Assisted Living Facilities

x

OUTLINE OF THE LAW

7. GOVERNMENT—Cont'd

**CIVIL SERVICE, OFFICERS, AND
INSTITUTIONS—Cont'd**

Attorney General
Coroners
District and Prosecuting Attorneys
Elections
Newspapers
Notaries
Officers and Public Employees
Prisons

Registers of Deeds
Sheriffs and Constables
United States Marshals

MILITARY AND NAVAL SERVICE
AND WAR

Armed Services
Military Justice
Militia
War and National Emergency

XI

§8.5 Legal encyclopedias

Legal encyclopedias are books that recite principles of law supported by footnote references to pertinent cases from throughout the United States. The law topics are arranged alphabetically. The principal encyclopedias used in the United States are *Corpus Juris Secundum* (cited as C.J.S.) and *American Jurisprudence Second* (cited as Am. Jur. 2d). Legal encyclopedias are a good starting point for legal research on a topic. They provide a solid overview on areas of law, and are laden with footnotes directing the researcher to relevant primary and secondary legal sources. (See Illustration 8-3.)

Illustration 8-3

gence may be raised.[20] However, in the absence of primary negligence by the defendant, contributory negligence cannot exist.[21]

Nature and basis.

The doctrine of contributory negligence rests in the law of torts as applied to negligence[22] and is an application of the doctrine of proximate cause.[23]

§ 254 Contributory and comparative negligence distinguished from assumption of risk and other doctrines

Research References

West's Key Number Digest, Negligence ⟐502, 1282

Under certain circumstances, the same acts or conduct may render one guilty of contribu-

tory negligence or give rise to the defense of assumption of risk or incurred risk.

Under certain circumstances, the same acts or conduct may render one guilty of contributory negligence or give rise to the defense of assumption of risk or incurred risk.[1] The traditional defenses of contributory or comparative negligence and assumption of risk both look to the plaintiff's actions; each defense asks how the plaintiffs might be responsible for their own injuries.[2] However, the affirmative defenses of contributory negligence and assumption of the risk, although closely intertwined, are distinct concepts.[3] Various statements of the distinction are that contributory negligence arises from lack of due care while assumption of risk will negative liability regardless of the fact that plaintiff may have acted with due

Mo.—Williams v. Ford Motor Co., 454 S.W.2d 611 (Mo. Ct. App. 1970).

Or.—Furrer v. Talent Irr. Dist., 258 Or. 494, 466 P.2d 605 (1970).

[20]Ohio—Malley v. Youngstown State Univ., 74 Ohio Misc. 2d 1, 658 N.E.2d 333, 105 Ed. Law Rep. 277 (Ct. Cl. 1995).

[21]Va.—Williams v. Harrison, 255 Va. 272, 497 S.E.2d 467 (1998).

[22]U.S.—Powell v. U.S. Steel Corp., 305 F. Supp. 645 (S.D. W. Va. 1969).

[23]N.M.—Le Doux v. Peters, 82 N.M. 661, 486 P.2d 70 (Ct. App. 1971), aff'd in part, 83 N.M. 307, 491 P.2d 524 (1971) (holding modified on other grounds by, Madrid v. Shryock, 106 N.M. 467, 745 P.2d 375 (1987)).

Proximate cause, generally, see §§ 188 et seq.

[Section 254]

[1]Md.—Maryland Sales & Service Corp. v. Howell, 19 Md. App. 352, 311 A.2d 432 (1973).

Assumption of risk, generally, see §§ 386 et seq.

Defenses not inconsistent

Ind.—Kroger Co. v. Haun, 177 Ind. App. 403, 379 N.E.2d 1004 (1978).

Neb.—Circo v. Sisson, 193 Neb. 704, 229 N.W.2d 50 (1975).

Tenn.—Duncan v. Ferrell, 58 Tenn. App. 133, 427 S.W.2d 36 (1967).

Vt.—Sunday v. Stratton Corp., 136 Vt. 293,

390 A.2d 398 (1978).

Conduct not mutually exclusive

Ohio—Dunn v. Higgins, 14 Ohio St. 2d 239, 43 Ohio Op. 2d 368, 237 N.E.2d 386 (1968).

Party may be contributorily negligent and have assumed risk

Ariz.—Hildebrand v. Minyard, 16 Ariz. App. 583, 494 P.2d 1328 (Div. 1 1972).

Doctrines frequently overlap

Cal.—Sperling v. Hatch, 10 Cal. App. 3d 54, 88 Cal. Rptr. 704 (4th Dist. 1970).

Failure to comprehend consequences as contributory negligence

Ariz.—Hildebrand v. Minyard, 16 Ariz. App. 583, 494 P.2d 1328 (Div. 1 1972).

A.L.R. Library: Applicability of comparative negligence principles to intentional torts, 18 A.L.R. 5th 525.

Products liability: contributory negligence or assumption of risk as defense in negligence action based on failure to provide safety device for product causing injury, 75 A.L.R.4th 443.

[2]Alaska—Shaw v. State, Dept. of Admin., 861 P.2d 566 (Alaska 1993).

Comparative negligence, generally, see §§ 316 et seq.

A.L.R. Library: Effect of adoption of comparative negligence rules on assumption of risk, 16 A.L.R.4th 700.

[3]Md.—Union Memorial Hosp. v. Dorsey, 125 Md. App. 275, 724 A.2d 1272 (1999).

28

Excerpt taken from 65A Corpus Juris Secundum 253

§ 8.6 Legal texts and treatises

Legal texts and *treatises* are books prepared by legal scholars and practice experts that cover specific areas of law. Legal texts usually deal with a single topic, such as contracts, torts, bankruptcy, trusts, evidence, and civil and criminal law and practice. Information about texts and treatises may be obtained through the catalog of a law library.

§ 8.7 Legal periodicals

Articles from legal periodicals also discuss specific areas of the law and are particularly useful for prediction and analysis of trends in the law. Treatment of the subject ranges from scholarly to practical to news reporting. Information about articles can be located by subject, author, or title through legal periodical indexes, such as *Index to Legal Periodicals*, current *Law Index*, or *Legaltrac*.

§ 8.8 Restatements

Restatements are publications setting out and explaining, by practical examples, the law in particular fields. Restatements covering various areas of law, including agency, conflict of laws, contracts, judgments, products liability, property, restitution, security, torts, trusts, and unfair competition have been published. The purpose of the American Law Institute, the prestigious group responsible for the restatements, is to restate the common law (as reflected both by case decisions and statutory interpretation). To that end, the institute appoints committees to study and draft restatements covering assigned law topics. Eminent legal scholars are appointed to be reporters for each one of the restatements being prepared, and, as a practical matter, they principally prepare the drafts. The restatements are not adopted in whole by the highest appellate courts in the states, but they are referred to, and in many instances are approved on, a section-by-section basis in the written opinion. Therefore, to that extent, they do become law. Information about court opinions that have interpreted restatement provisions is contained in the appendix volumes of the restatement set.

§ 8.9 Uniform laws annotated

Individual lawyers, judges, and law professors are selected as commissioners to sit with the National Conference of Commissioners on Uniform State Laws. They then research and draft model legislation covering law topics dealing with specific legal problems. Their goal is to make uniform, as far as possible, many of the major areas of the law that can be codified. The state legislatures may or may not adopt the law, but the books are valuable for a comparison of case law interpretations from various states. Many of the uniform laws, such as the Uniform Commercial Code, have been adopted by practically all of the states.

§ 8.10   Other research aids

Law book publishers offer additional aids to legal researchers, the most important of which are discussed. (See Illustration 8-4.)

§ 8.11   Annotated statutes

An official statutory code is typically published by the governmental entity. Thus, the federal government publishes the United States Code. Individual states typically publish their own codes.

In addition, private legal publishers such as Thomson Reuters and LexisNexis publish annotated codes. Annotated codes provide the text of the official code as well as other commentary helpful to understanding individual code sections, including comments on legislative history, summaries of relevant judicial decisions, citations to legal scholarship concerning the law, etc. Generally speaking, a privately published code will be more current than its official counterparts. For example, the official United States Code is published every six years. By contrast, Thomson Reuters' United States Code Annotated (cited as U.S.C.A.) and United States Code Service (cited U.S.C.S. and published by LexisNexis) are supplemented annually to keep the practitioner up to date on recent changes in the law. Both sources are available online on Westlaw and Lexis.com.

Illustration 8-4

Ch. 9   FOOD, DRUG AND COSMETIC ACT   21 § 355

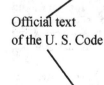

Official text
of the U. S. Code

(b) Labeling and advertising

A veterinary feed directive drug and any feed bearing or containing a veterinary feed directive drug shall be deemed to be misbranded if their labeling fails to bear such cautionary statement and such other information as the Secretary may by general regulation or by order prescribe, or their advertising fails to conform to the conditions and indications for use published pursuant to section 360b(i) of this title or fails to contain the general cautionary statement prescribed by the Secretary.

(c) Nonprescription status

Neither a drug subject to this section, nor animal feed bearing or containing such a drug, shall be deemed to be a prescription article under any Federal or State law.

(June 25, 1938, c. 675, § 504, as added Oct. 9, 1996, Pub.L. 104–250, § 5(b), 110 Stat. 3155.)

HISTORICAL AND STATUTORY NOTES

Revision Notes and Legislative Reports
  1996 Acts. House Report No. 104–823, see 1996 U.S. Code Cong. and Adm. News, p. 3540.

Prior Provisions
  A prior section 354, Act June 25, 1938, c. 675, § 504, 52 Stat. 1052, which re-

quired the Secretary to promulgate regulations for the listing of coal-tar colors for drugs and is covered by section 376 of this title, was repealed by Pub.L. 86–618, Title I, § 103(a)(2), July 12, 1960, 74 Stat. 398.

LIBRARY REFERENCES

Texts and Treatises
  Business and Commercial Litigation in Federal Courts § 70.2.

WESTLAW ELECTRONIC RESEARCH

See WESTLAW guide following the Explanation pages of this volume.

§ 355. New drugs

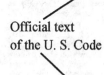

Official text
of the U. S. Code

(a) Necessity of effective approval of application

No person shall introduce or deliver for introduction into interstate commerce any new drug, unless an approval of an application filed pursuant to subsection (b) or (j) of this section is effective with respect to such drug.

(b) Filing application; contents

(1) Any person may file with the Secretary an application with respect to any drug subject to the provisions of subsection (a) of this section. Such person shall submit to the Secretary as a part of the application (A) full reports of investigations which have been made to show whether or not such drug is safe for use and whether such drug

659

Meetings of the panel may be held using electronic communication to convene the meetings.

(8) Within 90 days after a scientific advisory panel makes recommendations on any matter under its review, the Food and Drug Administration official responsible for the matter shall review the conclusions and recommendations of the panel, and notify the affected persons of the final decision on the matter, or of the reasons that no such decision has been reached. Each such final decision shall be documented including the rationale for the decision.

(June 25, 1938, c. 675, § 505, 52 Stat. 1052; 1940 Reorg.Plan No. IV, § 12, eff. June 30, 1940, 5 F.R. 2422, 54 Stat. 1237; June 25, 1948, c. 646, § 32(b), 62 Stat. 991; May 24, 1949, c. 139, § 127, 63 Stat. 107; 1953 Reorg.Plan No. 1, § 5, eff. Apr. 11, 1953, 18 F.R. 2053, 67 Stat. 631; June 11, 1960, Pub.L. 86–507, § 1(18), 74 Stat. 201; Oct. 10, 1962, Pub.L. 87–781, Title I, §§ 102(b)–(d), 103(a), (b), 104(a)–(d)(2), 76 Stat. 781–783, 784, 785; Aug. 16, 1972, Pub.L. 92–387, § 4(d), 86 Stat. 562; Sept. 24, 1984, Pub.L. 98–417, Title I, §§ 101, 102(a)–(b)(5), 103, 104, 98 Stat. 1585, 1592, 1593, 1597; May 13, 1992, Pub.L. 102–282, § 5, 106 Stat. 161; Aug. 13, 1993, Pub.L. 103–80, § 3(n), 107 Stat. 777; Nov. 21, 1997, Pub.L. 105–115, Title I, §§ 115(a), (b), 117, 119, 120, 124(a), 111 Stat. 2313, 2315, 2316, 2318, 2324.)

Citations to original and amending Acts of Congress in U. S. Statutes at Large

HISTORICAL AND STATUTORY NOTES

Revision Notes and Legislative Reports

1949 Acts. Senate Report No. 303 and House Report No. 352, see 1949 U.S. Code Cong. Service, p. 1248.

Notes explaining historical development of Act

1960 Acts. Senate Report No. 1489, see 1960 U.S. Code Cong. and Adm. News, p. 2356.

1962 Acts. Senate Report No. 1744 and Conference Report No. 2526, see 1962 U.S. Code Cong. and Adm. News, p. 2884.

1972 Acts. Senate Report No. 92–924, see 1972 U.S. Code Cong. and Adm. News, p. 2963.

1984 Acts. House Report No. 98–857(Parts I and II), see 1984 U.S. Code Cong. and Adm. News, p. 2647.

1992 Acts. House Report No. 102–272, see 1992 U.S. Code Cong. and Adm. News, p. 103.

1997 Acts. House Conference Report No. 105–399, see 1997 U.S. Code Cong. and Adm. News, p. 2881.

Amendments

1997 Amendments. Subsec. (b)(1). Pub.L. 105–115, § 115(b), added "The Secretary shall, in consultation with the Director of the National Institutes of Health and with representatives of the drug manufacturing industry, review and develop guidance, as appropriate, on the inclusion of women and minorities in clinical trials required by clause (A)."

Subsec. (b)(4). Pub.L. 105–115, § 119(a), added par. (4).

Subsec. (c)(4). Pub.L. 105–115, § 124(a), added par. (4).

Subsec. (d). Pub.L. 105–115, § 115(a), added "If the Secretary determines, based on relevant science, that data from one adequate and well-controlled clinical investigation and confirmatory evidence (obtained prior to or after such investigation) are sufficient to establish effectiveness, the Secretary may consider such data and evidence to constitute substantial evidence for purposes of the preceding sentence."

Subsec. (i). Pub.L. 105–115, § 117(1), redesignated former pars. (1) to (3) as subpars. (A) to (C), respectively.

Subsec. (i)(1). Pub.L. 105–115, § 117(2), (3), inserted "(1)" after "(i)" and struck out, "Such regulations shall provide that such exemption shall be conditioned upon the manufacturer, or the sponsor of the investigation, requiring that experts using such drugs for investigational purposes certify to such manu-

§.8.12 Form and practice books

Form books are specialized publications that provide suggested text for various legal forms, such as contracts, leases, and procedural pleadings and papers. Large sets of form books cover an encyclopedic range of forms on virtually all subjects. Smaller sets can focus on particular areas of law. Although these forms are very useful for guidance in drafting legal documents, care must be taken to verify that the suggested language is in fact applicable to the specific case.

Many other practical publications exist to assist the lawyer in procedural, evidentiary, and trial practice areas. Some examples are *Am Jur Trials, Am Jur Proof of Facts* and *Causes of Action.*

§8.13 Keeping the library current

In order for a lawyer to be able to rely on the books in the library, they must be absolutely current. There are several services provided by law book publishers to help keep the library current.

§8.13.1 Keeping the library current—Pocket parts

Most law books are equipped with pockets in the inside back covers which accommodate pamphlet inserts. All statutes and codes are kept current in this manner, and new *pocket parts* are issued after each legislative session. In legal research it is very important to check the pocket parts for recent changes.

In many offices it is the responsibility of the lawyer's assistant to keep the pocket parts current. Generally, these are published once a year. When new pocket parts arrive, they should immediately be placed in the pertinent volumes and the old pocket parts destroyed according to the instructions that come with each new supplement. The pocket parts are clearly labeled, so there can be no mistake as to where they belong.

§8.13.2 Keeping the library current—Replacement volumes

When the pocket part becomes so bulky that the book no longer closes properly, the volume is replaced. Replacement volumes usually come with instructions on which book or books are being replaced. It is not unusual for one volume to be replaced by two. Be guided by the publisher's instructions, as they are usually very specific.

§8.13.3 Keeping the library current—Bound supplements

Bound supplements may be of a temporary nature, to be used because a pocket part would be too bulky or because the book is not equipped with a pocket parts or as permanent updates to the main volume. Here, again, rely on the publisher's instructions for guidance.

§8.13.4 Keeping the library current—Advance sheets

National Reporter System volumes are published as soon as there are a sufficient number of cases to fill a bound volume. Often, a lawyer

must know about the most current cases sooner than that. To alleviate the problem, Thomson Reuters issues *advance sheets* in a
paperback pamphlet weekly. The advance sheets carry the correct volume numbers and page numbers of the National Reporter volume of
which it will become a part. Once the bound volume arrives, the
advance sheets may be destroyed.

§ 8.13.5 Keeping the library current—Loose-leaf services

Loose-leaf services are used extensively in administrative law.
Changes occur at a rapid rate, and the materials must be kept current to be of any value.

These services are kept current by the publication of replacement
pages or additional pages. It is a good idea to replace substitute pages
as soon as they arrive, as it can be very confusing to attempt the
insertion of more than one group of changes. Be very careful to follow
the publisher's instructions about the replacements.

§ 8.14 Computer-assisted legal research

A substantial portion of the publications described in this chapter
are located in the large computer-assisted research systems of
lexisnexis.com and Westlaw. These two databases contain the full text
of federal and state case law (both current and historical), statutes
and regulations, legal periodicals, treatises, forms, news, public records, and other publications. Both systems use open-ended keyword
search techniques, which facilitate location of pertinent materials
without resorting to indexes, digests, and multiple sources for
updating. These computer systems can be a cost-effective approach to
legal research.

§ 8.14.1 Computer-assisted legal research—Westlaw

Westlaw is the online legal research service provided by Thomson
Reuters. Through Westlaw, the legal researcher can access all
published federal and state appellate cases (and numerous unpublished cases as well), all federal and state statutes, all federal
administrative regulations, the administrative codes for most states,
and a rich library of secondary research material (law review articles,
practice guides, treatises, and so forth).

In addition, Westlaw permits the researcher to search case law
databases using Thomson Reuters' Topic and Key Number System.
Thus, to search in Westlaw for cases involving the validity of wills executed under improper influence, for example, the researcher might
include in the query the topic and key number assigned to cases dealing with this issue. Topic 409 is *Wills*; Key Number 154 within this
topic is *undue influence*. So, the researcher will create a query including the phrase *409k154* to restrict the search to cases discussing this
issue.

§ 8.14.2 Computer-assisted legal research—Lexisnexis.com

Lexisnexis.com is another computer-assisted legal research service. Lexisnexis.com provides access to the primary law materials available on Westlaw. Like Westlaw, lexisnexis.com also offers a rich collection of secondary legal resources. Both services provide an assortment of nonlegal material such as news databases, company information, public records, etc.

§ 8.14.3 Computer-assisted legal research—The Internet as a legal research tool

The Internet is an important resource for the legal researcher. Official government websites provide access to almost all of the same federal and state statutory codes and administrative regulations available on Westlaw or lexisnexis.com. Websites maintained by individual federal and state courts provide convenient access to recent judicial opinions, court rules, etc. Official government websites offer material without charge. Thus, for certain primary law material, the Internet can represent a low-cost alternative to using a commercial online service.

Although these government-sponsored websites provide free access to a great deal of American primary law, they are currently no substitute for lexisnexis.com or Westlaw. A website may offer the text of the law itself, but it will not provide the editorial enhancements offered by these services. In many cases, the primary law available on the Internet is not as current as the same material available through a fee-based, online service. Statutory codes available on lexisnexis.com and Westlaw, for example, typically flag any section amended by a recent session law; no such warning appears on statutory material available on the web. The case law databases available on the Internet tend to have recent cases only; lexisnexis.com and Westlaw generally offer far more comprehensive coverage of each jurisdiction's case law. Finally, web-based search engines tend to be primitive by comparison with the search engines and robust searching capabilities employed by lexisnexis.com and Westlaw.

The Internet, however, outshines the commercial services in providing access to certain kinds of primary law. County and city municipal codes are increasingly available on the Internet; lexisnexis.com and Westlaw are increasing their collections, but neither offer a complete solution for these materials. There is a great deal more foreign law (in English and in the native language) on the Internet than is available through the commercial services. Finally, in certain cases, the Internet can actually be more current than the online services. Some recent judicial opinions, for example, appear at court websites before the cases are picked up by the commercial services (the lag, however, is seldom more than a matter of days).

Currently, the Internet's most important strength as a legal resource lies in its ability to deliver timely, free access to certain primary and secondary legal materials. For example, the federal government and most state governments have created websites for their respective legislative bodies. Through these sites, one can easily track current legislation, retrieve otherwise hard-to-locate committee reports, locate the text of recently enacted session laws, etc. Websites maintained by federal and state administrative agencies provide excellent access to otherwise hard-to-find guidance documents published by such agencies. Such documents can be crucial to the practitioner but are generally not available on lexisnexis.com or Westlaw because they are not primary law. A number of academic law journals also offer online access to recent articles.

§ 8.15   Learning the law library

To become an efficient researcher, the lawyer's assistant must become familiar with the books and other research tools in the law library. Knowing where the books and other research tools are and why they are there makes the lawyer's assistant much more helpful to the lawyer.

The art of effective legal research requires concentrated study and practice. As the lawyer's assistant learns the way around the library, the assistant should:

- Take the time to study some of the books.
- Read the table of contents, introduction, and foreword of some of the books.
- Study the indexes. Try to find a key word listed for a current legal problem in the office.
- Study the topics of the Key Number System. Many legal indexes may use the same topic designations.
- Always check pocket parts or supplementary pamphlets.
- Read some of the headnotes in the state reporter. Try to find references to the same key number somewhere else.
- Find a case in a reporter and Shepardize or KeyCite it. Pull one of the cases referred to. Is it on the same point of law?
- Do the same for one of the statutes.
- If the law office has access to Lexis.com or Westlaw, become familiar with these databases.

§ 8.16   Law librarians

Law librarians are skilled information specialists that help judges, attorneys, professors, students, legal professionals, and members of the public find information on legal issues. Many hold master's degrees in Library and Information Science, and some also hold law and other advanced degrees. Law librarians perform a variety of duties relating to the organization and distribution of legal and nonlegal information, including:

- Providing specialized reference and research services;

- Executing online database searches;
- Teaching legal research and materials use;
- Training on the use of print and electronic legal information sources;
- Evaluating and collecting legal materials;
- Designing and maintaining information storage and retrieval systems; and
- Preparing fiscal reports and long-range plans.

Smaller firms generally do not have a designated full-time law librarian, but many midsize and large law firms do have one or more law librarians on staff. Many state and regional law library associations feature volunteer guest speakers who can teach group seminars on the fundamentals of legal research. Seminars on legal research basics may also be available to the public at the local county and state law library.

Chapter 9

The Courts

> **KeyCite®:** Cases and other legal materials listed in KeyCite Scope can be researched through the KeyCite service on Westlaw®. Use KeyCite to check citations for form, parallel references, prior and later history, and comprehensive citator information, including citations to other decisions and secondary materials.

§ 9.1   History of the law

It is difficult to point to a beginning date for the development of the law. In highly developed civilizations as early as 2100 B.C., codes of conduct were written and enforced. Religion played an important role in the history of the law after the decline of the Roman Empire, when the ecclesiastical courts handled most legal matters. Many ancient civilizations had relatively sophisticated written laws. Eventually all of the concepts embodied in these ancient laws evolved into the two legal systems, which dominate the Western world today—civil law and common law.

§ 9.1.1   History of the law—Civil law

Civil law derives from Roman law. Most of the countries in Western Europe today operate under civil law systems. In the United States, Louisiana operates under a civil law system greatly influenced by France's Code Napoleon. California and Texas law were heavily influenced by Spanish law. Some of the Spanish influence is evident also in New Mexico and Arizona law.

§ 9.1.2   History of the law—Common law

Except for a few civil law states as mentioned above, the remainder of our states operate under a ***common law*** system that is an adapta-

tion of England's common law. **Common law** evolved in England after the Norman Conquest. At that time, there were no written rules to
govern conduct. When disputes arose, the parties appeared before a
tribunal or a judge, and a decision was reached based upon the evidence and the facts at hand. Under that system two different courts
could reach completely different conclusions in a similar fact situation
because there was nothing in writing to guide the judge to a decision.

§9.1.3   History of the law—Distinction between civil law and common law

Civil law is based on a series of written codes or laws. These written codes are interpreted by courts when disputes arise, but it is the
written law itself that is binding. On the other hand, **common law**
has evolved from earlier decisions made by courts. To solve the
problem of inconsistency in decisions reached in similar fact situations, these decisions have been reduced to writing, and the courts are
generally bound by them. This concept is known as the **doctrine of
stare decisis** (to stand by decisions). For that reason, it is often said
that common law is based on the law of **precedent**. One court sets a
precedent, and courts making subsequent decisions relating to similar
fact circumstances are generally bound by that precedent. The primary distinction between the two systems is that civil law is based on
written codes, while common law is based on judicial precedent.

§9.2   The American judicial system

The distinction between civil law and common law is now primarily
a historic one, because the American legal system today is a fusion of
both systems. For example, no longer do any of the state court systems
rely exclusively upon common law or case decisions. All states,
whether their legal system is based on civil or common law, have
written laws. The Constitution of the United States was ratified in
1788 and, of course, is written law. Although civil law states use written law, case law has become a very important part of civil law. Tort
law is a common law concept, but in Louisiana (a civil law state), the
law of torts is applied much as it is in the rest of the United States.
Most commercial laws in force in the United States today, although
written in commercial codes, have their origin in common law.

§9.2.1   The American judicial system—The role of law

The law establishes rules of conduct that define what is legally
right and what is legally wrong. Laws are nothing more than rules of
human behavior enforced by the state or federal government by means
of penalties for their violation. To a great extent, laws are influenced
by moral and social habits or customs. Therefore, as society changes
its customs and traditions, laws change. These changes are accomplished when new laws are enacted by the legislative branch of
government or when the judiciary interprets existing laws.

§ 9.2.2   The American judicial system—Significance of the law

Many people do not realize the extent to which laws affect their daily lives. Common events, such as a birth, a death, applying for a driver's license, buying or selling a house or a car, paying taxes, buying a bus or airplane ticket, banking, and using electricity or other utilities are all governed by specific laws. Many lay people have the mistaken impression that laws apply only to those who commit crimes. That simply is not the case. The law affects everyone, and everyone should have some idea of legal rights so he or she can know when to consult a lawyer.

§ 9.2.3   The American judicial system—Criminal actions

Criminal actions generally are brought by the people through a government (either federal, state, or local) against the person or persons accused of a crime. Because society is wronged by the commission of a crime, the government prosecutes the wrongdoer on behalf of society. Therefore, in a criminal action a governmental entity is typically the plaintiff.

§ 9.2.4   The American judicial system—Civil actions

Civil actions generally are brought by one party against another to resolve a controversy. These actions, broadly speaking, include any kind of legal action that is not a criminal action, but they typically seek one of the following remedies:

- Money, generally referred to as damages
- Specific performance of some conduct
- Restrictions on some conduct

In actions for performance or restrictions, the relief usually requested is in the form of a restraining order or an injunction.

§ 9.3   Substantive vs. procedural law

Law is categorized based upon its nature (substantive law) or how it is applied in deciding issues of substantive law (procedural law). *Substantive law* is the statutory or written law that governs rights and obligations of those who are subject to it. It tells what a person can or cannot legally do. *Procedural law* defines and describes the process that must be followed to enforce substantive law. The most common source of procedural law is court rules adopted and published by the courts or procedures required by constitutionally mandated due process.

§ 9.4   Source of the law

Law is often classified on the basis of where it is found. *Constitutional law* is set out in the Constitution of the United States and in the state constitutions. The Constitution of the United States carries the greatest degree of dignity of any law in this country. No other law—whether adopted by Congress or by a state legislature—can conflict with the United States Constitution. Each state has its own constitution. However, those constitutions may not contain any provision that is contrary to a provision in the United States Constitution. *Statutory law* is that body of laws passed by the United States Congress, the state legislatures, and local governments. In addition, the rules and regulations generated by governmental agencies and commissions that are empowered by statutory law also have the force of statutory law. *Case law* is that body of court decisions resulting from legal controversies over interpretations of substantive and procedural law. Any law can be considered from several different viewpoints. A law can be classified as constitutional, statutory, substantive, procedural, or case law. (See Illustration 9-1.)

Illustration 9-1

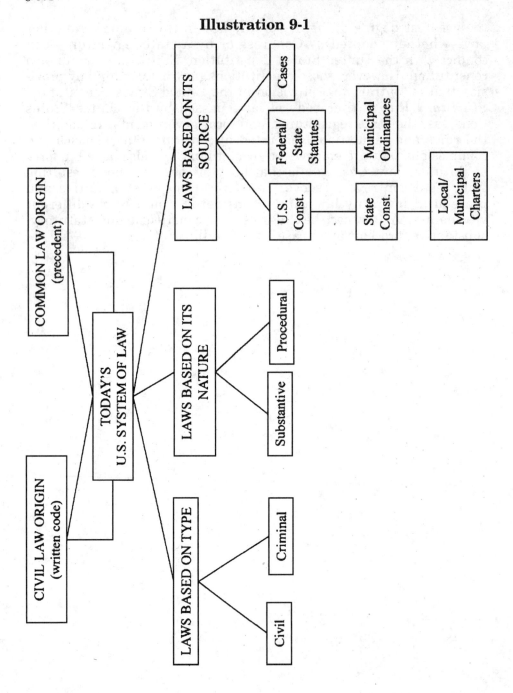

§ 9.5 Creation of court systems in the United States

Courts are created by constitutional authority. The Constitution of the United States is the primary source of the judicial powers of federal courts. The basis of the judicial authority of federal courts is found largely in Article III, § 2 of the United States Constitution. The state constitutions create courts for their states, and the legislative bodies, both federal and state, have the power to create courts and give judicial authority to those courts subject to any restrictions set forth in the state constitutions or the United States Constitution. Regardless of what authority establishes a court, that court has authority to decide only those cases which the United States Constitution or state constitution ultimately gives it authority to decide.

Without authority granted in the state's constitution, a legislative body may not alter, abolish, or restructure a constitutional court, but it may alter, abolish, or restructure any court that it has created pursuant to constitutional authority. State courts are not under the authority and control of Congress, but Congress may authorize state courts to enforce federal laws. Both federal and state legislative bodies may increase, decrease, create, or change the number of judicial districts or circuits as long as they act under constitutional authority. They also may divide a court into divisions or departments. A court so divided remains a single court, and any decisions or judgments rendered by that division or department are considered as having been rendered by the whole court.

Courts, whether federal or state, apply the laws created by constitutions, legislative bodies, and administrative agencies having authority to enact rules and regulations. They do this in two ways: they *adjudicate* or settle controversies and disputes between parties, and they decide which laws are applicable to the cases that are before them. Once their decisions are final, they are binding.

In addition to the application and interpretation of laws, courts may adopt rules that affect procedural law within their jurisdiction. These court rules cannot conflict with the Constitution of the United States, the state's constitution, or any law enacted by Congress or the respective state legislatures.

§ 9.6 Jurisdiction

Jurisdiction is the power of a court to hear and decide certain cases. There are many limitations on that power, and very often those limitations are the product of constitutional or legislative restrictions.

§ 9.6.1 Jurisdiction—Original jurisdiction

Original jurisdiction is the authority granted a court to hear and determine a matter for the first time. Actions are begun in courts of original jurisdiction. It is in the court of original jurisdiction that the lawsuit is filed and the trial is held or the matter is otherwise resolved.

§ 9.6.2   Jurisdiction—Subject matter jurisdiction

Subject matter jurisdiction is authority given a court to render binding decisions over the matter in dispute. Lack of subject matter jurisdiction cannot be waived by the court or by the parties. In fact, if a court lacks jurisdiction over the subject matter, any judgment it renders is void.

EXAMPLE:

Patent disputes are heard exclusively by federal courts. If a patent dispute were to be filed in state court, the matter would be dismissed for lack of subject matter jurisdiction.

§ 9.6.3   Jurisdiction—Jurisdiction *in personam*

Jurisdiction in personam (personal jurisdiction) is the power of a court to render a judgment against a person or to subject the disputing parties to the decisions and rulings made by it. Ordinarily, this means that a defendant has the right to be tried only in those states where he or she has sufficient contacts. This is only a general rule, however, and other types of *in personam* jurisdiction may preempt that general rule. A person may be subjected to the jurisdiction of a court by statute, by agreement, or if he or she does not file a formal objection to the court's personal jurisdiction. In order for the judgment to be valid in such an instance, however, the court must also have subject matter jurisdiction.

EXAMPLES:

A lives in Dallas, Texas, and made a contract with *B*, who lives in Oklahoma City, Oklahoma, to pay *B* $10,000 for delivery of certain merchandise. The contract was made in Texas and all negotiations took place in Texas. *A* now refuses to pay *B*. The state courts of Oklahoma have authority to hear and decide this type of case (breach of contract) because the state courts have subject matter jurisdiction to hear contract disputes. However, the state courts of Oklahoma probably do not have personal jurisdiction over *A* because he has insufficient contacts with that state. *B* therefore cannot sue *A* in Oklahoma.

Assume the same facts. *B* sues *A* in Oklahoma City, where *A* now spends a lot of time on business. *A* employs the services of an Oklahoma City lawyer to defend the suit that *B* files. When *A* makes an appearance in that matter through his lawyer and does not dispute the jurisdiction, he has subjected himself to the jurisdiction of the Oklahoma City court. Therefore, the Oklahoma court can render a valid judgment against *A*.

§ 9.6.4   Jurisdiction—Jurisdiction *in rem*

Jurisdiction in rem is the authority of a court to render a judgment concerning property over which it has jurisdiction. Ordinarily, this means that the court and the property are in the same geographic location, even if the owner of the property is not subject to personal jurisdiction in that court. When a court renders an *in rem* judgment, that judgment affects only the property which is the subject of the court's jurisdiction. The judgment does not apply to the owner of the property if the court does not have personal jurisdiction over the owner. This means that any such judgment would have to be satisfied only from the property subject to the court's jurisdiction. Other personal assets and property of the owner which are located elsewhere beyond the court's jurisdiction could not be seized by a court which did not have personal jurisdiction over the owner.

EXAMPLE:

A lives in Dallas and owes *B*, who lives in Oklahoma City, $10,000, which is secured by a mortgage on property located in Oklahoma City. *B* must sue *A* in Oklahoma City if he wishes to regain possession of the property in payment of the mortgage, since only the Oklahoma City court has jurisdiction *in rem*. However, if *B* is not interested in the property but only wants to get his money back, he may sue *A* in a Dallas court that has *in personam* jurisdiction over *A* so that once he has a judgment he can seize other assets owned by *A* to satisfy his judgment, if such assets are located in Texas.

§ 9.6.5   Jurisdiction—Limited jurisdiction

A court of *limited jurisdiction* is one that is restricted in the type of case it can hear or in the amount of money involved in the litigation.

EXAMPLE:

A juvenile court, probate court, or a family court can hear only cases involving that particular subject matter if their jurisdiction is limited by state statute.

Many municipal courts (or other state courts) are limited by the amount of money involved in a particular lawsuit.

EXAMPLE:

A owes *B* $10,000. *B* wishes to sue *A*. If the municipal court where *A* lives does not have monetary jurisdiction of $10,000, *B* must sue *A* in the appropriate court having monetary jurisdiction of that amount.

§ 9.6.6   Jurisdiction—Exclusive jurisdiction

Exclusive jurisdiction is the authority granted to a court to hear certain matters to the exclusion of all other courts. No other court within the same territorial limits may hear any matter for which there is a court with exclusive jurisdiction. The court also may be restricted to that type of case.

EXAMPLE:

Patent litigation or litigation under the National Labor Relations Act is exclusively vested in federal court. No state court may hear such matters.

§ 9.6.7   Jurisdiction—Territorial jurisdiction

Territorial jurisdiction applies to the actual geographic area over which the court has authority. Both the federal and state court systems have various divisions which limit jurisdiction to specific geographic areas.

§ 9.6.8   Jurisdiction—General jurisdiction

If a court has *general jurisdiction*, this usually means that the court has no limitation as to the types of cases it can hear and no limitation on its monetary jurisdiction. Since there is no limit as to subject matter or as to the amount in controversy, it is often referred to as a court of general or *unlimited jurisdiction*. However, courts are limited in some regards, because most court systems contain courts of special, exclusive jurisdiction; courts of general jurisdiction cannot hear cases over which special courts have exclusive jurisdiction.

§ 9.6.9   Jurisdiction—Concurrent jurisdiction

Concurrent jurisdiction refers to jurisdiction granted to different courts at the same time over the same matters and within the same territorial limit. This means that in certain situations, the plaintiff has a choice of the court in which to file suit. This is particularly true, for example, where municipal or small claims courts are established to alleviate crowding in the courts of general jurisdiction. Usually, the jurisdiction of the small claims court is concurrent with that of the court of general jurisdiction. The whole purpose of the small claims court is to give claimants a more efficient and economical court than the court of general jurisdiction in which to process claims that do not involve large sums of money.

§ 9.6.10   Jurisdiction—Monetary jurisdiction

Monetary jurisdiction refers to the limitation on dollar amounts that a court may award. Usually, courts of general jurisdiction are not limited by monetary jurisdiction, but municipal courts and small claims courts are. Federal district courts have jurisdiction in diversity of citizenship cases only when the amount in dispute is more than a set amount, currently $75,000.

§ 9.6.11   Jurisdiction—Appellate jurisdiction

Appellate jurisdiction grants authority to a court to review cases tried in lower courts. Some courts have both original and appellate jurisdiction.

Very often, a judgment of a municipal or small claims court can be appealed to a court of general or unlimited jurisdiction. In that instance, therefore, the court of general jurisdiction, which is usually a trial court, becomes an appellate court.

Most states have a court of last resort (often called the supreme court). Often, these courts have a right to decide whether or not they will even hear an appeal. In addition, it is often the court of last resort that handles disbarment cases against lawyers. In that instance, the court may act as a trial court of original jurisdiction, although it is usually an appellate court.

§ 9.6.12 Jurisdiction—Venue

Venue refers to the proper location where a case may be heard by a court of law. For example, in a state having a trial court of general jurisdiction encompassing four counties, the court has the same subject matter jurisdiction and thus can hear the same type of disputes in all four counties, but venue differs from one county to the next. Even if the four counties share one judge, each county has its own courthouse and personnel. Venue determines in which county that particular dispute is to be tried. Generally, but subject to many exceptions, venue is based on the residence of the defendant. In federal court, a civil action based on diversity of citizenship is proper where the defendant resides if all defendants reside in the same state. Otherwise, venue is generally proper where the events giving rise to the claim occurred.

§ 9.7 Dual system of courts

Although there are many similarities in the federal and state court systems, they operate independently. There are instances in which the United States Supreme Court might review a judgment rendered by a state court, but those instances are rare, occurring only when there has been a final judgment or decree of the highest court of the state involving a substantial federal question. Lawsuits that are initiated in either the state or federal system usually are not switched from one system to the other. There are exceptions to this rule, because some state actions can be removed to federal court.

Historically, certain types of legal matters are exclusively reserved to state courts. Federal courts are very hesitant to intervene in matters of marriage, divorce, custody, probate proceedings, and property. On the other hand, there are matters over which federal courts have exclusive jurisdiction, such as criminal matters involving violation of federal laws; admiralty and maritime matters; United States copyright matters; bankruptcy proceedings; and proceedings against ambassadors, consuls, and ministers.

§ 9.7.1 Dual system of courts—Concurrent jurisdiction of state and federal courts

There are times when state courts and federal courts have concurrent jurisdiction. The most common instance is a case with diversity of citizenship (the parties are from different states or one is from a foreign country) in which the amount in dispute is more than a certain amount, currently $75,000. In such a situation, if a lawsuit is filed in the federal court, the federal court applies state substantive law. Since the federal court and the state court have concurrent jurisdiction, however, the plaintiff may file suit in either court, but once the court is selected, the suit is usually brought to conclusion in that court. That said, a change in circumstances in the action may warrant a *remand* of the action to state court (for example, if a new non-diverse party joints the action or a settlement of one or more of the claims has the effect of reducing the amount in controversy to less than $75,000).

§ 9.8   Federal court system

The federal court system includes the federal district courts located in each state, the United States Courts of Appeals, the Supreme Court, and a number of specialized courts with limited jurisdiction, which are discussed below.

§ 9.8.1   Federal court system—The United States Supreme Court

The United States Supreme Court is the only court specifically created by the United States Constitution. Its jurisdiction is varied, but usually appellate. There are three principal ways in which a case can be heard by the United States Supreme Court:

- When a decision has been handed down in a trial court and in an appellate court, the losing party may petition the United States Supreme Court for a *writ of certiorari* or review. If the Supreme Court wishes to hear the case, it grants the writ and assumes jurisdiction of the case. If it does not, the writ is denied and jurisdiction remains with the lower court. No reasons need be stated for the Court's decision. Once the writ is denied, the litigant generally has no more avenues of relief.
- There are some cases the Supreme Court is obligated to hear. These cases come to the Supreme Court on appeal.
- There are a few instances in which the United States Supreme Court has original jurisdiction.

EXAMPLE:
   Texas and Louisiana have a dispute over their common boundary along the Sabine River. Only the United States Supreme Court has jurisdiction to hear this dispute.

Since it has original jurisdiction over disputes between states, the United States Supreme Court is a trial court in this instance. Because it is the highest court in America, there would be no right to appeal from its decision in this type of case.

§ 9.8.2   United States Courts of Appeals

These courts hear appeals from various federal district courts, bankruptcy courts, and tax courts. They also review decisions of federal administrative agencies. In many cases that are appealed to a United States Court of Appeals, the losing party may petition the United States Supreme Court for a ***writ of certiorari*** which means the Supreme Court will hear the appeal. Very few cases are granted certiorari. There are 13 circuit courts of appeals, including one for Washington, D.C., and the Federal Circuit, which is devoted, irrespective of geography, to appeals arising from particular types of subject matter disputes. (See Illustration 9-2.)

Illustration 9-2

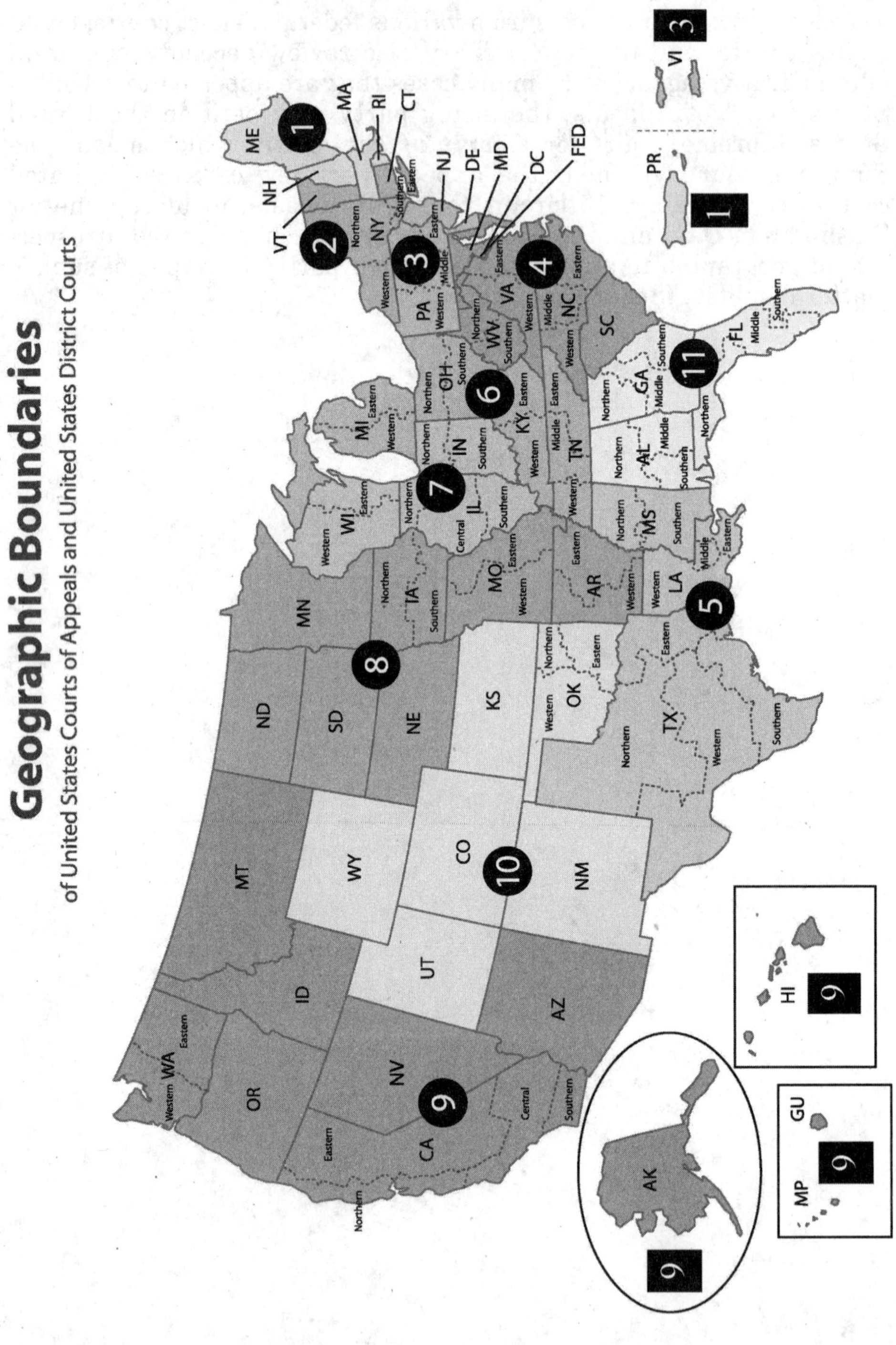

Geographic Boundaries
of United States Courts of Appeals and United States District Courts

§ 9.8.3 United States District Courts

These federal courts have both civil and criminal subject matter jurisdiction. They have original jurisdiction in the following types of actions:

- Civil actions arising under the United States Constitution, laws, or treaties of the United States.
- Actions where the matter in controversy exceeds a set sum (currently $75,000), exclusive of interest and costs, and is between citizens of different states; citizens of a state and foreign states or their citizens or subjects; or citizens of different states in which foreign states or their citizens or subjects are additional parties (diversity jurisdiction).
- All criminal offenses against the laws of the United States.
- Admiralty, maritime, and prize cases.
- Bankruptcy matters and proceedings.
- Actions of interpleader involving money or property of a value equal to or greater than the dollar amount set forth in the current rules claimed by citizens of different states.
- Actions to enforce, enjoin, set aside, annul, or suspend, in whole or in part, any order of the Interstate Commerce Commission.
- Actions or proceedings arising under any act of Congress regulating commerce or protecting trade and commerce against restraints and monopolies.
- Any civil action arising under any act of Congress relating to the postal service.
- Actions arising under any act of Congress providing for internal revenue or revenue from imports or tonnage except matters within the jurisdiction of the Court of International Trade.
- Any civil action authorized by federal law to be commenced by any person dealing with civil rights, election disputes, and voting rights.
- All civil actions, suits, or proceedings commenced by the United States or by any agency or officer thereof.
- Actions for recovery of taxes levied by the Internal Revenue Service or actions not exceeding the current monetary limit set forth in the rules, founded upon the Constitution, any act of Congress, or any regulation of any executive department (the United States Claims Court has concurrent jurisdiction in those actions).
- Actions for the partition of lands where the United States is one of the tenants in common or joint tenants.
- Actions involving banks and other corporations.
- Actions involving labor disputes by specific statute.
- Aliens' actions for torts.
- Actions and proceedings against consuls or vice consuls of foreign states.

- Actions on bonds executed under any law of the United States (state courts have concurrent jurisdiction in those actions).
- Actions involving allotments for Native Americans and land grants from different states.
- Actions involving injuries under federal laws.
- All proceedings to condemn real estate for the use of the United States or its departments or agencies.

§ 9.8.4   Other federal courts

United States Court of Appeals for the Federal Circuit. This court replaced the United States Court of Customs and Patent Appeals effective October 1, 1982. It hears appeals from the United States Claims Court, the United States Court of International Trade, the Merit Systems Protection Board, and appeals in cases relating to patents, copyrights and trademarks, among others. Its decisions may be reviewed by the United States Supreme Court on *certiorari*. (The Federal Circuit is one of the 13 circuit courts of appeals referred to in § 9.8.2. above.)

United States Court of Appeals for the Armed Forces. This court hears appeals from court martial decisions. Its decisions may be reviewed by the Supreme Court by writ of *certiorari* in certain cases.

United States Court of Federal Claims. This court, formerly called the United States Court of Claims, hears actions against the United States Government. These cases may be appealed to the United States Court of Appeals for the Federal Circuit.

United States Tax Court. This court, formerly called the Tax Court of the United States, hears cases concerning federal tax laws. Its decisions may be appealed to the United States Circuit Courts of Appeals (other than the Court of Appeals for the Federal Circuit).

United States Court of International Trade. This court hears cases concerning federal tariff laws. Its decisions may be appealed to the United States Court of Appeals for the Federal Circuit.

United States Bankruptcy Courts. These courts are units of the United States district courts and hear bankruptcy and reorganization matters referred to bankruptcy judges by the district courts. Their decisions may be appealed to the United States district court and, in some cases, to the United States Circuit Courts of Appeals or a bankruptcy appellate panel, if one has been established in that circuit.

§ 9.9   State court system

Because each state has the authority to create its own courts, there are more differences among state courts than federal courts.

Generally, each state has:

- A court of last resort, the highest court in the state from which there is no appeal, except when a decision may be reviewed by the United States Supreme Court.

- An intermediate appellate court or courts to which most appeals are brought before reaching the court of last resort.
- Courts of original jurisdiction having general unlimited jurisdiction. These courts may also have a division that has appellate jurisdiction to hear appeals from lower courts of limited power.
- On a level with these courts, there may be courts with limited jurisdiction, such as a court for family matters, a separate court to handle estate matters, and perhaps a separate criminal court. There also may be a court of claims to hear and determine claims by or against the state.
- The lowest courts in a state are typically courts with lesser monetary and territorial jurisdictions, such as municipal courts, civil courts, district courts, county courts, criminal courts, and even small claims and traffic courts.

§ 9.10   Terminology of the court

Technically, the word *court* means a tribunal with judicial authority to handle the administration of justice. That administration requires a meeting place, a system for meeting at particular times, and administrative personnel. Therefore, when a person is said to be "in court," that phrase usually means that the person is attending a formal court hearing. However, day-to-day usage of the word "court" also includes:

- Reference to a hearing date or place.

  EXAMPLE:
  "Court will be held on June 10" or "Court will recess and reconvene at 2 p.m."

- Reference to the judge who presides at a hearing or over a particular court.

  EXAMPLE:
  "The Court believes," "May it please the Court," or "With the Court's permission." (All spoken by or to the presiding judge.)

- Reference to the physical facility that houses the court (the courtroom or the courthouse).
- Reference to a specific court.

  EXAMPLE:
  Court of Common Pleas or Probate Court, Tulsa County.

§ 9.10.1   Terminology of the court—Term of court

Court rules sometimes designate the period of time during which a court sits to conduct business. This is known as a *term of court*. A term may be divided into different periods which are referred to as sessions. These terms are often given names such as spring term, October term, general term, or trial term.

§ 9.10.2   Terminology of the court—The bar

The *bar* refers to all the lawyers who have been admitted to practice law in a particular state or court system. Their organization is known as the *bar association*. Being licensed to practice law is known as being *admitted to the bar*.

§ 9.10.3   Terminology of the court—The bench

The raised podium at the front of a courtroom behind which the judge sits is known as *the bench*, and the term *the bench* is often used to refer to the judge in a given courtroom. For instance, a *bench-tried case* is tried in front of a judge instead of a jury. During a trial, lawyers may request permission to "approach the bench," meaning they wish to confer with the judge out of the hearing of the jury.

§ 9.10.4   Terminology of the court—In chambers

A judge may sometimes meet with the lawyers and parties in chambers, or in the judge's office, rather than in the courtroom. These meetings usually are less formal than hearings in court. Proceedings in chambers are generally not recorded unless the lawyers make a specific request for a record.

§ 9.10.5   Terminology of the court—In open or closed court

Hearings conducted in the courtroom at which members of the general public may be present as spectators are said to be open. In contrast, hearings that exclude members of the general public as spectators are closed hearings. A judge may exercise discretion whether to close a hearing. Generally, however, unless a closed hearing is required by law, court hearings are open to members of the public.

§ 9.10.6   Terminology of the court—*Ex parte* communications

Ex parte communication is communication to the court that does not include all parties to the matter. *Ex parte* communication is generally prohibited and under most circumstances is considered an ethical violation. However, there are exceptions.

The prevention of injury or harm may necessitate *ex parte* communication; the party who was not included will be informed in due time by service of process. For example, a petition for a restraining order or a personal protection order may be permitted *ex parte*. An order granting *ex parte* generally makes provision for a date and time at which the opposing side may appear before the court to present arguments against the continuation of such order.

If a party has not yet been served in a lawsuit, an application for an extension of time to effect service would also be an *ex parte* communication that could be permitted. Note, however, that the party is not involved in the communication because they have not yet been served.

§ 9.10.7 Terminology of the court—Contempt of court

When an individual refuses to obey a written or oral order of the judge, the judge may find that person in **contempt of court**. The judge usually has the option of levying a fine, imposing a jail sentence, or both upon the person who is found in contempt of court.

§ 9.10.8 Terminology of the court—*Pro se*

When a person represents himself or herself without a lawyer, that person is said to be appearing **pro se** (literally *for myself*) or *in proper person*. (In some courts, such as those in New York, such litigants are now formally referred to as "self-represented litigants"—which terminology is thought to be more respectful.) The *pro se* party also uses that designation when signing pleadings. Generally, corporations, partnerships, and other legal entities cannot appear *pro se* and must appear through a lawyer.

§ 9.10.9 Terminology of the court—Law and motion day

A court often sets aside a specific time or day to hear routine matters, such as motions for purely procedural matters (extension of time, exclusion of evidence, etc.). Hearings at which the lawyers, but not the parties, need appear or which will be of short duration are often set for law or motion days or dockets.

§ 9.10.10 Terminology of the court—Attorneys vs. lawyers

In court, lawyers are always referred to as attorneys, often as attorneys of record, attorney for plaintiff, or attorney for defendant.

§ 9.10.11 Terminology of the court—Docket

The term **docket** refers to a calendar of cases to be tried in a certain term of court or a specific courtroom. Often attorneys who spend much time in court will tend to refer to their own schedule as a **docket**. In a law office, the docket is the day's agenda, including appointments, hearings, and files to be handled. The word docketing is also used to refer to the act of scheduling a case or hearing.

§ 9.11   Officers of the court

Most of the people involved in the administration of justice are known as *officers of the court*.

§ 9.11.1   Officers of the court—Judge

The *judge* is the presiding officer of the court. Most state judges are elected, although some are appointed. All federal judges are appointed. A judge's principal duties are to preside over hearings and the trial of cases and to rule on issues that come up during hearings or trials. The judge instructs the jury on matters of law in jury trials.

§ 9.11.2   Officers of the court—Clerk of court

The *court clerk* is the administrator or chief clerical officer of the court. The clerk is responsible for the clerical details of a case. In most jurisdictions, the court clerk is the custodian of all public records filed with the court. In some jurisdictions, the court clerk is also a recorder of conveyances and of mortgages, and in this capacity, the clerk may keep records of sales and mortgages on property.

§ 9.11.3   Officers of the court—Deputy clerk or law clerk or court attorney

Most judges have at least one *deputy clerk* or *law clerk* or *court attorney*. This person may function as a secretary, assistant, and researcher for the judge. The deputy clerk may attend court sessions and may be responsible for the judge's calendar, files, and exhibits filed with the court. Judges in federal courts and in the higher state courts usually have at least one law clerk in addition to a secretary.

§ 9.11.4   Officers of the court—Court reporter

A court, as circumstances may require, may have a *court reporter* attend in-court sessions and record all legal proceedings verbatim with some type of recording equipment. The court also may have a courtroom deputy clerk to keep track of files, exhibits, and proceedings and to administer oaths. Many courts are using video recording systems to replace actual court reporting.

§ 9.11.5   Officers of the court—Bailiff

The *bailiff* or *court officer* is the peace officer of the court and is responsible for keeping order. The bailiff or court officers is also responsible for the protection of everyone in the courtroom and for maintaining appropriate decorum during proceedings.

§ 9.11.6   Officers of the court—Sheriff or marshal

The *sheriff* is a county officer, and the *marshal* is the law enforcement officer for federal court. Their duties are similar. The sheriff and marshal may serve summonses, complaints, subpoenas, orders of court, garnishments, and executions. The marshal is responsible for transportation of federal prisoners and protection of federal judicial officers. The marshal makes civil seizures to satisfy judgments, holds public auctions, and reports the results to the court regarding these matters. In a few jurisdictions, sheriffs are designated specifically to serve with regard to civil or criminal matters, but not both. In some states, private citizens may be designated as a local "marshal" to undertake many of the civil tasks usually handled by the sheriff.

§ 9.11.7 Officers of the court—Lawyers

Each lawyer is also an officer of the court and as such is obligated to uphold the dignity of the court and to abide by the rules of the court.

§ 9.12 Contact with courts

In performing daily tasks, the lawyer's assistant in litigation practice will often need to talk with court personnel. Having an amicable relationship with these people can make the job much easier. Because they are thoroughly familiar with the procedural aspects of court matters, the savvy assistant will seek guidance from them when he or she is uncertain of court procedures. In a smaller town or county court system, the assistant should get to know the court personnel by name, keeping a file or listing of each contact, what they do, how to reach them directly, and so forth. In a city-based court system, the staff will likely be too large to allow that degree of personal interaction, but the assistant should note which department handles which types of court events. For example, a case initiation department may be responsible for filing new cases and issuing summonses, while the judge's clerk or assistant is responsible for setting up hearings in the individual court divisions. Contacting the correct department will greatly speed the process of getting information and accomplishing the necessary tasks.

§ 9.13 Court records

Courts, both federal and state, generally must keep a record of all judicial proceedings. The record is the written history of all proceedings in a legal matter, regardless of whether the matter is tried. A court record is opened when the complaint or petition is filed. All subsequent pleadings in that case, all actions taken by the court, all written material filed for discovery or evidence, and the transcript of the trial, if there is one, are filed in the record. If an appeal is taken, the appeal also forms part of the record. In the event of an appeal, the entire record, or some designated portion, is sent to the appellate court; the proceedings in the appellate court become part of the record; and when all appeals have been exhausted, the record on appeal is sent back to the trial court, where it remains. Some courts, such as justice of the peace courts, however, do not keep written records of all proceedings, because these are not courts of record.

§ 9.14 Rules of court

Each court, whether federal or state, has its own *court rules* and procedures that govern the conduct of court business. These rules have the effect of law and are very important to the efficient preparation of pleadings or documents, as well as interaction with the court. It is essential that the lawyer and lawyer's assistant both have access to a copy of the court rules for each court in which the lawyer appears. Copies of these rules are usually available from the clerk of court's office. Many law firms subscribe to Thomson-Reuter publications, and each year they will receive a publication that gives the court rules of the United States Supreme Court, the United States Courts of Appeals for the state, the federal district courts for the state, and the major state courts. Most courts also publish their rules on their web pages.

The rules of court provide the court's requirements as to the number of copies of pleadings which must be filed, costs and fees for filing, information about getting orders signed by the judge, priority of cases, how to get on the trial docket, and other useful information. It is important for the lawyer's assistant to consult the rules whenever he or she is unsure how to proceed in a matter pending in court.

As well as the official Federal Rules of Court, which are adopted by Congress, and the state rules, which are generally adopted by the Supreme Court of a given state, local courts often adopt their own rules that tend to fill in the gaps found in the federal and state rules. Therefore, the lawyer and lawyer's assistant should also have a copy of the local rules as well.

§ 9.15 Summary

Although the subject of courts is very broad and sometimes difficult to comprehend, it is essential for a lawyer's assistant to have a good understanding of court structure and procedure. Court rules and procedures change constantly. The lawyer's assistant can keep current by reading bar association publications and by attending workshops and seminars sponsored by NALS® and by local and state bar associations. Often notice of changes in court rules and procedures comes through the mail from law book publishers. The lawyer's assistant should study these changes after they have been routed to the lawyer, noting any important changes.

Chapter 10

Administrative Agencies

KeyCite®: Cases and other legal materials listed in KeyCite Scope can be researched through the KeyCite service on Westlaw®. Use KeyCite to check citations for form, parallel references, prior and later history, and comprehensive citator information, including citations to other decisions and secondary materials.

---

§ 10.1   Introduction

Administrative agencies are created by the legislative branch of government to administer a specific law or group of similar laws. Generally, the three main functions of administrative agencies are (1) rulemaking; (2) regulating individuals and entities subject to their jurisdiction; and (3) enforcement and adjudication. Federal agencies are created by Congress, and state agencies are created by state legislatures. Many federal and state agencies address areas of law that may relate to legal practice requiring familiarity on the part of legal assistants. Some federal and state agencies allow paralegals to represent clients before them, thereby offering career development opportunities.

§ 10.2   Federal agencies

Lawyer's assistants in larger cities are often able to secure needed information from local branches of the agencies and the public library. Local offices were once listed government offices in telephone directories. Now that information is more readily available on an agency's website. For some kinds of information, it may still be necessary to communicate directly with the agency's main office. A useful Internet site is www.USA.gov.

Some of the agencies that a lawyer's assistant may be more apt to have a need to interact with include:

Bureau of Land Management (BLM)
www.blm.gov

The Bureau of Land Management has jurisdiction over approximately 245 million surface acres of public lands and 700 million subsurface acres located primarily in the West and Alaska. Its objective is to maximize public benefit from these public lands. Among the reasons that BLM land may be opened for public use may be for grazing for sheep cattle or for leasing the rights to mineral resources or timber. Among the reason that BLM land may be withdrawn from public use is to conserve natural resources, prevent soil erosion, or protect watershed areas.

Consumer Product Safety Commission (CPSC)

www.cpsc.gov

The CPSC was established to protect the public against unreasonable risks of injury and death from consumer products. The CPSC issues and enforces mandatory standards; issues recalls; conducts research; and informs and educates consumers; and responds to consumer complaints.

Customs and Border Protection (CBP)

www.cbp.gov

As part of the Department of Homeland Security, Customs and Border Protection incorporates the functions of U.S. Customs Service as well as the Border Patrol in collecting revenue from imports and ensuring border security, including the quarantine of agricultural and other products.

Department of Veterans Affairs (VA)

www.va.gov

The Department of Veterans Affairs (formerly the Veterans Administration) provides for the care and benefits of veterans. Among these benefits are compensation for service-connected disability or death; pensions for non-service-connected disability or death, based on age and financial need; medical benefits including nursing home, domiciliary, or hospital care; burial benefits; and life insurance. Benefits may extend to dependents and survivors.

Environmental Protection Agency (EPA)

www.epa.gov

The EPA was established to protect human health and safeguard the natural environment. Among its ongoing efforts is working with state and local governments to abate and control pollution.

Equal Employment Opportunity Commission (EEOC)

www.eeoc.gov

The EEOC was established to eliminate discrimination in all areas of employment and to promote voluntary compliance by employers. The EEOC enforces federal laws that make it illegal to discriminate against a job applicant or an employee because of the person's race, color, religion, sex, national origin, age, disability, or genetic information.

Federal Aviation Administration (FAA)

www.faa.gov

The FAA is charged with regulating air commerce to promote aviation safety.

Federal Bureau of Investigation (FBI)

www.fbi.gov

The FBI's primary purpose is to protect and defend the United States against terrorist and foreign-intelligence threats acting inside the United States; to uphold and enforce the criminal laws of the United States; and to provide leadership and criminal justice services to federal, state, municipal, and international agencies.

The FBI investigates all violations of federal criminal laws except those specifically assigned to other federal agencies. Some of the areas in which the FBI is involved are espionage, sabotage, kidnapping, extortion, bank robbery, civil rights matters, interstate gambling violations, and assault or attack on the President or a federal officer.

Federal Communications Commission (FCC)

www.fcc.gov

The FCC licenses and regulates interstate and foreign communications by radio, television, wire, satellite, and cable.

Federal Deposit Insurance Corporation (FDIC)

www.fdic.gov

The FDIC is an independent agency within the executive branch that provides insurance coverage for depositors' accounts in banks and savings and loans up to a specific amount in the event of the failure of a financial institution. The FDIC also examines and supervises financial institutions for safety and soundness to protect consumers and manages receiverships when required.

Federal Mediation and Conciliation Service (FMCS)

www.fmcs.gov

The FMCS provides mediation services to industry, community, and other governmental agencies. The FMCS offers its services upon request or in disputes affecting interstate commerce, including mediation of labor-management relationships, work stoppages, threatened work stoppages, and other labor-management disputes.

Federal Trade Commission (FTC)

www.ftc.gov

The primary objective of the FTC is to protect consumers and prevent anticompetitive business practices. The FTC enforces those laws over which it has enforcement authority. One important task of the FTC is to protect franchisees by dictating the types of disclosures required by franchisors.

Food and Drug Administration (FDA)

www.fda.gov

FDA activities are directed toward protecting the public against unsafe drugs, food, cosmetics, and medical devices. The FDA is also responsible for helping to speed innovations that make medicines and foods safer, more affordable, and, in the case of medicines, more effective. The FDA also has jurisdiction over biopharmaceuticals, animal feeds, and veterinary products.

Government Printing Office (GPO)

www.gpo.gov

The GPO is responsible for the gathering, cataloguing, producing, authenticating, and preserving published information for the federal government. There are approximately a quarter of a million titles available to the public at www.gpo.gov/fdsys, and another half million titles are available through the GPO's partner websites. A free informational brochure designed to familiarize the public with the material, *Consumers Guide to Federal Publications,* is available from the GPO.

Internal Revenue Service (IRS)

www.irs.gov

The IRS is a federal agency that administers all federal tax laws except those relating to alcohol, tobacco, firearms, and explosives as well as tariffs.

National Labor Relations Board (NLRB)

www.nlrb.gov

The NLRB administers the National Labor Relations Act, a law that governs relations between unions and employers in the private sector. NLRB is vested with the power to safeguard employees' rights to form bargaining units and to prevent and remedy unfair labor practices.

Occupational Safety and Health Administration (OSHA)

www.osha.gov

OSHA develops and regulates occupational safety and health standards, including the investigation and adjudication of whistleblower complaints. OSHA also encourages states to develop and operate their own job safety and health programs and approves and monitors state plans.

Securities and Exchange Commission (SEC)

www.sec.gov

The SEC regulates the securities industry by enforcing the securities laws as they relate to companies subject to its jurisdiction. This includes rulemaking, monitoring activities of companies subject to its jurisdiction, and undertaking investigations and administrative actions.

Small Business Administration (SBA)

www.sba.gov

The SBA provides various types of assistance, including loans or loan guarantees, for small businesses.

Social Security Administration (SSA)

www.ssa.gov

This Social Security Administration administers Social Security, Retirement, Medicare, and Disability programs.

U.S. Marshals Service

www.usmarshalls.gov

The U.S. Marshals Service shares the responsibility for ensuring the security of court facilities and judicial personnel. The Marshals Service has the primary responsibility for the tracking and apprehension of fugitives.

United States Citizenship and Immigration Services (US-CIS)

www.uscis.gov

As part of the Department of Homeland Security, USCIS oversees the administration and enforcement of the immigration laws of the United States. Among its areas of responsibility are those previously overseen by the Immigration and Naturalization Service (INS).

United States Patent and Trademark Office (USPTO)

www.uspto.gov

The Patent and Trademark Office reviews and registers trademarks and service marks. The existence of this agency is derived directly from the U.S. Constitution Its jurisdiction over trademarks is derived indirectly from the Constitution's Commerce Clause.

United States Postal Service (USPS)

www.usps.gov

The Postal Service provides mail processing and delivery to individuals and entities within the United States. It also processes mail for delivery to areas outside of the United States.

§ 10.3 State agencies

Each state government and many local governments have their own administrative agencies. Depending upon the state and local government, it is often quite common for contacts to occur between law firms and these state and local agencies.

EXAMPLES:

- Public service or public utilities commissions regulate utilities (oil, gas, water, telephone, and electricity).
- Workers' compensation boards or industrial commissions handle claims of workers injured on their jobs.
- Civil service commissions regulate the hiring of government employees.
- Licensing boards regulate the issuance of licenses for any profession designated by the law that create these boards.
- Boards of health regulate matters concerning public health.
- Zoning commissions regulate the use of property under their jurisdiction.
- School boards regulate matters involving the public school systems.
- Banking boards regulate certain aspects of banking subject to their jurisdiction.

§ 10.4 Establishing and maintaining a contact and good relations with an agency

When a lawyer's assistant calls an administrative agency, he or she may be transferred repeatedly before reaching someone who may be able to provide the needed information. Because further contact with this person may be needed, it is important to document the name, title, telephone number and extension, fax number, address, and e-mail address (or as much of this information as can be obtained). Retention of such information within a file is also recommended so that future calls on the same matter can then be handled more efficiently.

It is important to maintain a positive relationship with all agency contacts even when needed information is not immediately forthcoming or the person with whom you are speaking is difficult. The person contacted may not be able to help in the short run but may be able to turn a problematic situation around on another occasion. It all depends on maintaining goodwill with the contact. Further, all such contacts should be handled professionally as the lawyer's assistant represents the lawyer and his or her firm.

Whether through a publication or website, may state and local governments publish a directory or manual that lists the various agencies and their functions. The Secretary of State may be able to provide such a directory or advise where such a list may be found. The time invested in locating this information may save a great deal of time over the long run.

Chapter 11

Litigation

KeyCite®: Cases and other legal materials listed in KeyCite Scope can be researched through the KeyCite service on Westlaw®. Use KeyCite to check citations for form, parallel references, prior and later history, and comprehensive citator information, including citations to other decisions and secondary materials.

---

§ 11.1 Litigation

Simply stated, litigation practice is the handling, preparation, and trial of lawsuits. This chapter offers a discussion of the steps in a civil lawsuit.

The American legal system provides that any person injured by another may bring a civil suit seeking damages for any legal wrong. The reason for the lawsuit, then, arises when one party suffers an injury or damage as a result of a legal wrong committed by another.

§ 11.2   Opening the litigation file

Before a suit can be filed, the lawyer and client need to meet, agree on the terms of representation, and do preliminary paperwork.

§ 11.2.1   Opening the litigation file—Initial client interview

The lawyer's first interview with the client is to determine whether there is a *cause of action*, or a wrong for which relief can be sought in court. In the early stages of the first interview, the lawyer must learn the names of all parties and whether an insurance company is involved. An initial or preliminary conflicts check should be completed before the lawyer delves too deeply into the case. The lawyer may sometimes be able to decide during the initial interview whether to accept the case. Other times, more research may need to be done first. During the initial interview, the lawyer will also answer the client's questions, explain how the case will be handled, estimate how long it may take to resolve the case, and explain the fee arrangement.

§ 11.2.2   Opening the litigation file—The fee arrangement

Legal management experts and state ethical rules emphasize the need for the lawyer and client to have a full understanding of the fee arrangement between them. Most lawyers make it a point to obtain a signed fee agreement during the first interview.

Contingency fees. When a client's case involves a personal injury for which damages may be recovered, a *contingency fee arrangement* is often used. Under a contingency fee arrangement, the client pays a specified percentage of the total recovery as a fee. Usually the percentage is less if the case is settled before suit is filed or before trial begins. If there is no recovery, there is no fee.

Flat fees. Depending on the kind of case involved, the fee may be a *flat fee*, a set amount covering all work to be done.

Hourly billing. Often the client is billed hourly in legal matters for which it is difficult to assess how much time will be billed.

Costs. The client is responsible for the costs of litigation, regardless of the type of fee arrangement chosen. The ethical rules and statutes do not permit the lawyer to pay costs for the client, although the lawyer can advance costs on behalf of the client for later repayment. Costs include expenses such as copy costs, filing fees, witness fees, and so forth.

§ 11.2.3   Opening the litigation file—Authorization forms

Depending upon the nature of the case, there are probably several forms the client will need to sign. It is usually most convenient to do this at the initial interview.

Medical authorizations. These forms are necessary to secure medical reports, x-rays, and other medical data from doctors and hospitals. Typically the lawyer has the client sign a medical authorization with the healthcare provider's name left blank so that it can be used for each doctor who treated the client and for each hospital or clinic in which the client was a patient.

Employer authorization. Employers need an authorization to release payroll information, and it may be necessary to have this information to establish lost wages.

Income tax authorizations. Income tax returns may also be needed to establish damages or lost wages. State taxing agencies and the Internal Revenue Service have special forms for this purpose.

Authorization to settle the case. The client sometimes signs an authorization for the lawyer to settle the claim for a specified amount. The case cannot be settled without client authorization.

General authorizations. General authorizations are written to suit a particular need. The lawyer usually dictates the contents of these documents.

§ 11.2.4 Opening the litigation file—Organizing the file

One of the most valuable services the lawyer's assistant can render in litigation matters is to organize the contents of the client's file. From the information obtained during the initial interview, the lawyer's assistant should generate a contact information sheet including the client's information and a new matter report, if one has not already been prepared.

If the law office has no preferred litigation file structure, the subfile structure discussed below may be useful.

Correspondence. All correspondence is arranged in reverse chronological order, with the most recent letter in front.

Attorney notes. Attorney notes should be arranged in reverse chronological order, ideally with each set of notes bearing the date on the front page.

Authorization files. A subfile or subfiles should be created for authorizations and requests for documents from sources such as health-care practitioners, employers, income tax agencies, and so forth. If there are a number of authorizations and records requests, a separate subfile can be set up for each agency from which records are being requested.

Pleadings. Pleadings files should be maintained in reverse chronological order, and the pleadings file should have an index indicating the date, party filing, and title of each pleading. The pleadings are filed behind numbered tabs, which are noted in the index for quick reference.

Discovery pleadings. A discovery pleadings subfile should be created to hold discovery documents. There are different philosophies about what should be in discovery subfiles. The most common practice is to place discovery pleadings and certificates of mailing together in one subfile. A less common practice is to include all court motions regarding discovery in the same file—this practice is most helpful when there are a number of discovery disputes. A separate subfile can be created for discovery requests going out and discovery requests coming in, or separate subfiles can be created for discovery coming from each different party in the case, when there are more than two parties. If needed, a discovery pleadings subfile can be indexed just as the pleadings file is.

Investigation. The investigation subfile can include accident reports, police reports, investigation reports, statements, and other items related to investigation.

Legal research. A subfile may be created for all legal research, with tabs separating different cases or topics and an index referencing each item, or separate subfiles may be created for each individual topic.

Fact witnesses. It may be useful to create a subfile for each fact witness. The file can include any documentation provided regarding the witness's potential testimony, the witness's statement and deposition transcript, and any other information developed regarding the witness.

Expert witnesses. Expert witnesses will provide a curriculum vitae or résumé describing their professional experience, prepare an expert report prior to trial, and may give a deposition prior to the trial. All of this information can be gathered in a separate subfile for each expert witness.

Exhibits. It may be helpful to create a subfile for trial exhibits, including photographs, drawings, documents, and so forth.

Billing and Costs. Some firms restrict the use of a firm billing file to only those documents sent to the client by the firm. Where that is the case, a separate costs subfile should be created to contain documentation of all case expenses, check requests, and other cost information related to the case. Where the firm is less strict in the use of a billing subfile, the cost information can be kept with the billing memoranda.

Careful organization will keep the file ready for the lawyer's review at any time. By following a consistent system in maintaining litigation files, when trial time arrives, the file will be in excellent condition, and the lawyer will have everything available needed to present the case.

§ 11.3 Before suit is filed

Before filing the lawsuit, the lawyer must be sure the matter cannot reasonably be settled without litigation. Then, when the lawyer decides to file suit, he or she must be certain that the lawsuit is filed by the correct parties, in the proper court within the statute of limitations requirements.

§ 11.3.1 Before suit is filed—The demand letter

The first step in settlement negotiation in many trials is the demand letter, which details the plaintiff's injuries and makes a demand for settlement upon the prospective defendant, typically threatening a lawsuit if the demands are not met. The amount demanded is based on the lawyer's experience with similar claims and injuries and is calculated to cover the plaintiff's costs including attorney's fees and a settlement amount for the plaintiff over and above the costs. The prospective defendant often contacts a lawyer to handle the demand letter and any subsequent litigation. The prospective defendant's counsel will consider the potential cost of litigation and the perceived validity of the plaintiff's demand. It is not unusual for offers and counteroffers to go back and forth several times before litigation is filed, and some cases are settled before the case is filed. Each time a new offer or counteroffer is received by either attorney, he or she is required to notify the client of the offer.

§ 11.3.2 Before suit is filed—Who may sue

The injured **party** (the *plaintiff*) is the person best able to determine whether to seek a recovery through the legal system for the alleged wrong done to them, so only the injured party has **standing** to bring a civil suit. The rule of standing is designed to control the amount of litigation that might arise from one incident or wrong by letting only the injured parties sue.

A **party or *person*** in litigation includes many legal entities, including corporations and partnerships, and is not limited to a human being. To have standing, the person or entity must have the legal capacity to sue.

Legal capacity refers to whether a person may sue in the person's own right without the assistance of someone else. Until a person reaches *majority* (usually 18 to 21 years of age), that person is a minor whose legal affairs must be handled by a parent or guardian. If a minor is emancipated, the minor has the legal capacity and authority to handle the minor's own legal affairs.

An adult who is mentally incapacitated cannot sue except through a guardian who has been appointed by the court to handle the legal affairs of that person. A deceased person's estate has standing to be a party to a lawsuit only through a *fiduciary* (*administrator, executor*, or *personal representative*) appointed by a court.

§ 11.3.3 Before suit is filed—Jurisdiction

The *jurisdiction* of the courts is set forth by Congress or by state legislature and is the authority of a court to hear a matter. If the complaint or petition is filed in a court that does not have jurisdiction, any action taken by the court in the lawsuit is void. *Venue*, often referred to as geographical jurisdiction, is the county or parish where the incident giving rise to the lawsuit occurred or where the parties reside. An important difference between jurisdiction and venue is the parties may waive venue, but jurisdiction is conveyed only by law and cannot be altered by the parties.

Jurisdiction covers the parties, the subject matter, the amount of damages in controversy, and other relevant factors. A new lawsuit may be brought only in a court of original jurisdiction, or a court that has jurisdiction to hear the matter for the first time.

Often, courts have *concurrent jurisdiction*; that is, an action may be filed properly in more than one court. For instance, some suits may be filed either in a state court or in a United States district court, provided the jurisdictional requirements of both courts are met. (For a more complete discussion of jurisdiction and venue, see Chapter 9, The Courts.)

§ 11.3.4   Before suit is filed—Statutes of limitation

Statutes of limitation set out, in both state and federal courts, how quickly litigation must be filed after the incident giving rise to the litigation occurs. If an action is filed after the statute of limitations expires, the defendant can ask to have the suit dismissed. Most statutes of limitations have exceptions that "toll" or delay the running of the statute of limitations. Such tolling can create an extension of time in which to file the suit. However, if a defendant can show that the case is not covered by such an exception, the suit will probably be dismissed. Note that the statute of limitations does not require that the litigation be completed within the time period set by statute; it simply must be filed.

Statutes of limitation vary considerably from state to state; within the states, they vary considerably among the types of claims. The statute of limitations might be one year, for example, on a worker's compensation case and five years on a fraud case.

Many legal malpractice claims arise out of missed statute of limitations dates. The lawyer's assistant can play a significant role in not allowing the statute of limitations to expire by keeping an accurate reminder system. As each file is opened, the lawyer's assistant should ask the lawyer to determine the statute of limitations date so it can be entered on the calendar. (See Chapter 3, The Law Office, for a detailed discussion of reminder systems.)

§ 11.4   Pleadings

Written statements called *pleadings* are prepared by the attorneys on each side of a lawsuit concerning the respective claims and defenses that will be tried in court. In some courts, the term *pleading* only refers to documents that contain statements or denials of fact, such as the complaint or petition, the answer, the reply, an answer to a cross-claim or counterclaim, or a third-party complaint and answer. Other papers filed in court may include orders, motions, memoranda, and affidavits. These documents may not be included within the term *pleading* under court rules. However, outside the courts, virtually all documents that bear a case style and are filed with a court or used in discovery during litigation are referred to generically as *pleadings*.

§ 11.4.1 Pleadings—Parties

Often, the natural persons, corporations, or other legal entities involved in a lawsuit are referred to as *parties*.

The term *plaintiff* is most commonly used to refer to the party who files a lawsuit. The term *petitioner* is more often used to refer to a party who files a nonlitigious proceeding (such as an adoption or probate matter) or the party who initiates dissolution proceedings in states having no-fault divorce laws. The *defendant* is the party who is sued. In states having no-fault divorce laws, the party being sued is often called the *respondent*.

§ 11.4.2 Pleadings—Filing

When a pleading is stamped and placed in the court file by the clerk or deputy clerk, the pleading is considered "filed". If it is the first pleading in the case, the clerk opens a new file and issues a case number (also sometimes known as a civil number, a docket number, or an index number). The case number is used on all future pleadings and documents filed in that case. Most courts assign case numbers in numerical order, but sometimes the numbering systems are divided into various subject matters, such as civil, criminal, family court, and others.

The original complaint, along with enough copies to meet court requirements and a copy for each defendant, the client, and the file, are filed with the clerk of the court. A filing fee is required at the time of filing the complaint. The clerk "file-stamps" the original pleading and all copies and returns the extra copies to the filer.

Some courts charge a fee only for commencing the action when the first pleading (complaint) is filed; others charge a fee for each additional pleading initiating action (such as counterclaims). Still other courts charge for filing certain other documents (such as jury demands). Most courts require the correct filing fee to be paid at the time the applicable document is filed.

In most state courts, a new case can be filed in person or by mail, provided all the needed documents are included and the proper fee is enclosed. When pleadings are filed by mail, the filer should enclose a self-addressed envelope with sufficient postage for all stamped copies to be returned. A fairly large number of state courts permit filing by facsimile, but court rules vary widely. The lawyer's assistant should always research court rules before fax filing.

All federal courts of original jurisdiction now require electronic filing. See § 4.19 for a more detailed explanation of electronic filing procedures.

§ 11.5 Complaint or petition

The pleading filed to initiate an action is usually called a complaint or a petition. In some jurisdictions, the term *complaint* is used in litigated matters, and the term *petition* is reserved for legal proceedings that do not involve a contest, such as petitions for adoption. In other jurisdictions, the term *petition* is used for all types of cases.

§ 11.5.1 Complaint or petition—Caption

The *caption* or *style* of the case is the title of the case. The actual form of the caption varies from jurisdiction to jurisdiction, but it usually sets out:

- The full name of the court in which the action is filed.
- The full names of the parties, with the plaintiff's name listed first. The Federal Rules of Civil Procedure and some state courts require the caption of the complaint to include the full names of all parties. An abbreviated style is acceptable on subsequent pleadings if there are multiple plaintiffs, listing only the name of the first plaintiff, followed by *et al.* to indicate there are other plaintiffs. The same procedure is used for cases having multiple defendants.
- The number of the case.
- The name of the pleading.

Illustration 11-1

IN THE DISTRICT COURT OF THE SIXTH JUDICIAL
DISTRICT OF THE STATE OF IDAHO, IN AND
FOR BANNOCK COUNTY

```
JOHN DOE, FRED WHEELER,          )
SAM SMITH, GEORGE                )
ALCOTT, ACE LINCOLN,             )   Civil No. ___
and JOHN BRYAN,                  )
                    Plaintiffs,  )   COMPLAINT
vs.                              )
                                 )
JANE X. BROWN,                   )
                    Defendant.   )
```

§ 11.5.2 Complaint or petition—Opening paragraphs

After an introductory paragraph introduces the plaintiff(s) and defendant(s) and briefly notes the nature of the case, all remaining paragraphs are numbered for ease of reference. In the complaint, such numbered paragraphs are called *allegations*.

§ 11.5.3   Complaint or petition—Allegations or claims

The first group of allegations usually provides information establishing the legal capacity of the plaintiff, the domicile of the parties, and the legal basis for jurisdiction and venue of the court. Depending on the complexity of the case, the pleading may be presented without further subdivision, ending with a paragraph that begins with the word "wherefore" and sets out the plaintiff's request for relief.

§ 11.5.4   Complaint or petition—Counts

If the case is complex, the complaint may first state the facts of the case, sometimes under a heading such as "Background", followed by a series of numbered counts which set forth various types of claims, such as breach of contract, quantum meruit, or others. Each count begins with an allegation stating that all prior allegations are included in the count as if fully set forth therein. Following that is listed a series of brief allegations that establish the legal basis for the specific count. Each count ends with a "wherefore" paragraph.

§ 11.5.5   Complaint or petition—Prayer

Each wherefore paragraph contains a **prayer** or a request for relief that sets forth a summary of what the plaintiff or petitioner is asking the court to do with respect to the specific count. Every complaint, whether individual counts are listed or not, ends with a wherefore paragraph that states a summary of the relief requested for the entire complaint. Sometimes the wherefore paragraphs under each count are tailored to the losses enumerated within the count, and sometimes they are identical to the final prayer for relief, depending on the lawyer's taste and training, the demands of the court, and the traditions in that venue. Wherefore paragraphs are not numbered.

§ 11.5.6   Complaint or petition—Verification

A complaint must be signed by the plaintiff's lawyer and must contain the lawyer's address, telephone number, and state bar number. In addition, many courts now require the lawyer to include an email address. In some jurisdictions the complaint may contain a statement by the plaintiff asserting that the allegations are true and correct to the best of the plaintiff's knowledge and belief. This is called a **verification** and is placed at the end of the complaint following the lawyer's signature. (See Illustration 11-2.) A verified complaint may also, in many cases, be used as an affidavit in later proceedings in the case. The verification must be signed before a notary public in some states.

Illustration 11-2

NO. ____

JANE DOE,	) IN THE DISTRICT COURT
Plaintiff,	)
v.	) ____ JUDICIAL DISTRICT
	)
ALEX PRINCE,	) BEXAR COUNTY, TEXAS
Defendant.	)

COMPLAINT

Plaintiff makes the following complaint:

1. The plaintiff is a resident of the City of ____, County of ____, State of ____, and the defendant is a resident of ____ County, residing at ____ Street, ____, ____. *[If either party is a corporation, give place and where incorporated.]*

2. On or about the ____ day of ____, *[Year]*, a ____ automobile owned by plaintiff was being driven by ____ in a ____ direction on ____ Street, in the City of ____. *[Set out facts upon which the plaintiff bases her cause of action.]*

3. The defendant was negligent in the operation of his automobile at the time of the collision in the following particulars: *[State facts indicating negligence].*

Each of the foregoing acts of omission and of commission were negligent, and each was a proximate cause of the accident which is the basis of the suit.

4. As a result of the collision, plaintiff has been forced to spend the sum of $____ in order to repair her automobile.

5. Plaintiff's automobile prior to said collision had a reasonable market value of $____, and just after the collision it had a reasonable market value of $____. Therefore, the plaintiff has been damaged in the amount of $____.

WHEREFORE, plaintiff prays that upon final hearing, the plaintiff recover her damages as alleged above, together with all costs; and for such other, further, and general relief to which she may be entitled.

_____
(name and address of lawyer)
Attorney for Plaintiff

VERIFICATION

STATE OF TEXAS	)
	) ss.
COUNTY OF ____	)

JANE DOE, being duly sworn, deposes and states she is the plaintiff in the above entitled action, she has read the foregoing complaint and every statement contained in the complaint is within her personal knowledge and is true and correct.

_____

JANE DOE

Subscribed and sworn to before me the ____ day of ____, *[Year]*.

_____

Notary Public, State of Texas

My commission expires:

§ 11.5.7 Complaint or petition—Suit for money damages

A damage suit seeks an award of money. Some examples of suits seeking **money damages** are automobile accident cases, slip-and-fall cases, contract disputes, title actions (boundary disputes and other land matters), consumer actions, civil antitrust actions, and professional malpractice cases.

§ 11.5.8 Complaint or petition—Suit for equity relief

Although most lawsuits seek awards of money, some seek other types of relief.

EXAMPLES:

Assume *A* and *B* entered into a contract in which *B* agreed to begin building a residence for *A* within 90 days after execution of the contract. *B* does not begin the work as he promised. *A* sues *B* for **specific performance**, which means he wants *B* to perform the terms of the contract.

A is demolishing a building in a residential area using explosives. *B* is concerned that his building next to *A*'s also will be demolished by the explosion. *B* may seek **injunctive relief**, asking the court to issue an injunction preventing *A* from using explosives to demolish his building.

Injunctive relief also may be sought to require that something be done rather than that something be stopped.

EXAMPLE:

A and the phone company are involved in a dispute over the nonpayment of a commercial account, a portion of which *A* guaranteed. *A* refuses to pay the disputed portion of the bill, so the phone company terminates *A*'s phone service at his residence. *A* seeks injunctive relief to require the phone company to restore his service.

§ 11.5.9   Complaint or petition—Alternative relief

In suits that seek one type of relief, it is not uncommon to ask for alternative relief as well.

EXAMPLE:

Assuming the facts in the house construction contract example above, *A*'s complaint could contain a plea in the alternative that if the court decides he is not entitled to specific performance, then he should be awarded a sum of money damages for the harm he sustained in not having his residence timely built.

§ 11.6   The civil cover sheet

The federal courts and most state courts now require a civil cover sheet be filed with each new case. The civil cover sheet contains basic information about the case for the court's case records. The names and addresses of the first named parties (some civil cover sheets ask for the names and addresses of all parties, continued on a separate sheet if needed); the name, address, phone number, and bar number of the attorney; information regarding opposing counsel, if known; the type of case; the amount of damages; and a very brief statement of the matters at issue in the case are among the information that is required on most civil cover sheets. Some civil cover sheets require the attorney's signature.

§ 11.7   The summons and service

A defendant must be served with the complaint and must be officially notified that suit has been filed. The official notification of a suit being filed is called a **summons**. The summons also advises the defendant that there is a time limit within which an appearance in court—which can be established by filing a pleading in response to the complaint—must be made.

After a complaint has been filed, the clerk in some states will sign and issue a summons. In other states, the summons may be issued by the plaintiff's lawyer after it is file-stamped with the case number by the clerk. The lawyer's assistant must prepare sufficient copies of the complaint and summons for service upon each defendant and extra copies if the lawyer is required to provide a copy for the return of service. The summons and a copy of the complaint, if required, may be served by the sheriff, the deputy, or by any other authorized person who is over the age of 18 and not a party to the action.

In some jurisdictions, the suit is not considered filed until the defendant has been served with the summons and complaint, because it is the service upon the defendant that brings him or her under the jurisdiction of the court. Failure to make proper service on the defendant within a prescribed time period can cause the complaint to be dismissed. This could cause the plaintiff to lose the right to sue if, by that time, the statute of limitations has run.

In a few states, a summons is not used. The lawyer's assistant must be aware of the procedures required in each jurisdiction where the lawyer practices.

§ 11.7.1   The summons and service—Information for service

The lawyer's assistant should be certain the process server has sufficient information to help him or her locate the defendant promptly. As a rule, the following information should be provided: complete name, gender, race, home address, and place of employment, including address, work hours, and telephone number. Any other information, such as type of car and places frequented, is helpful.

§ 11.7.2   The summons and service—Service of process

Service is obtained by delivering a copy of the summons and complaint to each defendant. The process server then completes the return of service on the original or a copy of the summons (depending upon the jurisdiction), which shows the name of the person served, and the place, date, and time of service. (See Illustration 11-3.) The summons showing the return of service is then filed with the court. In some jurisdictions, the process server prepares a separate certificate or affidavit of return of service.

Illustration 11-3

RETURN OF SERVICE

STATE OF ____   )
) ss.
COUNTY OF ____)

____, being duly sworn, states that he is a person of suitable age and discretion and that on the ____ day of ____, *[Year]*, he served the Summons and the Complaint, a copy of which is attached hereto, upon _____*(name of defendant)*, at ____, by personally delivering same to said defendant.

_____

Subscribed and sworn to before me
this ____ day of ____, *[Year]*.

_____

Notary Public

My commission expires:

§ 11.7.3　The summons and service—Service on a nonresident

For service of a nonresident defendant, a process server in the defendant's area can be used. The process server should be provided with a copy of the rules of service for the jurisdiction in which the case is filed. Many states have a long-arm statute, under which service may be obtained through the secretary of state, who forwards the service documents by certified mail, return receipt requested, to the defendant's last known address. A small fee is usually charged by the secretary of state. In some states, long-arm statute service can be obtained by the lawyer, using certified mail.

§ 11.7.4　The summons and service—Service on corporations

Service on corporations is obtained through a service agent, who may be a corporate officer, at the corporate offices in the state where suit has been filed, or upon a service agent registered with the state corporate division, commonly known as a ***registered agent***. Check the website of the state corporate division (often a division of the secretary of state's or lieutenant governor's office) to learn whether there is an agent for service in the state.

The defendant corporation is often a foreign corporation, particularly in the case of insurance companies. A foreign corporation is a corporation domiciled in another state. It is important to determine whether the company has designated a registered agent to accept service of process in the state where suit has been filed.

§ 11.7.5　The summons and service—Other types of service

Some states also provide, under certain circumstances, for:
- Service on a third party at the residence of defendant.
- Service by posting the summons on the door of the defendant's residence or in a public place.
- Service by publication of a notice in a newspaper of general circulation for a specific period of time.

Affidavits as to the need for service by one of these methods are sometimes required, and a court order granting permission to serve by one of these methods is needed.

§ 11.8　Delivery of complaint or petition to the court clerk

In preparing the complaint for filing with the clerk, confirm that the original complaint is signed by the lawyer; the verification of the client is attached, signed, and notarized, if applicable; a civil cover sheet has been prepared and signed by the attorney, if needed; there are sufficient copies for service and return of service; there are an appropriate number of summonses prepared for issuance by the clerk, if appropriate; and there is a check for the filing fee.

§ 11.9   Request for jury trial

In most jurisdictions, the lawyer must request a jury trial well in advance of the trial date. A jury fee sometimes accompanies the request for a jury trial. See Illustration 11-4 for a sample jury request. Failure to make a timely request for a jury trial may later prevent the parties from having a jury trial, resulting in a trial before the judge. In some jurisdictions, the request for jury trial is filed with or as a part of the complaint or answer.

Illustration 11-4

NO. ____

JOHN W. BROWN,	)	IN THE DISTRICT COURT
Plaintiff	)	
v.	)	____ JUDICIAL DISTRICT
	)	
CHARLES M. WHITE,	)	____ COUNTY, TEXAS
Defendant	)	

DEMAND FOR JURY TRIAL

Now comes CHARLES M. WHITE, defendant in the above-referenced cause, and demands a trial by jury.

_____
(Name and address of lawyer)
ATTORNEY FOR DEFENDANT,
CHARLES M. WHITE

CERTIFICATE OF SERVICE

I certify that a true and correct copy of the foregoing Demand for Jury Trial was served on the attorney for plaintiff, Mr. Jack Jones, 717 Main Street, Your town, Your State, by certified mail, return receipt requested, on this ____ day of ____, *[Year]*.

_____
(Defendant's Lawyer)

§ 11.10   Appearance of counsel

After receiving the summons and complaint, most defendants hire an attorney. The first thing an attorney will generally do is file a short pleading called an ***entry of appearance*** with the court. This tells the court and the plaintiff that the defendant is represented by counsel and all contact with defendant must be through defendant's attorney.

§ 11.11   Objections to the complaint

The defendant may object to the form of the complaint on several grounds as described below.

§ 11.11.1   Objections to the complaint—Lack of jurisdiction

A motion objecting to the jurisdiction is filed in lieu of an answer. It alleges that the court has no jurisdiction over the party filing it and states the reason for such lack of jurisdiction. Its purpose is to prevent the entering of a default judgment pending a decision by the court on jurisdiction. Usually this pleading must be sworn to and filed before any answer is filed or the defendant may waive the right to file it.

§ 11.11.2   Objections to the complaint—Motion to quash service

If service is improperly made, the wrong party is served, or the summons does not show the date of service, a motion may be made to *quash service*, or declare the service invalid. This requires the plaintiff's lawyer to have the summons reissued and new service attempted.

§ 11.11.3   Objections to the complaint—Motion to change venue

A *motion to change venue*, sometimes called a *plea to the venue*, must be filed before an answer is filed, must be sworn to, and must give reasons why the case should be transferred to another county or parish.

EXAMPLES:

The incident occurred in a different county from where the suit is filed, so the court does not have venue.

The residence of the parties is in a different county, so the court does not have venue.

The plaintiff, within a time set out by statute, may file a responsive pleading setting out any statutory conditions that would allow the lawsuit to remain in the county where it was originally filed. If the plaintiff does not timely file such a response, the order of transfer is prepared by the defendant's lawyer and submitted to the court for entry. Unlike the other responses discussed here, an answer to the complaint must be filed in addition to the motion to change venue. Such answer should state that the answer is subject to the motion to change venue and does not waive such issue.

§ 11.12   Answer

After being served, the defendant has a specific time within which to file an *answer* or other response to the complaint. The time varies from state to state and even from court to court within a state. In the federal courts, the time is usually 30 days if the defendant resides within the same state, unless the United States is a party defendant, in which case the answer date is 60 days.

In federal court, extensions of time are obtained only with permission of the court. In some instances, an answer may never be filed because the defendant never appears in the case or the case has been settled out of court. A trial cannot be held until the answer is filed.

The answer is a pleading in which the defendant responds to the allegations of the complaint, paragraph by paragraph. The defendant's answer tells the defendant's version of the lawsuit. Often the defendant simply denies all allegations of the complaint.

EXAMPLES:

The defendant John Good, by and through his attorney of record, for answer to the complaint filed herein, denies each and every allegation as though his denials were set out at length herein.

The defendant John Good, by and through his attorney of record, for answer to the complaint filed herein, denies the allegations of paragraphs 1 through 10, inclusive, as though his denials were set out at length herein.

Sometimes the allegations contain information about which the defendant has no knowledge. However, each of the allegations must be answered. In this situation, those allegations are denied for lack of information sufficient to justify a belief as to the truth or falsity of the specific allegation.

EXAMPLE:

The defendant denies the allegations of paragraphs 5, 6, 7, 9, and 10 and states he lacks sufficient information or belief to answer those allegations.

Note that in federal court and most state courts, each specific allegation of the plaintiff's complaint must be either denied or admitted. Those allegations not specifically denied are deemed admitted unless the defense counsel can show good cause why they can neither be admitted nor denied. It is good practice to include a general denial: "All allegations not specifically admitted herein are denied."

§ 11.12.1 Answer—Affirmative defenses

There are special defenses available by law to certain types of actions. These special defenses are called *affirmative defenses*, and to be considered by the court, they must be specifically asserted in the answer. In most courts, if they are not included, many affirmative defenses are waived and may not be asserted later.

Contributory negligence. *Contributory negligence* means the injuries and damages complained of by the plaintiff were caused, in whole or in part, by the plaintiff's own negligence. Contributory negligence is an all-or-nothing defense; if proved, it completely negates the plaintiff's claims.

Comparative negligence. *Comparative negligence* means that if an accident were caused in part by the negligence of plaintiff, any award to the plaintiff should be diminished in the proportion to the plaintiff's negligence. Comparative negligence was adopted by statute in many states and by judicial precedent in others as a means of acknowledging the plaintiff's possible negligence while considering the defendant's role in the claim. Comparative negligence, when proven, creates a result in which plaintiff and defendant are deemed both to be responsible to a certain percentage, and the damages due the plaintiff are adjusted accordingly.

Assumption of risk. *Assumption of risk* means the plaintiff was capable of assessing a situation and willingly assumed the inherent risks and therefore should be responsible for the consequences. For example, the defendant might allege that the plaintiff was fully aware of the icy condition of a sidewalk and made a conscious decision to use it anyway.

Statute of limitations. A statute of limitations defense applies only to situations in which a time limit exists within the statute that would bar plaintiff's filing the case.

Laches. An affirmative defense of *laches* alleges there was an inexcusable delay in filing suit and defendant is prejudiced because of it. The affirmative defense of laches works in a similar way to a statute of limitations defense but does not require the expiration of a statute of limitations.

Failure to state a claim. The affirmative defense of *failure to state a claim* asserts the plaintiff has failed to state a claim for which relief could be granted by the court against that defendant.

§ 11.13   Service of pleadings

Court rules require that each party to an action must be provided with copies of all court documents filed in the lawsuit. Except for summonses, complaints, and subpoenas, which usually must be served personally, service is obtained by mailing, faxing, delivering, or, in some jurisdictions, emailing copies to the attorneys of record or the defendant if there is no attorney of record.

A certificate of service, which is typed at the end of the document and also filed as a separate document for discovery service, states that the appropriate copies have been provided to the lawyers for the parties and gives the method and date of service. A copy of the certificate of service is filed with the court.

EXAMPLE:

I certify on the _____ day of _____ *[Year]*, I mailed (or hand delivered) a copy of the foregoing Answer to John Q. Jones, Esq., 999 Tudor Avenue, Salt Lake City, Utah 84111, Attorney for Plaintiff.

———————————————

(name of lawyer)
Attorney for Defendant

§ 11.14 At issue

A case is said to be *at issue* or the issues are said to be *joined* when the complaint and a responsive pleading (usually an answer) have been filed. This means that the plaintiff has pleaded its claims, and the defendant has pleaded its or her defenses to those claims. There now exists a preliminary indication of which facts or issues are in dispute.

§ 11.15 Default

If the defendant does not file an answer or other responsive pleading within the time required by the court rules, the defendant is in *default*. Generally, a court will set aside a default if a defendant asks the court to do so and has a reasonable explanation for failure to file an answer and can show a meritorious defense. If the default is not set aside, the plaintiff is generally entitled to a *default judgment* granting the relief requested in the complaint. Usually a default judgment requires a hearing in which the plaintiff offers minimal evidence to support the allegations stated in the complaint.

§ 11.16 Removal to federal court

If the plaintiff's action was filed in a state court, jurisdiction would be valid in that district's federal court. If the defendant is from a different state and other requirements are met, the defendant may, within 30 days of service of first filing, file a petition to *remove* the case to the appropriate United States district court. A defendant may also file a petition for removal if the case involves a question of federal law. If the plaintiff's lawyer desires, a motion to remand or return the case to state court may be filed. The federal court then determines whether the case should remain in federal court. If so, the defense lawyer must then file an answer and a demand for jury trial, if desired, and the case is handled as any other federal court case.

§ 11.17 Third-party complaint

During the preparation of the defense of the lawsuit, it may become evident that a party not named as a defendant may be responsible for the cause of action. The defendant files a third-party action against the additional party. In some jurisdictions leave of court may be required. The defendant (now also the third-party plaintiff) files the third-party complaint, and the new party (the third-party defendant) is served with a summons in the same manner as the original defendant. Within the time limit shown on the summons, the third-party defendant must file a responsive pleading. This situation occurs frequently in products liability cases.

EXAMPLE:

A buys a car from B, a car dealer. The car simply will not run, and B's service department cannot get it to run. A sues B to rescind the sale and get his money back. When B answers A's suit against him, he admits that he sold A the car, but since he did not manufacture the car, he files a third-party complaint against C, the manufacturer of the car.

§ 11.18   Leave of court

In the course of a lawsuit, it may become necessary to obtain permission of the court to take some action, such as permission to amend a complaint or to extend the time within which to answer. This permission is termed *leave of court*. Usually, applicable rules of civil procedure dictate when leave is required. Leave is often required to file amended pleadings and certain types of motions, such as motions for extension of time to file a brief.

§ 11.19   Counterclaim

The defendant may file an action for damages (*counterclaim*) against the plaintiff, who then also becomes a *counter-defendant*; the defendant is then also called a *counter-plaintiff*. A counterclaim is usually a claim that would reduce the amount owed by the defendant to the plaintiff if the defendant is successful in establishing the claim.

EXAMPLE:

A hires B to install bathroom plumbing and agrees to pay $500. A pays $250 and does not pay the rest. B sues A for the $250. A counterclaims against B for $1,000, stating that the plumbing leaks and has destroyed his flooring worth $750 and he should have the $250 back.

§ 11.20   Cross-claim

Where there is more than one defendant, any defendant may file an action against any other defendant alleging that another defendant was responsible for the matter which is the subject of the complaint. The action is called a *cross-claim*. The filing defendant is also called a *cross-plaintiff*; the defendant the action is filed upon is then also called a *cross-defendant*. When a defendant files a cross-claim, the position taken is that if the defendant owes the plaintiff any money, then the cross-defendant owes the defendant-cross-plaintiff the same amount (or some portion of it).

EXAMPLE:

 A owns a building that he leases to *B* for $30,000 per year, payable in monthly installments. After *B* has been in the building two months, he subleases the building to *C* for the same rental. *C* pays the rent for one month and moves out of the building. *A* sues *B* and *C* for all unpaid rent under the lease. *B* files a cross-claim against *C*. *A* gets a judgment against *B* and *C*, and *B* gets a judgment against *C* on his cross-claim. *B* must pay *A*, but he can collect from *C*.

The difference between cross-claims and counterclaims is that cross-claims are litigated by parties on the same side of the litigation, while counterclaims are litigated between opposing parties in the principal action.

§ 11.21   Amended and supplemental pleadings

Under the Federal Rules of Civil Procedure and in most state courts, a change in pleadings can be made once without court order at any time before responsive pleadings are filed. Afterward, either leave of court or consent of opposing counsel is usually needed to amend or supplement pleadings.

An *amendment* to a pleading involves correction of the pleading. The content of the amendment was in existence at the time the original pleading was filed. A *supplemental* pleading involves events that were not known or not in existence at the time the original pleading was filed.

§ 11.22   Interventions

An additional party (intervenor) having an interest in the outcome of the lawsuit may attempt to intervene by filing a written *petition in intervention*, setting out the reasons why the intervenor has an interest and the amount the intervenor seeks.

EXAMPLES:

 An insurance company, which has paid money damages to the plaintiff for injuries growing out of the same cause of action, may seek to recover its payment.

 Where several parties claim injuries in the same incident and only one party has filed suit, others may petition to intervene, claiming they also were damaged and thus are entitled to recover damages.

 In wrongful death cases which are usually filed by the spouse or an heir at law of the deceased, other heirs may intervene, claiming a legal interest in the estate of the decedent. This often happens in cases in which children of a prior marriage intervene for a portion of the recovery.

§ 11.23   Discovery

Discovery is the vehicle by which one party to a lawsuit obtains certain facts, documents, and other information from the opposing party to help the first party prepare for trial. The purposes of discovery are to clarify the issues, to eliminate surprise in the courtroom, and to avoid wasting the judge's time.

Filing procedures. Discovery procedures include requests for admissions, interrogatories, requests for production of documents, and depositions. Discovery documents, including requests for admissions, interrogatories, requests for production of documents, and responses to those documents, are often not filed with the court unless there is a discovery dispute that requires the documents to be filed. Instead, a certificate of service or certificate of mailing is filed; the certificate contains the affirmation of the filing attorney that the original discovery document and any required copies were served upon other counsel, giving the method and date of service. Deposition transcripts are filed or presented as evidence when required to support the claims of the parties. Deposition notices are filed if required by local rules, if the attorney prefers to file them, or when there is a discovery dispute regarding the scheduling of depositions.

Electronic discovery requirements. The local rules in many courts require that interrogatories, requests for admission, and requests for document production be served both in hard copy and in electronic form on disk or by email.

Continuing discovery. Most discovery documents, particularly interrogatories and requests for production of documents, are continuing in nature. The initial responses are due within a set period of time, but any additional information which is responsive to the discovery requests and is obtained after the due date must be supplemented.

Discovery deadlines. Discovery documents, such as interrogatories, requests for admissions, and requests for production of documents, must be responded to within a set period of time. An objection is considered a valid response until the objection is dealt with either by agreement between counsel or by ruling from the judge. Absent any objection, the requested responses or documents must be provided when due, or the counsel requesting them can file a *motion for sanctions* requesting disciplinary action or motion to compel requesting the court compel the other party to respond.

§ 11.23.1   Discovery—Request for admissions

Either party may request the other party to admit or deny certain facts not in dispute. The primary reason for using *requests for admissions* is to avoid having to prove undisputed facts at the trial.

EXAMPLES:

1. Admit you were the owner of a blue automobile, license No. 0000, on the date of the incident that is the basis of this suit.
2. Admit you were the operator of that vehicle on the occasion in question.

OR:

1. Admit that you were a partner in the firm of Smith & Smith on August 1, 1997.
2. Admit that the firm of Smith & Smith entered into a contract (a copy of which is attached as Exhibit A) on August 1, 1997, with Jones Construction Company.

OR:

1. Admit that Exhibit A attached hereto is a true and correct copy of the contract entered into between A and B on March 1, 1997.

NOTE: In each of the sample requests, the admissions requested are easily established by testimony. However, to call witnesses at trial and ask them a series of questions designed to show those facts would be needlessly time-consuming and expensive. Note that the first two sample requests do not ask whether an accident took place and that the second two requests do not ask whether there was a problem concerning the contract because these likely would involve disputed facts. The requests resolve basic, undisputed issues.

Requests for admissions are served on counsel for the opposing party and consist of:

- The caption or style of the case.
- The title of the pleading.
- The name of the party to whom such requests are directed.
- An opening paragraph setting out the state or federal rule under which the requests are made and the time within which to respond.
- The requests.
- The signature of the lawyer requesting the admissions.
- A certificate that the requests were served on the opposing lawyer and the date and method of service.

A certificate of mailing or service often appears at the bottom of a discovery request; many attorneys prefer to include this in addition to the certificate filed with the court.

§ 11.23.2   Discovery—Responses to request for admissions

When the lawyer receives a request for admissions, the lawyer's assistant should stamp it with the date it is received and place a note in the calendar in advance of the date the response is due. This is very important, because failure to respond (usually within 30 days) results in a finding that the requests are admitted. There are several possible responses to such requests, but each separate request must be answered. For example, the lawyer responding may:

- Admit any statement.
- Deny any statement.
- Neither admit nor deny. (This must be done specifically and a reason given for the refusal to admit or deny must be given; this typically is due to lack of sufficient information with which to respond.)
- Omit answering a particular statement in the request. (This

last method is not an oversight, but is consciously chosen by the lawyer, because failure to respond to any statement in the request results in the statement being deemed admitted.)

The response may be short and need contain only the caption, title, and the responses, which may be shortened. Examples of responses might be:

- Admitted.
- Denied.
- Neither admitted nor denied due to lack of information at this time with which to respond.

The response must be signed by the lawyer, and a verification by the person making the response may need to be attached, depending on local rules. A certificate that the response has been served on opposing counsel is necessary.

Requests for admission are often used strategically. An attorney may bury a controversial request for admission in a group of innocuous ones in hopes that opposing counsel will forget to respond on time, thus admitting the controversial statement. Again, reminders must be calendared to prevent this occurrence.

§ 11.23.3　Discovery—Interrogatories

One of the simplest and most economical discovery tools is *interrogatories* (questions). At any time after the suit is filed, either party may propound, or serve, interrogatories upon the opposing party. Interrogatories include:

- The caption or style of the case.
- The title of the pleading.
- The name of the party to whom the interrogatories are directed.
- An opening paragraph setting out the state or federal rule under which the interrogatories are propounded and the time within which to answer.
- The interrogatories.
- A statement that the interrogatories are ongoing and the answering party must supply additional information as it becomes available.
- The signature of the party serving the interrogatories.
- A certificate of service on the opposing lawyer, giving the method and date of service.

Some states require that sufficient space be left after each question for the opposing party to fill in the answer, which may then be photocopied and returned. The local rules in many areas require that interrogatories be served with one original and two copies.

Parties generally are not limited in the types of interrogatories that may be asked, but the number of interrogatories may be limited.

Some states, however, allow only certain interrogatories to be asked. Some typical interrogatories, in a personal injury case, include questions about:

- Name
- Address
- Marital status
- Previous marriages
- Social security and driver's license numbers
- Previous accidents
- Version of the incident
- What is claimed by the other party as the cause of the incident
- Injuries
- Amount of time lost from work
- Whether the injured party has returned to work
- Lost wages
- Names of doctors
- Location and custodian of records
- Names of hospitals
- Amount of medical expenses to date
- The existence and limits of coverage on insurance policies
- Names of witnesses to be called at trial
- Names of experts consulted and their fields of expertise

§ 11.23.4 Discovery—Answers to interrogatories

On receipt of interrogatories, the lawyer's assistant should calendar both the date received and the date answers are due. The client should be contacted and arrangements made for the client to provide answers to the interrogatories, in person or by mail. The lawyer's assistant should provide a date by which the client must respond so that the lawyer may timely file the answers. Some states require the answers to be signed by the answering party, while other states permit the lawyer to respond for the client. When the answers to interrogatories are served on the other attorney, a certificate of service must be filed with the court.

§ 11.23.5 Discovery—Objections to interrogatories

The lawyer may file objections to some of the interrogatories. Any interrogatory that is objected to is not required to be answered until the opposing counsel has responded to the objection. Often, opposing counsel will explain the interrogatory in more detail, limit it as to scope or time, or make other revisions to resolve the objection. However, if objections cannot be resolved, the dispute will have to be ruled upon by the judge. A good-faith effort must be made to answer all interrogatories that have not been objected to within the time allowed.

§ 11.23.6 Discovery—Request for production of documents

There are numerous documents, photographs, and other materials that may be obtained through discovery. This is accomplished by serving a *request for production of documents* upon opposing counsel. Samples of discoverable documents include: photographs, contracts, corporate records, income tax records, and drawings and plans of equipment or buildings involved in the litigation. The request should be addressed to the party from whom the materials are requested, show the federal or state rule under which the request is filed, specify the time within which to respond, and list each item requested. This discovery document is sometimes called a request for production of documents and things, because it is common to request physical evidence, such as a videotape, that is not in document form.

§ 11.23.7 Discovery—Responses to request for production of documents

As soon as such a request is received, the lawyer's assistant should make a calendar entry noting the date the response is due. A letter to the client should then be drafted for the lawyer's approval, enclosing a copy of the request, with instructions to produce the requested documents.

Clients are not always able to judge which documents are responsive to a request for production. The lawyer may receive a number of client documents which should not be produced in discovery. Once a decision has been made which documents should be produced, any client documents not produced should be segregated in a separate subfile clearly labeled "Client Documents Not Produced." This helps prevent the accidental production of the wrong documents and may make it easier to locate needed documents later.

§ 11.23.8 Discovery—Objections to request for production of documents

The party on whom the request is served may file objections, for example, the requests are unduly burdensome or the materials requested are irrelevant. Upon motion, the court rules on the validity of the objections. If the objections are overruled, the materials must be produced within a specified period of time. If the objections are sustained, those particular documents need not be produced.

§ 11.23.9 Discovery—Privileged documents

Certain documents are protected from discovery. The two most common forms of protection are *attorney-client privilege* and the *work product doctrine*. As noted earlier, all communications between lawyer and client that are not disclosed to a third party are privileged. Sometimes attorneys will prepare letters or memos to the client labeled "Attorney-Client Privileged" or "Attorney Work Product".

These designations are used any time a document discusses strategy or matters that the lawyer does not want brought out in discovery, deposition, or trial.

The work product doctrine protects attorney work; for example, attorney notes or memos regarding strategy, evaluating evidence or case value, or developing trial outlines or arguments, from being revealed. The attorney's thoughts about the case, when laid out on paper, are protected from discovery through the work product doctrine.

Not all attorney documents are considered privileged, even if they typically are exchanged only between the attorney and client. An obvious example is the attorney bill. The bill may be considered all or partially privileged if the descriptions of the attorney's work reveal case strategy, but such determinations usually have to be made by the judge. Simply labeling the bill "Attorney-Client Privileged" or "Attorney Work Product" is not enough to keep the bill from being brought into evidence.

Where one counsel believes the other is wrongly withholding documents under attorney-client privilege or work product doctrine, the other counsel is typically required by the court to make a list of privileged documents called a *privilege log*, briefly describing the document and its contents, so the disputed documents can be ruled admissible or inadmissible for discovery by the judge.

§ 11.23.10 Discovery—Depositions

One of the most useful discovery tools is the *deposition*. Each side in a lawsuit has the right to question the parties on the other side, as well as other persons who are not parties, such as eyewitnesses, doctors, and experts employed by either side to investigate and give an opinion in the case.

Either party may take an oral deposition that consists of sworn testimony in the presence of counsel for all parties before a court reporter, who transcribes the testimony verbatim. The testimony is as binding as any testimony given at the actual trial of the case, and often entire depositions or portions of depositions are read into the record during the course of trial.

§ 11.23.11 Discovery—Setting the depositions

Depositions are usually set by agreement between the lawyers as to time and place. It is the lawyer's assistant's responsibility to calendar the setting. The lawyer's assistant should draft a follow-up letter to the opposing lawyer confirming the date and time. In addition, the lawyer's assistant should inform the *deponent*, the witness to be deposed, and the deponent's lawyer, if represented, by telephone and letter of the time and place of the deposition. The party requesting the deposition usually makes arrangements for the court reporter. If the deposition is to be taken in the office, the lawyer's assistant should reserve a conference room or other suitable place for the deposition. The room should be large enough to accommodate the lawyers for each side, the person whose deposition is being taken, and the court reporter. Shortly before the scheduled time of the deposition, the lawyer's assistant should check the room where the deposition will be taken to be sure it is ready.

Many firms prefer to set up a conference room for depositions with coffee, water, ice, soda, and even juice in sufficient quantities for all the attendees. In some firms, conference room setups are considered a subtle show of strength. It may be necessary to place documents to be used in the room or audiovisual equipment in some cases; pens, pencils, and legal pads may also be needed. It is important to escort the participants to the conference room and make sure that opposing counsel are not allowed to wander the halls and the parties the lawyer represents are not left alone in a conference room with opposing counsel. It may later be necessary to provide lunch for some or all of the parties. When the deposition is over, the conference room needs to be restored to its normal condition, with coffee and water dumped out, unused soda returned to proper storage, trash cleaned up, and any deposition materials or documents returned to their proper location. It is extremely important that no documents are left in any conference room after a deposition.

§ 11.23.12   Discovery—Notice of depositions

If the state requires it, a notice to take the deposition is filed, setting out the time and place of the deposition, and any subpoenas (for the depositions of nonparties to the action) or **subpoenas duces tecum** (commanding the deponent to produce specified items) are issued. The notice is served on opposing counsel well in advance of the date of the deposition. State rules on notices of depositions vary widely.

§ 11.23.13   Discovery—Subpoena *duces tecum*

The **subpoena duces tecum** is authorized by the Federal Rules of Civil Procedure, and most states have a similar provision. A **subpoena duces tecum** is issued to custodians of certain documents to appear at a designated time and place with certain records described in the subpoena. A **subpoena duces tecum** can be attached to the deposition notice of a fact witness, requiring they bring personal or corporate documents. The term *duces tecum* means, essentially, *bring with you.*

In other instances, the **subpoena duces tecum** is used to subpoena the ordinary business records (e.g., medical records) of the custodian, and the records may simply be copied and supplied to the requesting party with a records affidavit, or they may be produced and the records custodian may be required to testify. Some health care providers will not produce any type of records without a subpoena.

§11.23.14 Discovery—Witness summonses

The clerk of court can issue subpoenas summoning witnesses to testify at depositions or at trial. These subpoenas usually are prepared by the lawyer for issuance by the clerk. In some states, lawyers can issue subpoenas in a pending case without the approval of the clerk.

§11.23.15 Discovery—Use of checklists

Many lawyers use a checklist or a detailed list of questions during depositions to make certain all pertinent information is obtained. This checklist should be placed in the file shortly before the deposition for the lawyer's use.

§11.23.16 Discovery—Meeting with client and opposing lawyer

Time should be allotted prior to the deposition for the lawyer to discuss the case with the deponent to explain the procedures and purpose of the deposition. (Important witnesses are sometimes prepared at length a day or two before the deposition.) To prepare the deponent properly, the lawyer should explain the manner and method of responding to questions and the necessity of answering such questions. One common attorney instruction to prospective deponents is to tell them to take their time in answering questions; a long pause while they think about their answer will not show up in a deposition transcript as it would in trial testimony. Only the well-considered answer will show.

Following a deposition, the lawyers sometimes discuss the possibility of settlement. Therefore, the lawyer's calendar for the date of deposition should allow sufficient time for the deposition and a discussion with the opposing lawyer afterward.

§11.23.17 Discovery—Transcript of depositions

The transcript of the deposition is prepared by the court reporter. The original copy is sent to the deponent's lawyer or directly to the deponent if not represented. The deponent may be asked to read the transcript, make any corrections, sign it, and have the signature notarized. This right is commonly waived by deponent's attorney. If the deponent does not review the transcript, it is assumed to be correct as filed. It is then returned to the court reporter who, in some jurisdictions, files it with the clerk of the court and also provides copies of the transcript to the parties who requested them.

§11.23.18 Discovery—Videotaped depositions

Use of videotaped depositions is extremely valuable when it is expected that a witness will be unavailable to testify at trial. This is especially appropriate if the client or witness is due to leave the country or is terminally ill. Use of a videotaped deposition enables the trier of fact to see the demeanor of the witness and thus evaluate the witness's credibility. There are some jurisdictions, however, where videotaped depositions are not admissible.

§ 11.23.19 Discovery—Written depositions

Written depositions may also be taken and generally are less expensive than oral depositions. Notice of taking a written deposition, together with a list of the questions to be asked by the reporter, must be sent to all opposing counsel, and sufficient time must be allowed (usually 10 to 15 days, according to the rules of the jurisdiction) for the opposing lawyer to submit cross-questions. These questions are mailed to the reporter, who sometimes obtains any necessary subpoenas, contacts the witness, and makes an appointment with them. At the time of the appointment, the reporter asks the questions and obtains any requested records. The answers are sworn to by the witness and are filed by the reporter in the same manner as an oral deposition.

Written depositions are often used to obtain a doctor's testimony, employment records, income tax records, and other information, but they also may be used in the case of a witness who is in a distant city or state, thereby avoiding the expense of the lawyers for all parties traveling to the deposition.

§ 11.24 Mediation

Mediation is a nonbinding and voluntary settlement discussion between the parties. A neutral third party assists with the negotiations and promotes reconciliation, settlement, or understanding among the parties. A mediator makes no decisions for the parties. If settlement is reached, it is a voluntary act taken by the parties. The mediator must hold in confidence all information received during a mediation. Presuit mediation is not intended as a substitute for trial, but as a method of settling a claim before trial starts, if possible. Mediation is often ordered by the court at a pretrial conference. It is usually done while the case is pending and after discovery is underway, as discovery can be very helpful in the evaluation and settlement of a case.

§ 11.25 Motions prior to trial

During the course of discovery, various facts may come to light which require motions to be filed. Some courts require supplementary documents supporting the request, such as an affidavit, memorandum of law, or legal brief. In some jurisdictions, a courtesy copy of the motion must be delivered to the judge in addition to the original being filed with court. In some jurisdictions, judges may require the hearing date and time be placed on the motion or the motion will automatically be denied. Some common pretrial motions are discussed below.

§ 11.25.1 Motions prior to trial—Notices

Whenever a hearing is scheduled, such as a hearing on a motion by one of the parties, all parties must be informed of the date, time, place, and subject matter. This is accomplished by sending a notice of hearing to all counsel. The lawyer requesting the hearing prepares and sends the notice. Notices are generally required to be filed at least ten days before the date of the hearing, and notices going out at the last minute are often served by facsimile. Federal courts set the time for motions and notify unrepresented parties. State courts have varied requirements for setting hearings. The lawyer's assistant should check local rules, and, when in doubt, call the court to confirm its procedures.

§ 11.25.2 Motions prior to trial—Orders

When a motion and notice of hearing are filed, the judge may hold a hearing and issue an order on the motion. In some instances, no hearing is held because the motion is routine, opposing counsel does not object, or the particular court does not hold motion hearings. The order is usually prepared for the judge's signature by the prevailing lawyer, although in federal court, the judges generally prepare their own orders.

§ 11.25.3 Motions prior to trial—Motion for continuance

A *motion for continuance* is a motion to postpone a trial date or hearing date. The term *continue* is used to refer to postponement to a later date, and the court or clerk's order approving the postponement describes it as a *continuance*. The content of the motion and requirements for filing vary considerably from jurisdiction to jurisdiction. Most continuance motions do require reasons to be given for continuance. A statement that the continuance is not intended to delay—or stall—the handling of the case is often required. A statement that no party will be prejudiced or harmed by the continuance is included. Consent of opposing counsel is usually sought prior to filing the request for continuance and is noted in the motion if obtained.

§ 11.25.4 Motions prior to trial—Motion to compel

A *motion to compel* is filed to require the opposing party to perform some act, usually to respond to discovery requests. When the motion is heard in court, the judge may impose any one of a number of possible sanctions, including an order that the requested act (e.g., production of discovery documents) be performed. If this order is not obeyed, the noncomplying party may be held in contempt of court or pleadings of the noncomplying party may be stricken by the court. The threat to *strike a pleading* is serious. To *strike a pleading* means to remove it from the record and make it as if it were never filed. For example, if the answer is stricken, the plaintiff very likely will win the case, because the defendant's defenses have been erased. The court also may impose a money penalty on the noncomplying party and may require them to pay the costs of the hearing on the motion to compel, including a reasonable lawyer's fee, to the other side.

§ 11.25.5   Motions prior to trial—Motion for protective order

A *motion for protective order* is filed in response to some action by the opposing side, requesting the court to take some action. For example, such a motion can be filed regarding a notice to take a deposition if travel distance or shortness of time make it difficult or impossible for the deponent or the lawyer to appear at the deposition. It also may be used when interrogatories or requests for production are unduly burdensome. A protective order may also be used to specify who may see confidential documents, such as the proprietary records of a corporate defendant.

§ 11.25.6   Motions prior to trial—Motion to dismiss for want of jurisdiction

A defendant may file a *motion to dismiss* the case for *want of jurisdiction* to assert that the court does not have authority to hear or decide the case.

§ 11.25.7   Motions prior to trial—Motion to dismiss for lack of prosecution

A defendant's *motion to dismiss* a case *for lack of prosecution* may be made for failure to respond to discovery after a motion to compel is granted. Granting such a motion is within the discretion of the court; however, most judges are reluctant to grant such motions unless the case has been inactive for a very long time.

§ 11.25.8   Motions prior to trial—Motion for nonsuit

A *motion for nonsuit* is a plaintiff's motion that requests the court to dismiss the case either with or without prejudice and can be presented at any time before the case goes to the jury. In some states it is called a *voluntary dismissal*. When such a motion is granted *without prejudice*, the plaintiff may later refile the same action. However, if the case is dismissed *with prejudice*, the plaintiff is prevented from again filing the same cause of action. In federal court, this motion is known as a *motion for dismissal*.

§ 11.25.9   Motions prior to trial—Motion for summary judgment

If either party believes there is no real issue of fact to be decided at trial, a *motion for summary judgment* may be filed. This motion requests the court to grant judgment, in whole or in part, in favor of the party filing it. It is usually accompanied by affidavits or answers to discovery stating the undisputed facts that entitle the party to a judgment in their favor. In many jurisdictions, it is difficult to obtain a summary judgment, and the party filing such a motion has the burden of proving that there is no genuine issue of fact in dispute. The opposing party has time in which to respond, and the court usually holds a hearing. If the court determines there is no fact issue, it can grant judgment to the moving party. However, if in the court's opinion there is any factual question that is in dispute, the court may deny the motion, and the case is then tried on its merits.

§ 11.25.10   Motions prior to trial—Motion for order to show cause

A *motion for an order to show cause* requests relief and requires the opposition to appear and show cause why an order granting the relief sought should not be entered. The opposition must be served with a copy of the motion in advance of the hearing. At the hearing, the requested relief can be granted, denied or modified. A motion for an order to show cause may initially be made *ex parte*, but the opposing party must be served and have the opportunity to reply.

§ 11.26   Stipulations

A written stipulation is an agreement made and signed by the lawyers for both sides of a case regulating any matter pertaining to the proceeding or trial about which they can agree. This may be used to dispose of or narrow certain issues so that trial time and proof are not required for those issues. A stipulation can also be used to request that the court change a trial or hearing date or extend the response time for a pleading.

§ 11.27   Pretrial conferences

A *pretrial conference* is a meeting with the trial judge at which each lawyer states the basis of the client's case and discloses exhibits or witnesses to be used at trial. The scheduling of the case through discovery and trial is also planned. A pretrial conference establishes ground rules for the trial and helps to eliminate courtroom surprises and delays.

A pretrial order is usually agreed to by both sides and presented to the court for entry. In some cases, the court prepares a pretrial summary instead. Such pretrial orders typically contain a basic statement of the contested and uncontested issues and facts, a stipulation of agreed facts, a list of witnesses to be called by each side, exhibits to be introduced by each side, and a list of relevant discovery or motion deadlines, conference or hearing dates, and the date of trial.

§ 11.28   Trial notebooks

The lawyer's assistant may assist in preparing a *trial notebook*. The lawyer will likely include the following items:

- All pleadings filed in the case, indexed for easy access
- All depositions, indexed for easy access, along with any deposition summaries
- All interrogatories and answers, request for admissions, any other discovery materials and photographs
- Any other documents the lawyer will present for evidence during trial

Certain motions to be presented during the trial may be prepared in advance.

In addition, a list of witnesses and their telephone numbers should be placed in a convenient place for the lawyer's use. The witness list should enumerate the names in the order their testimony will be presented. Likewise, the documents to be presented as evidence should be placed in the order in which they will be introduced. If the court rules permit, the lawyer's assistant could mark the documents with appropriate exhibit stickers. (See Illustration 11-5 for a checklist that reviews the steps to be taken and materials to be included when preparing the trial notebook.)

Illustration 11-5

CLIENT_____

Our File No._____

TRIAL NOTEBOOK CHECKLIST

_____ Check pleadings for amendments.

_____ Pleadings amended.

_____ Amend prayer to: _____.

_____ Prepare subpoena for each witness.

_____ Basic information sheet prepared.

_____ All witnesses listed.

_____ List all expenses.

_____ Copies of all bills.

_____ Exhibits numbered and listed.

_____ Medical and/or other expert reports.

_____ All doctors and/or other expert witnesses alerted.

_____ Depositions read and marked.

_____ Case law, law notes inserted.

_____ Requested instructions prepared.

NOTE: This is a sample list and may be adjusted to include different items pertinent to a given case. It should be noted that,
depending on the complexity of the trial, the trial notebook
may become a group of trial notebooks, with each notebook
devoted to a separate topic, such as pleadings, discovery
responses, or depositions.

§ 11.29   Settlement

If the lawyers can reach settlement prior to trial, costs can be
minimized, and the plaintiff may realize a larger recovery than if the
case were tried and appealed. Even if financial savings are minimal,
in some situations, avoiding the emotional costs of trial may make
settlement more desirable.

Settlement negotiations are usually conducted up until the time the
trial begins or even during trial. It is not unheard of for a lawsuit to
result in settlement after the jury retires to deliberate, but before the
verdict is reached (often to the disappointment of the jury members).
Settlement may also be reached after judgment is entered and during
the course of an appeal.

Changes in the settlement value occur during the case because, for
example, the plaintiff incurs additional medical or other expenses,
such as an additional operation. If the plaintiff returns to work or presents a poor impression as a witness, the lawyer may recommend a
settlement offer. Other factors that affect settlement value could
include an extremely large verdict or a total loss by a plaintiff in a
similar case, favorable or unfavorable facts ascertained in a deposition, or new information revealed by discovery. Each factor influences
the lawyer's recommendation to the client. Occasionally, a client
insists the case be tried regardless of the lawyer's recommendation.

Once a settlement has been agreed to by all parties, the documents
reflecting the settlement must be prepared, usually by the defendant's
lawyer. These include a release of claims to be signed by the plaintiff
and a dismissal of the lawsuit. In some matters (workers' compensation and cases involving minor plaintiffs), court approval is necessary
and a hearing is held to approve the settlement. In some cases, the
court allows the use of interrogatories in place of a hearing to
determine the fairness of the settlement; these are filed by the
defendant's lawyer and answered by the plaintiff.

After releases are executed and the court enters judgment, the
settlement amount is paid to the prevailing party and counsel. The
case can then be closed. If the prevailing party is a minor, the award
is handled through a guardian and deposited according to the court
order for the use and benefit of the minor. The guardian may be
required to post a bond with the court to ensure proper handling of
the minor's funds. The court retains jurisdiction over the disbursement of funds, in most cases, until the minor reaches majority.

§ 11.30   The trial

At *trial*, the parties are given the opportunity to present their case. The judge presides in the courtroom and ensures that only proper evidence and arguments are presented. In a *jury trial*, the judge instructs the jury on issues it will consider. In a nonjury or **bench trial**, the judge serves the role of both judge and jury.

§ 11.30.1   The trial—Selection of the jury

A jury trial begins when the first prospective juror is called for **voir dire** (means "to speak the truth"). Both plaintiff's and defendant's lawyers have the right to examine the prospective jurors after they are sworn. The court may disqualify a prospective juror when any doubt exists as to the juror's competency to serve. After the juror is questioned, either lawyer may accept him or her, challenge for cause, or reject him or her using a peremptory challenge. In federal court, the judge conducts the *voir dire*.

During *voir dire*, either the plaintiff or defendant may **challenge for cause** when the prospective juror lacks a qualification required by law, is not impartial, is related to any of the parties, or will not accept the law as given to them by the court.

Each party has a given number of **peremptory challenges** established by law, which enable the lawyers to reject prospective jurors without cause. This decision is based on a subjective assessment that a prospective juror would be detrimental to the client's case. *Voir dire* continues until both sides have used all their peremptory challenges or a sufficient panel of jurors has been agreed upon by all lawyers. The jury is then impaneled.

§ 11.30.2   The trial—Opening statement

An opening statement is not argument but rather a highlight of the facts that will be presented at trial. After the jury is impaneled, each side may present an opening statement. The plaintiff has the burden of proving the alleged wrongdoing, damages suffered from such wrongdoing, and that the defendant caused such damages. The lawyer for the plaintiff is allowed to present the plaintiff's opening statement first. The opening statement of defendant's lawyer follows.

§ 11.30.3   The trial—Presentation of the case

After the opening statements, the receipt of testimony and documents begins. The plaintiff sometimes is the first person to testify and give a version of the incident, describes any injuries and damages, and relates any other matters upon questioning by the plaintiff's attorney. This is known as **direct examination**. The plaintiff's lawyer may present additional witnesses to support or prove plaintiff's case. The defense lawyer has an opportunity to **cross-examine** each witness after the plaintiff's lawyer has questioned them. The plaintiff's lawyer then has an opportunity to re-question each witness on the points covered by the defense lawyer. This re-questioning process is known as *redirect examination*.

After the plaintiff's case is presented, the defense lawyer may present witnesses on direct examination and introduce documents into evidence. The plaintiff's lawyer is allowed to cross-examine defendant's witnesses, and defendant's lawyer can redirect. After the defendant has presented evidence, the plaintiff may be allowed to present *rebuttal* testimony, to refute evidence introduced by the defendant.

§ 11.30.4   The trial—Impeachment of witnesses

On cross-examination, counsel may introduce documents to *impeach* or discredit the testimony of a witness. If a witness testifies to one fact and a statement or document in the files contradicts that testimony, the document can then be used to question the witness as to the accuracy of the statements or cast doubt on the witness's general credibility.

§ 11.30.5   The trial—Objections

An objection during trial by either lawyer is made in response to the preceding question or testimony. The usual purpose is to prevent the introduction of testimony or evidence about to be given and exclude it from the record. If the judge sustains the objection, that particular question, testimony, or evidence is excluded. If the objection is overruled, the question is asked and the testimony given. Often, the lawyers will approach the bench and present oral arguments for or against the objection. At this point, the judge usually sends the jury out of the courtroom while arguments are heard. Rulings on objections are often the basis for an appeal. The objection must be made at the time the question, testimony, or evidence is introduced during the trial in order to preserve the right to later appeal on that point. The court reporter must also be asked to include the objection and arguments in the record. This is called *preserving the record*.

§ 11.30.6   The trial—Motions during course of trial

Before the closing arguments and up until the time the case is sent to the jury for deliberation, certain motions may be made.

§ 11.30.7   The trial—Motion *in limine*

A *motion in limine* is presented before a jury hears a particular part of testimony. The moving party sets out certain facts, and requests the court to instruct opposing counsel and the client or other witnesses to refrain from mentioning such facts. Such facts might include the existence or content of any insurance policies, subsequent marriages, criminal records (if applicable), issuance of traffic citations, and other matters which are either not relevant to the case or might influence the jury unfairly.

§ 11.30.8   The trial—Motion for instructed or directed verdict

A *motion for instructed or directed verdict* is usually made by the defendant's lawyer at the close of evidence presented by the plaintiff and is based on the premise that the plaintiff has failed to prove their case. If granted, the court instructs the jury to render a verdict for the defendant and against the plaintiff, and the trial is concluded in the defendant's favor. If the court denies the motion, the defendant may present it again following the presentation of the evidence and again after closing arguments.

§ 11.30.9   The trial—Motion for mistrial

Either party may petition the court to declare a *mistrial* at any time during the course of the trial if matters not admissible as evidence are presented by any witness intentionally or unintentionally in the presence of the jury. For example, the mentioning of any items set out in a *motion in limine* granted by the court results in a mistrial. When the court grants a *motion for mistrial*, the jury is immediately dismissed, and the trial ends. The case must then be set for a new trial with a new jury.

§ 11.30.10   The trial—Closing arguments

Each side is given the opportunity to present *closing arguments*. Each party summarizes its case in a closing argument to the jury, giving the reasons why the jury should find in its favor. Time limits are set for closing arguments. The plaintiff's lawyer presents the plaintiff's closing argument first and may choose to reserve some of the allotted time for rebuttal of the defendant's argument.

§ 11.30.11   The trial—Deliberation of the jury

The jury listens to the testimony, reviews all the exhibits, and considers the arguments of counsel throughout the trial. The presiding judge delivers the charge to the jury after both sides have completed closing arguments. In some jurisdictions, the charge is in the form of written instructions prepared by the lawyers for both sides and approved or modified by the court. Some jurisdictions permit the lawyers to prepare specific questions that the jury is asked to answer. The jury then retires to deliberate what has been presented to them and arrives at a verdict. After returning to the jury box, the jury foreman announces the verdict to the court.

§ 11.30.12   The trial—Hung jury

The jury may be unable to reach a verdict. In this event, the court declares a *mistrial*, and the case must be tried again before a new jury. A jury that cannot reach a verdict is usually referred to as a *hung jury*.

§ 11.30.13 The trial—Preparation of judgment

Following the jury's verdict, the judgment is prepared by the prevailing party and presented to the court for entry. Either side may give notice of its intention to appeal. The losing party may file post-trial motions before a judgment is entered. One such motion may be for a *judgment non obstante veredicto* or notwithstanding the verdict, setting out the reasons why the court should disregard the jury verdict and render judgment for the movant. The losing party may object to the prepared judgment and present its own version of the judgment in keeping with the jury verdict. There is a time period set by the rules within which all post-trial motions must be filed.

In a bench trial, the judgment may be prepared by the prevailing party and presented to the court in much the same manner as in a jury trial. The judgment is usually based on the findings of facts and conclusions of law reached by the court. Most courts provide written reasons for judgments entered on the merits of a case. This is a document signed by the judge that sets out the factual and legal reasons as to how the decision was reached. This document is generally known as the *memorandum opinion* or *opinion* of the court. When a court issues a decision, it is said that the court *renders judgment*. This generally occurs after a trial on the merits, though it could follow a motion, such as a motion for summary judgment. The procedure for preparing the judgment in final form for court entry varies from state to state, and local procedure should be followed.

§ 11.30.14 The trial—Costs

If the jury or the judge awarded costs to the prevailing party, it is necessary to prepare a *bill of costs* (a certified, itemized statement of the amount of costs incurred in the suit) for approval by the court. Rule or statute specifies allowable costs. Upon approval of the costs, the prevailing party is entitled to payment for those costs. Costs do not typically include attorney fees.

§ 11.31 Post-trial activities

As soon as possible after the trial, the lawyer may wish to prepare a complete written report of the trial for the client, together with results and recommendations. The final date for appeal must be calendared by both lawyers. If no appeal is filed by the losing side, a closing report and final bill for services is prepared. If the losing party files an appeal, the client should be notified immediately, advising the client of the procedures and costs of an appeal.

At this point negotiations for a settlement may be renewed, as both parties must determine whether or not it is advantageous to continue spending more time and money on the case.

§ 11.32   Motion for new trial

In most jurisdictions, the first step of an appeal is the filing of a *motion for new trial*, setting out the grounds why a new trial should be granted. Any alleged error by the trial judge that prevented a fair trial, such as overruling objections or allowing testimony, is set out in the motion. If the motion is denied, the appealing party then files an appeal.

§ 11.33   Appeals

When an *appeal* is filed, the party filing the appeal becomes the *appellant*, and the party against whom the appeal is filed is the *appellee*.

The function of the appellate court is to ensure that the trial court acted properly in its conduct of the trial and legal principles were recognized and applied correctly. Appeals are not based on the facts of the case but on questions of law. The appellate court considers whether the trial court committed error in conducting the trial, thus adversely affecting the outcome. Its review of the record is limited to determining whether the trial court erred in admitting or refusing to admit testimony, whether the court's instructions to the jury correctly reflected the law, whether the court correctly sustained or overruled the lawyers' objections, and whether there was jury misconduct.

The appeal usually requires:

- Notice of filing an appeal
- Bond for costs and filing fees, if required
- The record on appeal as designated by the parties
- Briefs
- Oral arguments (sometimes required)
- Trial court decision

Procedures for requesting the preparation of the record for the appellate court vary with different jurisdictions. The appealing party is responsible for initiating the requests. The record will consist of the transcript of the proceedings at trial and a transcript (sometimes called a *legal file*) of requested documents from the court file.

The appellant's lawyer notifies the court reporter to prepare a transcript of the proceedings. This is usually done by letter, along with payment for such transcript. The court reporter will forward the completed original transcript directly to the appellate court within the time allowed.

The appellant's lawyer also requests the clerk of court to provide legal file documents. The documents desired will be listed in the request. Some courts have a special form that must be used for this purpose. By copy of this request, the opposing counsel will be advised of the documents requested and be given an opportunity to add any other documents opposing counsel deems relevant. The transcript or legal file is prepared, sealed, and forwarded to the appellate court by the clerk of court.

§ 11.33.1   Appeals—Communication with the client

Effective communication between a client and the lawyer is as necessary after the trial as it is before the trial. After the trial, the prevailing party is often under the mistaken impression that what was granted in the trial, whether money, land, objects, or rights, will be received within a short period of time. While this may happen in some instances, it is not always the case. The losing party often appeals the decision. This means additional time and expenses before the decision is final. Until the appellate court renders an opinion, the execution of the terms of the judgment is on hold. The prevailing party in the trial court may lose the appeal. Lawyers for both parties must explain all the possible risks of an appeal to the clients. Statistically, appeals courts overwhelmingly support lower court decisions, barring a very severe departure from normal legal procedure. It is relatively rare for the appellant to win, and that risk must be taken into account when appeals are filed.

§ 11.33.2   Appeals—Time limits

The applicable rules of procedure, including local and federal rules, set out specific time limits within which each step on appeal must be taken. The time limits are jurisdictional requirements, and the appellate courts do not have the power to waive them. If a deadline has passed, the appellate court can only dismiss the appeal. Thus, a calendar notation of time limits is of vital importance in an appeal. The time limit begins to run on the date the judgment is entered in the trial court. The appellate court may, when good cause is shown in a written motion filed by either lawyer, grant an extension of time to file the record or briefs. However, the request for extension of time must be filed prior to the time limit expiration and must state a specific requested time for extension.

§ 11.33.3   Appeals—Briefs

Briefs are filed by both sides, with the *appellant's brief* due first. The appellee then responds. The *appellant's brief* is a written argument setting out the points of error alleged in the appeal. Relevant rules, statutes, and case law are cited and argued in the brief. The appellee's brief will respond to the appellant's points and arguments.

§ 11.33.4   Appeals—Oral argument

Once the briefs have been filed, assuming the lawyers have timely filed their requests, the appellate court may set a date for oral argument. If oral argument is allowed, both lawyers may present statements to support their case. No testimony is allowed. The lawyers can only address the law applied in their case. The panel of judges hearing the arguments may question either lawyer during oral argument or may simply listen. Oral arguments are limited to a specific amount of time. When oral arguments are not presented, the case is said to be **submitted on the record**.

§ 11.33.5   Appeals—Opinion

The opinion of the appellate court can:

- Uphold the judgment of the trial court
- Reverse and remand (overturn the judgment and order the trial court to retry the case or enter a new judgment)
- Reverse and render (overturn the judgment and enter a new judgment)
- Remand in part (some of the results were correct, but other points need to be clarified)

§ 11.33.6   Appeals—Courts of last resort

In states having intermediate courts of appeal, there is a court of last resort (most often called the *supreme court*) which has the right to review lower appellate court decisions. In those instances, however, that court usually has the right to decide whether it will review the decisions of the intermediate courts of appeal. The losing party in the intermediate appellate court applies to the supreme court for a **writ of certiorari** or review or petitions the court for leave to appeal. The supreme court, on the basis of the application, decides whether it will grant the writ or the petition and hear the case. If it does, the entire court record of the proceeding, from the initial pleading in the lawsuit to the decision of the intermediate appellate court, is sent to the supreme court. The same procedure as in the intermediate appellate court then is followed. The lawyers for all parties file briefs; there may be oral argument before a panel of judges; and after reviewing the entire record with the additional briefs and arguments, the supreme court reaches a decision, usually set forth in a written opinion. In some states, once the supreme court has reached its decision, a party may petition the court for a rehearing. Even when a court has the right to grant a rehearing, it rarely does. Rehearings are only granted if the losing party can convince the court that it made a grave error or failed to consider an important legal point.

If the court of last resort is a state court, a losing party may be able to seek review by the United States Supreme Court. Such review is limited to cases of the utmost significance, generally involving constitutional issues.

§ 11.33.7   Appeals—*Res judicata*

Once a legal matter has been heard by the court of last resort or once that court has refused a further hearing of a case, the judgment in that case is said to be *res judicata*. This means that the particular dispute has been resolved once and for all, and neither party to the suit can sue the other again regarding the same dispute.

§ 11.34 Collecting a judgment

Once all the appeals have been exhausted, if the defendant prevailed, the matter ends with no monetary payment from the defendant. If the plaintiff prevailed and was awarded a monetary sum, the plaintiff then becomes a *judgment creditor* and the defendant becomes a *judgment debtor*. Often, at this point, the amount of the judgment is paid by the judgment debtor, together with any interest accrued and court costs, if awarded.

Local or state rules dictate the time limit for collecting a judgment, as well as whether this time limit may be renewed and the process of renewal. The lawyer's assistant should note the calendar with the expiration date of all judgments for clients. The lawyer should then be advised of the time limits so judgments can be renewed in a timely manner.

If the judgment rendered is for a certain sum of money, in most jurisdictions, the plaintiff can seek satisfaction of judgment by seizing assets that belong to the defendant. The plaintiff might seize the defendant's bank account, wages, a car, or anything of value the defendant owns. There are many variations from state to state as to what property can be seized in satisfaction of a judgment and the procedures that must be followed.

The court provides for writs of execution and writs of garnishment to enforce collection of a judgment. A *writ of execution* instructs a court official, usually the sheriff, to seize the judgment debtor's property and sell it at auction. Any money collected from the sale is given to the judgment creditor. If this is not sufficient to satisfy the judgment, it remains in force for the balance due until it can be paid or collected.

A *writ of garnishment* enables the judgment creditor to seize property from other people who hold assets belonging to the debtor. Funds from a bank account or wages may be seized in this manner. The bank would be forced to release the funds in that account or the employer would withhold a percentage of the debtor's wages until the judgment could be satisfied.

Sometimes a judgment debtor is said to be *judgment-proof*, meaning there are no assets with which to satisfy the judgment. Some assets, such as a homestead, are exempt from judgment. These exemptions vary according to the jurisdiction, as do the methods of seizing property to satisfy a judgment.

In most states, a judgment may be recorded in the county where real estate owned by the defendant is located and becomes a lien attaching to any property owned by the defendant in that county. This means that the defendant will be unable to dispose of the property until the lien is satisfied.

Once a judgment has been paid, it is said to have been satisfied, and evidence of satisfaction is filed with the court so the judgment can be canceled. The procedures for filing and canceling judgments vary considerably from state to state.

§ 11.35 Billing

The method for billing a lawsuit depends upon the fee arrangement made with the client. When a contingent fee case is settled or tried, the lawyer is reimbursed for advanced expenses from the award or settlement funds, and the contingent fee is calculated from the remaining balance of the judgment recovered. The remainder of the funds is paid to the client, and the lawyer then receives payment for fees incurred. All funds are deposited in the firm's trust account until ready for distribution.

If the fee arrangement is hourly, careful records of the time spent by the lawyer are maintained. The client is billed according to office procedure and the agreement with the client. The bill should include the time spent, rate charged for fees, and the expenses incurred or advanced by the lawyer for the client.

§ 11.36 The team concept in litigation

Many law firms use a team strategy for handling cases. This concept can be very effective in litigation practice. Usually the team consists of one or more lawyers, lawyer's assistants, and paralegals or legal assistants. Proper use of the lawyer's assistant and legal support staff can help keep the cost of litigation down. Each member of the team is important and contributes to the effective preparation and trial of the lawsuit.

§ 11.36.1 The team concept in litigation—Lawyer

It is the lawyer who first examines the claim and decides whether to accept the case. The lawyer, at various stages while the case is pending, evaluates the case and offers the client an opinion of the possible outcome based on the law and other factors. The lawyer is responsible for the preparation of briefs and makes all necessary court appearances and ultimately tries the lawsuit. Since the ultimate responsibility for the case belongs to the lawyer, all members of the trial team are under the direct supervision of the lawyer. The lawyer assigns tasks and corrects work when necessary.

§ 11.36.2 The team concept in litigation—Paralegal or legal assistant

The paralegal or legal assistant works under the supervision of the lawyer. Based upon this supervision, the paralegal may question witnesses, prepare discovery documents, and obtain information with which to answer interrogatories. The paralegal can gather and index evidentiary documents. The paralegal can do basic legal research and write memoranda concerning the results. If the lawyer uses a trial notebook, the paralegal can gather the materials for the book, prepare indexes, and have it ready for the lawyer's use at trial.

§ 11.36.3 The team concept in litigation—Lawyer's assistant

The lawyer's assistant works closely with each member of the team to maintain files and gather information needed for trial. Often docket control and the calendar are the lawyer's assistant's responsibility. The lawyer's assistant reminds the lawyer and the paralegal of deadlines and appointment dates; keeps time records for the lawyer and, depending on firm policy, for the paralegal; and may prepare or supervise the billing. The lawyer's assistant schedules depositions, arranges for the court reporter, sets a deposition location, and makes travel arrangements for lawyers and deponents. When a paralegal is not assigned to the team, the lawyer's assistant assumes both roles and completes both sets of tasks.

§ 11.37 Summary

The lawyer's assistant involved in litigation will be responsible for organizing and maintaining the litigation file, calendaring key discovery and trial dates, gathering the documents for and assembling the trial notebook, preparing a variety of pleadings, perhaps completing legal research, organizing records received, and doing a variety of other tasks important to the successful completion of a trial. The variety of work, the intensity of a trial, and the opportunity of working together with a team of dedicated professionals make litigation an exciting specialty.

Chapter 12

Contracts

KeyCite®: Cases and other legal materials listed in KeyCite Scope can be researched through the KeyCite service on Westlaw®. Use KeyCite to check citations for form, parallel references, prior and later history, and comprehensive citator information, including citations to other decisions and secondary materials.

---

§ 12.1   The Statute of Frauds

The law of contracts is a broad, general area upon which many other areas of law hinge. Contract law evolved from the British *Statute of Frauds* passed in 1676 and pre-existing common law. The Statute of Frauds required that certain contracts be in writing and further provided that such contracts could not be changed merely by an oral agreement. The statute of frauds, in somewhat altered form, remains in place today. The types of contracts required to be in writing by the statute of frauds are:

- Contracts by executors or administrators to pay an estate's debts out of their own funds
- Contracts to answer for the debt or default of another
- Contracts made in consideration of marriage
- Certain contracts creating an interest in land
- Contracts that by their terms cannot be performed within one year
- Certain contracts for the sale of goods of $500 or more

§ 12.2   Definition of contract

A *contract* is an enforceable agreement between two or more competent parties that creates an obligation to do or not to do a particular thing. Contracts may be oral or written, but prudence usually calls for written contracts.

Much of contract law relates to the sale of goods, either for cash or on credit. The *Uniform Commercial Code* (U.C.C.), which has been enacted in all states except Louisiana (Louisiana has enacted a code that includes many comparable provisions), governs most of these transactions.

§ 12.3   Essential elements

There are four elements essential to a valid contract. Unless all four are present, no contract exists.

- Mutual assent (offer and acceptance)
- Competent parties
- Lawful consideration
- Lawful subject matter

§ 12.3.1   Essential elements—Mutual assent

Both parties must agree to the aspect of contract performance required of each. To meet this requirement, there must be both a valid *offer* by one party (known as the *offeror*) and a valid *acceptance* by the party to whom the offer was made (the *offeree*).

EXAMPLES:

A offers to wash B's windows for $10. B agrees to pay $10 for that service. There is both an offer and an acceptance, so there is mutual assent.

A offers to wash B's windows for $10. B thinks the price is too high and does not accept. There is no mutual assent.

The offer must be clear and definite, and made in such a way that it will be taken seriously. An offer that is made in jest or is too vague may not be deemed an offer under the law.

EXAMPLES:

At a party one evening, A pulls out a very expensive ring and says, "Anyone who can guess what I actually paid for this ring can have it for $15." This would not be considered a serious offer.

B is very desirous of purchasing A's house at any price. A finally tells B, "Okay, I'll sell you my house someday." The word *someday* is too vague to consider the statement an offer.

Some contracts call for the offer to remain open for a specified period of time in exchange for which the offeree pays a sum of money. This is called an **option contract**.

EXAMPLE:

A wants to lease a portion of B's property to construct a new factory; however, A does not want to enter into the lease until A completes all of the details for financing. A agrees to pay $1,000 to B in exchange for B's promise that B will not lease the property to anyone else for a period of six months and will permit A to execute the option and obtain a lease within that period. This is an *option* to lease.

Offers can be made specifying a time limit during which the offer must be accepted. If the offer is not accepted within that period, the offer is automatically withdrawn. Offers for sale of real estate are good examples of this.

Where no time limit is specified, the offer remains open until any one of these events occur:

- Acceptance of the offer by the offeree
- Rejection of the offer by the offeree
- Revocation or withdrawal of the offer by the offeror
- Passage of a reasonable length of time without any of the previous three actions by the parties

(Death or insanity of the offeror or offeree may also cause an offer to terminate automatically, especially where personal services are involved.)

EXAMPLES:

A offers to wash B's windows for $10; B accepts. There is no longer an offer, but rather mutual assent and therefore a contract.

A offers to wash B's windows for $10 but B refuses. Later B changes his mind and wants to accept A's offer. Acceptance is not valid now, since the offer terminated when B originally refused it.

A offers to wash B's windows for $10 and B wants to think about it. In the meantime, A withdraws the offer. There is no longer a valid offer, so there can be no acceptance.

A offers to wash B's windows for $10, but B wants to think about it. One year later, B decides it would be a good bargain. The offer is generally not considered valid, since a year is more time than is reasonable under the circumstances to hold the offer open.

A offers to wash B's windows for $10, but before B has a chance to accept, A dies. The offer terminates, since it was based upon personal services.

Advertisements by retailers, mail circulars, auctions, and so forth do not generally constitute offers. Instead, they are characterized as *invitations to offer*. Parties who bid on or respond to an invitation to offer are typically characterized as the offerors.

Typically, acceptance by an offeree must be in total agreement with the offer, point for point, or it is not an acceptance. This principle is referred to as the *mirror image rule*. If the acceptance changes any of the terms of the offer, it actually becomes an independent offer or *counteroffer*.

EXAMPLE:

A offers to wash B's windows for $10. B is willing to accept but only if A will also wash the screens for that amount. There is no acceptance, since B has changed the terms of the offer and has made a counteroffer to A. If A agrees to the new terms, it is A who makes the acceptance.

Silence does not generally constitute acceptance. The exception to this rule is where prior dealings of the parties have incorporated silence as part of their normal method of acceptance or if it is reasonable under the circumstances to infer that silence should constitute acceptance.

EXAMPLES:

A offers to wash B's windows for $10, but B makes no response. His silence would not generally be considered an acceptance.

A and B have had a mutual understanding over the years that periodically A would leave a note stating that he would be in the neighborhood on Saturday and would wash B's windows at that time, for which B would then pay him the usual $10 fee. As a part of the understanding, B would then contact A only on those occasions when he knew he would not be home on the day indicated by the note. They would then set another day. Because of the prior dealings between the parties over the years, silence on the part of B would constitute acceptance.

Unless the offer specifies the manner in which acceptance must be made, the acceptance is generally valid if communicated in the same way as the offer.

EXAMPLE:

An offer arrives by letter, stating that acceptance must be made within 24 hours. B immediately writes an acceptance letter and drops it in the mail during lunch. The letter is not received by the offeror until two days later.

The acceptance would be valid as soon as it was deposited in the mail. Since this was done within the 24-hour period specified, the acceptance is valid even though it was not actually received until two days later.

Though the parties have made both an offer and an acceptance, lack of mutual assent may be claimed to void the contract where any of the following factors can be proven:

- Mistake
- Fraud
- Misrepresentation
- Duress
- Undue influence

§ 12.3.2   Essential elements—Mistake

It is possible that what appears to be mutual assent will have been given based on a genuine misunderstanding. This would not include misunderstandings created because a party failed to reasonably investigate the facts or because a party was negligent in reading a document. The law would not recognize either of these *mistakes.* A genuine misunderstanding occurs when, even after the parties have exercised reasonable care, the end result of the contract is not what the parties intended.

EXAMPLES:

A wants to buy a lot on Poplar Street in Los Angeles and obtains the name of the owner from municipal authorities. *B* agrees to sell *B*'s lot to *A*, and they sign an agreement. Unknown to either party, there are two Poplar Streets in Los Angeles. *A* intended to purchase a lot on the other Poplar Street. There has been a mistake as to the subject matter, and the contract may be voided.

A has several cases of what he believes are apples in his warehouse. He sells them as apples to *B*. When B opens the cases, they contain oranges. There may be no contract because of the parties' mutual mistake.

§ 12.3.3   Essential elements—Fraud

To prove *fraud*, there must have been (1) a false statement (2) of a material fact (3) made with the intent to deceive (4) that is relied upon (5) and is intended to be relied upon (6) that causes a loss to the victim. If all six elements can be proven, the contract may be voided because of the fraud. (However, note that the precise requirements to prove fraud vary from state to state.)

EXAMPLE:

A, a jeweler, convinced *B*, a wholesale jeweler, that he was from St. Louis and that *A*'s credit was excellent. Relying on *A*'s intentional representation, *B* delivered $5,000 worth of jewelry to *A*. *B* later learned that *A* was actually from Kansas City and that he had a very poor credit rating. Once proved, this fact situation would constitute fraud by *A*.

§ 12.3.4   Essential elements—Misrepresentation

Misrepresentation differs from fraud in that it does not involve the intent to deceive. The other elements are the same, and if they are proven, the contract may be voided. Because misrepresentation can result from an honest mistake, it is often called *innocent misrepresentation*.

EXAMPLE:

A sells a block of stock in a certain corporation to *B*, representing it to be worth $10,000 based upon the corporation's net worth. It is later determined that losses of the corporation had reduced its net worth substantially, even though *A* honestly believed he had given the correct information to *B*. It is possible that the contract could be voided based on misrepresentation.

§ 12.3.5   Essential elements—Duress

Duress is the use of force or threatened force to gain consent. In either case, the consent would not be the voluntary act of the person giving consent, and that person could void the contract if duress were shown to exist. The person must be reasonably convinced the threat can be carried out. Where duress is claimed, the claim must be made reasonably soon after the force or threat of force is removed. Failure to make the claim promptly could be considered a waiver that would bar the claim.

EXAMPLES:

A paid a ridiculously high freight charge in order to take possession of some goods shipped to him. Six months later, he demanded a refund, claiming duress. Though duress was present, there may be some question of *A*'s right to claim it since he let so much time pass.

A, a city official, threatened to turn off *B*'s water unless *B* immediately paid an illegal license fee. *B* needed the water supply to operate his factory, so he paid the fee and immediately initiated an action to recover the money. Duress would apply, and *B* would probably recover his damages.

§ 12.3.6   Essential elements—Undue influence

Undue influence is the exercise of dominance by a stronger-willed person over a weaker-willed one. Constant pressure and persuasion may impair the will of a victim so that the victim's consent is not a voluntary act but is rather the expression of the will of the dominant person. A contract created under these circumstances is valid until the victim takes some action to void it. As with duress, whatever action the victim takes must be done within a reasonable amount of time.

Some relationships may create a presumption of undue influence because the parties are not on equal footing in the transaction. In those relationships, one party is presumed to be in a position to take advantage of the other. Guardian-ward, physician-patient, and lawyer-client relationships may give rise to the presumption of undue influence.

§ 12.3.7   Essential elements—Competent parties

Competent parties are persons having the legal capacity to enter into a contract. Those persons who do not generally have legal capacity are:

- Minors
- The mentally disabled
- Intoxicated persons
- Corporations (under certain circumstances)

Claims related to incompetence may be confusing because there are many instances in which hard and fast rules have not been established by the courts. For instance, a minor may be held liable for contracts entered into to obtain necessities of life provided such necessities could not be obtained from a parent or guardian. Those necessities would include food, shelter, clothing, and certain educational expenses. For most other contracts, the minor has the choice of disaffirming or avoiding a contract once the age of majority is reached, provided this is done within a reasonable length of time after the minor reaches the age of majority. If a minor marries, the minor is considered emancipated, and emancipation automatically makes the minor an adult for purposes of making a contract. A minor can be emancipated by a judicial proceeding and sometimes simply by leaving home and becoming self-supporting.

Contracts made by persons declared to be mentally disabled or by persons who are so intoxicated that they are temporarily incapacitated can be voided, but only if the disabled party wishes to do so. He or she must be legally competent at the time of disaffirming the contract. Until the claim is made, the contract is valid.

State statutes give corporations certain powers. Corporations can enter into contracts but only within the limitations upon their powers set forth by state law. Some contracts of corporations that exceed the limitations of such power (*ultra vires* **contracts**) can be voided. However, as long as the subject matter of the contract is not illegal, such contracts will typically be deemed valid.

In summary, the concept of competency may be complicated. Because there are a number of exceptions, a lawyer must review the facts of each case before determining what rules apply.

§ 12.3.8   Essential elements—Lawful consideration

Consideration is that thing that leads a party to do something he or she would not otherwise be obliged to do or to forgo doing something he or she would otherwise have the legal right to do. Basically, consideration represents a bargained-for exchange of value, and each party must benefit from some form of consideration for a contract to be valid. Common items of consideration include money, property, or a promise to do or not to do some act.

Common law presumes that if the consideration is acceptable enough for the party to make the contract, it is sufficient to bind that party to the contract terms.

The consideration must pass from one party to the other during the term of the contract. Past acts or promises of either party do not usually provide consideration for a new contract. If an individual makes a bad bargain, but some form of sufficient consideration exists, he or she generally may not claim lack of consideration to void the contract.

§ 12.3.9   Essential elements—Lawful subject matter

A contract cannot be based upon anything that is illegal or against public policy. Examples of illegal subject matter are:

- Wagers
- Usury
- Illegal drugs
- Unfair trade practices

Examples of contracts against the public policy are:

- Agreements requiring performance that violates criminal laws
- Agreements requiring performance that is a tort

If a thing or act is illegal outside the realm of the contract, then no legal contract can be made concerning it.

§ 12.4   Types of contracts

Once it is determined that all necessary elements are present and that a contract exists, the rights and duties of the parties are further clarified by determining the type of contract that exists. The contract can be unilateral or bilateral; executory or executed; express or implied; and valid, voidable, or void.

§ 12.4.1   Types of contracts—Unilateral and bilateral contracts

A *unilateral contract* is one in which a person makes a promise conditioned upon the performance of another. The contract is not binding until the performance occurs, because such performance is what constitutes the consideration provided by such party.

EXAMPLE:

A promises B to pay B a commission if B locates a buyer for A's house. When B finds a willing buyer, a contract forms and A must pay B.

A *bilateral contract* is one in which both parties make a promise.

If either party fails to keep the promise, the other may be entitled to recover damages.

EXAMPLE:

A promises to pay *B* 90 cents per dozen of eggs if *B* will deliver 50 dozen eggs by tomorrow morning. *B* promises to deliver them.

§ 12.4.2 Types of contracts—Executory and executed contracts

Executory contracts are those that have been partially performed, but with performance remaining to be completed by one or both of the parties.

EXAMPLE:

B delivers the 50 dozen eggs on time but *A* has not yet paid. At this point, the bilateral contract is also executory.

Executed contracts are those that have been fully performed by both parties. The transaction is complete and nothing remains to be done.

EXAMPLE:

Upon delivery of the 50 dozen eggs, *B* receives $45 from *A*. At this point, there is an executed bilateral contract.

§ 12.4.3 Types of contracts—Express and implied contracts

An *express contract* is one in which the terms are specifically stated and agreed to by both parties. Express contracts are generally written. An insurance policy is an express contract because it is written and specifies terms and conditions. Leases are also express contracts.

An *implied contract* is one created by law and imposed upon parties because of their actions or because of their relationship. The action of using electricity creates an implied contract with the power company.

§ 12.4.4 Types of contracts—Formal and informal contracts

A *formal contract* is one in which the format of the contract (the way it appears) must meet certain requirements established by law. Negotiable instruments, for instance, fall into the formal contract category. Note that all checks follow the same basic format, since checks are negotiable instruments and formal contracts.

An *informal contract* is any contract that is not formal. A contract may be written and still be an informal contract if its format is not as prescribed by law.

§ 12.4.5 Types of contracts—Valid, voidable, and void contracts

A *valid contract* is one that contains all the necessary elements of a contract.

A *voidable* contract is one that is potentially defective in some respect. If the defect is asserted, one of the parties could void the contract. Defects such as a failure to have mutual assent or competent parties could create a voidable contract, for example. Voidable contracts are treated as valid contracts until one of the parties asserts a defect.

Void contracts are those that do not comply with the law and are unenforceable from inception. Oral contracts for the sale of land are not enforceable because the law requires those contracts to be in writing. The same is true of a negotiable instrument that does not conform to the form prescribed by law. A contract to commit murder is void. The courts cannot enforce contracts that do not conform to the law.

§ 12.5 Assignment of contracts

To *assign* means to transfer. Contracts involving specialized skills, knowledge, or judgment may not be assignable. For example, a musician may not be able to assign another musician a contract to perform at a certain event without the consent of the party with whom he has contracted.

Generally, contracts involving money or property may be assigned to third persons without the specific consent of the other party to the original contract. The third person is called the *assignee*. The person who transfers interest in the contract to the assignee is called the *assignor*. The assignee usually has responsibility for notifying the other party to the original contract that the assignment was made.

Assignment is simply a substitution of one party for another in a contractual relationship. The assignee "stands in the shoes" of the assignor, having the same rights and duties as the assignor. If an assignee fails to perform under the contract terms, however, the responsibility falls back on the assignor to make that performance.

Assignments are not always voluntary. Bankruptcy requires that the property of the debtor be assigned to a trustee for the benefit of creditors. Probate proceedings have the effect of assigning property to the personal representative (sometimes called executor or administrator) of the deceased for distribution to heirs.

§ 12.6 Discharge of contracts

Discharge in contract law means the termination of the contract. There are many ways to discharge a contract, although only the ones used most often will be discussed.

§ 12.6.1 Discharge of contracts—Performance

The most obvious method of discharge is *performance* of all the contractual terms by both parties. Most contracts are discharged by performance.

EXAMPLE:

A offers to wash B's windows for $10. B accepts. A washes the windows, and B pays the $10. The contract is discharged.

§ 12.6.2 Discharge of contracts—Accord and satisfaction

Accord is the agreement of a contract party to accept another thing in place of the thing promised in the original contract (substitution). Once the substituted thing is given or the substituted act performed, it *satisfies* the original contract and the agreement for substitution. Accord and satisfaction occurs at that point.

EXAMPLE:

After receiving $10 to wash A's windows, B becomes concerned about working on a ladder and offers to clean the garage instead. A agrees. B cleans the garage.

It is not correct to say accord and satisfaction occurred at any point before B completed cleaning the garage.

§ 12.6.3 Discharge of contracts—Rescission

If both parties agree to cancel (rescind) a contract, it can be done by **rescission**. Rescission requires only the agreement to cancel or repeal the contract and to do whatever is necessary to restore both parties to their original condition. In effect, rescission is a contract to cancel the original contract.

EXAMPLE:

A offers B $10 to wash A's windows and B accepts. A then changes his mind and asks B to agree to cancel the deal. B agrees.

§ 12.6.4 Discharge of contracts—Novation

Discharge by **novation** involves the two original parties to a contract and a newcomer. One of the original parties is removed from the contract, and the newcomer takes the party's place absolutely. All three parties must consent. This should not be confused with assignment of contract, since the two have very different consequences.

EXAMPLE:

B agrees to wash A's windows for $10. B later realizes he does not want to wash windows and convinces C to do it. A, B, and C agree that A will pay C $10 to wash the windows.

In this situation, B is discharged from the contract by novation. The duty to A is ended. Because there is no legal duty, B cannot be held liable if C fails to wash the windows. Note, however, that if B had assigned only the duty to perform to C, and C later failed to wash the windows, B would have been ultimately liable to A for the failure to perform. Novation discharges B. Assignment does not.

§ 12.6.5   Discharge of contracts—Account stated

Suppose a debtor and creditor have had several transactions, and the creditor sends one statement as a summary of the transactions, with a price shown for each. If the debtor holds the bill for an unreasonable time, the creditor may use the summary statement as a basis for suit on **account stated**. This has the effect of discharging the underlying transactions or contracts in favor of the account stated. The debtor can object if done within a reasonable time. In that case, the creditor would be required to justify each transaction listed.

§ 12.6.6   Discharge of contracts—Release and covenant not to sue

This method of discharge is typically used for contracts that are not fully performed but are too far along for rescission. One party has performed all or part of such party's obligation, the other has not, but they both want to end the contract relationship.

§ 12.6.7   Discharge of contracts—Impossibility of performance

If a contract has been formed and an unforeseeable event occurs that makes performance of the contract impossible, the contract will be discharged. **Impossibility** means that no person could legally or physically perform the contract terms.

The city passes an ordinance requiring all those who wash windows to be licensed. While this places an unforeseen burden on B, it is not an impossibility. However, if the ordinance stated that no person could wash the windows of another, B would be discharged. Washing A's windows after the ordinance had passed would require B to do an illegal act.

Suppose that A's house burned down after the contract was formed. It would be impossible for B to wash windows after the house had been destroyed, and B would be discharged.

Suppose that B died before the windows were washed. Again, B's performance would no longer be possible, and B would be discharged.

This last situation may seem ridiculously obvious—one cannot perform an act after death—but not all legal obligations end at death. Recall the binding effect of a contract to sell land, for instance, on the estate of the deceased. Contracts for personal services, such as B's window washing, are discharged at death. The legal effect of the discharge is to free B's estate from performing the balance of the contract.

Discharge for impossibility of performance only means the rest of the contract does not have to be performed. It does not cancel any contract obligations for prior performance. Suppose B agrees to wash A's windows for a year, washed A's windows for three months, and then died. B's estate would be entitled to receive payment for three months of the work, even though the remaining nine months were discharged for impossibility.

§ 12.6.8   Discharge of contracts—Breach and remedy for breach

Once a contract is formed, both parties have a duty to comply fully with its terms. If either fails to do so, the noncomplying party is in breach of the contract. It is possible for both parties to breach the contract terms and therefore for each party to have a claim against the other for *breach of contract*.

The theory of contract law is simply to enforce binding promises people make to each other. If a person makes a binding promise and then fails to carry it out, the law will step in to require that person to either keep the promise or pay for the damage caused by the broken promise. There are several methods of doing this, called remedies for *breach of contract*:

- Specific performance
- Restitution
- Money damages
- Some combination of these

§ 12.6.9   Discharge of contracts—Specific performance

Specific performance is a legal remedy requiring the defendant to comply with the terms of an agreement. However, courts are usually reluctant to award specific performance unless money damages are inadequate. Contracts for the sale of real estate are the most notable exception to the general rule, as land is regarded as being unique.

§ 12.6.10   Discharge of contracts—Restitution

Restitution is the act of restoring a thing to its rightful owner. Restitution lends itself to those situations where personal property has changed hands, but payment has not been made. The wrongful possessor of the property could be ordered to return the property to the rightful owner.

§ 12.6.11   Discharge of contracts—Money damages

Money damages is a remedy which may be awarded in a court proceeding seeking a money judgment. Money damages represent the largest percentage of remedies awarded, simply because the harm caused by most breaches can be reduced to a dollar value. In assessing money damages, the loss must generally be *mitigated* (reduced) by the person making the claim, where he or she can do so. This ensures compensation is for the actual amount of loss.

EXAMPLE:

   B employs *A* under an employment contract for one year at $2,000 per month. After eight months, *A* is fired even though he has performed all the duties of his employment. *A* would not generally be permitted to sit at home during the remaining four months and recover money damages for that time. He would be expected to seek other employment. Suppose he found another job two months later at a salary of $1,500 a month. His actual damages would be computed:

Salary of $4,000 for two months unemployed and $1,000 ($2,000–$1,500) for two months employment at a lesser rate or a total of $5,000 actual damage for four months remaining under the contract.

Suppose A went to work the next day at a greater salary. He sustained no actual loss; however, it is very possible that, because B breached the contract, A could be awarded nominal damages simply because the breach had occurred.

§ 12.7   Summary

Nothing in this material is intended to imply that the area of contract law is simple. It can be highly complex and is usually a far cry from the simple dilemma of having B's windows washed. It is presented here to give the beginning lawyer's assistant a basic understanding of the concepts involved and to emphasize the importance of the lawyer's role in resolving contract disputes.

Chapter 13

Torts

KeyCite®: Cases and other legal materials listed in KeyCite Scope can be researched through the KeyCite service on Westlaw®. Use KeyCite to check citations for form, parallel references, prior and later history, and comprehensive citator information, including citations to other decisions and secondary materials.

---

§ 13.1 Definition

The law of torts is a broad general area of civil law that is very difficult to define. The Restatement of the Law (Second), Torts[1] devotes pages to its definition. The word ***tort*** comes from the Latin word *tortus*, meaning twisted or crooked, and from the French word *tort*, meaning injury or wrong. Generally, a tort is an act or omission causing an injury or wrong to someone else who is provided a legal remedy. The law of torts therefore deals with injuries or wrongs for which society permits compensation or remedy.

§ 13.2 Distinction between tort and contract law

Most civil actions arise out of contracts or torts. Contracts form the basis of rights and obligations of the parties. By entering into a contract, the parties commit to perform certain acts and usually acquire certain rights. A valid contract has the force of law between the parties. Without a contract, the rights and obligations that exist between people are found in the law of torts.

§ 13.3 Distinction between tort and criminal law

Torts are civil wrongs against individuals or entities. Criminal acts are wrongs against the state. Tort law deals with conduct of individual society members toward each other, and criminal law deals with conduct toward society as a whole. An act may be both a tort and a crime, but a tort is not necessarily a crime, and a crime is not necessarily a tort.

EXAMPLE:

An automobile driver runs a traffic light. An accident results in which the other driver is injured. Under the law of torts, the injured person could bring a civil action seeking compensation for his injuries, and the state could bring a criminal action against the driver for running a red light. If such were the case, however, the civil action filed by the injured driver would not necessarily involve the action brought by the state for the traffic violation. Different courts would probably hear them at different times, and the result in one case would not necessarily have any effect on the other.

§ 13.4 Kinds of torts

Since tort law provides a remedy for any injury or wrong not covered by contract law, it encompasses a large variety of cases. Some are more common than others, but they all arise out of three categories of torts: intentional torts, negligence, and strict liability.

[Section 13.1]

[1]American Law Institute, Restatement of the Law (Second), Torts. Thomson Reuters, St. Paul, Minnesota, 1979.

§ 13.5 Intentional torts

Intentional torts result from intentional interference with another's person or property. There are two broad categories of intentional torts:

- Those interfering with the person, such as battery, assault, and false imprisonment.
- Those interfering with property, such as trespass and conversion.

§ 13.5.1 Intentional torts—Battery

A *battery* is a harmful, offensive touching of another's person. The principle is that a person may expect freedom from harmful or offensive bodily contact from another.

EXAMPLES:

A intentionally pushes B off a sidewalk. A is liable in tort if B proves A intended for the pushing action to be offensive.

A punches B in the nose. A has committed a battery.

A taps B on the shoulder to get his attention. A has not committed a battery. Reasonable people would not be offended by this intrusion.

§ 13.5.2 Intentional torts—Assault

An **assault** is an act that creates in a person the immediate fear of an attempted battery. Assault need not involve actual contact—it only requires intent and the resulting fear. The legal principle is that a person may expect freedom from fear of immediate contact, whether harmful or merely offensive.

EXAMPLES:

A throws a brick at B. B sees the brick coming at him and steps aside to avoid being hit. Although B is not injured, A may be liable in tort.

A puts his hand in his pocket so it appears to B that A has a gun. A tells B to give him his money or his life. A has committed an assault. Any reasonable person would believe the danger was real and immediate.

A tells B that if it were not a holiday, he would punch him in the nose. A has not committed an assault. Threats alone are not an immediate danger.

A tells B he is going to punch him in the nose and then draws back his fist. A has committed an assault. B believes A has the ability to carry out his threat.

§ 13.5.3 Intentional torts—False imprisonment

False imprisonment is holding a person against a person's will without legal authority. The principle is that if a person is held against the person's will by threats, intimidation, or physical force, the person is entitled to be compensated for time, physical discomfort, inconvenience, and any resulting illness, mental anguish, or emotional distress.

EXAMPLES:

A shopper in a department store triggers an alarm as the shopper is leaving the store. The shopper is detained by the security guard, who searches the shopper's packages. It is discovered that the clerk failed to remove a security tag from one of the purchases. The department store may be liable to the shopper.

A, a police officer, stops B's automobile, asks to see B's driver's license, and tells B not to leave until A clears B through telephone contact with police headquarters. This is not false imprisonment. A is authorized to do this to preserve society's safety.

A offers B a ride home, and B accepts. A then refuses to take B to his house or to stop the car so B can get out. This is false imprisonment. B cannot escape a moving vehicle without risking serious injury.

§ 13.5.4   Intentional torts—Trespass to land

Trespass to land occurs when a person directly enters upon the land of another without permission or remains upon the land or places or projects any object upon the land. The principle in law is that a landowner has the right to keep the land intact (the surface, air space above it, and the minerals below it), so anyone violating such right is liable in tort.

EXAMPLES:

If a person enters the land of another person without permission and cuts the timber, such person is liable to the owner for the value of the timber.

The airline flight pattern of A calls for its plane to travel above B's land. This is not trespass.

§ 13.5.5   Intentional torts—Conversion

Conversion is taking another's property and using it as one's own. The legal principle is that only the owner of a thing is entitled to possess, use, and control.

EXAMPLES:

Some of A's cattle stray into B's field. B knows A owns the cattle, but instead of returning them, B sells them at a cattle market as his own. B is liable to A for the fair market value of the cattle.

A borrows B's boat intending to return the boat within the hour. A, however, is in a boating accident and B's boat is wrecked. A is liable to B for the fair market value of the boat.

§ 13.5.6   Intentional torts—Proving damages

In most intentional torts, it is not necessary for the plaintiff to prove actual damages. The plaintiff must only prove nominal damages.

In other areas of tort law, it is usually necessary for a plaintiff to prove actual damages were suffered. It is sometimes difficult for a layman to understand there can be tort liability without damage. To recover for an intentional tort, the plaintiff need only convince the court the defendant intended the act in question.

EXAMPLE:

If one person intentionally strikes another, battery results. One can distinguish this from a person accidentally striking another by carelessly waving his arms. In the latter, there was no intent to cause harmful or offensive touching, so there is no battery.

As noted earlier, however, only a judge or jury can decide the defendant's intent, and in making the decision, the finder of fact must apply many technical elements.

§ 13.6 Negligence

Unintentional torts, not controlled by the doctrine of strict liability (discussed later), fall under the broad category of negligence. In establishing *negligence*, a plaintiff must prove the defendant owed a duty to the plaintiff. This duty falls into two categories:

- That which a reasonable person owes to another in the particular circumstances—called "duty of due care."
- A special duty or care required by a specific statute or by case law. This special duty may be in addition to or in place of the duty of due care.

Ordinarily, due care is the care a reasonable, prudent person would exercise in a particular situation. To determine what a reasonable action is, the court weighs the act's usefulness against the foreseeability and severity of any harm that might result. Society is constantly changing, and what constitutes a reasonable act also changes. Therefore, an act, which was reasonable 20 years ago, may be considered unreasonable today. The lawyer must look to current case law to evaluate the client's claim. Examples of some common torts resulting from negligence follow.

§ 13.6.1 Negligence—Personal injury cases

A suit filed to recover damages for physical injury is considered a personal injury suit. If one person's negligence causes injury to another, the negligent person is said to be liable in tort.

EXAMPLE:

A driver fails to obey a traffic signal, causing an accident. Someone is injured in that accident. The injured person is entitled to compensation.

However, the injured person may not always recover damages if the injuries are not determined to be serious enough by a judge or jury. In New York, for example, the injured person must meet a "serious injury threshold," which means that the injuries suffered must meet one of the following criteria: (1) death; (2) dismemberment; (3) significant disfigurement; (4) a fracture; (5) loss of a fetus; (6) permanent loss of use of a body organ, member, function or system; (7) permanent consequential limitation of use of a body organ or member; (8) significant limitation of use of a body function or system; or (9) a medically determined injury or impairment of a non-permanent nature which prevents the injured person from performing substantially all of the material acts which constitute such person's usual and customary daily activities for not less than ninety days during the one hundred eighty days immediately following the occurrence of the injury or impairment.[1]

§ 13.6.2 Negligence—Defamation (libel and slander)

Damage to a person's reputation caused by the publication or repetition of false information is libel or slander. (The defamation is *libel* if the information is written or published and *slander* if the information is spoken.) A person who publishes an untruthful statement that is defamatory of someone is held liable for any damage to that person's reputation or business.

§ 13.6.3 Negligence—Malpractice

Malpractice applies to doctors, lawyers, ministers, counselors, teachers, realtors, and almost any other professionals or quasi-professionals. In general, malpractice is a negligence action with the standard of performance measured by what is expected of a similar professional rendering services based on geographical area, level of expertise, and what was represented to the client. Simply put, malpractice is a departure from an accepted standard of care or practice. A tremendous rise in the cost of malpractice insurance has prompted the statutory creation in some jurisdictions of procedural prerequisites to suit, such as peer review boards, arbitration, notice requirements, and caps on the damages the injured person can receive.

§ 13.7 Strict liability

Strict liability is imposed by law to provide a remedy for injuries received as a result of certain accidents or situations regardless of the degree of care exercised by the defendant. Under strict liability, neither negligence, nor intent is considered. The plaintiff need only establish that strict liability applies to the case. This theory is most often used in real estate or products liability cases, and in New York, it also applied to labor law cases.

[Section 13.6.1]

[1]New York State Insurance Law Section 5102(d).

§ 13.7.1   Strict liability—Products liability

Cases in which a person sustains injuries as the result of an allegedly defective product are called ***products liability*** cases. Manufacturers are liable for damages caused by their defectively designed, manufactured, or labeled products. Liability is based on the theories of negligence or strict liability.

EXAMPLE:

An automobile accident occurs due to a defective steering mechanism in the car. The driver of the car is injured. The car manufacturer is liable in tort to the injured person, who is entitled to compensation. It is assumed the product was fit to be used for its intended purpose.

In New York, however, the burden of proof is on the injured person to show that the serious injury threshold has been met, or no recovery may be obtained.[1]

§ 13.7.2   Strict liability—Animal cases

For purposes of tort law, ***animal cases*** involve injuries or damages caused by animals, including all kinds of livestock, domesticated wild animals, household pets, or farm animals. An owner is strictly liable for damage caused by livestock, domestic animals, or wild animals the owner keeps regardless of whether the owner exercises due care. Some states have statutes governing animal bite situations.

EXAMPLE:

A child is playing with the neighbor's dog when the dog bites the child. Regardless of whether the bite was playful, the neighbor is liable.

In New York, the above example is not always the case. The state's highest court ruled that "the owner of a domestic animal who either knows or should have known of that animal's vicious propensities will be held liable for the harm the animal causes as a result of those propensities. Vicious propensities include the propensity to do any act that might endanger the safety of the persons and property of others in a given situation."[1]

§ 13.7.3   Strict liability—Extrahazardous activities

An ***extrahazardous activity*** is one that carries the likelihood of causing some type of damage even if reasonable care is exercised. A person who maintains a dangerous thing or engages in a dangerous

---

[Section 13.7.1]

[1]See Footnote "1" of § 13.6.1.

[Section 13.7.2]

[1]Bard v. Jahnke, 6 NY3d 592 (N.Y. 2006), citation omitted.

activity which produces a high risk of harm to other persons or property is liable to those damaged or injured regardless of whether the person exercises due care.

EXAMPLE:

A demolition company is leveling a building by using carefully placed explosive charges. Every possible precaution is taken, but when the charges are detonated, flying debris breaks nearby windows. The demolition company is liable since explosives are inherently dangerous.

Some torts do not fall neatly into one of these broad categories. Recovery could be based on more than one kind of tort liability. A particular tort might sometimes be classified as falling under strict liability in one situation and as negligence in another. In those cases, the kind of tort liability depends upon the circumstances of the case.

The examples listed above are not all-inclusive and are given simply to provide the reader with a basic understanding of the most common torts. In fact, our courts continue to expand the realm of tort law by applying it to claims for which there is no other legal remedy.

§ 13.8   Defenses in intentional torts

The most important reason for classifying torts is to determine applicable defenses. The defenses available vary with the kind of tort. The defenses discussed here are the most common defenses. The most important defenses available to a defendant charged with an intentional tort are consent, self-defense, privilege, defense of property, legal process, and recapture of chattels.

§ 13.8.1   Defenses in intentional torts—Consent

A defendant sued for battery might take the position that although the defendant did cause the plaintiff's injuries, the plaintiff consented to the fistfight that resulted in the injuries, so plaintiff's *consent* bars recovery.

§ 13.8.2   Defenses in intentional torts—Self-defense

Using the same example, the defendant could take the position that the plaintiff provoked the fight, attacked the defendant, and the defendant injured the plaintiff in *self-defense*.

§ 13.8.3   Defenses in intentional torts—Privilege

As a defense to an action for trespass, a defendant might assert *privilege* to enter upon the land, alleging there was a written agreement authorizing the entry.

§ 13.8.4   Defenses in intentional torts—Defense of property

A defendant might also allege *defense of property* to an injury received by a plaintiff on the defendant's property that the defendant was forced to take action to protect the property.

§ 13.8.5   Defenses in intentional torts—Legal process

A defendant sued for an injury could use the **defense of *legal process*** if the defendant were a police officer who used force to keep the plaintiff, who had been charged with a crime, in custody.

Another example is if a driver was injured in an accident as a result of his failure to yield the right of way to an emergency vehicle with its emergency lights on and sirens blaring.

§ 13.8.6   Defenses in intentional torts—Recapture of chattels

In a personal injury action, the defendant could assert the plaintiff was injured when force was used to *recapture* money the plaintiff stole from defendant.

§ 13.9   Defenses to negligence

Two basic defenses to negligence are available—contributory negligence and assumption of risk.

Contributory negligence occurs when a negligent act by the plaintiff contributes to the plaintiff's damages or injury. In some jurisdictions, if a plaintiff is held to be contributorily negligent, the plaintiff cannot recover.

Many jurisdictions have now modified the contributory negligence doctrine by adopting the ***comparative negligence*** doctrine. Under comparative negligence theory, if the plaintiff is found to be contributorily negligent, the finder of fact decides in what percentage each party was negligent and awards damages accordingly.

EXAMPLE:

> In a suit involving an automobile accident where Driver A failed to obey a stop sign, but Driver B was traveling over the speed limit, the jury might decide Driver A was 80 percent at fault and Driver B was 20 percent at fault. If the court then determines Driver B's injuries are worth $50,000, Driver B is awarded 80 percent of $50,000, or $40,000.

The method of awarding damages varies in some jurisdictions. (*See* footnotes in sections 3.7.1 and 3.7.2 Contributory negligence is a defense only to negligence.)

An ***assumption of risk*** defense is employed when the defendant contends the plaintiff was aware of the risks involved and made a conscious decision to proceed in spite of them.

EXAMPLE:

> If A slips and falls on B's obviously icy driveway, is injured, and sues B, B can allege as a defense that A knew the driveway was icy but still took the risks involved.

§ 13.10   Defenses to strict liability actions

Traditional defenses cannot be employed in a strict liability action. The concept of strict liability is such that liability is intended under

specific circumstances. That is not to say a defendant cannot successfully defend this kind of lawsuit. It merely means the defenses available in other tort areas are not available in strict liability cases, and a
defendant must find other defenses to rebut the plaintiff's claim.

§ 13.11 Summary

Whether a defendant is found liable in tort depends upon whether
the plaintiff can prove the defendant's act or failure to act falls within
one of the three areas of liability discussed above and whether or not
the plaintiff can prove the severity of the injuries sustained. In general legal practice, litigation often involves torts, and the lawyer's assistant should refer to the chapter on litigation for an overview of
trial procedures and a general description of duties in litigation.

Chapter 14

Criminal Law and Procedure

§ 14.1 Introduction

An assistant employed by a lawyer who specializes in criminal law will find the job to be not only demanding and challenging but perhaps one of the most diversified, interesting, and sensitive in the legal field.

To be charged with a crime is one of the most significant events in a person's life. If he or she is convicted, the punishment may include a substantial fine, a prison term, or even the death penalty. Even if acquitted, the fact that an individual has been accused of a crime will undoubtedly affect the individual's personal and business relationships. The mere filing of a criminal charge may ruin a future business opportunity or political career. Frequently there are related civil suits and administrative proceedings that are conducted at the same time as a criminal investigation.

§ 14.2 Definition

In the early days of the English monarchy, every crime was a crime against the peace and dignity of the king, since he owned everything, and it was the duty of his subjects to live in peace. To some extent, this concept remains the basis of criminal charges today, and the government brings charges because the crimes are committed against the peace and dignity of the people of a political entity, such as a city or state.

A *crime* is usually defined as an act that violates the laws of a community, state, or country and for which a specific punishment is prescribed. A person convicted of a crime may be imprisoned, fined, or both. In some cases, capital punishment is also a possibility.

Federal criminal charges are prosecuted by the United States. State actions are brought by the state, generally in the county where the crime has occurred. The government is always the plaintiff in a criminal action.

§ 14.3 Initial client interview

The initial interview of the criminal client is very important. At that time, the lawyer must obtain from the client the details of the arrest to determine whether the client's rights may have been violated or any illegal acts may have been committed by the arresting officer.

The criminal client is frequently apprehensive, nervous, distraught, and/or irrational. Communicating with an illiterate client may be extremely difficult. That client requires special attention and understanding, regardless of the crime with which he or she may be charged. The lawyer's assistant should never divulge confidential information regarding a case.

§14.4 Jurisdictional differences

Because of the differences among the federal, state, and local governments, specific matters and procedures outlined in this chapter may relate to only some jurisdictions.

§14.5 Criminal law

Crimes are those offenses, either felonies or misdemeanors, which violate laws established by legislation.

EXAMPLE:

A man who murders another man threatens the safety of people in general, and therefore the community punishes him for his crime.

Historically, all crimes were considered torts or civil wrongs. Even murder was a private matter and was settled by the murderer and the family of the victim, either by the family's accepting payment from the murderer or by taking revenge on the murderer. Punishment was primarily a matter of revenge until people began to consider punishment as a deterrent to committing crimes. Later, the idea of crime as an offense against society led to the development of criminal laws. There are some acts, however, such as vehicular homicides and wrongful deaths, which may constitute both a crime and a civil tort.

EXAMPLE:

After having consumed several alcoholic drinks, A drives through a stop sign and hits B, a male pedestrian, who later dies of injuries sustained in the accident. The state charges A with vehicular homicide. B's wife also files a civil lawsuit against A seeking monetary compensation from A for the wrongful death of B.

§14.5.1 Criminal law—Scope

Criminal law includes matters involving the administration of criminal justice and encompasses such aspects as substantive criminal law, criminal procedure, and special problems in administering and enforcing criminal law.

§14.5.2 Criminal law—Substantive criminal law

Substantive criminal law is the law that defines what conduct is criminal and prescribes the type of punishment to be imposed for such conduct.

§14.6 Sources of criminal law

The rules that are enforced by the government are found in common law rules, constitutions, legislation, decisions of courts, and orders of administrative agencies, which are described below.

§ 14.6.1   Sources of criminal law—The United States Constitution and federal statutes

The United States Constitution is the supreme law of the land and establishes the basic rights and liberties of the American people. The Supreme Court of the United States is the final authority in interpreting the Constitution and can set aside any law—federal, state, or local—that conflicts with any provision of the Constitution. Congress enacts federal laws that prohibit certain conduct, e.g., price-fixing in violation of the federal antitrust laws or counterfeiting United States currency, in which the federal government is deemed to have an interest.

§ 14.6.2   Sources of criminal law—State constitutions and statutes

State constitutions and statutes enacted by state legislatures comprise state laws and are found in the various state codes. State law governs crimes such as robbery, murder, burglary, and other laws that have been established.

§ 14.6.3   Sources of criminal law—Common law

Common law rules are made by courts. These rules have developed from custom and usage and can vary widely from state to state because of the differences in local customs.

§ 14.6.4   Sources of criminal law—Administrative rulings

Administrative rules are made by bureaus of the government called administrative agencies. While administrative rulings rarely acquire the force of criminal law, some regulatory agencies, such as the Environmental Protection Agency, have the power to assess criminal penalties in specific circumstances.

§ 14.7   Classes of crime

A person accused of a crime is entitled to certain rights under the Constitution of the United States and the constitutions of the individual states, as well as under federal and state statutes. The criminal charges must be filed in the proper court before the statute of limitations has expired, and the case must be brought to trial on a reasonably speedy basis.

The two major classes of crimes are:

Felony A crime which generally carries a potential prison term of greater than one year, such as murder, grand larceny, arson, and rape. The penalty may include either a fine, imprisonment, or both, and in some jurisdictions, even the death penalty.

Misdemeanor A crime that generally carries a maximum potential jail term of one year or less, such as petty larceny, drunkenness, disorderly conduct, and vagrancy. As with a *felony*, the penalty may include a fine, jail, or both.

§ 14.8   Commencement of proceedings

Criminal proceedings are initiated by filing a criminal complaint, an information, or an indictment. A ***complaint*** is usually filed under oath in order to secure an arrest warrant. An ***information*** is an accusation filed in writing by the prosecutor, charging a person with an offense. An ***indictment*** is an accusation filed in writing by a grand jury, charging a person with an offense that is usually more serious than those offenses prosecuted by a complaint or information; however, some jurisdictions differ in their process.

§ 14.8.1   Commencement of proceedings—The grand jury

A ***grand jury*** is a body of citizens assembled to investigate complaints and accusations in criminal cases, to hear evidence, to determine whether probable cause exists that a crime has been committed and whether an indictment should be returned against a person for such a crime. If probable cause exists, the grand jury returns a ***true bill***. If probable cause does not exist, the grand jury returns a ***no bill***. A grand jury is usually comprised of more jurors than the ordinary trial jury or ***petit jury***. A grand jury does not decide guilt or innocence but decides only whether there is enough evidence to require an individual to stand trial. A grand jury's work is done in secrecy to avoid improper influence and to avoid harm to the reputation of those it may be investigating. The grand jury is assisted or directed by a prosecuting lawyer.

§ 14.8.2   Commencement of proceedings—Arrest

An *arrest* is an actual restraint of the person for submission to custody. An arrest may be made pursuant to a warrant signed by an appropriate judicial officer, such as a judge or magistrate. The arrest ***warrant*** indicates that the judge has found that probable cause exists to believe the named individual has committed an offense. The warrant authorizes any law enforcement officer to arrest the individual to be brought before the court. Under proper circumstances, an officer may be authorized to make an arrest without a warrant. Without an arrest warrant if the officer has reasonable cause to believe a crime has been committed and the person to be arrested has recently committed it. An arrest may also be made without a warrant if an offence, either a felony or misdemeanor, is committed or attempted in the officer's presence.

§ 14.8.3   Commencement of proceedings—Bail

Usually a person charged with a crime is entitled to be released on bail pending trial. ***Bail*** is security given for the release of a jailed person to ensure attendance at all required court appearances and the safety of the public. A person charged with an offense has a right to have bail set. Below are some of the considerations for determining bail:

- Financial condition of the accused
- Address of the accused and employment history
- Risk release will pose to the public
- Family situation and history
- Prior criminal record and pertinent facts of the particular offense

These factors may also be considered in determining the amount of bail.

A person who is granted bail may likewise be released on his or her own recognizance (without posting bail) at the discretion of the court. In certain limited circumstances, a person can be held without bail because of the seriousness of the offense and other considerations.

Since one purpose of bail is to ensure the attendance of the accused at all required court appearances, if the lawyer can show that the accused resides and works or owns property in the immediate area, the likelihood of that person being granted bail increases. At the discretion of the court, bail may be posted in cash or by a written guarantee called an **undertaking** or **bail bond**. The person who posts the bail bond is called a **surety**. A commercial surety is an insurance company that posts a bond for a premium. Individual sureties are persons who collectively own real or personal property within the jurisdiction with a net worth of at least the amount set in the order for bail. In some jurisdictions, the net worth of the sureties must be at least twice the amount of the bail bond. Each surety must sign an affidavit that the surety's net worth is sufficient to pay the bail bond. Each may also be examined under oath by the court or by the prosecuting lawyer in the presence of the court. The sureties who have signed the bail bond are then liable for all appearances required of the defendant up to and including the time when sentence, if any, is imposed. Upon approval of the bail bond by the court, the officer having custody releases the arrested person. Note that jurisdictions differ regarding bail issues.

§ 14.8.4 Commencement of proceedings—Reduction of bail

Sometimes the lawyer feels that the amount of bail set by the court is excessive, considering the accused person's financial status, the nature of the alleged offense, and other facts. If that is the case, the lawyer files a motion to reduce bail. (See Illustration 14-1.) The motion is an application to the court for an order reducing the bail, stating the grounds upon which it is made. It must be filed within the time prescribed by law.

The sample forms in this chapter are only a few of many that may be used during the course of a criminal proceeding. These are included primarily to acquaint the reader with some of the basic forms and should be used for guideline purposes only.

Illustration 14-1
[NAME OF COURT]

————,

	Plaintiff,	) MOTION FOR
vs.		) REDUCTION OF BAIL
————,		) No. ——
	Defendant.	)

Defendant moves the Court for an order reducing the bail which has been set in this matter in the sum of $—— for the reason that the amount is excessive, and for the further reasons *[here the lawyer will set out the facts concerning the defendant's financial condition, ties in the community, employment history and status, and prior criminal record or lack of it].*

DATED this —— day of ——, *[Year]*

———————————————

JOHN SMITH
[address]
Lawyer for Defendant

CERTIFICATE OF SERVICE

I certify that a copy of the foregoing Motion for Reduction of Bail was mailed, postage prepaid, to *[name and address of lawyer for plaintiff][or was personally served on lawyer for plaintiff]*, this —— day of ——, *[Year]*.

———————————————

§14.9 Misdemeanor cases

At the first appearance in court by both the defendant and defendant's lawyer, a written entry of appearance may be filed. (See Illustration 14-2.)

Illustration 14-2

[NAME OF COURT]

————,

	Plaintiff,	)
vs.		) ENTRY OF APPEARANCE
		) No. ——
————,		)
	Defendant.	)

JOHN SMITH enters his appearance as lawyer for defendant in this case.

DATED this ____ day of ____, *[Year]*

———————————————

JOHN SMITH
[address]
Lawyer for Defendant

CERTIFICATE OF SERVICE

[Similar to Illustration 14-1]

§ 14.9.1   Misdemeanor cases—Arraignment

The initial appearance in a misdemeanor case is usually the arraignment. An ***arraignment*** is conducted in open court, where the judge reads the criminal charges to the defendant or states the substance of the charge and gives the defendant a copy of the complaint or information before calling on the defendant to plead. At the arraignment, the defendant may plead not guilty or guilty. If the defendant enters a plea of guilty, the defendant is then scheduled for sentencing. If the defendant enters a plea of not guilty, a trial date is set.

§ 14.9.2   Misdemeanor cases—Trial

In all cases, the defendant has the right to appear and defend the charges levied, in person or by counsel. Depending on the maximum potential sentence, misdemeanors in some jurisdictions may be tried without a jury unless the defendant makes a written demand for a jury within the time prescribed by law prior to trial or unless otherwise ordered by the court. (See Illustration 14-3.)

Illustration 14-3

[NAME OF COURT]

————,		)	
	Plaintiff,	)	
vs.		)	DEMAND FOR JURY TRIAL
		)	No. ____
————,		)	
	Defendant.	)	

Defendant demands a trial by jury in this case.

DATED this ____ day of ____, *[Year]*

_____

JOHN SMITH
[address]
Lawyer for Defendant

CERTIFICATE OF SERVICE
[Similar to Illustration 14-1]

§ 14.9.3 Misdemeanor cases—Sentencing

Upon the entry of a plea or a verdict of guilty, the court sets a date for imposing sentence. Pending sentence, the court may commit the defendant to jail or may continue or alter the bail. At the time of sentencing, the court imposes sentence and enters judgment of conviction. There are several purposes for a sentence, including:

- Prevention
- Restraint
- Rehabilitation
- Deterrence
- Education
- Restitution

In many misdemeanor cases and some lesser felonies, probation may be granted as a sentence. **Probation** is an act by the court that suspends the imposition or execution of a sentence, generally under the supervision of a probation officer. The court may impose a number of terms as a part of the probation, including requirements that the defendant not violate laws, not engage in similar conduct to the conviction, attend treatment or counseling, pay fines, pay restitution to the victims of the crime, serve a jail sentence, have no contact with the victims (or even persons similar to them), or not drink or use drugs.

§ 14.10 Felony cases

When a person is arrested for a felony, the procedure is more complicated because the charge is more serious. After the arrest, the accused is brought before the court, where the defendant is advised of the charges against him/her, of the right to a preliminary hearing or examination, and a date for the hearing is set unless it is waived by the defendant. The preliminary hearing is to ascertain whether there is probable cause to believe a crime was committed and the defendant may have committed it. If the court believes there is probable cause, the defendant is bound over or transferred to the appropriate trial court of general jurisdiction to answer the charges. If the defendant is bound over to the trial court, the prosecuting lawyer will either file an information within the prescribed time or seek an indictment from the grand jury if state law requires an indictment for that particular offense.

§ 14.10.1 Felony cases—Arraignment in trial court of general jurisdiction

Upon the filing of an information by the prosecuting lawyer or the return of an indictment by the grand jury, the defendant is arraigned in the trial court. As in a misdemeanor case, an arraignment is conducted in open court, where the charge is read to the defendant or the substance of the charge is stated.

Upon arraignment, a defendant is usually represented by counsel, unless counsel is waived in open court. At the arraignment, or within a reasonably brief time thereafter, a defendant may plead guilty, not guilty, or *no contest*.

If the defendant wants to plead guilty, the court should make the following findings:

- If the defendant is not represented by counsel, that defendant has knowingly waived right to counsel and does not desire counsel.
- The plea is made voluntarily.
- The defendant knows his or her legal rights, including the right against compulsory self-incrimination, the right to a jury trial, the right to confront and cross-examine in open court the witnesses against the defendant, and that by entering the plea all of those rights are waived.
- The defendant understands the nature and elements of the offense to which the plea is being entered; that at a trial the prosecution would have the burden of proving each of those elements beyond a reasonable doubt; and that the plea is an admission of all those elements.
- The defendant knows the minimum and maximum sentences that may be imposed in the case for each offense to which a plea is entered, including the possibility of the imposition of consecutive sentences.
- Whether the tendered plea is a result of a prior plea discussion and plea agreement, and if so, what agreement has been reached.

If the defendant pleads guilty or no contest, the court sets a date for sentencing. If the defendant pleads not guilty or refuses to plead, the court enters a plea of not guilty and the case moves forward.

§ 14.10.2 Felony cases—Discovery and trial preparation

Even before a defendant's arraignment, the lawyer should have begun preparing for trial by interviewing witnesses and preparing them to be examined and cross-examined. Exhibits may be gathered and prepared for presentation as evidence in the trial, investigations may be made, and research done concerning the various issues pertinent to the case. In most jurisdictions, the government is required, by statute or rule, to provide certain basic information or discovery to the accused, e.g., results of scientific tests such as drug analyses, the defendant's own statement made to the police, etc.

Only by thorough preparation can the lawyer evaluate the nature and strength of the evidence that will be produced by the prosecution, and the lawyer then will be able to prepare and to properly present the best possible defense.

§ 14.10.3   Felony cases—Bill of particulars

An indictment or information may contain, in addition to the formal accusation, certain details of the alleged crime. If the indictment or information does not provide these details, the defendant may file a written motion for a *bill of particulars* asking for details concerning the offense charged. This enables the defendant to prepare a proper defense and to avoid double jeopardy, i.e., being tried more than once for the same offense. (See Illustration 14-4.)

Illustration 14-4

[NAME OF COURT]

————,	)	
Plaintiff,	)	MOTION FOR
vs.	)	BILL OF PARTICULARS
————,	)	No. ———
Defendant.	)	

Defendant moves the Court to direct the State to file a bill of particulars in this case, particularly setting forth the following:

[List items about which more particulars are sought, e.g., where and to whom does the State allege the defendant sold narcotics.]

DATED this ——— day of ———, *[Year]*

_____

JOHN SMITH
[address]
Lawyer for Defendant

CERTIFICATE OF SERVICE
[Similar to Illustration 14-1]

§ 14.10.4   Felony cases—Motion to dismiss

After the lawyer reviews the charging document (the information or indictment) against the provisions of the statute alleged to have been violated, a motion to dismiss based upon failure to have a speedy trial, lack of jurisdiction, or other grounds may be filed. Motions to dismiss must be filed within a specific time after the defendant is arraigned. Failure to file such a motion on time could result in a defendant's waiver of all such grounds other than lack of jurisdiction or failure of the charge to state an offense.

Whether a charge is sufficient to state an offense is generally governed by the rule that it is not sufficient unless it contains all necessary elements of the statute. In the event the statute does not specifically define the act or acts constituting the offense created thereby, the acts must be alleged sufficiently or the charge is deficient. Defenses and objections based on defects in the indictment or information other than that it fails to establish jurisdiction in the court or to charge an offense must usually be raised prior to trial by written motion. (See Illustration 14-5.)

Illustration 14-5

[NAME OF COURT]

_____,		)	MOTION TO DISMISS THE
	Plaintiff,	)	INDICTMENT FOR FAILURE
			TO STATE AN OFFENSE
vs.		)	
_____,		)	No. ____
	Defendant.	)	

Defendant moves the Court for an order dismissing the indictment in this case on the grounds that it fails to state a cause of action against defendant as set forth in *[cite the relevant statute]*.

DATED this ____ day of ____, *[Year]*

_____

JOHN SMITH
[address]
Lawyer for Defendant

CERTIFICATE OF SERVICE
[Similar to Illustration 14-1]

§ 14.10.5   Felony cases—Change of venue

The lawyer may also feel that the client cannot receive a fair and impartial trial in the county where the crime was committed. In cases receiving much publicity and notoriety, the lawyer may seek a ***change of venue*** by filing a motion for such change. A change of venue is a change in the location of the trial. This motion must be in writing, supported by facts demonstrating that the defendant cannot receive a fair trial in the county in which the crime is charged. (See Illustration

14-6.)

Illustration 14-6

[NAME OF COURT]

_____,	)	
Plaintiff,	)	MOTION FOR A
vs.	)	CHANGE OF VENUE
_____,	)	No. ____
Defendant.	)	

Defendant moves the Court for an order transferring this case to a court of competent jurisdiction in any county other than the county of ____. In support of this motion, defendant sets forth the following facts showing that by reason of extensive and prejudicial publicity regarding the offense herein charged, the defendant cannot receive a fair trial in the county of ____.

DATED this ____ day of ____, *[Year]*

_____

JOHN SMITH
[address]
Lawyer for Defendant

CERTIFICATE OF MAILING
[Similar to Illustration 14-1]

§ 14.10.6 Felony cases—Evidence illegally seized

If the lawyer feels there was not probable cause for the arrest of the defendant or that evidence was illegally seized, a motion to suppress evidence seized illegally should be filed. (See Illustration 14-7.)

Illustration 14-7

[NAME OF COURT]

_____,	)	
Plaintiff,	)	MOTION TO SUPPRESS
vs.	)	EVIDENCE
_____,	)	No. ____
Defendant.	)	

Defendant moves the Court to suppress as evidence against the defendant all items seized during the execution of a search warrant of the premises located at ____, executed on ____, including but not limited to the following items:

[List items seized]

and as a basis for this motion, defendant states the search and seizure of said evidence was illegal in the following respects:

A. The search warrant is insufficient on its face and fails to state probable cause for its issuance,

B. *[List other bases]*

Further, the search warrant is in violation of the rights of the defendant under the Fourth Amendment of the United States Constitution and a violation of *[here set forth state constitution section violated and section of the state statute violated]*.

DATED this ___ day of ___, *[Year]*

JOHN SMITH
[address]
Lawyer for Defendant

CERTIFICATE OF SERVICE

[Similar to Illustration 14-1]

§ 14.10.7   Felony cases—Plea bargaining

Plea bargaining agreements have received much attention in the administration of law and justice in our country. While the plea agreement system may need reform, the United States Supreme Court has expressly recognized the need for this system.

A plea agreement means the government and the defendant have agreed upon a resolution to the case and will not take the case to trial. The government and defense have grant latitude to reach an agreed upon resolution in a case, including, but not limited to, a reduction in charges, a dismissal of charges, or an agreement regarding the sentence. The judge presiding over the case must accept the agreement that the parties have made.

To protect the accused, the courts have held that there must be evidence in the record of the trial court that:

- The guilty plea is entered into knowingly and intelligently.
- The defendant is aware of the maximum penalty that may be imposed.
- The defendant is aware that by entering the plea a number of important rights, including the rights forbidding compulsory self-incrimination, to a trial, and to confront and cross-examine witnesses in open court are waived.

Although the client must make the final decision as to whether to plead guilty or go to trial, it is the defense lawyer's duty to advise and inform the client so that the client may make an informed choice.

§ 14.10.8   Felony cases—Jury trial

The defendant has the right to appear and defend against charges brought in person or by counsel and to be personally present during the trial.

A defendant has a right to be tried by a jury of peers. In most felony cases, including *capital cases*, i.e., felonies punishable by death, the jury is usually comprised of twelve persons. However the number of jurors depends upon the jurisdiction. The prosecution and defense may proceed to trial or complete a trial then in progress with any number of jurors less than otherwise required with the consent of the accused and the approval of the court.

After the jury has been impaneled and sworn, the trial proceeds in the following order:

1. The charge is read.
2. The prosecuting lawyer makes an opening statement. The defense lawyer may make an opening statement at that time or reserve it until the prosecution has rested.
3. The prosecution offers evidence in support of the charge, and the defendant may cross-examine the state's witnesses.
4. When the prosecution has finished its case or rested, the defense may present its case through witnesses.
5. Thereafter, the parties may offer only evidence to rebut or refute the other side's case, unless the court otherwise permits.
6. At the conclusion of the evidence, the defense lawyer and the prosecuting lawyer make closing arguments.
7. When the arguments are concluded, the court instructs the jury on what law to apply in deliberating on a verdict.
8. The jury deliberates or considers the case in secret and returns a unanimous verdict of guilty or a unanimous or non-unanimous verdict of not guilty.

If a judgment of not guilty (an *acquittal*) is returned by the jury, the defendant is discharged.

If a guilty verdict is returned, the court may order the defendant to be taken into custody to await judgment on the verdict or may permit the defendant to remain on bail.

Upon the entry of a verdict of guilty, the court sets a time for imposing sentence.

§ 14.10.9 Felony cases—Sentencing

Before imposing sentence, the court affords the defendant an opportunity to make a statement on his or her own behalf and to present any information to mitigate punishment (make it less severe) or to show any legal cause why sentence should not be imposed. The prosecuting lawyer is also given an opportunity to present any information material to the imposition of *sentence*. Most jurisdictions require notice to the victim(s) so that they may be heard.

If the judgment calls for imprisonment, the sheriff of the county or other appropriate custodial officer designated by the court, upon receipt of a certified copy of the judgment, delivers the defendant to the appropriate prison to serve the sentence.

When judgment of death is rendered, a warrant signed by the judge is delivered to the sheriff of the county where the defendant is convicted. The sheriff delivers the warrant and a certified copy of the judgment to the warden of the prison at the time of delivering the defendant to the prison. The warrant states the conviction and judgment and the appointed day on which the judgment is to be executed.

In capital cases, the case is automatically reviewed by the supreme court of the state.

§ 14.11   Posttrial proceedings

After a defendant has been convicted, a motion for a new trial may be filed. This motion is made in writing within a specified time and should be accompanied by affidavits or evidence of the essential facts in support of the motion. (See Illustration 14-8.)

Illustration 14-8

[NAME OF COURT]

_____, Plaintiff,	)))	
vs.	)	MOTION FOR NEW TRIAL
	)	No. ____
_____, Defendant.	)))	

Defendant moves the Court for an order granting a new trial in this case, based on the grounds that *[set forth grounds]*.

DATED this ____ day of ____, *[Year]*

_____

JOHN SMITH
[address]
Lawyer for Defendant

CERTIFICATE OF SERVICE
[Similar to Illustration 14-1.]

The court may, upon motion or its own initiative, grant a new trial in the interest of justice if there is any error or impropriety that had a substantial adverse effect on the rights of a party.

If a new trial is granted, the defendant is in the same position as if no trial had been held, and the former verdict cannot be used or mentioned either in evidence or in argument.

§ 14.11.1   Posttrial proceedings—Appeals

Following imposition of sentence, the court advises the defendant of the right to appeal and the time within which any appeal must be filed.

After the court has imposed sentence, the defendant may file a motion for a correction or reduction of the sentence within the time period specified in the local rules. In considering a motion to reduce or correct the sentence, the court has virtually unlimited discretion to reduce or modify the sentence.

If the defendant takes an appeal from the conviction, the defendant must file a brief setting forth the facts and law upon which the conviction should be reversed. After the defendant has filed this brief, the state is given an opportunity to file a brief in opposition to the defendant's brief. Thereafter, the defendant may file a reply brief to the state's brief in opposition.

§ 14.11.2 Posttrial proceedings—Collateral attack

After the defendant has exhausted the so-called direct appellate remedies, the defendant may still seek to make a *collateral attack* upon the conditions of confinement, or indirectly attack the conviction. Many states and the federal government have provisions by which inmates may seek to have their conviction set aside or conditions of confinement changed. In some cases, a defendant convicted in a state court may also file a motion in federal court seeking to have a federal court review the conviction on constitutional grounds.

§ 14.11.3 Posttrial proceedings—Parole

At some point during confinement, a defendant may come up for periodic review by the state or federal parole board. If the parole board determines to release the defendant upon certain conditions, the defendant will be released on parole. If the defendant commits or is even arrested for another offense during parole, parole may be revoked and the defendant may be ordered back to the institution to complete the sentence. In certain cases, the defendant will also face additional incarceration resulting from parole revocation on top of the original sentence.

Chapter 15

Family Law

KeyCite®: Cases and other legal materials listed in KeyCite Scope can be researched through the KeyCite service on Westlaw®. Use KeyCite to check citations for form, parallel references, prior and later history, and comprehensive citator information, including citations to other decisions and secondary materials.

---

§ 15.1 Introduction

Family law encompasses all areas of the law pertaining to the family: abortion, adoption, child custody, duties to disabled people, juvenile, civil and criminal support enforcement, parentage and paternity, and marriage and divorce laws. In many areas the term ***domestic relations*** refers to family law.

§ 15.2 Influence of uniform acts

Although state law controls family law, the state laws have been greatly influenced by several uniform acts. Many state legislatures have used these acts as models and modified or expanded them. Some of the uniform acts pertinent to this chapter are the Uniform Marriage and Divorce Act, the Uniform Adoption Act, the Uniform Interstate Family Support Act, the Uniform Child Custody Jurisdiction Enforcement Act, the Uniform Parentage Act, the Uniform Duties to Disabled Persons Act, the Parental Kidnapping Prevention Act, and the Uniform Collaborative Law Act.

§ 15.3 Marriage

Marriage is a civil contract governed by state law. All states have laws regulating the licensing, solemnization, and registration of a marriage. There are two types of marriages:

- The *ceremonial marriage*, authorized by legislative action and validated according to statute for licensing, solemnization, and registration.
- The *common-law marriage*, which is an agreement between two people to marry, followed by their living together and representing themselves to the public as husband and wife. Common-law marriages are recognized in only a few states.

§ 15.4 Ceremonial marriage

Each state has its own rules and regulations concerning application for a marriage license, the license itself, and the registration of a marriage.

§ 15.4.1 Ceremonial marriage—Prohibited marriages

Marriage by a person before the dissolution or invalidity of a previous marriage is prohibited. Marriage between people within specific degrees of blood relationship is also prohibited. A prohibition of this type often includes people who are adopted, since in most cases they are treated as blood children of the adopting family. The exact prohibitions are set out in state statutes. The licensing clerk requires satisfactory proof that any proposed marriage is not prohibited.

§ 15.4.2 Ceremonial marriage—Application for license

The application for a marriage license usually requires biographical data for the couple, such as:

- Names, ages, and sexes
- Addresses
- Birthdates and birthplaces
- Occupations
- Race

- Names and birthplaces of the couple's parents
- Information on previous marriages
- Method of termination of previous marriages
- Whether the couple is related and, if so, how
- Social security numbers

§ 15.4.3   Ceremonial marriage—Blood tests

Many states require applicants to have blood tests taken prior to applying for the license. The tests are to assure that neither person has a venereal disease and to verify immunity to rubella. Certification of these tests is supplied to the couple at the time they take the test on a form prescribed by the appropriate state agency. This certification must be presented at the time of application for the license.

§ 15.4.4   Ceremonial marriage—Marriage of minors

In the event either party is a minor, the party's parents or guardians must consent to the marriage. Many states require only one parent to consent. The consent of the court is also sometimes required. The minimum age at which a license may be obtained is commonly 16, but this varies. Pregnancy is not necessarily an automatic reason for licensing an under aged applicant.

Some states require the couple to have professional counseling prior to issuance of the license if either party is a minor. This counseling may be done by someone appointed by the court or by an ordained minister (depending upon state law). After the required counseling has been completed, the counselor then files a written statement with the court indicating the counseling requirement has been met.

§ 15.4.5   Ceremonial marriage—The license

The clerk of court or deputy clerk usually issues the marriage license. There is a fee for the license, which must be paid before the license is issued.

§ 15.4.6   Ceremonial marriage—The waiting period

Sometimes there is a waiting period after issuance of the license before the marriage can be legally solemnized. In some jurisdictions, the court has the authority to shorten or waive the waiting period. There is often also a maximum period during which the license must be used (usually around 180 days).

§ 15.4.7   Ceremonial marriage—Solemnization

The clerk explains at the time of issuance that the license can be used only within a designated geographic area. A minister, judge, or other authorized state official performs the marriage ceremony. At the time the marriage is solemnized, the license is signed by the couple, the officiating minister or state official, and the witnesses. The officiating minister or state official forwards the marriage certificate to the appropriate state office for registration. Once the marriage is registered, the original license is usually returned to the husband and wife.

§ 15.5 Common-law marriage

A common-law marriage is usually contracted by a couple cohabiting and representing to the public that they are husband and wife. This is the basic requirement for a common-law marriage relationship in those states that recognize common-law marriages.

A person who lives with another of the opposite sex and believes in good faith that they have a common-law marriage is referred to as a *putative spouse* until information is received to indicate that a marriage relationship does not exist. A putative spouse has the rights of a legal spouse; however, in the event there is more than one putative spouse or if there is a legal spouse, the court in its discretion generally apportions marital assets, maintenance, and support among the parties making claim.

Many people believe that by living together for seven years, a couple contracts a common-law marriage. This is not necessarily true. In some states that recognize common-law marriages, the relationship of husband and wife is deemed to exist as soon as the parties represent to the public that they are husband and wife. On the other hand, in those states that do not recognize common-law marriages, neither a representation that the couple are husband and wife nor their living together for any length of time constitutes a marriage.

A couple that is common-law married sometimes wishes to file in the public records a declaration of marriage to protect the putative spouse's rights in the event of the other's death or disability. Such declarations are usually in the form of affidavits by people who have known the couple for a number of years and know that a marriage relationship exists.

A divorce is required to terminate common-law marriages in those states that recognize them.

§ 15.6 Termination of marriage

Although the spiritual and emotional intent of most couples is that marriage lasts a lifetime, since marriage is a civil contract governed by state law, state law can terminate it by several methods:

- Death of one of the parties
- Divorce or dissolution
- Annulment or invalidity

§ 15.7 Annulment or invalidity

Although annulment and invalidity are referred to as means of terminating a marriage, in the strict sense, they are not. An *annul-*

ment establishes that a marriage never existed. *Invalidity* describes a marriage that was invalid or void from its inception. In some states, the term *annulment* includes *invalidity*, and a court declaration of annulment indicates the marriage never existed, regardless of the reason.

§ 15.7.1   Annulment or invalidity—Grounds

The grounds for a declaration of invalidity or annulment include:

- Either of the parties lacked legal capacity to consent to the marriage, e.g., one of the parties was still married to another or both parties were drunk or incapacitated at the time of the marriage.
- Either of the parties was under duress.
- Fraudulent pretenses were used to induce the marriage.
- Either of the parties was underage and did not have proper consent or approval.
- The marriage was prohibited under state laws.
- In some states, lack of capacity to consummate the marriage was not known to the other party prior to or at the time of the marriage.

§ 15.7.2   Annulment or invalidity—Statute of limitations

States have time limitations after the discovery of one or more of the above circumstances within which an annulment or invalidity action may be filed. Persons other than the parties to the marriage can file for the annulment. The classic example of this is a parent who institutes an annulment proceeding because a minor child did not have consent to marry. Special circumstances must exist, however, for another party to initiate the proceeding.

§ 15.7.3   Annulment or invalidity—Children of an annulled or invalid marriage

Generally, the children of an annulled or invalid marriage are considered legitimate. Whether an invalidity decree is retroactive to the date of the marriage usually depends upon the circumstances and the wishes of the parties. Since children and property rights are often involved, the invalidity decree may be effective on the date it is granted rather than retroactively.

§ 15.8   Divorce or dissolution

Divorce or dissolution is the legal termination of a marriage relationship. The terms *dissolution* and *divorce* are used interchangeably in this chapter, although there is a technical difference between the two terms in some states.

§ 15.8.1   Divorce or dissolution—Grounds

The grounds for divorce may include one or more of the following:

- Cruel treatment of one spouse by the other.
- Abandonment of one spouse by the other (leaving home with no intention of returning).
- Living separate and apart from each other for a specified period of time.
- Adultery.

The foregoing list is not exhaustive, but it is representative.

§ 15.8.2 Divorce or dissolution—No-fault divorce

No-fault divorce means that neither spouse need be accused of the traditional grounds in order for a divorce to be granted, so neither spouse carries the stigma of any of the traditional grounds. Consequently, the no-fault concept relieves much of the mental and emotional stress experienced by the parties and their families during a dissolution proceeding. Two bases for a no-fault divorce are irretrievable breakdown and irreconcilable differences.

One of the purposes of the Uniform Marriage and Divorce Act is to make *irretrievable breakdown* a basis for dissolution. Many states have adopted irretrievable breakdown as the sole ground for filing a dissolution action. In some states, the term *irreconcilable differences* or insupportability carry the same meaning.

§ 15.8.3 Divorce or dissolution—Division of property

The termination of a marriage naturally requires division of the property accumulated during the marriage. How a division of the couple's property is accomplished is controlled by state law. A primary consideration is the contribution made by each party, monetary or otherwise, toward acquisition of the property. This would not be the case, however, in community-property states, where the property of the couple is owned one-half by each. It is often possible for the couple to reach an agreement regarding the division of property, but in many states the court must still approve the division of property.

§ 15.8.4 Divorce or dissolution—Child custody and support

An action for dissolution includes determination of custody or control of any minor children. In addition, it is customary as part of the same proceeding to set an amount to be paid by the noncustodial parent for child support. The court in which the action for dissolution is brought is typically the court that has jurisdiction over the children.

§ 15.8.5 Divorce or dissolution—Determination of custody

Many parents are able to reach an amicable agreement on which parent is to have custody of the children. If the parents are unable to reach an amicable agreement, then the court makes the determination.

The criteria for the award of child custody vary sufficiently from state to state that it would be impossible to list them here. The general rule is that the court is to act in the best interests of the minor children. This leaves the court with a great deal of discretion.

§ 15.8.6 Divorce or dissolution—Disputed custody cases

In disputed cases, the court takes testimony of the parties and their witnesses just as in any other trial. Sometimes the court requires and considers reports from investigative agencies. The judge also has the discretion to interview the children to ascertain their wishes and feelings, but the court is not bound to follow the wishes of the children. In some jurisdictions a lawyer, *guardian ad litem*, or **attorney ad litem** may be appointed to represent the children in the custody hearing.

§ 15.8.7 Divorce or dissolution—Legal and physical custody

In some states, a distinction is made between legal and physical custody; both types can be solely vested in either parent or be shared (*joint* custody). *Physical custody* refers to the actual physical residence of the child or children with one or both parents. The parent having physical custody makes the day-to-day decisions for the children, including meals, clothing, playmates, bedtime, and so forth. In joint physical custody arrangements, parents may alternate weeks or months with the children, or the children's time may be divided equally in a manner that meets the needs of the family. Generally, the parents work out physical custody arrangements, as they can be more creative than the courts.

Legal custody refers to the right and responsibility of making important long-term decisions affecting the children's welfare, including education, religion, and medical care decisions. Legal custody may also be joint or divided in appropriate cases. Joint custody, legal or physical, may not be appropriate in every case and requires the parents to work together for the welfare of their children.

§ 15.8.8 Divorce or dissolution—Visitation

Regardless of which parent is awarded custody of the children, the noncustodial parent has the right to visit the children, except in rare instances. Therefore, the custody award is usually subject to the right of reasonable *visitation* (sometimes called *access* or *secondary physical custody*) by the noncustodial parent. The intent of a reasonable visitation provision is that the parents cooperate and act in the best interests of the children. The court establishes specific times for visitation if the parties cannot agree. In most states, there are guidelines that suggest reasonable visitation, usually depending on the age of the children and subject to modification by the court.

§ 15.8.9   Divorce or dissolution—Child support

In determining support for the children, the resources of both the custodial and noncustodial parent, as well as the child's resources, are considered although in some states only the resources of the noncustodial parent are relevant. The child who has special needs— physical, emotional, or mental—may be entitled to a higher degree of support for a longer term than other children, including support and maintenance for special education to allow the child to function independently.

§ 15.8.10   Divorce or dissolution—Child custody and support agreements

When the parties are not in dispute as to custody and are able to agree upon support, they enter into a written agreement. Often the agreement recites that while both parents are fit and proper persons to have the care, custody, and control of the children, they deem it in the best interests of the children to place them in the custody of one of the parties. Visitation privileges are also provided for in this agreement. The court will generally approve an agreement reached by the parties, subject to the guidelines of the state.

§ 15.8.11   Divorce or dissolution—Alimony

Alimony, sometimes referred to as *spousal maintenance*, is an allowance that a spouse pays for the support of the other party, usually by court order. Most states have a provision for *alimony pendente lite*, that is, an allowance made during the pendency of an action for dissolution of marriage. Whether the spouse is entitled to alimony after the divorce is granted may depend upon other factors. However, this is an area in which the trial judge is allowed great discretion. Generally, the court considers the entire financial status of the parties, including individual incomes, debts, and the earning history and potential of the parties, in setting alimony. Often, if the parties reach an agreement on the division of property and child custody and support, they can also reach an amicable agreement as to whether and how much alimony or maintenance is to be paid.

Traditionally, only wives were entitled to alimony and maintenance. Some state statutes providing alimony for wives only have been declared unconstitutional. Most states are therefore amending their statutes to provide for alimony and spousal maintenance for either spouse. The following factors may be considered:

- The financial resources of the spouse seeking maintenance (payee), including marital property apportioned to the payee and the ability to meet needs independently and the extent to which a provision for support of a child living with the payee includes a sum for the payee as custodian.
- The time necessary to acquire sufficient education or training to

enable the payee to find appropriate employment, taking into account the payee's age, skills, and the ability to complete education or training to become fully or partially self-supporting. This is sometimes referred to as rehabilitative alimony.

- The standard of living during the marriage.
- The duration of the marriage and, in the case of a homemaker, the length of absence from employment and the extent to which any education, skills, or experience have become outdated and earning capacity has become permanently diminished.
- The loss of earnings, seniority, retirement benefits, and other employment opportunities forgone by the spouse seeking spousal maintenance.
- The age and physical and emotional condition of the spouse seeking maintenance.
- The ability of the maintenance payor to meet payor's own reasonable needs while meeting those of the payee.
- The contribution of each party in the acquisition, preservation, depreciation, or appreciation in the amount or value of the marital property, as well as the contributions of a spouse as a homemaker or in the furtherance of the payor's employment, business, or education.

In setting alimony or maintenance and child support, there are tax consequences to be considered. Often, in an amicable settlement, a larger portion of the alimony and child support is classified as alimony in the agreement. This is because, although alimony is considered income to the payee, it is deductible to the payor for income tax purposes. Therefore, if the wife is in a much lower tax bracket than the husband, for example, a higher income might not result in a substantial increase in taxes for the wife, but it might result in a substantial deduction and savings for the husband. The lawyer considers the tax consequences to ensure that the decree or agreement will satisfy the requirements of the Internal Revenue Service. Child support is not deductible, but arrangements must be made according to federal law concerning who will claim any child as a dependent for tax purposes.

§ 15.9 Procedures in termination of marriage

The increasing use of the no-fault concept of dissolution of marriage has reduced the paperwork necessary for traditional divorce actions. It also makes drafting legal pleadings simpler. The lawyer's assistant can draft a simple petition of this type for the lawyer's review.

Since the procedural structure of invalidity parallels that of dissolution, only dissolution is covered here. In instances in which the parties agree, the procedure is simpler than most civil litigation. When there is a dispute, the litigation follows the same course as any other litigation, with a petition, an answer or waiver, discovery, and a trial.

§ 15.9.1 Procedures in termination of marriage—Pleadings forms file

The lawyer's assistant can learn many of the pleadings requirements for dissolutions of marriage by referring to the forms file in the law office. If there is none, the assistant should begin to develop one. A good forms file can relieve the lawyer of the burden of dictating every pleading. However, forms must be individualized to the given situation. Each time a new situation arises or unique language is used, the assistant should put a copy of the appropriate portion of the document in the forms file for future reference. Document creation computer programs are also available.

§ 15.9.2 Procedures in termination of marriage—Client interview sheet

Preparation of dissolution pleadings can be streamlined using a detailed interview sheet. The lawyer's assistant can soon learn how to prepare initial documents from the information on the interview sheet completed by the lawyer.

§ 15.9.3 Procedures in termination of marriage—The pleadings

In traditional termination proceedings, the initiating party may be called either the *plaintiff* or the *petitioner*, and the spouse is the *defendant* or the *respondent*, depending on the custom of the court. Sometimes no party designation is used in the caption, e.g., "In the Matter of Susie Que and Curley Que Applying for Dissolution." In states where a joint petition for dissolution is allowed, the caption may read, "Susie Que and Curley Que, Joint Petitioners."

The initial document is called a *petition* or a *complaint*, and a summons or citation is issued as in any other civil litigation. Even in no-fault dissolutions, it is still necessary to prepare a petition. Some jurisdictions allow one of the spouses to waive service.

§ 15.9.4 Procedures in termination of marriage—The petition

The petition for a dissolution normally contains at least:

- The age, address, occupation, residence, and any prior names of each party and length of time residence has been continuously maintained within the state by each party.
- A statement that at least one of the parties has resided within the state of jurisdiction for the required length of time.
- The city, county, and state where the parties were married, the date of the marriage, and the office or governmental agency where the marriage was registered. This is particularly important under the uniform law, as a statistical report is sent to this office or governmental agency after the decree is entered.

439

- A statement as to whether or not state conciliation laws apply to the action and, if so, a statement that the provisions have been met.
- A statement that the marriage relationship is irretrievably broken.
- The names, ages, addresses, and birthdates of the children are required.
- A statement that the wife is or is not pregnant.
- The date the parties separated or ceased living together as man and wife.
- A reference to the division of property. If a division has been reached, it is described. The description may be included in the petition, or it may be a separate document referenced or incorporated in the petition.
- A statement of custody, support, and visitation rights regarding minor children. If an agreement has been reached, the provisions of the agreement are referenced.

The prayer of the petition is typed just as in any other civil litigation and gives a summary of the relief sought by the petitioner:

- That the marriage be dissolved.
- That the court approve the provisions of the agreement regarding the property rights or that the court determine the parties' respective property rights.
- That custody, support, visitation, temporary or permanent maintenance, and lawyers' fees be ordered as set forth in the petition or that these matters be determined by the court.
- That the wife's former or maiden name be restored, if desired.

The lawyer for the petitioner usually signs the petition. The petition may also need to be signed or verified by the petitioner.

Once the petition has been prepared and is ready to be filed, the lawyer's assistant will proceed just as in any other type of civil litigation. Refer to state laws and local rules of court for details on what specific documents must be included and served with the petition.

§ 15.9.5   Procedures in termination of marriage—Service

It is common in divorce proceedings for the defendant or respondent to accept service. A simple statement on the face of the summons acknowledging receipt of the summons on a certain date at a certain place usually does this. It is dated and signed by the defendant or respondent and returned to the originating lawyer for filing with the court. The respondent can accept service through the respondent's lawyer, through the mail, or in person.

Some jurisdictions require the serving party, e.g., the sheriff's office, to complete the return of service on the summons. It is important to learn the service requirements in the state where the dissolution is to be filed and comply with them.

§ 15.9.6 Procedures in termination of marriage—Answer or response

Just as in any other civil litigation, the defendant or respondent has a specified period of time within which to answer the petition. If the parties are in agreement, the respondent may file a verified response admitting the allegations of the petition and requesting that the decree be entered as prayed for in the petition. An alternative is that the respondent makes no appearance and the petitioner takes a *default judgment*. The defendant's first pleading may be called an *answer* or *response*.

§ 15.9.7 Procedures in termination of marriage—Importance of calendaring

The date that a response or an answer is due must be calendared, as in all forms of litigation. This is particularly crucial if the lawyer represents the defendant or respondent, as a response is essential to prevent a default judgment from being taken.

§ 15.9.8 Procedures in termination of marriage—The decree

When the decree is entered, whether in an amicable action or a disputed one, it may set forth findings of fact, conclusions of law, and the decision of the court. In some states, if the matter is a disputed one, the lawyer for the prevailing party drafts the judgment and submits it to the opposing lawyer for approval before presenting it to the judge for signature and entry. In other states, one of the parties appears to "prove-up" the decree.

Testimony is taken by the court, and at the conclusion of the testimony, the judge signs the decree that has been prepared by the lawyer prior to the court hearing.

Regardless of how the decree is obtained, it contains substantially the same information:

- The names of the parties.
- The summons was served and the default entered or that the summons was served and a response filed and whatever other action resulted.
- The date of the hearing or the date of the decree.
- A statement that witnesses were sworn and testified and that from the evidence presented the court makes the findings of fact contained in the decree.
- The findings of fact.
- A statement that from the findings the court draws the conclusions set out in the decree.
- The conclusions of law.

- The fact that the marriage is dissolved.
- The parties have entered into an agreement regarding distribution and disposition of their property that is incorporated by reference into the decree and approved.
- Full provisions for child custody, support, and visitation.
- Provisions regarding alimony or spousal maintenance.

It is also possible in some states to obtain the actual marriage dissolution in advance, reserving the property settlement, child custody, and support matters for consideration later. This is known as a *bifurcated* hearing or decree. The original decree should conform to this structure, with a final decree being entered when the remaining issues are settled or have been heard.

When the decree has been entered, copies should be served on the parties as required by appropriate state laws. The state may require a notice of entry of decree, and the lawyer's office may be responsible for preparing that notice, although it may be served by the clerk or by the sheriff. It is a good practice to see that each party receives a certified copy of the decree.

§ 15.9.9   Procedures in termination of marriage—Appeals

Appeals in these actions generally follow the same rules and procedures as in any other type of civil litigation.

§ 15.10   Appointment of guardian *ad litem*

In some jurisdictions, either parent may petition the court to appoint a disinterested lawyer to represent the interests of minor or disabled children who are affected by the custody, support, and property settlement of the parties. This lawyer then enters the case as **guardian *ad litem*** or **attorney *ad litem***. Depending upon the jurisdiction, the attorney or guardian *ad litem* may be responsible for representing to the court what the child wants. In other jurisdictions, the attorney or guardian *ad litem* represents to the court what the attorney thinks is in the child's best interest.

§ 15.10.1   Appointment of attorney or guardian *ad litem*— Petition to appoint

The petition to appoint simply requests that the court appoint a lawyer to represent special parties. Depending upon the procedural rules of the jurisdiction, generally the best interests of the children are sufficient reason to seek an appointment. The fees of the guardian *ad litem* are fixed by the court and taxed to the parties accordingly.

§ 15.10.2   Appointment of guardian *ad litem*—Mentally disabled party

When one of the parties to the dissolution action is mentally disabled, the court may appoint a guardian *ad litem* to act in the place of the mentally disabled spouse. The guardian *ad litem* then retains the services of a lawyer to represent the mentally disabled party.

In most states, mental disability for a specific duration constitutes grounds for a divorce or dissolution. This type of action might be used when a spouse must be institutionalized, placing a financial burden on the family. The dissolution action may enable the mentally disabled spouse to receive Medicaid or another subsidy to pay for the institutionalization and enable the family to remain financially intact.

§15.11 Uncontested proceedings

In *uncontested proceedings*, the marriage partners have decided that they no longer wish to remain married, and they have reached an amicable decision on property, custody, child support, visitation, and alimony. Often the lawyer prepares a proposed agreement for execution by the parties prior to filing the action. This agreement recites basically the following facts and provisions:

- Names of the parties.
- Date and place of the marriage.
- The parties are currently husband and wife.
- The parties have separated or will be separated for whatever reason and date the separation occurred.
- The name, age, sex, and birthdate of any minor children.
- The name of each lawyer representing each party; if one is not represented by a lawyer, a statement that the unrepresented party understands he or she is free to seek legal representation and has been advised to do so.
- Statement that the parties intend by the agreement to set forth in writing their mutual promises.
- The agreement is mutual.
- The provisions for the division of property and debts.
- Provisions for child custody, support, and visitation, with a statement that the parties feel these are in the best interests of the children.
- If child custody is to be joint, the controlling provisions.
- Alimony or spousal maintenance provisions.
- How tax returns for the year of dissolution will be handled, including who gets any refund or pays any taxes due.
- How the dependent tax deductions for minor children will be allocated.
- Provisions for modification of the agreement.
- Provisions for lawyers' fees.
- Provisions for effecting transfer of title of the assets.
- Statement that the parties have fully disclosed all property, debts, and agreements to each other and to their lawyers.
- The parties have read and understand the agreement.
- The agreement is voluntary.

- The name of the court having jurisdiction over the dissolution proceedings, any future modification of the agreement, and future child custody and support proceedings.

The agreement, when finalized, is sometimes signed in triplicate by the parties and notarized. Each party then retains one original, and the third original is filed with the court when the petition for dissolution is filed. This eliminates the necessity of having to set forth the agreement in the petition. It also saves time when the decree is granted, as the agreement can be made a part of the decree by reference if an original is in the court record.

§ 15.12   Collaborative divorce

A new trend in family law is the *collaborative divorce*, in which the parties agree to settle the divorce rather than try it in court. Attorneys are retained on the contract basis that they will assist the couple in resolving the issues associated with divorce or dissolution, but if the couple is not able to reach agreement and goes to court, the attorneys from the collaborative process will withdraw representation. Collaborative divorces also often enlist professionals, such as an accountant or financial adviser to assist in division of property and other financial interests, to assist in creating an agreement between the parties. Therapists may be recruited to counsel the couple and any children. The goal of collaborative divorce is to resolve the differences between the parties and assist in healing the wounds that are created by the termination of the marriage.

Collaborative divorce is not yet recognized or practiced in a number of states. The attorneys who participate in collaborative divorce are encouraged to obtain specialized training. Although the principle of collaborative divorce is lofty, in practice, the number of experts required to assist in the process can make it costly. For a couple with substantial property and resources, the cost of an amicably negotiated settlement may be considerably less than the cost of protracted litigation—which is one of the advantages of collaborative divorce. But it is also a significant disadvantage for the couple whose resources are too limited to permit them to retain additional professionals for the divorce process.

§ 15.13   Modification of a decree

State laws usually set a time within which a dissolution decree, including custody and support provisions, cannot be modified after it is entered. The Uniform Marriage and Divorce Act recommends two years. During this time, the decree cannot be modified unless there is a substantial change in circumstances such as severe disability of the custodial parent affecting the children, inability of noncustodial parent to continue support payments in the amount ordered, or circumstances that have changed greatly since the entry of the decree affecting the best interests of the minor children.

§ 15.14   Uniform Interstate Family Support Act

The Uniform Interstate Family Support Act (UIFSA) provides a means for enforcing duties of support in foreign jurisdictions. In this context *foreign jurisdiction* means a state other than the one where the child and custodial parent live. UIFSA has now been adopted by a majority of states.

§ 15.14.1   Uniform Interstate Family Support Act— Jurisdiction

Actions under UIFSA are initiated in the jurisdiction of the custodial parent and child to whom support is due. An attorney initiates the proceedings. The action is then transferred to the county and state where the respondent lives for service on the respondent.

Sometimes a custodial parent initiates the petition hoping to avoid becoming dependent on state aid. Sometimes the parent seeks support when the couple is still married but separated—a noncustodial parent still has an obligation to support the child whether or not the parents are divorced.

A state department of welfare that has provided support to the custodial parent often initiates a petition for enforcement of support. Usually, a condition to receiving financial aid or support from a state department is the assignment by the custodial parent of all support payments to which they are entitled. The state then initiates an action on behalf of the custodial parent to enforce support obligations and recover welfare or other payments made to the custodial parent. Sometimes the state is given custody of children because of emotional, physical, or mental disabilities or because of neglect by the parents. In those instances, the state often initiates a UIFSA action against the parents for support to offset the cost to the state for the child's care.

It is also common in cases in which unwed mothers seek welfare aid for their children for the state department of welfare to file an action to enforce support from the father. In order to receive such aid, the unwed mothers are usually required to provide the name of the putative father of the child. The state then seeks to have the parentage of the child determined legally and seeks to enforce support obligations of the father.

§ 15.14.2   Uniform Interstate Family Support Act—Verified testimony

The verified testimony of the custodial parent containing the following information is an essential element of the UIFSA action:

- Full names and addresses of both parties.
- Date and place of marriage and dissolution or separation, or date and court where paternity was established.
- Names, ages, and addresses of the minor children.

- Amount of support ordered monthly.
- Amount of arrearages, together with date and amount of last payment.
- Respondent's employment, property, income, etc., as known to petitioner.
- Petitioner's monthly expenses, broken down into housing, food, utilities, health care costs, gasoline, and other expenses for the petitioner and the children.
- Whether the petitioner is currently on welfare or will have to seek welfare assistance if support payments are not made.
- A description of the respondent, including age and distinguishing marks.
- Respondent's last known address and usual occupation, as well as other occupations in which he or she may be engaged.
- Any other information that might aid authorities to find the respondent.

§ 15.14.3   Uniform Interstate Family Support Act—Certificate of transfer

Another essential element to a UIFSA action is a request of the court to enter a certificate for the transfer of the action to the appropriate jurisdiction. Occasionally when the action is started by the state, the petition and testimony are a combined document; the important thing is that all information required be presented.

§ 15.14.4   Uniform Interstate Family Support Act—Defenses to the action

The respondent must present testimony as to the defenses for the alleged failure to provide support. When the respondent has been unemployed or otherwise unable to meet the obligations of support, the court takes the circumstances into consideration and sometimes reduces the amount of support requested in the UIFSA action.

§ 15.14.5   Uniform Interstate Family Support Act—Action by the court

After consideration of the evidence and the respondent's testimony, the court enters its order. The order may require the respondent to make all payments through the clerk of court in the jurisdiction where the hearing is held. When that is done, that clerk of court then forwards the funds to the clerk of court in the originating jurisdiction for disbursement. Sometimes the court simply orders regular support payments be made to the custodial parent and a specified amount reimbursed to the welfare department.

The pleadings generally required by the lawyer for the petitioner are the petition, the verification of the testimony, and the certificate of the originating court to have the action transferred to the respondent's jurisdiction. The petition is one for which the law office likely has a standard form. If not, once the lawyer has dictated one, new cases can be conformed to the same format. A very important aspect of the pleading is the sworn testimony of the petitioner, which sets out the information recited in the section on verified testimony; a client interview sheet can provide this information. The certificate of transfer must also be prepared.

§ 15.14.6 Uniform Interstate Family Support Act— Forwarding pleadings to respondent's jurisdiction

The petition, testimony, and certified copies of the UIFSA filing, as adopted in the state of origin, are forwarded to the respondent's jurisdiction. The clerk forwards the entire filing to the appropriate jurisdiction with the correct number of copies. Upon receipt of the action in the responding jurisdiction, the clerk files it immediately and turns it over to the prosecuting attorney. A citation for the respondent to appear is issued and served, advising respondent of the hearing date, together with a complete copy of the documents on file.

§ 15.14.7 Uniform Interstate Family Support Act—Failure to appear

Failure to appear before the court may cause the respondent to be held in contempt and punished accordingly. If the respondent has a history of fleeing after being served with process in a UIFSA action, the initiating court may request that the respondent be arrested and held until an appearance can be made before the judge.

§ 15.14.8 Uniform Interstate Family Support Act—Inability to locate respondent

In the event the parent against whom the action has been filed cannot be located, the prosecuting attorney immediately notifies the initiating court. In this event, it may be necessary for the lawyer's assistant to help locate the respondent. Telephone directories, police records, income tax offices, and social security records may help to trace the respondent and effect service. Agencies such as the Internal Revenue Service and the Social Security Administration will usually help as much as they legally can in a child support matter.

§ 15.14.9 Uniform Interstate Family Support Act— Representing the respondent

The assistant to the lawyer for the respondent has a somewhat different role in the UIFSA action. The assistant will help the client gather and categorize support payments made, employment records, income tax returns, and other financial records. This can be a time-consuming process. The lawyer's assistant should verify, through the court where support was due, the actual payments ordered and the amount the client has paid.

All financial records of the respondent, as well as medical records and other pertinent information that would show a change in circumstances substantially affecting the respondent's ability to contribute to the support of the children should be organized for presentation to the court.

If respondent denies paternity, copies of birth certificates and other public records that may substantiate the denial should be obtained. The lawyer's assistant may also be responsible for arranging that blood tests be made available for use at a hearing.

§ 15.15   Uniform Civil Liability for Support Act

The Uniform Civil Liability for Support Act sets forth the duties of support between spouses and parents and children. This act and UIFSA were both enacted to help enforce court-ordered support obligations.

The custodial parent may also initiate civil actions against obligors for support. These actions are filed much the same as any other civil suit, with a complaint initiating the action and the issuance of a summons. Judgments are obtained and enforced through execution and foreclosure proceedings.

If the defendant to a civil support action resides in another state, the judgment entered may also be registered in that state to ensure enforcement. It is also generally recognized that even when children have reached their majority, the noncustodial parent still owes the obligation to the custodial parent for support payments in arrears. Some states allow a child who has reached majority to pursue the noncustodial parent for support arrearages.

§ 15.16   Adoption

Adoption is the legal process by which a child is taken into one's family and given all rights and privileges of a natural child and heir.

§ 15.16.1   Adoption—Uniform Adoption Act

Although the Uniform Adoption Act has been adopted by only a few states, it still serves as a suitable basis for discussing the requirements of adoption. Many of the states adopting the act have greatly modified it. As always, the lawyer's assistant should be familiar with local and state requirements.

§ 15.16.2   Adoption—Jurisdiction

Adoption matters may be filed in the probate division of a state court. However, some states have separate family courts or juvenile courts that have jurisdiction over adoption proceedings.

§ 15.16.3   Adoption—Closed hearings

Adoption files are sealed. If a client is adopted from an agency, even the parents are not allowed access to these files. Discretion on the part of the lawyer's assistant is imperative in adoption proceedings. Usually, adoption agencies request that the lawyer somehow prevent the adoptive parent from even seeing the last name of the child when signing the requisite documents and pleadings. The adoption hearing itself is a closed hearing. There is continuing controversy over whether an adopted child should be allowed to find the biological parents or whether parents should be allowed to find their children placed for adoption. Many times whether a child is allowed to see the adoption file is left to the discretion of the presiding judge.

§ 15.16.4 Adoption—Adoption of stepchildren

When a stepparent adopts stepchildren:

- The stepparent files a petition in the proper court.
- The spouse of the stepparent consents to the adoption by joining in the petition.
- In some cases, the noncustodial parent consents to the adoption releasing all parental rights. In other cases, the noncustodial parent's rights have been terminated.
- Depending on the state, there is an investigation by a state agency, such as a department of social services.
- The agency reports to the court.
- There is a closed court hearing, usually in the judge's chambers. Assuming the judge finds the record of the case to be in proper form, the decree is granted.

In most states, adults may be adopted; however, the prospective adoptee and spouse, if any, must also consent to the adoption.

From the initial client interview, the lawyer determines the eligibility of the prospective adopting parent and who must receive notice and consent to the adoption. If the office uses a detailed interview sheet, the lawyer's assistant should have little difficulty drafting the petition. The following information is usually included in the petition.

- Full name, age, and place and length of residence of the petitioner.
- Petitioner's interest (the reason for the petition for adoption, such as marriage to the natural, custodial parent).
- Full name of the minor child, sex, date and place of birth, relationship to petitioner, and request for name change.
- If petitioner is married to custodial parent, date and place of marriage.
- How long child has been in physical custody of petitioner.
- That petitioner is a fit and proper person and has the capability, resources, and facilities to provide for the care, support, and maintenance of the child; that petitioner desires to do so and to establish the relationship of a natural parent and child.
- Name of natural parent of the child and any other person from whom consent might be necessary or the reason why consent from someone else is not necessary.

- Value and description of any property the child has.
- Signature of the petitioner with a verification.
- Name, address, and signature of petitioner's lawyer.

Usually the custodial parent joins in the petition for adoption. This joinder, with the consent, can be in affidavit form and should contain the following information:

- Name of parent and relationship to child.
- Restatement of child's full name, age, sex, date and place of birth.
- Former name of parent (as shown on birth certificate) if applicable.
- Name of other natural parent, if known, or statement that other parent is deceased or other reason why consent from that parent is not necessary.
- Statement of free consent to adoption and of joining in petition to adopt.
- Statement that parent, by joining in adoption petition, does not relinquish rights as natural parent.

When the petition and consent have been prepared and signed, they are filed in the proper court. A certified copy of the petition and attached consent are served upon the state agency responsible for conducting the investigation regarding the proposed adoption.

§ 15.16.5   Adoption—Consent to a stepchild's adoption

While the investigation by the state agency is conducted, any required consents to the adoption can be obtained and filed. Even if the child is illegitimate, the natural father's consent should be obtained to avoid future actions to invalidate the adoption. If consent from someone who cannot be located is required, an order to show cause why the adoption should not be granted may be served by publication in a newspaper of general circulation in the jurisdiction where that person was last known to reside. Service of this type will vary greatly among jurisdictions, but the lawyer will supervise any such notice.

If the noncustodial parent or other person from whom consent is necessary refuses to give consent, he or she may be personally served with an order to appear and show cause why the adoption should not be granted, especially if there is a legal reason why consent may not be necessary.

After service of the petition and investigation by the investigative agency and a report by that agency is given to the court, the matter is set for hearing. Notice of the hearing is given in accordance with applicable state laws.

At the time of the hearing, the court, in its discretion, may enter a summary decree that waives all time requirements and declares the adoption final at that time. The court may also enter an interlocutory decree to be in effect for a specific period of time, usually six months, at which time another hearing is held prior to entry of a final decree of adoption.

It is important to know the local court rules and the attitudes of the presiding judge for the final hearing. Often one judge will require that an interlocutory decree be entered in all adoptions, while another judge usually enters a final decree at the initial hearing. The judge will usually expect a decree prepared and ready for him or her to sign at the time of the hearing.

As the lawyer's assistant is usually responsible for seeing that the adopting parents and child are notified of the hearing date, the assistant should also be aware of others whom the judge wishes to attend. Many judges like to have the adopting parents and their other children present in order to assess the family situation and determine the feelings of other family members toward the adoption. Of course, the lawyer will also be at the hearing. Since the hearings are closed, no one is allowed except those who are required to be present. In the event of a contested adoption, parties having a direct and vested interest are allowed to participate at the hearing.

When the adoption has been finalized, the lawyer's assistant should obtain certified copies of the decree with one copy given to the adoptive parent, one copy sent to the agency that conducted the investigation, and one copy sent (with appropriate fee) to the state bureau of vital statistics requesting a new birth certificate. This birth certificate should be delivered to the adopting parents, with a copy retained in the office files. A copy of the final decree is likewise retained for the office files.

Special note should be given to private or nonagency adoptions. These adoptions have come under close scrutiny because of adverse publicity. Most states have adopted legislation that either outlaws private adoptions or strictly regulates them.

§ 15.17 Uniform Child Custody Jurisdiction Enforcement Act

A majority of states have adopted the Uniform Child Custody Jurisdiction Enforcement Act (UCCJEA). The primary purpose of this act is the protection of the child in child custody litigation or when the child has been abducted by the noncustodial parent. The act establishes procedure on jurisdictional questions. If the lawyer specializes in this type of action, the beginning lawyer's assistant will soon become familiar with the procedures. This is still a changing area of the law, and new decisions are being granted frequently in cases of this type.

§ 15.17.1 Uniform Child Custody Jurisdiction Enforcement Act—Procedures

With certain exceptions, preparation of pleadings in a UCCJEA action is much the same as in any other civil suit. However, it is not uncommon in these types of cases for out-of-state service to be required. Litigation can sometimes be avoided by designating in the custody and support agreement what court is to have jurisdiction over the child for future custody and support purposes.

Child custody decrees entered by out-of-state courts may be filed with the clerk in another state and transferred much the same as any other decree or judgment. A decree filed in this manner has the same force and effect as a decree entered in the state where the decree was entered, provided the state in which it is filed has adopted statutes recognizing out-of-state decrees.

It is important for the lawyer's assistant to be aware of the existence of the UCCJEA action in the event of a child custody action. Initial information obtained from the client should include:

- The court where an original order of custody was entered.
- How the client obtained custody of the child.
- Who was awarded custody in the original order, and when or how that has been changed since.
- Residence of the child since the decree was entered.
- Any other information with regard to the custody of the child which might be helpful.

§ 15.18   Grandparent visitation rights

Increasingly in recent years, grandparents are seeking judicial determination of their visitation rights with grandchildren subject to a custody agreement. Some state statutes now recognize the rights of grandparents to visit with their grandchildren under custody and visitation privileges. Setting out these rights in the original agreement, as well as in the decree, can save the client the time, money, and emotional distress involved in litigation with grandparents for visitation privileges later. In some cases, persons other than grandparents or noncustodial parents may seek, and be granted, visitation rights.

§ 15.19   Alternate birth options

Alternate options to birth, such as *in vitro* (test tube) babies, surrogate mothering, open adoption (where the natural parents know the adoptive parents), artificial insemination, and international adoptions are becoming increasingly popular and have raised a myriad of legal issues not yet fully resolved. Some of these issues are the rights of the surrogate mother who changes her mind, malpractice involving sperm donors, and forms of contracts between the various parties. While these issues can be similar to adoption, they are presently approached in large part through contract law.

§ 15.20   Uniform Parentage Act

The Uniform Parentage Act defines, among other things, the parent-child relationship and how it is established. It also provides who may bring actions to establish paternity and when such actions may be initiated. The use of blood tests and the preservation of records are also provided for in this act.

These actions are usually brought by state prosecuting attorneys on behalf of a mother receiving welfare aid against the purported father of a child to enforce support obligations. The child is usually made a party to the action and represented by a guardian *ad litem*. The mother and purported father are also made parties to the action.

§ 15.21   Parentage and paternity procedure

Ordinarily, this type of action is much the same as in any other civil suit, except that the proceedings are closed to the public. Initial pretrial proceedings are generally informal. Some lawyers prefer to avoid a formal court action by interacting with the purported father through his attorney. Information needed for the paternity action may include the likelihood that the mother engaged in sexual activity with another man during the period when conception most likely occurred. The lawyer's assistant may help arrange for blood tests or locate experts to testify at the hearing.

The civil proceeding for determination of paternity brought by a mother or a child for support is usually also conducted in a closed courtroom with no jurors or spectators, but the evidence is similar to that brought by a prosecutor to enforce support obligations. A paternity suit can also be brought by a possible father seeking visitation and a relationship with a child. Any judgment or order granted by the court usually includes an order that the birth certificate be amended or reissued to conform to the order of the court.

After paternity is determined, support must be acted upon. As in other support proceedings, the abilities of both parents, the child's resources and any special needs, as well as other pertinent information are used to determine the amount of support required. Visitation is also generally established, and may, depending on the circumstances, include a familiarization period.

§ 15.22   Abortion

The legal definition of *abortion* is the intentional termination of a pregnancy. Abortion law is still changing rapidly amid considerable controversy. The Uniform Abortion Act was developed in an effort to standardize abortion law. The most common cases the lawyer's assistant is likely to encounter are those involving medical malpractice with regard to abortion, parental consent for abortion performed on minors, and the rights of the father in an abortion situation. There are still criminal penalties for illegal abortions that vary from state to state.

§ 15.23   Duties to disabled persons

A disabled person is one who lacks legal capacity or one who is physically or mentally disabled from acting on the person's own behalf or pursuing a normal occupation. The Uniform Duties to Disabled Persons Act provides for duties of police officers, medical practitioners, and others to disabled persons; it also provides for the use of identifying devices for the disabled person. Persons with specific disabilities— epilepsy, diabetes, medicinal allergies—are encouraged (but not required) to wear identifying devices to aid police, doctors, and others in the event the person is unable in an emergency to communicate these conditions. On the other hand, police officers and medical practitioners especially have a duty to make reasonable searches of disabled or injured persons to ascertain whether or not they are in possession of such identifying devices. The lawyer's assistant is likely to become acquainted with this area of the law when a disabled person or the disabled person's family brings suit against others for their failure to perform duties required under this act. Whether the lawyer is prosecuting or defending the action, the pleadings and procedures are similar to any other civil action.

§ 15.24 Address confidentiality programs

In the course of working with domestic clients, the lawyer's assistant may encounter those who are victims of domestic violence, sexual abuse, rape, or stalking who may need more information about how to protect themselves. Promoted through the National Association of Secretaries of State, address confidentiality programs (called *Safe at Home* in some states and *Address Confidentiality Program* or *ACP* in others) are now active or being organized in 35 states and the trend continues to grow. These programs prevent the use of government documents to allow abusers to locate their victims and serve to safely forward First Class and Certified Mail and provide service of legal documents to an undisclosed address for individuals who have been the victims of domestic violence, sexual abuse, rape, or stalking. The programs currently are state-based and do not provide address confidentiality outside the state. It is hoped that national legislation enabling address confidentiality programs that work across state lines will be developed soon. In the meantime, it may be helpful to know whether such a program operates in the state where the lawyer's assistant's employer practices family law.

§ 15.25 Summary

Family law is rapidly changing. The lawyer's assistant who works for a lawyer who practices family law needs to keep current with changes in family law. Often the changes are procedural and localized to a specific county or court. Local and state professional associations, such as those affiliated with NALS®, may be helpful in keeping the lawyer's assistant up to date on such procedural changes. Articles from bar associations and other publications to which the law firm subscribes may contain useful material on changes in state laws.

The beginning lawyer's assistant may also wish to read some of the uniform acts to become familiar with them. *American Jurisprudence Second* and *Corpus Juris Secundum* contain the uniform acts, and many of them are also published in the **Martindale-Hubbell Law Directory**. The law firm that specializes in family law may subscribe to *The Family Law Reporter*, published weekly by The Bureau of National Affairs. This publication highlights important cases in all areas of family law; reading it may help the lawyer's assistant stay up to date on family law decisions.

Chapter 16

Business Organizations

KeyCite®: Cases and other legal materials listed in KeyCite Scope can be researched through the KeyCite service on Westlaw®. Use KeyCite to check citations for form, parallel references, prior and later history, and comprehensive citator information, including citations to other decisions and secondary materials.

---

§ 16.1 Introduction

The challenge of structuring a business organization to meet the needs of the owners and allow the business to function effectively is considerable. Business organizations can help separate business finances from the owners' personal finances; they can help protect the owners from personal liability for business problems; and they can assist the owners in avoiding excessive taxes. However, no business structure meets all of these needs perfectly, and it is the responsibility of the lawyer in corporate practice to assist clients to form a business structure that allows the best mix of these components.

§ 16.2 Corporations

A *corporation* is a legal entity created under the laws of a state or nation. For most legal purposes, a corporation is considered a person domiciled in its state of incorporation and is considered a separate and distinct legal entity from its owners. Corporations typically may enter into contracts, own property, sell property, sue, and be sued.

§ 16.2.1 Corporations—Domestic and foreign corporations

A corporation created or organized in the state in which it does business is known as a *domestic corporation* in that state.

EXAMPLE:

If a corporation is organized and doing business in Vermont, it is a domestic corporation in Vermont.

The term *foreign corporation* is used to describe a corporation doing business in a state or country other than the state or country in which it was organized.

EXAMPLE:

A corporation organized and incorporated in Vermont conducts business in Kentucky. In Kentucky, the corporation would be characterized as a foreign corporation.

§ 16.2.2 Corporations—Types of corporations

Corporations are generally classified as one of the following types:

- *Business corporations*, organized to make a profit.
- *Nonprofit corporations*, organized typically for charitable, religious, educational, scientific, and other similar purposes.
- *Public corporations*, organized for governmental purposes, such as city or county governments.
- *Professional corporations*, organized to permit a professional or group of professionals to practice their profession.

State laws differ regarding the organization and operation of corporations. The majority of corporations the lawyer's assistant will encounter will be business corporations, and the discussion here will focus on business corporations.

§ 16.2.3 Corporations—Advantages and disadvantages

One reason for incorporating a business is limitation of liability to its owners. Since the corporation is itself a legal entity, the corporation is legally responsible for its acts and debts. The officers, directors, and shareholders of a corporation have no personal liability for debts and other obligations incurred by the corporation, provided they act in good faith and keep their personal business completely separate from that of the corporation. When an officer, employee, or director commits a tort while acting on behalf of a corporation, both the individual committing the tort and the entity will be liable. The limitation of liability will still protect other owners and individuals not involved in the tort.

As a separate legal entity, the corporation can continue to do business in the event one of its officers, directors, or shareholders dies. The ownership of the corporation can change without interrupting its day-to-day business operations.

Because the corporation has the power to hold property in its own name, it is sometimes a useful vehicle for estate planning. The ownership interest in an incorporated business may pass down from generation to generation through gifts of shares of stock in the corporation to family members.

There are a variety of corporate structures available to adjust the ways in which corporate income is taxed. Some result in income being taxed at the corporate level; others pass taxable income to the owners. When income is taxed at the corporate level, it will also be taxed as the owner's personal income. There are a number of requirements and restrictions associated with corporate tax elections. It may be necessary to enlist the assistance of a tax accountant or tax attorney to determine what structure is best for the client.

Disadvantages of incorporation include greater expenses of organization, greater governmental regulation, and sometimes tax disadvantages.

§ 16.2.4   Corporations—Corporate structure and operation

The management and operation of the corporation depend upon three groups of people: the shareholders, the board of directors, and the officers. A data sheet listing the parties involved is helpful in preparing corporate documents. (See Illustration 16-1.)

Illustration 16-1
CORPORATION DATA SHEET

Name of Corporation: _____

Date of Corporation: _____

Directors: Address: Office:

_____

_____

_____

_____

_____

_____

Maximum Number:_____   Quorum: _____   ,   Terms: _____

Capitalization: _____

Common Shares: _____   Par Value: _____

Voting Shares

Non Voting Shares

Preferred Shares

Issued Shares:

    Name: _____   Number Issued: _____   Consideration: _____

    Address: _____   Soc. Sec. No: _____

Principal Place of Business: _____

_____

Purpose: _____

_____

Registered Agent and Office: _____

_____

Accountant/CPA:_____

Preemptive Rights: _____

Indemnification Allowed: _____

Cumulative Voting Allowed: _____

Executive Committee: _____

Annual Meeting:

    Date: _____

    Place: _____

Fiscal Year: _____

First Meeting:

    Date: _____

    Place: _____

    Attendance: _____

Bank:
  Who Signs: _____
  Limitations: _____
  Limitations on Borrowing: _____

Salaries: _____
1244: _____
Subchapter S: _____
Employer ID #: _____
Actions Taken: _____

Documents: (strike any not needed)	Prepared	Executed	Filed
Reservation of Corporate Name	_____	_____	_____
Articles	_____	_____	_____
Bylaws	_____	_____	_____
Minutes of 1st Directors Meeting	_____	_____	_____
Minutes of 1st Shareholders Meeting	_____	_____	_____
1244 Plan	_____	_____	_____
Subchapter S Election	_____	_____	_____
Assumed Name Certificate	_____	_____	_____
Certificate of Authority for Other States	_____	_____	_____
Shareholder Purchase Agreement	_____	_____	_____
Medical Reimbursement Plan	_____	_____	_____
Securities Filing	_____	_____	_____
Other	_____	_____	_____

Stock and Seal Ordered: _____

§ 16.2.5 Corporations—Shareholders

The **shareholders** (also known as **stockholders**) are the persons (either individuals or other legal entities) who own shares of stock in the corporation and therefore own the corporation. A **share** is a proportionate ownership interest in the corporation evidenced by a certificate issued by the corporation.

The initial sale of stock by the corporation to the shareholders often provides the initial operating capital for the corporation. Before the corporation is formed, prospective shareholders may agree to purchase a specific number of shares by executing a subscription agreement. (See Illustration 16-2.)

The shareholders have the right to vote on major corporate issues, including the right to elect the board of directors, to merge with other corporations, to sell substantially all the corporation's assets, and to dissolve the corporation. Shareholders also have the right to share in the profits made by the corporation and in the net assets distributed upon dissolution of the corporation.

Illustration 16-2
SUBSCRIPTION AGREEMENT

THE UNDERSIGNED hereby subscribes to 2900 shares of the no par value common stock of A.B.C. Corporation, a _____[*state of incorporation*] corporation. The undersigned agrees to pay the A.B.C. Corporation the sum of $____ for said shares.

Dated: ____

_____

(name of subscriber)

§ 16.2.6   Corporations—Board of directors

The **board of directors** is the governing body of the corporation and is composed of individuals elected by the shareholders. The board of directors establishes policies and oversees officers' actions. It acts by resolution adopted at directors' meetings or by written consent.

§ 16.2.7   Corporations—Officers

Corporate **officers** are elected by the board of directors and are subject to its control. Officers typically include the president, vice president(s), treasurer, and secretary. The officers conduct the day-to-day business of the corporation and implement policies established by the board of directors.

§ 16.2.8   Corporations—Meetings

The corporate documents, such as articles of incorporation or bylaws, provide for meetings of shareholders and the board of directors to be held at specified times throughout the year. Additionally, there is generally a provision under state law and/or the corporation's bylaws to permit special meetings of both the shareholders and the board of directors.

It is the duty of the corporate secretary to notify the shareholders or the board members of these meetings. Often the lawyer or lawyer's assistant will generate these notices for corporate clients. The bylaws typically provide for the manner in which the notices must be sent. It is important to follow the provisions in the corporate documents and state statute in providing notices. Notices of meetings of directors and shareholders must be in writing unless notice is waived or all directors or shareholders attend the meetings. It is not unusual for the shareholders or board members to waive notice of a corporate meeting. The waivers must be prepared in accordance with the corporate bylaws and state statute and be signed by each director or shareholder.

BASIC MANUAL FOR THE LEGAL PROFESSIONAL

§ 16.2.9 Corporations—Quorum

The corporate bylaws and state statutes give the number of persons required to constitute a quorum for shareholders and board of directors meetings. A quorum is required in order for the meeting to be validly held. In most corporations, a majority of the stock ownership constitutes a quorum for a meeting of shareholders. This means that if a corporation has five shareholders who own more than half of the stock, when those five shareholders attend a meeting that constitutes a quorum, regardless of the total number of shareholders. A majority of the board of directors usually constitutes a quorum for the board of directors meeting.

§ 16.2.10 Corporations—Proxies

A *proxy* is the authority given by one shareholder to another to vote his or her shares of stock. This practice is particularly common in large corporations because it is difficult for all shareholders to attend meetings. In the case of publicly traded corporations, the Securities and Exchange Commission (SEC) requires a proxy form be sent with the notice of meeting so the shareholder can name a proxy. The term *proxy* is used to mean both the authority given and the form used to accomplish it.

§ 16.2.11 Corporations—Securities registration and regulation

A corporation's stock is a type of security, the offering and sale of which is regulated by federal and state law. The SEC administers federal securities laws and issues rules and regulations with respect to those laws. In addition, each state has its own laws that regulate the offering and sale of securities (often referred to as *blue sky laws*). The federal and state securities laws include requirements to register securities and rules to prevent fraud. Violations of these laws can result in significant fines for the corporations and fines or criminal convictions for the individuals involved, including lawyers.

Certain types of securities and certain sales of securities are exempt from various securities laws, such as the registration requirements. Such exemptions often apply to the stock of small business corporations and to sales of stock not made to the general public. Some exemptions require certain actions to be taken (e.g., filing with the SEC or applicable state securities agency) before the exemption is effective. In other cases, proof might be required from the corporation or purchasers of the stock that the exemption requirements have been satisfied. In cases where exemptions apply, stock certificates often bear a legend that the shares have not been registered and may not be transferred unless they are registered or an exemption from registration applies.

Securities laws are complex and may have very serious ramifications if violated. Lawyers often engage the services of a securities law specialist to make sure these laws are complied with.

§ 16.3   Incorporation process

The incorporation process includes a number of steps and, while it is not required that the process be completed by a lawyer, it often is given the complexity of the process and the need to comply with state laws. The lawyer first meets with the client to determine the client's needs and to obtain the information to begin the incorporation process. Most lawyers use a checklist for this purpose. (See Illustration 16-1.)

§ 16.3.1   Incorporation process—Reservation of corporate name

One piece of information the lawyer secures at the initial client interview is the corporate name the client proposes to use. Since most states do not allow a new business to use a name that is deceptively similar to an existing one, it is necessary to check the availability of the name in each state where the corporation will do business. (The term *deceptively similar* refers to a name sufficiently like that of an existing business entity where outsiders might confuse the two, with the possibility that the new corporation might either inadvertently or intentionally take advantage of the existing business's reputation.) Note that most states require the words "Corporation," "Incorporated," "Company," or "Limited," in full or abbreviated, to be part of the corporate name.

Most states provide a method by which the proposed corporate name may be reserved for a specific time period. During that time, no one else is allowed to use that name. The name is usually reserved by filing the proper form together with the reservation fee with the state agency responsible for business registrations (e.g., corporation commission, secretary of state, or lieutenant governor). Reserving the name allows the incorporator time to prepare the necessary documents without fear of losing the name.

§ 16.3.2   Incorporation process—Articles of incorporation

The legal document required to form a corporation is called the *articles of incorporation,* or the *certificate of formation*. The articles of incorporation state, among other things, what a corporation is authorized to do. In some states it is permissible to form a corporation for "any legal purpose." In states where such general authority is not allowed, the articles of incorporation provide more detail as to what the corporation may do. Lawyers often prefer to state corporate purposes very generally to avoid overly restricting the corporation's activities.

The corporation laws of each state specify what information must be contained in the articles of incorporation. The *Martindale-*

Hubbell Law Directory contains a summary of the requirements that must be met in each state. A set of typical articles would contain:

- The name of the corporation
- The date of incorporation
- The principal place of business
- The duration of the corporation
- Whether stockholders have cumulative or preemptive rights
- The total number of shares the corporation is allowed to issue, the classes of stock, and the par value of each share
- The registered agent and office address

A statement as to the corporation's initial capitalization or stock ownership may be required. Many other provisions may be in the articles depending upon state law.

§ 16.3.3 Incorporation process—Close corporation

The incorporators may limit the sale or transfer of stock by having a *close corporation* provision in the articles of incorporation. The purpose of this provision is to give the initial shareholders the right to decide whether they want to allow any additional shareholders. Usually this provision specifies that in the event a shareholder proposes a sale of stock, the shareholder must first offer the stock on the same terms as the proposed sale to the other shareholders or to the corporation itself. The corporation or shareholders are allowed a specific period of time within which to buy the stock, and if they fail to do so, the selling shareholder has the right to sell such stock to a third party.

§ 16.3.4 Incorporation process—Preemptive rights

A *preemptive right provision* gives the shareholders the right to maintain their original, proportionate share of the corporation in the event the corporation should issue additional shares of stock. The articles of incorporation specify the number of shares that the corporation is authorized to issue. It is possible for the corporation to increase the number later by amendment to the articles of incorporation. In the event of an increase in the number of authorized shares of stock issued, a preemptive right provision means that the original shareholders are given the first option to buy enough additional shares to maintain their proportionate share of ownership.

EXAMPLE:

If the corporation originally authorized 200 shares of stock with four shareholders each owning 50 shares, and the corporation authorizes an additional 200 shares, a preemptive right provision would allow each shareholder the right to buy another 50 shares. This would allow each shareholder to maintain a 25 percent interest in the corporation. (See Illustration 16-3.)

Illustration 16-3

ARTICLES OF INCORPORATION OF A.B.C. CORPORATION

We, the undersigned natural persons of the age of twenty-one years or more, acting as incorporators of the corporation under the Business Corporation Act, adopt the following Articles of Incorporation for the corporation.

ARTICLE I: (The name of the corporation; *Corporation, Incorporated, Inc., Company,* or *Limited* may be required in the name)

ARTICLE II: (The period of the corporation's duration)

ARTICLE III: (The purposes for which the corporation is organized)

ARTICLE IV: (The capitalization structure of the corporation, e.g., dollar amount of capital stock, aggregate number of shares authorized, par value per share, voting rights of shares, designation of class or classes of shares)

ARTICLE V: (The corporation will not commence business until consideration of the value of at least $1,000 has been received for the issuance of the shares)

ARTICLE VI: (Provisions limiting or denying to shareholders the preemptive right to acquire additional or treasury shares of the corporation)

ARTICLE VII: (Provisions pertaining to the manner of voting in the election of directors)

ARTICLE VIII: (The post office address of the corporation and the name of its initial registered agent for service of process at said address)

ARTICLE IX: (The number, names, and addresses of the persons who shall serve as the initial Board of Directors of the corporation)

ARTICLE X: (Provisions eliminating or limiting the liability of directors and/or officers to the corporation or its shareholders)

ARTICLE XI: (Provisions pertaining to indemnification of directors and/or officers by the corporation)

ARTICLE XII: (The name and address of each of the incorporators of the corporation)

DATED this _____ day of _____, *[Year].*

INCORPORATORS:

_____

_____

_____

STATE OF   )

_____

)   ss.

COUNTY OF   )

_____

467

On the ____ day of ____, *[Year]*, personally appeared before me John Doe, George Doe, and Charles Doe, who duly acknowledged to me they executed the foregoing Articles of Incorporation as the incorporators of A.B.C. Corporation.

_____

Notary Public
Residing at:

My Commission Expires:

§ 16.3.5   Incorporation process—Filing of articles of incorporation

After the articles of incorporation have been prepared, they must be executed by the incorporator. If the state requires more than one incorporator, all incorporators must sign. Many states require that the signatures be notarized. Once the articles are executed, they are filed with the state agency responsible for business registrations, together with the filing fee. The state agency issues a charter or certificate that evidences the incorporation. It may also be necessary to file duplicate originals in the office of the county clerk where the corporation is to do business and own property.

§ 16.3.6   Incorporation process—First meeting of shareholders

Although filing the articles of incorporation with the state creates a corporation, other steps must be taken for a corporation to do business. In most states these matters are handled in an ***organizational meeting***. The organizational meeting may also be known as a *shareholders, stockholders, incorporators,* or *subscribers meeting*. A few states do not require an organizational meeting, and in those states the matters handled in the organizational meeting may be handled by the board of directors in its first meeting. A unanimous written consent may be signed by all directors in lieu of actually holding an organizational meeting. Typical items handled at this meeting would include:

- Election of the initial board of directors
- Adoption of bylaws for the corporation
- Issuance of the capital stock

§ 16.3.7   Incorporation process—First meeting of board of directors

The first meeting of the board of directors is usually held immediately following the execution of the articles of incorporation and the organizational meeting, if there is one. Typical items handled at this meeting include:

- Election of officers of the corporation
- Adoption of the corporate seal
- Approval of the form of stock certificate
- Selection of a bank for the corporation and a decision who will sign checks
- Action on corporate tax structure elections, as needed
- Acceptance of subscriptions for shares

(See Illustration 16-4.)

Illustration 16-4

MINUTES OF FIRST MEETING OF BOARD OF DIRECTORS OF

A.B.C. CORPORATION

The first meeting of the Board of Directors of A.B.C. CORPORA-TION was held at _____ at _____ _.m. on _____, *[Year]*, in *[city and state]*, in accordance with the following Waiver of Notice:

WAIVER OF NOTICE FOR FIRST MEETING OF DIRECTORS

The undersigned, being all of the Directors of A.B.C. CORPORA-TION do hereby waive notice and publication of notice of the first meeting of the Directors of the Corporation. We do hereby assent and agree to the holding of the first meeting of the Directors of the Corporation at the offices of _____ at *[Time]* on the _____ day of _____, *[Year]*, for the purposes of establishing the corporation in business, organizing the board of directors, electing officers, and the transacting of such other business as may properly come before this meeting, and we do further agree that any business transacted at this meeting shall be as valid and binding and of the same legal force and effect as though said meeting had been held after call and notice duly given.

_____
_____
_____

PROCEEDINGS

_____ called the meeting to order and upon motion duly made and seconded was appointed Temporary Chairman, and _____ was appointed Temporary Secretary.

The election of officers was thereupon declared to be in order. The following were named and duly elected:

President, TODD PAUL

Vice President, MYLES DAVID

Vice President, LOUIS BERNARD

Secretary, LISA WYNNE

Treasurer, LINDA GREEN

The Chairman announced that the Certificate of Incorporation had been filed in the office of the Secretary of State of _____ on the _____ day of _____, *[Year]*, and that a certified copy thereof would be recorded in the office of the County Clerk and Recorder of _____ County, state of _____. The Secretary was instructed to cause a copy of the Certificate of Incorporation to be inserted in the Minute Book of this Corporation.

The Secretary presented a form of bylaws for the regulation of the internal affairs of the Corporation, which were read by all present, section by section.

On motion duly made, seconded, and carried, it was:

RESOLVED that the Bylaws submitted to and read at this meeting be, and the same hereby are, adopted as the Bylaws of this Corporation. The Secretary is instructed to cause said Bylaws to be inserted in the Minute and Bylaws Book of this Corporation which shall be held open for inspection by the shareholders at all reasonable times.

On motion duly made, seconded, and carried, it was:

RESOLVED that the seal, an impression of which is herewith affixed, be adopted as the Corporate Seal of this Corporation.

A form of stock certificate was presented and upon motion duly made, seconded, and carried, was unanimously approved.

The Secretary was authorized and directed to procure the proper Corporate Book.

On motion duly made, seconded, and carried, it was:

RESOLVED that the _____ Bank of _____ be designated as the depository of the Corporation and that funds deposited therein be withdrawn upon a check, draft, note, or order of the Corporation.

FURTHER RESOLVED that all checks, drafts, notes, or orders drawn against said account or evidencing indebtedness of this Corporation be signed by one of the five named officers of this Corporation.

It was agreed by the Board that each person desiring to transfer equipment and property in return for stock proceed to do so through the Secretary of this Corporation, with the Secretary keeping a record of all property transferred and its agreed valuation upon transfer, said agreed valuation to be consistent with the current market value attributed to each item transferred. The Board acknowledged that the acquisition of property and equipment would be necessary and essential for Corporate operations.

Upon motion duly made, seconded, and carried unanimously, it was:

RESOLVED that the Corporation acquire property and equipment from those persons who desire to transfer property and equipment at market value as may be desired by the Corporation in exchange for the issuance of Corporate stock as payment in full, said stock to be without par value, and to constitute full payment; it being further stipulated that in the event any property transferred is encumbered by mortgage or other indebtedness, the Corporation assumes such indebtedness, if any.

FURTHER RESOLVED that the Secretary be instructed to maintain a list of the property transferred and the valuation attributed thereto.

On motion duly made, seconded, and carried unanimously, it was:

RESOLVED that the proper officers of this Corporation be authorized and directed to take all steps necessary to execute and complete issuance of the stock and deliver all papers, including certificates of shares of stock of this Corporation, as such officers so acting may deem appropriate to effect the objectives and purposes of this Corporation, whether or not the same are subject to specific reference in this first meeting.

On motion duly made, seconded, and carried unanimously, it was:

RESOLVED that the Treasurer be authorized to pay all fees and expenses incident to the incorporation and organization of this Corporation.

On motion duly made, seconded, and carried unanimously, it was:

RESOLVED that ____, ____, ____, ____, and ____ constitute an executive committee in accordance with the Articles of Incorporation to act while the Board of Directors is not in session, said Executive Committee to have the same complete and unrestricted powers while so acting as would the Board of Directors acting in session.

There was discussion concerning salaries, following which, on motion duly made, seconded, and carried unanimously, it was:

RESOLVED that the following salaries be fixed to be paid to the individuals indicated until further action by the Board of Directors:

____$ per year to each officer.

There being no further business to come before the meeting, on motion duly made, seconded, and carried unanimously, the meeting adjourned at ____ __m.

_____
Secretary

§16.3.8 Incorporation process—Bylaws

The *bylaws* are the rules and regulations under which the corporation will operate. They are adopted by the shareholders or the board of directors at their first meeting. Unlike the articles of incorporation, the bylaws are typically not filed with the state. The officers, directors, and shareholders are bound by these bylaws, which may contain provisions for the management of the corporation that are lawful and consistent with the articles of incorporation. Every corporation has the power to adopt, alter, and amend bylaws. The bylaws may be a brief document or a long, detailed one. Most law offices have their own form of bylaws that they individualize for each corporation. (See Illustration 16-5 for the index of provisions usually contained in bylaws.)

Illustration 16-5
BYLAWS
TABLE OF CONTENTS

§ 16.3.9   Incorporation process—Corporate minutes

As part of the incorporation process, the lawyer's office generally takes responsibility for the preparation of the *record book*. The record book should contain copies of the articles of incorporation, bylaws, minutes of the first meeting of shareholders, and minutes of the first board of directors meeting, as well as any other documents prepared in the incorporation process. The record book will either be turned over to the secretary of the corporation or maintained by the law firm. *Minutes* are simply a written record of who attended a meeting and what transpired there. However, it is essential that the record book be kept up to date. In fact, some states impose a fine if the corporation fails to do so. An incomplete record book could also result in serious tax consequences in the event of a tax audit.

§ 16.3.10   Incorporation process—Corporate seal

In some states it is necessary for a corporation to have a corporate seal. A law firm in a state where a seal is required may order the seal as a part of the incorporation process. The *corporate seal* is a stamp that makes an embossed impression on a document and, combined with the signature of a corporate officer, verifies corporate authority.

§ 16.3.11   Incorporation process—Stock certificates

The lawyer's office often takes responsibility for issuing the original shares of stock and opening a *stock register* or *stock book*. Either a bound stock book or individual blank stock certificates may be used.

The articles of incorporation provide for the number of shares the corporation is authorized to issue. The minutes of the organizational meeting lists the number of shares of stock purchased by each stockholder. From this list, the lawyer's assistant should be able to prepare the stock certificates. Each stock certificate should include:

- The name of the corporation
- The domicile of the corporation (city and state)
- The name of the shareholder
- The number of shares purchased by the shareholder
- The par value of each share of stock
- The number of the stock certificate (starting with number 1)
- The notation that the stock is issued under Section 1244 of the Internal Revenue Code (if applicable)

Each stock certificate is attached to a receipt which contains the same information as the stock certificate, together with a notation that the stock is the original issue. (See Illustration 16-6.) The shareholder signs the receipt, which is detached from the certificate. The shareholder is given the stock certificate, and the receipt is retained in the stock register. The stock register contains a continuing record of the stock ownership of a corporation. The stock register must be kept up to date and show all changes in stock ownership. Anyone should be able to look at a corporation's stock register at any time and tell who the shareholders of the corporation are and how many shares of stock each shareholder owns.

Illustration 16-6

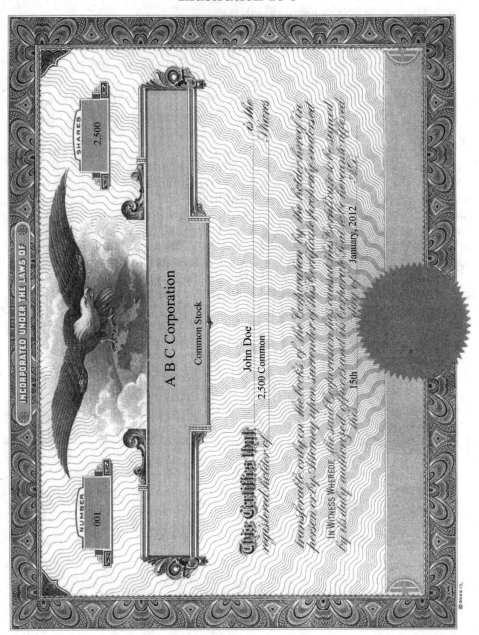

An assignment form is printed on the reverse of each stock certificate; the shareholder may transfer his or her shares of stock by executing the assignment. (See Illustration 16-7.) When the assigned stock certificate is handed to the secretary of the corporation, the secretary issues a stock certificate to the new shareholder, writes "canceled" across the face of the transferred stock certificate, and attaches it to the receipt of that certificate in the stock register. The receipt of the new stock certificate shows that it is a transfer of shares from the original certificate.

Illustration 16-7

§ 16.3.12　Incorporation process—Assumed or fictitious name

If the corporation wishes to do business under a name other than its own, the lawyer's assistant may be asked to prepare a certificate of assumed business name or a fictitious name registration. These forms can usually be found on the website of the state agency responsible for business registrations.

§ 16.3.13　Incorporation process—Application for employer identification number

The law office may complete the corporation's application for an employer identification number (EIN), IRS Form No. SS-4. The IRS offers several methods of filing the SS-4, but prefers the application to be filed on the Internet. The information is validated during the session, and an EIN is issued immediately. If a corporation is being filed in a set of entities (i.e., the general partner of a limited partnership is the managing partner of a limited liability company), the IRS does restrict the application based upon the Applicant's social security number to one application per day. (See Illustration 16-8.)

Current versions of this and other IRS forms are available on the Internet at www.irs.gov/forms-pubs.

Illustration 16-8

Form **SS-4**	**Application for Employer Identification Number**	OMB No. 1545-0003

Form SS-4
(Rev. December 2017)
Department of the Treasury
Internal Revenue Service

Application for Employer Identification Number
(For use by employers, corporations, partnerships, trusts, estates, churches, government agencies, Indian tribal entities, certain individuals, and others.)
► Go to *www.irs.gov/FormSS4* for instructions and the latest information.
► See separate instructions for each line. ► Keep a copy for your records.

EIN

Type or print clearly.

1 Legal name of entity (or individual) for whom the EIN is being requested

2 Trade name of business (if different from name on line 1)

3 Executor, administrator, trustee, "care of" name

4a Mailing address (room, apt., suite no. and street, or P.O. box)

5a Street address (if different) (Do not enter a P.O. box.)

4b City, state, and ZIP code (if foreign, see instructions)

5b City, state, and ZIP code (if foreign, see instructions)

6 County and state where principal business is located

7a Name of responsible party

7b SSN, ITIN, or EIN

8a Is this application for a limited liability company (LLC) (or a foreign equivalent)? . . . . ☐ Yes ☐ No

8b If 8a is "Yes," enter the number of LLC members . . . . . . ►

8c If 8a is "Yes," was the LLC organized in the United States? . . . . ☐ Yes ☐ No

9a **Type of entity** (check only one box). **Caution.** If 8a is "Yes," see the instructions for the correct box to check.

☐ Sole proprietor (SSN) _____
☐ Partnership
☐ Corporation (enter form number to be filed) ► _____
☐ Personal service corporation
☐ Church or church-controlled organization
☐ Other nonprofit organization (specify) ► _____
☐ Other (specify) ►

☐ Estate (SSN of decedent) _____
☐ Plan administrator (TIN) _____
☐ Trust (TIN of grantor) _____
☐ Military/National Guard ☐ State/local government
☐ Farmers' cooperative ☐ Federal government
☐ REMIC ☐ Indian tribal governments/enterprises
Group Exemption Number (GEN) if any ►

9b If a corporation, name the state or foreign country (if applicable) where incorporated

State

Foreign country

10 **Reason for applying** (check only one box)
☐ Started new business (specify type) ► _____
☐ Hired employees (Check the box and see line 13.)
☐ Compliance with IRS withholding regulations
☐ Other (specify) ►

☐ Banking purpose (specify purpose) ► _____
☐ Changed type of organization (specify new type) ► _____
☐ Purchased going business
☐ Created a trust (specify type) ► _____
☐ Created a pension plan (specify type) ► _____

11 Date business started or acquired (month, day, year). See instructions.

12 Closing month of accounting year

13 Highest number of employees expected in the next 12 months (enter -0- if none). If no employees expected, skip line 14.

Agricultural	Household	Other

14 If you expect your employment tax liability to be $1,000 or less in a full calendar year **and** want to file Form 944 annually instead of Forms 941 quarterly, check here. (Your employment tax liability generally will be $1,000 or less if you expect to pay $4,000 or less in total wages.) If you do not check this box, you must file Form 941 for every quarter. ☐

15 First date wages or annuities were paid (month, day, year). **Note:** If applicant is a withholding agent, enter date income will first be paid to nonresident alien (month, day, year) . . . . ►

16 Check one box that best describes the principal activity of your business.
☐ Construction ☐ Rental & leasing ☐ Transportation & warehousing
☐ Real estate ☐ Manufacturing ☐ Finance & insurance
☐ Health care & social assistance ☐ Wholesale-agent/broker
☐ Accommodation & food service ☐ Wholesale-other ☐ Retail
☐ Other (specify) ►

17 Indicate principal line of merchandise sold, specific construction work done, products produced, or services provided.

18 Has the applicant entity shown on line 1 ever applied for and received an EIN? ☐ Yes ☐ No
If "Yes," write previous EIN here ►

Third Party Designee

Complete this section **only** if you want to authorize the named individual to receive the entity's EIN and answer questions about the completion of this form.

Designee's name

Designee's telephone number (include area code)

Address and ZIP code

Designee's fax number (include area code)

Under penalties of perjury, I declare that I have examined this application, and to the best of my knowledge and belief, it is true, correct, and complete.

Name and title (type or print clearly) ►

Applicant's telephone number (include area code)

Signature ► Date ►

Applicant's fax number (include area code)

For Privacy Act and Paperwork Reduction Act Notice, see separate instructions.

Cat. No. 16055N

Form **SS-4** (Rev. 12-2017)

Do I Need an EIN?

File Form SS-4 if the applicant entity does not already have an EIN but is required to show an EIN on any return, statement, or other document.[1] See also the separate instructions for each line on Form SS-4.

IF the applicant...	AND...	THEN...
Started a new business	Does not currently have (nor expect to have) employees	Complete lines 1, 2, 4a–8a, 8b–c (if applicable), 9a, 9b (if applicable), and 10–14 and 16–18.
Hired (or will hire) employees, including household employees	Does not already have an EIN	Complete lines 1, 2, 4a–6, 7a–b (if applicable), 8a, 8b–c (if applicable), 9a, 9b (if applicable), 10–18.
Opened a bank account	Needs an EIN for banking purposes only	Complete lines 1–5b, 7a–b (if applicable), 8a, 8b–c (if applicable), 9a, 9b (if applicable), 10, and 18.
Changed type of organization	Either the legal character of the organization or its ownership changed (for example, you incorporate a sole proprietorship or form a partnership)[2]	Complete lines 1–18 (as applicable).
Purchased a going business[3]	Does not already have an EIN	Complete lines 1–18 (as applicable).
Created a trust	The trust is other than a grantor trust or an IRA trust[4]	Complete lines 1–18 (as applicable).
Created a pension plan as a plan administrator[5]	Needs an EIN for reporting purposes	Complete lines 1, 3, 4a–5b, 9a, 10, and 18.
Is a foreign person needing an EIN to comply with IRS withholding regulations	Needs an EIN to complete a Form W-8 (other than Form W-8ECI), avoid withholding on portfolio assets, or claim tax treaty benefits[6]	Complete lines 1–5b, 7a–b (SSN or ITIN optional), 8a, 8b–c (if applicable), 9a, 9b (if applicable), 10, and 18.
Is administering an estate	Needs an EIN to report estate income on Form 1041	Complete lines 1–6, 9a, 10–12, 13–17 (if applicable), and 18.
Is a withholding agent for taxes on non-wage income paid to an alien (i.e., individual, corporation, or partnership, etc.)	Is an agent, broker, fiduciary, manager, tenant, or spouse who is required to file Form 1042, Annual Withholding Tax Return for U.S. Source Income of Foreign Persons	Complete lines 1, 2, 3 (if applicable), 4a–5b, 7a–b (if applicable), 8a, 8b–c (if applicable), 9a, 9b (if applicable), 10, and 18.
Is a state or local agency	Serves as a tax reporting agent for public assistance recipients under Rev. Proc. 80-4, 1980-1 C.B. 581[7]	Complete lines 1, 2, 4a–5b, 9a, 10, and 18.
Is a single-member LLC (or similar single-member entity)	Needs an EIN to file Form 8832, Classification Election, for filing employment tax returns and excise tax returns, or for state reporting purposes[8], or is a foreign-owned U.S. disregarded entity and needs an EIN to file Form 5472, Information Return of a 25% Foreign-Owned U.S. Corporation or a Foreign Corporation Engaged in a U.S. Trade or Business (Under Sections 6038A and 6038C of the Internal Revenue Code)	Complete lines 1–18 (as applicable).
Is an S corporation	Needs an EIN to file Form 2553, Election by a Small Business Corporation[9]	Complete lines 1–18 (as applicable).

[1] For example, a sole proprietorship or self-employed farmer who establishes a qualified retirement plan, or is required to file excise, employment, alcohol, tobacco, or firearms returns, must have an EIN. A partnership, corporation, REMIC (real estate mortgage investment conduit), nonprofit organization (church, club, etc.), or farmers' cooperative must use an EIN for any tax-related purpose even if the entity does not have employees.

[2] However, do not apply for a new EIN if the existing entity only (a) changed its business name, (b) elected on Form 8832 to change the way it is taxed (or is covered by the default rules), or (c) terminated its partnership status because at least 50% of the total interests in partnership capital and profits were sold or exchanged within a 12-month period. The EIN of the terminated partnership should continue to be used. See Regulations section 301.6109-1(d)(2)(iii).

[3] Do not use the EIN of the prior business unless you became the "owner" of a corporation by acquiring its stock.

[4] However, grantor trusts that do not file using Optional Method 1 and IRA trusts that are required to file Form 990-T, Exempt Organization Business Income Tax Return, must have an EIN. For more information on grantor trusts, see the Instructions for Form 1041.

[5] A plan administrator is the person or group of persons specified as the administrator by the instrument under which the plan is operated.

[6] Entities applying to be a Qualified Intermediary (QI) need a QI-EIN even if they already have an EIN. See Rev. Proc. 2000-12.

[7] See also Household employer on page 4 of the Instructions. Note: State or local agencies may need an EIN for other reasons, for example, hired employees.

[8] See Disregarded entities on page 4 of the instructions for details on completing Form SS-4 for an LLC.

[9] An existing corporation that is electing or revoking S corporation status should use its previously-assigned EIN.

§ 16.3.14 Incorporation process—Miscellaneous forms

There are other forms, such as applications for state and city business and sales tax licenses, withholding tax registration, unemployment insurance, and workers' compensation forms, that may be required. Most corporations handle the preparation and filing of these themselves, but other documents may be required to complete the legal work for the corporation.

§ 16.4 Professional corporations

A *professional corporation* is a business corporation formed for the purpose of professional practice; its incorporators or shareholders must be natural persons duly licensed or admitted to practice their profession by a court, department, board, commission, or other government agency. For example, lawyers, doctors, and certified public accountants must be licensed by the state in which they practice. Many states also permit licensed professionals to form professional limited liability companies and partnerships (including professional LPs, LLPs, and LLLPs).

§ 16.4.1 Professional corporations—Differences between business and professional corporations

The formation, structure, and operation of a professional corporation are generally similar to a business corporation, but there are some significant differences. The articles of incorporation must contain a specific statement that the corporation is a professional corporation, and the license number of the incorporator may be required by some states.

A *professional corporation* is formed only for the purpose of rendering a professional service and may not engage in any business other than the rendering of the professional service. Nevertheless, it may own real estate, make investments, and do other acts incidental to its primary purpose.

Each professional corporation must acquire a certificate of registration from the state board regulating that particular profession. The shareholder(s) must be licensed in the profession, e.g., only lawyers can be shareholders of a professional corporation organized for the practice of law. Generally, shares in a professional corporation can be delivered, issued, traded, etc., only to a third person licensed in the same profession in the same state or to the corporation. Officers and directors of the corporation may not need to be licensed professionals, depending on state law and the corporation's organizational documents.

A professional corporation may use any name not prohibited by law, by the ethical rules of the profession in which the corporation is engaged, or by a rule or regulation of the court, department, board, commission, or agency regulating such profession. For instance, a professional corporation engaged in the practice of law cannot use the name "Divorce Mill, Inc." because the ABA Model Rules of Professional Conduct and similar rules adopted by the states would not permit such a name.

Although Corporation, Company, Limited, or Incorporated, in full or abbreviated, must be used in the name of a corporation, the name of a professional corporation typically need not contain any of these words. The name may use the word *Associate(s)* or consist solely of the name of one or more of the shareholders of the corporation. Some professional corporations use *P.C.* instead of *Inc.*

§ 16.4.2　Professional corporations—Advantages and disadvantages

The advantages and disadvantages of a professional corporation are similar to those of other types of corporations. However, the corporate entity cannot shield the licensed professional from liability for direct breach of professional ethical standards or negligence in performing services.

§ 16.5　Partnerships

A *partnership* is a voluntary association of two or more persons to carry on a business for profit as co-owners; the partners contribute capital, labor, skills, and/or property. Partnerships are governed by each state's laws regarding partnerships. Nearly all states have adopted the Uniform Partnership Act and the Uniform Limited Partnership Act with some modifications. There are four primary types of partnerships: general partnerships, limited partnerships, limited liability partnerships, and limited liability limited partnerships.

§ 16.5.1　Partnerships—General partnerships

General partnerships are formed by two or more persons for the purpose of carrying on a business for profit as co-owners. The Uniform Partnership Act defines a person as an individual, partnership, corporation, or other association. A partnership may be comprised of any two or more such persons, provided the entity is properly constituted and each person is competent to enter into the partnership.

§ 16.5.2　Partnerships—Partnership agreement

While no formal written agreement is required by law to establish a general partnership, to avoid problems and misunderstandings as to rights, duties, and liabilities, a written agreement is usually entered into by the partners. The names and addresses of the partners are listed in the agreement. There are no restrictions on the name the general partnership selects, except that it does not infringe upon an existing name.

Unlike corporations, partnerships cannot exist perpetually, and the partnership agreement generally states a termination date and provides that the partnership will terminate upon specified events, such as the death or bankruptcy of a partner. However, the partners may desire the partnership to be formed for an indefinite period. In such event, the partnership agreement does not state a termination date and the partnership exists at will.

The nature of the business the partnership will transact and the address from which it will operate are set forth in the partnership agreement. Sometimes there is no specific business address and the address of one of the partners is used.

§ 16.5.3   Partnerships—Financial structure

Contributions by a partner to the partnership may be in cash, property, skills, and/or services; the initial contributions are recorded in the partnership agreement. The agreement may call for additional contributions to be made at a future date or additional services to be performed.

In the absence of different provisions in the partnership agreement, all of the partners share equally in the profits and losses of the partnership. The agreement also sets forth the responsibilities of the partners in the event losses are sustained and additional funds are required from the partners to sustain the partnership. Agreements specifically allocating profit and loss can be complex and require special expertise in preparation particularly with respect to tax issues.

The method of keeping the partnership account, who will be responsible for keeping the account, and where the partnership records will be located are set forth in the agreement. The method of valuing a partner's contribution or partnership interest also may be set forth in this section.

To avoid having several partners withdraw money from the partnership at the same time, rules and procedures are typically set forth specifying when and in what amounts partners may withdraw funds. All income is deposited to and expenses paid from a central partnership account.

Additional partners may be admitted to the partnership on terms and conditions specified in the agreement. The incoming partner becomes a member upon execution of an amendment to the partnership agreement. To avoid dissolution of the partnership by operation of law, the partnership agreement must provide for its continuation in the event of the admission of a new member.

§ 16.5.4   Partnerships—Commencement of existence

A general partnership commences at the time any one of the following occurs:

- Execution of the partnership agreement

- Commencement of the partnership business
- The filing of any document required by state law to commence its existence

The partnership agreement may provide for a different event to cause commencement of the partnership business.

§ 16.5.5   Partnerships—Ownership of partnership property

Property brought into the partnership as a contribution becomes the property of the partnership. State law and the partnership agreement govern whether a partner may assign or encumber his or her interest in partnership property. Title to partnership property may be held in the partnership name or in the names of all of the individual partners.

§ 16.5.6   Partnerships—Partners' liability

In general, all of the partners in a general partnership are each fully liable for losses or damages arising out of the partnership. A new partner is responsible for liabilities incurred prior to the new partner's admission, but only to the extent of the partner's share of partnership property. If a deficit occurs, the partners are required to satisfy the deficit, generally in proportion to their share of profits. If one partner cannot completely satisfy its share, the other partners must make up the defaulting partner's share and then seek reimbursement from the defaulting partner.

§ 16.5.7   Partnerships—Tax returns

The partnership itself is not taxed, but an information return must be filed by the partnership with state and federal tax authorities. The partners are taxed on the income attributed to their partnership interests under the partnership agreement as part of their individual income tax returns, and the partners are also entitled to the benefit of any partnership losses that may occur.

§ 16.5.8   Partnerships—Dissolution

Dissolution under state law ends the right of a partnership to continue to do business. The partnership goes through a winding-up process and is then terminated as a legal entity. The partnership may be terminated by operation of law or by dissolution caused by the actions of the partners. Partnership agreements may express that certain actions cause dissolution of the partnership. Actions of the partners that may cause dissolution include:

- The express action of any one partner
- The consent of all of the partners
- The expulsion of a partner

Events that may automatically cause dissolution of the partnership include:

- The occurrence of an event making it unlawful to continue the partnership business
- The death or bankruptcy of a partner or bankruptcy of the partnership

The partnership also automatically dissolves at the termination of the definite time for which it was formed.

After dissolution, the affairs of the partnership are wound up. The partnership agreement may indicate which partners will be responsible for winding up the affairs of the partnership. Winding up consists of collecting and preserving the partnership assets, paying debts, and distributing any remaining assets. Creditors of the partnership have first claim on partnership assets, with the partners sharing any remaining assets after repayment of their capital contribution. After dissolution and during the winding-up process, the liabilities of the partners continue, so where dissolution of a partnership is caused by the death of a partner, the partner's estate inherits such partner's liability. While liabilities remain, however, the partners' authority ceases upon dissolution except for any acts they are required to perform to wind up the partnership. Notice of dissolution must be given to the partners and to any persons who have dealt with the partnership.

§ 16.5.9 Partnerships—Classification of partners

Within a partnership, partners can be further classified as follows:

- A partner who takes no active part in the management of the business and is not known to the public as a partner is a dormant, sleeping, silent, or secret partner.
- A person who permits others to believe or behaves so people believe he or she is a partner of a partnership may be required to answer for certain partnership debts. Such a person is known as a ***partner by estoppel*** or an ***ostensible partner***.
- A person who is named as a partner is a nominal partner.

Additional types of partners are found in other forms of partnership.

§ 16.6 Limited partnerships

Limited partnerships (**LPs**) are regulated considerably more than general partnerships and, unlike general partnerships, must be created by a written agreement. Any two or more persons may form a limited partnership, but there must be at least one general partner and at least one limited partner. The ***general partner*** has unlimited liability for the obligations of the partnership; the ***limited partner***'s liability is limited to such partner's contributions to the partnership. While a general partner may contribute management services, cash, and/or property, a limited partner may contribute only cash or property. A limited partner has no voice in the operation or management of the partnership, except to the extent permitted in the limited partnership agreement. Limited partners performing acts outside of the limited scope detailed in a limited partnership agreement may be considered general partners and thus forfeit their limited liability status. Natural persons, partnerships, limited partnerships, trusts, estates, associations, or corporations may be partners in LPs.

§ 16.6.1 Limited partnerships—Partnership name

There are restrictions on the name under which a limited partnership does business. *Ltd.* or *Limited Partnership* must generally be included in the limited partnership name. In some states, the limited partnership's name may not include the name of a limited partner unless it is the same as a general partner's or the business operated under a name in which the limited partner's name appeared prior to becoming a limited partnership.

§ 16.6.2 Limited partnerships—Existence

A limited partnership begins its existence by filing a certificate of limited partnership with the state agency responsible for business registrations. The name of the partnership must be registered or a statement filed with the state agency stating who is doing business under the partnership name and where the business is located. The certificate must be amended whenever there is any change to it. On dissolution, a cancellation of the certificate must be filed for the public record. All of the partners named in a certificate of limited partnership must execute the original certificate, but in the case of amendment, fewer signatures may be required.

§ 16.6.3 Limited partnerships—Right of inspection of books and records

Even though limited partners are not involved in the day-to-day activities of the partnership, they have the right to inspect and copy any of the partnership's records, which it is required by law to maintain at the partnership office.

§ 16.6.4 Limited partnerships—Financial structure

Limited partners must contribute cash or property or perform certain tasks to the extent provided by law and as agreed in the limited partnership agreement. If property or services are required but a limited partner is unable to contribute, a contribution of cash equal to the portion of the required contribution may be necessary.

The ratio in which the limited and general partners share in the profits and losses of the partnership is set forth in the limited partnership agreement. This agreement also states the amount of and manner in which future contributions will become due.

§ 16.7 Limited liability partnerships

A *limited liability partnership* (**LLP**), as opposed to a limited partnership, is a general partnership that has elected to be treated as an LLP and has adopted a name disclosing its limited liability (generally by adding *LLP* to its name and filing a disclosure and election document as required by state laws). LLPs afford insulation for partners from liability for certain acts of the partnership or another partner. The LLP form does not generally protect partners from liability for partnership business debts or liability arising from their own actions. The extent to which such limitation of liability may be available to a limited liability partnership organized in one state for liabilities arising in another state must be determined under the applicable state law.

§ 16.8 Limited liability limited partnerships

A *limited liability limited partnership (LLLP)* is a limited partnership that has elected to be treated as a limited liability partnership in addition to being a limited partnership. To become an LLLP, the limited partnership must qualify under state law, file any necessary disclosure and election documents, and adopt a name that indicates its status as an LLLP. The liability of general partners of LLLPs is limited to the same extent as the liability of partners of LLPs.

§ 16.9 Other partnerships

Other partnership associations include joint ventures, joint stock companies, syndicates, cooperatives, trading and nontrading associations, and mining partnerships. These are described below.

§ 16.9.1 Other partnerships—Joint venture

A *joint venture* is similar to a general partnership in formation, but its duration is generally only for the accomplishment of the specific purpose for which it was formed. The duties owed by the joint venturers are the same as those owed by general partners. While one joint venturer might perform the major portion of the management duties, all joint venturers share in the profits, losses, and obligations, typically as set forth in an agreement between the parties.

§ 16.9.2 Other partnerships—Syndicate

A *syndicate* is an association of persons formed to conduct a specific—generally financial—business transaction. The most common type of syndicate is one formed by an investment bank to market stocks and bonds.

§ 16.9.3 Other partnerships—Cooperative

A *cooperative* is comprised of a group of people who pool their products or resources for mutual advantage. Many states have enacted regulations concerning cooperatives. In some states incorporation is permitted.

§ 16.9.4   Other partnerships—Business or Massachusetts trust

A *business* or *Massachusetts trust* permits the ownership of property to be transferred by the owners to trustees who run the business for the owners' benefit. To evidence the ownership of the property, the trustees issue shares or certificates to the trustors showing their original ownership or interest in the property. The shares or certificates may be freely transferred, but the trustors do not have the control over the trustees that corporate shareholders have over directors. One possible benefit of this form of organization is that the trustors avoid liability by transferring responsibility for operating the trust to the trustees.

§ 16.9.5   Other partnerships—Joint stock company

A *joint stock company* is somewhat like a combined partnership and corporation. Shares of stock are issued to evidence each partner's ownership, and the shares are transferable. Management of the business is delegated to a small group of partners because there are usually many partners in a joint stock company. There is no restriction on the transfer of the shares or who may purchase them, and any person to whom such shares are transferred or sold becomes a member of the joint stock company upon such sale or transfer.

§ 16.9.6   Other partnerships—Trading partnership

A *trading partnership* is specifically engaged in buying and selling merchandise. The partners have authority to bind the partnership and obtain loans in the partnership name.

§ 16.9.7   Other partnerships—Nontrading partnership

A *nontrading partnership* is engaged in performing legal, accounting, medical, or other services. The partners have no authority to bind the partnership, and the success of the partnership is more dependent upon the results of the partners than on the capital they may contribute.

§ 16.9.8   Other partnerships—Mining partnership

A *mining partnership* is formed when two or more people join together to work a mining claim to extract minerals. While similar to a general partnership, a mining partnership is not dissolved when a partner's interest is transferred, and such interest is freely transferable. The partners share in the profits and losses in the ownership ratio.

§ 16.9.9 Other partnerships—Unincorporated associations

Unincorporated associations are formed when persons combine either to make a profit or for a nonprofit charitable purpose. Generally, unless a member ratifies or authorizes an act, the member is not liable for the association's actions. The association has no existence apart from its members and cannot sue or be sued in its name. The association might, however, be taxable as a corporation.

§ 16.10 Limited liability company

A *limited liability company* (LLC) is a business form first available under the laws of Wyoming. It is now available in all fifty states and has become popular because of its relative flexibility. It seeks to blend the advantages of limited liability for equity owners found in corporations and the tax advantages found in partnerships.

State laws generally provide that the owners and managers of an LLC are not personally liable for any debt, obligation, or liability of the LLC solely by reason of their association with it, except to the extent of their capital contribution.

The IRS adopted rules effective January 1, 1997, which cause an entity such as an LLC with two or more members to be treated as a partnership, unless it elects to be treated otherwise. A corporation generally must pay taxes on its income and the shareholders must pay taxes on the dividends and distributions they receive from the corporation, which results in the taxation of the same income twice. Entities that are treated like partnerships for tax purposes, however, are not taxed on income at the entity level because all of the partnership's income is passed through to the partners, and the partners pay taxes on their share of the partnership's income. An LLC with only one member is taxed like a sole proprietorship.

§ 16.10.1 Limited liability company—Formation and operation

Although state laws vary, generally an LLC may be formed for any business purpose. Some states have exceptions for banking and insurance businesses. An LLC is formed by filing an organizational document with the state agency responsible for registration of businesses. An LLC's name must typically contain one of the following: *Limited Liability Company, Limited Liability Co.,* or *LLC*.

Unless an LLC's certificate of formation states otherwise, it will be managed by all of its members. The members, however, may elect to have the LLC managed by one or more managers who need not be members. Generally, unless an LLC agreement provides otherwise, members are entitled to vote in proportion to their respective percentage interests.

§ 16.10.2   Limited liability company—Personal liability of members and managers

Generally, members and managers are not personally liable for the obligations and liabilities of the LLC. State laws allow some exceptions, however, such as provisions in which a creditor can enforce a member's contractual obligation to contribute cash, property, or perform services for the LLC to the extent the creditor reasonably relied on such obligation. Another type of exception is provided where a member may be obligated to return an LLC distribution that the member knew was made in violation of the state law's limitations on distributions by an insolvent LLC.

LLC members may also be liable for the LLC's debts under circumstances that would expose a corporation's shareholders to liability. Generally, a corporation's shareholders are liable for the corporation's obligations only if it is shown that the corporation was intentionally used to violate or evade a duty that is owed to another and such personal liability is necessary to prevent an unjustified loss to a third party.

§ 16.10.3   Limited liability company—Financial structure

Contributions to an LLC may be in the form of cash, property, or services rendered. Unless otherwise specified in an LLC agreement, profits, losses, and distributions are allocated to the members based on each member's percentage ownership interest. Distributions are often prohibited if they would cause the LLC not to be able to pay its debts or if the LLC's liabilities would then exceed the fair market value of its assets.

§ 16.10.4   Limited liability company—Assignment of interest in an LLC

An LLC member does not have an interest in any specific property of an LLC; he or she simply has an ownership interest in the entity as a whole. Unless prohibited by an LLC agreement, a member may transfer the member's interest in the LLC's profits and losses and right to receive distributions. An assignee, however, cannot become a member or participate in the management of the LLC until all the other members have given consent, unless the LLC agreement provides otherwise.

§ 16.10.5   Limited liability company—Dissolution

State laws typically provide that an LLC will dissolve upon the occurrence of specified events including:

- expiration of its term or a period of statutorily established years from the date of formation
- an event of dissociation or withdrawal of any member
- written consent of all of the members

- entry of a decree of judicial dissolution

Often an LLC agreement may alter the events of dissociation, withdrawal, and dissolution.

§ 16.10.6 Limited liability company—Comparison with other business entities

Corporation. While it is possible to structure a corporation to allow pass-through of taxable income, the requirements for such an election are rigid and any violation terminates the election.

Limited Partnership. Unlike an LLC, at least one partner of a limited partnership (the general partner) will be personally liable for the obligations of the partnership. While the use of a corporate general partner can reduce the risk of such liability, this practice involves another layer of complexity and expense.

Limited Liability Limited Partnership. Qualification as an LLLP provides limited liability protection to the general partners of limited partnerships, thus reducing or eliminating the reason to have a corporate general partner. LLLPs are comparable to LLCs in that taxable income is passed through to the owners in both, and both provide limited liability for all their owners.

§ 16.11 Sole proprietorship

A person who solely owns a business and is solely responsible for its day-to-day operation of a business is a *sole proprietor*. No formal documentation is required to form a sole proprietorship. A sole proprietorship is not a legal entity separate from the sole proprietor and does not limit the sole proprietor's personal liability related to obligations of the business.

Depending on the type of business and local, state, and federal requirements, permits or licenses may be required to operate the business. If the business is conducted under a name other than the owner's, it may be necessary to file documents similar to the fictitious name registrations used for other business entities.

Except for required licenses or permits, there are no restrictions on transfer of ownership of the business. Upon the death of the owner, the business ceases to exist.

Chapter 17

Real Estate

KeyCite®: Cases and other legal materials listed in KeyCite Scope can be researched through the KeyCite service on Westlaw®. Use KeyCite to check citations for form, parallel references, prior and later history, and comprehensive citator information, including citations to other decisions and secondary materials.

---

§ 17.1   Introduction

Real estate law offers the lawyer's assistant many opportunities to assist the lawyer in documenting real estate transactions. To handle preliminary workups, closing documents, and gathering necessary information, the lawyer's assistant must understand the basic elements of real estate law.

§ 17.2   History of real estate law

Many property rights laws come from England. In medieval times, English kings often granted real estate to an individual who supported the king during a war or performed some other valuable service. After the Revolutionary War, the United States found itself with a great deal of land and a lot of debt. The government opted to sell land to retire the debt. Unfortunately, much of the land was undeveloped and in many cases totally unexplored and devoid of landmarks. The government had no way to describe the property it was selling. Thus, in 1785, the government ordered a survey to be taken. This was the beginning of the United States Government Survey. A majority of states still use this system for legal descriptions. The remaining states retain control over original surveys of land that form the basis for all legal descriptions.

§17.3 Definition of real estate

Real estate, also called *real property* or *realty*, is defined as land and anything permanently attached to it. It includes items attached to the land naturally, such as grass, shrubs, or trees and items attached to the land artificially, such as buildings, fences, certain fixtures, and other improvements.

§17.3.1 Definition of real estate—Fixtures

Fixtures are those items firmly affixed to buildings. Whether or not an item is a fixture has been the subject of much litigation.

EXAMPLE:

A built-in dishwasher is a fixture that has become a part of the real estate. It has a specially-created opening for its installation, and its removal would leave an obvious unfinished area in the kitchen not easily used for other purposes. On the other hand, a portable dishwasher that is moved about the kitchen on wheels would not be considered a fixture.

The distinction is often not so easily made as in this example, so great care is exercised by lawyers in defining the fixtures to be included in a given transaction.

§17.3.2 Definition of real estate—Improvements

Improvements include buildings, curbs, gutters, sidewalks, street lights, and sewer systems. Any permanent item constructed upon real estate may be referred to as an improvement.

§17.4 Elements of real estate law

The general elements of real estate law that play a significant role in the practice of real estate law are:
- Ownership of real estate
- Evidence of title to real estate
- Examination of title to real estate
- Encumbrances of real estate
- Transfer of real estate
- Financing the acquisition of real estate
- Preparation of real estate documents
- Closing of real estate transactions

§ 17.5 Ownership of real estate

Although there are many forms of ownership, this chapter deals only with the most common:
- Fee simple or fee simple absolute
- Joint tenancy
- Tenancy in common
- Community property
- Tenancy by the entireties

§ 17.5.1 Ownership of real estate—Fee simple or fee simple absolute

Ownership of real estate in *fee simple* or *fee simple absolute* gives the owner the absolute legal possession of the property. The vast majority of real estate transactions involve ownership in fee simple, although there are other, more complicated forms of lesser ownership. The phrase *in fee simple* means that the owner named owns it all without reservation. Fee simple ownership of real estate may be acquired by corporations, partnerships, individuals, trusts, or estates. Individuals may acquire fee simple ownership either alone or with others. If two or more individuals own real estate together, they may own it either as joint tenants or as tenants in common.

§ 17.5.2 Ownership of real estate—Joint tenancy

Joint tenancy is ownership by two or more persons with the right of survivorship. It means that upon the death of one of the joint tenants, the property automatically and immediately becomes the property of the surviving joint tenant without the necessity of probate proceedings. This right of survivorship is considered by many to be the principal advantage of joint tenancy. In some states, the right of survivorship is not inherent to joint tenancy and must be established by including additional language creating survivorship rights. A joint tenant may not change the right of survivorship in the other joint tenant by will. Frequently, husbands and wives hold title to real estate in joint tenancy, but joint tenancy is not limited to married couples. On the other hand, just because a husband and wife have occupied certain premises jointly does not necessarily mean that they are owners in joint tenancy. The form of ownership is specified in the deed by which the owners acquired ownership of the property. Therefore, it is clearly delineated in the records. There are circumstances in which joint tenancy ownership is not advisable for a husband and wife.

If it has been determined that the buyers will hold title as joint tenants, the deed contains language similar to the following:

> . . . CONVEY and WARRANT to JOHN SMITH and MARY SMITH, husband and wife, as joint tenants, with right of survivorship . . .

or

> . . . CONVEY and WARRANT to JOHN SMITH and MARY SMITH, husband and wife, as joint tenants and not as tenants in common . . .

or when the parties are not related:

> . . . CONVEY and WARRANT to JOHN SMITH and MARY JONES, as joint tenants and not as tenants in common . . .

In most states, if the deed does not clearly indicate how title is to be held, title passing only to "John Smith and Mary Smith" is presumed to be tenancy in common. In some states, special forms are used for each form of tenancy. If this is the case, the lawyer's assistant should be careful to use the correct form.

§ 17.5.3 Ownership of real estate—Tenancy in common

Tenancy in common means the tenants of the property hold undivided fractional interests in the same property, with each having the right to possess. The interest is a fraction of the whole, as there is no tangible division of the property. Therefore, none of the tenants in common can claim any specific portion of the property, such as the north half or the east half. Interests of tenants in common may be equal or unequal, and each has a separate legal title to an undivided fractional interest. Each tenant can sell the tenant's interest or provide for its distribution by will. In the event a tenant in common dies without a will, the undivided interest passes to that tenant's heirs according to the laws of intestacy. These heirs become tenants in common with the other owners. The language in such a deed might read as follows:

> . . . CONVEY and WARRANT to JOHN SMITH and MARY SMITH, husband and wife, as tenants in common, each to an undivided one-half interest, and not as joint tenants . . .

§ 17.5.4 Ownership of real estate—Community property

Community property exists in some states, and it is the presumption in those states that any property acquired during a marriage by either the husband or the wife, except property acquired by gift or inheritance, belongs one-half each equally to husband and wife.

§ 17.5.5 Ownership of real estate—Tenancy by the entirety

Another form of ownership by a husband and wife is known as *tenancy by the entirety*. This form of ownership provides that neither party may convey such party's share of the property individually nor neither share can be attached by creditors. In some states, this form of ownership has been abolished, while in others a conveyance to a husband and wife is presumed to be a tenancy by the entirety unless some other form of ownership is clearly indicated.

§ 17.6   Evidence of title to real estate

Regardless of the form of ownership, when a parcel of real estate changes ownership, the owner, or in some instances the buyer, is required to furnish evidence of title. The form of title evidence varies from state to state, so the lawyer's assistant must determine the methods used locally. Most commonly, evidence of title is in the form of an abstract, a Torrens certificate, or a title insurance policy.

§ 17.6.1   Evidence of title to real estate—Abstracts

The *abstract* is a summary of all transactions pertaining to the parcel from the time of governmental entry (when the real estate was first recorded in formal land records) up to and including the current transaction.

Some areas deal almost exclusively with voluminous abstracts in real estate transactions. When such abstracts are used, they are updated for each transaction affecting the particular property covered by the abstract. The updating of an abstract is commonly referred to as a *continuation* or *extension of abstract*. The continuation may be attached to an existing abstract so that the abstract remains as one large document. On the other hand, the continuation might be done for each new transaction involving the real estate. The result would be several pieces of abstract, frequently referred to as *stub abstracts*. The cover sheet or first page of a continuation, called the *caption*, gives the legal description of the property covered by the abstract. The caption may sometimes describe a larger parcel of real estate from which the property involved in the transaction was taken. The final page of the continuation, called the *abstracter's certificate*, contains several items of information needed for the real estate transaction. If the caption on the abstract refers to a larger parcel of land, the abstracter's certificate indicates the entry at which the legal description for which the abstract has been extended can be found.

The extension or continuation of an abstract may be done by a lawyer. More commonly, it is done by a *title company* specializing in such work. In some states, a title company can examine and assist in the search of records, insure the title to the property, and act as an escrow or closing agent. The extent to which a title company participates in these services depends upon state laws and local customs. The lawyer's assistant should become familiar with the information a title company must have in order to perform its services rapidly and efficiently. The assistant must also be aware of the special services title companies have developed to provide specific limited title information to lawyers. Because the contribution and cooperation of the title company's staff are an integral part of the efficient real estate transaction, rapport should be developed with the title company's staff members. The duties of the lawyer's assistant often include arranging for continuations of an abstract on pending real estate transactions. The lawyer's assistant must know how to place an order for such a continuation.

An abstract must be treated as a valuable legal document, as it is very expensive and time consuming to replace. Most firms use receipts in all transfers of an abstract. The lawyer's assistant should be able to draft such receipts. (See Illustration 17-1.)

Illustration 17-1

ABSTRACT RECEIPT

September 15, *[Year]*

RECEIVED OF Jones and Jones, Lawyers, the Abstract of Title to the following real estate:

Lot 2, Block 1, Red Rose Addition, Any County, Any State.

_____

John K. Smith

Client/File Reference: *S-6948*

§ 17.6.2   Evidence of title to real estate—Torrens certificate

Real estate having a Torrens certificate or owner's duplicate certificate of title is formally referred to as *registered property*. Under the Torrens Act, which has been adopted by some states, a county may establish a system of title registration indemnified by a security or assurance fund backed by county assets. All transactions concerning a parcel of real estate registered under the Torrens system must be recorded in the office of the registrar of titles. The registrar of titles issues a certificate of title for each parcel of real estate registered under the Torrens system. A *Torrens certificate* is considered to be conclusive evidence of the present ownership and status of title. Liens, mortgages, and other encumbrances in existence are listed on the certificates. These entries are called *memorials*. The original certificate of title is kept in the office of the registrar of titles and may not be removed for any reason. In some states, an *owner's duplicate certificate of title* is also issued and is delivered to the owner. This duplicate should be treated as an important legal document, as it must be surrendered to the registrar of titles upon change of ownership or when new encumbrances are memorialized. If the owner cannot produce the owner's duplicate at such times, a court order must be obtained to have it replaced. In a transaction involving registered property, the lawyer's assistant may be requested to order a *registered property abstract* from a title company. This type of abstract summarizes the information contained on the certificate of title. In some instances, the law firm may conduct an independent examination of Torrens records either in place of or as a supplement to a registered property abstract. In some states, a mortgagee's duplicate certificate of title may also be issued. Receipts should always be used in the transfer of duplicate certificates of title.

§ 17.6.3   Evidence of title to real estate—Title policy

A *title insurance policy* is issued by a title insurance company and insures that a certain parcel of real estate is titled to certain parties. There are several kinds of title insurance available that insure differing interests. In ordinary real estate transactions, however, the lawyer's assistant will be dealing with owner's and mortgagee's insurance policies, also known as lender's insurance policies. An *owner's title insurance policy* gives the owner the right to recover any loss suffered from a covered title defect. How much the owner can recover depends upon the amount of coverage afforded by the title insurance policy. The amount of coverage on an owner's policy is usually the purchase price of the real estate.

A *mortgagee's title policy* is separate insurance coverage which insures the mortgagee's lien on the real estate. Normally, any institution lending money for the purchase of real estate will require title insurance in the amount of its loan. Mortgagee's coverage does not insure an owner's interest but guarantees only that the mortgagee will be paid in the event of any title defect. Mortgagee's coverage may be issued in conjunction with an owner's policy or by itself. If both an owner's policy and a mortgagee's policy are issued simultaneously, the insured parties are both the owner and the mortgagee, but a separate premium is charged for each insured party. A title insurance policy may be issued by itself even when no abstract of title exists or if the abstract of title has been lost or destroyed. A title insurance policy may be issued in addition to an abstract if a title defect emerges and the title company is willing to insure over such defect. Registered property may also be covered by title insurance.

In a real estate transaction, the lawyer's assistant may be required to order the title insurance policy by delivering the necessary information to the title insurance company. The names of the sellers, the names and marital status of the buyers, the amount of coverage, a legal description of the property, and in some cases the abstract of title, if one exists, are commonly provided to the title insurance company. The title insurance company then issues a commitment for title insurance for the lawyer to examine prior to issuing the title insurance policy.

§ 17.6.4   Evidence of title to real estate—Examination of title

The buyer relies upon the lawyer to certify that the prospective seller is in a position to convey a clear, merchantable, and marketable title. *Clear and merchantable title* is the term applied to ownership of property that is free from any type of legal defect or encumbrance. Therefore, when a lawyer certifies to a buyer that the property has a clear and merchantable title, it means that a prudent person need have no fear of accepting it, as it would be readily transferable on the open market. If a defect in the title does exist, it is referred to as a *cloud on the title* or a *defect in the title*. Therefore, prior to the closing of a real estate transaction, the buyer has the evidence of title examined by a lawyer. In lieu of or in addition to such an examination, the buyer may secure title insurance. At the conclusion of the title examination, the lawyer issues a *title opinion*. In some areas, if title insurance is obtained, the lawyer does not issue a title opinion. The title opinion or the commitment for title insurance advises the client as to the condition of the title. If there are defects or clouds on the title, the title opinion or title insurance commitment describes what action is required to correct them. Typically, the items that affect the title are:

- Encumbrances
- Easements
- Encroachments
- Tax sales
- Irregularities

§ 17.6.5 Evidence of title to real estate—Encumbrances

An *encumbrance* is a recorded document placing the public on notice that a third person may have a claim against the property that might diminish the value of the property. In such cases, the closing lawyer would hold back sufficient funds to pay any such encumbrance so that the buyer ultimately gets full value for the purchase price or would ensure that encumbrances are removed before or simultaneously with closing.

§ 17.6.6 Evidence of title to real estate—Mortgages

A *mortgage* is a security instrument against real estate given by a debtor to a creditor to guarantee the payment of a debt. In granting a mortgage to a creditor, a debtor pledges property to guarantee to the creditor that the debt will be paid. If the debtor does not pay, then under the terms of the mortgage, the creditor may foreclose on the property. This means that upon meeting any applicable legal requirements, the creditor may seize the property and have it sold to pay the debt owed the creditor by the seller.

EXAMPLE:

The seller borrowed $10,000 against his home and has not paid back any of the money. He gave a mortgage as security for the loan. He immediately decided to sell the property and has found a buyer who has agreed to pay $80,000 for the property. In examination of the title, the buyer's lawyer discovers the mortgage, which is an encumbrance against the property. He contacts the creditor to determine how much money the seller owes. That amount is deducted from the seller's proceeds, and the creditor is paid the amount owed through escrow in exchange for a satisfaction of mortgage at closing.

§ 17.6.7 Evidence of title to real estate—Judgments

A *judgment* is a court order or decree. There are many kinds of judgments rendered by courts as a result of litigation. The type most likely to be encountered in real estate law is the *money judgment*, which awards a sum of money to the plaintiff. The plaintiff who is awarded the money judgment is the *judgment creditor*, and the debtor against whom the judgment is rendered is the *judgment debtor*. Plaintiffs file a certificate making the judgment a lien on all of the debtor's real estate, wherever located.

EXAMPLE:

The seller in the example above might also have a judgment recorded against him. That judgment creates a lien against the property owned by the seller. Its payment is handled much the same way as payment of a mortgage is handled. The closing lawyer contacts the lawyer for the judgment creditor to find out how much money is owed on the judgment. This amount is then paid from the escrow funds in order to receive confirmation that the judgment will be satisfied shortly after closing.

§ 17.6.8 Evidence of title to real estate—Materialman's or mechanic's liens

A *materialman's* or *mechanic's lien* is a right created in a person who has done work on or delivered materials to property which, if perfected, creates a right enforceable against the property. (The manner in which liens are perfected is governed by state law.) If such a lien is found to be recorded against the property being sold, it must be paid by the seller and an appropriate formal satisfaction delivered at closing if the buyer is to receive clear title.

§ 17.6.9 Evidence of title to real estate—Tax liens

Local, state, and federal governments may use the *tax lien* as a vehicle to collect taxes. They attach by virtue of law; no court action is necessary. These taxes include real estate taxes, income taxes, sales taxes, federal unemployment taxes, and so forth. A seller must pay any tax lien to give the buyer a clear title and deliver a formal satisfaction at closing. In many states, the lien of unpaid real estate taxes is superior to all other liens.

§ 17.6.10 Evidence of title to real estate—Easements

An *easement* is a right granted to someone by a property owner to come upon or use the land for a specified purpose. The terms *easement* and *servitude* are sometimes used interchangeably. An easement may be created by the act of the parties involved through negotiation and agreement. Easements are usually custom-drafted by the lawyers of the respective parties. An example of an easement would be the right of a utility company to install a gas line across an individual's property and thereafter to enter the land to maintain, repair, and service the line. The utility company would not have the right to enter the property for any other purpose except as set forth in the easement document.

§ 17.6.11   Evidence of title to real estate—Encroachments

An *encroachment* is the unlawful intrusion of one's buildings, improvements, or fixtures onto the land of another.

EXAMPLE:

If a neighbor builds a fence or a garage that extends over his property line onto his neighbor's property, that portion extending over the property line constitutes an encroachment when the owner of the land on which the encroachment exists does not consent to the encroachment.

The encroachment is usually discovered by the engineer who makes a survey of the property, and the buyer's lawyer discovers the encroachment when examining the survey in connection with title examination. If an encroachment continues unchallenged for a requisite number of years established by law, the property right can become permanent to the one encroaching; this is called *adverse possession*.

§ 17.6.12   Evidence of title to real estate—Restrictive covenants

When property is developed into a subdivision, the developer usually places restrictions on the use of the property. The *restrictive covenants* usually provide that the property will be used only for residential purposes and often provide for the size of the residences and the kinds of building materials permitted to be used. The reason for these covenants is to maintain the value of the property. By specifying the size and building materials, the developer ensures that the residences will cost generally the same to build.

EXAMPLE:

If it were possible for a homebuilder to build a $100,000 house next to a $600,000 house, the $600,000 house would lose some of its value based merely on the fact that it was located next to a $100,000 house.

Although restrictive covenants are most commonly seen in a residential context, they can also be placed on commercial or other property.

§ 17.6.13   Evidence of title to real estate—Tax sales

As a rule, both state and local governing bodies levy taxes against property to obtain revenue. The tax is usually computed by multiplying a rate in mills ($1 per $1,000) times the assessed value of the property. (In some jurisdictions, the assessed value may be some arbitrary percentage of the retail value.) Property taxes are collectible against the property. Therefore, if a property owner does not pay taxes, the tax authority may seize the property and sell it to a purchaser who pays the taxes. This is known as a *tax sale*. The title lawyer therefore routinely verifies that property taxes on the property have been paid. If they have not been paid and the property has been sold for taxes, it is necessary for the seller to redeem the property within a specified time. This is done by paying the taxes due, as well as interest, penalties, and costs.

§ 17.6.14   Evidence of title to real estate—Irregularities

Errors or variations in legal descriptions, errors in divorce or probate proceedings, and other types of problems must sometimes be corrected.

In most jurisdictions, the seller bears the cost of furnishing the evidence of title, while the buyer secures and pays for a title examination or title insurance policy. However, this custom varies by location.

In the event that title insurance is to be used in lieu of or in addition to a lawyer's opinion, the title company examines the title and issues its commitment or binder prior to the closing. This document contains a list of all defects or clouds on the title, such as those listed above. These defects are called **exceptions** to the policy. The title policy does not provide coverage for any loss resulting from the listed exceptions. The commitment also lists the requirements to be met prior to closing and the issuance of its final policy. The final policy is issued once all conditions are met and the transaction has been closed, subject only to customary exceptions and any exceptions approved by the buyer. Some **exceptions to title** are considered customary, and they appear on most title policies. Easements, for example, are essential to proper maintenance of electric, gas, telephone, and water services.

§ 17.7   Instruments of conveyance

Since any legal entity may own property, an individual, a corporation, a partnership, or a limited liability company may acquire an interest in real estate. There are a number of ways to acquire real estate. The most common are by sale or deed and by inheritance.

§ 17.7.1   Instruments of conveyance—Sale or deed

In a transfer by sale or deed, the **owner** (called *grantor, vendor,* or *seller*) conveys title to the buyer (called *grantee, vendee,* or *purchaser*) by the delivery of a deed. A **deed** is a formal written contract between the parties by which the seller sells the property to the buyer for agreed upon **consideration (the purchase price)**.

The law of each state outlines the requirements of a deed. Printed forms containing these legal requirements are usually available through a legal stationer or through the county clerk's office. Some states require that only their forms be used, while other states allow general usage of various types of deeds. The lawyer's assistant should use the most acceptable form in the state in which the property is located, taking care to comply with requirements for execution, such as witnesses or notary acknowledgments.

§ 17.7.2   Instruments of conveyance—The warranty deed

The *warranty deed* (sometimes called a *general warranty deed*) is the most desirable type of deed for the buyer. The seller gives the following warranties to the buyer:

- That at the time of the making and delivery of the deed, the seller owned a fee simple interest in the property and had the full right to convey it.
- That the title is free of all encumbrances, except any specifically listed in the deed.
- That the buyer and any successors in interest have the right to quiet and peaceable possession of the premises and are indemnified by the seller against the claims of all persons who may lawfully claim an interest other than those encumbrances.

§ 17.7.3   Instruments of conveyance—Special warranty deed

A *special warranty deed* or *limited warranty deed* warrants the title to the property being conveyed against any claims by, through, or under the seller or seller's heirs excepting encumbrances specifically listed in the deed. It does not guarantee against any claims that occurred prior to the time of the seller's acquisition.

§ 17.7.4   Instruments of conveyance—Quitclaim deed

A *quitclaim deed* from the seller conveys any claim, right, title, or interest that seller may have to the subject property. The seller on a quitclaim deed does not warrant the condition of the title. The quitclaim deed does not even warrant that seller has any interest in the property. It merely provides that if seller does own any interest in the property, that interest is being conveyed. Quitclaim deeds are often used to correct certain types of title defects and are often used when the grantor gifts property to the grantee for no consideration.

§ 17.7.5   Instruments of conveyance—Probate deed

If property is acquired from an estate or guardianship, the buyer receives a type of special warranty deed called a *probate deed* or a **guardian's** or *personal representative's deed*, which generally does not contain warranties. In some states, it is possible, however, to obtain a deed with warranties.

A *transfer by devise* occurs when the owner of real estate dies and leaves such property to a person or persons by a will. If the owner has left no will, it is distributed by operation of law to the owner's heirs at law. The method of conveyance is a decree, sometimes called a certificate of transfer, from the court of jurisdiction in probate matters. The decree or certificate is then recorded with the appropriate county office.

§ 17.8   Legal description of real estate

All real estate must have a means by which it can be uniformly described. This is known as the *legal description*. Do not confuse the legal description with the street address or tax identification number. A complete and accurate legal description is needed for every deed, mortgage, and other formal document required in a real estate transaction.

§ 17.8.1   Legal description of real estate—The government survey

The *government survey* is a description based upon the rectangular survey system, which divides land into a system of squares within squares. The squares are six miles long and six miles wide. These squares are resubdivided into 36 sections (although there are some irregular sections) with each section being one-mile square. Thirty-six sections make up one township. Each section contains 640 acres and is numbered from 1 to 36 running east to west. Townships are separated from each other by range lines which run north and south.

Illustration 17-2 is a diagram of the method of numbering a township.

Illustration 17-2

6	5	4	3	2	1
7	8	9	10	11	12
18	17	16	15	14	13
19	20	21	22	23	24
30	29	28	27	26	25
31	32	33	34	35	36

Township 8 South

Township 9 South

Township 10 South

Range 7 West   Range 6 West   Range 5 West

N

[C4052]

The following shows the relationships involved when the rectangular survey system is used:

1 Range	=	16 Townships
1 Township	=	36 Sections
1 Section	=	640 Acres
1/4 Section	=	160 Acres

Illustration 17-3 is a diagram of a government survey section, showing two methods of division.

Illustration 17-3

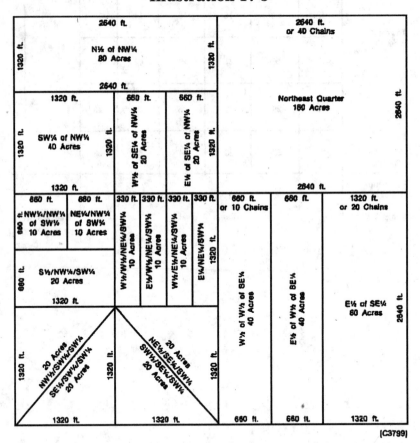

[C3799]

The description prescribed by these original surveys, whether government or state controlled, is the underlying basis for all legal descriptions in use today. For example, a typical original United States Government Survey description would be:

> The Northwest Quarter (NW 1/4) of Section Five (5), Township Fifteen (15) North, Range Three (3) West, Jones County, Any State.

Illustration 17-4

Sec. 5, Twp 15N, Rge. 3W

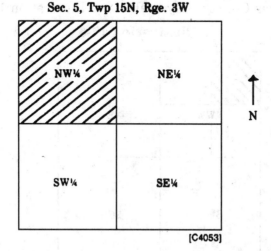

[C4053]

Illustration 17-5 shows the location of this property, a parcel that would consist of 160 acres (a quarter of a section or quarter section). Assume that this parcel is located in an urban area and is sold in increasingly smaller parcels.

EXAMPLE:

The description of a 40-acre tract in the northwest corner would be:

The Northwest Quarter of the Northwest Quarter (NW 1/4 of NW 1/4) of Section Five (5), Township Fifteen (15) North, Range Three (3) West, Jones County, Any State. (See Illustration 17-5.)

Illustration 17-5

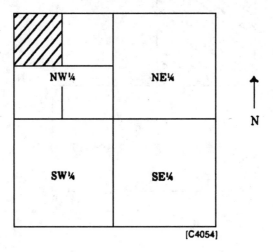

[C4054]

As increasingly smaller tracts are sold, particularly those having irregular boundaries, the legal descriptions become increasingly cumbersome. Simplified methods of describing real estate evolve. Also, as the tracts become smaller and irregularly shaped, it becomes very difficult to locate some of the parcels. Therefore, it is often necessary to have a registered land surveyor actually locate the property and draw a map of the location. To do this, the surveyor makes on-site measurements of the property being surveyed. If reference maps to help determine the physical location of the property cannot be found, property records must be searched to find all sales of parcels in a section and measure those on site before being able to measure the property being surveyed.

§ 17.8.2 Legal description of real estate—Metes and bounds description

The *metes and bounds description* begins at a designated point and proceeds to describe the parcel of land by reference to units of measurement and direction.

Assume that the purchaser of the NW 1/4 of the NW 1/4 in the illustration above erected some fencing that encloses a portion of the 40-acre tract and now wishes to sell that portion. A surveyor establishes a point of beginning and then follows the fencing around the property, carefully measuring distance and direction of each piece of fence until returning to the point of beginning. The description of the property would be as follows:

> Beginning at the Southeast corner of the Northwest Quarter of the Northwest Quarter (NW 1/4 of NW 1/4) of Section Five (5), Township Fifteen (15) North, Range Three (3) West, Jones County, Any State, according to the United States Government Survey thereof; thence proceed west along the south line of the NW 1/4 of NW 1/4 to an intersection with the east line of the west half of said NW 1/4 of NW 1/4; thence north along said east line 357.44 feet to a point and corner; thence south 66° 07'24" East to an intersection with the east line of said NW 1/4 of NW 1/4; thence south along the quarter line 56.7 feet to the point of beginning.

Illustration 17-6 shows where this property is located. The entire quarter section is shown so the property described can be placed in context. An actual survey plat would show only the property enclosed within the fence that is being sold.

Illustration 17-6

Sec. 5, Twp 15 N, Rge. 3 W

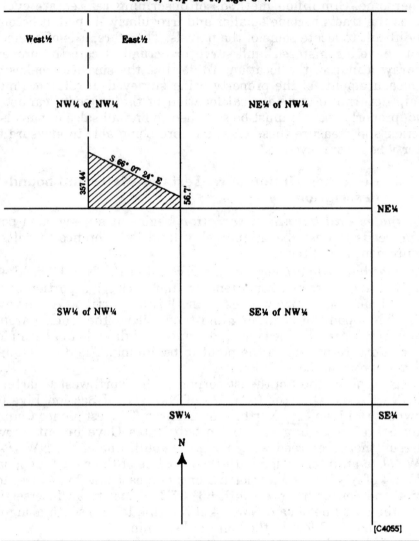

A *metes and bounds* description uses angles or *vectors* (a vector is a direction and distance of a line) to describe the line segments that represent the boundaries of the property being described. The description is actually a group of *calls*, each call describing one line segment. Each call has length and direction. The length is usually given in feet, but it is not unusual to find other units of linear measurement. The direction is given in one of two ways. If the line segment's direction is exactly north, south, east, or west, then N, S, E, or W will accurately describe the direction of the line. If the direction is NE, NW, SE, or SW, then the angle between the line segment and the north-south line must be known. That angle is measured in degrees, minutes, and seconds. If, for instance, the line direction is northwest and the angle between the line and the north-south line is 40, then the description of the line is N 40° W. Note that N 40° W generally describes the direction of the line, and by including *40°* the line is identified uniquely. There is only one line that fits the description. (See Illustration 17-7.)

Illustration 17-7

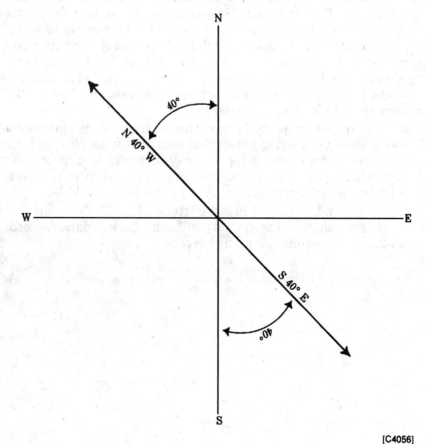

[C4056]

It is interesting to note that a line can be described in either direction. The same line can also be described as S 40°. A metes and bounds property description always proceeds from the point of beginning, around the property (usually clockwise) and back to the point of beginning, carefully and accurately describing each line segment. Once the direction of travel around the property is determined, then each line can no longer be described two ways. It must be described in the direction of travel.

In Illustration 17-6, the fencing that formed the northerly boundary of the property described made an angle of just over 66 degrees with the north/south line. Going around the property clockwise, the call the surveyor used was S 66° 07'24" E. This call did not have a dimension in feet. Nevertheless, the distance can be found because it referred to a quarter-quarter line, which has a specific length.

§ 17.8.3   Legal description of real estate—Recorded plat of subdivision

A *subdivision* is a division of one tract into two or more smaller lots or parcels. The word *subdivision* is also used to designate a development of similar lots for the purpose of constructing residences. A property owner who decides to subdivide property for this purpose is often called a *developer*. The services of a civil engineer may be engaged to map out the subdivision. The map is recorded in the county clerk's office, and the recorded map is then used as the basis for describing the lots in that subdivision.

Since most urban property is now subdivided, this is the predominant means used to describe urban real estate. It is much simpler and less cumbersome than describing property by metes and bounds or by government survey. A typical subdivision plat is shown in Illustration 17-8. A typical legal description in that subdivision would be:

> Lot Twenty-five (25), Block Fourteen (14), Linden Park Addition Division No. 6 to the city of Idaho Falls, Idaho, according to the recorded plat or plan thereof.

Illustration 17-8

LINDEN PARK ADDITION

DIVISION NO. 6
TO
THE CITY OF IDAHO FALLS, IDAHO
Part of
NE 1/4 of Sec. 20 T. 2 N., R. 38 E.B.M.

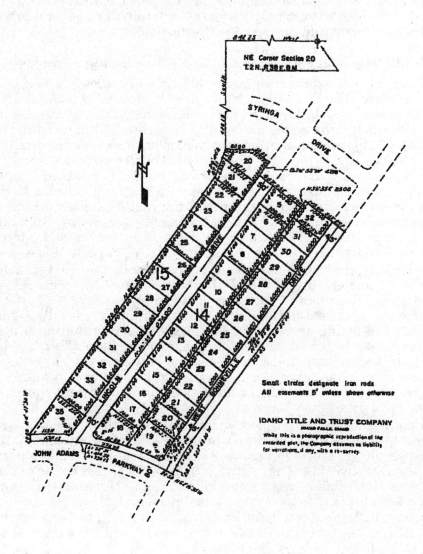

Small circles designate iron rods
All easements 5' unless shown otherwise

IDAHO TITLE AND TRUST COMPANY
IDAHO FALLS, IDAHO
While this is a photographic reproduction of the
recorded plat, the Company assumes no liability
for variations, if any, with a re-survey.

§ 17.9   The real estate transaction

Real estate transactions are frequently complex business transactions involving the buyer, the seller, and a host of supporting players (commercial real estate transactions sometimes involve dozens of buyers and sellers, each with their own supporting cast). The transactions proceed through several steps, can vary significantly with the types of financing involved, and require informed, skilled practitioners in every profession to complete them successfully. The general process and some of its variations are described below.

§ 17.9.1   The real estate transaction—The listing agreement

A typical real estate transaction begins when someone decides to sell property. The prospective seller may enlist the services of a real estate broker to help locate a buyer. Additionally, the real estate broker often helps the seller arrive at a proposed selling price for the property. The broker charges a commission for services, usually a fixed percentage of the sale price or occasionally a flat fee. Once the prospective seller and real estate broker reach an agreement on the terms of the commission, they enter into a contract, called a *listing agreement*, which describes in detail the real estate to be sold; the personal property to be included in the transaction, if any; the asking price; the terms of sale to which the seller is agreeable; and information concerning taxes, assessments, and existing encumbrances.

Ordinarily, the listing agreement is prepared by the real estate broker on a commercially printed form that contains the terms customarily used in that locale. The seller may, however, engage a lawyer to review the proposed listing agreement before it is actually signed. Usually the listing agreement is exclusive, meaning that even if the owner finds a buyer while the listing agreement is in effect, the broker must be paid a commission. When the listing agreement is nonexclusive, the broker only earns a commission if the broker procures the buyer. Thereafter, the broker advertises, promotes, and shows the property to prospective buyers.

It is not unusual for prospective buyers to seek the services of a real estate broker to help them find property. This is particularly true when people are moving to another state or are interested in a particular kind of investment property. In many areas, real estate brokers exchange information concerning all listings in the area (sometimes called a multiple listing service), thus broadening the exposure of the property. If the property is ultimately sold to a client of another broker, that broker is said to be the selling broker, while the original broker is the listing broker. The broker may act as the buyer's agent or as another agent of the seller.

§ 17.9.2   The real estate transaction—The purchase agreement

When a prospective buyer becomes interested in the property, an offer is made to the seller. If the property is exclusively listed with a real estate broker, the prospective buyer makes the offer through the broker, who then relays the offer to the seller. The purchaser's offer usually includes a proposed price and a method of proposed payment. If the prospective buyer and seller reach an agreement, that agreement is reduced to writing in the form of a ***purchase agreement***, also referred to as a ***memorandum sale agreement, purchase offer,* offer to purchase, or *earnest money contract***. This document may be prepared by a lawyer, a real estate broker, or by the parties themselves. The purchase agreement is a contract, and it must meet all legal requirements for a contract. It includes such information as:

- Full names and marital status of the seller(s)
- Full names of the buyer(s)
- Addresses of the parties
- Legal and common (street address) description of the property
- Personal property to be included in the transaction (draperies, appliances, or similar items)
- Sale price
- Terms and conditions of the sale including financing arrangements or contingencies
- Type of deed required
- Evidence of title to be provided

The closing and possession dates and any other special provisions or conditions of the transaction should be clearly set forth in the purchase agreement. A down payment, referred to as ***earnest money***, is usually required from the buyer. The down payment typically is deposited in the trust account of either the lawyer for the seller or the broker or in an escrow account at an escrow or title company pending the closing of the transaction. As the parties negotiate the terms, the purchase agreement may be revised extensively before its final execution, since this document controls the consummation of the transaction. Frequently, lawyers for both parties review it and suggest changes. If a real estate broker is involved in the transaction, most of the basic information concerning the property will be provided by the broker. A broker may also assist the buyer with financing arrangements.

§ 17.9.3 The real estate transaction—Financing arrangements

Once a seller and buyer have reached an agreement on the terms of the transaction, the buyer must get the money to buy the property. It is not uncommon for a purchase agreement to be conditioned upon the purchaser's ability to secure financing. The buyer usually arranges financing either through a commercial lending institution. However, in some transactions, the buyer may arrange financing directly with the seller.

§ 17.9.4   The real estate transaction—Conventional financing

Local banks and savings institutions often have funds available for residential purchase financing. This type of financing is referred to as conventional financing. Some *conventional financing* allows for assumption of the financing by a subsequent purchaser of the property, subject to the bank's approval.

§ 17.9.5   The real estate transaction—FHA and VA financing

Assuming a buyer qualifies, financing through government agencies, such as the *Department of Veterans Affairs* (VA) or the *Federal Housing Administration* (FHA), can be secured. These loans require little or no cash down payment and have less restrictive financial qualifications than conventional loans. VA loans are available only to veterans and to surviving spouses of servicemen who died while on active duty.

VA and FHA loans are processed through local lending institutions, but the guarantee extended by the VA or FHA ensures that the local lender suffers no financial loss in the event the buyer defaults on the loan. The *Federal National Mortgage Association* (FNMA) offers a similar guarantee to local lenders on qualified conventional loans.

§ 17.9.6   The real estate transaction—The loan application

Regardless of the type of loan, the buyer's application for the loan is processed through a lending institution. To process a homebuyer's application, the lender accumulates financial and personal data to determine whether the homebuyer qualifies for the kind and amount of loan desired.

§ 17.9.7   The real estate transaction—Private financing

It is possible for the buyer to arrange for payment of the purchase price without securing commercial financing. Sometimes the seller is in a position to help with the financing. It is common for some type of financing already to be in existence on the property. In such a case, the buyer may be able to assume the existing financing. The existing financing is most commonly found in the form of a commercial loan the seller made when originally purchasing the property. That loan would be guaranteed by a mortgage on the property.

The most common methods of private financing are:

- Assumption of an existing mortgage
- Installment real estate contract, with or without an escrow
- Purchase money mortgage
- Deed of trust

§ 17.10   Documenting the real estate transaction

Under the statute of frauds, all real estate transactions must be in writing. As a practical matter, however, there is very little risk that a real estate transaction could be done any other way. The documents required in real estate transactions vary greatly. The lawyer's assistant should develop a checklist of items required in various types of transactions. A commercial real estate transaction, such as an apartment complex or office building, could easily require more than 25 different documents, while a transaction involving a home or vacant land could involve fewer than five. All real estate transactions require some form of conveyance document and a closing statement. All except cash transactions require financing documents.

If a real estate broker is involved, the broker's firm may have a closing department that submits drafts of documents to lawyers for both the buyer and the seller. The real estate firm may also act as an intermediary with any lending institution. In some states, lending institutions or title insurance companies prepare the loan documentation, while in other states, lawyers prepare all loan documents.

§ 17.10.1 Documenting the real estate transaction—The cash transaction

If a purchaser is buying the property for cash, no financing documents need to be prepared. A deed, typically a warranty deed, is prepared. This is a fill-in-the-blank form that can be computer-generated or purchased at a legal stationer. The printed language in the form is important, and the lawyer should verify that the correct form is used.

The other key document to prepare for the cash transaction is the closing statement. It will be a much simpler form than the example shown in Illustration 17-9 because of the nature of a cash transaction, but the same principles apply to the preparation of all closing statements.

§ 17.10.2 Documenting the real estate transaction—The sale with assumption of mortgage

In a transaction involving an assumption, the buyer pays cash down equal to the sales price less the balance of the existing mortgage and thereafter makes all payments under the terms of the mortgage. For example, if a buyer pays $50,000 for a house having a $15,000 mortgage, the earnest money and cash at closing total $35,000.

If an assumption is planned, the lawyer or broker verifies prior to the closing that an assumption is possible. Most commercial mortgages specifically prohibit assumption, and even if the purchase agreement provides for assumption of the mortgage, the sale may not be possible if this is the case. Although the lawyer often determines this fact during the examination of the title, it may come to light when the lawyer's or broker's office contacts the mortgage company for assumption information.

The lawyer's assistant helping to process this type of sale to closing will contact the mortgage company for the necessary assumption information. The law office may have a form letter developed for this purpose, but if not, the assistant should ask the lawyer to help develop such a form. The mortgage company will be requested for the balance due on the loan, the amount of the monthly payments, the balance being held by the company in any escrow accounts, and the status of both the monthly payment and any escrow accounts.

Since the sale documents cannot be prepared without this information, the request should be made as soon as possible. A good rule of thumb is to write the mortgage company when the file is opened and order whatever abstract work must be done. The lawyer will probably order the abstract work until the assistant becomes familiar with the procedures or will give instructions on how to do this. If the mortgage cannot be assumed, the mortgage company will advise the lawyer of this in response to the request for information. In most mortgages, the balance owed under the mortgage is due on sale of the property, and the lender reserves the right to approve any prospective buyer in the event of a sale with an assumption. Most real estate brokers know the local lenders that require this and often coordinate securing lender approval of the prospective buyer before the file reaches the lawyer's office. If the broker does not do this, the lender will notify the lawyer of this requirement in response to the request for an assumption statement.

§ 17.10.3 Documenting the real estate transaction—The assumption closing statement

There are a few elements of the closing statement that are peculiar to the assumption sale:

- Most lenders charge an assumption or transfer fee. The amount of the fee varies greatly, and the lender's assumption statement will indicate the amount.
- It is important to verify that the monthly installments on the loan are up to date, and if not, those payments must be collected from the seller.
- The escrow account is for the payment of property taxes and hazard and extended insurance (protection against fire, wind damage, hail, and other perils of nature). The monthly payments include one-twelfth of the property taxes and one-twelfth of the insurance policy premium. The lender directs the payment of property taxes and insurance from the money in the escrow account. Sometimes there is not enough money in the escrow account to pay the amount of the taxes or insurance, so the lender overdraws the account. This creates an escrow shortage, and the lender usually requires funds to bring this account current in the event of an assumption.

Although the buyer usually pays the transfer fee and lawyer's fees for an assumption and the seller must pay to bring the loan and escrow account current, all closing costs in connection with an assumption of mortgage are negotiable; therefore, it is necessary to refer to the purchase agreement to determine who is paying which costs. Since insurance is usually paid in advance, sometimes the amount of the insurance premium is prorated, and the buyer pays the seller for the unused portion of the insurance premium if the insurance policy is being transferred in the sale. Property taxes are handled the same way, but in most areas, property taxes are paid after they have accrued, and the taxes will be prorated accordingly. These items should be handled in keeping with local practice, and the lawyer will need to be closely involved in preparing the assumption closing statement.

§ 17.10.4 Documenting the real estate transaction— Installment real estate contract

An *installment real estate contract*, also called a *land contract* or a *contract for deed*, is an agreement between the seller and the buyer for the purchase of real estate over a period of time by making installment payments with interest. The buyer takes possession of the property and becomes responsible for payment of taxes, insurance coverage, maintenance of the property, and any other conditions set forth in the contract, but the seller retains title to the premises until the price is paid in full. The contract is recorded in order that anyone searching title can ascertain the buyer's interest in the property. Upon the buyer's completion of the contract, the buyer receives a deed giving them title to the property. In some states, to ensure the performance of the seller, the signed deed is placed in escrow until consummation of the contract.

The use of an installment contract provides the parties with a great deal of flexibility in structuring the financing for the real estate transaction. It often provides the seller with the opportunity for more favorable income tax treatment. Advantages to the buyer may include a lower interest rate than that available from commercial lending institutions and lower payments in the early years of ownership through the use of a balloon payment. A *balloon payment* is a provision that provides for payment in full of any unpaid balance a certain number of years from the date of the contract, typically five to ten years, but the payments are calculated as though the loan were for a longer period of time.

§ 17.10.5 Documenting the real estate transaction—Escrow agreement for installment real estate contract

The *escrow agent* (usually a bank, a title company, or an attorney) serves as a trustee for certain documents (warranty deed executed by the seller, fire and extended coverage insurance policy, or abstract of title). The escrow agent collects payments from the buyer and puts them in the seller's account. When the total due has been paid, all documents are delivered to the buyer, and the warranty deed that the agent was holding in trust is recorded. The escrow agent charges a monthly fee for this service. Who pays the fee is negotiable, but it is often paid one-half by the seller and one-half by the buyer. If payments are not made as required, the escrow agent gives notice of default to the buyer upon the request of the seller. The agreement often provides that if a lawyer is retained by the seller or the escrow agent to collect on the default, the buyer must pay the lawyer's fee.

All provisions of the agreement between the buyer and the seller are set out in an *escrow agreement* signed by all parties and acknowledged before a notary public. The escrow agreement contains provisions that generally protect both the seller and the buyer. When the contract is paid, the buyer does not have to locate the seller for execution of a deed. The seller is protected because title is retained until full payment for the property has been received.

§ 17.10.6   Documenting the real estate transaction—Purchase money mortgage

A *purchase money mortgage* is a mortgage given by a buyer to a seller to secure a portion of the purchase price. Although the buyer pays an agreed portion of the price in cash, this kind of sale is generally referred to as a credit sale. Since the seller does not receive full payment for the property until later, the property is considered sold on credit. The transaction is directly between the buyer and seller. The seller gives a deed to the buyer at closing, and the buyer gives the seller a mortgage just as if the loan were obtained from a commercial lending institution.

If the financing on the transaction is being handled by the seller, the lawyer's office will likely prepare the documentation for both the deed and the mortgage. The kind of instrument used in this kind of transaction varies a great deal, but the law firm will already have on hand the kind of form it prefers to use. Generally, the buyer pays the seller in monthly installments over a specified period of time just as if dealing with a commercial lender. The buyer executes a promissory note and a mortgage in favor of the seller. These evidence the debt to the seller and also provide the seller with security on the debt.

§ 17.10.7   Documenting the real estate transaction—Mortgage and note for purchase money mortgage

Once a buyer's loan application has been approved, the lender issues closing instructions that advise the closing lawyer or title company of its requirements in connection with the loan. The duties of the closing lawyer may include preparation of the security instruments required by the lender. The *promissory note*, a note for the amount of the purchase, and mortgage are prepared on preprinted or computer-generated forms provided by the lending institution or on commercially prepared forms. In the case of FHA or VA insured loans, the note and mortgage are prepared on forms provided by the FHA or

VA. Until the lawyer's assistant is able to differentiate among the various forms, he or she should request the lawyer to specify the forms needed for a particular transaction.

The person obligated to pay the amount of the promissory note is the *maker*, while the person or entity to whom the payment is made is the *payee*. Many of the terms of the promissory note are requirements of the lending institution and are provided to the lawyer in writing. The mortgage is prepared using the information contained in the promissory note and deed for the parties' names and the legal description. The mortgage secures payment of the promissory note by the maker. The person executing the mortgage and granting the security in the real estate is called the *mortgagor*, while the lending institution is the *mortgagee*. A lending institution usually requires that its mortgage be the first lien against the premises, so the mortgage is generally recorded immediately after the deed is recorded. Should the mortgagor grant a subsequent or second mortgage on the premises, another promissory note and mortgage would be executed in compliance with the terms set forth by the lending institution or the individual taking the second mortgage.

The preparation of the mortgage documents follows the same principles as set forth below for the preparation of deeds. In addition, the mortgage may contain the terms of the loan as they appear in the promissory note. A mortgage and promissory note are executed only by the mortgagor in the same manner as deeds are executed.

§ 17.10.8 Documenting the real estate transaction—Deed of trust

In some states, lending institutions hold a deed of trust to the property rather than a mortgage. They lend the money to the buyer. The buyer executes a deed of trust transferring the property in trust to the lending institution as security for the loan. In many states, only certain individuals or entities, such as a title company, bank, lending institution, or lawyer can serve as trustee. Normally the trustee is either an officer of or the lawyer for the lending institution. When the institution has been paid in full, the trustee executes a *deed of release and reconveyance*, returning title of the property to the buyer.

§ 17.11 Preparation of deeds

Regardless of the type of deed to be used in a given transaction, the preparation of deeds must be done precisely and with great attention to detail. Deeds should not contain any visible typographical corrections. In some jurisdictions, deeds containing such corrections are not recordable. The guidelines to be followed in the preparation of deeds are:

- The name of the seller must appear on the deed exactly as title was taken to the property. If the name of a seller appears in a different form on different documents, the preferred usage should be followed by the variant.

EXAMPLE:

John A. Smith a/k/a Jon A. Smith; or Florence A. Jones formerly Florence A. Smith.

- It may be necessary for the spouse of the seller to join in the conveyance and execute the deed even if the spouse is not listed as the title holder in the title evidence. (This requirement may vary from state to state.)
- The marital status of the seller must be shown.

EXAMPLE:

John A. Smith and Florence A. Smith, husband and wife; or John A. Smith, a single person.

- If the seller is a corporation or a partnership, its name should be used as set forth in its articles of incorporation or articles of partnership.

EXAMPLE:

A.B.C. Inc., an Any State corporation; or Jones and Smith Company, an Any State general partnership.

- If the seller is a trust, that fact should be shown.

EXAMPLE:

Jack Smith, Trustee under Agreement with Donald Smith, dated January 15, 1986.

- The buyer's name should appear exactly as the buyer desires to take title. The lawyer's assistant should verify the correct spelling of the names of all buyers.
- The deed must contain the exact legal description of the property being conveyed. The legal description should be taken from the title opinion or title insurance binder or commitment. Never rely upon a legal description taken from a tax statement. The legal description should be carefully proofread, preferably by reading it out loud to another lawyer's assistant, and all punctuation and capitalization must be exact. The lawyer's assistant should not alter a single character of any legal description, even if it appears to be incorrect, without discussing the change with the lawyer first.
- A deed is signed only by the seller. The name of the seller should be typed beneath the appropriate signature line. In some states this is mandatory.

- Some states require that witnesses sign the deed as well. It is helpful if the witnesses' names are printed beneath their signatures.
- A deed must be acknowledged by a notary public or other authorized person. The name of the grantor must appear in the acknowledgment exactly as it appears in the body of the deed. The notary public must date, sign, and affix the official notary seal to the deed. Some states also require that the notary's area of commission and the expiration date of the commission appear on the deed.
- Many states require that the deed indicate the name and address of the person or firm drafting the deed and the name and address of the person or entity to whom future tax statements should be directed. Since this is often the buyer, the address can be placed after the buyer's name.
- Some states require that the consideration shown on the warranty deed be the amount of the purchase price. In other states, a nominal consideration (usually $10) is stated along with the phrase "and other good and valuable consideration," but for tax purposes, the total consideration must be disclosed.
- Consideration on a quitclaim deed is usually a nominal amount, such as $1.

§ 17.12   The real estate closing

The **closing** is the formal meeting of all parties to the transaction at which documents are executed and funds disbursed. In some states, closings are handled by title companies in their offices. In other states, they are handled by law firms, lending institutions, or closers employed by a real estate broker. Occasionally, there is no formal closing with all parties being in attendance at the same time; rather, the parties individually deposit other closing deliveries, together with a closing instruction letter addressed to the title company or lawyers handling the transaction that details the conditions under which the deliveries may be released to the other party or for filing. When all title matters are resolved, documents prepared, and financing arrangements finalized, a time for the closing is set. The lawyer carefully explains the meaning of each of the documents, supervises their execution, and sometimes disburses sale funds to the client through their trust account if a closing or escrow agent is not involved.

The **closing statement** is a detailed accounting of the credits and charges to the buyer and seller. In preparing the closing statement, the purchase agreement serves as the guideline for determining prorations and payoff figures. Illustrations 17-9 and 17-10 are sample buyer's and seller's closing statements. It should be noted that the earnest money or down payment is deducted from the purchase price. It is held in the trust account of the real estate broker or by the lawyer for the seller if no real estate broker is involved or by the title company and released to seller or buyer in accordance with the terms of the purchase agreement.

Probably the most commonly used closing statement form is the HUD-1 Settlement Statement issued by the United States Department of Housing and Urban Development. It is designed to meet the requirements of the federal Real Estate Procedures Act (RESPA). (See Illustration 17-11.)

Illustration 17-9

BUYER'S CLOSING STATEMENT

Seller: John Doe
Buyer: David Smith
Property: Lot 1, Block 2, Marigold Addition
Date: September 15, 20xx

Item	Debits	Credits
Purchase Price	$50,000.00	$
Earnest Money		5,000.00
First Mortgage Assumed		35,000.00
Interest		
15 days at $7.67		115.05
Transfer tax		33.00
Abstracting charges		56.00
20xx real estate tax adjustment $750.00 ÷ 365 × 107 days =		219.35
Cash at closing		9,576.60
	$50,000.00	$50,000.00

Accepted:

_____   _____
Buyer   Seller

Note: The foregoing represents a simple buyer's closing statement and accordingly would not reflect such items as broker's commissions, and so forth. These would be contained in a separate seller's closing statement.

Buyer's credits against the purchase price may include adjustments for:

- Accrued real estate taxes for the year in which the transaction occurs (as designated in the purchase agreement).
- Special assessments (as provided for in the purchase agreement).
- Unearned rent for the remainder of the month (if the property is a rental unit).
- The amount to be carried on contract or the balance of the mortgage (if the transaction involves an installment contract or a mortgage assumption).
- Services rendered in repairing certain items on the premises or improvements made prior to closing.
- Discount points that the seller may be required to pay in order for buyer to obtain financing.

Buyer's expenses (debits) may include adjustments for:
- Lawyer's fees for examination of the title and preparation of title opinion.
- Preparation of the promissory note, mortgage, and other financing documents required for the closing.
- Closing services.
- Recording fees for the deed and mortgage.
- Mortgage registration tax.
- Abstracting expenses.
- Origination charge or service fee imposed by the lending institution according to the terms of the loan.
- Interest on the new loan should the lending institution require it.

EXAMPLE:

A transaction is closed on January 20. The first mortgage payment is due on March 1. The lender may require that interest accruing on the loan from January 20 through January 31 be paid at closing. (February interest is paid in the March 1 payment.)

- Any other expenses incurred by the buyer prior to closing

Illustration 17-10

SELLER's CLOSING STATEMENT

Seller:	John Doe
Buyer:	David Smith
Property:	Lot 1, Block 2, Marigold Addition, Street Address, City, State
Date:	September 15, 20xx

Item	Debits	Credits
Purchase Price	$	$50,000.00
Existing Mortgage Assumed	35,000.00	
Interest adjustment 15 days at $7.67	115.05	
Transfer tax	33.00	
Abstracting charges	56.00	
20xx real estate tax adjustment $750.00 ÷ 365 × 107 days =	219.35	
Real estate commission	3,500.00	
Balance due Seller	11,076.60	
	$50,000.00	$50,000.00

Accepted:

_____   _____

Buyer   Seller

Note: Earnest money paid by the buyer is normally held in the broker's trust account pending closing. In this example, the seller will receive $9,576.60 from the buyer and the balance from the broker's trust account after deduction is made for the real estate commission.

The seller might receive credit for:
- Unearned insurance premiums (should a buyer assume existing insurance coverage).
- Insurance reserves or escrows being held by a lending institution (on a mortgage assumption).

The seller's expenses usually include:
- The broker's commission.
- Abstracting charges.
- Recording charges for a release of mortgage or any documents necessary to clear title defects.

- Lawyer's fees applicable to seller for preparing a contract, deed, closing statement, and attendance at the closing.
- Transfer tax, if required by the city, county, or state in which the transaction is being closed.
- The balance due on any outstanding contract, including interest up to the date of payment, or the balance due on a mortgage, including interest up to the date of payoff.
- Any other expenses or liens as outlined or required by the purchase agreement, such as inspection fees, repair costs, and similar items.

A contract payoff is obtained from the contract seller or his agent, and a mortgage payoff with per diem interest is available from the lending institution holding the mortgage.

Other adjustments might be necessary to a closing statement, depending upon the particular transaction and the terms of the purchase agreement.

Illustration 17-11

OMB Approval No. 2502-0265

 A. **Settlement Statement (HUD-1)**

B. Type of Loan				
1. ☐ FHA 2. ☐ RHS 3. ☐ Conv. Unins.	6. File Number:	7. Loan Number:	8. Mortgage Insurance Case Number:	
4. ☐ VA 5. ☐ Conv. Ins.				

C. Note: This form is furnished to give you a statement of actual settlement costs. Amounts paid to and by the settlement agent are shown. Items marked "(p.o.c.)" were paid outside the closing; they are shown here for informational purposes and are not included in the totals.

D. Name & Address of Borrower:	E. Name & Address of Seller:	F. Name & Address of Lender:
G. Property Location:	H. Settlement Agent:	I. Settlement Date:
	Place of Settlement:	

J. Summary of Borrower's Transaction		K. Summary of Seller's Transaction	
100. Gross Amount Due from Borrower		**400. Gross Amount Due to Seller**	
101. Contract sales price		401. Contract sales price	
102. Personal property		402. Personal property	
103. Settlement charges to borrower (line 1400)		403.	
104.		404.	
105.		405.	
Adjustment for items paid by seller in advance		**Adjustment for items paid by seller in advance**	
106. City/town taxes to		406. City/town taxes to	
107. County taxes to		407. County taxes to	
108. Assessments to		408. Assessments to	
109.		409.	
110.		410.	
111.		411.	
112.		412.	
120. Gross Amount Due from Borrower		**420. Gross Amount Due to Seller**	
200. Amount Paid by or in Behalf of Borrower		**500. Reductions In Amount Due to seller**	
201. Deposit or earnest money		501. Excess deposit (see instructions)	
202. Principal amount of new loan(s)		502. Settlement charges to seller (line 1400)	
203. Existing loan(s) taken subject to		503. Existing loan(s) taken subject to	
204.		504. Payoff of first mortgage loan	
205.		505. Payoff of second mortgage loan	
206.		506.	
207.		507.	
208.		508.	
209.		509.	
Adjustments for items unpaid by seller		**Adjustments for items unpaid by seller**	
210. City/town taxes to		510. City/town taxes to	
211. County taxes to		511. County taxes to	
212. Assessments to		512. Assessments to	
213.		513.	
214.		514.	
215.		515.	
216.		516.	
217.		517.	
218.		518.	
219.		519.	
220. Total Paid by/for Borrower		**520. Total Reduction Amount Due Seller**	
300. Cash at Settlement from/to Borrower		**600. Cash at Settlement to/from Seller**	
301. Gross amount due from borrower (line 120)		601. Gross amount due to seller (line 420)	
302. Less amounts paid by/for borrower (line 220)	( )	602. Less reductions in amounts due seller (line 520)	( )
303. Cash ☐ From ☐ To Borrower		**603. Cash** ☐ To ☐ From Seller	

The Public Reporting Burden for this collection of information is estimated at 35 minutes per response for collecting, reviewing, and reporting the data. This agency may not collect this information, and you are not required to complete this form, unless it displays a currently valid OMB control number. No confidentiality is assured; this disclosure is mandatory. This is designed to provide the parties to a RESPA covered transaction with information during the settlement process.

L. Settlement Charges		
	Paid From Borrower's Funds at Settlement	Paid From Seller's Funds at Settlement
700. Total Real Estate Broker Fees		
Division of commission (line 700) as follows :		
701. $ to		
702. $ to		
703. Commission paid at settlement		
704.		
800. Items Payable in Connection with Loan		
801. Our origination charge $ (from GFE #1)		
802. Your credit or charge (points) for the specific interest rate chosen $ (from GFE #2)		
803. Your adjusted origination charges (from GFE #A)		
804. Appraisal fee to (from GFE #3)		
805. Credit report to (from GFE #3)		
806. Tax service to (from GFE #3)		
807. Flood certification to (from GFE #3)		
808.		
809.		
810.		
811.		
900. Items Required by Lender to be Paid in Advance		
901. Daily interest charges from to @ $ /day (from GFE #10)		
902. Mortgage insurance premium for months to (from GFE #3)		
903. Homeowner's insurance for years to (from GFE #11)		
904.		
1000. Reserves Deposited with Lender		
1001. Initial deposit for your escrow account (from GFE #9)		
1002. Homeowner's insurance months @ $ per month $		
1003. Mortgage insurance months @ $ per month $		
1004. Property Taxes months @ $ per month $		
1005. months @ $ per month $		
1006. months @ $ per month $		
1007. Aggregate Adjustment -$		
1100. Title Charges		
1101. Title services and lender's title insurance (from GFE #4)		
1102. Settlement or closing fee $		
1103. Owner's title insurance (from GFE #5)		
1104. Lender's title insurance $		
1105. Lender's title policy limit $		
1106. Owner's title policy limit $		
1107. Agent's portion of the total title insurance premium to $		
1108. Underwriter's portion of the total title insurance premium to $		
1109.		
1110.		
1111.		
1200. Government Recording and Transfer Charges		
1201. Government recording charges (from GFE #7)		
1202. Deed $ Mortgage $ Release $		
1203. Transfer taxes (from GFE #8)		
1204. City/County tax/stamps Deed $ Mortgage $		
1205. State tax/stamps Deed $ Mortgage $		
1206.		
1300. Additional Settlement Charges		
1301. Required services that you can shop for (from GFE #6)		
1302. $		
1303. $		
1304.		
1305.		
1400. Total Settlement Charges (enter on lines 103, Section J and 502, Section K)		

531

Comparison of Good Faith Estimate (GFE) and HUD-1 Charges		Good Faith Estimate	HUD-1
Charges That Cannot Increase	HUD-1 Line Number		
Our origination charge	# 801		
Your credit or charge (points) for the specific interest rate chosen	# 802		
Your adjusted origination charges	# 803		
Transfer taxes	# 1203		

Charges That In Total Cannot Increase More Than 10%		Good Faith Estimate	HUD-1
Government recording charges	# 1201		
	#		
	#		
	#		
	#		
	#		
	#		
	Total		
Increase between GFE and HUD-1 Charges		$ or %	

Charges That Can Change		Good Faith Estimate	HUD-1
Initial deposit for your escrow account	# 1001		
Daily interest charges $ /day	# 901		
Homeowner's insurance	# 903		
	#		
	#		
	#		

Loan Terms

Your initial loan amount is	$
Your loan term is	years
Your initial interest rate is	%
Your initial monthly amount owed for principal, interest, and any mortgage insurance is	$ includes ☐ Principal ☐ Interest ☐ Mortgage Insurance
Can your interest rate rise?	☐ No ☐ Yes, it can rise to a maximum of % . The first change will be on and can change again every after . Every change date, your interest rate can increase or decrease by %. Over the life of the loan, your interest rate is guaranteed to never be **lower** than % or **higher** than %.
Even if you make payments on time, can your loan balance rise?	☐ No ☐ Yes, it can rise to a maximum of $
Even if you make payments on time, can your monthly amount owed for principal, interest, and mortgage insurance rise?	☐ No ☐ Yes, the first increase can be on and the monthly amount owed can rise to $. The maximum it can ever rise to is $
Does your loan have a prepayment penalty?	☐ No ☐ Yes, your maximum prepayment penalty is $
Does your loan have a balloon payment?	☐ No ☐ Yes, you have a balloon payment of $ due in years on
Total monthly amount owed including escrow account payments	☐ You do not have a monthly escrow payment for items, such as property taxes and homeowner's insurance. You must pay these items directly yourself. ☐ You have an additional monthly escrow payment of $ that results in a total initial monthly amount owed of $. This includes principal, interest, any mortgage insurance and any items checked below: ☐ Property taxes ☐ Homeowner's insurance ☐ Flood insurance ☐ ☐ ☐

Note: If you have any questions about the Settlement Charges and Loan Terms listed on this form, please contact your lender.

§ 17.12.1 The real estate closing—Recording of documents

Transfer of title occurs at the time an executed deed is delivered to and accepted by the buyer or agent. A security interest (mortgage or other financing arrangement) becomes effective at the time the documents are executed and the funds disbursed. Recording is not necessary to complete the transfer of title between the parties; however, it is necessary to protect the buyer against a second fraudulent sale by the seller and against any liens that may accrue against the property while it is still recorded in the seller's name. Likewise, the mortgagee will want to have its security interest recorded to protect it from subsequent security interests. Hence, the time of recording becomes essential in determining the priority of each of the liens or claims against the real estate. It is important, therefore, to record documents as soon as possible after the completion of a transaction.

The recording of documents is a function that will frequently be delegated to the lawyer's assistant. The requirements for recording and fees charged for recording vary greatly from state to state and county to county. In some states, documents are returned to the person filing them after the recording process is complete, while in other states they are not. Documents filed under the Torrens system are never returned to the filer.

§ 17.12.2 The real estate closing—The role of the investor

Although the majority of residential financing is originated on the local level, unless the financing is arranged through a local lender, once the loan has been made and the legal work completed, the loan is often sold to an investor. This is particularly common with VA and FNMA loans. The investor may retain the local lender to service the loan or collect the monthly payment from the buyer and handle any day-to-day problems that arise. Most mortgagors are not even aware that their loans are not owned by the lender servicing them.

§ 17.13 Other areas of real estate practice

The practice of real estate law is not limited to the representation of clients buying or selling property. Other common real estate law issues include real estate exchanges, leases, and litigation.

§ 17.13.1 Other areas of real estate practice—Exchanges of real estate

To delay the payment of taxes, sometimes owners of real estate will exchange one piece of real estate for another. These transactions are referred to as *like-kind exchanges* or *1031 exchanges*. Real estate can be exchanged directly between owners, but more often an intermediary is used to facilitate a like-kind exchange. The tax code governs the timing and methods of like-kind exchanges.

§ 17.13.2　Other areas of real estate practice—Leases

A *lease* is a contract between the *landlord* (*lessor*) and the *tenant* (*lessee*) whereby the landlord conveys the use of real estate to another for a specific term at a particular rent subject to certain conditions. Many commercially printed lease forms are available from legal stationers. These forms may be used in their entirety or may be used in part to create custom-drafted instruments, depending upon the needs of the client. A lawyer drafts the lease to protect the client and includes those clauses and phrases beneficial to the client. Commercially printed lease forms generally favor the landlord. Certain statutory provisions and court decisions also govern the rights of the landlord and tenant in such contracts. A lease also contains specific provisions relating to the permitted use of the premises during the term of the lease.

§ 17.13.3　Other areas of real estate practice—Real estate in litigation

Real estate may also become the subject of litigation. One of the most common reasons a lawsuit is brought is to establish the proper ownership of a parcel of real estate that has not been registered. Usually such a lawsuit has its basis in a title defect. A lawsuit of this kind is called an *action to quiet title*. Lawsuits may also result from boundary disputes, fraudulent conveyances, or misrepresentations made during a sale.

§ 17.14　Summary

The foregoing is by no means exhaustive of all real estate matters the lawyer's assistant will encounter. With the economic upheavals in late 2008 and early 2009 and the continuing economic difficulties, some of which centered on mortgage transactions and investments, increased and continued government regulation of real estate transactions and their financing is likely. At the same time, continuing concern with the needs of homeowners and the condition of the housing industry has generated and is likely to continue to generate a number of programs to assist the homebuyer in purchasing or refinancing a home. Every transaction in which a lawyer's assistant is involved may involve new procedures. As the assistant's skills and knowledge increase, the lawyer's assistant can become highly valuable to the real estate lawyer.

Chapter 18

Estate Planning

> **KeyCite®:** Cases and other legal materials listed in KeyCite Scope can be researched through the KeyCite service on Westlaw®. Use KeyCite to check citations for form, parallel references, prior and later history, and comprehensive citator information, including citations to other decisions and secondary materials.

§ 18.1 Introduction

The area of law dealing with the disposition of a person's property after a person's death is known as *estate planning*. The estate planning lawyer can tailor a plan to achieve the client's desired distribution of property while minimizing estate taxes and administration expenses.

The most common document used in estate planning is the last will and testament, or more simply, a *will*. However, many people create living trusts which enable them to avoid probate of their assets upon death and the necessity of having to establish a guardianship or conservatorship during their lifetime, should they become incapacitated. The trust agreement can minimize estate taxes and meet the special needs of the trustor or trustor's family. Both wills and trusts have their places in estate planning, and even if a trust is executed and funded, it is still important for the testator to execute a will to take care of any assets that may not have been transferred to the trust.

§ 18.2 Importance of accuracy and proper execution

A will or trust agreement is one of the most important legal documents prepared in the law office. Not only is it extremely important that it be prepared properly, but it must be executed with care to protect the party making the will or trust. An error or omission could result in a lawsuit and expenditures of large sums for lawyer's fees and court costs, and even worse, the wishes of the decedent might not be carried out.

§ 18.3 Terminology

A *will* is a legal document in which a person provides for the disposition of their property to take effect after death. A *testator* is a person who makes a will.

Those persons named in a will to receive property are *beneficiaries*. Gifts of real estate by will are *devises*, and the recipients of such gifts are *devisees*. Personal property transferred by will is known as a *bequest*. Money passing under a will is known as a *legacy* and the recipient as a *legatee*; however, the words *legacy* and *legatee* are commonly used to refer to gifts of other kinds of personal property as well. In states that have adopted the Uniform Probate Code, all recipients of property under a will are referred to as *devisees*, regardless of whether they receive real or personal property. More information concerning the Uniform Probate Code is given in Chapter 19, Estates and Guardianships.

If a testator gives away specific property in testator's will but no longer owns the property at the time of death, an *ademption* occurs. This means that legacy is extinguished, and that provision of the will can be ignored. The remainder of the will is not affected by the ademption.

In addition to the distribution of the property, the testator also names a person or persons or an entity (usually a bank with a trust department or independent trust company) to administer the terms of the will and distribute the estate. That person or entity is called the *executor*. Under the Uniform Probate Code, the person or entity is referred to as the *personal representative*. If the testator has minor children, he or she may also designate a guardian for those children. The supervision of an estate by an administrator or executor is called an *administration*.

A person who dies having made no will is referred to as having died *intestate*. If a person dies without a will, the court probate process is called an *administration*, and the fiduciary appointed by the court is called an *administrator*.

A trust creates a fiduciary relationship with regard to property wherein the legal title is in the trustee, but the benefit of ownership is in another person. A trust must be intentionally created. The person who benefits from the trust is called the *beneficiary*. The maker of the trust is called a *grantor, trustor*, or *settlor*. The administration of a trust imposes fiduciary duties on the trustee.

§ 18.4   Power and capacity to make a will

In order for a will to be valid, the testator must have both the power and capacity to make a will. In most states, a person who has reached legal age has the power to make a will. Generally, minors and adults under legal disability (incapacitated or incompetent) do not possess the power to make a will. Possession of the requisite capacity to make a will means that the testator is of sound mind, knows the extent of the testator's assets, who their natural heirs are, the disposition to be made of any personal assets, and that the testator intends to make a will.

§ 18.5   Characteristics of a will

Certain requirements control the preparation of all wills:

- Opening clause (preamble) stating domicile and declaring document to be the testator's last will. It is not required that the will state it is the "last" will of a testator as a person may execute several wills before their death. It is sufficient to state that it is the testator's will.
- Clause identifying spouse and children.
- Clause(s) relating to the payment of testator's debts, estate taxes, expenses of administration, etc.

- Clause(s) directing the disposition of the testator's property.
- Clause nominating the estate's personal representative.
- Signature and attestation clause (for testator and witnesses).

All wills prepared by lawyers will contain these basic elements. There may be many additional provisions, and these basic elements may be expanded to accommodate the testator's individual needs.

§ 18.5.1   Characteristics of a will—Opening and domicile clause

The opening clause or preamble of a will gives the testator's name and domicile and revokes any earlier wills or codicils that may exist. The revocation clause should be a part of every will, whether or not the testator remembers executing a previous will.

The place of the decedent's domicile should not be confused with the place of residence. It is quite possible to have several residences, but one may have only one domicile. The place of domicile at the time of death determines the location of the primary probate proceeding as well as the state that collects the major portion of state estate taxes. A classic example of the dilemma of domicile is the estate of the late billionaire, Howard Hughes. Mr. Hughes died without a will and lived in several states, apparently without firmly establishing domicile in any one. Three different states alleged that his domicile was in their state. Millions of dollars in state death taxes were at stake, and the matter was in litigation for several years.

§ 18.5.2   Characteristics of a will—Identification of family

In some states if the testator fails to name and specifically make provisions for the spouse, this voids the will as to the spouse, who then takes the inheritance by intestate succession according to the laws of descent in the state of domicile. If children are not named, they may claim a portion of the estate as a pretermitted heir if there is no surviving spouse.

§ 18.5.3   Characteristics of a will—Payment of debts clause

The clause relating to the payment of debts, expenses, and taxes gives the estate's personal representative specific direction as to whether the general estate or specific gifts will pay these items. The direction relating to death taxes is of particular importance, as it can determine whether such taxes will be paid from estate funds or charged to the beneficiaries of the estate.

§ 18.5.4   Characteristics of a will—Disposition of property clause

The disposition of property is divided into two basic kinds—specific bequests or devises and residuary bequests or devises.

§ 18.5.5 Characteristics of a will—Specific bequest clause of a will

A *specific bequest* (also called a *preresiduary gift*) is a gift of an identified asset or stated amount of money.

EXAMPLE:

I give and bequeath to my daughter, Jane Doe, my sterling silver flatware.

I give and bequeath to my friend, John Smith, the sum of $10,000.

Some states allow the disposition of tangible personal property by reference in the will to a separate written document.

§ 18.5.6 Characteristics of a will—Residuary bequest clause

A *residuary bequest* is a gift of the remaining assets of the estate.
EXAMPLE:

All of the rest, residue, and remainder of my property, real, personal, or mixed, wherever situated, I give, devise, and bequeath to my daughters, Jane Doe and Mary Doe, in equal shares, or to the survivor of them.

The *residue* of an estate is what is left over after the payment of debts, expenses, taxes, and specific bequests. If the estate's assets are depleted entirely by payment of the debts, expenses, taxes, and specific bequests, there is no residue to distribute, so the residuary beneficiaries receive nothing.

§ 18.5.7 Characteristics of a will—Appointment of personal representative

The clause relating to the testator's choice of personal representative may also include statements as to the specific powers granted to the representative. A testator may give the representative the full range of possible powers under the law. This enables the representative to go about the business of administering the estate without requesting the power from the court for each transaction. A will may designate that the representative need not provide a bond with surety. Some states now provide that representatives have statutory powers, regardless of whether or not they are set forth in the will. This clause usually includes the nomination of alternates to the first choice of personal representative, in case he or she is unwilling or unable to serve.

§ 18.5.8 Characteristics of a will—Signature lines

The signature area of the will is an important one, since virtually all jurisdictions require a will be signed by the testator. The date of the signing is also important since, if more than one will is found after the testator's death, the one bearing the most recent date controls.

§ 18.5.9   Characteristics of a will—Attestation clause

The *attestation clause* is the section where the witnesses sign the will. Most states require that wills be executed in the presence of at least two witnesses. In addition to the act of witnessing the execution, the witnesses also usually attest to the fact that the testator declared that this is the testator's will and requested the individuals present to witness it.

All wills drafted by lawyers contain these basic elements, although many are a great deal more sophisticated than the will shown in Illustration 18.1.

§ 18.5.10   Characteristics of a will—Self-proving affidavit

Most states acknowledge the addition of an affidavit at the end of the will that is signed by the witnesses and acknowledged by a notary at the time the will is signed by the testator. This affidavit will allow the will to be admitted into probate without having to have one of the attesting witnesses sign and file a separate affidavit or testify in court. In some states this may be accomplished by attaching a separate affidavit of attesting witnesses to the will. Other states have a one-step process allowing the signatures of the witnesses and notary to appear within the will itself.

§ 18.5.11   Characteristics of a will—Possession of the will

One important characteristic of a will is that it is the personal possession of the testator. The testator may designate who shall hold the will and may request possession of the document at any time. Because of the very personal nature of a will, should the testator desire to revoke the will, the testator must do so personally. A will may be revoked by mutilation, cancellation, destruction, or execution of a new will. A revoked will must be destroyed by the person making it.

§ 18.6   Types of wills

There are many types of wills used for different purposes. Many of the more sophisticated wills are written to achieve favorable estate tax consideration and involve the use of various kinds of trusts. A will may also contain trust provisions for minor children to avoid distributing estate assets into a guardianship for a minor child or to a child when the child attains majority because the testator may feel that the child is not ready to handle large sums of money.

§ 18.6.1   Types of wills—Simple will

The wills the lawyer's assistant prepares will be drafted by lawyers. This chapter deals primarily with those wills, although more unusual kinds of wills are defined. A typical simple will is shown in Illustration 18-1. This will contains all of the necessary elements mentioned earlier in the chapter.

Illustration 18-1

LAST WILL AND TESTAMENT OF JANE A. DOE

I, Jane A. Doe, domiciled in Any County, State of Anystate, do hereby make, with complete testamentary intent and capacity, my Last Will and Testament, hereby revoking all former wills and codicils.

ARTICLE I
Identification of Family

My immediate family now consists of my husband, John J. Doe, and my three (3) children: Paul Doe, born March 3, 1973; Elizabeth Doe, born July 14, 1975; and Ryan Doe, born October 7, 1977.

ARTICLE II

I direct my executor to pay all funeral expenses, expenses of administration, and my just debts, if any, except such as are at the time of my death specific liens upon property holdings, which my executor is authorized to continue in force if and for so long as, in his judgment, it is necessary or desirable.

ARTICLE III

I direct that all estate, inheritance, legacy, and estate taxes imposed on account of my death, whether or not accruing against property or insurance proceeds not part of my probate estate, be paid from the residue of my estate passing under Article VI, without apportionment. There shall be no obligation resting on anyone to contribute to the payment of said taxes, and my Personal Representative shall have no duty to secure reimbursement to my estate on account of taxes so paid.

ARTICLE IV

I give and devise any homestead, including contiguous land used in connection therewith, which I may own at the time of my death to my husband, John J. Doe, outright. Should my husband not survive me, this devise shall lapse, and said homestead shall be added to and be distributed with the residue of my estate. [Optional unless required by statute.]

ARTICLE V

I give and bequeath to my husband, John J. Doe, all of the household furniture and furnishings, automobiles, musical instruments, books, pictures, jewelry, watches, silverware, wearing apparel, and all other articles of household or personal use or adornment that I own at my date of death. In the event he shall not survive me, then I give all of said property to my children or to the survivor or survivors of them, in equal shares.

ARTICLE VI

All the rest, residue, and remainder of my property, real, personal or mixed, wheresoever situated, I give and devise to my husband, John J. Doe; but if he does not survive me, I direct that my Personal Representative distribute said property to my children, Paul Doe, Elizabeth Doe, and Ryan Doe, in equal shares, or to their issue by right of representation.

ARTICLE VII

I nominate, constitute, and appoint my husband, John J. Doe, personal representative of my estate to serve without bond. If my husband predeceases me or is unable or unwilling to serve, then I appoint Brian Doe as personal representative. I grant my personal representative the power to do without court order any of the acts permitted a personal representative pursuant to the statutes of that state of Anywhere.

ARTICLE VIII

In the event my husband and I die under such circumstances that the order of our deaths may not be conveniently determined, I direct that the distribution of my estate under this Will shall be made as if my husband predeceased me.

IN WITNESS WHEREOF, I have hereunto set my hand to this my Last Will and Testament this ____ day of ____, *[Year]*.

_____
Jane A. Doe

This instrument, consisting of ____ typewritten pages, including this certificate, each bearing the signature of the above named Jane A. Doe, was signed by her on the date hereof. We believe her to be of sound and disposing mind and memory and have hereunto subscribed our names as witnesses.

_____   Residing at _____

_____   Residing at _____

STATE OF _____
COUNTY OF _____

We, Jane A. Doe, ____, and ____, the Testator and the witnesses, respectively, whose names are signed to the attached or foregoing instrument, being first duly sworn, do hereby declare to the undersigned authority that the Testator signed and executed the instrument as her last will and that she had signed willingly or directed another to sign for her, and that she executed it as her free and voluntary act for the purposes therein expressed; and that each of the witnesses, in the presence and hearing of the Testator, signed the will as witness and that to the best of their knowledge the Testator was at that time 18 or more years of age, of sound mind, and under no constraint or undue influence.

_____

Testator

_____

Witness

_____

Witness

[Signature of Testator not required on the affidavit in many states.]

Subscribed, sworn to and acknowledged before me by Jane A. Doe, the Testator, and subscribed and sworn to before me by ____ and ____ witnesses, this ____ day of ____, *[Year]*.

_____

Notary Public

My commission expires:

This is a sample of a simple will. Often additional paragraphs will be added to provide for the appointment of a guardian or a trust for minor children. Trust provisions for minor children do not have to be complicated and can continue beyond the time a minor child comes of age. If funds are not left to a trust but are distributed to a guardianship for the estate of a minor child, then the funds must be distributed to the child upon attaining majority, whether the child understands handling money or not.

§ 18.6.2 Types of wills—Holographic will

A **holographic will** is one completely handwritten by the testator and signed without the benefit of statutory formalities. State laws regarding the circumstances under which holographic wills are valid vary greatly, although many states provide for holographic wills under certain circumstances.

§ 18.6.3 Types of wills—Oral wills (nuncupative and soldiers' and sailors')

Two kinds of oral wills are recognized by some states—**nuncupative wills** and **soldiers' and sailors' wills**. A **nuncupative will** is spoken by a person in peril of imminent death. Usually, the witnesses to whom it was spoken must reduce it to writing within a limited time. **Soldiers' and sailors' wills** are oral dispositions made by soldiers in actual military service or sailors at sea.

Again, the requirements and recognition of these wills vary greatly in the states in which they are permitted. Since oral wills offer the open opportunity for fraud, all states in which they are recognized restrict severely the value of assets to pass under them and restrict it to personal property. In those states in which the Uniform Probate Code has been adopted, only written wills are permitted.

§ 18.6.4   Types of wills—Contingent or conditional wills

Contingent or conditional wills do not take effect unless a specific event occurs. Therefore, if the event does not occur, it is as though there were no will. Most states do not recognize contingent wills.

§ 18.6.5   Types of wills—Joint wills

Sometimes two or more persons execute a **joint will**, that is, they execute the same document. These are not widely used, since problems often arise if circumstances change and one testator desires to change the terms or revoke the instrument. Some states do not recognize joint wills.

§ 18.6.6   Types of wills—Codicils

A **codicil** to a will literally means a "little will." It is an amendment, afterthought, postscript, addition, supplement, or change to the original will. It must be prepared, executed, and witnessed with all the formality of the original will.

§ 18.7   Preparation of wills

A person's will is a very personal matter, and it must be drafted to meet the individual needs of the client. Most law offices will have a compilation of standard will clauses in their computer forms file. Some clauses are not standard and need to be dictated by the lawyer.

§ 18.7.1   Preparation of wills—Will paper

Many law firms use special paper, manuscript covers, and envelopes in preparing wills.

§ 18.7.2   Preparation of wills—Printed forms

Occasionally the lawyer's assistant may encounter an online or printed form of will. Such wills should be used with caution as the forms available through mail order houses or online obviously cannot be adapted easily to the needs of a particular testator. Such wills also may not comply with the laws of the state in which they are executed. It is very important the executed will be entirely valid so the testator's wishes will be honored. A will that is successfully contested or proved invalid is inadmissible to probate, and the decedent's assets will be disposed of according to the laws of descent in the state of domicile.

§ 18.7.3   Preparation of wills—Corrections to wills

The will must be absolutely free of spelling, typographical, numerical, or grammatical errors that could change the meaning of the will. If percentages or fractions are used, they must equal 100 percent or a whole unit. If the will must be corrected at the time of execution, the correction should be written out by the testator and initialed by the testator and witnesses. This type of correction could include changing the year at the beginning of a new year, a middle initial, etc. The best way to make corrections, however, is to revise and reprint the page before the testator signs.

§ 18.7.4   Preparation of wills—Numbering paragraphs and pages

Within the body of the will, each clause should be numbered with a roman numeral or other designation consistent with local practice. The pages should be numbered. At the bottom of each page there may be a signature line for the testator or there may be places for the testator and witnesses to initial each page. If used, the will should include lines for the testator's signature, initials, etc., in the footer of the will.

§ 18.7.5   Preparation of wills—Ending a page

It is best not to complete an item at the bottom of a page. The signature or attestation clause should never be typed on a page separate from the remainder of the will. Following this procedure will safeguard against the possibility of someone substituting a changed page in an executed will. The self-proving affidavit of attesting witnesses can be on a separate page as long as the witnesses will be signing the affidavit.

§ 18.7.6   Preparation of wills—Execution of wills

Wills should be executed under the supervision of a lawyer. The lawyer's assistant may, however, be called upon to serve as a witness.

The testator should declare that the instrument is, in fact, their will. It is preferable, and in some states mandatory, that none of the witnesses be beneficiaries or parties with a financial interest in the estate. Usually, the witnesses need not be aware of the contents of the will. Each witness should sign his or her name and address in the presence of the testator and should initial each page, if requested. Most states require the witnesses and the testator sign in the presence of each other, so it is a good practice not to leave the room or attend to other business while executing a will. Only the necessary parties—the testator, the lawyer, the witnesses, and the notary public—should be in the room during the execution process. Once these people enter the room, the door should be closed, and no one should be permitted to leave until the task of execution is complete. The will should be dated correctly and checked after execution as to the accuracy and completeness of the execution. Only the original of the will should be executed, although file copies should be conformed to reflect the date of execution, witnesses, etc., or copies made for the lawyer's file. The procedures described here are merely illustrative. The lawyer's assistant working in estate planning should learn the formal requirements for execution of wills in the assistant's state. The formal requirements do vary and are important, as a will could be contested for failure to meet those requirements.

§ 18.8   Trusts

There are two types of trusts—revocable and irrevocable. A *revocable trust* is one that can be revoked or amended by the trustor at any time prior to death. An *irrevocable trust* cannot be revoked by the trustor and cannot be materially changed once it is executed. A trust is presumed to be irrevocable unless it is expressly stated to be revocable. A trust can be established between the trustor and the trustee during the lifetime of the trustor, or it can be established through the trustor's will to take effect upon the trustor's death. In order to establish a trust, the trustor must have the legal capacity to transfer the property to the trustee.

Irrevocable trusts are generally made for tax reasons, and the trustor transfers all ownership rights in and all power over property to the trustee so that the assets in the trust will not be included as part of the taxable estate for estate tax purposes at the time of the trustor's death. There are numerous types of irrevocable trusts used in sophisticated estate planning techniques beyond the scope of this chapter.

In a revocable trust, the trustor generally maintains some power over the trust as long as he or she is alive and not incapacitated. Once the trustor dies or becomes incapacitated, the terms of the trust become irrevocable and cannot be changed without court order.

The trustor can be more than one person, and the trustee can be more than one person, or it can be an entity, such as the trust department of a bank.

§ 18.8.1   Trusts—Classifications of trusts

Most trusts are active trusts in which the trustee has some additional duty other than just transferring the property to the beneficiary.

Testamentary trusts are created under a will, and *inter vivos* or *living trusts* are created during the lifetime of the trustor.

Express restrictions are usually included in a trust to limit the access to trust assets by a beneficiary and existing creditors. These restrictions are referred to as *spendthrift provisions*.

In revocable trusts, standby trust provisions permit the trustor to retain control over the trust assets during trustor's lifetime, unless the trustor becomes disabled or requests the trustee to assume management of the trust. Income is taxed to the trustor, and the assets are included in the trustor's estate for federal estate tax purposes at the time of death. No gift tax liability is created.

A *joint interest trust* is created when two trustors place jointly held assets in a trust. The income and principal are distributed by the trustee according to the terms of the trust. This type of trust is quite often used for a husband and wife so that they do not have to establish two separate trusts. When one of the trustors dies, that share of the trust property passes as the trust agreement dictates.

When the trustor and trustee of a revocable trust are the same person, the trust does not need to file separate fiduciary income tax returns, and the income is included on the trustor's individual income tax returns. If the trustor and trustee are not the same person, the Internal Revenue Code requires that the trust obtain a federal identification number and file its own fiduciary income tax returns.

A *qualified terminable interest provision* in a trust (or even in a will) permits property to qualify for a marital deduction, if the spouse has use of the property for life and other Internal Revenue Code requirements are met. The personal representative or trustee is given the option to make this election, and the election is made on the decedent's federal estate tax return. If the election is not made on a return which is timely filed, the election is lost and not available.

§ 18.8.2 Trusts—Powers and duties of trustee

The powers, duties, and liabilities of a trustee are interrelated. The trust instrument usually sets forth the trustee's powers. Most states have statutory laws that regulate a trustee's powers, duties, and liabilities. Generally it is not necessary for a trustee to post a bond or make accountings to a court, such as may be required by a personal representative. A trustee is accountable to the trustor and beneficiaries during the trustor's lifetime and to the beneficiaries after the trustor's death.

§ 18.8.3 Types of trusts—Funding the trust

A trust agreement can be executed by the trustor, but until the assets are actually placed in the trustee's name and delivered to the trustee, the trust is not activated. In other words, if the trustor makes a trust agreement but does not deed any real property to the trust or place existing bank accounts, securities, and other personal property in the trustee's name, then these assets remain in the individual's name and are not subject to the terms of the trust. If these assets have not been transferred to the trust, they are treated like any other asset at the time of the trustor's death and may have to be probated. That is why it is important that a trustor also execute a will. In the event there are any assets that are not in the trust, they can be distributed to the trust and become a part of the trust estate. This type of will is often referred to as a **pourover will** because it simply pours the decedent's assets over to the trust.

It is a good idea for the lawyer to keep in a client's file a letter, memorandum, or other written evidence of what assets the lawyer has assisted the client in transferring to the trust and what assets the client is going to handle personally. This could be very beneficial to the lawyer after the trustor's death if the beneficiaries bring a claim against the lawyer for not transferring estate assets to the trust.

§ 18.8.4   Types of trusts—Trust termination

The trustor can revoke a trust, so long as the power of revocation is according to the trust terms. Generally a trust is terminated in accordance with the trust provisions, although it can be terminated differently, with the consent of all of the beneficiaries, if no material trust purpose is defeated by such termination.

§ 18.9   Other estate planning documents

Many other documents may be executed by the client at the time of signing the will or trust agreement. Many people now desire to execute **health care powers of attorney**. This kind of power of attorney permits the attorney-in-fact to make health care decisions on behalf of the maker in the event the maker is unable to make these decisions personally. A health care power of attorney should not be confused with a living will. In an **advance health care directive** or a **living will**, the maker instructs the physician or medical supplier not to keep the maker alive by the use of life-supporting procedures. The living will is an essential document, as most courts will enforce the provisions of a valid living will.

A **durable power of attorney** is used quite often in estate planning. A durable power of attorney is given to another, usually a spouse, adult child, or entity, which empowers that person to act on behalf of the maker, even if the maker has become incapacitated. If the maker has established a trust and has not transferred all existing assets to the trust, a general durable power of attorney would permit the agent to transfer the assets, so the assets would become part of the trust estate and subject to the trust provisions. It is important that the power of attorney include language that it will be effective even if the maker is incapacitated, or it will not qualify as a durable power of attorney, and the agent will not be able to continue to act under the provisions of the power of attorney.

§ 18.10   Elder law

The area of **elder law** developed as a response to the changing demographics of American society. It is sometimes defined as a practice of law focused on the unique concerns of that particular segment of the population over the age of 50. Lawyers who practice in this area are attuned to the social, medical, and legal aspects of complex issues facing the elderly and their families. Such issues include:

- Planning for disability
- Estate planning and management
- Estate tax and gift tax issues
- Medicaid and Medicare issues
- Age discrimination in housing and employment
- Personal injury
- Guardianships
- Living wills or advance health care directives
- Durable power of attorney
- Health care power of attorney

§ 18.11   The role of the lawyer's assistant

The lawyer's assistant's role in estate planning law is important. He or she can assist the lawyer by making sure estate planning documents are prepared as accurately as possible and that the file contains documentation of what the lawyer has agreed to do for the client. If the assistant thinks a paragraph in a will or trust agreement does not make sense, it should be brought to the lawyer's attention. If the lawyer's assistant does not believe the will or trust agreement includes all of the provisions it should, he or she should address their concerns with the lawyer. The lawyer's assistant can act as a second set of eyes to ensure that the estate planning documents contain all the necessary language in order to carry out the client's wishes. Most of the time estate planning documents are not used until the client is either deceased or incapacitated, and then it is too late to make corrections that should have been included prior to signing.

Chapter 19

Estates and Guardianships

KeyCite®: Cases and other legal materials listed in KeyCite Scope can be researched through the KeyCite service on Westlaw®. Use KeyCite to check citations for form, parallel references, prior and later history, and comprehensive citator information, including citations to other decisions and secondary materials.

---

§ 19.1 Introduction

When a person dies, it is necessary that an orderly disposition be made of that person's property. The person who dies is called the *decedent*. The property the decedent owned at death is referred to as the decedent's *estate*. The decedent's estate usually consists of both probate and nonprobate assets.

Probate property consists of property owned solely by the decedent, property owned by the decedent as a tenant in common, the decedent's interest in community property, and life insurance proceeds payable to the personal representative of the decedent's estate.

Estate administration or *probate proceedings* are the terms most often used to refer to proceedings used to distribute the estate. The persons or entities that become owners of the decedent's estate under a will and after the completion of probate proceedings are called *beneficiaries*. The persons or entities that become owners of the decedent's estate if no will exists and after the completion of an administration are called *heirs*. The persons or institutions who manage money or property for another and who must exercise a standard of care imposed by law, i.e., personal representative or executor of an estate, trustee, etc., are called *fiduciaries*. Fiduciaries also handle the affairs of living persons, such as wards and minors.

Nonprobate property consists of assets owned by the decedent and others in joint tenancy, life insurance, and other property payable under contract to specific beneficiaries other than the decedent's estate, and property titled in *inter vivos* and **Totten** trusts. All of these are transferred automatically to the recipient without passing through probate. An *inter vivos* trust is created by the decedent and becomes operative during the decedent's lifetime.

A *Totten trust* is created upon the deposit by the decedent of money into the decedent's own name as trustee for another. It may be revoked at will until the decedent's death, when it automatically becomes the property of the named beneficiary. These nonprobate assets, however, are subject to claims of creditors of the decedent.

Laymen tend to find the legal process involved in handling a decedent's estate tedious and burdensome, but the legal process is actually very orderly and can save the heirs many tax dollars. Probate is often the first contact the survivors have with the court system. The event that necessitates this kind of proceeding is also traumatic— the death of a loved one. It is very important that the lawyer's assistant have an understanding of estate administration and be able to deal intelligently and compassionately with the bereaved client.

§ 19.2   The Uniform Probate Code

The Uniform Probate Code adopted by the National Conference of Commissioners on Uniform State Laws has been adopted by most states. Some states have adopted the code with modifications or have adopted only parts of it. The purpose of the Uniform Probate Code is to make it possible for estates to be administered the same way in all states and to streamline procedures. There has been much criticism from the public that the probate process is too complicated and permits the courts to become involved in matters in which they need not be involved.

The Uniform Probate Code provides for informal proceedings in some cases that can be handled without the assistance of a lawyer or with only minimal lawyer involvement. This greatly reduces the expense of administering an estate. The code also provides for traditional court proceedings. Accordingly, the heirs, personal representative, lawyer, and court have the option of determining whether the estate should be administered under informal or formal provisions of the code.

§ 19.3   Classification

For purposes of handling the decedent's probate estate, the estate is classified as testate or intestate.

If the decedent had a will, the decedent died **testate**. A **will** is a document by which an individual provides for the disposition of property after death. Those persons named in the will to receive some portion of the estate are beneficiaries. Gifts of real estate by a will are known as **devises**, and the recipients of such gifts are **devisees**. Personal property (property other than real estate) transferred by will is a **legacy**, and the recipient of the property is a **legatee**. The terms **legacy** and **devise** and **legatee** and **devisee** are used interchangeably in many jurisdictions. Under the Uniform Probate Code, all gifts made by will are known as devises, and the recipient is the devisee, regardless of whether the gifts consist of real or personal property.

§ 19.3.1   Classification—Locating the will

If the decedent died testate, it is necessary to locate the original will so it can be presented to the court for probate. Probate of the will is its presentation to the court to have it declared valid. Note, however, that the word **probate** is now used to describe all estate administration proceedings.

If the decedent was a client of the law firm, all of the client's files should be reviewed, as they may contain information that will be needed for estate administration. The files may contain a copy of the decedent's will. If so, copies should be available at the initial conference with the personal representative, together with information about the location of the original.

It is customary for the lawyer to hold the original will for the client. Some lawyers hesitate to do this, since one important characteristic of a will is that it is the personal possession of the **testator**, person who makes the will. The testator may designate who will hold the will and may request possession of the document at any time. Because of the very personal nature of a will, should the testator desire to revoke the will, it must be done personally. A will may be revoked by mutilation, cancellation, destruction, or execution of a new will. A will must be destroyed by the testator. In many wills, the first paragraph is a revocation of all prior wills. A will that was unintentionally destroyed by the testator may still be probated if the contents can be established to the satisfaction of the court. Marriage or divorce subsequent to the date of the will, however, may modify the terms.

Some people place their wills in their safe deposit boxes, home safes, or even desk drawers at home. If the family believes the decedent left a will, it is incumbent upon them to search through decedent's personal belongings until they find it. When the will is stored in a safe deposit box, the box may be sealed upon the decedent's death, requiring the lawyer and family to follow special procedures to obtain the will.

An amendment, addition, or supplement to a will is known as a *codicil* or literally a "little will." If there are one or more codicils in existence, they will be subject to the same treatment as wills in the probate proceedings.

If the decedent did not leave a will, the decedent is said to have died *intestate*. The estate is then administered and distributed according to the laws of the state of domicile.

§ 19.3.2   Classification—Determination of heirship

Proof of heirship is the judicial determination of the identity of those persons who are entitled to inherit the decedent's property if the decedent dies intestate. In many states, this proof is an essential part of the probate proceeding. It is also necessary in some states to notify all possible heirs of the pending probate proceeding, regardless of whether they are named as beneficiaries. This notice is extremely important, since it affords any heir at law not named as a beneficiary an opportunity to object to the admission of the will to probate. There is a statutory time period within which an objection to the will must be made. In the case of an intestate proceeding, the heirs at law must be notified, since they will ultimately share in the distribution of the estate.

§ 19.3.3   Classification—Proof of heirship

In many jurisdictions, heirship is proved by the filing of an affidavit of death and heirship. This is simply an affidavit executed by one or two family members (heirs are not allowed to sign this affidavit in some states) or close friends who attest to their knowledge of:

- The date of the decedent's death.
- The decedent's address at the time of death.
- The decedent's age at the time of death.
- Facts about the decedent's marriages, surviving spouse, and children.

The affidavit is specific about the number of times the decedent was married and the children who were born of each marriage. Additionally, if there were children who died before the decedent, the names of these children, as well as their issue, are listed. In the case of intestacy, these children would probably inherit their parent's share.

§ 19.3.4 Classification—Minor heirs

When minor children are heirs, the court in most states appoints a guardian to protect the minor's interests. The appointment of a guardian of the estate varies from jurisdiction to jurisdiction and may be a lawyer disinterested in the proceeding, the natural guardian (parent), or the legally appointed guardian of the child. The court may also require that the inherited funds of a minor be deposited with the court until the minor becomes of legal age.

§ 19.4 Functions of estate administration

Probate serves three main functions:

- Identification of assets so they can be distributed to beneficiaries of the decedent
- Protection of creditors of the decedent
- Determination of the tax liability of the estate

§ 19.4.1 Functions of estate administration—Protection of creditors

Since distribution cannot be made to heirs without paying debts of the decedent, it is necessary to determine what debts exist. Usually the family members are aware of the debts, and if they are not, creditors can notify either the lawyer or a family member of their claim. Most states also have a procedure by which creditors may protect their claims against estates. Most states also require the personal representative to publish notice to creditors and give notice of the claims filing procedure to known creditors.

All states make legal provisions to protect claims of creditors of an estate. While the method for making the claim varies from state to state, there is always a specific time period within which a creditor must assert a claim. Generally, a claim is filed by presenting it either to the court or to the personal representative or lawyer.

In some states, a claim must be made for such items as expenses of the last illness and funeral expenses, as well as for ordinary debts. In other states, the expenses of the last illness and funeral expenses are paid routinely as expenses of administration.

In some states, the executor or representative may pay any debts presented on a routine basis; while in other states, the executor must advertise intent to pay the debts and must have court approval. Generally, if an executor or representative wishes to disallow a particular debt submitted by a creditor, it is necessary to file an intent to disallow the claim with the court within a specific period of time after the claim is presented. The principal purpose of these provisions is to ensure that the creditor does not suffer a loss from having extended credit to the decedent.

§ 19.4.2 Functions of estate administration—Estate or inheritance taxes

The federal government, the District of Columbia, and most states have some form of *estate or inheritance tax*. This means that either the decedent's estate or its beneficiaries are taxed in connection with the distribution of the decedent's property. There are three types of these taxes:

- Estate taxes, a tax on the property constituting the estate
- Inheritance (or succession) taxes, a tax on the transfer of property
- Pickup taxes equal to the state's tax credit allowed on the federal estate tax return

§ 19.4.3 Functions of estate administration—Estate tax

An *estate tax* is a tax imposed by the federal government upon the privilege of transmitting property at death and thus is payable upon the entire amount of the taxable estate, which is the gross estate of probate and nonprobate assets less deductions and exemptions. Some exceptions to basic estate tax procedures are discussed in Chapter 18. Recent legislation has created new exemptions. No federal estate tax return is required to be filed if the gross estate is:

- $5 million or less in 2011 and 2012
- $5 million or less in 2013, adjusted for inflation
- $11.18 million or less in 2018.

If a return must be filed, it is filed within nine months from the date of death. As of 2018, an IRS Form 706 must be filed if the decedent's gross estate plus adjusted taxable gifts given during the lifetime of the decedent are valued at more than $11,180,000. It is very important that the lawyer's assistant calendar the date that the federal estate tax return is due, because severe penalties and interest are imposed if the estate tax return is not filed and taxes paid on time. Deferral of payment or an extension of time to file the return are available in special circumstances upon proper application.

Many states also levy an estate tax, either alone or in conjunction with a pickup tax.

§ 19.4.4 Functions of estate administration—Inheritance tax

An *inheritance tax* is another type of state tax. Inheritance taxes are imposed upon the amount received by each beneficiary. Generally, certain beneficiaries are granted an exemption based upon the family relationship to the decedent (the closer the relationship, the larger the exemption). The balance is taxed in accordance with a rate schedule provided by state laws. In addition, the rates often vary depending upon the relationship between the beneficiary and the decedent. The deadline for this return, if required, should also be calendared.

§ 19.4.5 Functions of estate administration—Pickup tax

Some states have what is commonly referred to as a *pickup* tax. In computing federal estate taxes, the government allows a credit for state taxes based on a graduated table. In the states having a pickup tax, this credit then becomes the required amount of state taxes paid to the state. Under federal law, the state tax credit was eliminated and replaced with a deduction for state estate taxes. However, if that law expires, the state tax credit will come back into play. Changes to state estate tax statutes should be closely monitored as states decide how to deal with this change to the federal law.

§ 19.4.6 Functions of estate administration—Final personal income tax return

The decedent's final personal income tax year ends on the date of death. The decedent's spouse, if any, is entitled to file a joint return for the year in which the decedent dies if that spouse remains unmarried at the end of the year. The personal representative is responsible for assisting the surviving spouse in the preparation of this return.

§ 19.4.7 Functions of estate administration—Fiduciary income tax returns

At the time of death, the decedent's estate becomes a separate entity for income tax purposes, and all income derived from probate assets must be reported on a fiduciary income tax return. The first tax year starts on the date of decedent's death and may end on any date chosen by the personal representative, provided that the first tax year may be no more than 12 months long and must end on the last day of a month. The choice of a tax year for the estate depends upon when the most favorable tax treatment of the income can be obtained. For second and subsequent years, the 12-month tax year starts on the first of the month following the end of the first return.

§ 19.5 Identification of assets

The assets of the decedent are things of value the decedent owned. Not all of a decedent's assets are necessarily included in the probate estate. The decedent's property that forms the probate estate is specifically set forth by law. It is dependent also upon the form of ownership of the property.

EXAMPLES:

A. If a decedent owned property with anyone else in joint tenancy with right of survivorship, that property would automatically belong to the other owner upon the decedent's death. It would not form a part of the probate estate, but all or part of it might be a part of decedent's gross estate for death tax purposes. On the other hand, if the decedent owned property as a tenant in common with someone else or as community property with decedent's spouse, then the undivided interest decedent owned in the property would form a part of decedent's probate estate.

B. If the decedent owned a life insurance policy payable to a named beneficiary, that policy would not be part of the probate estate, but would be part of the estate for estate tax purposes. On the other hand, if the decedent owned a life insurance policy payable to the estate, that policy would form part of the probate estate.

C. If the decedent owned property that was titled to beneficiaries other than the estate, particularly in certain types of trusts, that property would not be included in the probate estate, but might be included for estate tax purposes.

Regardless of whether the decedent died testate or intestate, it is necessary for the lawyer to develop a list of the decedent's assets, both probate and nonprobate. The lawyer needs to know whether at the time of death the decedent owned or had an interest in any of the following:

- Real estate (the form of ownership of each parcel must also be known)
- Mortgages, promissory notes, or real estate installment sale contracts payable to decedent
- Stocks, bonds, and other types of securities
- Life insurance on decedent's life
- Life insurance owned by decedent on the life of another
- Oil, mineral, timber, and gas interests
- Cash, bank accounts, savings certificates, etc.
- Interests in unincorporated businesses or partnerships
- Annuities, IRAs, and Keogh plans
- Pension, profit sharing, and other employee benefit plans
- Assets in certain types of trusts
- Farm equipment, livestock, and crops
- Powers of appointment
- Large amounts of jewelry
- Coin or stamp collections
- Antiques
- Art objects
- Household goods
- Vehicles
- Death benefits
- Uncashed checks in decedent's possession
- Payroll checks receivable
- Accounts receivable
- Tax refunds for decedent's final tax year
- Military benefits

This list does not include all possible types of assets but gives an idea of their diversity.

The form of ownership of each item must be known to determine whether it is a probate or nonprobate asset. Often compiling an accurate list of all assets is the most time-consuming step in administration of the estate. It may be necessary to have several conferences with the family members before a complete list is compiled. It is also usually necessary to correspond with banks, savings and loan associations, stockbrokers, the former employer of the decedent, and insurance companies to get all of the information needed to administer the estate.

It is also necessary to determine the value of the assets as of the date of death. This process can be quite complicated. For some assets, such as bank accounts, this can be accomplished by writing to the bank and requesting the date of death balance plus accrued interest to that date. However, many assets do not have such a clearly obtainable value and require the use of formulas and guidelines used by the Internal Revenue Service or professional appraisers. The exact procedures may also vary depending upon the jurisdiction and the size of the estate.

§ 19.6   The personal representative

The person who handles estate administration is known as the *personal representative*. This term is used in the Uniform Probate Code to mean anyone who handles the administration regardless of whether the appointment is by will or by the court in cases of intestacy. In many jurisdictions the formal designation of the personal representative depends upon whether the estate is testate or intestate and whether a representative is named in the will.

In the case of testate succession, the will usually designates someone to serve as the estate's representative. That person is referred to as the *executor*, whether male or female.

However, if the executor named is unable or unwilling to serve and no alternative is designated, the court appoints a representative known as the *administrator c.t.a.* (the Latin abbreviation for *cum testamento annexo*, meaning "with will annexed") or an **executor *de bonis non***. If the decedent died intestate, then the representative appointed by the court is the administrator. Each of these persons serves the same function and has basically the same duties. These terms are often used interchangeably, although in the legal documents, the appropriate designation should be used.

A testator may give the executor a great deal of leeway and fully outline in the will the powers accorded the executor. This enables the executor to administer the estate without requesting authority from the court to handle transactions such as the sale of assets. A will may also provide that the executor need not provide a surety bond. The surety bond is required for the protection of both the heirs and the creditors. The surety bond is often in the form of a commercial bond (similar to an insurance policy) issued by an insurance company which, for a premium, insures that the executor will properly perform all duties. The court may in some states override the waiver of the bond by the testator and require the executor to post bond. Some states now give executors certain statutory powers whether or not they are specifically set out in the will.

There are certain requirements (in addition to posting bond) that the representative must meet to be qualified to serve as the representative. Once the requirements are met, the court issues *letters testamentary* (in testate matters) or *letters of administration* (in intestate matters) to the representative. These letters give the representative authority to act.

Usually, the representative acts under court supervision. The will or state statute may give the representative some freedom as to how much court authority is necessary to perform certain acts (such as paying bills or selling assets). These powers are referred to as nonintervention powers in some states. However, it may be necessary for the representative to make periodic accountings to the court concerning the administration of the estate. A decedent may provide, within the will, that the executor may act independently and without court supervision other than the returning of an inventory to the court.

There are alternatives to probate that do not require the appointment of a representative. These kinds of proceedings are usually reserved for small estates passing to close relatives or having limited types of assets or community property agreements in community property states. It is not possible to discuss every conceivable alternative in this chapter.

§ 19.7   Initial client interview

One or more of the decedent's closest relatives generally make the initial contact with the law firm. An appointment is usually scheduled as soon as practicable after the funeral.

The initial interview generally includes the lawyer and the decedent's spouse, children, or other close relatives. It may also include the personal representative if it is someone other than a family member. The lawyer's assistant should also be included in the initial conference to take notes as information is obtained.

Most firms have client interview forms for probate matters to ensure that they secure all needed information. (See Illustration 19-1.)

If the will is available for the initial conference, it is read then. The reading of the will, however, is not nearly as dramatic as is depicted in the movies. In fact, the family usually is familiar with the contents of the will before the conference with the lawyer. At that time the lawyer answers any questions any member of the family might have concerning the terms of the will and the probate process.

It may also be useful to locate a copy of any printed obituaries appearing in the local newspapers, as they will list survivors and relationships. This will help the legal assistant and lawyer to become familiar with the family structure prior to the interview. Since the lawyer must secure biographical data concerning the decedent's family, everyone benefits if some of the information can be obtained from the files.

Illustration 19-1
CLIENT INTERVIEW FORM
GENERAL INFORMATION

Estate of _____

Known aliases _____

Date of birth _____ Place of birth _____

Date of death _____ Place of death _____

Name of spouse _____ Date of birth of spouse _____

If spouse is deceased, state date of death _____

Decedent's social security no. _____

Spouse's social security no. _____

Date of marriage to surviving spouse _____

Domicile at date of marriage _____

Year domicile established in this state _____

For each devisee, heir or other interested person, state:

Full name and relationship to decedent	**Address**	**Date of birth**	**Social Security No.**

Decedent's business or occupation _____

Employer identification number, if any _____

Name and address of personal representative _____

_____

Business phone _____ Home phone _____

Address of decedent at date of death _____

_____

Did the decedent have a safe deposit box? _____

_____

If so, state: Name of bank _____ and joint depositor(s), if any_____

_____

ASSET INFORMATION

It is suggested that sheets similar to the following should be prepared for each type of asset. In some cases, a separate sheet will be needed for every item of property within that category while for others several may be listed on the same sheet. These forms can be easily modified to meet specific information requirements of the state. If all information is not available, the forms can be given to the personal representative and family members to gather the information.

REAL ESTATE

Estate of _____

Probate _____

Nonprobate _____

Legal description of property _____

_____

Name or names in which title stands and form of ownership _____

_____

Homestead? Yes _____   No _____

Abstract _____   Torrens _____

Location of abstract of title or Torrens certificate _____

_____

Value at Date of Death $ _____

Mortgages or other encumbrances:

Payee _____

Loan No. _____

Balance of encumbrance on date of death $_____

Payee _____

Loan No. _____

Property identification number _____

NOTE: It is helpful to obtain a copy of the most recent real estate
tax statement and the deed to the present owner.

BANK ACCOUNTS

Estate of _____

Probate _____

Nonprobate _____

Name of bank _____

Type of account _____

No. of account _____

Approximate balance $_____

Date of death balance $_____

Name or names in which account stands and form of ownership _____

_____

LIFE INSURANCE

Estate of _____

Probate _____

Nonprobate _____

Name of company _____

Policy No. _____

Date of issuance _____

Face amount of policy _____

Value at Date of Death _____

Beneficiary and relationship _____

Policy owner _____

Date established _____

Any known loans _____

NOTE: Form 712 should be requested from the insurance company for each policy of life insurance on the decedent's life.

STOCKS AND BONDS

Estate of _____

Probate _____

Nonprobate _____

Name of company _____

Certificate No. _____ Dated _____

Issued to _____ for _____ shares

Transfer Agent _____

Value at Date of Death $_____ Source _____

CUSIP number _____

U.S. SAVINGS BONDS

Estate of _____

Probate _____

Nonprobate _____

Joint Owner _____

Date of issuance	Denomination	Serial number	Value at Date of Death
_____	_____	_____	_____
_____	_____	_____	_____
_____	_____	_____	_____

MISCELLANEOUS SECURITIES & INVESTMENTS

Estate of _____

Probate _____

Nonprobate _____

Complete description of security, including type, numbers, date, approximate value, maturity date, if any, etc.

_____

Name or names in which security stands and form of ownership ____

MISCELLANEOUS PERSONAL PROPERTY

Estate of _____

Probate _____

Description	Joint owner or beneficiary, if any	Value
Federal income tax refund		
State income tax refund		
Household goods and furnishings		
Automobile		

Year and make _____

Vehicle ID or serial # _____
Final payroll check

Company _____
Cash in decedent's possession
Uncashed checks in decedent's possession (List) _____
Jewelry or other personal property of intrinsic value (List) _____

Retirement and/or deferred compensation plans (obtain copy of plan)
Interests in partnerships
IRA and Keogh Plans

PROPERTY TRANSFERRED PRIOR TO DEATH

Estate of _____
Description _____
Transferee _____
Relationship to decedent _____
Date of transfer _____
Value of transfer _____
Were gift tax returns filed? _____
NOTE: If gift tax returns were filed, copies should be obtained.

EXPENSES OF ADMINISTRATION

Estate of _____

Expenses of last illness:

_____ $_____
_____   _____
_____   _____
_____   _____

Funeral expenses:
    Mortuary _____ $_____
    Cemetery _____ $_____
    Flowers _____ $_____
    Marker _____ $_____
    Honorariums _____ $_____
    Other _____ $_____
Debts of decedent:

_____ $_____
_____   _____
                         _____
Taxes:
_____ $_____
Attorney's fees:
_____ $_____
Miscellaneous
_____ $_____

§ 19.8   Probate procedures

The domicile of the decedent at the time of death generally controls where a proceeding must be filed. A domicile does not have the same legal meaning as a residence. A person may maintain many residences but can be domiciled at only one address.

The pleadings needed will depend upon whether the estate is testate or intestate and whether informal proceedings may be used. The pleadings vary with the jurisdiction. The lawyer's assistant should become familiar with the pleadings used in the assistant's state for each kind of proceeding. Most firms will have sample forms of pleadings in a forms file or procedures manual.

A petition is generally used to begin probate—the petition may be a printed form or a formal pleading, depending upon state requirements. The affidavit of death and heirship, if required, will probably be filed at the same time as the petition. Pleadings regarding proof of the will and notice to creditors and heirs may also be filed at that time.

In the event there is more than one validly executed will in existence at the time of a decedent's death, the will bearing the most recent date usually controls.

In most states at least one court hearing is required to admit the will to probate, establish heirship, and appoint a representative for the estate. The major exception to the hearing requirement is in informal proceedings under the Uniform Probate Code where only a conference with a registrar is necessary. The registrar is either a judge or a person such as the clerk of court designated as a registrar by the court.

§ 19.8.1   Probate procedures—Proof of will

Proof of will is the process by which a decedent's will is validated and admitted to probate. In some states, this is done by one or more of the witnesses filing an affidavit stating that they witnessed execution of the will and the testator was of sound mind when the will was made. In other states, one or more of the witnesses may have to appear in open court and give oral testimony as to the circumstances under which the will was executed.

§ 19.8.2   Probate procedures—The self-proved will

The *self-proved will* was introduced by the Uniform Probate Code and contains not only the signatures of the testator and witnesses but also a notary public's acknowledgement of the signatures, the soundness of the testator's mind, and the testator's intention to declare the will testator's last will and testament. In those states in which the Uniform Probate Code has been adopted, a self-proved will needs no further proof. Even if the code has not been adopted, a state can make statutory provisions allowing self-proved wills.

§ 19.8.3   Probate procedures—Contesting the will

Any heir who is disgruntled because the heir was omitted from the will or did not receive the full bequest to which the heir felt entitled may file a petition to contest the will. Most states have a specific time period within which this must be done. Such a contest follows the standard procedures of civil litigation. Notice and service on the parties are required. The petitioner must allege the reasons for the contest and prove undue influence, fraud, or mistake in the making of the will. If the petitioner receives a favorable decision, the will is declared invalid, is not admitted to probate, and the laws of intestacy apply.

§ 19.8.4   Probate procedures—Administering the assets

In administering the estate, the representative collects assets; liquidates assets if necessary or prudent; pays debts, funeral and administration expenses, taxes, and claims; and determines the distributions to be made. *Liquidation* is the process of converting assets into cash for easier distribution when the estate is closed. If property is not liquidated and is distributed in the same form received, it is said to have been *distributed in kind*.

The estate of a decedent is generally administered in the state of domicile; however, if the decedent owned any real estate or tangible property in another state, a probate proceeding may be required in that state. This is known as an *ancillary proceeding*.

As soon as feasible after appointment and prior to the statutory deadline date, the representative must file a complete inventory of the property owned by the decedent, including appraised or approximate values as required by law. An accurate inventory is important, as it serves as the basis for taxation and accounting. It is sometimes necessary to amend the inventory or file an addendum to it if additional property is discovered after the inventory is filed.

§ 19.8.5   Probate procedures—Accounting and distribution

In all except informal probate matters, settlement of the estate is accomplished by the representative's filing a final account with the court; this account summarizes all of the transactions involved in the administration. At the same time, the representative petitions the court for distribution of the remaining assets. In some states, a hearing is required on this account, while in others the hearing may be waived by consent of the heirs or by statute. The court, after submission of these documents and the hearing (if required), approves the account and orders the distribution of assets. At the time distribution is made, the representative must obtain a receipt from each devisee or legatee to file with the court. Thereafter, the representative is discharged from all responsibilities. If a surety bond was required, it is ordered terminated.

To keep costs down, most estates are settled informally when the personal representative presents the beneficiaries with an accounting disclosing all the assets of the estate, all distributions and disbursements, and all income. In informal proceedings, the beneficiaries review the accounting and execute an approval and release without court involvement.

In informal proceedings, a statement is sometimes filed to close the estate. However, without accounting and release being presented, no discharge is given releasing the personal representative; however, a statutory time period begins to run on the liability of the personal representative for the representative's actions.

§ 19.9   Guardianships or conservatorships

Since minors do not have the legal capacity to act for themselves, the court appoints someone to act for them concerning their legal affairs. The same is true of adults who do not possess either the mental or physical capacity to care for themselves or who may be deemed to be *vulnerable adults*. Someone must be appointed to handle their affairs. These persons are sometimes considered wards of the court, and the court appoints one or more guardians or conservators to protect the ward's personal needs and preserve any financial resources.

Terminology, when referring to these persons, varies from jurisdiction to jurisdiction. The term *minor* usually means someone under the age of legal majority (usually 18 to 21 years of age). The terms incompetent, incapacitated, or disabled adult are applied to adults. Although state laws vary, guardianships generally may be initiated for both minors and adults, while conservatorships are generally limited to disabled adults.

When it is necessary to appoint a guardian for a minor, a parent is often appointed, since a parent is usually the natural guardian of the child. If the court determines that the interests of the natural guardian may conflict with the interests of the minor, the court may appoint a **guardian** *ad litem* to represent the minor in that particular legal proceeding only.

When it is necessary to appoint a guardian or conservator for a disabled adult, it is necessary to present detailed proof to the court that the adult is in fact disabled. The disabled adult is usually served with a copy of the petition seeking the guardianship, limited guardianship, or conservatorship, although in some states physically disabled adults may petition for conservatorship on their own behalf voluntarily. A lawyer or a **guardian *ad litem*** may be appointed to represent the disabled adult. The court then receives testimony from a physician and the lawyer appointed to represent the adult as to the adult's inability to manage his or her own affairs and physical care.

Some states use the terms guardianship and conservatorship interchangeably. In other states, guardianships and conservatorships are separate and distinct proceedings. The basic difference in these states is that a person under guardianship is declared incompetent to manage his or her own affairs. A person under conservatorship or limited guardianship does not lose any civil rights and, thus, is free to execute a will, marry, vote, etc. Conservatorships and guardianships of adults can be terminated when the ward regains mental or physical capacity or upon death. Guardianships of minors terminate when the ward reaches legal age. In both instances, a final accounting and hearing are usually required before termination.

In both guardianships and conservatorships, bonds are usually required of the guardian or conservator. These bonds are typically in the form of commercial insurance policies and guarantee the property of the ward under the guardian's or conservator's control.

It is necessary for the guardian or conservator to file an inventory of the assets of the ward, obtain court authorization to make expenditures, and to keep detailed accounts of administration. Periodic accountings must be filed with the court, and when the guardianship or conservatorship terminates, a final accounting must be filed before the bond may be terminated and the guardian or conservator discharged.

§ 19.10 Summary

Many of the tasks of probate work, conservatorships, and guardianships are paper-intensive and fairly routine. As the lawyer's assistant gains experience in these fields, the assistant can assume considerable responsibility for gathering information, preparing court forms for attorney review and signature, documenting necessary information, and the like. The more experienced the assistant, the easier the lawyer's job. At the same time, an experienced and compassionate assistant can be of enormous help in working with family members who are either bereaved or who may have had to make difficult decisions regarding conservatorship or guardianship of their loved ones.

Chapter 20

Bankruptcy

§ 20.1 Introduction

A *bankruptcy* is a proceeding in which an individual or legal entity requests protection under Title 11 of the United States Code. The protection given a debtor under the bankruptcy code provides the opportunity for financial rehabilitation and a fresh start.

§ 20.2 History

Under the Constitution, Congress has the power to establish "uniform laws on the subject of bankruptcies throughout the United States" (Article 1, Section 8). Prior to 1978, these laws encompassed several bankruptcy acts. The present bankruptcy code was enacted November 6, 1978, and amended in 1982, 1984, 1986, 1988, and 1994. In 2001, bankruptcy reform was attempted by Congress, but a vote scheduled for mid-September was preempted by the tragic events of September 11, 2001, and the attempt was temporarily abandoned. In 2005, bankruptcy reform legislation called the **Bankruptcy Abuse Prevention and Consumer Protection Act (BAPCPA)** was finally passed, which affects cases filed on and after October 17, 2005. BAPCPA instituted significant changes, most notably means testing and a requirement that debtors receive credit counseling before filing bankruptcy and take an approved financial management course after filing.

In addition to the changes in the bankruptcy code, procedural changes were instituted beginning in 2001, when the federal courts undertook an initiative to put all bankruptcy courts on an electronic case management and case filing system. Today the bankruptcy courts in all fifty states, the District of Columbia, Guam, Puerto Rico, and the Virgin Islands are on the Case Management/Electronic Case Filing (CM/ECF) system. The bankruptcy court in the Northern Mariana Islands is currently in the process of implementing a CM/ECF system. Bankruptcy documents can be accessed online and documents are filed electronically. Local rules provide for the needs of *pro se* bankruptcy filers (those who are representing themselves) who may not have access to electronic filing methods.

§ 20.3 The bankruptcy code

When the first bankruptcy law was established, a person seeking relief under the law was known as a *bankrupt*. The 1978 code abolished the term *bankrupt*. A person or entity filing for relief under the bankruptcy code now is called a *debtor*. Persons who are owed money by the debtor are generally called *claimants* or *creditors*.

§ 20.3.1   The bankruptcy code—Options available under the code

Under the bankruptcy code, a debtor can obtain a fresh start through liquidation of its nonexempt assets (Chapter 7) or make arrangements to repay its creditors from income in future years under Chapter 11 (reorganization), Chapter 13 (wage earner payment plan), or Chapter 12 (family farmer and fisherman plan). There is also a chapter for bankrupt municipalities (Chapter 9).

§ 20.4   The bankruptcy code—Purpose for seeking bankruptcy protection

The primary purpose of bankruptcy is to give a debtor a chance to make a fresh start by relieving the debtor of the burden of dischargeable debt. When filing Chapter 7, as a condition for receiving this relief, the debtor must turn over to the bankruptcy court all nonexempt property the debtor owns. This property is converted into money and is used to pay costs of administration and creditors to the extent funds are available.

§ 20.4.1   The bankruptcy code—Need for a lawyer

A debtor contemplating filing for relief under the bankruptcy code will generally benefit from the services of a lawyer. A lawyer can:

- Advise a client whether bankruptcy is the best solution to financial problems
- Prepare the necessary legal papers
- Provide representation during the course of the bankruptcy proceedings
- Give advice on exemptions, taxes, and other rights
- Negotiate on behalf of the debtor with counsel for creditors or the trustee

§ 20.5   Bankruptcy courts and jurisdiction

The court of exclusive jurisdiction for bankruptcy is the United States bankruptcy court for each United States district court. This court has jurisdiction over the debtor; all of the debtor's property, no matter where it is located; and all lawsuits by or against the debtor. Bankruptcy law, as federal law, has supremacy over state law, but the bankruptcy court can look to state law when there is no governing bankruptcy law.

§ 20.5.1   Bankruptcy courts and jurisdiction—Venue

A debtor can file for bankruptcy only in the district where that debtor has resided or had a primary place of business for the majority of the preceding 180 days.

§ 20.5.2 Bankruptcy courts and jurisdiction—Bankruptcy court officers

The bankruptcy court has officers whose job it is to administer an estate. They include:

- Bankruptcy judge—The judge presides over the bankruptcy court and hears all litigation pertaining to the case. It is the bankruptcy judge who determines whether a debtor is entitled to a discharge.
- Clerk of court—The clerk has identical duties to those of a federal district clerk of court. In some districts, the clerk is the presiding officer at the first meeting of creditors.
- Chapter 7 trustee—A trustee is appointed at the commencement of a bankruptcy case and serves in the capacity of interim trustee until the first meeting of creditors where he qualifies as permanent trustee unless a new trustee is elected in accordance with the Code. It is the duty of the trustee to recover all nonexempt assets of the debtor and liquidate those assets for the benefit of the creditors. Trustees in most districts are chosen from a panel of private individuals appointed by the United States Trustee.
- United States Trustee—The United States Trustee is a division of the Department of Justice that monitors performance of bankruptcies, ensuring they proceed to resolution; monitors the performance of Chapter 7 trustees; supervises the appointment of creditors' committees; and assists in the appointment of examiners and Chapter 11 and 12 trustees.
- Chapter 13 trustee—Most districts have one standing Chapter 13 trustee.

§ 20.6 Definitions of bankruptcy terms

The following terms are commonly used in bankruptcy law. A list of defined words and their legal definition under the bankruptcy code can be found at 11 U.S.C. § 101.

- Adversary proceedings—individual lawsuits brought within a bankruptcy case.
- Automatic stay—is subject to exceptions—see § 362 (b) and (c)—an injunction or court order that takes effect when a bankruptcy petition is filed, prohibiting all creditors from taking any action against the debtor, property of the debtor, or property of the bankruptcy estate.
- Business bankruptcy—a bankruptcy filed by a business entity.
- Claim—a right to payment asserted by another.
- Consumer bankruptcy—a bankruptcy filed by an individual (or husband and wife) who is not in business with primarily consumer debts.
- Consumer debt—a debt incurred by an individual or family primarily for a personal, household, or family use.

- Creditor—a person or entity that has claim to be owed money by the debtor.
- Debt relief agency—anyone who provides bankruptcy assistance to an assisted person.
- Debtor—the person or entity seeking relief under the bankruptcy code.
- Debtor-in-possession—the entity or individual retaining possession of the assets of the bankruptcy estate in a Chapter 11 bankruptcy.
- Discharge—when all payments under a plan have been made or the debtor has been relieved of its debts.
- Estate—all of a debtor's nonexempt property.
- Exempt property—all of the property of a debtor which is, by the bankruptcy code or state statute, not attachable in a bankruptcy.
- Family farmer—an individual, corporation, or partnership owned by one or more farmers engaged in a farming operation with a regular annual income.
- Family fisherman—an individual, corporation, or partnership owned by one or more fishermen engaged in a fishing operation with a regular annual income.
- Insolvent—when the total debt of a person or entity is greater than the total value of its property or when a person or entity is unable to pay its debts as they come due.
- Judicial lien—a lien obtained by judgment or other judicial process.
- Lien—a legally enforceable claim against property of a debtor to secure repayment of a debt or obligation.
- Liquidation—the sale of all of a debtor's nonexempt property.
- Median family income—the median family income calculated and reported by the Bureau of Census in the most recent year.
- Proof of claim—statement under oath filed in a bankruptcy proceeding by a creditor in which the creditor sets forth the amount owed in sufficient detail to identify the basis for the claim.

§ 20.7 Filing a bankruptcy

A bankruptcy case can be started by filing a voluntary petition or an involuntary petition. In a *voluntary* case, a debtor seeks relief under the code. In an *involuntary* case, creditors ask the court to place a debtor in bankruptcy. The creditors must satisfy certain requirements to file an involuntary bankruptcy, depending on the size and nature of the debtor.

§ 20.7.1 Filing a bankruptcy—Conditions to file voluntary Chapter 7 cases

An individual voluntarily seeking a discharge of debts under Chapter 7 of the bankruptcy code must meet certain conditions:

- Only a person who resides, has a place of business, or owns property in the United States can file bankruptcy.
- One or more debts must be owed, although there is no minimum or maximum as to the amount of debts owed. (Interestingly, there is no requirement that the individual be insolvent. Normally, however, the individual seeking a discharge in bankruptcy is insolvent or is unable to pay debts as they come due.)
- BAPCPA requires a debtor to pass *means testing*. The means test formula is based on the median family income for the area and household size of the debtor. It is complex. It is a major part of the BAPCPA legislation.
- BAPCPA requires a debtor to receive approved credit counseling before filing bankruptcy and take an approved financial management instructional course after filing.
- A debtor may not file for Chapter 7 bankruptcy if previously granted a discharge in a Chapter 7 or Chapter 13 proceeding commenced within eight years before the date of filing bankruptcy, with limited exceptions.

§ 20.7.2 Filing a bankruptcy—Filing the petition

Bankruptcy begins with the filing of a petition for an order for relief in the United States bankruptcy court having jurisdiction.

Additional papers called *schedules* must also be filed by the debtor. The information required in the schedules is set forth in official bankruptcy forms. (See Illustration 20-1.) The forms are available online. Virtually every law office that practices bankruptcy law today has software that allows for the computer generation of bankruptcy forms and schedules that can be corrected as often as needed until they are precisely correct and then converted to pdf documents for filing with the court. The debtor's lawyer is responsible for proper preparation of the forms using information first obtained from the debtor. The lawyer's assistant prepares the forms under the lawyer's supervision. Careful attention in preparation of the forms is very important. Errors or omissions often necessitate amendments to the pleadings and cause delays in the discharge. The debtor must swear, under penalty of perjury, to the accuracy of the schedules.

The schedules and statements, other than the statement of intention, are filed with the petition in a voluntary case, or if the petition is accompanied by a list of all the debtor's creditors and their addresses, can be filed within 14 days (with some exceptions) (see Illustration 20-1).

If an individual debtor's schedule of assets and liabilities includes consumer debts which are secured by property of the estate, the debtor must also file a statement of intention (see Illustration 20-1) within 30 days after filing the petition or on or before the date of the meeting of creditors, whichever is earlier, and must serve a copy on the trustee and the creditors named in the statement.

Preparation of the petition, schedules, and other supporting documents should be completed with as much information as possible. The more detail and information presented in the filed documents, the less time the debtor will need to spend with the trustee at the meeting of creditors.

The voluntary petition is completed for all types of bankruptcies and is signed and dated by the lawyer and debtor. Husband and wife debtors are allowed to file jointly and must both sign everywhere a single debtor would sign. If the debtor is a business organization, an authorized representative signs on behalf of the business everywhere the debtor is required to sign.

Exhibit A to the voluntary petition is only used by corporations filing under Chapter 11 of the Code.

The schedules include general instructions which should be reviewed before completing the forms to ensure that all the necessary information is available.

The first page of the debtor's schedules and of any amendments must contain the name of the court, debtor, and case number. Subsequent pages should be identified with the debtor's name and case number. If the schedules are filed with the petition, the case number is left blank.

The summary of schedules indicates which schedules are attached and states the number of pages in each schedule. The totals from each schedule are listed in the appropriate box. The total number of sheets of all schedules is added and inserted in the box at the bottom of the column entitled *No. of Sheets*.

Schedule A/B. The first section of the Schedule lists all real property in which the debtor has any legal, equitable, or future interest, including all property owned as a cotenant, community property, or in which the debtor has a life estate. The values of the property should reflect the debtor's best estimate of true market value. The remainder of the Schedule lists all personal property of the debtor of whatever kind and is separated into 33 different categories. If the debtor does not own any property in a category, the column entitled None is checked. The values should reflect the debtor's best estimate of true market value.

Schedule C lists the property claimed as exempt by the debtor. In some states, it may be best to select state instead of federal exemptions. The property claimed as exempt should be listed individually, each item should be valued separately, and the specific exemption by subsection should be indicated. The bankruptcy rules allow debtors to amend schedules at any time.

Schedule D lists all creditors holding secured claims. If the debtor has no secured creditors, the box provided on the form must be checked to indicate that. On this and all following schedules, if a continuation page is used, the number of continuation pages must be entered on the appropriate line at the bottom of the first page and the page number and total number of continuation sheets must be completed on continuation pages.

Schedule E/F. The first section of the Schedule lists creditors holding unsecured priority claims and the types of the priority claims. If the debtor has no unsecured creditors holding priority claims, the box provided on the first page must be checked to indicate that. The first page also contains other statements that must be answered, and on the next page or the continuation page the creditors are listed. The remainder of the Schedule lists creditors holding unsecured nonpriority claims. For each creditor listed, the amount of the claim, the date incurred, and the reason for the claim (e.g., credit card debt, medical service, etc.) must be identified. If the debtor has no unsecured creditors, the box provided on the first page must be checked to indicate that.

It is important that all creditors be listed on the appropriate schedules. Any creditor omitted from the schedules may not be discharged, and, if the omission is a result of error in preparation by the lawyer or lawyer's assistant, the error could result in a claim against the lawyer.

Schedule G lists executory contracts and unexpired leases. If the debtor is not a party to any such contracts, the box must be checked to indicate this fact.

Schedule H lists codebtors (an entity that may also be liable on any debts listed in the schedule of creditors), other than a spouse in a joint proceeding. Again, if there are no codebtors, the box must be checked to indicate this fact.

Schedule I lists the current income of the debtor. If the debtor is self-employed, a detailed listing of the debtor's business income and expenses must be submitted with Schedules I and J.

Schedule J lists the current expenditures of the debtor.

The declaration concerning debtor's schedules is signed by the debtor under penalty of perjury.

The statement of financial affairs must be completed by every debtor. It contains instructions and definitions at the beginning of the form that should be reviewed prior to completion of the form. Each question must be answered. If the answer is *None* or the question is not applicable, mark the box labeled *None*. If the answer space provided is not sufficient, attach a separate sheet identified with the case name, case number (if known), and the number of the question. It is signed by the debtor.

The disclosure of compensation paid to counsel for the debt or pursuant to Rule 2016(b) form is signed by the lawyer and is filed and transmitted to the United States Trustee within 14 days after the order for relief or at another time if the court directs.

§ 20.7.3   Filing a bankruptcy—Filing fee

A filing fee must be paid to the clerk at the time the petition is filed unless by local court rule it may be paid in installments or waived.

This fee is in addition to the fees charged by the lawyer and generally cannot be advanced by the lawyer. The debtor may not receive a discharge unless the filing fee is paid in full. Under the bankruptcy code, a husband and wife may file under a single petition and pay one filing fee.

§ 20.7.4 Filing a bankruptcy—Effect of filing

The act of the debtor in filing a petition in bankruptcy has far-reaching significance:

- The petition serves as the application by the debtor for an order of relief discharging any debts.
- The petition operates as an automatic stay, applicable to almost all creditors of the debtor, prohibiting further collection efforts.
- An estate is created by law consisting of any property and interests possessed by the debtor that are not exempt under applicable federal or state law. The estate is used for repayment to creditors.

§ 20.7.5 Filing a bankruptcy—Notice to creditors

Within a reasonable time after the petition is filed, the bankruptcy court sends out notice (with at least 21 days' notice) (the *341 notice*) by mail to all creditors listed by the debtor on the schedules of a meeting of creditors (the *341 meeting*). Creditors are entitled, but not required, to attend the 341 meeting and question the debtor. In the same notice, they are given information about filing claims, as well as deadlines for filing objections to discharge or dischargeability and to exemptions claimed by the debtor.

§ 20.7.6 Filing a bankruptcy—First meeting of creditors

The debtor must attend this meeting (normally with the lawyer). The bankruptcy judge is not permitted to attend the meeting of creditors. An interim trustee presides at the meeting. At the first meeting of creditors, the debtor is questioned under oath by the presiding clerk or trustee and by any interested creditors. The debtor is required to be completely truthful and cooperative in answering questions concerning personal financial matters. Failure to cooperate or providing inaccurate information can be the basis for dismissal of the case; denial of discharge; or under the most extreme circumstances, referral to the United States Attorney for prosecution.

§ 20.7.7 Filing a bankruptcy—Types of claims

Creditors' claims are generally classified as secured or unsecured. *Secured claims* concern those debts supported by some kind of collateral. Liens are not usually affected by the bankruptcy filing.

EXAMPLE:

The debtor bought a car, borrowing the money from a bank. The bank took a security interest in the car, reflected by a lien. The debtor purchased a home, again borrowing the money from the bank. The bank took a mortgage on the house as security. The debtor borrowed money from a finance company to consolidate other debts. The finance company took a security interest in all of the furniture and appliances. The bank and finance company are secured creditors.

Unsecured claims are those claims that have no collateral or other lien. For example, open accounts such as credit card or trade accounts, personal loans, or claims where the amount of security is less than the debt (for instance, $10,000 is owed on a car worth $7,000; partly secured and partly unsecured).

EXAMPLE:
The debtor has charge cards at a number of local department stores. The debtor has an American Express card and a MasterCard. The debtor has outstanding obligations to a plumber or a lawyer.

These are unsecured debts and the creditors are unsecured creditors, since none of the obligations are secured by collateral.

A third classification of claim is a *priority claim*. Section 567 of the bankruptcy code provides a list of the types of claims and expenses that may be designated priority claims. One type of priority claim is an *administrative claim*. Administrative claims are related to the bankruptcy administration, e.g., payment of taxes, accountants, or lawyers, and are given priority treatment.

When the debtor files a petition, the debtor is required to list all creditors, identifying whether the claim is secured, unsecured, or priority. If the creditor disagrees with either the classification or the amount of the debt listed by the debtor, it must notify the court by filing a claim.

§ 20.7.8   Filing a bankruptcy—Filing of claims by creditors

Creditors in Chapter 7 cases, other than for taxes, must file their claims with the bankruptcy court within the time set by the court or be barred from participating in any distribution that might be declared. There is a prescribed form for submitting *proofs of claim* which may be obtained from the bankruptcy court. If the creditor fails to file a claim, the trustee or a codebtor may file a claim for the creditor. Often a creditor is advised in the 341 Notice not to file a claim at that time, awaiting a determination of whether there are any nonexempt assets available to pay creditors.

§ 20.8   The debtor's estate

At the time a Chapter 7 bankruptcy petition is filed, the debtor's nonexempt property comes under the control of the bankruptcy court. It is the responsibility of the trustee to liquidate the estate in the best interests of the creditors. There are many factors the trustee must consider in liquidation of the estate, and in many consumer cases, the trustee will determine that there are no assets available to pay creditors, because the debtor has only exempt assets or the value of the debtor's nonexempt assets is so low it is uneconomical to liquidate. This is called a *no asset case*.

§ 20.8.1   The debtor's estate—Liquidation of the estate

The trustee examines the economics of the debtor's entire financial situation. The trustee is interested in how much money can be raised for the benefit of creditors and at what cost. In determining whether there are assets to liquidate, the trustee will consider whether assets are exempt and whether there is equity in the asset.

§ 20.8.2   The debtor's estate—Exempt property

Although in theory the debtor surrenders all property for the benefit of the creditors, the debtor is entitled by law to keep certain items of property. Such property is called **exempt property**. The bankruptcy code identifies certain exemptions under federal law. Most states have their own exemption system. Unless dictated by state law, a debtor must choose whether to use the federal or state exemption system. The federal exemption law is adjusted every three years.

There are various other exempt items, insurance, retirement, alimony, and so forth, specifically itemized in Section 522 of the code. State exemptions vary significantly and should be evaluated by the debtor and lawyer to determine whether state or federal exemptions are more favorable.

§ 20.8.3   The debtor's estate—Equity

Equity is the value of a property or of an interest in it in excess of claims against it.

EXAMPLE:

The debtor has a house worth $30,000. The mortgage balance is $18,000. The debtor's equity is $12,000, assuming there are no other liens (judgment, tax, etc.) on the house.

It would seem that if the trustee sold the house, the debtor's estate would realize a profit of $12,000. However, the net amount available to pay creditors is reduced both by the cost of sale (often estimated at ten percent of the sale price), plus the debtor's homestead exemption, if the property sold qualifies as a homestead. The value of the homestead exemption (whether state or federal) is generally distributed to the debtor on sale, reducing the net benefit to the estate. Accordingly, the trustee, when analyzing equity, may determine there is no value available to creditors, and thus no point to liquidating the property. In this example, the house sells for $30,000, the underlying mortgage is $18,000, and the cost to sell is $3,000, leaving net proceeds of $15,000. Since the debtor's federal homestead exemption is $21,625, the estate would receive nothing. Alternatively, in areas where property values have increased, a debtor may have accumulated significant equity in property, which can be liquidated to pay creditors.

§ 20.8.4   The debtor's estate—Abandoned property

When, as in the example above, the estate will receive nothing from the sale of an asset, such asset will generally be abandoned by the trustee. When the trustee abandons the property, the debtor becomes the owner again, subject to valid liens against it. The trustee may abandon any property which is burdensome or of inconsequential value to the estate, with certain exceptions to contaminated property. In addition, a party in interest may request the court to order the trustee to abandon property.

§ 20.8.5   The debtor's estate—Sale of property

There are many instances when there is sufficient equity in property over and above the debtor's exemptions to make a sale profitable for the estate. In those instances, the trustee offers the property for sale. Sales of property have to be approved by the court.

§ 20.9   Dischargeable and nondischargeable debts

The filing of a petition for relief under Chapter 7 acts as a request for a discharge of all of a person's debts. If no objection to the dischargeability of a debt is filed by a creditor or if no objection to discharge is filed by a creditor or the trustee within the time set by the bankruptcy court, then a discharge will be entered, relieving the debtor of all prebankruptcy debts except those secured by a lien (to the extent of the value of the lien) and certain obligations the legislature has determined, for public policy reasons, should not be eligible for discharge. Debtors may only discharge debts in Chapter 7 once every eight years.

§ 20.9.1   Dischargeable and nondischargeable debts— Nondischargeable debts

Debts not discharged by the Chapter 7 bankruptcy are itemized in the code in Section 523 and include:
- Certain taxes and loans to pay taxes
- Alimony, child support, and maintenance obligations
- Certain debts related to luxury goods
- Debts arising from fines, penalties, or forfeitures payable to a governmental unit
- Personal injury or other claims arising from drunk driving or for willful or malicious injury
- Educational loans, absent a showing of extreme hardship

- Debts incurred through false pretenses, false representation, or fraud
- Debts not listed by the debtor on the schedules filed with the bankruptcy court (but a case can be reopened to include debts inadvertently omitted)

Some of the obligations nondischargeable in Chapter 7 may be discharged in a Chapter 13 proceeding.

§ 20.9.2 Dischargeable and nondischargeable debts— Complaint to have debt declared nondischargeable

If a creditor or the trustee believes that a debt is not dischargeable, it has the right to file a complaint with the court to find a particular debt nondischargeable under Section 523 of the code or the debtor should be denied a discharge in its entirety under Section 727 of the code. The complaint is called an *adversary proceeding* and is conducted as a separate lawsuit within the bankruptcy proceeding. If the bankruptcy court agrees that a discharge should be denied, or, in the event only one debt is found nondischargeable, the creditor may seek a judgment for the amount owed, which will survive the bankruptcy.

§ 20.9.3 Dischargeable and nondischargeable debts— Discharge

A debtor will generally be granted a discharge under Chapter 7, absent an objection. The bankruptcy code requires the bankruptcy court to hold a trial to determine whether or not to discharge the debt. Otherwise the debtor remains liable for all debts.

Once a debtor has been granted a discharge, all creditors are enjoined from commencing or continuing any action against the debtor or the exempt property to collect their debt, with the exception of debts reaffirmed which are subsequently defaulted on by the debtor or nondischargeable debts. Debtors can voluntarily repay a discharged debt at any time.

§ 20.9.4 Dischargeable and nondischargeable debts— Reaffirmation of a debt

Debtors are often encouraged by creditors to *reaffirm* a debt, effectively negating the benefit of the discharge granted by a bankruptcy. The debtor would sign a Reaffirmation Agreement whereby the debtor agrees to continue making payments to the creditor in the same manner prior to filing bankruptcy in order to keep the asset subject to the lien. Reaffirmation is appropriate only in limited situations, and courts often refuse to allow a debtor to reaffirm a debt if the court believes it will interfere with the debtor's fresh start. When seeking reaffirmation, either the lawyer for the debtor must sign the reaffirmation stating that the debtor fully understood what they were doing and the lawyer believes that the reaffirmation does not impose an undue hardship on the debtor or any dependents, or the debtor must appear in court and explain to the bankruptcy judge why it is in the debtor's best interests to do so. Many courts have local rules and requirements for reaffirmation agreements, so the local rules should be checked before any agreement is executed or submitted to the court.

§ 20.9.5   Dischargeable and nondischargeable debts—Closing out the estate

The administration of the estate is carried on by the trustee in accordance with specific duties set out in the bankruptcy code. Additionally, the trustee makes periodic accountings to the bankruptcy court and a final report to the court of the liquidation, including a detailed accounting of the money realized and disbursed and all property sold and disburses all funds on hand to the creditors in accordance with the bankruptcy court's order.

§ 20.10   Chapter 11 reorganization

Chapter 11 of the bankruptcy code is available to businesses and individual debtors who seek to reorganize their affairs rather than liquidate. Many major U.S. corporations have sought protection under Chapter 11. In *Chapter 11*, the business continues to be operated by the debtor and its management as a ***debtor-in-possession***, rather than a trustee, unless the court rules a trustee is necessary. Procedures under Chapter 11 are quite different from those described in this chapter.

§ 20.11   Chapter 12 for a family farmer or fisherman

The 1986 amendments to the bankruptcy code created a new chapter, **Chapter 12**, for use by family farmers or fishermen, including partnerships and corporations consisting of owner farmers and fishermen operating a farming or fishing operation. Only a family farmer or fisherman with regular annual income may be a debtor under Chapter 12. A Chapter 12 case may only be initiated voluntarily.

Once a plan has been filed, a Chapter 12 trustee will supervise the debtor's operation for a period of from three to five years, but once the plan has been confirmed, the debtor retains possession of the assets of the estate, including operating the debtor's farm or fishing business.

§ 20.12   Chapter 13 relief

Under **Chapter 13** of the bankruptcy code, the debtor files a plan agreeing to pay a certain percentage of future earnings or cash from sales of assets to a trustee to pay off the debts within a reasonable period of time, three to five years. If the court accepts the plan, the debtor has the protection of the court while the debts are paid. At the conclusion of the plan, all debts not repaid are discharged. Thus, in

Chapter 13, a debtor uses future earnings, not current assets, to satisfy creditors.

Further advantages of a Chapter 13 plan are:

- Discharge of criminal fines and penalties (but not restitution)
- Discharge of debts for fraud and malicious injury (excluding death or personal injury caused while driving intoxicated)
- Payment of tax arrearages without further penalties and interest
- Payment of mortgage arrearages over the objection of the mortgage lender
- Ability to change the terms of a secured loan (other than a mortgage secured only by the residence). A debtor can change the interest rate, length of loan, monthly payment, etc.

Chapter 13 or *wage earner* bankruptcies are an alternative to liquidation for an individual consumer with a regular source of income. The debtor must also have noncontingent, liquidated, unsecured debt of less than $360,475, and noncontingent, liquidated, secured debt of less than $1,081,400.

Illustration 20-1
Complete Petition Package

B1 (Official Form 1) (12/11)

UNITED STATES BANKRUPTCY COURT _____ District of_____	VOLUNTARY PETITION
Name of Debtor (if individual, enter Last, First, Middle):	Name of Joint Debtor (Spouse) (Last, First, Middle):
All Other Names used by the Debtor in the last 8 years (include married, maiden, and trade names):	All Other Names used by the Joint Debtor in the last 8 years (include married, maiden, and trade names):
Last four digits of Soc. Sec. or Individual-Taxpayer I.D. (ITIN)/Complete EIN (if more than one, state all):	Last four digits of Soc. Sec. or Individual-Taxpayer I.D. (ITIN)/Complete EIN (if more than one, state all):
Street Address of Debtor (No. and Street, City, and State): ZIP CODE	Street Address of Joint Debtor (No. and Street, City, and State): ZIP CODE
County of Residence or of the Principal Place of Business:	County of Residence or of the Principal Place of Business:
Mailing Address of Debtor (if different from street address): ZIP CODE	Mailing Address of Joint Debtor (if different from street address): ZIP CODE
Location of Principal Assets of Business Debtor (if different from street address above):	ZIP CODE

Type of Debtor
(Form of Organization)
(Check one box.)

☐ Individual (includes Joint Debtors)
   See Exhibit D on page 2 of this form.
☐ Corporation (includes LLC and LLP)
☐ Partnership
☐ Other (If debtor is not one of the above entities, check this box and state type of entity below.)

Nature of Business
(Check one box.)

☐ Health Care Business
☐ Single Asset Real Estate as defined in 11 U.S.C. § 101(51B)
☐ Railroad
☐ Stockbroker
☐ Commodity Broker
☐ Clearing Bank
☐ Other

Chapter of Bankruptcy Code Under Which the Petition is Filed (Check one box.)

☐ Chapter 7
☐ Chapter 9
☐ Chapter 11
☐ Chapter 12
☐ Chapter 13
☐ Chapter 15 Petition for Recognition of a Foreign Main Proceeding
☐ Chapter 15 Petition for Recognition of a Foreign Nonmain Proceeding

Chapter 15 Debtors

Country of debtor's center of main interests:

Each country in which a foreign proceeding by, regarding, or against debtor is pending:

Tax-Exempt Entity
(Check box, if applicable.)

☐ Debtor is a tax-exempt organization under title 26 of the United States Code (the Internal Revenue Code).

Nature of Debts
(Check one box.)

☐ Debts are primarily consumer debts, defined in 11 U.S.C. § 101(8) as "incurred by an individual primarily for a personal, family, or household purpose."
☐ Debts are primarily business debts.

Filing Fee (Check one box.)

☐ Full Filing Fee attached.

☐ Filing Fee to be paid in installments (applicable to individuals only). Must attach signed application for the court's consideration certifying that the debtor is unable to pay fee except in installments. Rule 1006(b). See Official Form 3A.

☐ Filing Fee waiver requested (applicable to chapter 7 individuals only). Must attach signed application for the court's consideration. See Official Form 3B.

Chapter 11 Debtors

Check one box:
☐ Debtor is a small business debtor as defined in 11 U.S.C. § 101(51D).
☐ Debtor is not a small business debtor as defined in 11 U.S.C. § 101(51D).

Check if:
☐ Debtor's aggregate noncontingent liquidated debts (excluding debts owed to insiders or affiliates) are less than $2,343,300 (*amount subject to adjustment on 4/01/13 and every three years thereafter*).

- -

Check all applicable boxes:
☐ A plan is being filed with this petition.
☐ Acceptances of the plan were solicited prepetition from one or more classes of creditors, in accordance with 11 U.S.C. § 1126(b).

Statistical/Administrative Information

☐ Debtor estimates that funds will be available for distribution to unsecured creditors.
☐ Debtor estimates that, after any exempt property is excluded and administrative expenses paid, there will be no funds available for distribution to unsecured creditors.

THIS SPACE IS FOR COURT USE ONLY

Estimated Number of Creditors

☐	☐	☐	☐	☐	☐	☐	☐	☐	☐
1-49	50-99	100-199	200-999	1,000-5,000	5,001-10,000	10,001-25,000	25,001-50,000	50,001-100,000	Over 100,000

Estimated Assets

☐	☐	☐	☐	☐	☐	☐	☐	☐	☐
$0 to $50,000	$50,001 to $100,000	$100,001 to $500,000	$500,001 to $1 million	$1,000,001 to $10 million	$10,000,001 to $50 million	$50,000,001 to $100 million	$100,000,001 to $500 million	$500,000,001 to $1 billion	More than $1 billion

Estimated Liabilities

☐	☐	☐	☐	☐	☐	☐	☐	☐	☐
$0 to $50,000	$50,001 to $100,000	$100,001 to $500,000	$500,001 to $1 million	$1,000,001 to $10 million	$10,000,001 to $50 million	$50,000,001 to $100 million	$100,000,001 to $500 million	$500,000,001 to $1 billion	More than $1 billion

B1 (Official Form 1) (12/11) Page 2

Voluntary Petition *(This page must be completed and filed in every case.)*	Name of Debtor(s):	
All Prior Bankruptcy Cases Filed Within Last 8 Years (If more than two, attach additional sheet.)		
Location Where Filed:	Case Number:	Date Filed:
Location Where Filed:	Case Number:	Date Filed:
Pending Bankruptcy Case Filed by any Spouse, Partner, or Affiliate of this Debtor (If more than one, attach additional sheet.)		
Name of Debtor:	Case Number:	Date Filed:
District:	Relationship:	Judge:

<table>
<tr>
<td>

Exhibit A

(To be completed if debtor is required to file periodic reports (e.g., forms 10K and 10Q) with the Securities and Exchange Commission pursuant to Section 13 or 15(d) of the Securities Exchange Act of 1934 and is requesting relief under chapter 11.)

☐ Exhibit A is attached and made a part of this petition.

</td>
<td>

Exhibit B

(To be completed if debtor is an individual whose debts are primarily consumer debts.)

I, the attorney for the petitioner named in the foregoing petition, declare that I have informed the petitioner that [he or she] may proceed under chapter 7, 11, 12, or 13 of title 11, United States Code, and have explained the relief available under each such chapter. I further certify that I have delivered to the debtor the notice required by 11 U.S.C. § 342(b).

X _____

  Signature of Attorney for Debtor(s)   (Date)

</td>
</tr>
</table>

Exhibit C

Does the debtor own or have possession of any property that poses or is alleged to pose a threat of imminent and identifiable harm to public health or safety?

☐   Yes, and Exhibit C is attached and made a part of this petition.

☐   No.

Exhibit D

(To be completed by every individual debtor. If a joint petition is filed, each spouse must complete and attach a separate Exhibit D.)

☐   Exhibit D, completed and signed by the debtor, is attached and made a part of this petition.

If this is a joint petition:

☐   Exhibit D, also completed and signed by the joint debtor, is attached and made a part of this petition.

Information Regarding the Debtor - Venue
(Check any applicable box.)

☐   Debtor has been domiciled or has had a residence, principal place of business, or principal assets in this District for 180 days immediately preceding the date of this petition or for a longer part of such 180 days than in any other District.

☐   There is a bankruptcy case concerning debtor's affiliate, general partner, or partnership pending in this District.

☐   Debtor is a debtor in a foreign proceeding and has its principal place of business or principal assets in the United States in this District, or has no principal place of business or assets in the United States but is a defendant in an action or proceeding [in a federal or state court] in this District, or the interests of the parties will be served in regard to the relief sought in this District.

Certification by a Debtor Who Resides as a Tenant of Residential Property
(Check all applicable boxes.)

☐   Landlord has a judgment against the debtor for possession of debtor's residence. (If box checked, complete the following.)

_____
(Name of landlord that obtained judgment)

_____
(Address of landlord)

☐   Debtor claims that under applicable nonbankruptcy law, there are circumstances under which the debtor would be permitted to cure the entire monetary default that gave rise to the judgment for possession, after the judgment for possession was entered, and

☐   Debtor has included with this petition the deposit with the court of any rent that would become due during the 30-day period after the filing of the petition.

☐   Debtor certifies that he/she has served the Landlord with this certification. (11 U.S.C. § 362(l)).

B1 (Official Form 1) (12/11)	Page 3
Voluntary Petition *(This page must be completed and filed in every case.)*	Name of Debtor(s):

Signatures

Signature(s) of Debtor(s) (Individual/Joint)	Signature of a Foreign Representative

I declare under penalty of perjury that the information provided in this petition is true and correct.
 [If petitioner is an individual whose debts are primarily consumer debts and has chosen to file under chapter 7] I am aware that I may proceed under chapter 7, 11, 12 or 13 of title 11, United States Code, understand the relief available under each such chapter, and choose to proceed under chapter 7.
 [If no attorney represents me and no bankruptcy petition preparer signs the petition] I have obtained and read the notice required by 11 U.S.C. § 342(b).
 	
 I request relief in accordance with the chapter of title 11, United States Code, specified in this petition.
 	
 X _____
     Signature of Debtor
 	
 X _____
     Signature of Joint Debtor
 	
     Telephone Number (if not represented by attorney)
 	
     Date
	I declare under penalty of perjury that the information provided in this petition is true and correct, that I am the foreign representative of a debtor in a foreign proceeding, and that I am authorized to file this petition.
	
	 (Check only one box.)
	
	 ☐ I request relief in accordance with chapter 15 of title 11, United States Code. Certified copies of the documents required by 11 U.S.C. § 1515 are attached.
	
	 ☐ Pursuant to 11 U.S.C. § 1511, I request relief in accordance with the chapter of title 11 specified in this petition. A certified copy of the order granting recognition of the foreign main proceeding is attached.
	
	 X _____
	     (Signature of Foreign Representative)
	
	     (Printed Name of Foreign Representative)
	
	     Date

Signature of Attorney*
 	
 X _____
     Signature of Attorney for Debtor(s)
 	
     Printed Name of Attorney for Debtor(s)
 	
     Firm Name
 	
     Address
 	
     Telephone Number
 	
     Date
 	
 *In a case in which § 707(b)(4)(D) applies, this signature also constitutes a certification that the attorney has no knowledge after an inquiry that the information in the schedules is incorrect.
	Signature of Non-Attorney Bankruptcy Petition Preparer
	
	 I declare under penalty of perjury that: (1) I am a bankruptcy petition preparer as defined in 11 U.S.C. § 110; (2) I prepared this document for compensation and have provided the debtor with a copy of this document and the notices and information required under 11 U.S.C. §§ 110(b), 110(h), and 342(b); and, (3) if rules or guidelines have been promulgated pursuant to 11 U.S.C. § 110(h) setting a maximum fee for services chargeable by bankruptcy petition preparers, I have given the debtor notice of the maximum amount before preparing any document for filing for a debtor or accepting any fee from the debtor, as required in that section. Official Form 19 is attached.
	
	     Printed Name and title, if any, of Bankruptcy Petition Preparer
	
	     Social-Security number (If the bankruptcy petition preparer is not an individual, state the Social-Security number of the officer, principal, responsible person or partner of the bankruptcy petition preparer.) (Required by 11 U.S.C. § 110.)

Signature of Debtor (Corporation/Partnership)
 	
 I declare under penalty of perjury that the information provided in this petition is true and correct, and that I have been authorized to file this petition on behalf of the debtor.
 	
 The debtor requests the relief in accordance with the chapter of title 11, United States Code, specified in this petition.
 	
 X _____
     Signature of Authorized Individual
 	
     Printed Name of Authorized Individual
 	
     Title of Authorized Individual
 	
     Date
	Address
	
	 X _____
	     Signature
	
	     Date
	
	 Signature of bankruptcy petition preparer or officer, principal, responsible person, or partner whose Social-Security number is provided above.
	
	 Names and Social-Security numbers of all other individuals who prepared or assisted in preparing this document unless the bankruptcy petition preparer is not an individual.
	
	 If more than one person prepared this document, attach additional sheets conforming to the appropriate official form for each person.
	
	 A bankruptcy petition preparer's failure to comply with the provisions of title 11 and the Federal Rules of Bankruptcy Procedure may result in fines or imprisonment or both. 11 U.S.C. § 110; 18 U.S.C. § 156.

B 1D (Official Form 1, Exhibit D) (12/09)

UNITED STATES BANKRUPTCY COURT

_____ District of _____

In re_____   Case No._____
      Debtor   (if known)

EXHIBIT D - INDIVIDUAL DEBTOR'S STATEMENT OF COMPLIANCE WITH CREDIT COUNSELING REQUIREMENT

Warning: You must be able to check truthfully one of the five statements regarding credit counseling listed below. If you cannot do so, you are not eligible to file a bankruptcy case, and the court can dismiss any case you do file. If that happens, you will lose whatever filing fee you paid, and your creditors will be able to resume collection activities against you. If your case is dismissed and you file another bankruptcy case later, you may be required to pay a second filing fee and you may have to take extra steps to stop creditors' collection activities.

Every individual debtor must file this Exhibit D. If a joint petition is filed, each spouse must complete and file a separate Exhibit D. Check one of the five statements below and attach any documents as directed.

❒ 1. Within the 180 days **before the filing of my bankruptcy case**, I received a briefing from a credit counseling agency approved by the United States trustee or bankruptcy administrator that outlined the opportunities for available credit counseling and assisted me in performing a related budget analysis, and I have a certificate from the agency describing the services provided to me. _Attach a copy of the certificate and a copy of any debt repayment plan developed through the agency._

❒ 2. Within the 180 days **before the filing of my bankruptcy case**, I received a briefing from a credit counseling agency approved by the United States trustee or bankruptcy administrator that outlined the opportunities for available credit counseling and assisted me in performing a related budget analysis, but I do not have a certificate from the agency describing the services provided to me. _You must file a copy of a certificate from the agency describing the services provided to you and a copy of any debt repayment plan developed through the agency no later than 14 days after your bankruptcy case is filed._

B 1D (Official Form 1, Exh. D) (12/09) – Cont.

☐ 3. I certify that I requested credit counseling services from an approved agency but was unable to obtain the services during the seven days from the time I made my request, and the following exigent circumstances merit a temporary waiver of the credit counseling requirement so I can file my bankruptcy case now. *[Summarize exigent circumstances here.]*

_____
_____
_____
_____

If your certification is satisfactory to the court, you must still obtain the credit counseling briefing within the first 30 days after you file your bankruptcy petition and promptly file a certificate from the agency that provided the counseling, together with a copy of any debt management plan developed through the agency. Failure to fulfill these requirements may result in dismissal of your case. Any extension of the 30-day deadline can be granted only for cause and is limited to a maximum of 15 days. Your case may also be dismissed if the court is not satisfied with your reasons for filing your bankruptcy case without first receiving a credit counseling briefing.

☐ 4. I am not required to receive a credit counseling briefing because of: *[Check the applicable statement.] [Must be accompanied by a motion for determination by the court.]*

☐ Incapacity. (Defined in 11 U.S.C. § 109(h)(4) as impaired by reason of mental illness or mental deficiency so as to be incapable of realizing and making rational decisions with respect to financial responsibilities.);
☐ Disability. (Defined in 11 U.S.C. § 109(h)(4) as physically impaired to the extent of being unable, after reasonable effort, to participate in a credit counseling briefing in person, by telephone, or through the Internet.);
☐ Active military duty in a military combat zone.

☐ 5. The United States trustee or bankruptcy administrator has determined that the credit counseling requirement of 11 U.S.C. § 109(h) does not apply in this district.

I certify under penalty of perjury that the information provided above is true and correct.

Signature of Debtor: _____

Date: _____

B 3A (Official Form 3A) (12/07)

UNITED STATES BANKRUPTCY COURT
_____ District Of _____

In re _____,   Case No. _____
                   Debtor

                                               Chapter _____

APPLICATION TO PAY FILING FEE IN INSTALLMENTS

1.   In accordance with Fed. R. Bankr. P. 1006, I apply for permission to pay the filing fee amounting to $_____ in installments.

2.   I am unable to pay the filing fee except in installments.

3.   Until the filing fee is paid in full, I will not make any additional payment or transfer any additional property to an attorney or any other person for services in connection with this case.

4.   I propose the following terms for the payment of the Filing Fee.*

        $ _____   Check one ☐   With the filing of the petition, or
                                         ☐   On or before _____

        $ _____ on or before _____

        $ _____ on or before _____

        $ _____ on or before _____

*   The number of installments proposed shall not exceed four (4), and the final installment shall be payable not later than 120 days after filing the petition. For cause shown, the court may extend the time of any installment, provided the last installment is paid not later than 180 days after filing the petition. Fed. R. Bankr. P. 1006(b)(2).

5.   I understand that if I fail to pay any installment when due, my bankruptcy case may be dismissed and I may not receive a discharge of my debts.

_____   _____   _____   _____
Signature of Attorney   Date   Signature of Debtor   Date
                                                (In a joint case, both spouses must sign.)

_____   _____   _____
Name of Attorney   Signature of Joint Debtor (if any)   Date

DECLARATION AND SIGNATURE OF NON-ATTORNEY BANKRUPTCY PETITION PREPARER (See 11 U.S.C. § 110)

I declare under penalty of perjury that: (1) I am a bankruptcy petition preparer as defined in 11 U.S.C. § 110; (2) I prepared this document for compensation and have provided the debtor with a copy of this document and the notices and information required under 11 U.S.C. §§ 110(b), 110(h), and 342(b); (3) if rules or guidelines have been promulgated pursuant to 11 U.S.C. § 110(h) setting a maximum fee for services chargeable by bankruptcy petition preparers, I have given the debtor notice of the maximum amount before preparing any document for filing for a debtor or accepting any fee from the debtor, as required under that section; and (4) I will not accept any additional money or other property from the debtor before the filing fee is paid in full.

_____   _____
Printed or Typed Name and Title, if any, of Bankruptcy Petition Preparer   Social-Security No. (Required by 11 U.S.C. § 110.)
If the bankruptcy petition preparer is not an individual, state the name, title (if any), address, and social-security number of the officer, principal, responsible person, or partner who signs the document.

_____

Address

x_____   _____
Signature of Bankruptcy Petition Preparer   Date

Names and Social-Security numbers of all other individuals who prepared or assisted in preparing this document, unless the bankruptcy petition preparer is not an individual:

If more than one person prepared this document, attach additional signed sheets conforming to the appropriate Official Form for each person.
A bankruptcy petition preparer's failure to comply with the provisions of title 11 and the Federal Rules of Bankruptcy Procedure may result in fines or imprisonment or both. 11 U.S.C. § 110; 18 U.S.C. § 156.

B 3A (Official Form 3A) (12/07) - Cont.

UNITED STATES BANKRUPTCY COURT
_____ District Of _____

In re _____,   Case No. _____
                Debtor

                                                       Chapter _____

ORDER APPROVING PAYMENT OF FILING FEE IN INSTALLMENTS

    ☐   IT IS ORDERED that the debtor(s) may pay the filing fee in installments on the terms proposed in the foregoing application.

    ☐   IT IS ORDERED that the debtor(s) shall pay the filing fee according to the following terms:

$ _____   Check one ☐ With the filing of the petition, or
                                    ☐ On or before _____

$ _____   on or before _____

$ _____   on or before _____

$ _____   on or before _____

    ☐   IT IS FURTHER ORDERED that until the filing fee is paid in full the debtor(s) shall not make any additional payment or transfer any additional property to an attorney or any other person for services in connection with this case.

                                                               BY THE COURT

Date: _____

                                                     _____
                                                    United States Bankruptcy Judge

B3B (Official Form 3B) (11/11)

APPLICATION FOR WAIVER OF THE CHAPTER 7 FILING FEE
FOR INDIVIDUALS WHO CANNOT PAY THE FILING FEE
IN FULL OR IN INSTALLMENTS

The court fee for filing a case under chapter 7 of the Bankruptcy Code is $306.

If you cannot afford to pay the full fee at the time of filing, you may apply to pay the fee in installments. A form, which is available from the bankruptcy clerk's office, must be completed to make that application. If your application to pay in installments is approved, you will be permitted to file your petition, generally completing payment of the fee over the course of four to six months.

If you cannot afford to pay the fee either in full at the time of filing or in installments, you may request a waiver of the filing fee by completing this application and filing it with the Clerk of Court. A judge will decide whether you have to pay the fee. By law, the judge may waive the fee only if your income is less than 150 percent of the official poverty line applicable to your family size and you are unable to pay the fee in installments. You may obtain information about the poverty guidelines at www.uscourts.gov or in the bankruptcy clerk's office.

Required information. Complete all items in the application, and attach requested schedules. Then sign the application on the last page. If you and your spouse are filing a joint bankruptcy petition, you both must provide information as requested and sign the application.

B3B (Official Form 3B) (11/11) -- Cont.

United States Bankruptcy Court
_____ District of _____

In re: _____   Case No. _____
         Debtor(s)   (if known)

APPLICATION FOR WAIVER OF THE CHAPTER 7 FILING FEE
FOR INDIVIDUALS WHO CANNOT PAY THE FILING FEE IN FULL OR IN INSTALLMENTS

Part A. Family Size and Income

1. Including yourself, your spouse, and dependents you have listed or will list on Schedule I (Current Income of Individual Debtors(s)), how many people are in your family? (Do not include your spouse if you are separated AND are not filing a joint petition.) _____

2. Restate the following information that you provided, or will provide, on Line 16 of Schedule I. Attach a completed copy of Schedule I, if it is available.

    Total Combined Monthly Income (Line 16 of Schedule I): $_____

3. State the monthly net income, if any, of dependents included in Question 1 above. Do not include any income already reported in Item 2. If none, enter $0.

                                                                      $_____

4. Add the "Total Combined Monthly Income" reported in Question 2 to your dependents' monthly net income from Question 3.

                                                                      $_____

5. Do you expect the amount in Question 4 to increase or decrease by more than 10% during the next 6 months? Yes ___ No ___

    If yes, explain.

Part B. Monthly Expenses

6. EITHER (a) attach a completed copy of Schedule J (Schedule of Monthly Expenses), and state your total monthly expenses reported on Line 18 of that Schedule, OR (b) if you have not yet completed Schedule J, provide an estimate of your total monthly expenses.

                                                              $_____

7. Do you expect the amount in Question 6 to increase or decrease by more than 10% during the next 6 months? Yes ___ No ___
    If yes, explain.

Part C. Real and Personal Property

EITHER (1) attach completed copies of Schedule A (Real Property) and Schedule B (Personal Property), OR (2) if you have not yet completed those schedules, answer the following questions.

8. State the amount of cash you have on hand. $_____

9. State below any money you have in savings, checking, or other accounts in a bank or other financial institution.

Bank or Other Financial Institution:	Type of Account such as savings, checking, CD:	Amount:
		$_____
_____	_____	
		$_____
_____	_____	

B3B (Official Form 3B) (11/11) -- Cont.

10. State below the assets owned by you. **Do not list ordinary household furnishings and clothing**.

Home   Address:

Value: $ _____

_____

Amount owed on mortgages and liens: $ _____

_____

Other real estate   Address:

Value: $ _____

_____

Amount owed on mortgages and liens: $ _____

_____

Motor vehicle   Model/Year: _____

Value: $ _____

_____

Amount owed: $ _____

Motor vehicle   Model/Year: _____

Value: $ _____

_____

Amount owed: $ _____

Other   Description_____

Value: $ _____

_____

Amount owed: $ _____

11. State below any person, business, organization, or governmental unit that owes you money and the amount that is owed.

Name of Person, Business, or Organization that Owes You   Amount Owed
Money

_____ $ _____

_____ $ _____

Part D. Additional Information.

12. Have you paid an **attorney** any money for services in connection with this case, including the completion of this form, the bankruptcy petition, or schedules? Yes ___ No ___
If yes, how much have you paid? $ _____

13. Have you promised to pay or do you anticipate paying an **attorney** in connection with your bankruptcy case? Yes ___ No ___
If yes, how much have you promised to pay or do you anticipate paying? $ _____

14. Have you paid **anyone other than an attorney** (such as a bankruptcy petition preparer, paralegal, typing service, or another person) any money for services in connection with this case, including the completion of this form, the bankruptcy petition, or schedules? Yes ___ No ___
If yes, how much have you paid? $ _____

15. Have you promised to pay or do you anticipate paying **anyone other than an attorney** (such as a bankruptcy petition preparer, paralegal, typing service, or another person) any money for services in connection with this case, including the completion of this form, the bankruptcy petition, or schedules?
Yes ___ No ___
If yes, how much have you promised to pay or do you anticipate paying? $ _____

16. Has anyone paid an attorney or other person or service in connection with this case, on your behalf?
Yes ___ No ___

If yes, explain.

B3B (Official Form 3B) (11/11) -- Cont.

17. Have you previously filed for bankruptcy relief during the past eight years? Yes ___ No ___

Case Number (if known)	Year filed	Location of filing	Did you obtain a discharge? (if known)		
_____	_____	_____	Yes ____	No ____	Don't know ____
_____	_____	_____	Yes ____	No ____	Don't know ____

18. Please provide any other information that helps to explain why you are unable to pay the filing fee in installments.

19. I (we) declare under penalty of perjury that I (we) cannot currently afford to pay the filing fee in full or in installments and that the foregoing information is true and correct.

Executed on: _____

          Date   Signature of Debtor

          Date   Signature of Codebtor

DECLARATION AND SIGNATURE OF BANKRUPTCY PETITION PREPARER (See 11 U.S.C. § 110)

I declare under penalty of perjury that: (1) I am a bankruptcy petition preparer as defined in 11 U.S.C. § 110; (2) I prepared this document for compensation and have provided the debtor with a copy of this document and the notices and information required under 11 U.S.C. §§ 110(b), 110(h), and 342(b); and (3) if rules or guidelines have been promulgated pursuant to 11 U.S.C. § 110(h) setting a maximum fee for services chargeable by bankruptcy petition preparers, I have given the debtor notice of the maximum amount before preparing any document for filing for a debtor or accepting any fee from the debtor, as required under that section.

_____   _____
Printed or Typed Name and Title, if any, of Bankruptcy Petition Preparer   Social-Security No. (Required by
                                                          11 U.S.C. §110.)
If the bankruptcy petition preparer is not an individual, state the name, title (if any), address, and social-security number of the officer, principal, responsible person, or partner who signs the document.

_____

_____
Address

x_____   _____
Signature of Bankruptcy Petition Preparer   Date

Names and Social-Security numbers of all other individuals who prepared or assisted in preparing this document, unless the bankruptcy petition preparer is not an individual:

If more than one person prepared this document, attach additional signed sheets conforming to the appropriate Official Form for each person.
A bankruptcy petition preparer's failure to comply with the provisions of title 11 and the Federal Rules of Bankruptcy Procedure may result in fines or imprisonment or both. 11 U.S.C. § 110; 18 U.S.C. § 156.

B3B (Official Form 3B) (11/11) -- Cont.

United States Bankruptcy Court
_____ District of _____

In re: _____   Case No. _____
     Debtor(s)

ORDER ON DEBTOR'S APPLICATION FOR WAIVER OF THE CHAPTER 7 FILING FEE

Upon consideration of the debtor's "Application for Waiver of the Chapter 7 Filing Fee," the court orders that the application be:

[   ] GRANTED.

> This order is subject to being vacated at a later time if developments in the administration of the bankruptcy case demonstrate that the waiver was unwarranted.

[   ] DENIED.

> The debtor shall pay the chapter 7 filing fee according to the following terms:
>
> $ _____ on or before _____
>
> $ _____ on or before _____
>
> $ _____ on or before _____
>
> $ _____ on or before _____
>
> Until the filing fee is paid in full, the debtor shall not make any additional payment or transfer any additional property to an attorney or any other person for services in connection with this case.
>
> IF THE DEBTOR FAILS TO TIMELY PAY THE FILING FEE IN FULL OR TO TIMELY MAKE INSTALLMENT PAYMENTS, THE COURT MAY DISMISS THE DEBTOR'S CASE.

[   ] SCHEDULED FOR HEARING.

> A hearing to consider the debtor's "Application for Waiver of the Chapter 7 Filing Fee" shall be held on _____ at _____ am/pm at _____.
>   (address of courthouse)

IF THE DEBTOR FAILS TO APPEAR AT THE SCHEDULED HEARING, THE COURT MAY DEEM SUCH FAILURE TO BE THE DEBTOR'S CONSENT TO THE ENTRY OF AN ORDER DENYING THE FEE WAIVER APPLICATION BY DEFAULT.

                                    BY THE COURT:

DATE: _____   _____
                                    United States Bankruptcy Judge

FORM 6. SCHEDULES

Summary of Schedules
Statistical Summary of Certain Liabilities and Related Data (28 U.S.C. § 159)

Schedule A - Real Property
Schedule B - Personal Property
Schedule C - Property Claimed as Exempt
Schedule D - Creditors Holding Secured Claims
Schedule E - Creditors Holding Unsecured Priority Claims
Schedule F - Creditors Holding Unsecured Nonpriority Claims
Schedule G - Executory Contracts and Unexpired Leases
Schedule H - Codebtors
Schedule I - Current Income of Individual Debtor(s)
Schedule J - Current Expenditures of Individual Debtors(s)

Unsworn Declaration Under Penalty of Perjury

GENERAL INSTRUCTIONS: The first page of the debtor's schedules and the first page of any amendments thereto must contain a caption as in Form 16B. Subsequent pages should be identified with the debtor's name and case number. If the schedules are filed with the petition, the case number should be left blank.

Schedules D, E, and F have been designed for the listing of each claim only once. Even when a claim is secured only in part or entitled to priority only in part, it still should be listed only once. A claim which is secured in whole or in part should be listed on Schedule D only, and a claim which is entitled to priority in whole or in part should be listed on Schedule E only. Do not list the same claim twice. If a creditor has more than one claim, such as claims arising from separate transactions, each claim should be scheduled separately.

Review the specific instructions for each schedule before completing the schedule.

B6 Summary (Official Form 6 - Summary) (12/07)

United States Bankruptcy Court
_____ District Of _____

In re _____,   Case No. _____
          Debtor

          Chapter _____

SUMMARY OF SCHEDULES

Indicate as to each schedule whether that schedule is attached and state the number of pages in each. Report the totals from Schedules A, B, D, E, F, I, and J in the boxes provided. Add the amounts from Schedules A and B to determine the total amount of the debtor's assets. Add the amounts of all claims from Schedules D, E, and F to determine the total amount of the debtor's liabilities. Individual debtors also must complete the "Statistical Summary of Certain Liabilities and Related Data" if they file a case under chapter 7, 11, or 13.

NAME OF SCHEDULE	ATTACHED (YES/NO)	NO. OF SHEETS	ASSETS	LIABILITIES	OTHER
A - Real Property			$		
B - Personal Property			$		
C - Property Claimed as Exempt					
D - Creditors Holding Secured Claims				$	
E - Creditors Holding Unsecured Priority Claims (Total of Claims on Schedule E)				$	
F - Creditors Holding Unsecured Nonpriority Claims				$	
G - Executory Contracts and Unexpired Leases					
H - Codebtors					
I - Current Income of Individual Debtor(s)					$
J - Current Expenditures of Individual Debtors(s)					$
TOTAL			$	$	

599

B 6 Summary (Official Form 6 - Summary) (12/07)

United States Bankruptcy Court
_____ District Of _____

In re _____,   Case No. _____
                    Debtor

                                                            Chapter _____

STATISTICAL SUMMARY OF CERTAIN LIABILITIES AND RELATED DATA (28 U.S.C. § 159)

If you are an individual debtor whose debts are primarily consumer debts, as defined in § 101(8) of the Bankruptcy Code (11 U.S.C. § 101(8)), filing a case under chapter 7, 11 or 13, you must report all information requested below.

☐ Check this box if you are an individual debtor whose debts are NOT primarily consumer debts. You are not required to report any information here.

This information is for statistical purposes only under 28 U.S.C. § 159.

Summarize the following types of liabilities, as reported in the Schedules, and total them.

Type of Liability	Amount
Domestic Support Obligations (from Schedule E)	$
Taxes and Certain Other Debts Owed to Governmental Units (from Schedule E)	$
Claims for Death or Personal Injury While Debtor Was Intoxicated (from Schedule E) (whether disputed or undisputed)	$
Student Loan Obligations (from Schedule F)	$
Domestic Support, Separation Agreement, and Divorce Decree Obligations Not Reported on Schedule E	$
Obligations to Pension or Profit-Sharing, and Other Similar Obligations (from Schedule F)	$
TOTAL	$

State the following:

Average Income (from Schedule I, Line 16)	$
Average Expenses (from Schedule J, Line 18)	$
Current Monthly Income (from Form 22A Line 12; **OR**, Form 22B Line 11; **OR**, Form 22C Line 20)	$

State the following:

1. Total from Schedule D, "UNSECURED PORTION, IF ANY" column		$
2. Total from Schedule E, "AMOUNT ENTITLED TO PRIORITY" column.	$	
3. Total from Schedule E, "AMOUNT NOT ENTITLED TO PRIORITY, IF ANY" column		$
4. Total from Schedule F		$
5. Total of non-priority unsecured debt (sum of 1, 3, and 4)		$

B6A (Official Form 6A) (12/07)

In re _____,   Case No. _____
                    Debtor   **(If known)**

SCHEDULE A - REAL PROPERTY

Except as directed below, list all real property in which the debtor has any legal, equitable, or future interest, including all property owned as a co-tenant, community property, or in which the debtor has a life estate. Include any property in which the debtor holds rights and powers exercisable for the debtor's own benefit. If the debtor is married, state whether the husband, wife, both, or the marital community own the property by placing an "H," "W," "J," or "C" in the column labeled "Husband, Wife, Joint, or Community." If the debtor holds no interest in real property, write "None" under "Description and Location of Property."

Do not include interests in executory contracts and unexpired leases on this schedule. List them in Schedule G - Executory Contracts and Unexpired Leases.

If an entity claims to have a lien or hold a secured interest in any property, state the amount of the secured claim. See Schedule D. If no entity claims to hold a secured interest in the property, write "None" in the column labeled "Amount of Secured Claim."

If the debtor is an individual or if a joint petition is filed, state the amount of any exemption claimed in the property only in Schedule C - Property Claimed as Exempt.

DESCRIPTION AND LOCATION OF PROPERTY	NATURE OF DEBTOR'S INTEREST IN PROPERTY	HUSBAND, WIFE, JOINT, OR COMMUNITY	CURRENT VALUE OF DEBTOR'S INTEREST IN PROPERTY, WITHOUT DEDUCTING ANY SECURED CLAIM OR EXEMPTION	AMOUNT OF SECURED CLAIM
		Total▶		

(Report also on Summary of Schedules.)

B 6B (Official Form 6B) (12/07)

In re _____,   Case No. _____
                    Debtor   **(If known)**

SCHEDULE B - PERSONAL PROPERTY

Except as directed below, list all personal property of the debtor of whatever kind. If the debtor has no property in one or more of the categories, place an "x" in the appropriate position in the column labeled "None." If additional space is needed in any category, attach a separate sheet properly identified with the case name, case number, and the number of the category. If the debtor is married, state whether the husband, wife, both, or the marital community own the property by placing an "H," "W," "J," or "C" in the column labeled "Husband, Wife, Joint, or Community." If the debtor is an individual or a joint petition is filed, state the amount of any exemptions claimed only in Schedule C - Property Claimed as Exempt.

Do not list interests in executory contracts and unexpired leases on this schedule. List them in Schedule G - Executory Contracts and Unexpired Leases.

If the property is being held for the debtor by someone else, state that person's name and address under "Description and Location of Property."
If the property is being held for a minor child, simply state the child's initials and the name and address of the child's parent or guardian, such as "A.B., a minor child, by John Doe, guardian." Do not disclose the child's name. See, 11 U.S.C. §112 and Fed. R. Bankr. P. 1007(m).

TYPE OF PROPERTY	N O N E	DESCRIPTION AND LOCATION OF PROPERTY	HUSBAND, WIFE, JOINT, OR COMMUNITY	CURRENT VALUE OF DEBTOR'S INTEREST IN PROPERTY, WITH-OUT DEDUCTING ANY SECURED CLAIM OR EXEMPTION
1. Cash on hand.				
2. Checking, savings or other financial accounts, certificates of deposit or shares in banks, savings and loan, thrift, building and loan, and homestead associations, or credit unions, brokerage houses, or cooperatives.				
3. Security deposits with public utilities, telephone companies, landlords, and others.				
4. Household goods and furnishings, including audio, video, and computer equipment.				
5. Books; pictures and other art objects; antiques; stamp, coin, record, tape, compact disc, and other collections or collectibles.				
6. Wearing apparel.				
7. Furs and jewelry.				
8. Firearms and sports, photographic, and other hobby equipment.				
9. Interests in insurance policies. Name insurance company of each policy and itemize surrender or refund value of each.				
10. Annuities. Itemize and name each issuer.				
11. Interests in an education IRA as defined in 26 U.S.C. § 530(b)(1) or under a qualified State tuition plan as defined in 26 U.S.C. § 529(b)(1). Give particulars. (File separately the record(s) of any such interest(s). 11 U.S.C. § 521(c).)				

B 6B (Official Form 6B) (12/07) -- Cont.

In re _____,   Case No. _____
                 Debtor   (If known)

SCHEDULE B - PERSONAL PROPERTY
(Continuation Sheet)

TYPE OF PROPERTY	N O N E	DESCRIPTION AND LOCATION OF PROPERTY	HUSBAND, WIFE, JOINT, OR COMMUNITY	CURRENT VALUE OF DEBTOR'S INTEREST IN PROPERTY, WITH-OUT DEDUCTING ANY SECURED CLAIM OR EXEMPTION
12. Interests in IRA, ERISA, Keogh, or other pension or profit sharing plans. Give particulars.				
13. Stock and interests in incorporated and unincorporated businesses. Itemize.				
14. Interests in partnerships or joint ventures. Itemize.				
15. Government and corporate bonds and other negotiable and non-negotiable instruments.				
16. Accounts receivable.				
17. Alimony, maintenance, support, and property settlements to which the debtor is or may be entitled. Give particulars.				
18. Other liquidated debts owed to debtor including tax refunds. Give particulars.				
19. Equitable or future interests, life estates, and rights or powers exercisable for the benefit of the debtor other than those listed in Schedule A – Real Property.				
20. Contingent and noncontingent interests in estate of a decedent, death benefit plan, life insurance policy, or trust.				
21. Other contingent and unliquidated claims of every nature, including tax refunds, counterclaims of the debtor, and rights to setoff claims. Give estimated value of each.				

B 6B (Official Form 6B) (12/07) -- Cont.

In re _____,   Case No. _____
           Debtor   (If known)

SCHEDULE B - PERSONAL PROPERTY
(Continuation Sheet)

TYPE OF PROPERTY	N O N E	DESCRIPTION AND LOCATION OF PROPERTY	HUSBAND, WIFE, JOINT, OR COMMUNITY	CURRENT VALUE OF DEBTOR'S INTEREST IN PROPERTY, WITHOUT DEDUCTING ANY SECURED CLAIM OR EXEMPTION
22. Patents, copyrights, and other intellectual property. Give particulars.				
23. Licenses, franchises, and other general intangibles. Give particulars.				
24. Customer lists or other compilations containing personally identifiable information (as defined in 11 U.S.C. § 101(41A)) provided to the debtor by individuals in connection with obtaining a product or service from the debtor primarily for personal, family, or household purposes.				
25. Automobiles, trucks, trailers, and other vehicles and accessories.				
26. Boats, motors, and accessories.				
27. Aircraft and accessories.				
28. Office equipment, furnishings, and supplies.				
29. Machinery, fixtures, equipment, and supplies used in business.				
30. Inventory.				
31. Animals.				
32. Crops - growing or harvested. Give particulars.				
33. Farming equipment and implements.				
34. Farm supplies, chemicals, and feed.				
35. Other personal property of any kind not already listed. Itemize.				

_____ continuation sheets attached   Total▶ $ _____

(Include amounts from any continuation
sheets attached. Report total also on
Summary of Schedules.)

B 6C (Official Form 6C) (04/10)

In re _____,   Case No. _____
            Debtor   *(If known)*

SCHEDULE C - PROPERTY CLAIMED AS EXEMPT

Debtor claims the exemptions to which debtor is entitled under: ☐ Check if debtor claims a homestead exemption that exceeds
(Check one box) $146,450.*
☐   11 U.S.C. § 522(b)(2)
☐   11 U.S.C. § 522(b)(3)

DESCRIPTION OF PROPERTY	SPECIFY LAW PROVIDING EACH EXEMPTION	VALUE OF CLAIMED EXEMPTION	CURRENT VALUE OF PROPERTY WITHOUT DEDUCTING EXEMPTION

* *Amount subject to adjustment on 4/1/13, and every three years thereafter with respect to cases commenced on or after the date of adjustment.*

B 6D (Official Form 6D) (12/07)

In re _____, Case No. _____
           Debtor   **(If known)**

SCHEDULE D - CREDITORS HOLDING SECURED CLAIMS

State the name, mailing address, including zip code, and last four digits of any account number of all entities holding claims secured by property of the debtor as of the date of filing of the petition. The complete account number of any account the debtor has with the creditor is useful to the trustee and the creditor and may be provided if the debtor chooses to do so. List creditors holding all types of secured interests such as judgment liens, garnishments, statutory liens, mortgages, deeds of trust, and other security interests.

List creditors in alphabetical order to the extent practicable. If a minor child is the creditor, state the child's initials and the name and address of the child's parent or guardian, such as "A.B., a minor child, by John Doe, guardian." Do not disclose the child's name. See, 11 U.S.C. §112 and Fed. R. Bankr. P. 1007(m). If all secured creditors will not fit on this page, use the continuation sheet provided.

If any entity other than a spouse in a joint case may be jointly liable on a claim, place an "X" in the column labeled "Codebtor," include the entity on the appropriate schedule of creditors, and complete Schedule H – Codebtors. If a joint petition is filed, state whether the husband, wife, both of them, or the marital community may be liable on each claim by placing an "H," "W," "J," or "C" in the column labeled "Husband, Wife, Joint, or Community."

If the claim is contingent, place an "X" in the column labeled "Contingent." If the claim is unliquidated, place an "X" in the column labeled "Unliquidated." If the claim is disputed, place an "X" in the column labeled "Disputed." (You may need to place an "X" in more than one of these three columns.)

Total the columns labeled "Amount of Claim Without Deducting Value of Collateral" and "Unsecured Portion, if Any" in the boxes labeled "Total(s)" on the last sheet of the completed schedule. Report the total from the column labeled "Amount of Claim Without Deducting Value of Collateral" also on the Summary of Schedules and, if the debtor is an individual with primarily consumer debts, report the total from the column labeled "Unsecured Portion, if Any" on the Statistical Summary of Certain Liabilities and Related Data.

☐   Check this box if debtor has no creditors holding secured claims to report on this Schedule D.

CREDITOR'S NAME AND MAILING ADDRESS INCLUDING ZIP CODE AND AN ACCOUNT NUMBER *(See Instructions Above.)*	CODEBTOR	HUSBAND, WIFE, JOINT, OR COMMUNITY	DATE CLAIM WAS INCURRED, NATURE OF LIEN, AND DESCRIPTION AND VALUE OF PROPERTY SUBJECT TO LIEN	CONTINGENT	UNLIQUIDATED	DISPUTED	AMOUNT OF CLAIM WITHOUT DEDUCTING VALUE OF COLLATERAL	UNSECURED PORTION, IF ANY
ACCOUNT NO.								
			VALUE $					
ACCOUNT NO.								
			VALUE $					
ACCOUNT NO.								
			VALUE $					
_____ continuation sheets attached			Subtotal ▶ (Total of this page)				$	$
			Total ▶ (Use only on last page)				$	$
							(Report also on Summary of Schedules.)	(If applicable, report also on Statistical Summary of Certain Liabilities and Related Data.)

B 6D (Official Form 6D) (12/07) – Cont.   2

In re _____,   Case No. _____
                Debtor   **(if known)**

SCHEDULE D - CREDITORS HOLDING SECURED CLAIMS
(Continuation Sheet)

CREDITOR'S NAME AND MAILING ADDRESS INCLUDING ZIP CODE AND AN ACCOUNT NUMBER (See Instructions Above.)	CODEBTOR	HUSBAND, WIFE, JOINT, OR COMMUNITY	DATE CLAIM WAS INCURRED, NATURE OF LIEN , AND DESCRIPTION AND VALUE OF PROPERTY SUBJECT TO LIEN	CONTINGENT	UNLIQUIDATED	DISPUTED	AMOUNT OF CLAIM WITHOUT DEDUCTING VALUE OF COLLATERAL	UNSECURED PORTION, IF ANY
ACCOUNT NO.								
			VALUE $					
ACCOUNT NO.								
			VALUE $					
ACCOUNT NO.								
			VALUE $					
ACCOUNT NO.								
			VALUE $					
ACCOUNT NO.								
			VALUE $					

Sheet no._____of_____continuation sheets attached to Schedule of Creditors Holding Secured Claims

Subtotal (s)►
(Total(s) of this page) $ $

Total(s) ►
(Use only on last page) $ $

(Report also on Summary of Schedules.)

(If applicable, report also on Statistical Summary of Certain Liabilities and Related Data.)

B 6E (Official Form 6E) (04/10)

In re _____,   Case No._____
              Debtor   *(if known)*

SCHEDULE E - CREDITORS HOLDING UNSECURED PRIORITY CLAIMS

A complete list of claims entitled to priority, listed separately by type of priority, is to be set forth on the sheets provided. Only holders of unsecured claims entitled to priority should be listed in this schedule. In the boxes provided on the attached sheets, state the name, mailing address, including zip code, and last four digits of the account number, if any, of all entities holding priority claims against the debtor or the property of the debtor, as of the date of the filing of the petition. Use a separate continuation sheet for each type of priority and label each with the type of priority.

The complete account number of any account the debtor has with the creditor is useful to the trustee and the creditor and may be provided if the debtor chooses to do so. If a minor child is a creditor, state the child's initials and the name and address of the child's parent or guardian, such as "A.B., a minor child, by John Doe, guardian." Do not disclose the child's name. See, 11 U.S.C. §112 and Fed. R. Bankr. P. 1007(m).

If any entity other than a spouse in a joint case may be jointly liable on a claim, place an "X" in the column labeled "Codebtor," include the entity on the appropriate schedule of creditors, and complete Schedule H-Codebtors. If a joint petition is filed, state whether the husband, wife, both of them, or the marital community may be liable on each claim by placing an "H," "W," "J," or "C" in the column labeled "Husband, Wife, Joint, or Community." If the claim is contingent, place an "X" in the column labeled "Contingent." If the claim is unliquidated, place an "X" in the column labeled "Unliquidated." If the claim is disputed, place an "X" in the column labeled "Disputed." (You may need to place an "X" in more than one of these three columns.)

Report the total of claims listed on each sheet in the box labeled "Subtotals" on each sheet. Report the total of all claims listed on this Schedule E in the box labeled "Total" on the last sheet of the completed schedule. Report this total also on the Summary of Schedules.

Report the total of amounts entitled to priority listed on each sheet in the box labeled "Subtotals" on each sheet. Report the total of all amounts entitled to priority listed on this Schedule E in the box labeled "Totals" on the last sheet of the completed schedule. Individual debtors with primarily consumer debts report this total also on the Statistical Summary of Certain Liabilities and Related Data.

Report the total of amounts <u>not</u> entitled to priority listed on each sheet in the box labeled "Subtotals" on each sheet. Report the total of all amounts not entitled to priority listed on this Schedule E in the box labeled "Totals" on the last sheet of the completed schedule. Individual debtors with primarily consumer debts report this total also on the Statistical Summary of Certain Liabilities and Related Data.

☐ Check this box if debtor has no creditors holding unsecured priority claims to report on this Schedule E.

TYPES OF PRIORITY CLAIMS (Check the appropriate box(es) below if claims in that category are listed on the attached sheets.)

☐ **Domestic Support Obligations**

Claims for domestic support that are owed to or recoverable by a spouse, former spouse, or child of the debtor, or the parent, legal guardian, or responsible relative of such a child, or a governmental unit to whom such a domestic support claim has been assigned to the extent provided in 11 U.S.C. § 507(a)(1).

☐ **Extensions of credit in an involuntary case**

Claims arising in the ordinary course of the debtor's business or financial affairs after the commencement of the case but before the earlier of the appointment of a trustee or the order for relief. 11 U.S.C. § 507(a)(3).

☐ **Wages, salaries, and commissions**

Wages, salaries, and commissions, including vacation, severance, and sick leave pay owing to employees and commissions owing to qualifying independent sales representatives up to $11,725* per person earned within 180 days immediately preceding the filing of the original petition, or the cessation of business, whichever occurred first, to the extent provided in 11 U.S.C. § 507(a)(4).

☐ **Contributions to employee benefit plans**

Money owed to employee benefit plans for services rendered within 180 days immediately preceding the filing of the original petition, or the cessation of business, whichever occurred first, to the extent provided in 11 U.S.C. § 507(a)(5).

* Amount subject to adjustment on 4/01/13, and every three years thereafter with respect to cases commenced on or after the date of adjustment.

B 6E (Official Form 6E) (04/10) – Cont.

In re _____ ,   **Case No.**_____
                        Debtor   *(if known)*

☐ **Certain farmers and fishermen**

   Claims of certain farmers and fishermen, up to $5,775* per farmer or fisherman, against the debtor, as provided in 11 U.S.C. § 507(a)(6).

☐ **Deposits by individuals**

   Claims of individuals up to $2,600* for deposits for the purchase, lease, or rental of property or services for personal, family, or household use, that were not delivered or provided. 11 U.S.C. § 507(a)(7).

☐ **Taxes and Certain Other Debts Owed to Governmental Units**

   Taxes, customs duties, and penalties owing to federal, state, and local governmental units as set forth in 11 U.S.C. § 507(a)(8).

☐ **Commitments to Maintain the Capital of an Insured Depository Institution**

   Claims based on commitments to the FDIC, RTC, Director of the Office of Thrift Supervision, Comptroller of the Currency, or Board of Governors of the Federal Reserve System, or their predecessors or successors, to maintain the capital of an insured depository institution. 11 U.S.C. § 507 (a)(9).

☐ **Claims for Death or Personal Injury While Debtor Was Intoxicated**

   Claims for death or personal injury resulting from the operation of a motor vehicle or vessel while the debtor was intoxicated from using alcohol, a drug, or another substance. 11 U.S.C. § 507(a)(10).

* *Amounts are subject to adjustment on 4/01/13, and every three years thereafter with respect to cases commenced on or after the date of adjustment.*

_____ continuation sheets attached

B 6E (Official Form 6E) (04/10) – Cont.

In re _____,　Case No. _____
　　　　　　　Debtor　　　　　　　　　　　　　　　　　**(if known)**

SCHEDULE E - CREDITORS HOLDING UNSECURED PRIORITY CLAIMS
(Continuation Sheet)

Type of Priority for Claims Listed on This Sheet

CREDITOR'S NAME, MAILING ADDRESS INCLUDING ZIP CODE, AND ACCOUNT NUMBER *(See instructions above.)*	CODEBTOR	HUSBAND, WIFE, JOINT, OR COMMUNITY	DATE CLAIM WAS INCURRED AND CONSIDERATION FOR CLAIM	CONTINGENT	UNLIQUIDATED	DISPUTED	AMOUNT OF CLAIM	AMOUNT ENTITLED TO PRIORITY	AMOUNT NOT ENTITLED TO PRIORITY, IF ANY
Account No.									
Account No.									
Account No.									
Account No.									
Sheet no. ___ of ___ continuation sheets attached to Schedule of Creditors Holding Priority Claims					Subtotals▶ (Totals of this page)		$	$	
			Total▶ (Use only on last page of the completed Schedule E. Report also on the Summary of Schedules.)				$		
			Totals▶ (Use only on last page of the completed Schedule E. If applicable, report also on the Statistical Summary of Certain Liabilities and Related Data.)					$	$

B 6F (Official Form 6F) (12/07)

In re _____,   Case No. _____
                    Debtor   **(if known)**

SCHEDULE F - CREDITORS HOLDING UNSECURED NONPRIORITY CLAIMS

State the name, mailing address, including zip code, and last four digits of any account number, of all entities holding unsecured claims without priority against the debtor or the property of the debtor, as of the date of filing of the petition. The complete account number of any account the debtor has with the creditor is useful to the trustee and the creditor and may be provided if the debtor chooses to do so. If a minor child is a creditor, state the child's initials and the name and address of the child's parent or guardian, such as "A.B., a minor child, by John Doe, guardian." Do not disclose the child's name. See, 11 U.S.C. §112 and Fed. R. Bankr. P. 1007(m). Do not include claims listed in Schedules D and E. If all creditors will not fit on this page, use the continuation sheet provided.

If any entity other than a spouse in a joint case may be jointly liable on a claim, place an "X" in the column labeled "Codebtor," include the entity on the appropriate schedule of creditors, and complete Schedule H - Codebtors. If a joint petition is filed, state whether the husband, wife, both of them, or the marital community may be liable on each claim by placing an "H," "W," "J," or "C" in the column labeled "Husband, Wife, Joint, or Community."

If the claim is contingent, place an "X" in the column labeled "Contingent." If the claim is unliquidated, place an "X" in the column labeled "Unliquidated." If the claim is disputed, place an "X" in the column labeled "Disputed." (You may need to place an "X" in more than one of these three columns.)

Report the total of all claims listed on this schedule in the box labeled "Total" on the last sheet of the completed schedule. Report this total also on the Summary of Schedules and, if the debtor is an individual with primarily consumer debts, report this total also on the Statistical Summary of Certain Liabilities and Related Data..

☐   Check this box if debtor has no creditors holding unsecured claims to report on this Schedule F.

CREDITOR'S NAME, MAILING ADDRESS INCLUDING ZIP CODE, AND ACCOUNT NUMBER *(See instructions above.)*	CODEBTOR	HUSBAND, WIFE, JOINT, OR COMMUNITY	DATE CLAIM WAS INCURRED AND CONSIDERATION FOR CLAIM. IF CLAIM IS SUBJECT TO SETOFF, SO STATE.	CONTINGENT	UNLIQUIDATED	DISPUTED	AMOUNT OF CLAIM
ACCOUNT NO.							
ACCOUNT NO.							
ACCOUNT NO.							
ACCOUNT NO.							
				Subtotal▶			$

_____ continuation sheets attached

Total▶ $

(Use only on last page of the completed Schedule F.)
(Report also on Summary of Schedules and, if applicable, on the Statistical Summary of Certain Liabilities and Related Data.)

B 6F (Official Form 6F) (12/07) - Cont.

In re _____,   Case No. _____
           Debtor   **(if known)**

SCHEDULE F - CREDITORS HOLDING UNSECURED NONPRIORITY CLAIMS
(Continuation Sheet)

CREDITOR'S NAME, MAILING ADDRESS INCLUDING ZIP CODE, AND ACCOUNT NUMBER (See instructions above.)	CODEBTOR	HUSBAND, WIFE, JOINT, OR COMMUNITY	DATE CLAIM WAS INCURRED AND CONSIDERATION FOR CLAIM. IF CLAIM IS SUBJECT TO SETOFF, SO STATE.	CONTINGENT	UNLIQUIDATED	DISPUTED	AMOUNT OF CLAIM
ACCOUNT NO.							
ACCOUNT NO.							
ACCOUNT NO.							
ACCOUNT NO.							
ACCOUNT NO.							

Sheet no._____ of_____ continuation sheets attached to Schedule of Creditors Holding Unsecured Nonpriority Claims

Subtotal▶ $

Total▶ $
(Use only on last page of the completed Schedule F.)
(Report also on Summary of Schedules and, if applicable on the Statistical Summary of Certain Liabilities and Related Data.)

B 6G (Official Form 6G) (12/07)

In re _____ ,   Case No._____
          Debtor   **(if known)**

SCHEDULE G - EXECUTORY CONTRACTS AND UNEXPIRED LEASES

      Describe all executory contracts of any nature and all unexpired leases of real or personal property. Include any timeshare interests. State nature of debtor's interest in contract, i.e., "Purchaser," "Agent," etc. State whether debtor is the lessor or lessee of a lease. Provide the names and complete mailing addresses of all other parties to each lease or contract described. If a minor child is a party to one of the leases or contracts, state the child's initials and the name and address of the child's parent or guardian, such as "A.B., a minor child, by John Doe, guardian." Do not disclose the child's name. See, 11 U.S.C. §112 and Fed. R. Bankr. P. 1007(m).

☐ Check this box if debtor has no executory contracts or unexpired leases.

NAME AND MAILING ADDRESS, INCLUDING ZIP CODE, OF OTHER PARTIES TO LEASE OR CONTRACT.	DESCRIPTION OF CONTRACT OR LEASE AND NATURE OF DEBTOR'S INTEREST. STATE WHETHER LEASE IS FOR NONRESIDENTIAL REAL PROPERTY. STATE CONTRACT NUMBER OF ANY GOVERNMENT CONTRACT.

B 6H (Official Form 6H) (12/07)

In re _____ ,   Case No. _____
                        Debtor   **(if known)**

SCHEDULE H - CODEBTORS

    Provide the information requested concerning any person or entity, other than a spouse in a joint case, that is also liable on any debts listed by the debtor in the schedules of creditors. Include all guarantors and co-signers. If the debtor resides or resided in a community property state, commonwealth, or territory (including Alaska, Arizona, California, Idaho, Louisiana, Nevada, New Mexico, Puerto Rico, Texas, Washington, or Wisconsin) within the eight-year period immediately preceding the commencement of the case, identify the name of the debtor's spouse and of any former spouse who resides or resided with the debtor in the community property state, commonwealth, or territory. Include all names used by the nondebtor spouse during the eight years immediately preceding the commencement of this case. If a minor child is a codebtor or a creditor, state the child's initials and the name and address of the child's parent or guardian, such as "A.B., a minor child, by John Doe, guardian." Do not disclose the child's name. See, 11 U.S.C. §112 and Fed. R. Bankr. P. 1007(m).

☐   Check this box if debtor has no codebtors.

NAME AND ADDRESS OF CODEBTOR	NAME AND ADDRESS OF CREDITOR

B6I (Official Form 6I) (12/07)

In re _____ ,   Case No. _____
            Debtor   **(if known)**

SCHEDULE I - CURRENT INCOME OF INDIVIDUAL DEBTOR(S)

The column labeled "Spouse" must be completed in all cases filed by joint debtors and by every married debtor, whether or not a joint petition is filed, unless the spouses are separated and a joint petition is not filed. Do not state the name of any minor child. The average monthly income calculated on this form may differ from the current monthly income calculated on Form 22A, 22B, or 22C.

Debtor's Marital Status:	DEPENDENTS OF DEBTOR AND SPOUSE	
	RELATIONSHIP(S):	AGE(S):

Employment:	DEBTOR	SPOUSE
Occupation		
Name of Employer		
How long employed		
Address of Employer		

INCOME: (Estimate of average or projected monthly income at time case filed)

	DEBTOR	SPOUSE
	$_____	$_____
1. Monthly gross wages, salary, and commissions (Prorate if not paid monthly)	$_____	$_____
2. Estimate monthly overtime		
3. SUBTOTAL	$_____	$_____
4. LESS PAYROLL DEDUCTIONS		
a. Payroll taxes and social security	$_____	$_____
b. Insurance	$_____	$_____
c. Union dues	$_____	$_____
d. Other (Specify): _____	$_____	$_____
5. SUBTOTAL OF PAYROLL DEDUCTIONS	$_____	$_____
6. TOTAL NET MONTHLY TAKE HOME PAY	$_____	$_____
7. Regular income from operation of business or profession or farm (Attach detailed statement)	$_____	$_____
8. Income from real property	$_____	$_____
9. Interest and dividends	$_____	$_____
10. Alimony, maintenance or support payments payable to the debtor for the debtor's use or that of dependents listed above	$_____	$_____
11. Social security or government assistance (Specify):_____	$_____	$_____
12. Pension or retirement income	$_____	$_____
13. Other monthly income (Specify):_____	$_____	$_____
14. SUBTOTAL OF LINES 7 THROUGH 13	$_____	$_____
15. AVERAGE MONTHLY INCOME (Add amounts on lines 6 and 14)	$_____	$_____
16. COMBINED AVERAGE MONTHLY INCOME: (Combine column totals from line 15)	$_____	

(Report also on Summary of Schedules and, if applicable, on Statistical Summary of Certain Liabilities and Related Data)

17. Describe any increase or decrease in income reasonably anticipated to occur within the year following the filing of this document:

_____

_____

B6J (Official Form 6J) (12/07)

In re _____ ,   Case No. _____
                    Debtor   **(if known)**

SCHEDULE J - CURRENT EXPENDITURES OF INDIVIDUAL DEBTOR(S)

Complete this schedule by estimating the average or projected monthly expenses of the debtor and the debtor's family at time case filed. Prorate any payments made bi-weekly, quarterly, semi-annually, or annually to show monthly rate. The average monthly expenses calculated on this form may differ from the deductions from income allowed on Form22A or 22C.

☐   Check this box if a joint petition is filed and debtor's spouse maintains a separate household. Complete a separate schedule of expenditures labeled "Spouse."

1. Rent or home mortgage payment (include lot rented for mobile home) $ _____
    a. Are real estate taxes included?   Yes _____   No _____
    b. Is property insurance included?   Yes _____   No _____
2. Utilities: a. Electricity and heating fuel $ _____
          b. Water and sewer $ _____
          c. Telephone $ _____
          d. Other _____ $ _____
3. Home maintenance (repairs and upkeep) $ _____
4. Food $ _____
5. Clothing $ _____
6. Laundry and dry cleaning $ _____
7. Medical and dental expenses $ _____
8. Transportation (not including car payments) $ _____
9. Recreation, clubs and entertainment, newspapers, magazines, etc. $ _____
10. Charitable contributions $ _____
11. Insurance (not deducted from wages or included in home mortgage payments)
        a. Homeowner's or renter's $ _____
        b. Life $ _____
        c. Health $ _____
        d. Auto $ _____
        e. Other _____ $ _____
12. Taxes (not deducted from wages or included in home mortgage payments)
(Specify) _____ $ _____
13. Installment payments: (In chapter 11, 12, and 13 cases, do not list payments to be included in the plan)
        a. Auto $ _____
        b. Other _____ $ _____
        c. Other _____ $ _____
14. Alimony, maintenance, and support paid to others $ _____
15. Payments for support of additional dependents not living at your home $ _____
16. Regular expenses from operation of business, profession, or farm (attach detailed statement) $ _____
17. Other _____ $ _____
18. AVERAGE MONTHLY EXPENSES (Total lines 1-17. Report also on Summary of Schedules and, $ _____
    if applicable, on the Statistical Summary of Certain Liabilities and Related Data.)
19. Describe any increase or decrease in expenditures reasonably anticipated to occur within the year following the filing of this document:

20. STATEMENT OF MONTHLY NET INCOME
    a. Average monthly income from Line 15 of Schedule I $ _____
    b. Average monthly expenses from Line 18 above $ _____
    c. Monthly net income (a. minus b.) $ _____

B6 Declaration (Official Form 6 - Declaration) (12/07)

In re _____,   Case No. _____

          Debtor   (if known)

DECLARATION CONCERNING DEBTOR'S SCHEDULES

DECLARATION UNDER PENALTY OF PERJURY BY INDIVIDUAL DEBTOR

    I declare under penalty of perjury that I have read the foregoing summary and schedules, consisting of _____ sheets, and that they are true and correct to the best of my knowledge, information, and belief.

Date _____   Signature: _____

                                                            Debtor

Date _____   Signature: _____

                                                     (Joint Debtor, if any)

                                               [If joint case, both spouses must sign.]

DECLARATION AND SIGNATURE OF NON-ATTORNEY BANKRUPTCY PETITION PREPARER (See 11 U.S.C. § 110)

    I declare under penalty of perjury that: (1) I am a bankruptcy petition preparer as defined in 11 U.S.C. § 110; (2) I prepared this document for compensation and have provided the debtor with a copy of this document and the notices and information required under 11 U.S.C. §§ 110(b), 110(h) and 342(b); and, (3) if rules or guidelines have been promulgated pursuant to 11 U.S.C. § 110(h) setting a maximum fee for services chargeable by bankruptcy petition preparers, I have given the debtor notice of the maximum amount before preparing any document for filing for a debtor or accepting any fee from the debtor, as required by that section.

_____   _____
Printed or Typed Name and Title, if any,   Social Security No.
of Bankruptcy Petition Preparer   *(Required by 11 U.S.C. § 110.)*

If the bankruptcy petition preparer is not an individual, state the name, title (if any), address, and social security number of the officer, principal, responsible person, or partner who signs this document.

_____

_____

_____
Address

X_____   _____
Signature of Bankruptcy Petition Preparer   Date

Names and Social Security numbers of all other individuals who prepared or assisted in preparing this document, unless the bankruptcy petition preparer is not an individual:

If more than one person prepared this document, attach additional signed sheets conforming to the appropriate Official Form for each person.

A bankruptcy petition preparer's failure to comply with the provisions of title 11 and the Federal Rules of Bankruptcy Procedure may result in fines or imprisonment or both. 11 U.S.C. § 110; 18 U.S.C. § 156.

DECLARATION UNDER PENALTY OF PERJURY ON BEHALF OF A CORPORATION OR PARTNERSHIP

    I, the _____ [the president or other officer or an authorized agent of the corporation or a member or an authorized agent of the partnership] of the _____ [corporation or partnership] named as debtor in this case, declare under penalty of perjury that I have read the foregoing summary and schedules, consisting of _____ sheets *(Total shown on summary page plus 1)*, and that they are true and correct to the best of my knowledge, information, and belief.

Date _____

                      Signature: _____

                                    [Print or type name of individual signing on behalf of debtor.]

[An individual signing on behalf of a partnership or corporation must indicate position or relationship to debtor.]

Penalty for making a false statement or concealing property: Fine of up to $500,000 or imprisonment for up to 5 years or both. 18 U.S.C. §§ 152 and 3571.

B 7 (Official Form 7) (04/10)

UNITED STATES BANKRUPTCY COURT
_____ District of _____

In re:_____,   Case No. _____
                 Debtor   (if known)

STATEMENT OF FINANCIAL AFFAIRS

This statement is to be completed by every debtor. Spouses filing a joint petition may file a single statement on which the information for both spouses is combined. If the case is filed under chapter 12 or chapter 13, a married debtor must furnish information for both spouses whether or not a joint petition is filed, unless the spouses are separated and a joint petition is not filed. An individual debtor engaged in business as a sole proprietor, partner, family farmer, or self-employed professional, should provide the information requested on this statement concerning all such activities as well as the individual's personal affairs. To indicate payments, transfers and the like to minor children, state the child's initials and the name and address of the child's parent or guardian, such as "A.B., a minor child, by John Doe, guardian." Do not disclose the child's name. See, 11 U.S.C. §112 and Fed. R. Bankr. P. 1007(m).

Questions 1 - 18 are to be completed by all debtors. Debtors that are or have been in business, as defined below, also must complete Questions 19 - 25. **If the answer to an applicable question is "None," mark the box labeled "None."** If additional space is needed for the answer to any question, use and attach a separate sheet properly identified with the case name, case number (if known), and the number of the question.

DEFINITIONS

"In business." A debtor is "in business" for the purpose of this form if the debtor is a corporation or partnership. An individual debtor is "in business" for the purpose of this form if the debtor is or has been, within six years immediately preceding the filing of this bankruptcy case, any of the following: an officer, director, managing executive, or owner of 5 percent or more of the voting or equity securities of a corporation; a partner, other than a limited partner, of a partnership; a sole proprietor or self-employed full-time or part-time. An individual debtor also may be "in business" for the purpose of this form if the debtor engages in a trade, business, or other activity, other than as an employee, to supplement income from the debtor's primary employment.

"Insider." The term "insider" includes but is not limited to: relatives of the debtor; general partners of the debtor and their relatives; corporations of which the debtor is an officer, director, or person in control; officers, directors, and any owner of 5 percent or more of the voting or equity securities of a corporate debtor and their relatives; affiliates of the debtor and insiders of such affiliates; any managing agent of the debtor. 11 U.S.C. § 101.

---

    1.   Income from employment or operation of business

None
☐
    State the gross amount of income the debtor has received from employment, trade, or profession, or from operation of the debtor's business, including part-time activities either as an employee or in independent trade or business, from the beginning of this calendar year to the date this case was commenced. State also the gross amounts received during the **two years** immediately preceding this calendar year. (A debtor that maintains, or has maintained, financial records on the basis of a fiscal rather than a calendar year may report fiscal year income. Identify the beginning and ending dates of the debtor's fiscal year.) If a joint petition is filed, state income for each spouse separately. (Married debtors filing under chapter 12 or chapter 13 must state income of both spouses whether or not a joint petition is filed, unless the spouses are separated and a joint petition is not filed.)

           AMOUNT   SOURCE

2. Income other than from employment or operation of business

None
☐

State the amount of income received by the debtor other than from employment, trade, profession, operation of the debtor's business during the **two years** immediately preceding the commencement of this case. Give particulars. If a joint petition is filed, state income for each spouse separately. (Married debtors filing under chapter 12 or chapter 13 must state income for each spouse whether or not a joint petition is filed, unless the spouses are separated and a joint petition is not filed.)

AMOUNT   SOURCE

---

3. Payments to creditors

Complete a. or b., as appropriate, and c.

None
☐

a. *Individual or joint debtor(s) with primarily consumer debts:* List all payments on loans, installment purchases of goods or services, and other debts to any creditor made within **90 days** immediately preceding the commencement of this case unless the aggregate value of all property that constitutes or is affected by such transfer is less than $600. Indicate with an asterisk (*) any payments that were made to a creditor on account of a domestic support obligation or as part of an alternative repayment schedule under a plan by an approved nonprofit budgeting and credit counseling agency. (Married debtors filing under chapter 12 or chapter 13 must include payments by either or both spouses whether or not a joint petition is filed, unless the spouses are separated and a joint petition is not filed.)

NAME AND ADDRESS OF CREDITOR	DATES OF PAYMENTS	AMOUNT PAID	AMOUNT STILL OWING

None
☐

b. *Debtor whose debts are not primarily consumer debts: List each payment or other transfer to any creditor made within* **90 days** *immediately preceding the commencement of the case unless the aggregate value of all property that constitutes or is affected by such transfer is less than $5,850*.* If the debtor is an individual, indicate with an asterisk (*) any payments that were made to a creditor on account of a domestic support obligation or as part of an alternative repayment schedule under a plan by an approved nonprofit budgeting and credit counseling agency. (Married debtors filing under chapter 12 or chapter 13 must include payments and other transfers by either or both spouses whether or not a joint petition is filed, unless the spouses are separated and a joint petition is not filed.)

NAME AND ADDRESS OF CREDITOR	DATES OF PAYMENTS/ TRANSFERS	AMOUNT PAID OR VALUE OF TRANSFERS	AMOUNT STILL OWING

Amount subject to adjustment on 4/01/13, and every three years thereafter with respect to cases commenced on or after the date of adjustment.

None
☐

c. *All debtors:* List all payments made within **one year** immediately preceding the commencement of this case to or for the benefit of creditors who are or were insiders. (Married debtors filing under chapter 12 or chapter 13 must include payments by either or both spouses whether or not a joint petition is filed, unless the spouses are separated and a joint petition is not filed.)

NAME AND ADDRESS OF CREDITOR AND RELATIONSHIP TO DEBTOR	DATE OF PAYMENT	AMOUNT PAID	AMOUNT STILL OWING

4. Suits and administrative proceedings, executions, garnishments and attachments

None
☐

a. List all suits and administrative proceedings to which the debtor is or was a party within **one year** immediately preceding the filing of this bankruptcy case. (Married debtors filing under chapter 12 or chapter 13 must include information concerning either or both spouses whether or not a joint petition is filed, unless the spouses are separated and a joint petition is not filed.)

CAPTION OF SUIT AND CASE NUMBER	NATURE OF PROCEEDING	COURT OR AGENCY AND LOCATION	STATUS OR DISPOSITION

None
☐

b. Describe all property that has been attached, garnished or seized under any legal or equitable process within **one year** immediately preceding the commencement of this case. (Married debtors filing under chapter 12 or chapter 13 must include information concerning property of either or both spouses whether or not a joint petition is filed, unless the spouses are separated and a joint petition is not filed.)

NAME AND ADDRESS OF PERSON FOR WHOSE BENEFIT PROPERTY WAS SEIZED	DATE OF SEIZURE	DESCRIPTION AND VALUE OF PROPERTY

5. Repossessions, foreclosures and returns

None
☐

List all property that has been repossessed by a creditor, sold at a foreclosure sale, transferred through a deed in lieu of foreclosure or returned to the seller, within **one year** immediately preceding the commencement of this case. (Married debtors filing under chapter 12 or chapter 13 must include information concerning property of either or both spouses whether or not a joint petition is filed, unless the spouses are separated and a joint petition is not filed.)

NAME AND ADDRESS OF CREDITOR OR SELLER	DATE OF REPOSSESSION, FORECLOSURE SALE, TRANSFER OR RETURN	DESCRIPTION AND VALUE OF PROPERTY

6. Assignments and receiverships

None
☐

a. Describe any assignment of property for the benefit of creditors made within **120 days** immediately preceding the commencement of this case. (Married debtors filing under chapter 12 or chapter 13 must include any assignment by either or both spouses whether or not a joint petition is filed, unless the spouses are separated and a joint petition is not filed.)

NAME AND ADDRESS OF ASSIGNEE	DATE OF ASSIGNMENT	TERMS OF ASSIGNMENT OR SETTLEMENT

None
☐

b. List all property which has been in the hands of a custodian, receiver, or court-appointed official within **one year** immediately preceding the commencement of this case. (Married debtors filing under chapter 12 or chapter 13 must include information concerning property of either or both spouses whether or not a joint petition is filed, unless the spouses are separated and a joint petition is not filed.)

NAME AND ADDRESS OF CUSTODIAN	NAME AND LOCATION OF COURT CASE TITLE & NUMBER	DATE OF ORDER	DESCRIPTION AND VALUE Of PROPERTY

7. Gifts

None
☐

List all gifts or charitable contributions made within **one year** immediately preceding the commencement of this case except ordinary and usual gifts to family members aggregating less than $200 in value per individual family member and charitable contributions aggregating less than $100 per recipient. (Married debtors filing under chapter 12 or chapter 13 must include gifts or contributions by either or both spouses whether or not a joint petition is filed, unless the spouses are separated and a joint petition is not filed.)

NAME AND ADDRESS OF PERSON OR ORGANIZATION	RELATIONSHIP TO DEBTOR, IF ANY	DATE OF GIFT	DESCRIPTION AND VALUE OF GIFT

8. Losses

None
☐

List all losses from fire, theft, other casualty or gambling within **one year** immediately preceding the commencement of this case **or since the commencement of this case**. (Married debtors filing under chapter 12 or chapter 13 must include losses by either or both spouses whether or not a joint petition is filed, unless the spouses are separated and a joint petition is not filed.)

DESCRIPTION AND VALUE OF PROPERTY	DESCRIPTION OF CIRCUMSTANCES AND, IF LOSS WAS COVERED IN WHOLE OR IN PART BY INSURANCE, GIVE PARTICULARS	DATE OF LOSS

9.   Payments related to debt counseling or bankruptcy

None ☐

List all payments made or property transferred by or on behalf of the debtor to any persons, including attorneys, for consultation concerning debt consolidation, relief under the bankruptcy law or preparation of a petition in bankruptcy within **one year** immediately preceding the commencement of this case.

NAME AND ADDRESS OF PAYEE	DATE OF PAYMENT, NAME OF PAYER IF OTHER THAN DEBTOR	AMOUNT OF MONEY OR DESCRIPTION AND VALUE OF PROPERTY

---

10. Other transfers

None ☐

a.   List all other property, other than property transferred in the ordinary course of the business or financial affairs of the debtor, transferred either absolutely or as security within **two years** immediately preceding the commencement of this case. (Married debtors filing under chapter 12 or chapter 13 must include transfers by either or both spouses whether or not a joint petition is filed, unless the spouses are separated and a joint petition is not filed.)

NAME AND ADDRESS OF TRANSFEREE, RELATIONSHIP TO DEBTOR	DATE	DESCRIBE PROPERTY TRANSFERRED AND VALUE RECEIVED

None ☐

b.   List all property transferred by the debtor within **ten years** immediately preceding the commencement of this case to a self-settled trust or similar device of which the debtor is a beneficiary.

NAME OF TRUST OR OTHER DEVICE	DATE(S) OF TRANSFER(S)	AMOUNT OF MONEY OR DESCRIPTION AND VALUE OF PROPERTY OR DEBTOR'S INTEREST IN PROPERTY

---

11. Closed financial accounts

None ☐

List all financial accounts and instruments held in the name of the debtor or for the benefit of the debtor which were closed, sold, or otherwise transferred within **one year** immediately preceding the commencement of this case. Include checking, savings, or other financial accounts, certificates of deposit, or other instruments; shares and share accounts held in banks, credit unions, pension funds, cooperatives, associations, brokerage houses and other financial institutions. (Married debtors filing under chapter 12 or chapter 13 must include information concerning accounts or instruments held by or for either or both spouses whether or not a joint petition is filed, unless the spouses are separated and a joint petition is not filed.)

NAME AND ADDRESS OF INSTITUTION	TYPE OF ACCOUNT, LAST FOUR DIGITS OF ACCOUNT NUMBER, AND AMOUNT OF FINAL BALANCE	AMOUNT AND DATE OF SALE OR CLOSING

---

12. Safe deposit boxes

None
☐

List each safe deposit or other box or depository in which the debtor has or had securities, cash, or other valuables within **one year** immediately preceding the commencement of this case. (Married debtors filing under chapter 12 or chapter 13 must include boxes or depositories of either or both spouses whether or not a joint petition is filed, unless the spouses are separated and a joint petition is not filed.)

NAME AND ADDRESS OF BANK OR OTHER DEPOSITORY	NAMES AND ADDRESSES OF THOSE WITH ACCESS TO BOX OR DEPOSITORY	DESCRIPTION OF CONTENTS	DATE OF TRANSFER OR SURRENDER, IF ANY

13. Setoffs

None
☐

List all setoffs made by any creditor, including a bank, against a debt or deposit of the debtor within **90 days** preceding the commencement of this case. (Married debtors filing under chapter 12 or chapter 13 must include information concerning either or both spouses whether or not a joint petition is filed, unless the spouses are separated and a joint petition is not filed.)

NAME AND ADDRESS OF CREDITOR	DATE OF SETOFF	AMOUNT OF SETOFF

14. Property held for another person

None
☐

List all property owned by another person that the debtor holds or controls.

NAME AND ADDRESS OF OWNER	DESCRIPTION AND VALUE OF PROPERTY	LOCATION OF PROPERTY

15. Prior address of debtor

None
☐

If debtor has moved within **three years** immediately preceding the commencement of this case, list all premises which the debtor occupied during that period and vacated prior to the commencement of this case. If a joint petition is filed, report also any separate address of either spouse.

ADDRESS	NAME USED	DATES OF OCCUPANCY

16. Spouses and Former Spouses

None
☐   If the debtor resides or resided in a community property state, commonwealth, or territory (including Alaska, Arizona, California, Idaho, Louisiana, Nevada, New Mexico, Puerto Rico, Texas, Washington, or Wisconsin) within **eight years** immediately preceding the commencement of the case, identify the name of the debtor's spouse and of any former spouse who resides or resided with the debtor in the community property state.

NAME

---

17. Environmental Information.

For the purpose of this question, the following definitions apply:

"Environmental Law" means any federal, state, or local statute or regulation regulating pollution, contamination, releases of hazardous or toxic substances, wastes or material into the air, land, soil, surface water, groundwater, or other medium, including, but not limited to, statutes or regulations regulating the cleanup of these substances, wastes, or material.

"Site" means any location, facility, or property as defined under any Environmental Law, whether or not presently or formerly owned or operated by the debtor, including, but not limited to, disposal sites.

"Hazardous Material" means anything defined as a hazardous waste, hazardous substance, toxic substance, hazardous material, pollutant, or contaminant or similar term under an Environmental Law.

None
☐   a. List the name and address of every site for which the debtor has received notice in writing by a governmental unit that it may be liable or potentially liable under or in violation of an Environmental Law. Indicate the governmental unit, the date of the notice, and, if known, the Environmental Law:

SITE NAME AND ADDRESS	NAME AND ADDRESS OF GOVERNMENTAL UNIT	DATE OF NOTICE	ENVIRONMENTAL LAW

None
☐   b. List the name and address of every site for which the debtor provided notice to a governmental unit of a release of Hazardous Material. Indicate the governmental unit to which the notice was sent and the date of the notice.

SITE NAME AND ADDRESS	NAME AND ADDRESS OF GOVERNMENTAL UNIT	DATE OF NOTICE	ENVIRONMENTAL LAW

None
☐   c. List all judicial or administrative proceedings, including settlements or orders, under any Environmental Law with respect to which the debtor is or was a party. Indicate the name and address of the governmental unit that is or was a party to the proceeding, and the docket number.

NAME AND ADDRESS OF GOVERNMENTAL UNIT	DOCKET NUMBER	STATUS OR DISPOSITION

---

18 . Nature, location and name of business

None
☐   a. *If the debtor is an individual*, list the names, addresses, taxpayer-identification numbers, nature of the businesses, and beginning and ending dates of all businesses in which the debtor was an officer, director, partner, or managing

executive of a corporation, partner in a partnership, sole proprietor, or was self-employed in a trade, profession, or other activity either full- or part-time within **six years** immediately preceding the commencement of this case, or in which the debtor owned 5 percent or more of the voting or equity securities within **six years** immediately preceding the commencement of this case.

If the debtor is a partnership, list the names, addresses, taxpayer-identification numbers, nature of the businesses, and beginning and ending dates of all businesses in which the debtor was a partner or owned 5 percent or more of the voting or equity securities, within **six years** immediately preceding the commencement of this case.

If the debtor is a corporation, list the names, addresses, taxpayer-identification numbers, nature of the businesses, and beginning and ending dates of all businesses in which the debtor was a partner or owned 5 percent or more of the voting or equity securities within **six years** immediately preceding the commencement of this case.

NAME	LAST FOUR DIGITS OF SOCIAL-SECURITY OR OTHER INDIVIDUAL TAXPAYER-I.D. NO. (ITIN)/ COMPLETE EIN	ADDRESS	NATURE OF BUSINESS	BEGINNING AND ENDING DATES

None ☐   b. Identify any business listed in response to subdivision a., above, that is "single asset real estate" as defined in 11 U.S.C. § 101.

NAME   ADDRESS

The following questions are to be completed by every debtor that is a corporation or partnership and by any individual debtor who is or has been, within **six years** immediately preceding the commencement of this case, any of the following: an officer, director, managing executive, or owner of more than 5 percent of the voting or equity securities of a corporation; a partner, other than a limited partner, of a partnership, a sole proprietor, or self-employed in a trade, profession, or other activity, either full- or part-time.

*(An individual or joint debtor should complete this portion of the statement **only** if the debtor is or has been in business, as defined above, within six years immediately preceding the commencement of this case. A debtor who has not been in business within those six years should go directly to the signature page.)*

---

19. Books, records and financial statements

None ☐   a. List all bookkeepers and accountants who within **two years** immediately preceding the filing of this bankruptcy case kept or supervised the keeping of books of account and records of the debtor.

NAME AND ADDRESS   DATES SERVICES RENDERED

None ☐   b. List all firms or individuals who within **two years** immediately preceding the filing of this bankruptcy case have audited the books of account and records, or prepared a financial statement of the debtor.

NAME   ADDRESS   DATES SERVICES RENDERED

None
☐
c. List all firms or individuals who at the time of the commencement of this case were in possession of the books of account and records of the debtor. If any of the books of account and records are not available, explain.

NAME   ADDRESS

None
☐
d. List all financial institutions, creditors and other parties, including mercantile and trade agencies, to whom a financial statement was issued by the debtor within **two years** immediately preceding the commencement of this case.

NAME AND ADDRESS   DATE ISSUED

---

20. Inventories

None
☐
a. List the dates of the last two inventories taken of your property, the name of the person who supervised the taking of each inventory, and the dollar amount and basis of each inventory.

| | | DOLLAR AMOUNT OF INVENTORY |
| DATE OF INVENTORY | INVENTORY SUPERVISOR | (Specify cost, market or other basis) |

None
☐
b. List the name and address of the person having possession of the records of each of the inventories reported in a., above.

| | NAME AND ADDRESSES OF CUSTODIAN |
| DATE OF INVENTORY | OF INVENTORY RECORDS |

---

21. Current Partners, Officers, Directors and Shareholders

None
☐
a. If the debtor is a partnership, list the nature and percentage of partnership interest of each member of the partnership.

NAME AND ADDRESS   NATURE OF INTEREST   PERCENTAGE OF INTEREST

None
☐
b. If the debtor is a corporation, list all officers and directors of the corporation, and each stockholder who directly or indirectly owns, controls, or holds 5 percent or more of the voting or equity securities of the corporation.

| | | NATURE AND PERCENTAGE |
| NAME AND ADDRESS | TITLE | OF STOCK OWNERSHIP |

---

22 . Former partners, officers, directors and shareholders

None
☐ a.   If the debtor is a partnership, list each member who withdrew from the partnership within **one year** immediately preceding the commencement of this case.

NAME   ADDRESS   DATE OF WITHDRAWAL

None
☐ b.   If the debtor is a corporation, list all officers or directors whose relationship with the corporation terminated within **one year** immediately preceding the commencement of this case.

NAME AND ADDRESS   TITLE   DATE OF TERMINATION

---

23 . Withdrawals from a partnership or distributions by a corporation

None
☐ If the debtor is a partnership or corporation, list all withdrawals or distributions credited or given to an insider, including compensation in any form, bonuses, loans, stock redemptions, options exercised and any other perquisite during **one year** immediately preceding the commencement of this case.

NAME & ADDRESS OF RECIPIENT, RELATIONSHIP TO DEBTOR	DATE AND PURPOSE OF WITHDRAWAL	AMOUNT OF MONEY OR DESCRIPTION AND VALUE OF PROPERTY

---

24. Tax Consolidation Group.

None
☐ If the debtor is a corporation, list the name and federal taxpayer-identification number of the parent corporation of any consolidated group for tax purposes of which the debtor has been a member at any time within **six years** immediately preceding the commencement of the case.

NAME OF PARENT CORPORATION   TAXPAYER-IDENTIFICATION NUMBER (EIN)

---

25. Pension Funds.

None
☐ If the debtor is not an individual, list the name and federal taxpayer-identification number of any pension fund to which the debtor, as an employer, has been responsible for contributing at any time within **six years** immediately preceding the commencement of the case.

NAME OF PENSION FUND   TAXPAYER-IDENTIFICATION NUMBER (EIN)

* * * * * *

[If completed by an individual or individual and spouse]

I declare under penalty of perjury that I have read the answers contained in the foregoing statement of financial affairs and any attachments thereto and that they are true and correct.

| | | Signature | |
| Date | _____ | of Debtor | _____ |

		Signature of	
		Joint Debtor	
Date	_____	(if any)	_____

[If completed on behalf of a partnership or corporation]

I declare under penalty of perjury that I have read the answers contained in the foregoing statement of financial affairs and any attachments thereto and that they are true and correct to the best of my knowledge, information and belief.

| | | Signature | |
| Date | _____ | | _____ |

| | | Print Name and | |
| | | Title | _____ |

[An individual signing on behalf of a partnership or corporation must indicate position or relationship to debtor.]

___continuation sheets attached

Penalty for making a false statement: Fine of up to $500,000 or imprisonment for up to 5 years, or both. 18 U.S.C. §§ 152 and 3571

DECLARATION AND SIGNATURE OF NON-ATTORNEY BANKRUPTCY PETITION PREPARER (See 11 U.S.C. § 110)

I declare under penalty of perjury that: (1) I am a bankruptcy petition preparer as defined in 11 U.S.C. § 110; (2) I prepared this document for compensation and have provided the debtor with a copy of this document and the notices and information required under 11 U.S.C. §§ 110(b), 110(h), and 342(b); and, (3) if rules or guidelines have been promulgated pursuant to 11 U.S.C. § 110(h) setting a maximum fee for services chargeable by bankruptcy petition preparers, I have given the debtor notice of the maximum amount before preparing any document for filing for a debtor or accepting any fee from the debtor, as required by that section.

| _____ | _____ |
| Printed or Typed Name and Title, if any, of Bankruptcy Petition Preparer | Social-Security No. (Required by 11 U.S.C. § 110.) |

If the bankruptcy petition preparer is not an individual, state the name, title (if any), address, and social-security number of the officer, principal, responsible person, or partner who signs this document.

_____
Address

| _____ | _____ |
| Signature of Bankruptcy Petition Preparer | Date |

Names and Social-Security numbers of all other individuals who prepared or assisted in preparing this document unless the bankruptcy petition preparer is not an individual:

If more than one person prepared this document, attach additional signed sheets conforming to the appropriate Official Form for each person

A bankruptcy petition preparer's failure to comply with the provisions of title 11 and the Federal Rules of Bankruptcy Procedure may result in fines or imprisonment or both. 18 U.S.C. § 156.

B 8 (Official Form 8) (12/08)

UNITED STATES BANKRUPTCY COURT

_____ District of _____

In re _____,   Case No. _____
                    Debtor   Chapter 7

CHAPTER 7 INDIVIDUAL DEBTOR'S STATEMENT OF INTENTION

PART A – Debts secured by property of the estate. *(Part A must be fully completed for **EACH** debt which is secured by property of the estate. Attach additional pages if necessary.)*

Property No. 1

Creditor's Name:	**Describe Property Securing Debt:**

Property will be *(check one)*:
  ❑ Surrendered   ❑ Retained

If retaining the property, I intend to *(check at least one)*:
  ❑ Redeem the property
  ❑ Reaffirm the debt
  ❑ Other. Explain _____ (for example, avoid lien using 11 U.S.C. § 522(f)).

Property is *(check one)*:
  ❑ Claimed as exempt   ❑ Not claimed as exempt

Property No. 2 *(if necessary)*

Creditor's Name:	**Describe Property Securing Debt:**

Property will be *(check one)*:
  ❑ Surrendered   ❑ Retained

If retaining the property, I intend to *(check at least one)*:
  ❑ Redeem the property
  ❑ Reaffirm the debt
  ❑ Other. Explain _____ (for example, avoid lien using 11 U.S.C. § 522(f)).

Property is *(check one)*:
  ❑ Claimed as exempt   ❑ Not claimed as exempt

PART B – Personal property subject to unexpired leases. *(All three columns of Part B must be completed for each unexpired lease. Attach additional pages if necessary.)*

Property No. 1		
Lessor's Name:	**Describe Leased Property:**	Lease will be Assumed pursuant to 11 U.S.C. § 365(p)(2): ☐ YES ☐ NO

Property No. 2 *(if necessary)*		
Lessor's Name:	**Describe Leased Property:**	Lease will be Assumed pursuant to 11 U.S.C. § 365(p)(2): ☐ YES ☐ NO

Property No. 3 *(if necessary)*		
Lessor's Name:	**Describe Leased Property:**	Lease will be Assumed pursuant to 11 U.S.C. § 365(p)(2): ☐ YES ☐ NO

_____ continuation sheets attached *(if any)*

I declare under penalty of perjury that the above indicates my intention as to any property of my estate securing a debt and/or personal property subject to an unexpired lease.

Date: _____   _____
                                        Signature of Debtor

                                        _____
                                        Signature of Joint Debtor

B 8 (Official Form 8) (12/08)

CHAPTER 7 INDIVIDUAL DEBTOR'S STATEMENT OF INTENTION
(Continuation Sheet)

PART A - Continuation

Property No.	
Creditor's Name:	**Describe Property Securing Debt:**

Property will be *(check one)*:
  ☐ Surrendered   ☐ Retained

If retaining the property, I intend to *(check at least one)*:
  ☐ Redeem the property
  ☐ Reaffirm the debt
  ☐ Other. Explain _____ (for example, avoid lien
using 11 U.S.C. § 522(f)).

Property is *(check one)*:
  ☐ Claimed as exempt   ☐ Not claimed as exempt

PART B - Continuation

Property No.		
Lessor's Name:	**Describe Leased Property:**	Lease will be Assumed pursuant to 11 U.S.C. § 365(p)(2): ☐ YES ☐ NO

Property No.		
Lessor's Name:	**Describe Leased Property:**	Lease will be Assumed pursuant to 11 U.S.C. § 365(p)(2): ☐ YES ☐ NO

B 4 (Official Form 4) (12/07)

UNITED STATES BANKRUPTCY COURT

_____ District Of _____

In re _____,   Case No. _____
　　　　　　　　Debtor

　　　　　　　　　　　　　　　　　　　　　　　　　Chapter _____

LIST OF CREDITORS HOLDING 20 LARGEST UNSECURED CLAIMS

　　　　Following is the list of the debtor's creditors holding the 20 largest unsecured claims. The list is prepared in accordance with Fed. R. Bankr. P. 1007(d) for filing in this chapter 11 [*or* chapter 9] case. The list does not include (1) persons who come within the definition of "insider" set forth in 11 U.S.C. § 101, or (2) secured creditors unless the value of the collateral is such that the unsecured deficiency places the creditor among the holders of the 20 largest unsecured claims. If a minor child is one of the creditors holding the 20 largest unsecured claims, state the child's initials and the name and address of the child's parent or guardian, such as "A.B., a minor child, by John Doe, guardian." Do not disclose the child's name. See, 11 U.S.C. §112 and Fed. R. Bankr. P. 1007(m).

(1)	(2)	(3)	(4)	(5)
Name of creditor and complete mailing address, including zip code	*Name, telephone number and complete mailing address, including zip code, of employee, agent, or department of creditor familiar with claim who may be contacted*	*Nature of claim (trade debt, bank loan, government contract, etc.)*	*Indicate if claim is contingent, unliquidated, disputed or subject to setoff*	*Amount of claim [if secured also state value of security]*

Date: _____

_____
　　　　　Debtor

[Declaration as in Form 2]

B 22A (Official Form 22A) (Chapter 7) (12/10)

In re _____
                 Debtor(s)

Case Number: _____
                 (If known)

According to the information required to be entered on this statement
(check one box as directed in Part I, III, or VI of this statement):

☐ **The presumption arises.**
☐ **The presumption does not arise.**
☐ **The presumption is temporarily inapplicable.**

CHAPTER 7 STATEMENT OF CURRENT MONTHLY INCOME
AND MEANS-TEST CALCULATION

In addition to Schedules I and J, this statement must be completed by every individual chapter 7 debtor. If none of the exclusions in Part I applies, joint debtors may complete one statement only. If any of the exclusions in Part I applies, joint debtors should complete separate statements if they believe this is required by § 707(b)(2)(C).

Part I. MILITARY AND NON-CONSUMER DEBTORS

1A	**Disabled Veterans.** If you are a disabled veteran described in the Declaration in this Part IA, (1) check the box at the beginning of the Declaration, (2) check the box for "The presumption does not arise" at the top of this statement, and (3) complete the verification in Part VIII. Do not complete any of the remaining parts of this statement. ☐ **Declaration of Disabled Veteran.** By checking this box, I declare under penalty of perjury that I am a disabled veteran (as defined in 38 U.S.C. § 3741(1)) whose indebtedness occurred primarily during a period in which I was on active duty (as defined in 10 U.S.C. § 101(d)(1)) or while I was performing a homeland defense activity (as defined in 32 U.S.C. §901(1)).
1B	**Non-consumer Debtors.** If your debts are not primarily consumer debts, check the box below and complete the verification in Part VIII. Do not complete any of the remaining parts of this statement. ☐ **Declaration of non-consumer debts.** By checking this box, I declare that my debts are not primarily consumer debts.

1C	**Reservists and National Guard Members; active duty or homeland defense activity.** Members of a reserve component of the Armed Forces and members of the National Guard who were called to active duty (as defined in 10 U.S.C. § 101(d)(1)) after September 11, 2001, for a period of at least 90 days, or who have performed homeland defense activity (as defined in 32 U.S.C. § 901(1)) for a period of at least 90 days, are excluded from all forms of means testing during the time of active duty or homeland defense activity and for 540 days thereafter (the "exclusion period"). If you qualify for this temporary exclusion, (1) check the appropriate boxes and complete any required information in the Declaration of Reservists and National Guard Members below, (2) check the box for "The presumption is temporarily inapplicable" at the top of this statement, and (3) complete the verification in Part VIII. **During your exclusion period you are not required to complete the balance of this form, but you must complete the form no later than 14 days after the date on which your exclusion period ends, unless the time for filing a motion raising the means test presumption expires in your case before your exclusion period ends.**
	
	 ☐ **Declaration of Reservists and National Guard Members.** By checking this box and making the appropriate entries below, I declare that I am eligible for a temporary exclusion from means testing because, as a member of a reserve component of the Armed Forces or the National Guard
	
	        a. ☐ I was called to active duty after September 11, 2001, for a period of at least 90 days and
	            ☐ I remain on active duty /or/
	            ☐ I was released from active duty on _____, which is less than 540 days before this bankruptcy case was filed;
	
	           OR
	
	        b. ☐ I am performing homeland defense activity for a period of at least 90 days /or/
	            ☐ I performed homeland defense activity for a period of at least 90 days, terminating on _____, which is less than 540 days before this bankruptcy case was filed.

633

B 22A (Official Form 22A) (Chapter 7) (12/10)   2

Part II. CALCULATION OF MONTHLY INCOME FOR § 707(b)(7) EXCLUSION			
2	**Marital/filing status.** Check the box that applies and complete the balance of this part of this statement as directed. a. ☐ Unmarried. **Complete only Column A ("Debtor's Income") for Lines 3-11.** b. ☐ Married, not filing jointly, with declaration of separate households. By checking this box, debtor declares under penalty of perjury: "My spouse and I are legally separated under applicable non-bankruptcy law or my spouse and I are living apart other than for the purpose of evading the requirements of § 707(b)(2)(A) of the Bankruptcy Code." **Complete only Column A ("Debtor's Income") for Lines 3-11.** c. ☐ Married, not filing jointly, without the declaration of separate households set out in Line 2.b above. **Complete both Column A ("Debtor's Income") and Column B ("Spouse's Income") for Lines 3-11.** d. ☐ Married, filing jointly. **Complete both Column A ("Debtor's Income") and Column B ("Spouse's Income") for Lines 3-11.**			
	All figures must reflect average monthly income received from all sources, derived during the six calendar months prior to filing the bankruptcy case, ending on the last day of the month before the filing. If the amount of monthly income varied during the six months, you must divide the six-month total by six, and enter the result on the appropriate line.		**Column A** Debtor's Income	**Column B** Spouse's Income
3	**Gross wages, salary, tips, bonuses, overtime, commissions.**		$	$
4	**Income from the operation of a business, profession or farm.** Subtract Line b from Line a and enter the difference in the appropriate column(s) of Line 4. If you operate more than one business, profession or farm, enter aggregate numbers and provide details on an attachment. Do not enter a number less than zero. **Do not include any part of the business expenses entered on Line b as a deduction in Part V.**			
	a.	Gross receipts	$	
	b.	Ordinary and necessary business expenses	$	
	c.	Business income	Subtract Line b from Line a	$	$
5	**Rent and other real property income.** Subtract Line b from Line a and enter the difference in the appropriate column(s) of Line 5. Do not enter a number less than zero. **Do not include any part of the operating expenses entered on Line b as a deduction in Part V.**			
	a.	Gross receipts	$	
	b.	Ordinary and necessary operating expenses	$	
	c.	Rent and other real property income	Subtract Line b from Line a	$	$
6	**Interest, dividends and royalties.**		$	$
7	**Pension and retirement income.**		$	$
8	**Any amounts paid by another person or entity, on a regular basis, for the household expenses of the debtor or the debtor's dependents, including child support paid for that purpose.** Do not include alimony or separate maintenance payments or amounts paid by your spouse if Column B is completed. Each regular payment should be reported in only one column; if a payment is listed in Column A, do not report that payment in Column B.		$	$
9	**Unemployment compensation.** Enter the amount in the appropriate column(s) of Line 9. However, if you contend that unemployment compensation received by you or your spouse was a benefit under the Social Security Act, do not list the amount of such compensation in Column A or B, but instead state the amount in the space below:			
	Unemployment compensation claimed to be a benefit under the Social Security Act	Debtor $ _____ Spouse $ _____	$	$

10	**Income from all other sources.** Specify source and amount. If necessary, list additional sources on a separate page. **Do not include alimony or separate maintenance payments paid by your spouse if Column B is completed, but include all other payments of alimony or separate maintenance.** Do not include any benefits received under the Social Security Act or payments received as a victim of a war crime, crime against humanity, or as a victim of international or domestic terrorism.		
	a. $		
	b. $		
	Total and enter on Line 10	$	$
11	**Subtotal of Current Monthly Income for § 707(b)(7).** Add Lines 3 thru 10 in Column A, and, if Column B is completed, add Lines 3 through 10 in Column B. Enter the total(s).	$	$
12	**Total Current Monthly Income for § 707(b)(7).** If Column B has been completed, add Line 11, Column A to Line 11, Column B, and enter the total. If Column B has not been completed, enter the amount from Line 11, Column A.	$	

Part III. APPLICATION OF § 707(b)(7) EXCLUSION

13	**Annualized Current Monthly Income for § 707(b)(7).** Multiply the amount from Line 12 by the number 12 and enter the result.	$
14	**Applicable median family income.** Enter the median family income for the applicable state and household size. (This information is available by family size at www.usdoj.gov/ust/ or from the clerk of the bankruptcy court.) a. Enter debtor's state of residence: _____ b. Enter debtor's household size: _____	$
15	**Application of Section 707(b)(7).** Check the applicable box and proceed as directed. ☐ **The amount on Line 13 is less than or equal to the amount on Line 14.** Check the box for "The presumption does not arise" at the top of page 1 of this statement, and complete Part VIII; do not complete Parts IV, V, VI or VII. ☐ **The amount on Line 13 is more than the amount on Line 14.** Complete the remaining parts of this statement.	

Complete Parts IV, V, VI, and VII of this statement only if required. (See Line 15.)

Part IV. CALCULATION OF CURRENT MONTHLY INCOME FOR § 707(b)(2)

16	**Enter the amount from Line 12.**	$
17	**Marital adjustment.** If you checked the box at Line 2.c, enter on Line 17 the total of any income listed in Line 11, Column B that was NOT paid on a regular basis for the household expenses of the debtor or the debtor's dependents. Specify in the lines below the basis for excluding the Column B income (such as payment of the spouse's tax liability or the spouse's support of persons other than the debtor or the debtor's dependents) and the amount of income devoted to each purpose. If necessary, list additional adjustments on a separate page. If you did not check box at Line 2.c, enter zero.	
	a. $	
	b. $	
	c. $	
	Total and enter on Line 17.	$
18	**Current monthly income for § 707(b)(2).** Subtract Line 17 from Line 16 and enter the result.	$

B 22A (Official Form 22A) (Chapter 7) (12/10)　　　　　　　　　　　　　　　　　　　　4

Part V. CALCULATION OF DEDUCTIONS FROM INCOME

Subpart A: Deductions under Standards of the Internal Revenue Service (IRS)

19A	**National Standards: food, clothing and other items.** Enter in Line 19A the "Total" amount from IRS National Standards for Food, Clothing and Other Items for the applicable number of persons. (This information is available at www.usdoj.gov/ust/ or from the clerk of the bankruptcy court.) The applicable number of persons is the number that would currently be allowed as exemptions on your federal income tax return, plus the number of any additional dependents whom you support.	$
19B	**National Standards: health care.** Enter in Line a1 below the amount from IRS National Standards for Out-of-Pocket Health Care for persons under 65 years of age, and in Line a2 the IRS National Standards for Out-of-Pocket Health Care for persons 65 years of age or older. (This information is available at www.usdoj.gov/ust/ or from the clerk of the bankruptcy court.) Enter in Line b1 the applicable number of persons who are under 65 years of age, and enter in Line b2 the applicable number of persons who are 65 years of age or older. (The applicable number of persons in each age category is the number in that category that would currently be allowed as exemptions on your federal income tax return, plus the number of any additional dependents whom you support.) Multiply Line a1 by Line b1 to obtain a total amount for persons under 65, and enter the result in Line c1. Multiply Line a2 by Line b2 to obtain a total amount for persons 65 and older, and enter the result in Line c2. Add Lines c1 and c2 to obtain a total health care amount, and enter the result in Line 19B.	

Persons under 65 years of age		Persons 65 years of age or older		
a1.	Allowance per person	a2.	Allowance per person	
b1.	Number of persons	b2.	Number of persons	
c1.	Subtotal	c2.	Subtotal	$

20A	**Local Standards: housing and utilities; non-mortgage expenses.** Enter the amount of the IRS Housing and Utilities Standards; non-mortgage expenses for the applicable county and family size. (This information is available at www.usdoj.gov/ust/ or from the clerk of the bankruptcy court). The applicable family size consists of the number that would currently be allowed as exemptions on your federal income tax return, plus the number of any additional dependents whom you support.	$
20B	**Local Standards: housing and utilities; mortgage/rent expense.** Enter, in Line a below, the amount of the IRS Housing and Utilities Standards; mortgage/rent expense for your county and family size (this information is available at www.usdoj.gov/ust/ or from the clerk of the bankruptcy court) (the applicable family size consists of the number that would currently be allowed as exemptions on your federal income tax return, plus the number of any additional dependents whom you support); enter on Line b the total of the Average Monthly Payments for any debts secured by your home, as stated in Line 42; subtract Line b from Line a and enter the result in Line 20B. **Do not enter an amount less than zero.**	

a.	IRS Housing and Utilities Standards; mortgage/rental expense	$	
b.	Average Monthly Payment for any debts secured by your home, if any, as stated in Line 42	$	
c.	Net mortgage/rental expense	Subtract Line b from Line a.	$

21	**Local Standards: housing and utilities; adjustment.** If you contend that the process set out in Lines 20A and 20B does not accurately compute the allowance to which you are entitled under the IRS Housing and Utilities Standards, enter any additional amount to which you contend you are entitled, and state the basis for your contention in the space below:	
		$

22A	**Local Standards: transportation; vehicle operation/public transportation expense.** You are entitled to an expense allowance in this category regardless of whether you pay the expenses of operating a vehicle and regardless of whether you use public transportation. Check the number of vehicles for which you pay the operating expenses or for which the operating expenses are included as a contribution to your household expenses in Line 8. ☐ 0 ☐ 1 ☐ 2 or more. If you checked 0, enter on Line 22A the "Public Transportation" amount from IRS Local Standards: Transportation. If you checked 1 or 2 or more, enter on Line 22A the "Operating Costs" amount from IRS Local Standards: Transportation for the applicable number of vehicles in the applicable Metropolitan Statistical Area or Census Region. (These amounts are available at www.usdoj.gov/ust/ or from the clerk of the bankruptcy court.)	$
22B	**Local Standards: transportation; additional public transportation expense.** If you pay the operating expenses for a vehicle and also use public transportation, and you contend that you are entitled to an additional deduction for your public transportation expenses, enter on Line 22B the "Public Transportation" amount from IRS Local Standards: Transportation. (This amount is available at www.usdoj.gov/ust/ or from the clerk of the bankruptcy court.)	$

23	**Local Standards: transportation ownership/lease expense; Vehicle 1.** Check the number of vehicles for which you claim an ownership/lease expense. (You may not claim an ownership/lease expense for more than two vehicles.) ☐ 1 ☐ 2 or more. Enter, in Line a below, the "Ownership Costs" for "One Car" from the IRS Local Standards: Transportation (available at www.usdoj.gov/ust/ or from the clerk of the bankruptcy court); enter in Line b the total of the Average Monthly Payments for any debts secured by Vehicle 1, as stated in Line 42; subtract Line b from Line a and enter the result in Line 23. **Do not enter an amount less than zero.**		
	a.	IRS Transportation Standards, Ownership Costs	$
	b.	Average Monthly Payment for any debts secured by Vehicle 1, as stated in Line 42	$
	c.	Net ownership/lease expense for Vehicle 1	Subtract Line b from Line a. $

24	**Local Standards: transportation ownership/lease expense; Vehicle 2.** Complete this Line only if you checked the "2 or more" Box in Line 23. Enter, in Line a below, the "Ownership Costs" for "One Car" from the IRS Local Standards: Transportation (available at www.usdoj.gov/ust/ or from the clerk of the bankruptcy court); enter in Line b the total of the Average Monthly Payments for any debts secured by Vehicle 2, as stated in Line 42; subtract Line b from Line a and enter the result in Line 24. **Do not enter an amount less than zero.**		
	a.	IRS Transportation Standards, Ownership Costs	$
	b.	Average Monthly Payment for any debts secured by Vehicle 2, as stated in Line 42	$
	c.	Net ownership/lease expense for Vehicle 2	Subtract Line b from Line a. $

25	**Other Necessary Expenses: taxes.** Enter the total average monthly expense that you actually incur for all federal, state and local taxes, other than real estate and sales taxes, such as income taxes, self-employment taxes, social-security taxes, and Medicare taxes. **Do not include real estate or sales taxes.**	$
26	**Other Necessary Expenses: involuntary deductions for employment.** Enter the total average monthly payroll deductions that are required for your employment, such as retirement contributions, union dues, and uniform costs. **Do not include discretionary amounts, such as voluntary 401(k) contributions.**	$
27	**Other Necessary Expenses: life insurance.** Enter total average monthly premiums that you actually pay for term life insurance for yourself. **Do not include premiums for insurance on your dependents, for whole life or for any other form of insurance.**	$
28	**Other Necessary Expenses: court-ordered payments.** Enter the total monthly amount that you are required to pay pursuant to the order of a court or administrative agency, such as spousal or child support payments. **Do not include payments on past due obligations included in Line 44.**	$

B 22A (Official Form 22A) (Chapter 7) (12/10)   6

29	**Other Necessary Expenses: education for employment or for a physically or mentally challenged child.** Enter the total average monthly amount that you actually expend for education that is a condition of employment and for education that is required for a physically or mentally challenged dependent child for whom no public education providing similar services is available.	$
30	**Other Necessary Expenses: childcare.** Enter the total average monthly amount that you actually expend on childcare—such as baby-sitting, day care, nursery and preschool. **Do not include other educational payments.**	$
31	**Other Necessary Expenses: health care.** Enter the total average monthly amount that you actually expend on health care that is required for the health and welfare of yourself or your dependents, that is not reimbursed by insurance or paid by a health savings account, and that is in excess of the amount entered in Line 19B. **Do not include payments for health insurance or health savings accounts listed in Line 34.**	$
32	**Other Necessary Expenses: telecommunication services.** Enter the total average monthly amount that you actually pay for telecommunication services other than your basic home telephone and cell phone service—such as pagers, call waiting, caller id, special long distance, or internet service—to the extent necessary for your health and welfare or that of your dependents. **Do not include any amount previously deducted.**	$
33	**Total Expenses Allowed under IRS Standards.** Enter the total of Lines 19 through 32.	$

	Subpart B: Additional Living Expense Deductions **Note: Do not include any expenses that you have listed in Lines 19-32**	
34	**Health Insurance, Disability Insurance, and Health Savings Account Expenses.** List the monthly expenses in the categories set out in lines a-c below that are reasonably necessary for yourself, your spouse, or your dependents. a. Health Insurance $ b. Disability Insurance $ c. Health Savings Account $ Total and enter on Line 34 **If you do not actually expend this total amount**, state your actual total average monthly expenditures in the space below: $ _____	$
35	**Continued contributions to the care of household or family members.** Enter the total average actual monthly expenses that you will continue to pay for the reasonable and necessary care and support of an elderly, chronically ill, or disabled member of your household or member of your immediate family who is unable to pay for such expenses.	$
36	**Protection against family violence.** Enter the total average reasonably necessary monthly expenses that you actually incurred to maintain the safety of your family under the Family Violence Prevention and Services Act or other applicable federal law. The nature of these expenses is required to be kept confidential by the court.	$
37	**Home energy costs.** Enter the total average monthly amount, in excess of the allowance specified by IRS Local Standards for Housing and Utilities, that you actually expend for home energy costs. **You must provide your case trustee with documentation of your actual expenses, and you must demonstrate that the additional amount claimed is reasonable and necessary.**	$
38	**Education expenses for dependent children less than 18.** Enter the total average monthly expenses that you actually incur, not to exceed $147.92* per child, for attendance at a private or public elementary or secondary school by your dependent children less than 18 years of age. **You must provide your case trustee with documentation of your actual expenses, and you must explain why the amount claimed is reasonable and necessary and not already accounted for in the IRS Standards.**	$

*Amount subject to adjustment on 4/01/13, and every three years thereafter with respect to cases commenced on or after the date of adjustment.

39	**Additional food and clothing expense.** Enter the total average monthly amount by which your food and clothing expenses exceed the combined allowances for food and clothing (apparel and services) in the IRS National Standards, not to exceed 5% of those combined allowances. (This information is available at www.usdoj.gov/ust/ or from the clerk of the bankruptcy court.) **You must demonstrate that the additional amount claimed is reasonable and necessary.**	$
40	**Continued charitable contributions.** Enter the amount that you will continue to contribute in the form of cash or financial instruments to a charitable organization as defined in 26 U.S.C. § 170(c)(1)-(2).	$
41	**Total Additional Expense Deductions under § 707(b).** Enter the total of Lines 34 through 40	$

Subpart C: Deductions for Debt Payment

42	**Future payments on secured claims.** For each of your debts that is secured by an interest in property that you own, list the name of the creditor, identify the property securing the debt, state the Average Monthly Payment, and check whether the payment includes taxes or insurance. The Average Monthly Payment is the total of all amounts scheduled as contractually due to each Secured Creditor in the 60 months following the filing of the bankruptcy case, divided by 60. If necessary, list additional entries on a separate page. Enter the total of the Average Monthly Payments on Line 42.

	Name of Creditor	Property Securing the Debt	Average Monthly Payment	Does payment include taxes or insurance?	
a.			$	☐ yes ☐ no	
b.			$	☐ yes ☐ no	
c.			$	☐ yes ☐ no	
			Total: Add Lines a, b and c.		$

43	**Other payments on secured claims.** If any of debts listed in Line 42 are secured by your primary residence, a motor vehicle, or other property necessary for your support or the support of your dependents, you may include in your deduction 1/60th of any amount (the "cure amount") that you must pay the creditor in addition to the payments listed in Line 42, in order to maintain possession of the property. The cure amount would include any sums in default that must be paid in order to avoid repossession or foreclosure. List and total any such amounts in the following chart. If necessary, list additional entries on a separate page.

	Name of Creditor	Property Securing the Debt	1/60th of the Cure Amount	
a.			$	
b.			$	
c.			$	
			Total: Add Lines a, b and c	$

44	**Payments on prepetition priority claims.** Enter the total amount, divided by 60, of all priority claims, such as priority tax, child support and alimony claims, for which you were liable at the time of your bankruptcy filing. **Do not include current obligations, such as those set out in Line 28.**	$

B 22A (Official Form 22A) (Chapter 7) (12/10)   8

45	**Chapter 13 administrative expenses.** If you are eligible to file a case under chapter 13, complete the following chart, multiply the amount in line a by the amount in line b, and enter the resulting administrative expense.	

45	a.	Projected average monthly chapter 13 plan payment.	$
	b.	Current multiplier for your district as determined under schedules issued by the Executive Office for United States Trustees. (This information is available at www.usdoj.gov/ust/ or from the clerk of the bankruptcy court.)	x
	c.	Average monthly administrative expense of chapter 13 case	Total: Multiply Lines a and b $

46	**Total Deductions for Debt Payment.** Enter the total of Lines 42 through 45.	$

Subpart D: Total Deductions from Income

47	**Total of all deductions allowed under § 707(b)(2).** Enter the total of Lines 33, 41, and 46.	$

Part VI. DETERMINATION OF § 707(b)(2) PRESUMPTION

48	**Enter the amount from Line 18 (Current monthly income for § 707(b)(2))**	$
49	**Enter the amount from Line 47 (Total of all deductions allowed under § 707(b)(2))**	$
50	**Monthly disposable income under § 707(b)(2).** Subtract Line 49 from Line 48 and enter the result	$
51	**60-month disposable income under § 707(b)(2).** Multiply the amount in Line 50 by the number 60 and enter the result.	$
52	**Initial presumption determination.** Check the applicable box and proceed as directed. ☐ **The amount on Line 51 is less than $7,025*.** Check the box for "The presumption does not arise" at the top of page 1 of this statement, and complete the verification in Part VIII. Do not complete the remainder of Part VI. ☐ **The amount set forth on Line 51 is more than $11,725*.** Check the box for "The presumption arises" at the top of page 1 of this statement, and complete the verification in Part VIII. You may also complete Part VII. Do not complete the remainder of Part VI. ☐ **The amount on Line 51 is at least $7,025*, but not more than $11,725*.** Complete the remainder of Part VI (Lines 53 through 55).	
53	**Enter the amount of your total non-priority unsecured debt**	$
54	**Threshold debt payment amount.** Multiply the amount in Line 53 by the number 0.25 and enter the result.	$
55	**Secondary presumption determination.** Check the applicable box and proceed as directed. ☐ **The amount on Line 51 is less than the amount on Line 54.** Check the box for "The presumption does not arise" at the top of page 1 of this statement, and complete the verification in Part VIII. ☐ **The amount on Line 51 is equal to or greater than the amount on Line 54.** Check the box for "The presumption arises" at the top of page 1 of this statement, and complete the verification in Part VIII. You may also complete Part VII.	

Part VII: ADDITIONAL EXPENSE CLAIMS

56	**Other Expenses.** List and describe any monthly expenses, not otherwise stated in this form, that are required for the health and welfare of you and your family and that you contend should be an additional deduction from your current monthly income under § 707(b)(2)(A)(ii)(I). If necessary, list additional sources on a separate page. All figures should reflect your average monthly expense for each item. Total the expenses.	

	Expense Description	Monthly Amount
a.		$
b.		$
c.		$
	Total: Add Lines a, b and c	$

Amounts are subject to adjustment on 4/01/13, and every three years thereafter with respect to cases commenced on or after the date of adjustment.

B 22A (Official Form 22A) (Chapter 7) (12/10) 9

Part VIII: VERIFICATION
I declare under penalty of perjury that the information provided in this statement is true and correct. *(If this is a joint case, both debtors must sign.)*

57

Date: _____   Signature: _____
                                                            (Debtor)

Date: _____   Signature: _____
                                                            (Joint Debtor, if any)

B 22B (Official Form 22B) (Chapter 11) (12/10)

In re _____
                    Debtor(s)

Case Number: _____
                    (If known)

CHAPTER 11 STATEMENT OF CURRENT MONTHLY INCOME

In addition to Schedules I and J, this statement must be completed by every individual chapter 11 debtor, whether or not filing jointly. Joint debtors may complete one statement only.

	Part I. CALCULATION OF CURRENT MONTHLY INCOME			
1	**Marital/filing status.** Check the box that applies and complete the balance of this part of this statement as directed. a. ☐ Unmarried. **Complete only Column A ("Debtor's Income") for Lines 2-10.** b. ☐ Married, not filing jointly. **Complete only Column A ("Debtor's Income") for Lines 2-10.** c. ☐ Married, filing jointly. **Complete both Column A ("Debtor's Income") and Column B ("Spouse's Income") for Lines 2-10.**			
	All figures must reflect average monthly income received from all sources, derived during the six calendar months prior to filing the bankruptcy case, ending on the last day of the month before the filing. If the amount of monthly income varied during the six months, you must divide the six-month total by six, and enter the result on the appropriate line.		**Column A** **Debtor's** **Income**	**Column B** **Spouse's** **Income**
2	**Gross wages, salary, tips, bonuses, overtime, commissions.**		$	$
3	**Net income from the operation of a business, profession, or farm.** Subtract Line b from Line a and enter the difference in the appropriate column(s) of Line 3. If more than one business, profession or farm, enter aggregate numbers and provide details on an attachment. Do not enter a number less than zero. a. Gross receipts — $ b. Ordinary and necessary business expenses — $ c. Business income — Subtract Line b from Line a.		$	$
4	**Net rental and other real property income.** Subtract Line b from Line a and enter the difference in the appropriate column(s) of Line 4. Do not enter a number less than zero. a. Gross receipts — $ b. Ordinary and necessary operating expenses — $ c. Rent and other real property income — Subtract Line b from Line a.		$	$
5	**Interest, dividends, and royalties.**		$	$
6	**Pension and retirement income.**		$	$
7	**Any amounts paid by another person or entity, on a regular basis, for the household expenses of the debtor or the debtor's dependents, including child support paid for that purpose.** Do not include alimony or separate maintenance payments or amounts paid by the debtor's spouse if Column B is completed. Each regular payment should be reported in only one column; if a payment is listed in Column A, do not report that payment in Column B.		$	$
8	**Unemployment compensation.** Enter the amount in the appropriate column(s) of Line 8. However, if you contend that unemployment compensation received by you or your spouse was a benefit under the Social Security Act, do not list the amount of such compensation in Column A or B, but instead state the amount in the space below: Unemployment compensation claimed to be a benefit under the Social Security Act Debtor $ _____ Spouse $ _____		$	$

B 22B (Official Form 22B) (Chapter 11) (12/10)   2

9	**Income from all other sources**. Specify source and amount. If necessary, list additional sources on a separate page. Total and enter on Line 9. **Do not include alimony or separate maintenance payments paid by your spouse if Column B is completed, but include all other payments of alimony or separate maintenance. Do not include** any benefits received under the Social Security Act or payments received as a victim of a war crime, crime against humanity, or as a victim of international or domestic terrorism.			
	a.	$		
	b.	$	$	$
10	**Subtotal of current monthly income.** Add Lines 2 thru 9 in Column A, and, if Column B is completed, add Lines 2 through 9 in Column B. Enter the total(s).		$	$
11	**Total current monthly income.** If Column B has been completed, add Line 10, Column A to Line 10, Column B, and enter the total. If Column B has not been completed, enter the amount from Line 10, Column A.		$	
	Part II: VERIFICATION			

12	I declare under penalty of perjury that the information provided in this statement is true and correct. *(If this a joint case, both debtors must sign.)*
	
	Date: _____ Signature: _____
	
	                                                    (Debtor)
	
	Date: _____ Signature: _____
	
	                                                    (Joint Debtor, if any)			

B 22C (Official Form 22C) (Chapter 13) (12/10)

In re _____
                Debtor(s)

Case Number: _____
              (If known)

According to the calculations required by this statement:
☐ **The applicable commitment period is 3 years.**
☐ **The applicable commitment period is 5 years.**
☐ **Disposable income is determined under § 1325(b)(3).**
☐ **Disposable income is not determined under § 1325(b)(3).**
(Check the boxes as directed in Lines 17 and 23 of this statement.)

CHAPTER 13 STATEMENT OF CURRENT MONTHLY INCOME
AND CALCULATION OF COMMITMENT PERIOD AND DISPOSABLE INCOME

In addition to Schedules I and J, this statement must be completed by every individual chapter 13 debtor, whether or not filing jointly. Joint debtors may complete one statement only.

Part I. REPORT OF INCOME		
1	**Marital/filing status.** Check the box that applies and complete the balance of this part of this statement as directed. a. ☐ Unmarried. **Complete only Column A ("Debtor's Income") for Lines 2-10.** b. ☐ Married. **Complete both Column A ("Debtor's Income") and Column B ("Spouse's Income") for Lines 2-10.**		

	All figures must reflect average monthly income received from all sources, derived during the six calendar months prior to filing the bankruptcy case, ending on the last day of the month before the filing. If the amount of monthly income varied during the six months, you must divide the six-month total by six, and enter the result on the appropriate line.	**Column A** **Debtor's** **Income**	**Column B** **Spouse's** **Income**
2	**Gross wages, salary, tips, bonuses, overtime, commissions.**	$	$
3	**Income from the operation of a business, profession, or farm.** Subtract Line b from Line a and enter the difference in the appropriate column(s) of Line 3. If you operate more than one business, profession or farm, enter aggregate numbers and provide details on an attachment. Do not enter a number less than zero. **Do not include any part of the business expenses entered on Line b as a deduction in Part IV.** a. Gross receipts $ b. Ordinary and necessary business expenses $ c. Business income Subtract Line b from Line a	$	$
4	**Rent and other real property income.** Subtract Line b from Line a and enter the difference in the appropriate column(s) of Line 4. Do not enter a number less than zero. **Do not include any part of the operating expenses entered on Line b as a deduction in Part IV.** a. Gross receipts $ b. Ordinary and necessary operating expenses $ c. Rent and other real property income Subtract Line b from Line a	$	$
5	**Interest, dividends, and royalties.**	$	$
6	**Pension and retirement income.**	$	$
7	**Any amounts paid by another person or entity, on a regular basis, for the household expenses of the debtor or the debtor's dependents, including child support paid for that purpose.** Do not include alimony or separate maintenance payments or amounts paid by the debtor's spouse. Each regular payment should be reported in only one column; if a payment is listed in Column A, do not report that payment in Column B.	$	$

644

B 22C (Official Form 22C) (Chapter 13) (12/10) 2

8	**Unemployment compensation.** Enter the amount in the appropriate column(s) of Line 8. However, if you contend that unemployment compensation received by you or your spouse was a benefit under the Social Security Act, do not list the amount of such compensation in Column A or B, but instead state the amount in the space below: Unemployment compensation claimed to be a benefit under the Social Security Act Debtor $ _____ Spouse $ _____	$	$
9	**Income from all other sources.** Specify source and amount. If necessary, list additional sources on a separate page. Total and enter on Line 9. **Do not include alimony or separate maintenance payments paid by your spouse, but include all other payments of alimony or separate maintenance. Do not include** any benefits received under the Social Security Act or payments received as a victim of a war crime, crime against humanity, or as a victim of international or domestic terrorism. a. _____ $ _____ b. _____ $ _____	$	$
10	**Subtotal.** Add Lines 2 thru 9 in Column A, and, if Column B is completed, add Lines 2 through 9 in Column B. Enter the total(s).	$	$
11	**Total.** If Column B has been completed, add Line 10, Column A to Line 10, Column B, and enter the total. If Column B has not been completed, enter the amount from Line 10, Column A.	$	

Part II. CALCULATION OF § 1325(b)(4) COMMITMENT PERIOD

12	**Enter the amount from Line 11.**	$
13	**Marital adjustment.** If you are married, but are not filing jointly with your spouse, AND if you contend that calculation of the commitment period under § 1325(b)(4) does not require inclusion of the income of your spouse, enter on Line 13 the amount of the income listed in Line 10, Column B that was NOT paid on a regular basis for the household expenses of you or your dependents and specify, in the lines below, the basis for excluding this income (such as payment of the spouse's tax liability or the spouse's support of persons other than the debtor or the debtor's dependents) and the amount of income devoted to each purpose. If necessary, list additional adjustments on a separate page. If the conditions for entering this adjustment do not apply, enter zero. a. _____ $ _____ b. _____ $ _____ c. _____ $ _____ Total and enter on Line 13.	$
14	**Subtract Line 13 from Line 12 and enter the result.**	$
15	**Annualized current monthly income for § 1325(b)(4).** Multiply the amount from Line 14 by the number 12 and enter the result.	$
16	**Applicable median family income.** Enter the median family income for applicable state and household size. (This information is available by family size at www.usdoj.gov/ust/ or from the clerk of the bankruptcy court.) a. Enter debtor's state of residence: _____ b. Enter debtor's household size: _____	$
17	**Application of § 1325(b)(4).** Check the applicable box and proceed as directed. ☐ **The amount on Line 15 is less than the amount on Line 16.** Check the box for "The applicable commitment period is 3 years" at the top of page 1 of this statement and continue with this statement. ☐ **The amount on Line 15 is not less than the amount on Line 16.** Check the box for "The applicable commitment period is 5 years" at the top of page 1 of this statement and continue with this statement.	

Part III. APPLICATION OF § 1325(b)(3) FOR DETERMINING DISPOSABLE INCOME

18	**Enter the amount from Line 11.**	$

B 22C (Official Form 22C) (Chapter 13) (12/10)   3

19	**Marital adjustment.** If you are married, but are not filing jointly with your spouse, enter on Line 19 the total of any income listed in Line 10, Column B that was NOT paid on a regular basis for the household expenses of the debtor or the debtor's dependents. Specify in the lines below the basis for excluding the Column B income (such as payment of the spouse's tax liability or the spouse's support of persons other than the debtor or the debtor's dependents) and the amount of income devoted to each purpose. If necessary, list additional adjustments on a separate page. If the conditions for entering this adjustment do not apply, enter zero.

a.		$
b.		$
c.		$

Total and enter on Line 19. $

20	**Current monthly income for § 1325(b)(3).** Subtract Line 19 from Line 18 and enter the result.	$
21	**Annualized current monthly income for § 1325(b)(3).** Multiply the amount from Line 20 by the number 12 and enter the result.	$
22	**Applicable median family income.** Enter the amount from Line 16.	$
23	**Application of § 1325(b)(3).** Check the applicable box and proceed as directed. ☐ **The amount on Line 21 is more than the amount on Line 22.** Check the box for "Disposable income is determined under § 1325(b)(3)" at the top of page 1 of this statement and complete the remaining parts of this statement. ☐ **The amount on Line 21 is not more than the amount on Line 22.** Check the box for "Disposable income is not determined under § 1325(b)(3)" at the top of page 1 of this statement and complete Part VII of this statement. **Do not complete Parts IV, V, or VI.**	

Part IV. CALCULATION OF DEDUCTIONS FROM INCOME

Subpart A: Deductions under Standards of the Internal Revenue Service (IRS)

24A	**National Standards: food, apparel and services, housekeeping supplies, personal care, and miscellaneous.** Enter in Line 24A the "Total" amount from IRS National Standards for Allowable Living Expenses for the applicable number of persons. (This information is available at www.usdoj.gov/ust/ or from the clerk of the bankruptcy court.) The applicable number of persons is the number that would currently be allowed as exemptions on your federal income tax return, plus the number of any additional dependents whom you support.	$
24B	**National Standards: health care.** Enter in Line a1 below the amount from IRS National Standards for Out-of-Pocket Health Care for persons under 65 years of age, and in Line a2 the IRS National Standards for Out-of-Pocket Health Care for persons 65 years of age or older. (This information is available at www.usdoj.gov/ust/ or from the clerk of the bankruptcy court.) Enter in Line b1 the applicable number of persons who are under 65 years of age, and enter in Line b2 the applicable number of persons who are 65 years of age or older. (The applicable number of persons in each age category is the number in that category that would currently be allowed as exemptions on your federal income tax return, plus the number of any additional dependents whom you support.) Multiply Line a1 by Line b1 to obtain a total amount for persons under 65, and enter the result in Line c1. Multiply Line a2 by Line b2 to obtain a total amount for persons 65 and older, and enter the result in Line c2. Add Lines c1 and c2 to obtain a total health care amount, and enter the result in Line 24B.	

Persons under 65 years of age			Persons 65 years of age or older			
a1.	Allowance per person		a2.	Allowance per person		
b1.	Number of persons		b2.	Number of persons		
c1.	Subtotal		c2.	Subtotal		$

25A	**Local Standards: housing and utilities; non-mortgage expenses.** Enter the amount of the IRS Housing and Utilities Standards; non-mortgage expenses for the applicable county and family size. (This information is available at www.usdoj.gov/ust/ or from the clerk of the bankruptcy court). The applicable family size consists of the number that would currently be allowed as exemptions on your federal income tax return, plus the number of any additional dependents whom you support.	$

B 22C (Official Form 22C) (Chapter 13) (12/10)　　　　　　　　　　　　　　　　　　　　　　　4

25B	**Local Standards: housing and utilities; mortgage/rent expense.** Enter, in Line a below, the amount of the IRS Housing and Utilities Standards; mortgage/rent expense for your county and family size (this information is available at www.usdoj.gov/ust/ or from the clerk of the bankruptcy court) (the applicable family size consists of the number that would currently be allowed as exemptions on your federal income tax return, plus the number of any additional dependents whom you support); enter on Line b the total of the Average Monthly Payments for any debts secured by your home, as stated in Line 47; subtract Line b from Line a and enter the result in Line 25B. **Do not enter an amount less than zero.**	

	a.	IRS Housing and Utilities Standards; mortgage/rent expense	$	
	b.	Average Monthly Payment for any debts secured by your home, if any, as stated in Line 47	$	
	c.	Net mortgage/rental expense	Subtract Line b from Line a.	$

26	**Local Standards: housing and utilities; adjustment.** If you contend that the process set out in Lines 25A and 25B does not accurately compute the allowance to which you are entitled under the IRS Housing and Utilities Standards, enter any additional amount to which you contend you are entitled, and state the basis for your contention in the space below: _____ _____ _____	$

27A	**Local Standards: transportation; vehicle operation/public transportation expense.** You are entitled to an expense allowance in this category regardless of whether you pay the expenses of operating a vehicle and regardless of whether you use public transportation. Check the number of vehicles for which you pay the operating expenses or for which the operating expenses are included as a contribution to your household expenses in Line 7. ☐ 0 ☐ 1 ☐ 2 or more. If you checked 0, enter on Line 27A the "Public Transportation" amount from IRS Local Standards: Transportation. If you checked 1 or 2 or more, enter on Line 27A the "Operating Costs" amount from IRS Local Standards: Transportation for the applicable number of vehicles in the applicable Metropolitan Statistical Area or Census Region. (These amounts are available at www.usdoj.gov/ust/ or from the clerk of the bankruptcy court.)	$

27B	**Local Standards: transportation; additional public transportation expense.** If you pay the operating expenses for a vehicle and also use public transportation, and you contend that you are entitled to an additional deduction for your public transportation expenses, enter on Line 27B the "Public Transportation" amount from IRS Local Standards: Transportation. (This amount is available at www.usdoj.gov/ust/ or from the clerk of the bankruptcy court.)	$

28	**Local Standards: transportation ownership/lease expense; Vehicle 1.** Check the number of vehicles for which you claim an ownership/lease expense. (You may not claim an ownership/lease expense for more than two vehicles.) ☐ 1 ☐ 2 or more. Enter, in Line a below, the "Ownership Costs" for "One Car" from the IRS Local Standards: Transportation (available at www.usdoj.gov/ust/ or from the clerk of the bankruptcy court); enter in Line b the total of the Average Monthly Payments for any debts secured by Vehicle 1, as stated in Line 47; subtract Line b from Line a and enter the result in Line 28. **Do not enter an amount less than zero.**	

	a.	IRS Transportation Standards, Ownership Costs	$	
	b.	Average Monthly Payment for any debts secured by Vehicle 1, as stated in Line 47	$	
	c.	Net ownership/lease expense for Vehicle 1	Subtract Line b from Line a.	$

29	Local Standards: transportation ownership/lease expense; Vehicle 2. Complete this Line only if you checked the "2 or more" Box in Line 28. Enter, in Line a below, the "Ownership Costs" for "One Car" from the IRS Local Standards: Transportation (available at www.usdoj.gov/ust/ or from the clerk of the bankruptcy court); enter in Line b the total of the Average Monthly Payments for any debts secured by Vehicle 2, as stated in Line 47; subtract Line b from Line a and enter the result in Line 29. **Do not enter an amount less than zero.**		
	a.	IRS Transportation Standards, Ownership Costs	$
	b.	Average Monthly Payment for any debts secured by Vehicle 2, as stated in Line 47	$
	c.	Net ownership/lease expense for Vehicle 2	Subtract Line b from Line a.	$

30	**Other Necessary Expenses: taxes.** Enter the total average monthly expense that you actually incur for all federal, state, and local taxes, other than real estate and sales taxes, such as income taxes, self-employment taxes, social-security taxes, and Medicare taxes. **Do not include real estate or sales taxes.**	$
31	**Other Necessary Expenses: involuntary deductions for employment.** Enter the total average monthly deductions that are required for your employment, such as mandatory retirement contributions, union dues, and uniform costs. **Do not include discretionary amounts, such as voluntary 401(k) contributions.**	$
32	**Other Necessary Expenses: life insurance.** Enter total average monthly premiums that you actually pay for term life insurance for yourself. **Do not include premiums for insurance on your dependents, for whole life or for any other form of insurance.**	$
33	**Other Necessary Expenses: court-ordered payments.** Enter the total monthly amount that you are required to pay pursuant to the order of a court or administrative agency, such as spousal or child support payments. **Do not include payments on past due obligations included in Line 49.**	$
34	**Other Necessary Expenses: education for employment or for a physically or mentally challenged child.** Enter the total average monthly amount that you actually expend for education that is a condition of employment and for education that is required for a physically or mentally challenged dependent child for whom no public education providing similar services is available.	$
35	**Other Necessary Expenses: childcare.** Enter the total average monthly amount that you actually expend on childcare—such as baby-sitting, day care, nursery and preschool. **Do not include other educational payments.**	$
36	**Other Necessary Expenses: health care.** Enter the total average monthly amount that you actually expend on health care that is required for the health and welfare of yourself or your dependents, that is not reimbursed by insurance or paid by a health savings account, and that is in excess of the amount entered in Line 24B. **Do not include payments for health insurance or health savings accounts listed in Line 39.**	$
37	**Other Necessary Expenses: telecommunication services.** Enter the total average monthly amount that you actually pay for telecommunication services other than your basic home telephone and cell phone service—such as pagers, call waiting, caller id, special long distance, or internet service—to the extent necessary for your health and welfare or that of your dependents. **Do not include any amount previously deducted.**	$
38	**Total Expenses Allowed under IRS Standards.** Enter the total of Lines 24 through 37.	$

Subpart B: Additional Living Expense Deductions Note: Do not include any expenses that you have listed in Lines 24-37

39	Health Insurance, Disability Insurance, and Health Savings Account Expenses. List the monthly expenses in the categories set out in lines a-c below that are reasonably necessary for yourself, your spouse, or your dependents.			
	a.	Health Insurance	$	
	b.	Disability Insurance	$	
	c.	Health Savings Account	$	
	Total and enter on Line 39			$
	If you do not actually expend this total amount, state your actual total average monthly expenditures in the space below: $ _____			
40	**Continued contributions to the care of household or family members.** Enter the total average actual monthly expenses that you will continue to pay for the reasonable and necessary care and support of an elderly, chronically ill, or disabled member of your household or member of your immediate family who is unable to pay for such expenses. **Do not include payments listed in Line 34.**			$
41	**Protection against family violence.** Enter the total average reasonably necessary monthly expenses that you actually incur to maintain the safety of your family under the Family Violence Prevention and Services Act or other applicable federal law. The nature of these expenses is required to be kept confidential by the court.			$
42	**Home energy costs.** Enter the total average monthly amount, in excess of the allowance specified by IRS Local Standards for Housing and Utilities that you actually expend for home energy costs. **You must provide your case trustee with documentation of your actual expenses, and you must demonstrate that the additional amount claimed is reasonable and necessary.**			$
43	**Education expenses for dependent children under 18.** Enter the total average monthly expenses that you actually incur, not to exceed $147.92 per child, for attendance at a private or public elementary or secondary school by your dependent children less than 18 years of age. **You must provide your case trustee with documentation of your actual expenses, and you must explain why the amount claimed is reasonable and necessary and not already accounted for in the IRS Standards.**			$
44	**Additional food and clothing expense.** Enter the total average monthly amount by which your food and clothing expenses exceed the combined allowances for food and clothing (apparel and services) in the IRS National Standards, not to exceed 5% of those combined allowances. (This information is available at www.usdoj.gov/ust/ or from the clerk of the bankruptcy court.) **You must demonstrate that the additional amount claimed is reasonable and necessary.**			$
45	**Charitable contributions.** Enter the amount reasonably necessary for you to expend each month on charitable contributions in the form of cash or financial instruments to a charitable organization as defined in 26 U.S.C. § 170(c)(1)-(2). **Do not include any amount in excess of 15% of your gross monthly income.**			$
46	**Total Additional Expense Deductions under § 707(b).** Enter the total of Lines 39 through 45.			$

Subpart C: Deductions for Debt Payment

47	**Future payments on secured claims.** For each of your debts that is secured by an interest in property that you own, list the name of the creditor, identify the property securing the debt, state the Average Monthly Payment, and check whether the payment includes taxes or insurance. The Average Monthly Payment is the total of all amounts scheduled as contractually due to each Secured Creditor in the 60 months following the filing of the bankruptcy case, divided by 60. If necessary, list additional entries on a separate page. Enter the total of the Average Monthly Payments on Line 47.				
		Name of Creditor	Property Securing the Debt	Average Monthly Payment	Does payment include taxes or insurance?
	a.			$	☐ yes ☐ no
	b.			$	☐ yes ☐ no
	c.			$	☐ yes ☐ no
				Total: Add Lines a, b, and c	$

B 22C (Official Form 22C) (Chapter 13) (12/10)   7

48	**Other payments on secured claims.** If any of debts listed in Line 47 are secured by your primary residence, a motor vehicle, or other property necessary for your support or the support of your dependents, you may include in your deduction 1/60th of any amount (the "cure amount") that you must pay the creditor in addition to the payments listed in Line 47, in order to maintain possession of the property. The cure amount would include any sums in default that must be paid in order to avoid repossession or foreclosure. List and total any such amounts in the following chart. If necessary, list additional entries on a separate page.	
		Name of Creditor	Property Securing the Debt	1/60th of the Cure Amount	
	a.			$	
	b.			$	
	c.			$	
				Total: Add Lines a, b, and c	$

| 49 | **Payments on prepetition priority claims.** Enter the total amount, divided by 60, of all priority claims, such as priority tax, child support and alimony claims, for which you were liable at the time of your bankruptcy filing. **Do not include current obligations, such as those set out in Line 33.** | $ |

50	**Chapter 13 administrative expenses.** Multiply the amount in Line a by the amount in Line b, and enter the resulting administrative expense.		
	a.	Projected average monthly chapter 13 plan payment.	$	
	b.	Current multiplier for your district as determined under schedules issued by the Executive Office for United States Trustees. (This information is available at www.usdoj.gov/ust/ or from the clerk of the bankruptcy court.)	x	
	c.	Average monthly administrative expense of chapter 13 case	Total: Multiply Lines a and b	$

| 51 | **Total Deductions for Debt Payment.** Enter the total of Lines 47 through 50. | $ |

| **Subpart D: Total Deductions from Income** | | |
| 52 | **Total of all deductions from income.** Enter the total of Lines 38, 46, and 51. | $ |

Part V. DETERMINATION OF DISPOSABLE INCOME UNDER § 1325(b)(2)		
53	**Total current monthly income.** Enter the amount from Line 20.	$
54	**Support income.** Enter the monthly average of any child support payments, foster care payments, or disability payments for a dependent child, reported in Part I, that you received in accordance with applicable nonbankruptcy law, to the extent reasonably necessary to be expended for such child.	$
55	**Qualified retirement deductions.** Enter the monthly total of (a) all amounts withheld by your employer from wages as contributions for qualified retirement plans, as specified in § 541(b)(7) and (b) all required repayments of loans from retirement plans, as specified in § 362(b)(19).	$
56	**Total of all deductions allowed under § 707(b)(2).** Enter the amount from Line 52.	$
57	**Deduction for special circumstances.** If there are special circumstances that justify additional expenses for which there is no reasonable alternative, describe the special circumstances and the resulting expenses in lines a-c below. If necessary, list additional entries on a separate page. Total the expenses and enter the total in Line 57. **You must provide your case trustee with documentation of these expenses and you must provide a detailed explanation of the special circumstances that make such expenses necessary and reasonable.**	
		Nature of special circumstances	Amount of expense	
	a.		$	
	b.		$	
	c.		$	
			Total: Add Lines a, b, and c	$

58	**Total adjustments to determine disposable income.** Add the amounts on Lines 54, 55, 56, and 57 and enter the result.	$
59	**Monthly Disposable Income Under § 1325(b)(2).** Subtract Line 58 from Line 53 and enter the result.	$

Part VI: ADDITIONAL EXPENSE CLAIMS

	Other Expenses. List and describe any monthly expenses, not otherwise stated in this form, that are required for the health and welfare of you and your family and that you contend should be an additional deduction from your current monthly income under § 707(b)(2)(A)(ii)(I). If necessary, list additional sources on a separate page. All figures should reflect your average monthly expense for each item. Total the expenses.	
60	Expense Description	Monthly Amount
	a.	$
	b.	$
	c.	$
	Total: Add Lines a, b, and c	$

Part VII: VERIFICATION

61	I declare under penalty of perjury that the information provided in this statement is true and correct. *(If this is a joint case, both debtors must sign.)*

Date: _____   Signature: _____
                                                          (Debtor)

Date: _____   Signature: _____
                                                          (Joint Debtor, if any)

B 23 (Official Form 23) (12/10)

UNITED STATES BANKRUPTCY COURT
_____ District of _____

In re _____,   Case No._____

  _____ *Debtor*

                                                   Chapter _____

DEBTOR'S CERTIFICATION OF COMPLETION OF POSTPETITION INSTRUCTIONAL
COURSE CONCERNING PERSONAL FINANCIAL MANAGEMENT

Every individual debtor in a chapter 7, chapter 11 in which § 1141(d)(3) applies, or chapter 13 case must file this certification. If a joint petition is filed, each spouse must complete and file a separate certification. Complete one of the following statements and file by the deadline stated below:

☐ I, _____, the debtor in the above-styled case, hereby

        (Printed Name of Debtor)

certify that on _____ *(Date)*, I completed an instructional course in personal financial management

provided by _____, an approved personal financial

                        (Name of Provider)

management provider.

Certificate No. *(If any)*:_____.

☐ I, _____, the debtor in the above-styled case, hereby

        (Printed Name of Debtor)

certify that no personal financial management course is required because of *[Check the appropriate box.]*:

        ☐ Incapacity or disability, as defined in 11 U.S.C. § 109(h);

        ☐ Active military duty in a military combat zone; or

        ☐ Residence in a district in which the United States trustee (or bankruptcy administrator) has determined that the approved instructional courses are not adequate at this time to serve the additional individuals who would otherwise be required to complete such courses.

Signature of Debtor: _____

Date: _____

Instructions: Use this form only to certify whether you completed a course in personal financial management. (Fed. R. Bankr. P. 1007(b)(7).) Do NOT use this form to file the certificate given to you by your prepetition credit counseling provider and do NOT include with the petition when filing your case.

Filing Deadlines: In a chapter 7 case, file within 60 days of the first date set for the meeting of creditors under § 341 of the Bankruptcy Code. In a chapter 11 or 13 case, file no later than the last payment made by the debtor as required by the plan or the filing of a motion for a discharge under § 1141(d)(5)(B) or § 1328(b) of the Code. (See Fed. R. Bankr. P. 1007(c).)

B19 (Official Form 19) (12/07)

United States Bankruptcy Court

_____ District Of _____

In re _____,   Case No. _____
                Debtor

                            Chapter _____

DECLARATION AND SIGNATURE OF NON-ATTORNEY
BANKRUPTCY PETITION PREPARER (*See* 11 U.S.C. § 110)

I declare under penalty of perjury that: (1) I am a bankruptcy petition preparer as defined in 11 U.S.C. § 110; (2) I prepared the accompanying document(s) listed below for compensation and have provided the debtor with a copy of the document(s) and the attached notice as required by 11 U.S.C. §§ 110(b), 110(h), and 342(b); and (3) if rules or guidelines have been promulgated pursuant to 11 U.S.C. § 110(h) setting a maximum fee for services chargeable by bankruptcy petition preparers, I have given the debtor notice of the maximum amount before preparing any document for filing for a debtor or accepting any fee from the debtor, as required by that section.

Accompanying documents: Printed or Typed Name and Title, if any, of
_____   Bankruptcy Petition Preparer:
_____   _____
_____   Social-Security No. of Bankruptcy Petition
_____   Preparer (Required by 11 U.S.C. § 110):
_____   _____

If the bankruptcy petition preparer is not an individual, state the name, title (if any), address, and social-security number of the officer, principal, responsible person, or partner who signs this document.

_____

_____
Address
X_____   _____
Signature of Bankruptcy Petition Preparer   Date

Names and social-security numbers of all other individuals who prepared or assisted in preparing this document, unless the bankruptcy petition preparer is not an individual:

If more than one person prepared this document, attach additional signed sheets conforming to the appropriate Official Form for each person.

A bankruptcy petition preparer's failure to comply with the provisions of title 11 and the Federal Rules of Bankruptcy Procedure may result in fines or imprisonment or both. 11 U.S.C. § 110; 18 U.S.C. § 156.

NOTICE TO DEBTOR BY NON-ATTORNEY BANKRUPTCY PETITION PREPARER
[Must be filed with any document(s) prepared by a bankruptcy petition preparer.]

I am a bankruptcy petition preparer. I am not an attorney and may not practice law or give legal advice. Before preparing any document for filing as defined in § 110(a)(2) of the Bankruptcy Code or accepting any fees, I am required by law to provide you with this notice concerning bankruptcy petition preparers. Under the law, § 110 of the Bankruptcy Code (11 U.S.C. § 110), I am forbidden to offer you any legal advice, including advice about any of the following:

- whether to file a petition under the Bankruptcy Code (11 U.S.C. § 101 et seq.);
- whether commencing a case under chapter 7, 11, 12, or 13 is appropriate;
- whether your debts will be eliminated or discharged in a case under the Bankruptcy Code;
- whether you will be able to retain your home, car, or other property after commencing a case under the Bankruptcy Code;
- the tax consequences of a case brought under the Bankruptcy Code;
- the dischargeability of tax claims;
- whether you may or should promise to repay debts to a creditor or enter into a reaffirmation agreement with a creditor to reaffirm a debt;
- how to characterize the nature of your interests in property or your debts; or
- bankruptcy procedures and rights.

[The notice may provide additional examples of legal advice that a bankruptcy petition preparer is not authorized to give.]

In addition, under 11 U.S.C. § 110(h), the Supreme Court or the Judicial Conference of the United States may promulgate rules or guidelines setting a maximum allowable fee chargeable by a bankruptcy petition preparer. As required by law, I have notified you of this maximum allowable fee, if any, before preparing any document for filing or accepting any fee from you.

_____   _____
Signature of Debtor   Date   Joint Debtor (if any)   Date

[In a joint case, both spouses must sign.]

B 201A (Form 201A) (11/11)

UNITED STATES BANKRUPTCY COURT

NOTICE TO CONSUMER DEBTOR(S) UNDER §342(b)
OF THE BANKRUPTCY CODE

In accordance with § 342(b) of the Bankruptcy Code, this notice to individuals with primarily consumer debts: (1) Describes briefly the services available from credit counseling services; (2) Describes briefly the purposes, benefits and costs of the four types of bankruptcy proceedings you may commence; and (3) Informs you about bankruptcy crimes and notifies you that the Attorney General may examine all information you supply in connection with a bankruptcy case.

You are cautioned that bankruptcy law is complicated and not easily described. Thus, you may wish to seek the advice of an attorney to learn of your rights and responsibilities should you decide to file a petition. Court employees cannot give you legal advice.

Notices from the bankruptcy court are sent to the mailing address you list on your bankruptcy petition. In order to ensure that you receive information about events concerning your case, Bankruptcy Rule 4002 requires that you notify the court of any changes in your address. If you are filing a **joint case** (a single bankruptcy case for two individuals married to each other), and each spouse lists the same mailing address on the bankruptcy petition, you and your spouse will generally receive a single copy of each notice mailed from the bankruptcy court in a jointly-addressed envelope, unless you file a statement with the court requesting that each spouse receive a separate copy of all notices.

1. Services Available from Credit Counseling Agencies

With limited exceptions, § 109(h) of the Bankruptcy Code requires that all individual debtors who file for bankruptcy relief on or after October 17, 2005, receive a briefing that outlines the available opportunities for credit counseling and provides assistance in performing a budget analysis. The briefing must be given within 180 days **before** the bankruptcy filing. The briefing may be provided individually or in a group (including briefings conducted by telephone or on the Internet) and must be provided by a nonprofit budget and credit counseling agency approved by the United States trustee or bankruptcy administrator. The clerk of the bankruptcy court has a list that you may consult of the approved budget and credit counseling agencies. Each debtor in a joint case must complete the briefing.

In addition, after filing a bankruptcy case, an individual debtor generally must complete a financial management instructional course before he or she can receive a discharge. The clerk also has a list of approved financial management instructional courses. Each debtor in a joint case must complete the course.

2. The Four Chapters of the Bankruptcy Code Available to Individual Consumer Debtors

Chapter 7: Liquidation ($245 filing fee, $46 administrative fee, $15 trustee surcharge: Total fee $306)
Chapter 7 is designed for debtors in financial difficulty who do not have the ability to pay their existing debts. Debtors whose debts are primarily consumer debts are subject to a "means test" designed to determine whether the case should be permitted to proceed under chapter 7. If your income is greater than the median income for your state of residence and family size, in some cases, the United States trustee (or bankruptcy administrator), the trustee, or creditors have the right to file a motion requesting that the court dismiss your case under § 707(b) of the Code. It is up to the court to decide whether the case should be dismissed.
Under chapter 7, you may claim certain of your property as exempt under governing law. A trustee may have the right to take possession of and sell the remaining property that is not exempt and use the sale proceeds to pay your creditors.
The purpose of filing a chapter 7 case is to obtain a discharge of your existing debts. If, however, you are found to have committed certain kinds of improper conduct described in the Bankruptcy Code, the court may deny

Form B 201A, Notice to Consumer Debtor(s)   Page 2

your discharge and, if it does, the purpose for which you filed the bankruptcy petition will be defeated.

Even if you receive a general discharge, some particular debts are not discharged under the law. Therefore, you may still be responsible for most taxes and student loans; debts incurred to pay nondischargeable taxes; domestic support and property settlement obligations; most fines, penalties, forfeitures, and criminal restitution obligations; certain debts which are not properly listed in your bankruptcy papers; and debts for death or personal injury caused by operating a motor vehicle, vessel, or aircraft while intoxicated from alcohol or drugs. Also, if a creditor can prove that a debt arose from fraud, breach of fiduciary duty, or theft, or from a willful and malicious injury, the bankruptcy court may determine that the debt is not discharged.

Chapter 13: Repayment of All or Part of the Debts of an Individual with Regular Income ($235 filing fee, $46 administrative fee: Total fee $281)

Chapter 13 is designed for individuals with regular income who would like to pay all or part of their debts in installments over a period of time. You are only eligible for chapter 13 if your debts do not exceed certain dollar amounts set forth in the Bankruptcy Code.

Under chapter 13, you must file with the court a plan to repay your creditors all or part of the money that you owe them, using your future earnings. The period allowed by the court to repay your debts may be three years or five years, depending upon your income and other factors. The court must approve your plan before it can take effect.

After completing the payments under your plan, your debts are generally discharged except for domestic support obligations; most student loans; certain taxes; most criminal fines and restitution obligations; certain debts which are not properly listed in your bankruptcy papers; certain debts for acts that caused death or personal injury; and certain long term secured obligations.

Chapter 11: Reorganization ($1000 filing fee, $46 administrative fee: Total fee $1046)

Chapter 11 is designed for the reorganization of a business but is also available to consumer debtors. Its provisions are quite complicated, and any decision by an individual to file a chapter 11 petition should be reviewed with an attorney.

Chapter 12: Family Farmer or Fisherman ($200 filing fee, $46 administrative fee: Total fee $246)

Chapter 12 is designed to permit family farmers and fishermen to repay their debts over a period of time from future earnings and is similar to chapter 13. The eligibility requirements are restrictive, limiting its use to those whose income arises primarily from a family-owned farm or commercial fishing operation.

3. Bankruptcy Crimes and Availability of Bankruptcy Papers to Law Enforcement Officials

A person who knowingly and fraudulently conceals assets or makes a false oath or statement under penalty of perjury, either orally or in writing, in connection with a bankruptcy case is subject to a fine, imprisonment, or both. All information supplied by a debtor in connection with a bankruptcy case is subject to examination by the Attorney General acting through the Office of the United States Trustee, the Office of the United States Attorney, and other components and employees of the Department of Justice.

WARNING: Section 521(a)(1) of the Bankruptcy Code requires that you promptly file detailed information regarding your creditors, assets, liabilities, income, expenses and general financial condition. Your bankruptcy case may be dismissed if this information is not filed with the court within the time deadlines set by the Bankruptcy Code, the Bankruptcy Rules, and the local rules of the court. The documents and the deadlines for filing them are listed on Form B200, which is posted at http://www.uscourts.gov/bkforms/bankruptcy_forms.html#procedure.

BTXN 094 (rev. 5/04)

UNITED STATES BANKRUPTCY COURT
NORTHERN DISTRICT OF TEXAS

In Re:

§
§
§   Case No.:
§
§
Debtor(s) §
§

VERIFICATION OF MAILING LIST

The Debtor(s) certifies that the attached mailing list (*only one option may be selected per form*):

   ☐ is the first mail matrix in this case.

   ☐ adds entities not listed on previously filed mailing list(s).

   ☐ changes or corrects name(s) and address(es) on previously filed mailing list(s).

   ☐ deletes name(s) and address(es) on previously filed mailing list(s).

In accordance with N.D. TX L.B.R. 1007.2, the above named Debtor(s) hereby verifies that the attached list of creditors is true and correct.

_____
Date

_____
Signature of Attorney (if applicable)

_____
Signature of Debtor

_____
Debtor's Social Security *(last four digits only)* /Tax ID No.

_____
Signature of Joint Debtor (if applicable)

_____
Joint Debtor's Social Security *(last four digits only)* /Tax ID No.

B 201B (Form 201B) (12/09)

UNITED STATES BANKRUPTCY COURT

_____ District Of _____

In re _____   Case No. _____
               Debtor

                                                      Chapter _____

CERTIFICATION OF NOTICE TO CONSUMER DEBTOR(S)
UNDER § 342(b) OF THE BANKRUPTCY CODE

Certification of [Non-Attorney] Bankruptcy Petition Preparer

    I, the [non-attorney] bankruptcy petition preparer signing the debtor's petition, hereby certify that I delivered to the debtor the attached notice, as required by § 342(b) of the Bankruptcy Code.

_____   Social Security number (If the bankruptcy petition
Printed name and title, if any, of Bankruptcy Petition Preparer   preparer is not an individual, state the Social Security
Address: number of the officer, principal, responsible person, or
          partner of the bankruptcy petition preparer.) (Required
X_____   by 11 U.S.C. § 110.)

Signature of Bankruptcy Petition Preparer or officer,
principal, responsible person, or partner whose Social
Security number is provided above.

Certification of the Debtor

    I (We), the debtor(s), affirm that I (we) have received and read the attached notice, as required by § 342(b) of the Bankruptcy Code.

_____   X_____
Printed Name(s) of Debtor(s)   Signature of Debtor   Date

Case No. (if known) _____   X_____
          Signature of Joint Debtor (if any)   Date

_____

Instructions: Attach a copy of Form B 201A, Notice to Consumer Debtor(s) Under § 342(b) of the Bankruptcy Code.

Use this form to certify that the debtor has received the notice required by 11 U.S.C. § 342(b) **only** if the certification has **NOT** been made on the Voluntary Petition, Official Form B1. Exhibit B on page 2 of Form B1 contains a certification by the debtor's attorney that the attorney has given the notice to the debtor. The Declarations made by debtors and bankruptcy petition preparers on page 3 of Form B1 also include this certification.

APPENDICES

APPENDIX 1

The Constitution of the United States: A Transcription

Provided by the U.S. National Archives and Records Administration

The following text is a transcription of the Constitution as it was inscribed by Jacob Shallus on parchment (the document on display in the Rotunda at the National Archives Museum.) *The spelling and punctuation reflect the original.*

We the People of the United States, in Order to form a more perfect Union, establish Justice, insure domestic Tranquility, provide for the common defence, promote the general Welfare, and secure the Blessings of Liberty to ourselves and our Posterity, do ordain and establish this Constitution for the United States of America.

ARTICLE I.

Section. 1.

All legislative Powers herein granted shall be vested in a Congress of the United States, which shall consist of a Senate and House of Representatives.

Section. 2.

The House of Representatives shall be composed of Members chosen every second Year by the People of the several States, and the Electors in each State shall have the Qualifications requisite for Electors of the most numerous Branch of the State Legislature.

No Person shall be a Representative who shall not have attained to the Age of twenty-five Years, and been seven Years a Citizen of the United States, and who shall not, when elected, be an Inhabitant of that State in which he shall be chosen.

Representatives and direct Taxes shall be apportioned among the several States which may be included within this Union, according to their respective Numbers, which shall be determined by adding to the whole Number of free Persons, including those bound to Service for a Term of Years, and excluding Indians not taxed, three fifths of all other Persons. The actual Enumeration shall be made within three Years after the first Meeting of the Congress of the United States, and within every subsequent Term of ten Years, in such Manner as they shall by Law direct. The Number of Representatives shall not exceed one for every thirty Thousand, but each State shall have at Least one Representative; and until such enumeration shall be made, the State of New Hampshire shall be entitled to chuse three, Massachusetts eight, Rhode-Island and Providence Plantations one, Connecticut five, New-York six, New Jersey four, Pennsylvania eight, Delaware one, Maryland six, Virginia ten, North Carolina five, South Carolina five, and Georgia three.

When vacancies happen in the Representation from any State, the Executive Authority thereof shall issue Writs of Election to fill such Vacancies.

The House of Representatives shall chuse their Speaker and other Officers; and shall have the sole Power of Impeachment.

Section. 3.

The Senate of the United States shall be composed of two Senators from each State, chosen by the Legislature thereof, for six Years; and each Senator shall have one Vote.

Immediately after they shall be assembled in Consequence of the first Election, they shall be divided as equally as may be into three Classes. The Seats of the Senators of the first Class shall be vacated at the Expiration of the second Year, of the second Class at the Expiration of the fourth Year, and of the third Class at the Expiration of the sixth Year, so that one third may be chosen every second Year; and if Vacancies happen by Resignation, or otherwise, during the Recess of the Legislature of any State, the Executive thereof may make temporary Appointments until the next Meeting of the Legislature, which shall then fill such Vacancies.

No Person shall be a Senator who shall not have attained to the Age of thirty Years, and been nine Years a Citizen of the United States, and who shall not, when elected, be an Inhabitant of that State for which he shall be chosen.

The Vice President of the United States shall be President of the Senate, but shall have no Vote, unless they be equally divided.

The Senate shall chuse their other Officers, and also a President pro tempore, in the Absence of the Vice President, or when he shall exercise the Office of President of the United States.

The Senate shall have the sole Power to try all Impeachments. When sitting for that Purpose, they shall be on Oath or Affirmation. When the President of the United States is tried, the Chief Justice shall preside: And no Person shall be convicted without the Concurrence of two thirds of the Members present.

Judgment in Cases of Impeachment shall not extend further than to removal from Office, and disqualification to hold and enjoy any Office of honor, Trust or Profit under the United States: but the Party convicted shall nevertheless be liable and subject to Indictment, Trial, Judgment and Punishment, according to Law.

Section. 4.

The Times, Places and Manner of holding Elections for Senators and Representatives, shall be prescribed in each State by the Legislature thereof; but the Congress may at any time by Law make or alter such Regulations, except as to the Places of chusing Senators.

The Congress shall assemble at least once in every Year, and such Meeting shall be on the first Monday in December, unless they shall by Law appoint a different Day.

Section. 5.

Each House shall be the Judge of the Elections, Returns and Qualifications of its own Members, and a Majority of each shall constitute a Quorum to do Business; but a smaller Number may adjourn from day to day, and may be authorized to compel the Attendance of absent Members, in such Manner, and under such Penalties as each House may provide.

Each House may determine the Rules of its Proceedings, punish its Members for disorderly Behaviour, and, with the Concurrence of two thirds, expel a Member.

Each House shall keep a Journal of its Proceedings, and from time to time publish the same, excepting such Parts as may in their Judgment require Secrecy; and the Yeas and Nays of the Members of either House on any question shall, at the Desire of one fifth of those Present, be entered on the Journal.

Neither House, during the Session of Congress, shall, without the Consent of the other, adjourn for more than three days, nor to any other Place than that in which the two Houses shall be sitting.

Section. 6.

The Senators and Representatives shall receive a Compensation for their Services, to be ascertained by Law, and paid out of the Treasury of the United States. They shall in all Cases, except Treason, Felony and Breach of the Peace, be privileged from Arrest during their Attendance at the Session of their respective Houses, and in going to and returning from the same; and for any Speech or Debate in either House, they shall not be questioned in any other Place.

No Senator or Representative shall, during the Time for which he was elected, be appointed to any civil Office under the Authority of the United States, which shall have been created, or the Emoluments whereof shall have been encreased during such time; and no Person holding any Office under the United States, shall be a Member of either House during his Continuance in Office.

Section. 7.

All Bills for raising Revenue shall originate in the House of Representatives; but the Senate may propose or concur with Amendments as on other Bills.

Every Bill which shall have passed the House of Representatives and the Senate, shall, before it become a Law, be presented to the President of the United States; If he approve he shall sign it, but if not he shall return it, with his Objections to that House in which it shall have originated, who shall enter the Objections at large on their Journal, and proceed to reconsider it. If after such Reconsideration two thirds of that House shall agree to pass the Bill, it shall be sent, together with the Objections, to the other House, by which it shall likewise be reconsidered, and if approved by two thirds of that House, it shall become a Law. But in all such Cases the Votes of both Houses shall be determined by yeas and Nays, and the Names of the Persons voting for and against the Bill shall be entered on the Journal of each House respectively. If any Bill shall not be returned by the President within ten Days (Sundays excepted) after it shall have been presented to him, the Same shall be a Law, in like Manner as if he had signed it, unless the Congress by their Adjournment prevent its Return, in which Case it shall not be a Law.

Every Order, Resolution, or Vote to which the Concurrence of the Senate and House of Representatives may be necessary (except on a question of Adjournment) shall be presented to the President of the United States; and before the Same shall take Effect, shall be approved by him, or being disapproved by him, shall be repassed by two thirds of the Senate and House of Representatives, according to the Rules and Limitations prescribed in the Case of a Bill.

Section. 8.

The Congress shall have Power To lay and collect Taxes, Duties, Imposts and Excises, to pay the Debts and provide for the common Defence and general Welfare of the United States; but all Duties, Imposts and Excises shall be uniform throughout the United States;

To borrow Money on the credit of the United States;

To regulate Commerce with foreign Nations, and among the several States, and with the Indian Tribes;

To establish an uniform Rule of Naturalization, and uniform Laws on the subject of Bankruptcies throughout the United States;

To coin Money, regulate the Value thereof, and of foreign Coin, and fix the Standard of Weights and Measures;

To provide for the Punishment of counterfeiting the Securities and current Coin of the United States;

To establish Post Offices and post Roads;

To promote the Progress of Science and useful Arts, by securing for limited Times to Authors and Inventors the exclusive Right to their respective Writings and Discoveries;

To constitute Tribunals inferior to the supreme Court;

To define and punish Piracies and Felonies committed on the high Seas, and Offences against the Law of Nations;

To declare War, grant Letters of Marque and Reprisal, and make Rules concerning Captures on Land and Water;

To raise and support Armies, but no Appropriation of Money to that

Use shall be for a longer Term than two Years;

To provide and maintain a Navy;

To make Rules for the Government and Regulation of the land and naval Forces;

To provide for calling forth the Militia to execute the Laws of the Union, suppress Insurrections and repel Invasions;

To provide for organizing, arming, and disciplining, the Militia, and for governing such Part of them as may be employed in the Service of the United States, reserving to the States respectively, the Appointment of the Officers, and the Authority of training the Militia according to the discipline prescribed by Congress;

To exercise exclusive Legislation in all Cases whatsoever, over such District (not exceeding ten Miles square) as may, by Cession of particular States, and the Acceptance of Congress, become the Seat of the Government of the United States, and to exercise like Authority over all Places purchased by the Consent of the Legislature of the State in which the Same shall be, for the Erection of Forts, Magazines, Arsenals, dock-Yards, and other needful Buildings;—And

To make all Laws which shall be necessary and proper for carrying into Execution the foregoing Powers, and all other Powers vested by this Constitution in the Government of the United States, or in any Department or Officer thereof.

Section. 9.

The Migration or Importation of such Persons as any of the States now existing shall think proper to admit, shall not be prohibited by the Congress prior to the Year one thousand eight hundred and eight, but a Tax or duty may be imposed on such Importation, not exceeding ten dollars for each Person.

The Privilege of the Writ of Habeas Corpus shall not be suspended, unless when in Cases of Rebellion or Invasion the public Safety may require it.

No Bill of Attainder or ex post facto Law shall be passed.

No Capitation, or other direct, Tax shall be laid, unless in Proportion to the Census or enumeration herein before directed to be taken.

No Tax or Duty shall be laid on Articles exported from any State.

No Preference shall be given by any Regulation of Commerce or Revenue to the Ports of one State over those of another: nor shall Vessels bound to, or from, one State, be obliged to enter, clear, or pay Duties in another.

No Money shall be drawn from the Treasury, but in Consequence of Appropriations made by Law; and a regular Statement and Account of the Receipts and Expenditures of all public Money shall be published from time to time.

No Title of Nobility shall be granted by the United States: And no Person holding any Office of Profit or Trust under them, shall, without the Consent of the Congress, accept of any present, Emolument, Office, or Title, of any kind whatever, from any King, Prince, or foreign State.

Section. 10.

No State shall enter into any Treaty, Alliance, or Confederation; grant Letters of Marque and Reprisal; coin Money; emit Bills of Credit; make any Thing but gold and silver Coin a Tender in Payment of Debts; pass any Bill of Attainder, ex post facto Law, or Law impairing the Obligation of Contracts, or grant any Title of Nobility.

No State shall, without the Consent of the Congress, lay any Imposts or Duties on Imports or Exports, except what may be absolutely necessary for executing it's inspection Laws: and the net Produce of all Duties and Imposts, laid by any State on Imports or Exports, shall be for the Use of the Treasury of the United States; and all such Laws shall be subject to the Revision and Controul of the Congress.

No State shall, without the Consent of Congress, lay any Duty of Tonnage, keep Troops, or Ships of War in time of Peace, enter into any Agreement or Compact with another State, or with a foreign Power, or engage in War, unless actually invaded, or in such imminent Danger as will not admit of delay.

ARTICLE II.

Section. 1.

The executive Power shall be vested in a President of the United States of America. He shall hold his Office during the Term of four Years, and, together with the Vice President, chosen for the same Term, be elected, as follows

Each State shall appoint, in such Manner as the Legislature thereof may direct, a Number of Electors, equal to the whole Number of Senators and Representatives to which the State may be entitled in the Congress: but no Senator or Representative, or Person holding an Office of Trust or Profit under the United States, shall be appointed an Elector.

The Electors shall meet in their respective States, and vote by Ballot for two Persons, of whom one at least shall not be an Inhabitant of the same State with themselves. And they shall make a List of all the Persons voted for, and of the Number of Votes for each; which List they shall sign and certify, and transmit sealed to the Seat of the Government of the United States, directed to the President of the Senate. The President of the Senate shall, in the Presence of the Senate and House of Representatives, open all the Certificates, and the Votes shall then be counted. The Person having the greatest Number of Votes shall be the President, if such Number be a Majority of the whole Number of Electors appointed; and if there be more than one who have such Majority, and have an equal Number of Votes, then the House of Representatives shall immediately chuse by Ballot one of them for President; and if no Person have a Majority, then from the five highest on the List the said House shall in like Manner chuse the President. But in chusing the President, the Votes shall be taken by States, the Representation from each State having one Vote; A quorum for this Purpose shall consist of a Member or Members from two thirds of the States, and a Majority of all the States shall be necessary to a Choice. In every Case, after the Choice of the President, the Person having the greatest Number of Votes of the Electors shall be the Vice President. But if there should remain two or more who have equal Votes, the Senate shall chuse from them by Ballot the Vice President.

The Congress may determine the Time of chusing the Electors, and the Day on which they shall give their Votes; which Day shall be the same throughout the United States.

No Person except a natural born Citizen, or a Citizen of the United States, at the time of the Adoption of this Constitution, shall be eligible to the Office of President; neither shall any Person be eligible to that Office who shall not have attained to the Age of thirty five Years, and been fourteen Years a Resident within the United States.

In Case of the Removal of the President from Office, or of his Death, Resignation, or Inability to discharge the Powers and Duties of the said Office, the Same shall devolve on the Vice President, and the Congress may by Law provide for the Case of Removal, Death, Resignation or Inability, both of the President and Vice President, declaring what Officer shall then act as President, and such Officer shall act accordingly, until the Disability be removed, or a President shall be elected.

The President shall, at stated Times, receive for his Services, a Compensation, which shall neither be encreased nor diminished during the Period for which he shall have been elected, and he shall not receive within that Period any other Emolument from the United States, or any of them.

Before he enter on the Execution of his Office, he shall take the following Oath or Affirmation:—"I do solemnly swear (or affirm) that I will faithfully execute the Office of President of the United States, and will to the best of my Ability, preserve, protect and defend the Constitution of the United States."

Section. 2.

The President shall be Commander in Chief of the Army and Navy of the United States, and of the Militia of the several States, when called into the actual Service of the United States; he may require the Opinion, in writing, of the principal Officer in each of the executive Departments, upon any Subject relating to the Duties of their respective Offices, and he shall have Power to grant Reprieves and Pardons for Offences against the United States, except in Cases of Impeachment.

He shall have Power, by and with the Advice and Consent of the

Senate, to make Treaties, provided two thirds of the Senators present concur; and he shall nominate, and by and with the Advice and Consent of the Senate, shall appoint Ambassadors, other public Ministers and Consuls, Judges of the supreme Court, and all other Officers of the United States, whose Appointments are not herein otherwise provided for, and which shall be established by Law: but the Congress may by Law vest the Appointment of such inferior Officers, as they think proper, in the President alone, in the Courts of Law, or in the Heads of Departments.

The President shall have Power to fill up all Vacancies that may happen during the Recess of the Senate, by granting Commissions which shall expire at the End of their next Session.

Section. 3.

He shall from time to time give to the Congress Information of the State of the Union, and recommend to their Consideration such Measures as he shall judge necessary and expedient; he may, on extraordinary Occasions, convene both Houses, or either of them, and in Case of Disagreement between them, with Respect to the Time of Adjournment, he may adjourn them to such Time as he shall think proper; he shall receive Ambassadors and other public Ministers; he shall take Care that the Laws be faithfully executed, and shall Commission all the Officers of the United States.

Section. 4.

The President, Vice President and all civil Officers of the United States, shall be removed from Office on Impeachment for, and Conviction of, Treason, Bribery, or other high Crimes and Misdemeanors.

ARTICLE III.

Section. 1.

The judicial Power of the United States, shall be vested in one supreme Court, and in such inferior Courts as the Congress may from time to time ordain and establish. The Judges, both of the supreme and inferior Courts, shall hold their Offices during good Behaviour, and shall, at stated Times, receive for their Services, a Compensation, which shall not be diminished during their Continuance in Office.

Section. 2.

The judicial Power shall extend to all Cases, in Law and Equity, arising under this Constitution, the Laws of the United States, and Treaties made, or which shall be made, under their Authority;—to all Cases affecting Ambassadors, other public Ministers and Consuls;—to all Cases of admiralty and maritime Jurisdiction;—to Controversies to which the United States shall be a Party;—to Controversies between two or more States;—between a State and Citizens of another State,—between Citizens of different States,—between Citizens of the same

State claiming Lands under Grants of different States, and between a State, or the Citizens thereof, and foreign States, Citizens or Subjects.

In all Cases affecting Ambassadors, other public Ministers and Consuls, and those in which a State shall be Party, the supreme Court shall have original Jurisdiction. In all the other Cases before mentioned, the supreme Court shall have appellate Jurisdiction, both as to Law and Fact, with such Exceptions, and under such Regulations as the Congress shall make.

The Trial of all Crimes, except in Cases of Impeachment, shall be by Jury; and such Trial shall be held in the State where the said Crimes shall have been committed; but when not committed within any State, the Trial shall be at such Place or Places as the Congress may by Law have directed.

Section. 3.

Treason against the United States, shall consist only in levying War against them, or in adhering to their Enemies, giving them Aid and Comfort. No Person shall be convicted of Treason unless on the Testimony of two Witnesses to the same overt Act, or on Confession in open Court.

The Congress shall have Power to declare the Punishment of Treason, but no Attainder of Treason shall work Corruption of Blood, or Forfeiture except during the Life of the Person attainted.

ARTICLE IV.

Section. 1.

Full Faith and Credit shall be given in each State to the public Acts, Records, and judicial Proceedings of every other State. And the Congress may by general Laws prescribe the Manner in which such Acts, Records and Proceedings shall be proved, and the Effect thereof.

Section. 2.

The Citizens of each State shall be entitled to all Privileges and Immunities of Citizens in the several States.

A Person charged in any State with Treason, Felony, or other Crime, who shall flee from Justice, and be found in another State, shall on Demand of the executive Authority of the State from which he fled, be delivered up, to be removed to the State having Jurisdiction of the Crime.

No Person held to Service or Labour in one State, under the Laws thereof, escaping into another, shall, in Consequence of any Law or Regulation therein, be discharged from such Service or Labour, but shall be delivered up on Claim of the Party to whom such Service or Labour may be due.

Section. 3.

New States may be admitted by the Congress into this Union; but no new State shall be formed or erected within the Jurisdiction of any other State; nor any State be formed by the Junction of two or more States, or Parts of States, without the Consent of the Legislatures of the States concerned as well as of the Congress.

The Congress shall have Power to dispose of and make all needful Rules and Regulations respecting the Territory or other Property belonging to the United States; and nothing in this Constitution shall be so construed as to Prejudice any Claims of the United States, or of any particular State.

Section. 4.

The United States shall guarantee to every State in this Union a Republican Form of Government, and shall protect each of them against Invasion; and on Application of the Legislature, or of the Executive (when the Legislature cannot be convened), against domestic Violence.

ARTICLE V.

The Congress, whenever two thirds of both Houses shall deem it necessary, shall propose Amendments to this Constitution, or, on the Application of the Legislatures of two thirds of the several States, shall call a Convention for proposing Amendments, which, in either Case, shall be valid to all Intents and Purposes, as Part of this Constitution, when ratified by the Legislatures of three fourths of the several States, or by Conventions in three fourths thereof, as the one or the other Mode of Ratification may be proposed by the Congress; Provided that no Amendment which may be made prior to the Year One thousand eight hundred and eight shall in any Manner affect the first and fourth Clauses in the Ninth Section of the first Article; and that no State, without its Consent, shall be deprived of its equal Suffrage in the Senate.

ARTICLE VI.

All Debts contracted and Engagements entered into, before the Adoption of this Constitution, shall be as valid against the United States under this Constitution, as under the Confederation.

This Constitution, and the Laws of the United States which shall be made in Pursuance thereof; and all Treaties made, or which shall be made, under the Authority of the United States, shall be the supreme Law of the Land; and the Judges in every State shall be bound thereby, any Thing in the Constitution or Laws of any State to the Contrary notwithstanding.

The Senators and Representatives before mentioned, and the Members of the several State Legislatures, and all executive and judicial Officers, both of the United States and of the several States, shall be bound by Oath or Affirmation, to support this Constitution; but no religious Test shall ever be required as a Qualification to any Office or public Trust under the United States.

ARTICLE VII.

The Ratification of the Conventions of nine States, shall be sufficient for the Establishment of this Constitution between the States so ratifying the Same.

AMENDMENT I

Congress shall make no law respecting an establishment of religion, or prohibiting the free exercise thereof; or abridging the freedom of speech, or of the press; or the right of the people peaceably to assemble, and to petition the Government for a redress of grievances.

AMENDMENT II

A well regulated Militia, being necessary to the security of a free State, the right of the people to keep and bear Arms, shall not be infringed.

AMENDMENT III

No Soldier shall, in time of peace be quartered in any house, without the consent of the Owner, nor in time of war, but in a manner to be prescribed by law.

AMENDMENT IV

The right of the people to be secure in their persons, houses, papers, and effects, against unreasonable searches and seizures, shall not be violated, and no Warrants shall issue, but upon probable cause, supported by Oath or affirmation, and particularly describing the place to be searched, and the persons or things to be seized.

AMENDMENT V

No person shall be held to answer for a capital, or otherwise infamous crime, unless on a presentment or indictment of a Grand Jury, except in cases arising in the land or naval forces, or in the Militia, when in actual service in time of War or public danger; nor shall any person be subject for the same offence to be twice put in jeopardy of life or limb; nor shall be compelled in any criminal case to be a witness against himself, nor be deprived of life, liberty, or property, without due process of law; nor shall private property be taken for public use, without just compensation.

AMENDMENT VI

In all criminal prosecutions, the accused shall enjoy the right to a speedy and public trial, by an impartial jury of the State and district wherein the crime shall have been committed, which district shall have been previously ascertained by law, and to be informed of the nature and cause of the accusation; to be confronted with the witnesses against him; to have compulsory process for obtaining witnesses in his favor, and to have the Assistance of Counsel for his defence.

AMENDMENT VII

In Suits at common law, where the value in controversy shall exceed twenty dollars, the right of trial by jury shall be preserved, and no fact tried by a jury, shall be otherwise re-examined in any Court of the United States, than according to the rules of the common law.

AMENDMENT VIII

Excessive bail shall not be required, nor excessive fines imposed, nor cruel and unusual punishments inflicted.

AMENDMENT IX

The enumeration in the Constitution, of certain rights, shall not be construed to deny or disparage others retained by the people.

AMENDMENT X

The powers not delegated to the United States by the Constitution, nor prohibited by it to the States, are reserved to the States respectively, or to the people.

AMENDMENT XI

Passed by Congress March 4, 1794. Ratified February 7, 1795.

Note: Article III, section 2, of the Constitution was modified by amendment 11.

The Judicial power of the United States shall not be construed to extend to any suit in law or equity, commenced or prosecuted against one of the United States by Citizens of another State, or by Citizens or Subjects of any Foreign State.

AMENDMENT XII

Passed by Congress December 9, 1803. Ratified June 15, 1804.

Note: A portion of Article II, section 1 of the Constitution was superseded by the 12th amendment.

The Electors shall meet in their respective states and vote by ballot for President and Vice-President, one of whom, at least, shall not be an inhabitant of the same state with themselves; they shall name in their ballots the person voted for as President, and in distinct ballots the person voted for as Vice-President, and they shall make distinct lists of all persons voted for as President, and of all persons voted for as Vice-President, and of the number of votes for each, which lists they shall sign and certify, and transmit sealed to the seat of the government of the United States, directed to the President of the Senate;—the President of the Senate shall, in the presence of the Senate and House of Representatives, open all the certificates and the votes shall then be counted;—The person having the greatest number of votes for President, shall be the President, if such number be a majority of the whole number of Electors appointed; and if no person have such majority, then from the persons having the highest numbers not exceeding three on the list of those voted for as President, the House of Representatives shall choose immediately, by ballot, the President.

But in choosing the President, the votes shall be taken by states, the representation from each state having one vote; a quorum for this purpose shall consist of a member or members from two-thirds of the states, and a majority of all the states shall be necessary to a choice. [And if the House of Representatives shall not choose a President whenever the right of choice shall devolve upon them, before the fourth day of March next following, then the Vice-President shall act as President, as in case of the death or other constitutional disability of the President.—]* The person having the greatest number of votes as Vice-President, shall be the Vice-President, if such number be a majority of the whole number of Electors appointed, and if no person have a majority, then from the two highest numbers on the list, the Senate shall choose the Vice-President; a quorum for the purpose shall consist of two-thirds of the whole number of Senators, and a majority of the whole number shall be necessary to a choice. But no person constitutionally ineligible to the office of President shall be eligible to that of Vice-President of the United States.

AMENDMENT XIII

Passed by Congress January 31, 1865. Ratified December 6, 1865.

Note: A portion of Article IV, section 2, of the Constitution was superseded by the 13th amendment.

Section 1.

Neither slavery nor involuntary servitude, except as a punishment for crime whereof the party shall have been duly convicted, shall exist within the United States, or any place subject to their jurisdiction.

Section 2.

Congress shall have power to enforce this article by appropriate legislation.

Superseded by section 3 of the 20th amendment.

AMENDMENT XIV

Passed by Congress June 13, 1866. Ratified July 9, 1868.

Note: Article I, section 2, of the Constitution was modified by section 2 of the 14th amendment.

Section 1.

All persons born or naturalized in the United States, and subject to the jurisdiction thereof, are citizens of the United States and of the State wherein they reside. No State shall make or enforce any law which shall abridge the privileges or immunities of citizens of the United States; nor shall any State deprive any person of life, liberty, or property, without due process of law; nor deny to any person within its jurisdiction the equal protection of the laws.

Section 2.

Representatives shall be apportioned among the several States according to their respective numbers, counting the whole number of persons in each State, excluding Indians not taxed. But when the right to vote at any election for the choice of electors for President and Vice-President of the United States, Representatives in Congress, the Executive and Judicial officers of a State, or the members of the Legislature thereof, is denied to any of the male inhabitants of such State, being twenty-one years of age,* and citizens of the United States, or in any way abridged, except for participation in rebellion, or other crime, the basis of representation therein shall be reduced in the proportion which the number of such male citizens shall bear to the whole number of male citizens twenty-one years of age in such State.

Section 3.

No person shall be a Senator or Representative in Congress, or elector of President and Vice-President, or hold any office, civil or military, under the United States, or under any State, who, having previously taken an oath, as a member of Congress, or as an officer of the United States, or as a member of any State legislature, or as an executive or judicial officer of any State, to support the Constitution of the United States, shall have engaged in insurrection or rebellion against the same, or given aid or comfort to the enemies thereof. But Congress may by a vote of two-thirds of each House, remove such disability.

Section 4.

The validity of the public debt of the United States, authorized by law, including debts incurred for payment of pensions and bounties for services in suppressing insurrection or rebellion, shall not be

---

Changed by section 1 of the 26th amendment.

questioned. But neither the United States nor any State shall assume or pay any debt or obligation incurred in aid of insurrection or rebellion against the United States, or any claim for the loss or emancipation of any slave; but all such debts, obligations and claims shall be held illegal and void.

Section 5.

The Congress shall have the power to enforce, by appropriate legislation, the provisions of this article.

AMENDMENT XV

Passed by Congress February 26, 1869. Ratified February 3, 1870.

Section 1.

The right of citizens of the United States to vote shall not be denied or abridged by the United States or by any State on account of race, color, or previous condition of servitude—

Section 2.

The Congress shall have the power to enforce this article by appropriate legislation.

AMENDMENT XVI

Passed by Congress July 2, 1909. Ratified February 3, 1913.

Note: Article I, section 9, of the Constitution was modified by amendment 16.

The Congress shall have power to lay and collect taxes on incomes, from whatever source derived, without apportionment among the several States, and without regard to any census or enumeration.

AMENDMENT XVII

Passed by Congress May 13, 1912. Ratified April 8, 1913.

Note: Article I, section 3, of the Constitution was modified by the 17th amendment.

The Senate of the United States shall be composed of two Senators from each State, elected by the people thereof, for six years; and each Senator shall have one vote. The electors in each State shall have the qualifications requisite for electors of the most numerous branch of the State legislatures.

When vacancies happen in the representation of any State in the Senate, the executive authority of such State shall issue writs of election to fill such vacancies: Provided, That the legislature of any State may empower the executive thereof to make temporary appointments until the people fill the vacancies by election as the legislature may direct.This amendment shall not be so construed as to affect the election or term of any Senator chosen before it becomes valid as part of the Constitution.

AMENDMENT XVIII

Passed by Congress December 18, 1917. Ratified January 16, 1919.

Repealed by amendment 21.

Section 1.

After one year from the ratification of this article the manufacture, sale, or transportation of intoxicating liquors within, the importation thereof into, or the exportation thereof from the United States and all territory subject to the jurisdiction thereof for beverage purposes is hereby prohibited.

Section 2.

The Congress and the several States shall have concurrent power to enforce this article by appropriate legislation.

Section 3.

This article shall be inoperative unless it shall have been ratified as an amendment to the Constitution by the legislatures of the several States, as provided in the Constitution, within seven years from the date of the submission hereof to the States by the Congress.

AMENDMENT XIX

Passed by Congress June 4, 1919. Ratified August 18, 1920.

The right of citizens of the United States to vote shall not be denied or abridged by the United States or by any State on account of sex. Congress shall have power to enforce this article by appropriate legislation.

AMENDMENT XX

Passed by Congress March 2, 1932. Ratified January 23, 1933.

Note: Article I, section 4, of the Constitution was modified by section 2 of this amendment. In addition, a portion of the 12th amendment was superseded by section 3.

Section 1.

The terms of the President and the Vice President shall end at noon on the 20th day of January, and the terms of Senators and Representatives at noon on the 3d day of January, of the years in which such terms would have ended if this article had not been ratified; and the terms of their successors shall then begin.

Section 2.

The Congress shall assemble at least once in every year, and such meeting shall begin at noon on the 3d day of January, unless they shall by law appoint a different day.

Section 3.

If, at the time fixed for the beginning of the term of the President, the President elect shall have died, the Vice President elect shall become President. If a President shall not have been chosen before the time fixed for the beginning of his term, or if the President elect shall have failed to qualify, then the Vice President elect shall act as President until a President shall have qualified; and the Congress may by law provide for the case wherein neither a President elect nor a Vice President shall have qualified, declaring who shall then act as President, or the manner in which one who is to act shall be selected, and such person shall act accordingly until a President or Vice President shall have qualified.

Section 4.

The Congress may by law provide for the case of the death of any of the persons from whom the House of Representatives may choose a President whenever the right of choice shall have devolved upon them, and for the case of the death of any of the persons from whom the Senate may choose a Vice President whenever the right of choice shall have devolved upon them.

Section 5.

Sections 1 and 2 shall take effect on the 15th day of October following the ratification of this article.

Section 6.

This article shall be inoperative unless it shall have been ratified as an amendment to the Constitution by the legislatures of three-fourths of the several States within seven years from the date of its submission.

AMENDMENT XXI

Passed by Congress February 20, 1933. Ratified December 5, 1933.

Section 1.

The eighteenth article of amendment to the Constitution of the United States is hereby repealed.

Section 2.

The transportation or importation into any State, Territory, or Possession of the United States for delivery or use therein of intoxicating liquors, in violation of the laws thereof, is hereby prohibited.

Section 3.

This article shall be inoperative unless it shall have been ratified as an amendment to the Constitution by conventions in the several States, as provided in the Constitution, within seven years from the date of the submission hereof to the States by the Congress.

AMENDMENT XXII

Passed by Congress March 21, 1947. Ratified February 27, 1951.

Section 1.

No person shall be elected to the office of the President more than twice, and no person who has held the office of President, or acted as President, for more than two years of a term to which some other person was elected President shall be elected to the office of President more than once. But this Article shall not apply to any person holding the office of President when this Article was proposed by Congress, and shall not prevent any person who may be holding the office of President, or acting as President, during the term within which this Article becomes operative from holding the office of President or acting as President during the remainder of such term.

Section 2.

This article shall be inoperative unless it shall have been ratified as an amendment to the Constitution by the legislatures of three-fourths of the several States within seven years from the date of its submission to the States by the Congress.

AMENDMENT XXIII

Passed by Congress June 16, 1960. Ratified March 29, 1961.

Section 1.

The District constituting the seat of Government of the United States shall appoint in such manner as Congress may direct:

A number of electors of President and Vice President equal to the whole number of Senators and Representatives in Congress to which the District would be entitled if it were a State, but in no event more than the least populous State; they shall be in addition to those appointed by the States, but they shall be considered, for the purposes of the election of President and Vice President, to be electors appointed by a State; and they shall meet in the District and perform such duties as provided by the twelfth article of amendment.

Section 2.

The Congress shall have power to enforce this article by appropriate legislation.

AMENDMENT XXIV

Passed by Congress August 27, 1962. Ratified January 23, 1964.

Section 1.

The right of citizens of the United States to vote in any primary or other election for President or Vice President, for electors for President or Vice President, or for Senator or Representative in Congress, shall not be denied or abridged by the United States or any State by reason of failure to pay poll tax or other tax.

Section 2.

The Congress shall have power to enforce this article by appropriate legislation.

AMENDMENT XXV

Passed by Congress July 6, 1965. Ratified February 10, 1967.

Note: Article II, section 1, of the Constitution was affected by the 25th amendment.

Section 1.

In case of the removal of the President from office or of his death or resignation, the Vice President shall become President.

Section 2.

Whenever there is a vacancy in the office of the Vice President, the President shall nominate a Vice President who shall take office upon confirmation by a majority vote of both Houses of Congress.

Section 3.

Whenever the President transmits to the President pro tempore of the Senate and the Speaker of the House of Representatives his written declaration that he is unable to discharge the powers and duties of his office, and until he transmits to them a written declaration to the contrary, such powers and duties shall be discharged by the Vice President as Acting President.

Section 4.

Whenever the Vice President and a majority of either the principal officers of the executive departments or of such other body as Congress may by law provide, transmit to the President pro tempore of the Senate and the Speaker of the House of Representatives their written declaration that the President is unable to discharge the powers and duties of his office, the Vice President shall immediately assume the powers and duties of the office as Acting President.

Thereafter, when the President transmits to the President pro tempore of the Senate and the Speaker of the House of Representatives his written declaration that no inability exists, he shall resume the powers and duties of his office unless the Vice President and a majority of either the principal officers of the executive department or of such other body as Congress may by law provide, transmit within four days to the President pro tempore of the Senate and the Speaker of the House of Representatives their written declaration that the President is unable to discharge the powers and duties of his office.

Thereupon Congress shall decide the issue, assembling within forty-eight hours for that purpose if not in session. If the Congress, within twenty-one days after receipt of the latter written declaration, or, if Congress is not in session, within twenty-one days after Congress is required to assemble, determines by two-thirds vote of both Houses that the President is unable to discharge the powers and duties of his office, the Vice President shall continue to discharge the same as Acting President; otherwise, the President shall resume the powers and duties of his office.

AMENDMENT XXVI

Passed by Congress March 23, 1971. Ratified July 1, 1971.

Note: Amendment 14, section 2, of the Constitution was modified by section 1 of the 26th amendment.

Section 1.

The right of citizens of the United States, who are eighteen years of age or older, to vote shall not be denied or abridged by the United States or by any State on account of age.

Section 2.

The Congress shall have power to enforce this article by appropriate legislation.

AMENDMENT XXVII

Originally proposed Sept. 25, 1789. Ratified May 7, 1992.

No law, varying the compensation for the services of the Senators and Representatives, shall take effect, until an election of representatives shall have intervened.

APPENDIX 2

Landmark Supreme Cases: Civil Liberties

Religion
1. *Epperson v. Arkansas*
2. *Edwards v. Aguillard*
3. *Engel v. Vitale*
4. *Lee v. Weisman*
5. *Zelman v. Simmons*
6. *Abington SD v. Schempp*
7. *Van Orden v. Perry*
8. *McCreary County (KY) v. ACLU*

Speech and Press
9. *Schenck v. U.S.*
10. *Texas v. Johnson*
11. *Miller v. California*
12. *Bradenburg v. Ohio*
13. *Tinker v. Des Moines*
14. *DeJonge v. Oregon*
15. *NY Times v. Sullivan*
16. *Hazelwood v. Kuhlmeier*

Privacy
17. *Katz v. U.S*
18. *Casey v. Planned Parenthood*
19. *Griswold v. Connecticut*
20. *Cruzan v. Missouri Dept. of Health*
21. *Gonzalez v. Carhart*
22. *Gonzalez v. Oregon*
23. *Georgia v. Randolph*
24. *Hudson v. Michigan*

Criminal Procedure
25. *Gideon v. Wainwright*
26. *Miranda v. Arizona*
27. *Escobedo v. Illinois*
28. *Atkins v. Virginia*
29. *Baze v. Rees*

30. *Mapp v. Ohio*
31. *Gregg v. Georgia*
32. *U.S. v. Leon*

Civil Rights

33. *McDonald v. Chicago*
34. *Korematsu v. U.S.*
35. *Dred Scott v. Sanford*
36. *Heart of Atlanta Motel v. U.S.*
37. *Swann v. Charlotte-Mecklenburg*
38. *Bakke v. California*
39. *Reed v. Reed*
40. *UAW v. Johnson Controls*
41. *Lawrence v. Texas*
42. *Gratz v. Bollinger / Grutter v. Bollinger*
43. *Romar v. Evans*
44. *Roskter v. Goldberg*

APPENDIX 3

Landmark Supreme Court Decisions

A Timeline and Summary

Marbury v. Madison, **1803 (4-0 decision)**
Established the Supreme Court's power of judicial review over Congress.

McCulloch v. Maryland, **1819 (7-0 decision)**
Established the federal government's implied powers over the states.

Dred Scott v. Sandford, **1857 (7-2 decision)**
Denied citizenship to African American slaves.

Plessy v. Ferguson, **1896 (7-1 decision)**
Upheld "separate but equal" segregation laws in states.

Korematsu v. United States, **1944 (6-3 decision)**
Upheld internment of Japanese Americans during World War II.

Brown v. Board of Education, **1954 (9-0 decision)**
Separating black and white students in public schools is unconstitutional.

Gideon v. Wainwright, **1963 (9-0 decision)**
Criminal defendants have a right to an attorney even if they cannot afford one.

New York Times v. Sullivan, **1964 (9-0 decision)**
Lawsuits based on libel or defamation must show intent or recklessness.

Miranda v. Arizona, **1966 (5-4 decision)**
Prisoners must be advised of their rights before being questioned by police.

Loving v. Virginia, **1967 (9-0 decision)**
Invalidated state laws prohibiting interracial marriage.

Roe v. Wade, **1973 (7-2 decision)**
Women have a constitutional right to an abortion during the first two trimesters.

United States v. Nixon, **1974 (8-0 decision)**
President cannot use executive privilege to withhold evidence from criminal trial.

Regents of the University of California v. Bakke, **1978 (5-4 decision)**
Upheld use of race as one of many factors in college admissions.

Bush v. Gore, **2000 (5-4 decision)**
No recount of the 2000 presidential election was feasible in a reasonable time period.

Lawrence v. Texas, **2003 (6-3 decision)**
Struck down state laws that prohibited sodomy between consenting adults.

District of Columbia v. Heller, **2008 (5-4 decision)**
Citizens have a right to possess firearms at home for self-defense.

Citizens United v. Federal Election Commission, **2010 (5-4 decision)**
Corporations and unions can spend unlimited amounts in elections.

National Federation of Independent Business v. Sebelius, **2012 (5-4 decision)**
Upheld the mandate that most Americans have health insurance.

Shelby County v. Holder, **2013 (5-4 decision)**
States and localities do not need federal approval to change voting laws.

United States v. Windsor, **2013 (5-4 decision)**
Federal government must provide benefits to legally married same-sex couples.

Obergefell v. Hodges, **2015 (5-4 decision)**
Same-sex marriage is legalized across all 50 states.

BIBLIOGRAPHY

Black's Law Dictionary With Pronunciations, Ninth Edition, Thomson Reuters, St. Paul, Minnesota, 2009.

NALS, Advanced Manual for the Lawyer's Assistant, 14th Edition, Thomson Reuters, 2017.

Martindale-Hubbell Law Directory, LexisNexis Martindale-Hubbell 2017.

Model Rules of Professional Conduct, American Bar Association, an amended 2009.

Rotunda, Ronald D., Professional Responsibility, 9th Ed., Thomson Reuters, 2011.

Sabin, William A., The Gregg Reference Manual, 11th ed., Glencoe/McGrawHill, Westerville, Ohio, 2011.

The Bluebook, A Uniform System of Citation, 20th ed., The Harvard Law Review Association, Annet House, Cambridge, Massachusetts, 2015.

United States Government Manual, U. S. Government Printing Office, Washington, D.C., 2009/2010.

GLOSSARY

341 meeting Often called the creditor's meeting. In bankruptcy, first meeting of creditors and equity security holders, at which time a trustee may be elected and the debtor examined under oath.

341 notice A notice given by the bankruptcy court to all creditors of a meeting of creditors; also known as the notice to creditors.

Abortion Intentional termination of pregnancy.

Abstract A summary of all transactions pertaining to the parcel of real estate from the time of governmental entity up to an including the current transaction. A condensed history of the title to the land.

Abstracter's certificate A certificate that is made a part of the abstract and signed by the abstracter verifying what the abstract covers; the final page of the continuation.

Acceptance In contracts, the situation occurring when the offeree is in total agreement with the offeror.

Access or secondary physical custody Also called visitation, the right of the noncustodial parent for reasonable access to the child or children.

Accord (and satisfaction) Accord is accepting a substituted item or service in place of the one promised in the original contract. Satisfaction occurs when the substitution is accepted.

Account stated A summarized statement of a debtor's account.

Accredited Legal Professional (ALP) The basic certification designed for the individual at the apprentice level of the legal support staff.

Acknowledgment Consists of a statement that the person who signed the document declared to and before the notary public that it was the person who signed the document.

Acquittal In criminal law, a finding of not guilty.

Action to quiet title Legal action taken by a property owner to have a court declare him the owner of a particular parcel.

Active voice Refers to the use of active voice and normal sentence structure.

Ademption When a testator gives specific property in a will but no longer owns the property at the time of death.

Adjective(s) Word which modifies, describes or limits nouns, pronouns, and gerunds.

Adjudicate (not defined in this chapter) To settle controversies and disputes between parties.

Administration The supervision of an estate by an administrator or executor; the court probate process when a person dies without a will.

Administrative agencies Agencies created by the legislative branch of government to administer laws pertaining to specific areas, such as the environment, taxes, transportation, and labor.

Administrative claim Under the bankruptcy code, a claim for costs related to administration of the bankruptcy.

Administrator A person appointed by a court to administer an intestate estate.

Administrator c.t.a When the named executor of a will is unable or unwilling to serve and no alternative is designated, the court appoints an administrator c.t.a., which means with will annexed.

Adoption The legal process by which a child is taken into one's family and given all rights and privileges of a natural child and heir.

Advance sheets Paperback pamphlets published weekly which contain reporter cases, including correct volume and page number.

Adverb(s) Word used to describe or limit a verb, adjective, or another adverb.

Adversary proceeding Individual lawsuits brought within a bankruptcy case.

Adverse possession A method of acquiring title to real property under certain conditions by possession for a statutory period.

Affiant The person who is making an affidavit.

Affidavit A written statement sworn to as being true before a notary public.

Affirmation A solemn or official declaration that the statements the person has just made or is about to make are true, but does not include an appeal to God or any supreme being.

Affirmative defenses A defense to the plaintiff's complaint raised in the defendant's answer.

Alimony (spousal maintenance) Allowance a spouse pays for the support of the other spouse after the final divorce decree is granted.

Alimony pendente lite Alimony allowance made during the pendency of an action for dissolution of marriage.

Allegations Numbered paragraphs setting forth the background and reasons for filing a suit.

Alphabetic filing A system of filing in which files are labeled and stored in alphabetical order, generally by the name of the client.

Alphanumeric filing A combination of an alphabetic filing system and a numeric system in which numbers are assigned to files in blocks according to the letter of the alphabet which identifies the client.

ALP™ The basic certification designed for the individual at the apprentice level of the legal support staff. See Accredited Legal Professional.

Amendment [to a pleading] An amended pleading is one that is corrected in regard to facts that existed at the time the original pleading was filed. Contrast to supplemental pleading.

Ancillary proceeding A proceeding that takes place outside the state of a decedent's domicile due to a probate requirement for real estate or tangible property in that state.

Animal cases Tort litigation involving injuries or damages caused by animals, including livestock, domesticated wild animals, household pets, or farm animals; these cases fall under strict liability tort law.

Annulment A proceeding that establishes that a marriage never existed.

Answer A formal, written statement by the defendant in a lawsuit that answers each allegation contained in the complaint. In family law, in a divorce action, the defendant's first pleading is called an answer; in a no-fault action, it may be called a response.

Apostrophe A punctuation mark used to form contractions of words and figures, in place of omitted letters or figure, to form possessives, to form plurals of lower case letters and upper case letters when the lack of an apostrophe may create confusion, to set off quoted material within a larger quotation, in names with the prefix "O."

Appeal A proceeding brought to a higher court to review a lower court's decision.

Appellant The party who takes an appeal from one court or jurisdiction to another.

Appellate jurisdiction Authority of a court to review cases tried in lower courts.

Appellee The party in a cause against whom an appeal is taken.

Append Allows the operator to gather or collect, in order, each item deleted and then insert them as a group in another location or document.

Application Term used to refer to the specific tasks a computer can do.

Arraignment The hearing at which the accused is brought before the court to plead to the criminal charge in the indictment.

Arrest The actual restraint of a person for submission to custody.

Articles of incorporation The basic instrument filed with the appropriate government agency to form a corporation.

Assault An act that creates in a person immediate fear of an attempted battery.

Assign (assignment) Assignment is a substitution of one party for another in a contractual relationship. If the assignee fails to perform under the terms, the contract responsibility falls back on the assignor.

Assignee A person to whom an assignment is made.

Assignor A person who assigns a right, whether or not he or she is the original owner thereof.

Assumption of risk The legal rule under which a person may not recover for an injury received when voluntarily exposed to a known danger.

At issue (joined) The term used to describe the status of litigation when the complaint and a responsive pleading have been filed.

Attestation clause The clause of a will immediately following the signature of a testator.

Attorney-client privilege The privilege that protects confidential communications, oral or written, between the attorney and a client in the course of the professional relationship that cannot be disclosed without the consent of the client.

Backup A second copy of computer data made to avoid data loss in the event of a computer outage.

Bail Security given for the release of a jailed person that guarantees his or her attendance at all required court appearances.

Bailiff The peace officer of the court (or court officer) responsible for keeping order and maintaining appropriate courtroom decorum.

Balance The difference between the total debits and total credits posted to an account.

Balloon payment A provision that requires payment in full of the unpaid balance of a loan a certain number of years from the date of initiation of the contract.

Bank draft A check issued by a bank upon its funds in another bank usually located in some other city.

Bankruptcy A proceeding in which an individual or legal entity requests protection under Title 11 of the United States Bankruptcy Code.

Bankruptcy Abuse Prevention and Consumer Protection Act (BAPCPA) The BAPCPA covers all bankruptcy cases filed on or after October 17, 2005, and institutes a number of changes, most notably means testing and required credit counseling and financial management courses for creditors.

Bar All attorneys admitted to practice law in a given state or court system.

Bar association Organization of attorneys admitted to practice law in a given state or court system.

Battery A harmful offensive touching of another's person.

Bench (the) The raised podium at the front of the courtroom behind which the judge sits, and also refers to the judge in a given court.

Bench trial Trial by a judge rather than a jury.

Beneficiary(ies) A person named to receive property in a will or trust.

Bequest Personal property transferred by will.

Bifurcated hearing The act of reserving the property settlement, child custody, and support matters for consideration later.

Bilateral contract A contract in which both parties make a promise.

Bill of costs A certified, itemized statement of the amount of costs in an action or suit.

Bill of particulars A motion by a criminal defendant that requests details concerning the offense charged.

Blank endorsement (endorsement in blank) The simple signature of the payee which makes the check payable to bearer.

Block billing A string of unrelated entries for the same client and on the same matter, put together in a block entry with semicolons between separate entries.

Blue sky laws State laws regulating the registration, offering and sale of securities.

Board of Directors Governing body of a corporation elected by the shareholders.

Breach of contract The failure of one party to carry out any condition of a contract.

Brief A memorandum of material facts, points of law, precedents, etc., prepared to familiarize the court with the facts and the law of a particular case.

Brief bank A law firm's collection, either in electronic form or in hard copy, of legal research, briefs, and forms that may be reviewed or reused for other projects.

Bureau of Land Management (BLM) The federal agency that has jurisdiction over and manages approximately 245 million acres of public land and 700 million subsurface acres located primarily in the west and Alaska.

Business corporations Corporations organized to make a profit.

Business or Massachusetts trust A business organization through which property is conveyed to trustees and managed for the benefit of the holders of certificates similar to corporate stock certificates.

Bylaws Rules and regulations under which the corporation will operate.

Byte Refers to the amount of space required to store one character of information. A kilobyte (KB) is one thousand bytes; a megabyte (MB) is one million bytes; a gigabyte (GB) is one billion bytes.

Calls One line segment of a property in a metes and bounds description.

Capital case(s) A felony case punishable by death.

Caption or style The title of the case, which usually includes the name of the court, the names of the parties, and the court number.

Case law That body of court decisions resulting from legal controversies over interpretations of substantive and procedural law.

Case Management/Electronic Case Filing (CM/ECF) The electronic filing system used in the federal court system.

Case number (civil number, docket number, index number) The number assigned to a new case and used on all pleadings and documents filed in a case.

Cashier's check A check drawn by a bank on its own funds.

Cause of action A wrong for which relief can be sought in court. The incident or facts that give a person a right to relief in court.

CD-ROM Compact Disk-Read Only Memory.

Central processing unit (CPU) Hardware and software are linked by the operations and calculations performed by the CPU.

Centralized filing A filing system in which the files are maintained at a single, central location and also include controlled access.

Ceremonial marriage A marriage authorized by legislative action and validated according to statutes for licensing, solemnization, and registration.

Certificate of mailing A receipt issued by the USPS that shows evidence of mailing.

Certified check A check issued by a bank that reduces the drawer's account by the amount of the check. The bank holds those funds for payment of the check and becomes responsible for its payment.

Certified mail A postal service that provides proof of delivery for First-Class Mail and Priority mail.

Challenge for cause A request by a plaintiff or defendant to a judge that a prospective juror not be allowed to be a member of the jury because of specified causes or reasons; see peremptory challenge.

Change of venue A change in the location of a trial,

Chapter 11 reorganization Available to businesses and individual debtors who seek to reorganize their affairs rather than liquidate.

Chapter 12 reorganization Under the bankruptcy code, an action that allows family farmers or fisherman to reorganize rather than liquidate debt.

Chapter 13 (or wage earner plan) A plan in bankruptcy which gives a salaried debtor or wage earner the protection of the court from creditors while he or she pays a percentage of his or her wages to a trustee to pay off his or her debts.

Citation A legal authority, such as a constitution, statute, case, or other authoritative source, which is used to support a written legal document.

Citators A resource that lists the citations to all of the judicial decisions that have cited a given case.

Civil cover sheet A cover sheet required by many courts listing the parties, the type of action, and other information related to the case that may be administratively useful to the court.

Civil law Law that is based on a series of written codes or laws.

Claimant The injured party in a litigation case. One who claims or asserts a right; persons who are owed money by the debtor.

Clear and merchantable title The term used to indicate that there are no outstanding liens or encumbrances of record against the property excepting only those of the type normally associated with the property to which most lawyers would not object.

Clerk of court Administrator or chief clerical officer of the court.

Close corporation Corporation whose shares are held by a single shareholder or a closely knit group of shareholders.

Closed hearing Hearings at which members of the general public are not allowed as spectators.

Closing arguments A summary presented by each party to a case that gives the jury reasons to find in the party's favor.

Cloud on the title A condition affecting the title of property that may render it unmarketable if not corrected, including encumbrances, easements, encroachments, and tax sales; also known as defect in the title.

Codicil An amendment to a will, either to add provisions or delete provisions of a will, which is executed with all the formalities of a will; this term means little will.

Collaborative divorce A form of divorce or dissolution of marriage that uses negotiation techniques and expert financial and counseling assistance as needed to mediate a divorce rather than trying it in the more hostile style of litigation.

Collateral attack The means by which a criminal defendant, after exhausting direct appellate remedies, seeks to attack the conditions of his or her confinement or otherwise indirectly attack his or her conviction.

Collective noun A collective noun names a group of persons or things and takes a singular verb.

Colon A punctuation mark used after a salutation, stating clock time, after introductory expressions preceding an enumeration, in a web address, may follow a verb, preposition, or conjunction when it introduces a list, or introduce a long quotation.

Comma A punctuation mark indicating a partial stop.

Common law Law that evolved from earlier decisions made by courts; law based on precedent; case law.

Common noun A noun that describes a general class of person, place, thing, or idea.

Common-law marriage An agreement to marry between two people, followed by their living together and presenting themselves to the public as husband and wife, in those states where permitted.

Community property Property acquired during a marriage that is owned by husband and wife, each having an undivided one-half interest.

Comparative negligence The rule under which negligence is measured by percentage and damages are diminished in proportion to the amount of negligence attributable to the plaintiff.

Comparative negligence doctrine Under this theory, if the plaintiff is found to be contributorily negligent, the finder of fact decides in what percentage each party was negligent and awards damages accordingly.

Competent parties In contract law, one of the essential elements of a contract is that both parties are competent--of legal age and not impaired.

Complaint The original pleading by which an action is filed in court.

Complex sentence Consists of one independent clause and one or more dependent clauses.

Compound adjective(s) An adjective that consists of two or more words that function as a unit and express a single thought.

Compound noun(s) A noun composed of two words and displayed as one work, two words with a hyphen between them, or two separate words.

Compound sentence Consists of two or more independent clauses connected by a coordinating conjunction, a semicolon, or a conjunctive verb.

Compound-complex sentence Consists of two or more independent clauses and one or more dependent clauses.

Concurrent jurisdiction Jurisdiction granted in different courts at the same time over the same matters and within the same territorial limit.

Conflict of interest Generally arises when the law firm (or the individual lawyers in the firm) places itself in the position of representing parties in adverse positions.

Conflicts check The procedure by which a law firm determines that there is no conflict in accepting work from a new client or on a new matter from an existing client.

Conform(ed)(ing) To insert on all copies of a document the information shown on the original so the copy will reflect dates, signatures, and corrections that were placed on the original.

Conjunctive adverbs Join clauses, words, and phrases that are grammatically equal.

Conjunction Word used to connect two or more words, phrases, or clauses.

Consecutive-number filing Filing system where numbers are assigned in straight sequential order and are filed in straight sequence.

Consent Agreement; voluntary acceptance of the wish of another.

Consideration (price) The contracted price paid for a promise, goods, or real estate.

Constitutional law Law set forth in the Constitution of the United States and in state constitutions.

Consumer Product Safety Commission (CPSC) The federal agency that protects the public against unreasonable risks of injury and death from consumer products; issues and enforces mandatory standards; issues recalls; conducts research; informs and educates consumers through the media, state, and local governments, private organizations; and responds to consumer inquiries.

Contempt of court The refusal to obey a court order.

Contingency fee arrangement A fee that is a percentage of the amount obtained in negotiation or litigation with another party.

Contingent or conditional will Also contingent will. One that does not take effect unless a specific event occurs. If the event does not occur, it is as though there were no will.

Continuation (or extension of abstract) The act of having the abstract of title brought to a current date through search of title records.

Continue or Continuance Refers to the postponement of a court date to a later date.

Contract An enforceable agreement between two or more competent parties that creates an obligation to do or not to do a particular thing.

Contributory negligence An affirmative defense that asserts the injuries and damages complained of by the plaintiff were caused in whole or in part by the plaintiff's own negligence.

Controlled access Means that only the file coordinator and file room staff members remove files from the file room.

Conventional financing Financing for home purchases funded by local bank and savings institutions.

Conversion Taking property that belongs to another and using it as one's own.

Cooperative A group of people who pool their products or resources for mutual advantage.

Coordinating conjunction Connect words, phrases, and clauses of equal value.

Corporate seal A seal used by a corporation to authenticate its corporate acts and execute legal instruments.

Corporation A legal entity created by authority of the laws of a state or nation.

Correlative conjunctions Words that join equal sentence elements (i.e. either/or and neither/nor).

Counterclaim A claim presented by a defendant in opposition to or for deduction from the claim of plaintiff, the defendant then becomes the counter-plaintiff and the plaintiff becomes the counter-defendant.

Counteroffer Response to an offer with different terms than the original offer; counterproposal.

Court Tribunal with judicial authority to handle the administration of justice; reference to a hearing date or place; reference to the judge presiding over a particular hearing or court; reference to the physical facility that houses the court.

Court clerk (in glossary as clerk of court) Administrator or chief clerical officer of the court.

Court reporter A person who usually sits in court while it is in session and records all proceedings verbatim.

Credit Recorded on the right side of an account.

Creditors (or claimants) Persons who are owed money by the debtor.

Crime An act in violation of the penal laws of a state or the United States for which a specific punishment is prescribed.

Cross-claim A pleading filed by a defendant that asserts a claim against another defendant arising out of the same action as the original complaint.

Cross-examine (examination) Questioning of a party by opposing counsel.

Data source The file that contains a set of names, addresses, phone numbers, and other types of individual information used for merging.

Database A compilation of data fields and records that is collected, stored, and organized for later retrieval through sorting, searches, queries, etc.

Database management system software Software that is used to collect, store, and organize data into a database.

Death tax The tax where an estate or its beneficiaries are taxed in connection with the distribution of the decedent's property.

Debit Recorded on the left side of an account.

Debtor One who owes a debt to another; a person or entity filing for relief under the bankruptcy code.

Debtor-in-possession Entity or individual retaining possession of the assets of the bankruptcy estate in a Chapter 11 bankruptcy case.

Decedent A person who has died.

Decentralized filing A filing system in which the lawyers store files in their own work areas and have total responsibility for and control of the files.

Deceptively similar In business organizations, a name sufficiently like the name of another business entity that outsiders might confuse the two is considered deceptively similar.

Decision The decision of the court.

Deed A formal written contract effectuating the sale and conveyance of property by the seller to the buyer for a price.

Deed or release and conveyance When an institution holding a deed of trust to secure a loan is paid in full, the trustee then executes a deed of release and reconveyance to return title of the property to the buyer.

Default In litigation, the failure of the defendant to appear and answer the summons and complaint in litigation. In contracts, the failure to comply with the terms of a contract.

Default judgment When a party fails to appear or respond to a petition or complaint, judgment can be granted to the opposing party by default.

Defendant or respondent (1) The person or entity defending or denying a suit. (2) The party against whom recovery is sought or the accused in a criminal case.

Defense of property Affirmative defense in criminal or tort law when force was used to protect one's property.

Demonstrative pronouns Used to modify a noun or take the place of a noun.

Department of Veterans Affairs (VA) The department of the executive branch of the United States Government that administers veteran's benefits.

Dependent clause A group of words including a subject and verb which do not form a complete sentence.

Deponent The witness or person to be deposed.

Deposition Testimony of a witness or a party taken under oath outside the courtroom.

Deputy clerk (or law clerk) An officer of the court who may function as a secretary, assistant, and researcher for the judge.

Devise(s) Also, preresiduary gift. A gift of real property by will. Under the Uniform Probate Code, a gift of personal or real property by will.

Devisee(s) The person to whom land or real property is given by will.

Digests A detailed index by subject on points of law covered by reported cases.

Digital versatile disk (DVD) Similar to a CD-ROM, they are available in write-once or re-recordable versions and can hold 4.7 gigabytes of data, or seven times the capacity of a CD-ROM.

Direct examination Questioning of a party to litigation conducted by the party's counsel.

Direct object The person, place, or thing receiving the action of a sentence.

Discharge In contract law, the termination of a contract.

Discovery The process by which a party to a lawsuit is entitled to obtain facts, documents, and information about the case.

Dissolution or divorce Legal termination of a marriage.

Distributed in kind In estate administration, property that is not liquidated and is distributed in the form in which it came into the estate.

Docket (1) A trial docket is a calendar of cases to be tried in a certain term of court or a specific courtroom; (2) In a law office, the docket is the day's agenda, including appointments, hearings, and files to be handled.

Docket Clerk (or docket coordinator) The employee who is responsible for reminding all lawyers of deadlines in advance.

Docket control system A system for keeping track of deadlines, court dates, and appointments. A docket control system may also include a mechanism for calendaring files to be reviewed or handled.

Doctrine of stare decisis A doctrine that requires courts to stand by earlier court decisions when hearing cases with similar fact situations.

Document management system A computerized mechanism for naming, storing, and labeling documents for ease and accuracy of later retrieval.

Domestic corporation Corporation created or organized in the state in which it does business.

Domestic relations The area of law dealing with family matters, including divorce, separation, custody, support, and adoption.

Domicile The place where a person has his or her true, fixed, and permanent home and principal establishment and to which, whenever he or she is absent, he or she has the intention of returning.

Dormant partner A partner who takes no active part in the management of a business and is not known to the public as a partner.

Drag and drop A word processing feature that simplifies the moving or copying procedure and is used when the text is being moved to a close location in the same file.

Drawee Person to whom a check is written.

Drawer Person by whom a check is written and upon whose funds the check is drawn.

Durable power of attorney A power given to another that empowers that person to act on behalf of the maker, even if the maker has become incapacitated.

Duress Force or threatened force used to gain consent.

Earnest money A down payment or deposit made by the buyer.

Easement (or servitude) A right to use the lands of another. See right of way.

Elder law A practice of law focused on the unique concerns of a segment of the population over the age of 50.

Electronic filing (efiling) A system used by courts, government agencies, attorneys, and the public to reduce paperwork and electronically filed documents over the Internet using a standard web browser.

Ellipses Used to indicate omission of a word or words in quoted material.

Em dash A punctuation mark the width of an "m." If no em dash symbol is available, two hyphens are used with no spaces on either side.

Email Electronic mail made possible through computer-based communications equipment.

Employer Identification Number (EIN) A number assigned to an employer by the Internal Revenue Service that must be used on all reports submitted to the IRS.

Encroachment An intrusion on the property of another.

Encumbrance A claim or lien on real property (real estate).

En dash A punctuation mark the width of an "n."

Entry of appearance Formal entry of an attorney into a case, presented to the court in pleading form.

Environmental Protection Agency (EPA) The federal agency that works to abate and control all forms of environmental pollution.

Equal Employment Opportunity Commission (EEOC) The federal commission charged with ending discrimination in all areas of employment and to promote voluntary compliance by employers.

Equity The value of a property or of an interest in it in excess of claims against it.

Escrow agreement Contains provisions that protect both the seller and the buyer; an escrow agent collects the purchase price and records the sale when all payments are made.

Estate A person's property. In bankruptcy, all of debtor's nonexempt property.

Estate administration (probate proceedings) Refers to proceedings used to distribute the estate.

Estate planning The area of the law dealing with arranging a person's property and estate by taking into account the laws of wills, taxes, property, and trusts to gain a maximum benefit under all laws while carrying out the person's own wishes for disposition of his or her property upon his or her death.

Estate tax A tax imposed by the federal government and some states on the right to transfer property by death based upon decedent's assets on date of death or an alternate valuation date.

Ethics Principles of conduct that govern an individual or profession.

Ex parte communication Referring to an action taken without the participation of both parties to litigation. In due course, the other party must be notified of the action. In some instances, ex parte actions are impermissible and disciplinable.

Exceptions The list of all defects or clouds on a title.

Exclamation point May be used internally in a sentence or at the end of a sentence; used to express strong feeling or emotion, or an excited exclamation.

Exclusive jurisdiction The authority granted to a court to hear certain matters to the exclusion of all other courts.

Execute(ing) To complete; to sign; to carry out according to its terms.

Executed contracts A contract that has been fully performed by both parties.

Executor A person or an entity appointed by a person to administer the terms of his or her will.

Executor de bonis non Representative appointed by the court when the named executor to the will is unable or unwilling to serve.

Executory contracts A contract that has been partially performed but with something remaining to be done by one or both parties.

Exempt property All of the property the debtor is entitled to keep by law.

Express contract A contract in which the terms are specifically stated and agreed to by both parties.

Extrahazardous activity An activity that carries the likelihood of causing some types of damage even if reasonable care is exercised.

Failure to state a claim Affirmative defense that alleges that the plaintiff failed to state a claim that the court can require the defendant to satisfy.

False imprisonment Holding a person against his or her will without legal authority.

Federal Aviation Administration (FAA) The federal agency that regulates air commerce to promote aviation safety.

Federal Bureau of Investigation (FBI) Protects and defends the United States against terrorist and foreign-intelligence threats acting inside the United States; upholds and enforces criminal laws of the United States; provides leadership and criminal justice services to federal, state, municipal, and international agencies. Investigates all violations of federal law except those assigned to other agencies.

Federal Communications Commission (FCC) The federal agency that licenses and regulates interstate and foreign communications by radio and television broadcast, wire, telephone, telegraphs, cable television operation, two-way radio and radio operators, microwave, and satellite communications.

Federal Deposit Insurance Corporation (FDIC) An independent agency within the executive branch of the federal government that insures, up to statutory limits, the deposits in national banks, state banks that are members of the Federal Reserve System, and state banks that apply for Federal Deposit Insurance. The FDIC also examines and supervises financial institutions for safety and soundness to protect consumers and manages receiverships when required.

Federal Mediation and Conciliation Service (FMCS) The agency which promotes the development of equitable and stable labor management relationships and assists in settling disputes in the event of work stoppages, threatened work stoppages, and labor management disputes.

Federal Register Published daily, contains federal administrative rules and regulations.

Federal Trade Commission (FTC) The agency which maintains a free and fair competitive enterprise system within the American economic system; also provides law enforcement, shares expertise with federal and state legislatures, and U.S. and foreign agencies; develops policy and research tools; and creates practical plain-language education programs for consumers and businesses.

Fee simple (or fee simple absolute) Absolute ownership of real property (real estate).

Felony Any offense punishable by death or by imprisonment for a term exceeding one year.

Fiduciary(ies) A person or institution that manages money or property of another and must exercise a standard of care imposed by law, e.g., personal representatives or executor of an estate, a trustee, etc.

Field One piece of information about a person or business used in a data source.

File management The control of each file in the office from the time it is opened to the time that it is ultimately closed and destroyed.

First-Class mail Postal service for letters, postcards, greeting cards, business reply mail, bills, and checks.

Fixtures An article of personal property permanently attached to real estate.

Flat fee A set fee based on a specific type of legal work.

Fonts Refers to the style or design of a collection of letters, numerals, symbols, and punctuation marks.

Food and Drug Administration (FDA) The agency which protects the public against impure and unsafe drugs, food, cosmetics, and medical devices. Also responsible for helping to speed investigations that make medicines and foods safer and more affordable, and in the case of medicines, more effective.

Footers Used in documents and pleadings to place the title and page number on each page.

For deposit only Restrictive endorsement used on checks to be deposited.

Foreign corporation A corporation that does business in a state or country other than the state or country in which it was created.

Foreign jurisdiction Means a state other than the one where the child and custodial parent live.

Formal contract A contact in which the format of the contract must meet certain requirements established by law.

Fraud A false statement of a material fact, intended to deceive, which statement is relied upon and intended to be relied upon to cause a loss to the victim.

General jurisdiction (also unlimited jurisdiction) A jurisdiction without limitation as to the types of cases or monetary limits on cases a court can hear (sometimes referred to as unlimited jurisdiction).

General partner Individual who has unlimited liability for the obligations of the partnership and may contribute management services, cash, or property.

General partnerships A partnership in which the parties carry on their trade or business for the joint benefit and profit of all parties.

Gerund Present participle form of the verb used in the sentence as a noun or part of a noun phrase.

Good law Persuasive or mandatory case law that has not been reversed or overruled and may be used to support arguments in pleadings.

Government Printing Office (GPO) The agency in charge of gathering, cataloguing, producing, authenticating, and preserving published information, including the production and destruction of information products and services for the federal government.

Government survey System adopted by government in 1785 for mapping out tracts of ground in townships and sections.

Grand jury A body of citizens assembled to receive complaints and accusations in criminal cases, to hear evidence, and to determine whether probable cause exists that a crime has been committed and whether an indictment should be issued.

Grantor, trustor, or settlor In real estate, the person who transfers property (the seller); in estate planning, the maker of a trust.

Graphical user interface (GUI) A system using icons and pictures to display menus and choices on a computer.

Guardian ad litem Person appointed by a court to represent a minor or incapacitated person in a legal proceeding.

Hardware The physical elements of a computer, such as a keyboard, monitor, printer, case or chassis, modem, scanner, and joy stick.

Headers Place text and graphics at the top of each page.

Headnotes Summary of each point of law contained in the court decision of a report case.

Health care power of attorney A power given to another permitting that person to make health care decisions on behalf of the maker.

Holographic will A will that is entirely handwritten, dated, and signed by the testator him- or herself.

Hung jury A jury that cannot reach a verdict; a hung jury results in a mistrial.

Hyphens A hyphen pulls words together into a single thought.

Impeach Discredit; as a witness for an opposing party.

Imperative mood A verb mood used to give an order, request, or command.

Implied contract A contract created by law and imposed upon parties because of their actions or their relationship.

Impossibility of performance In contract law, a discharge resulting from the inability to legally or physically fulfill the terms of an existing contract.

Improvements Such items as curbs, gutters, sidewalks, street lights, and sewer systems constructed to enhance development of real estate.

In chambers Meeting in the judge's office.

Indefinite pronouns Do not stand for a particular person or thing, some are always singular, some are always plural, others may be either singular or plural depending on the noun to which they refer.

Indicative mood A verb mood used to state a fact or ask a question.

Indictment A written accusation issued by a grand jury against a defendant.

Indirect object The person, place, or thing receiving the direct object.

Infinitive The unconjugated form of a verb, preceded by the word to. An infinitive may be used as a noun, adjective, or verb.

Informal contract A contract that is not formal, may be written and still be informal if its format is not as prescribed by law.

Information A written accusation against the defendant.

Inheritance tax A tax imposed by some states upon persons receiving property from an estate based upon individual shares, less exemptions, depending upon familial relationship between the decedent and recipient.

Injunctive relief A type of relief in equity in which a party is ordered not to perform an action or to perform an action.

Innocent misrepresentation When a misrepresentation results from an honest mistake.

Input device A means of getting information or data from the operator into the computer, either by keyboard, mouse, optical character reader, imaging scanner, or voice recognition system.

Installment real estate contract (land contract or contract for deed) Agreement between seller and buyer for the purchase of real estate by installment payments with interest. The buyer takes possession of the property and maintains it, but the seller retains title to the property until the buyer has paid the entire price.

Intentional torts Wrong perpetuated by one who intends to break the law.

Inter vivos or living trusts or Totten trusts A trust created during a decedent's lifetime that becomes operative during his life time.

Interjection A word used to express a strong feeling or emotion.

Internal Revenue Service (IRS) The federal agency that administers the tax laws of the United States, except taxes on alcohol, firearms, explosives, and tobacco.

Interrogative pronouns Used in asking questions.

Interrogatories A set or series of written questions served upon a party, witness, or other person having information or interest in a case; a discovery device.

Intestate Having died without making a will.

Intranet An in-house online web page used by firms as an internal bulletin board and can include directories, firm news, and general firm information.

Intransitive verb An action verb that is complete without a direct object upon which to act.

Invalidity (invalid marriage) A marriage that is invalid from its inception.

Invitations to offer Advertising or sales materials that do not present a true contract offer are considered invitations to offer.

Involuntary bankruptcy Creditors ask the court to place a debtor in bankruptcy.

Irregular verb A verb whose past tense and past participle are not formed according to normal verb forms.

Irretrievable breakdown or irreconcilable differences A grounds for dissolution of marriage that is functionally identical to irretrievable breakdown.

Irrevocable trust A trust which may not be revoked by the maker after its creation, generally made for tax reasons.

Joint custody In a divorce or dissolution, custody of a minor child or children by both parents. Joint custody can be joint legal custody, granting joint participation in major parental decision-making; it can be joint physical custody, granting extensive participation in the physical living circumstances of the child to both parents; or it can be both.

Joint interest trust A trust created by two persons placing jointly held assets in trust.

Joint stock company An unincorporated business enterprise with ownership represented by shares of stock.

Joint tenancy Property held by two or more persons, each with the same undivided interest in the property.

Joint venture A partnership engaged in the joint undertaking of a commercial enterprise.

Joint will A single will made by two or more persons.

Judge The presiding officer of the court.

Judgment The written decision of a court to an action or suit submitted to the court for determination.

Judgment creditor One who is owed money as a result of a judgment in his or her favor.

Judgment debtor One who owes money as a result of a judgment in favor of a creditor.

Judgment-proof A judgment debtor that has no assets to seize in satisfaction of a judgment is considered judgment-proof.

Jurisdiction The power and authority of a court to hear and try a case.

Jurisdiction in personam The authority of a court to render a judgment against a person or to subject the disputing parties to the decisions and rulings made by it.

Jurisdiction in rem The authority of a court to render a judgment concerning property over which it has jurisdiction.

Justification Refers to four types of text alignment, left justification, center justification, full justification, or right justification.

Laches An affirmative defense that alleges an inappropriate delay in filing suit that resulted in prejudice to the defendant.

Landlord (lessor) Also lessor. The owner of property who leases it to a person or business entity.

Law blank A printed legal form available for preparing documents.

Lawyer's assistant The term used to indicate the support person who serves a lawyer in a secretarial capacity, perhaps with expanded duties.

Lease A contract between the landlord and tenant whereby the landlord conveys the use of real estate to another for a specific term at a particular rent subject to certain conditions.

Leave of court Permission of court to take some action.

Legacy A disposition of personal property by will; a bequest.

Legal backing Heavy paper longer than the document and typically made of colored stock.

Legal cap Ruled legal paper.

Legal custody The parental right granted to one or both parents in dissolution or divorce actions that allows the parent to be extensively involved in major decision-making for the child's welfare.

Legal description A detailed description of real property that must be complete enough so the parcel can be located and identified.

Legal encyclopedias Books that state principles of law supported by footnote references to pertinent cases throughout the U.S.

Legal file A transcript of court proceedings submitted as part of an appeal.

Legal texts (or treatises) Books that cover specific areas of the law, usually dealing with a single topic.

Legatee The person to whom a legacy is given in a will.

Letter bank A collection of form letters, memos, messages, and other documents used as templates for routine correspondence.

Letters of administration Formal document issued by probate court appointing the administrator of an estate.

Letters testamentary The formal instrument of authority and administration given to a personal representative by the court in a testacy situation, empowering the personal representative to enter upon the discharge of his or her office as the personal representative.

Libel In torts, damage to a person's reputation by written or published information.

Like-kind exchanges (1031 exchanges) Exchange of one piece of real estate for another.

Limited jurisdiction Jurisdiction in which a court is restricted in the type of case it can hear or in the amount of money involved in the litigation.

Limited liability company (LLC) A business entity giving advantages of limited liability to equity owners and managers.

Limited liability limited partnership (LLLP) A limited partnership which has elected to be treated as a limited liability partnership in addition to being a limited partnership.

Limited liability partnership (LLP) A limited liability partnership is a general partnership that has elected to be treated as an LLP.

Limited partners A partner whose liability is limited to the extent of his or her contributions to the partnership, which are usually limited to cash or property.

Limited partnerships (LPs) A partnership consisting of one or more general partners who conduct the business and one or more limited partners who contribute cash payments as capital but are not liable for the debts of the partnership beyond the amount each contributes.

Linking verb Verb that expresses a state of being and is used to link the subject to words that identify the subject.

Links (hyperlinks, hypertext, hotspots, jumps) Web addresses that contain an activated linkage to another location or website on the Internet.

Liquidation The process of converting assets into cash for easier distribution when the estate is closed.

Listing agreement Agreement through which owners of real estate agree to have a broker represent them in the sale of real estate.

Living will (listed as Advanced health care directive) A document by which the maker instructs the physician or health care provider not to keep the maker alive by use of life-support procedures.

Local area network (LAN) Connects computers that are located close together (in the same building) and joined by cables or with a wireless connection.

Loose-leaf services Loose-leaf replacement pages provided by a publisher in areas of the law where changes occur at a rapid rate.

Macro(s) A computer feature that allows the operator to record keystrokes and then play them back with just a few keystrokes.

Mainframe computers Large, very expensive, high-speed machines that require trained operators and special temperature environments, used for scientific and engineering computations.

Majority Age at which a person is legally no longer a minor.

Maker The person obligated to pay the amount of a promissory note.

Malpractice Professional misconduct or unreasonable lack of skill; a violation of a standard of care.

Malware A general term referring to problems that can be transmitted from computer to computer through email or Internet access, such as viruses, Trojans, and keyboard scanners.

Mandatory legal authority Primary legal authority that the court is required to follow.

Marshal The law enforcement officer for a federal court.

Martindale-Hubbell Law Directory A resource that contains names, addresses, specialties, and ratings of lawyers listed at martindale.com.

Materialman's lien Also mechanic's lien. An instrument filed by a materialman or a mechanic who furnished material for or performed labor upon improvements to property but has not been paid for that work, creating an enforceable right against the property.

Matters Separate projects for a given client.

Means testing A formula based on the median family income for the area and household size of the debtor.

Mediation Nonbinding settlement discussions between the parties.

Memorandum opinion or opinion (renders judgment) A judgment in which the judge sets out the factual and legal reasons that the judge used to reach the conclusions given in his or her opinion.

Memorials In real estate, entries on a Torrens certificate which describe encumbrances (such as mortgages or liens) in existence on the property.

Merging The process of combining data from two files to make a third document.

Metadata Data stored in a computer that shows who created, accessed, or revised a document, what changes were made and by whom, and the dates and times when all of this occurred.

Metes and bounds description A form of legal description by listing compass directions and distances of each boundary edge surrounding a property.

Microcomputers Small-sized computers often called personal or desktop computers (PCs).

Minicomputers Mid-sized, powerful computers often used as network servers.

Mining partnership A partnership formed when two or more people join together to work a mining claim to extract minerals.

Minor A person under the age of legal competence.

Minute book The official book of corporate minutes kept by the secretary of the corporation.

Minutes Memorandum of a transaction or proceeding.

Mirror image rule In contract law, the offeree's acceptance must completely agree with, or create a mirror image, of the offeror's offer in order to be considered an acceptance.

Misdemeanor A criminal offense lesser than a felony and punishable by fine or by imprisonment for less than one year.

Misrepresentation A false statement of material fact that is relied upon and is intended to be relied upon to cause a loss to the victim.

Mistrial Declared when an event occurs that undoes the ability to conduct a fair trial. One cause might be the revelation of excluded information either deliberately or accidentally; another cause would be the inability of the jury to determine a verdict.

Mixed (standard) punctuation In a business letter, a colon follows the salutation and a comma follows the complimentary closing.

Monetary jurisdiction The limitation on dollar amounts that a court may award.

Money damages Damages in a case that can be reduced to financial claims.

Money judgment Usually found in real estate, a judgment that awards a sum of money to the plaintiff.

Money order A payment document that can be purchased at a United States post office, bank, and many stores to use in place of a check, paid for with cash.

Mortgage A written instrument that grants an interest in real property to provide security for the repayment of a debt.

Mortgagee The lending institution in a mortgage.

Mortgagee's policy A policy of insurance issued by a title insurance company to a lender insuring the lender from loss resulting from a defect of title.

Mortgagor The person executing the mortgage and granting the security in the real estate.

Motion for continuance A motion that seeks to postpone a trial or hearing date.

Motion for dismissal The term used in federal court to a motion for nonsuit.

Motion for instructed or directed verdict A motion typically made by the defendant's lawyer at the close of evidence presented by the plaintiff, based on the premise that the plaintiff has failed to prove his or her case.

Motion for mistrial A motion that requests immediate dismissal of a case because inadmissible evidence has been presented that irreparably damages on the parties' cases.

Motion for nonsuit (also voluntary dismissal) A motion requesting the court to dismiss the case for lack of action on the part of the opposing party. In various courts, the action is referred to as a voluntary dismissal or motion for dismissal.

Motion for order to show cause A motion that requests the court to issue specific relief for the filing party that requires the opposing party to appear and demonstrate, or show cause, why the relief should not be granted.

Motion for protective order A motion filed to protect one party from requests by the opposing party, such as a request to take depositions at too great a distance from the witness.

Motion for sanctions A motion filed when discovery responses are not delivered timely to request disciplinary action.

Motion for summary judgment A pleading that requests the court to grant judgment against the opposing party, where the party filing believes there is no real issue of fact to be decided at trial.

Motion in limine A motion which seeks to suppress revelation of certain information during litigation.

Motion to change venue (plea to the venue) A pleading filed before answering a petition or complaint that requests the case be transferred to another county or parish.

Motion to compel A motion seeking an order compelling the opposing party to perform some action relative to the litigation; often used to compel production of overdue discovery.

Motion to dismiss for lack of prosecution A motion made for failure to respond to discovery after a motion to compel is granted.

Motion to dismiss for want of prosecution A motion to assert that the court does not have authority to hear or decide the case.

Motion to quash service A motion seeking to have service declared invalid on the basis that service was improperly made, that the wrong party was served, or that the summons does not show the date of service.

NALS® The association for legal professionals, encourages the personal and professional growth of its members through education and the promotion of professional standards and ethics.

National Labor Relations Board (NLRB) The agency that administers the National Labor Relations Act which governs the relations between unions and employers in the private sector and is vested with the power to safeguard employees' rights to form bargaining units and to prevent and remedy unfair labor practices.

Negligence Failure to use care that a reasonable and prudent person would use under similar circumstances.

No bill The result returned by a grand jury when there is no probable cause to believe a crime has been committed.

No-fault divorce The dissolution of a marriage on the grounds of irreconcilable differences or that the marriage is irretrievably broken.

Non obstante veredicto (motion for judgment) A posttrial motion that asks the judge to disregard a jury's verdict.

Nonprofit corporations Corporations organized typically for charitable, religious, educational, or scientific purposes.

Nontrading partnership A partnership engaged in performing services; dependent on the work results of the partners rather than on capital they contribute.

Notary public A person authorized by law to administer oaths, attest to and certify depositions, and take acknowledgements of signatures on documents.

Noun Word that names a person, place, thing, or idea.

Noun clause Functions as a noun, serves as the subject, direct object, or object of the preposition.

Novation In contracts, the removal of one of the original parties to a contract and the substitution of a newcomer (all parties must consent).

Numeric filing Filing system in which numbers are assigned to client files, which are then filed in numerical order.

Nuncupative will A will spoken by a person in peril of imminent death.

Oath A solemn or official declaration that the statement the person has just made or is about to make are true.

Occupational Safety and Health Administration (OSHA) OSHA develops, regulates, and enforces occupational safety and health standards.

Offer An offer consists of an invitation to another to perform an action for compensation or to compensate another to perform an action.

Offeree The party to whom the offer is made.

Offeror The party making the offer.

Officers In corporations, the persons elected by the directors of said corporation to be responsible for the day-to-day operation and management of the corporation.

Officers of the court Individuals who are involved in the court system, including judges, clerks, attorneys, bailiffs, sheriffs, and marshals.

Open codes Codes that are invoked once to create a change in line spacing, margins, tab settings, font changes, justification, and page numbering.

Open hearing A hearing the public may attend.

Open punctuation In a business letter, no punctuation is used following the salutation or the complimentary closing.

Operating system Software that controls the flow of information to and from the central processing unit and to and from the input/output devices.

Optical character recognition (OCR) A scanner that converts an image into a character-based text file.

Ordinances (not defined in this chapter) A rule established by authority; may be a municipal statute of a city council regulating such matters as zoning, building, safety, matters of municipality, etc.

Organizational meeting Meeting of shareholders held as part of the incorporation process to handle routine matters necessary for the corporation to commence business.

Original jurisdiction The authority granted to a court to hear and determine a matter for the first time.

Orphan A single line at the bottom of a page.

Output device A computer device used to get information or data out of the computer and back to the operator, such as a monitor or printer.

Owner (grantor, vendor, or seller) In real estate, the person who transfers property (the seller); in estate planning, the maker of a trust.

Paired codes Codes that are turned on and off to invoke changes such as underlining, bold face, italics, and styles and affect only the text appearing between the paired codes.

Parentheses A strong mark of punctuation used when it is necessary to separate certain information from the rest of the sentence.

Participle A verb form that requires a helping verb to complete it.

Participle phrase Consists of the participle and words closely associated with it.

Partner by estoppel (also ostensible partner) An individual who permits or encourages others to believe he or she is a partner of a partnership; he or she may become liable for debts of the partnership.

Partnership A voluntary association of two or more persons to place their money, effects, labor, and skill in lawful commerce or business and to have a proportional share in profits and losses between them.

Party (or person) A legal person or entity engaged in litigation with another.

Passive voice Refers to the use of forms of to be plus the past participle of a verb; the passive voice creates an inverted and some what distorted sentence structure and contributes to wordiness.

Past participle The third principal part of the verb.

Patent and Trademark Office (PTO) The agency that registers trademarks, examines and issues design, plant, and utility patents.

Payee Person to whom a promissory note, bank draft or check is issued.

Peremptory challenges Request by a party that a judge not allow a prospective juror to serve as a member of the jury. No reason or cause need be given.

Perfect participle Formed by adding "having or having been" to the past participle.

Performance A method of discharge of all the contractual terms by both parties.

Period A type of punctuation indicating a full stop.

Peripherals Devices that are connected to a computer, such as terminals, tape drives, disk drives, modems, and printers.

Personal pronouns Words that are used to refer to a person speaking, being spoken to, or being spoken about.

Personal representative Term used by the Uniform Probate Code to designate the representative of an estate, replacing the terms executor, administrator, etc.

Persuasive legal authority Case law and analysis from other jurisdictions that may shed light on a case in which mandatory legal authority is ambiguous or nonexistent.

Petition (or complaint) First pleading filed in any lawsuit; also called complaint.

Petition in intervention An additional party with an interest in the outcome of a lawsuit may file a petition in intervention, setting out the details of the intevernor's interests and the relief the intervenor seeks.

Petitioner Initiating party in a dissolution of marriage proceeding.

Petty cash A fund used to pay small amounts for which a firm check is not apprporiate, either due to time constraints or when a check is not accepted.

Phrase A group of words, usually serve as modifiers in the sentence.

Physical custody The right granted to one or both parents to maintain the primary home for a child in a dissolution or divorce action.

Pickup tax The federal government allows a credit for state death taxes; in some states, the credit for state death taxes becomes the amount of the state death tax.

Plaintiff or petitioner A person or entity who brings the action; the party who complains or sues in a civil action.

Pleadings Written statement made by each side of a lawsuit concerning the various claims and defenses to be decided in court.

PLS® An advanced certification for legal support professionals with three or more years of legal experience and certifies the individual as one who possesses the foundation to perform substantive legal tasks, a mastery of office and people skills, and the ability to interact on a professional level with lawyers.

Pocket parts Supplements to law books in pamphlet form which are inserted in a pocket inside the back cover of the books to keep them current.

Portable computers Notebooks, laptops, tablets, and even smartphones qualify as portable computers.

Possessive pronouns Noun forms that indicate ownership.

Pourover will A type of will in which any assets that are not in a trust can be distributed to the trust and become a part of the trust estate.

PP® The certification for those with five or more years of experience for paralegal or legal assistants who wish to be identified as exceptional in all areas of law.

Prayer A paragraph containing a request for relief that sets forth a summary of what the plaintiff or petitioner is asking the court to do regarding a specific count.

Precedent Law created by case decisions previously made.

Predicate adjective The word that describes the subject and is connected to the subject by a linking verb.

Predicate nominative Means the same thing as the subject and is connected to the subject by a linking verb.

Preemptive right provision A provision under which the original shareholders are given the first option to buy enough additional issued shares of stock to maintain their proportionate share of ownership.

Preposition(s) A connective word that shows the relationship of the noun or pronoun that follows it to some other word in the sentence.

Present participle Word formed by adding "ing" to the present form of the verb.

Preserving the record A recording is made of testimony on disputed points in litigation, typically by a court recorder; the transcript can be used to support a later appeal.

Pretrial conference Conference among the lawyers and the judge called at the discretion of the court to review the issues to be tried and set discovery deadlines and hearing and trial dates.

Primary legal authority Constitutions, codes, statutes, ordinances, and case law.

Priority claims A claim designated as receiving priority over other claims in a bankruptcy action listed under Section 567 of the Bankruptcy Code.

Priority mail First-Class mail that weighs more than 13 ounces.

Privilege A benefit or advantage to certain persons beyond the advantages of other persons, e.g., an exemption, immunity, power, etc.

Privilege log A log describing discovery documents the production of which is objected to by the answering party.

Pro bono Describes legal work or services performed free of charge.

Pro se Term used to designate a person who represents himself in court.

Probate Court proceeding by which a will is proved valid or invalid. The term is also used to mean all proceedings pertaining to the administration of an estate.

Probate deed (guardian's or personal representative's deed) An instrument by which property is acquired from an estate or guardianship, generally without warranty. Sometimes referred to as executor's, fiduciary's, or trustee's deed.

Probation Sentence imposed for commission of crime in which a convicted criminal is released into the community under the supervision of a probation officer in lieu of incarceration.

Procedural law That body of laws which defines and describes the process to be followed to enforce substantive law.

Products liability Legal responsibility of manufacturers and sellers to buyers, users, and bystanders for damages or injuries suffered because of defects in goods.

Professional corporation(s) A corporation of licensed professionals rendering personal service to the public, e.g., lawyers, physicians, surgeons, dentists, certified public accountants, etc.

Promissory note A promise in writing to pay a certain sum of money at a future time.

Pronoun Words that replace a noun or name in order to avoid repetition.

Proof of heirship Judicial determination of the identity of those persons entitled to inherent a decedent's property when the decedent died without leaving a will.

Proof of will The process by which a decedent's will is validated or admitted to probate.

Proofs of claim Statement under oath filed in a bankruptcy proceeding by a creditor in which the creditor sets forth the amount owed and sufficient detail to identify the basis for the claim.

Proper noun The name of a particular person, place, thing, or idea.

Proxy The instrument authorizing one person to represent, act, and vote for another at a shareholders' meeting of a corporation.

Public corporations Corporations organized for governmental (typically city or county) purposes.

Purchase agreement (memorandum sale agreement, purchase offer, earnest money contract) Also sales agreement. Agreement between buyer and seller of property which sets forth in general the consideration and terms of a proposed sale.

Purchase money mortgage A mortgage given by a buyer to a seller to secure a portion of the purchase price.

Putative spouse A person who lives with another person of the opposite sex and believes in good faith that he or she has a common-law marriage.

Qualified terminable interest provision A type of property which is permitted to qualify for a marital deduction under federal estate tax if the spouse has use of the property for life and other Internal Revenue Code requirements are met.

Question mark A punctuation mark used after a direct question and after each of a series of questions in a single sentence.

Quitclaim deed A deed without warranty of title that passes whatever title the grantor has, if any, to another.

Quotation mark A punctuation mark used: to set off slang or coined words, for the title of a published article, or to indicate conversation.

Reaffirm An agreement in which the debtor agrees to continue payments to the creditor as prior to filing bankruptcy.

Real estate (or real property or realty) Land and whatever is attached or affixed to it. Generally synonymous with the words real property.

Rebuttal Evidence given by one party in litigation to refute evidence introduced by the other party.

Recapture of chattels A defense to personal injury claims that asserts the defendant was attempting to recover his or her own property that had been taken from him or her.

Reciprocal pronouns Pronouns that relate specifically to another person.

Record Made up of all the fields relating to one person or business in a data source.

Redirect examination Questioning of a party by the party's own counsel following a session of cross-examination of opposing counsel.

Redline (blacklines) The feature that allows the comparisons of one document to another.

Reflexive pronouns Used only to refer back to a noun in the sentence meaning the same person, ends in "self" or "selves."

Registered agent An individual named by a corporation to receive service of process on behalf of the corporation. The registered agent is listed with the state corporate division, along with his or her contact information for service.

Registered mail A postal service that provides the most secure possible delivery for First-Class or Priority mail.

Registered property Real property registered upon application of the owner under the Torrens title system.

Regular verb One that forms its past tense and past participle by adding "d" or "ed" to the present tense of the verb.

Relative pronoun Joins a dependent clause to an independent clause.

Remand To remand a case, brought into an appellate court or removed from one court into another, is to send it back to the court from which it came, so that further proceedings in the case, if any, may be taken there.

Remove (removal to federal court) Where the facts of a case permit either federal or state action, and the case is filed in state court, the opposing party can have the case removed to federal court for hearing under federal law and rules.

Repetitive strain (or stress) injuries (RSI) An injury caused by physical strain due to repetitive movement; carpal tunnel is a common RSI.

Reporters Books that contain published court decisions.

Request for production of documents A direction or command served upon another party, witness, or other person for production of specific documents and things for review with respect to a suit; a discovery device.

Requests for admissions Written statements of fact concerning a case that are submitted to an adverse party which that party must admit or deny.

Res judicata The principle that states that once there has been a judicial decision, the matter cannot be litigated again.

Rescission Agreement to cancel or repeal a contract with an exchange of whatever is necessary to restore both parties to their original condition as if the contract had never existed.

Residuary bequest A gift of the remaining assets of an estate.

Residue Pertains to what is left after the payment of specific bequests, devises, expenses, and taxes.

Respondent The party against whom a dissolution of marriage proceeding is initiated.

Restatements A publication that explains the law in a particular field.

Restitution Act of restoring a thing to its rightful owner. Restitution does not unmake any existing contract between the parties, and it is done by one party to mend a breach in the contractual relationship with the other. See rescission for contrast.

Restrictive covenants Regulations of record setting forth those things that are allowed and not allowed affecting property such as minimum building lines, etc.

Retainer An advance payment made to cover some of the expected costs of a legal action such as filing fees, fines, court costs, or other costs.

Revocable trust A trust in which the maker generally maintains some power over the trust as long as he or she is alive and not incapacitated; can be amended or revoked during maker's lifetime.

Safe at Home or Address Confidentiality Program (ACP) These programs, in existence or being organized in 35 states, allow victims of domestic violence, sexual abuse, rape, or stalking to safely receive First-Class mail and service of process at an undisclosed address.

Schedules Additional pleadings filed by a debtor under the Bankruptcy Code. The information required is set forth in the forms. The schedules are filed with the petition in a voluntary case, or, if the petition is accompanied by a list of all the debtor's creditors and their addresses, within 14 days (with some exceptions).

Secondary legal authority (1) Legal encyclopedias, treatises, legal texts, law review articles, restatements, and essays; (2) Writings which set forth the opinion of the writer as to the law.

Secured debts (claims) Debts that are supported by some kind of collateral.

Securities and Exchange Commission (SEC) The SEC monitors the securities industry by providing disclosure to the investing public and protects the interests of investors against malpractice in the securities and financial markets.

Self-defense The right of a person to defend his or her person, property, home, or family against anyone who intends to commit a forcible felony.

Self-proved will A will that does not require further proof to be admitted to probate.

Semicolon Punctuation mark used between parts of a sentence to separate phrases, clauses, and enumerations.

Sentence In grammar, a sentence expresses a complete thought. In criminal law, it is judgment on the verdict, usually in a criminal action.

Session laws The laws passed during a legislative session and compiled in volumes.

Share A proportionate ownership interest in the corporation evidenced by a certificate issued by the corporation.

Shareholders (or stockholders) The persons or other entities that own shares in a corporation and therefore indirectly own the corporation.

Shepardizing Checking the subsequent history of a reported court decision to make sure it has not been overturned by a higher court.

Sheriff The county officer for a court.

Shortcut keys Shortcut keys help provide the user with an easier and usually quicker method of navigating and using computer software programs, usually used in conjunction with the ALT, CTRL or SHIFT keys in conjunction with another key.

Sic Latin term placed in parentheses following any mistake in quoted material to indicate that the mistake appears in the original.

Slander Damage to a person's reputation by spoken information.

Small Business Administration (SBA) The federal agency that provides assistance of all kinds, including loans to small businesses.

Social Security Administration (SSA) The federal agency that administers the national social security and Medicare programs.

Software All programs needed to instruct, control, and operate the hardware of a computer system such as flowcharts, manuals, programs, routines, training, and the like.

Soldiers' and sailors' wills An oral disposition made by soldiers in actual military service or sailors at sea.

Sole proprietor A business owned and operated by a person who is solely responsible for its day-to-day operation.

Special warranty deed (limited warranty deed) Deed in which grantor pledges that he or she has done nothing to cloud or encumber title to the deeded property, but does not guarantee that no defects occurred before he or she owned the property.

Specific bequest (preresiduary gift) A gift in a will of an identified asset or stated amount of money.

Specific performance A type of relief in equity in which a defaulting party is ordered to perform the terms of the contract between the parties.

Spendthrift provisions A provision in a will to limit access to a trust by a beneficiary or his or her creditors.

Spike Allows the operator to select text and copy it to the end of an existing document without opening or retrieving that document to the screen.

Strict liability Concept applied by the courts in product liability cases that when a manufacturer presents its goods for public sale it is representing that the goods are suitable for their intended use.

Standard mail Primarily used by retailers, catalogers, and other advertisers who have large mailings.

Standing A concept requiring that the person injured is the one who must sue.

Statute of limitations The time period following an occurrence within which a lawsuit must be filed.

Statutes at Large Session laws enacted by Congress.

Statutory law Law enacted by Congress, state legislatures, and local governments.

Stock register or stock book A continuing record of the shares or stock ownership of a corporation.

Styles The tool used to create a consistent appearance in a word processing document, while reducing keystrokes required to format the document.

Subdivision The division of a tract or parcel of land or lot into two or more tracts, parcels, or lots for sale or development.

Subject matter jurisdiction The authority of a court to render a binding judgment over the matter in dispute.

Subjunctive mood Verb mood used to express conditions that are contrary to fact; doubtful; wished for but nonexistent; or requested, suggested, commanded, or proposed.

Submitted on the record An appeal in which no oral arguments are presented is considered submitted on the record of the case in the lower court.

Subordinating conjunction Joins dependent clauses to independent clauses.

Subpoenas duces tecum A command to appear at a certain time and place to give testimony and to bring items specified in the subpoena.

Substantive criminal law The law that defines what conduct is criminal and prescribes the type of punishment to be imposed for such conduct.

Substantive law The statutory or written law that governs rights and obligations of those who are subject to it.

Summons The official notification that suit has been filed.

Supplemental (pleading) A supplemental pleading is filed to address events that were not known or did not exist at the time the original pleading was filed.

Supremacy clause This clause of the United States Constitution establishes that neither Congress nor any state legislature may enact laws that conflict with the U.S. Constitution.

Surety A person or entity who posts bond for another.

Syndicate An association of individuals formed for the purpose of conducting and carrying out some particular business transaction, usually of a financial character, in which the members are mutually interested.

Table of Authorities A table of sources used in constructing a brief, including constitutions, statutes, case law, and other references structured according to strict rule about the order and display of each reference.

Tax lien A lien filed for nonpayment of property taxes or for nonpayment of federal, state, or local taxes such as income taxes, sales taxes, etc.

Tenancy by the entireties Type of ownership in which a husband and wife hold title to the entire property with the right of survivorship should one spouse die.

Tenancy in common The type of ownership by which each owner holds an undivided interest in the entire property with no right of survivorship to the parties. The owner's interest passes on to his or her heirs upon the owner's death.

Tenant (lessee) Also lessee. One who uses lands of another during the term of a lease.

Tense of verb Refers to the time an action or event takes place or the time of the state of being.

Term of court The term of court refers to a specific session in which a court is hearing cases.

Terminal-digit filing Filing system where numbers are broken down into groups of two digits and are filed in numerical order by the last two digits.

Territorial jurisdiction The actual geographic area over which the court has authority.

Testamentary trusts A trust created in a will, which takes effect upon the death of the decedent.

Testate Having died leaving a valid will.

Testator A person who makes a will.

Testimonium clause The clause of a deed or a legal instrument immediately preceding the signatures that reads: "In witness whereof the parties hereunto have caused this instrument to be properly executed the day and year first above written."

The bench A term that refers indirectly to the judge in a given court.

Title insurance policy Insurance against loss or damage resulting from defects in the title to a parcel of real estate.

Title opinion Written opinion of a lawyer that certifies to the validity and merchantability of title to property based on review of an abstract of title or other land records.

Torrens certificate A Torrens certificate is considered to be conclusive evidence of the present ownership and status of title.

Tort(s) A private or civil wrong or injury for which the court provides a remedy through an action for damages.

Trackpad A device found on many laptops that allows fingertip control of cursor movement.

Trackball A pointing device with a ball on top that is rolled with the fingertip to move the cursor while the base of the trackball device remains stationary.

Trading partnership A business whose nature is that of buying and selling merchandise.

Transfer by devise This describes a transfer when the owner of real estate dies and leaves a property to someone in his or her will.

Transitive verb An action verb that needs a direct object upon which to act.

Trespass to land This describes a transfer when the owner of real estate dies and leaves a property to someone in his or her will.

True bill The document generated by a grand jury if probable cause exists to believe a crime has been committed.

Ultra vires contract A contract entered into by a corporation that exceeds the limitations of its power; it can be voided.

Unauthorized practice of law (not defined) The practice of law by one not licensed to do so, definitions vary by state.

Uncontested proceedings Where the marriage partners have reached agreements regarding the issues in a divorce proceeding.

Undertaking or bail bond A written guaranty executed by a defendant and a surety to ensure the defendant will appear and make himself or herself available to the court.

Undue influence Dominance of a stronger-willed person over a weaker-willed person.

Uniform Resource Locator (URL) The address or code at which an Internet site can be located.

Unilateral contract A contract in which a person makes a promise conditioned on the performance of another.

Unincorporated associations An organization formed for a non-profit purpose that has no existence apart from its members and cannot sue or be sued in its name.

United States Citizenship and Immigration Services (US-CIS) The agency within the Department of Homeland Security that rules upon immigration and naturalization petitions and asylum and refugee applications; also establishes immigration services policies and procedures.

United States Customs and Border Protection (CBP) The agency formerly known as the United States Customs Service. It is organized under the Department of Homeland Security and administers and enforces customs laws (includes the collection of revenue from imports, and carries on the functions of the Border Patrol and former INS, Customs, and agricultural quarantine inspectors).

United States Marshals Service The agency that ensures the protection of court facilities, the personal safety of judges, has the primary responsibility of tracking and apprehending fugitives, is the principal contact for all international investigations, provides protection to witnesses, maintains custody of federal prisoners after arrest and during transport, houses unsentenced prisoners in federal, state, and local jails, and seizes, manages, and disposes of forfeited properties and assets from major drug and criminal cases.

United States Postal Service (USPS) The federal agency that provides mail processing and delivery to individuals and businesses within the United States.

Unsecured debts (claims) Claims that have no collateral or other lien, e.g. open accounts such as credit cards or trade accounts, personal loans, or claims where the amount of security is less than the debt.

USB drives (memory sticks, flash drives, thumb drives) Sometimes called memory sticks, flash drives, or thumb drives, these devices plug into USB drives on a computer and contain memory that functions like a hard drive.

Valid contract One which contains the four essential elements of a contract; i.e., mutual consent, competent parties, lawful consideration, and lawful subject matter.

Vector The direction and distance of a line used in a metes and bounds description.

Venue The geographic location of a lawsuit; authority of a court to hear a matter based on geographical location.

Verb Word or word group that tells what the subject does or is or what happens to the subject.

Verification A statement that the allegations in a complaint or discovery responses are true and correct.

Virus(es) Computer code that can be copied into an existing computer program and make itself known by impeding correct function of the program.

Void contracts A contract that does not comply with the law and is unenforceable from its inception.

Voidable contract A contract that is potentially defective in some respect (treated as a valid contract unless the defect is asserted).

Voir dire The preliminary examination in court of a witness or juror to determine his competency or interest in a matter. Literally, voir dire means "to speak the truth."

Voluntary bankruptcy A proceeding under which a debtor voluntarily seeks relief under the bankruptcy code.

Vulnerable adults Adults who lack the mental or physical capacity to care for themselves.

Warrant A warrant is issued by a judge when the judge finds that probable cause exists to believe the named individual has committed a criminal offense.

Warranty deed (general warranty deed) Also general warranty deed. A deed that guarantees that the title conveyed is good and nothing has been done to cloud or encumber title beyond the permitted encumbrances specified therein.

Web browser A program that allows a computer user to explore the Internet.

Web page or website A page found on an Internet site.

Webcam A small inexpensive device that functions like a camera, with its images being sent over the Internet.

Wide area network (WAN) The linking of computers that are located far apart, i.e., in different cities, through cables, fiber optics, or satellites.

Widow-orphan A single line at the top of a page.

Will (last will and testament) An instrument through which a person makes a disposition of his or her property, to take effect after death.

With prejudice A type of judgment that bars the right to bring or maintain an action on the same claim or cause.

Without prejudice A type of judgment that dismisses an action but does not bar the right to re-file the matter later.

Without recourse This endorsement relieves the endorser of any future liability on the check.

Work product doctrine A doctrine that protects the evaluations, strategy, and planning of the attorney from discovery by opposing counsel during litigation.

Writ of certiorari An order by the appellate court requiring the lower or trial court to surrender jurisdiction to the appellate court for the duration of the appeal.

Writ of execution An order of the court evidencing debt of one party to another and commanding the court officer to take property in satisfaction of the debt.

Writ of garnishment An order of the court in which property, money, or credits in the possession of a third party may be seized and applied to pay a debtor's debt. It is used as an incident to or auxiliary of a judgment rendered in a principal action.

Written down Time that is reduced or removed from a bill to create a discounted bill.

Zip drives A portable computer drive, now nearly obsolete due to the common usage of recordable CDs and DVDs.

Index